THE FRENCH COLONIAL MIND

....

VOLUME 2

FRANCE OVERSEAS
Studies in Empire and Decolonization
....
SERIES EDITORS:
A. J. B. Johnston, James D. Le Sueur,
and Tyler Stovall

THE FRENCH COLONIAL MIND

VOLUME 2

Violence, Military Encounters, and Colonialism

Edited and with an introduction by Martin Thomas

UNIVERSITY OF NEBRASKA PRESS : LINCOLN AND LONDON

© 2011 by the Board of Regents of the University of Nebraska

All rights reserved. Manufactured in the United States of America

∞

Library of Congress Cataloging-in-Publication Data

The French colonial mind, volume 2 : violence, military encounters, and colonialism / edited and with an introduction by Martin Thomas.
p. cm. — (France overseas : studies in empire and decolonization)
Includes bibliographical references and index.
ISBN 978-0-8032-2094-2 (paperback: alkaline paper)
ISBN (set) 978-0-8032-3815-2 (paperback: alkaline paper)
1. France—Colonies—Africa—History. 2. France—Colonies—Africa—Administration—History. 3. Africa, French-speaking West—Colonization—History. 4. Africa, French-speaking Equatorial—Colonization—History. I. Thomas, Martin, 1964–

DT33.F73 2011   325'.344—dc23   2011024159

Set in Sabon by Bob Reitz. Designed by A. Shahan.

Contents

Acknowledgments ix

Introduction:
Mapping Violence onto French Colonial Minds xi
MARTIN THOMAS

PART 1
Cultures of Violence in the Empire

1 Dahra and the History of Violence
  in Early Colonial Algeria 3
  WILLIAM GALLOIS

2 Losing Their Mind and Their Nation?
  Mimicry, Scandal, and Colonial Violence
  in the Voulet-Chanoine Affair 26
  BERTRAND TAITHE

3 Fear and Loathing in French Hanoi:
  Colonial White Images and Imaginings
  of "Native" Violence 52
  MICHAEL G. VANN

4 Anti-Semitism and the Colonial Situation
  in Interwar Algeria: The Anti-Jewish Riots
  in Constantine, August 1934 77
  JOSHUA COLE

5 Fascism and Algérianité: The Croix de Feu
   and the Indigenous Question in 1930s Algeria   112
   SAMUEL KALMAN

6 Colonial Minds and Colonial Violence:
   The Sétif Uprising and the Savage
   Economics of Colonialism   140
   MARTIN THOMAS

PART 2
Colonial Minds and Empire Soldiers

7 Conquest and Cohabitation: French Men's
   Relations with West African Women
   in the 1890s and 1900s   177
   OWEN WHITE

8 The French Colonial Mind and the Challenge
   of Islam: The Case of Ernest Psichari   202
   KIM MUNHOLLAND

9 French Race Theory, the Parisian Society
   of Anthropology, and the Debate over
   la Force Noire, 1909–1912   221
   JOE LUNN

10 Colonial Minds Confounded: French Colonial
   Troops in the Battle of France, 1940   248
   MARTIN S. ALEXANDER

11 The "Silent Native": *Attentisme*, Being
   Compromised, and Banal Terror during the
   Algerian War of Independence, 1954–1962   283
   NEIL MACMASTER

12 Exposing the "Paradoxical Citizenship":
French Authorities' Responses to the
Algerian Presence in Federal Germany
during the Algerian War, 1954–1962   304
MATHILDE VON BÜLOW

Conclusion: The Colonial Past
and the Postcolonial Present   334
ROBERT ALDRICH

List of Contributors   357
Index   361

Acknowledgments

In this second collection of essays on aspects of attitudinal formation, normative standards, and ways of thinking and doing among French colonial officials in the nineteenth and twentieth centuries, our focus is on violence, repression, and conflict. To be sure, the chapters treat these issues differently. Some do so singly and with reference to specific individuals, events, or crises. Others do so more broadly, considering how various forms of coercion became embedded in colonial practices over time. What unites them is their attempt to tease out the connections between colonialism and violence, whether physical and material or psychological and intangible.

Once again, it is my pleasure to thank all those who have helped bring this edited collection to fruition. This, and its partner volume, *The French Colonial Mind, Volume 1: Mental Maps of Empire and Colonial Encounters*, are products of a conference held at the University of Exeter's Institute of Arab and Islamic Studies in April 2007. The conference was hosted by the Centre for the Study of War, State, and Society, which received essential backing from the Leverhulme Trust and the University of Exeter's Department of History. My job as editor has been made much easier by the advice and generosity of others. Claire Keyte and Andrew Thorpe at Exeter helped make the conference possible. Heather Lundine, Bridget Barry, Joeth Zucco, and Jim Le Sueur at the University of Nebraska Press provided invaluable guidance. Jane Curran's copyediting was, once again, exemplary. Insights from the two anonymous readers helped us make essential improvements to individual chapters. Other friends and colleagues, among them Jennifer Sessions, Dan Branch, Ruth Ginio, Jim House, Patricia Lorcin, Peter Jackson, and Herman Lebovics, enriched the book by helping us think through the ideas discussed here. Finally, my thanks to the contributors: their hard work has made this book possible.

Introduction

Mapping Violence onto French Colonial Minds

MARTIN THOMAS

Mental Maps, Disorder, and Colonial Violence

It was political scientist Alan Henrikson who introduced us to the term "mental maps" as a determinant of social action.[1] The idea that the attitudinal outlooks embedded in minds as a result of cultural formation and past experience are integral to political choices has gained purchase ever since. Among the specialist communities quickest to recognize the usefulness of the "mental maps" idea have been Henrikson's fellow political scientists, international historians, and scholars of the "missing dimension" of intelligence service activity interested in processes of cognition—the way the world is understood—and resultant analytical thinking.[2] Historians of empire and colonialism have, by contrast, tended to use the idea of mental maps piecemeal, sometimes to explain the diffusion of Orientalist thinking, sometimes to account for (usually misguided) policy decisions, but more often in a rather nebulous way to illustrate the misapprehensions of European publics about the colonial empires held in their name.

The first volume of this collection on French "colonial minds" suggested that one issue uniting the various people and events described is that thought normally precedes action. But the actions of those in positions of colonial power in the French Empire were also, to a greater to lesser extent, reflective of established patterns of behavior. Furthermore, as the phrase implies, a pattern of behavior necessarily took shape over

Introduction

time through repetition and reinforcement of certain actions.[3] In the case of army or police organizations, such repetition and reinforcement could entrench certain patterns of behavior, sometimes disbarring consideration of alternative perspectives that cut against the grain of prevailing military assumptions about subject populations and how they were to be regarded, policed, or otherwise "controlled." The organizational cultures of France's colonial security forces, in other words, often acted as a barrier to reflective engagement with colonial peoples. As a result rarely were innovations, whether in operational practice or in military cultures, internally generated outside crisis conditions. Only after dramatic political failures or violent outbreaks were attitudes likely to change, which is part of what Edgar Schein, a leading theorist of organizational culture, terms the process of "trauma learning."[4] But were colonial military minds susceptible to such learning in less overtly violent times?

Here we come to perhaps the most challenging and often the most revealing aspect of colonial minds at work: those situations in which, it seems, thought hardly preceded action at all. Indeed, in some instances historians posit that the behavior of Europeans in unfamiliar colonial settings was anything but rational. Numerous colonial encounters, from initial contact to protracted exposure, have been described in terms of irrationality, mental disorder, even madness, or, less dramatically, as the abandonment of European norms and manners, the dread outcome of which was "going native."[5] A distinct subdiscipline of "colonial" psychiatry, many of whose practitioners and critics achieved lasting notoriety, looked on the racial differentiation inherent to colonial societies as pivotal to new delineations of mental disorder and supposed African inferiority that helped entrench colonial power.[6]

The metaphor of psychiatric disorder will also be familiar to anyone acquainted with the work of Martiniquan psychiatrist and anticolonial revolutionary Frantz Fanon, as well as to scholars of decolonization more generally. As Ann Laura Stoler has recently reminded us, Fanon's central concern with the lasting physical distress, the personal degradations, and psychological disorders left among Algerians scarred by French colonial rule was very much a study in the ruination of minds.[7] And as Benjamin Brower and Marnia Lazreg have emphasized in the same context, any study of colonial "official thinking," whether in the first phases of imperial conquest or in the final years of colonial collapse, must engage with the cruelties and coercion perpetrated as part of the imperial claim to govern groups and communities judged subordinate and inferior.[8]

If Fanon's primary purpose was to explain the injustices of colonialism in terms of their corruptive effects on the minds of colonizers and colonized alike, his preoccupation with violence—whether that perpetrated in the name of the colonial state or that demanded of colonial subjects freeing their bodies and purifying their minds through acts of insurrection—suggests that the study of colonialism must encompass the study of violence. Such investigation must attempt at least two things. First, we need to define what is meant by violence. The chapters to follow are dominated by physical acts of violence, most collective, some individual. But the authors recognize that violence could also be otherwise. It might be cultural—the denigration of established ways of life or particular ethnicities or religions, for instance. It could be social—and here one thinks of the destruction of customary practices, communal bonds, and economic relationships. And it was sometimes psychological—creating insecurity as a form of coercive practice. Violence, then, covers a wide spectrum from physical injury to societal disruption and the inculcation of fear.

Just as there were multifarious forms of violence, so, to paraphrase Benjamin Brower, colonial violence was informed by a "multiple logic." Violent acts imposed new forms of social exclusion. Destruction or seizure of resources created new economic hierarchies. Both provided physical evidence of imperial "reach" far beyond established centers of colonial power. The use of force, on some occasions, reflected presumptions about the impossibility or pointlessness of political compromise. It mirrored official understanding about how colonized communities understood displays of power. And it revealed deeply racist precepts about the nature of permissible killing in "uncivilized" societies.[9] Perhaps more familiar in the conquest period, these tendencies resurfaced during France's wars of decolonization during which anticolonial insurgents and their civilian backers were denied the rights accorded to enemy combatants.[10] State repression, at its most extreme during the Algerian War, brings us to another unsettling problem: the muting effects of violence on colonial minds—and voices. Colonial civil and military administrators imposed certain silences in respect of violent acts practiced for "reasons of state."[11] Their tendency to censor and censure was compounded by the efforts of their anticolonial opponents to expose the levels of violence practiced against them before the court of international opinion.[12]

Confronting the specificity of colonial coercion raises a second challenge: the need for a typology of violence to tease out its specifically "colonial" dimension. If this explains Fanon's near obsessive concern with the subject, it also indicates why most studies of colonial violence tend to concentrate primarily on the perpetrators of violence and their particular relationship with identifiable centers of colonial power, whether these were governments, regional administrations, police and army commands, or major corporate employers.[13] Putting French violence first takes us some way to identifying the colonial element in the subject, but it does not alone suffice. For the violent actions described above could be seen as simple variants of state violence practiced within acutely unequal societies and predicated on the control or conversion of a dominant social group. This does not mean, however, that we should reject the colonial state as a primary agent of colonial violence; far from it. Perhaps more than anything else, what makes the violence described in this volume different—and singularly colonial—is its duality. For colonial violence was both constitutive of colonial power and destructive of it. And these opposing processes often proceeded simultaneously. The contradiction here may be unraveled if we think in terms of conflicting short-term needs and longer-term goals. Violence as repression was typically applied to impose colonial order in the short term. But its prevalence undermined longer-term efforts to reconstruct colonized societies to suit the requirements of the colonizing power. Violence could silence opposition, but it was an insecure foundation on which to build a supposedly better society. The ways in which French colonial minds wrestled with this contradiction take us to the very essence of French imperialism.

Sometimes routine state violence or military repression provoked acts of spectacular counterviolence, which left entire army units wiped out. Catastrophic losses like the October 1950 "Cao Bang disaster" during the Indochina War, which left 4,800 troops either dead or missing, or the Palestro "massacre" southeast of Algiers in May 1956 in which 19 recently arrived *rappelés* and their section commander were fatally ambushed sent shock waves through metropolitan opinion. These transgressions of the usual asymmetry between state repression versus anticolonial violence seared themselves into official memories of colonialism.[14]

Confronted with such dilemmas, perhaps not surprisingly the rulers of empire increasingly conceptualized its stresses in literal terms. Once social and political disorder in colonial territory was addressed in terms of a psychological crisis afflicting those who ran the show, could the end of colonial dominion be very far off? This was precisely what happened in France's postwar colonial service when senior officials sought to diagnose and cure the alleged "malaise" among administrators trying to govern an empire they no longer entirely controlled or understood. On the other side of the colonial-anticolonial divide, Herman Lebovics has stressed how frequently the rulers of empire made use of psychological terms and diagnoses, albeit erroneously, to pathologize colonial rebellion and anticolonial activity more generally as evidence of antisocial behavior rather than as a logical reaction to years of discrimination.[15]

As the chapters in this volume indicate, it is in the realm of colonial violence that the apparent disjuncture between rationality and actions, between sanity and psychiatric disturbance, between order and disorder, is most striking. If, as Caroline Ford has argued, the boundaries between religious violence and organized political protest in France became more porous during the nineteenth century, so, too, with the horrendous exception of repression of the Paris Commune in 1870, instances of collective violence in French society were less Rabelaisian, less highly ritualized, less self-consciously hellish than they had been in early modern France, most notably during the protracted religious warring of the sixteenth century. Violence had not gone away, but the codes of violent public behavior had changed.[16] By the interwar period, political violence in metropolitan France, still recurrent and endemic, was nonetheless rationalized as either ideologically driven or part of the lingering, traumatic aftermath of the Great War.[17] Colonial violence was represented differently in France at the time, not as politically organized and functional and bound by certain accepted limits, but as culturally derived, dysfunctional, and potentially unlimited. What went generally unacknowledged was that such violence was often the result of colonial intervention or perpetrated by the French themselves.

The forms and scale of colonial violence, as well as the range of violent circumstances investigated here, confirm that French men and women both confronted and perpetrated violence in numerous ways. Some were products of rebellion, others the by-product of war. But what of less sensational occasions where the actions of Europeans appear, superficially at least, to have been unthinkingly violent? Was the casual violence meted out to a domestic servant, a plantation worker, or an intrusive street hawker carefully thought through, or was it merely a conditioned, almost reflex, response? Michael Vann's chapter in this second volume of the collection suggests, for instance, that French violence in colonial Hanoi was as casual as it was habitual. Were the stereotypical characterizations of indigenous traits the result of personal evaluation or merely the repetition of attitudes prevalent in the colonial milieu of the officers' club, the settler's home, or even the governor's residence? How far was colonial stereotyping derivative of the prevalent French biomedical thinking and masculine honor codes to which Robert Nye's work has alerted us? If, as seems likely, a readiness to use violence was essential to the socialization of young European men serving or working in colonial territories, then perhaps we may be able to discern distinctly colonialist attitudes to violence itself.[18] Bringing these viewpoints together, it is tempting to suggest that colonial violence reflected the predominantly masculine—and often highly macho—worlds of white colonial society, and that violence was also integral to the fabric of productive relations in colonial economies marked by labor-intensive industries, coercive practices, and, at least until 1936, official resistance to legal recognition of workers' rights.[19]

Sociologies of Violence

Consideration of the parameters of colonial violence is made easier by engaging with the ideas of French sociologist Pierre Bourdieu. Originally brought to prominence by his ethnographical research into Algeria's Kabyle Berber and Arab communities in the latter stages of the Algerian War, Bourdieu had much to say about forms of violence.[20] To appreciate this, one needs to dwell a little on his ideas of "capital" and "symbolic violence." Rejecting Marxist materialism and structuralism, Bourdieu conceptualized capital as the various currencies of power in any given social arena or field. Individuals and groups seek to accumulate such capital to enhance their social status and power. This capital could be material and economic—tangible assets and resources—but it could also be intangible: the cultural capital conferred by linguistic ability, specialist knowledge, and academic qualification; or the "symbolic capital" conferred by high office, career achievement, or public reputation. This search for prestige, for elevated social status, while not uniquely colonial, was clearly manifest among officials, traders, settlers, and missionaries whose capacity to dominate or influence others rested, in part, on their acquisition of such symbolic capital.[21]

Bourdieu's theories are doubly relevant to us here because of his suggestion that possession of such capital also enhanced the ability of social actors to undertake acts of "symbolic violence," that is, to impose their own normative standards and social meanings on other sections of society. In other words, armed with their advantages in capital—be it material, cultural, or symbolic—dominant social actors could legitimate their own prevailing standards and expectations about individuals' behavior and deference to colonial authority as the normal way of things, as the way the world should be. Herein lay the ultimate irony: for the very success of symbolic violence such as this derived from the fact that those inculcated to accept these normative standards as superior and unchallengeable rarely perceived such domination as an act of violence in itself.[22]

In this sense the art of successful domination is subterfuge. To take a couple of examples, each from colonial Vietnam: evolving statist conceptions of socioeconomic development, or *mise en valeur* in the Vietnamese territories, justified French control in terms of heightened productivity, increased national output, and, in consequence, the amelioration of poverty.[23] Yet the prevailing modes of colonial production, from plantation agriculture to rubber extraction and mining, remained labor intensive, highly exploitative, and always poorly paid. The entire modernization project had labor coercion and continued impoverishment at its core.[24] At the same time, French imposition of educational curricula that systematically denigrated precolonial cultures while lauding France's historic achievements illustrated Bourdieu's conception of symbolic violence in practice.[25] If we can see forms of violence in the printed word of the schoolroom, then surely it was also present in the adult world of colonial workplaces and private lives. Put simply, how should we read such quotidian facets of colonial rule: the low-level but persistent colonial violence, the petty prejudice, or the ingrained racism of some colonial minds? Were they born of the colonial encounter, or were they products of attitudes and assumptions developed over time, sometimes in France itself? Was colonial violence part of European efforts to sustain order, or did it reflect the breakdown of order whether at the national, local, or even familial level?

Again, other sociological approaches may help us here. Expanding on the work of Donald Black and Roberta Senechal de la Roche, the social theorist David Sciulli draws a conceptual distinction between consensual and nonconsensual types of "orderly behavior." He suggests on the one hand that orderliness may reflect individuals' capacity for social control, but on the other hand that orderly behavior may also be the outcome of social integration. As Sciulli explains it, "Individuals are controlled when it is not possible for them simply to recognize and understand in common what is expected of them; in their fear and anxiety, they are supine. By contrast, individuals' orderliness may be a product of their possible social integration when the rules or duties orienting their behavior are at least kept recognizable and understandable."[26] Sciulli's ideas are useful when considering violent interactions between colonial overseers and colonized subjects because they suggest that external imposition of "orderly behavior" amounted to a form of social engineering built on the premise that the colonial subjects to be made "orderly" were incapable of integration into a colonial order that was alien to them. Colonial subjugation, in other words, stemmed from the institutionalization of repressive social control within the bureaucratic and legal fabric of the colonial state. Whether or not colonial control stemmed directly from military conquest, it seems reasonable to suggest that violence was integral to the structures of colonialism: its economic foundations, its institutions, and its governing precepts.[27]

The full implications of this argument bear amplification. Just as the organized use of violence might be constitutive of order, in this case the consolidation of the administrative apparatus of the colonial state, its demands and its practices, so resistance to it might be destructive of that order.[28] To borrow sociological terminology, collective violence, or the coordinated inflicting of physical damage by a group, is not abnormal or "deviant"; rather it is a form of social control capable of coherent explanation. As the leading social theorist Charles Tilly has warned us, while it is rash to claim that such violence conforms to any generic laws or theories, discrete patterns of collective violence may be discerned nonetheless.[29] We have, it seems, come a long way from Gustave Le Bon's elaboration of "crowd theory" in the 1890s. Far from being symptomatic of mass hysteria or the derangement of a collective "crowd mind" as Le Bon suggested, group violence may be justified, either as a form of social protest in the absence of permitted nonviolent alternatives, or, on the opposing side of the political divide, as a means to suppress such protest.[30] Its form and frequency is also conditioned by the "conflict structure" that pertains in the society in question; in other words it is substantially contingent on the extent of social division, economic iniquity, and perceived cultural difference between the parties involved.[31] To use the language of political psychology, levels of political violence are likely to reflect patterns of socialization in a particular community as well as the form and extent of centralized state control over that community.[32] To paraphrase Jeff Goodwin's work on revolutionary movements after 1945, violent protest is typically pursued by groups that discern "no other way out" of their societal condition.[33] If we take these indicators as our yardstick, endemic violence in colonial societies is unsurprising both because the socialization of dependent peoples as colonial subjects denied them basic rights and resources, and because, paradoxically, colonial state control was typically too weak or remote to enforce rigid popular compliance in all circumstances. Furthermore, the sense of embattlement among colonial elites nurtured threat perceptions about the local populations around them that became manifest in heightened levels of repression whenever the colonial state seemed especially vulnerable to dissent or overthrow.[34]

Yet, as Roberta Senechal de la Roche has argued convincingly—if provocatively—a double standard lurks in much of the sociological literature on collective violence in sharply unequal societies. While the violence perpetrated by those suffering discrimination or oppression has been rationalized and in many cases defended or excused, that of the dominant groups in such societies is usually depicted as not only indefensible but irrational too.[35] Adapted to our analytical context, the violence of the colonial oppressed is commonly depicted by academics as a normative response—maybe even a laudable one, but the counter-violence it triggered from state authorities is typically seen as both unjust and abnormal. Looking back from a post-empire perspective, we are therefore confronted with an exact inversion of the way in which colonial minds viewed the violence of colonizers and colonized. If Senechal de la Roche is right, then surely it is incumbent on us to exercise particular care when interpreting the violent actions of the rulers of empire and the outlooks and normative standards that lay behind them.

Rationalizing Colonial Violence

Such actions signified a reflection and a reinforcement of behaviors commonly observed in intercommunal colonial relations. This is not to reduce the Frenchmen and Frenchwomen of empire to mere "colonizer" stereotype. Not all resorted to violence. Not all denigrated indigenous society or, to use their own parlance, the *indigènes* they employed, they knew, or, in many cases, they lived alongside. Take, for instance, Albert Memmi, the Tunis-born novelist and teacher who first articulated the supposedly binary opposition between rulers and ruled in his 1957 book, *The Colonizer and the Colonized*, and who conceded that those on each side of his equation were trapped there by circumstance, not choice.[36] Memmi drew on his childhood experiences as a Jew in a predominantly Muslim colonial city and was writing just as Tunisia neared independence from France. He found himself trapped between the opposing categories he described. He recognized, nonetheless, that colonizers sustained their privileged position by accepting and sometimes working for a fundamentally racist political system, and a system upheld by coercing and excluding those that it identified as inferior. Colonialism, in other words, was inherently violent, and its wrongs could only be rectified by destroying it.[37]

Memmi's insight was to accept that there could be no halfway house on the road to decolonization. Yet others before him genuinely believed in the progressive potential of colonialism and aspired to contribute to it. Individuals such as these sought to cultivate dependent populations rather than to expropriate from them, albeit on their own terms.[38] Indeed, some of the bitterest critics of colonial coercion and racial abuses emerged from settler communities or colonial careers. But one thing remains inescapable. The European populations spread across the French empire inhabited societies in which the differential treatment and the differential characterization of people were fundamental to the functioning of the colony. And, whatever its roots in colonial conquest, in the political forms of the colonial state, in the economic structures of empire, such differentiation was deeply embedded in colonial minds. This was not a uniquely French phenomenon. Nor was it reducible to a single, generic racism derived from particular racial theories.[39] Nor were discriminatory actions explicable simply as the product of a long-standing foreign occupation. Yet, for all that, differential treatment of people according to their ethnicity, gender, or sexuality, whether actual or presumed, was prevalent among settlers, officials, and missionaries; in short, among Europeans in the colonies.

Institutionalized discrimination and the high incidence of low-level, banal violence across racial and communal divides cannot be reduced to a simplistic binary characterization of hegemonic colonial violence versus determined anticolonial popular resistance. For one thing, the colonial "presence" in many of the dependent territories colored blue, pink, or orange on the European classroom walls of the late nineteenth and early twentieth centuries was far less entrenched and altogether more fleeting than imperialist publics "back home" were led to believe. In many places the "colonial state" hardly amounted to any kind of functioning administrative provision at all.[40] For another, European colonial bureaucrats such as those vying for influence across late nineteenth-century tropical Africa typically justified the violence of conquest not as enforced subjugation but as transient pacification, as the displacement of the apparently endemic feuding between what veteran anthropologist Jack Goody describes as "acephalous 'tribal' groups" by the orderliness of fixed state boundaries, new legal regimens, and white-officered constabularies.[41] Perhaps most important of all, an accretion of rules, regulations, and customary practices made the use of violence routine.

What one historian has recently termed "the banality of brutality" was a sedimentary process in which arbitrary arrest, collective punishments, coercive interrogation techniques, and denial of basic rights of redress were all layers on which endemic security force violence was built. To those acculturated to practice it, such violence was not exceptional or inexcusable, but the logical outcome of past precedent—the way "to get things done."[42]

Even the use of corporal punishment, whipping and caning in particular, to coerce African labor or mete out instant discipline to alleged wrongdoers was frequently excused by Europeans in the late nineteenth and early twentieth centuries as not only expedient but readily understood by those who experienced or witnessed it. According to the defenders of such practices, inflicting physical pain helped bring order both to colonial society and to naive, disorderly African minds. It was no coincidence that whereas flogging was banned in the British Army during the 1870s, whipping and caning persisted within Britain's colonial forces in Africa until 1946.[43] The institutionalization of colonial violence through legal procedure and regimens of punishment was thus depicted as progressive and modern, part of the transition from precolonial disorder to colonial order. Progressive it may have been claimed to be, but colonial violence was also clearly systemic. It was in part bound up with the political obligations, social structures, and economic processes imposed by European rule, in part facilitated by European understandings of how order in dependent societies could and should be maintained.[44] Moreover, as international efforts to codify binding laws of war gathered momentum during the late nineteenth and early twentieth centuries, the imperial nations ensured that colonial rule was exempted from putative restrictions on the rights and actions of occupying powers.[45] Not until the composition of the United Nations General Assembly was transformed by an influx of formerly colonized Afro-Asian states in the 1950s were levels of colonial violence finally exposed to sustained and hostile international scrutiny.[46] Prior to this, as we shall see, just as violence was writ large in colonial experience, so it was integral to the attitudes and cultures of practice of numerous colonial authority figures.

A number of the chapters in this volume also show that the colonies were laboratories for organized violence, where new forms of suppression, punishment, and political control were practiced and refined. Colonial borrowing of metropolitan policing methods and the interplay between colonial and metropolitan ideas of urban planning and social regulation in cities indicate that experimentation in forms of social control was an interactive process between the empire and mainland France.[47] Innovation in organized colonial violence, whether in terms of legal restrictions and punishments, policing dissent, or reconfiguring colonial cities to facilitate segregation and surveillance, was necessarily a continuous process, but it reached a new intensity in the years immediately after World War I. There were several reasons for this. One was population movement. While the French never colonized their empire with Anglo-Saxon enthusiasm, economic pressure, the greater accessibility of colonial territory, and the expansion of colonial bureaucracy and commerce in the interwar years sent tens of thousands of new colonists to the empire. The new arrivals soon registered their presence in material change such as the growth of settler-inhabited *nouvelles villes* in the cities of French North Africa and Vietnam, which gave concrete expression to the economic and cultural hierarchies of colonialism.[48] Also apparent after 1918 was a growing tension among politicians, legislators, and officials over the long-term direction of colonial policy in the aftermath of a conflict so shockingly destructive that it rendered formulaic rhetoric about the civilizing potential of European cultures outmoded and trite. Genuine antipathy to empire remained a minority interest, the preoccupation of Communist activists, colonial students resident in France, and surrealist artists determined to demythologize received wisdom about French imperial benevolence.[49] Yet in the political mainstream too, French colonial minds were adjusting to different currents of opinion about the long-term justifications for empire. Numerous government members, senior officials, academics, writers, and other social commentators, none of them anticolonialists, recognized that France's imperial purpose required some measure of reinvention, perhaps even more radical revaluation. This rethinking underpinned major colonial policy shifts informed by reconfigurations of race, ideas of colonial citizenship, and the essence of French identity.[50]

For others, empire remained an unimpeachable project, but one whose fixity could only be sustained with the new technologies of coercive power more readily available after the Great War. It was no coincidence that imperial conflicts of the 1920s became at once the preferred sites of experimentation for new weapons of war—military aircraft, armored vehicles, poison gas—and the dumping ground for surplus military hardware left over from the years 1914-18. Colonial rebels, dissentient colonial communities, and even recalcitrant colonial taxpayers faced lethal violence delivered on an unprecedented scale by airplanes, tanks, and machine guns.[51] This trend toward greater lethality in repressive violence was prefigured before 1914 in more widespread use by colonial security forces of weaponry considered unacceptable in intra-European conflict. The dumdum bullet, designed to maximize bodily trauma and blood loss, stands as a ghastly exemplar of this shift.[52] Using high-technology weapons (by the standards of the day) to assure even greater asymmetry in colonial violence (keeping white casualties down while killing as many opponents as possible) became still more prevalent as European militaries built on their experiences of the Great War. Nowhere was this more apparent than in the widespread turn to "air policing" as a cheap but deadly form of colonial control. In the expanded French and British colonial empires that took shape after World War I newly available apparatus of imperial coercion made the open skies—the very air—over the North African Maghreb and the Fertile Crescent of the Middle East a new type of political, military, and cultural space. Politically, mastery of the air emphasized the apparent superiority of Western industrial modernism, underscoring the right to rule of imperial nations. Militarily, the airplane offered new possibilities of force projection, destructive power, and consequent strategic advantage. Politically, coercive bombardment transcended the temporal divide between initial imposition of colonial authority through the threat, or use, of indiscriminate violence and the subsequent maintenance of imperial power through more selective violence targeted against dissident populations, whether as an end in itself or as an instrument of broader deterrence.[53]

Other key post–World War I changes help us understand what made such repressive violence appear natural and unavoidable to its European practitioners. To adapt Zara Steiner's comment about the peacemaking of 1919, none of the usual bases for state identity—language, religion, ethnicity, geography, ideology—commanded universal assent as a basis either for individual colonial statehood or for common identity across the French Empire as a whole.[54] Concepts of what it was to be truly, authentically French, whether citizen or worker, and not some ersatz, colonial alternative were also fast becoming more ethnically and culturally exclusive.[55] The year 1919 marked a moment of huge significance in the crystallization of racist attitudes in France for another reason: the mass expulsion of factory workers, as well as other unskilled and semiskilled laborers, recruited from the colonies to assist the war effort in metropolitan France.[56] As Tyler Stovall notes, "The vaunted exoticism and fascination with empire of the interwar years arose not just from the colonial presence in wartime France, but also from its abrupt termination once the war was over. . . . In sending imperial subjects back home, the French inadvertently gave racial distinctions a new, and permanent, place in the metropole itself." In Stovall's pithy summary, "the very nature of Frenchness was conditioned by race." The inescapable conclusion is that one of the most critical factors in making early twentieth-century minds "colonial" was a sense of "whiteness" that became synonymous with a more exclusive, ethnocentric idea of French national identity in the 1920s and beyond.[57]

It is also worth remembering, however, that French colonial minds did not solely define the limits of social inclusion and exclusion in terms of whiteness. Officials and settlers were often suspicious of colonial fellow travelers, individuals who may have been employed by the colonial state or French commercial enterprises, but who remained either ideologically hostile to, or profoundly disillusioned with, the imperial project. The colonies, after all, were sometimes a refuge for the escapee, the outsider, or the felon, let alone the adventurer or the dissident. From 1895 onward in French West Africa, for example, police surveillance of white Europeans was sometimes as rigorous as that of African colonial subjects. Indeed, transgression of acceptable norms of European behavior, whether culturally or politically, carried with it the threat of expulsion, incarceration, or even, in extreme cases, more violent criminal punishment.[58] Nor were settler communities homogeneous. Ethnic tensions, particularly among the various Latin communities of French North Africa, were by the 1920s intensifying amid the ideological frictions spilling over from southern Europe. Here, too, suspicion, stereotyping, even sedition, infected European colonial minds.[59]

The accumulated experiences of the 1930s Depression, the upheavals of defeat, regime changes, and "liberation" in World War II, and the proliferation of anticolonial violence as pressure for national independence gathered momentum after 1945 inevitably swayed colonialist outlooks. But neither local disorder nor extraneous factors proved sufficient to decolonize colonial minds to the extent that peaceful transitions from empire to nation-state became possible in French Africa or Southeast Asia.[60] Rather, the violence of colonialism entered its last and bloodiest phase. In a quantum leap from the protests and containable rebellions of the pre-1939 period, wars of decolonization and unprecedented violence gripped Indochina, Madagascar, and French North Africa. Cumulatively, these conflicts spanned generations. Their immediate origins were evident in the disputed colonial heritage of World War II, in arguments over precisely who or what would resume the levers of power throughout the empire and with what longer-term objectives. Their final acts were part of the supposedly postcolonial international order of the 1960s. In many cases, sites of colonial violence would morph into sites of internationalized conflict as Cold War pressures, regional rivalries, and contested political successions provoked renewed struggles for power in which the French found themselves largely observers.[61]

Violence, then, was as intrinsic to imperial decline as it was to imperial expansion. But was it merely the unprecedented breadth and scale of decolonization's violence that marked it out as different from its prewar antecedents? Or are the patterns of collective violence in French colonies after 1945 much the same as before? At the geopolitical level, new elements might be sought in the intrusion of Cold War rivalry and the growing part played by foreign proxies that arose from it.[62] The consolidation of stronger organized nationalist groups and the fundamental changes promised by Fourth Republic reformism each altered the terrain on which contested colonial politics were fought. Deeper socioeconomic changes also made empire something of a powder keg in the postwar world. Industrial concentration and attendant labor disputes, urbanization and heightened demographic pressure, plus the reconfiguration of trade between the colonial world, France, and the capitalist West: all presented harder challenges to colonial authorities.[63] Rapidly changing cultural expectations in the colonies and in France about permissible interventionism and permissible levels of violence—about what colonial administrations could or should be doing—added to the weight on official minds.[64] Also striking after 1945 were the growing regional imbalances within French colonial violence, between what became war zones—in Southeast Asia, Madagascar, and North Africa—and wide swathes of territory, principally in West and Equatorial Africa and the island territories, where organized political violence remained rare. The settler presence, proximity to Cold War front lines, the amount of French capital—human and commercial—at stake: each played a role in such variation. But none is sufficient to explain it outright. In those regions where colonial impasse prevailed, oppositional violence and counter-violence gained intensity meanwhile. The result was to warp colonialist attitudes into grotesque self-parody. For some, most infamously in the upper reaches of the colonial military, erstwhile imperial ideals of sacrifice, public service, and cultural transmission became twisted into a last-ditch defense of the colonial presence, seemingly at any price. Exploring diehard colonial minds in the age of decolonization resolves itself into a disturbing exploration of how political circumstances, cultural misreading, authoritarian impulses, and closed organizational cultures give rise to extreme violence.[65]

Chapter Content: Volume 2

The first of this volume's two sections is focused on "cultures of violence in the French Empire." The Algerian colonial experience is writ large here, as it is throughout the volume, and it is to France's premier African colony that we turn in William Gallois's essay, the first of the six essays in this section. His is a careful reconsideration of changing depictions of the French Army's bloody work of Algerian conquest from the 1830s to the 1850s. Creeping southward colonization, first into the fertile lands beyond the coast, then toward the Sahara's northern reaches, was never the "peaceful penetration" initially promised by its advocates. Punitive raids or *razzias*, collective punishments, even the slaughter of entire town populations and quiet toleration of slavery, all would mark out the Algerian conquest for decades ahead.[66] Gallois suggests that this process, through which mass violence entered the normative practice of Algerian colonial rule, gave rise to multiple French "mental maps," each with distinctive perspectives on whether and how the conquest should proceed. Far from being united and supportive, French political opinion emerges as diffuse and dissentient in Gallois's account. Thus, the policy of settler colonization adopted in the late 1830s stirred powerful, Enlightenment-inspired intellectual opposition, which drew on the anti-imperialism of writers such as Montesquieu. Division was also apparent between French liberals, who were quick to identify the colonial army with the suppression of domestic liberal dissent, and a broader popular culture, exemplified by pamphlets, pictures, cartoons, and songs, which venerated the Armée d'Afrique as a colonial reincarnation of Napoleon's *grand armée*.

Gallois then turns to consideration of this army, its leadership, and its recourse to increasingly brutal forms of violence and collective punishment. Forever identified with General Thomas Bugeaud, the infamous methods used to terrorize Algeria's population hinged on the *razzia*—the destructive raid in which civilians were terrorized, their property burned, their livestock killed, and their crops seized or destroyed. Devised as a form of deterrence, this strategy also deliberately blurred the line between civilian and combatant, the noncommittal and the insurgent.[67] Sexual violence was also part of the repertoire of French terror, holding a mirror to the darkest reaches of colonial minds as military commanders essentialized the Algerian population as an undifferentiated enemy against which violent acts of whatever sort were justified as, at once, instrumental in hastening subjugation and outside the realms of warfare between "civilized" cultures. The brutality of the conquest also became inscribed on the minds of its perpetrators in other ways. Gallois describes how officers' writings and reflections on their participation in massacre returned time and again to metaphors of madness and of a dystopian universe made real in Algeria. Thus, the leading colonial minds of the Armée d'Afrique increasingly cast themselves as victims, not instigators, of the violence and societal breakdown they described.

Metaphorical madness is meshed with actual evidence of mental disorder in Bertrand Taithe's searing analysis of the Voulet-Chanoine Affair, one of the ghastliest and bloodiest episodes of colonial conquest run riot in black Africa. The "affair" achieved notoriety in 1890s France, not because of the horrendous levels of violence perpetrated against the affected population of Upper Nigeria by a roving French military column, but because two of the junior officers in charge of this expedition murdered their French commanding officer before wreaking still more widespread havoc. Taithe shows that much may be learned about French colonial minds from the three themes that dominated French popular representation and political discussion of the Voulet-Chanoine Affair.

First, as mentioned above, a military expedition gone disastrously wrong only became a political scandal because of the murder of one officer by two others who were apparently driven to insanity by their personal encounters with colonialism. Linked to this, the second theme was a propensity to employ psychological and psychiatric explanations to explain the course of events. This Taithe identifies as a tendency to pathologize the French colonial mind, something that, as we have seen, would recur until the closing events of decolonization. Behind this lay a deeper assumption: namely, that the unfamiliarity of African colonial environs had an inherent capacity to derange European minds.[68] The third theme was also perhaps the most telling. For all its savagery and casual violence, the story of the Voulet-Chanoine column's gory progress across the African interior still lies *within* the spectrum of colonial conquest violence, albeit at the extreme end of that spectrum. In other words, this descent into the heart of darkness was not all that exceptional, its Conradian horror notwithstanding. Only the murder of a French officer by others made it so. Taithe's vivid and shocking account of the Voulet-Chanoine expedition reminds us that colonial conquest could be the very antithesis of the selfless heroism in the face of horrific local violence portrayed in the popular press of the day.

Routine violence, admittedly of less severity, also lies at the heart of Michael Vann's discussion of daily life in the settler districts of colonial Hanoi. As Vann describes it, French settlement in Hanoi was born in violence, nurtured in violence, and died in violence. Even where actual assaults did not occur, the threat of native attacks was omnipresent in Europeans' lives.[69] This is what Milton Osborne called the "background anxiety" of settler existence.[70] Vann concedes, however, that the paucity of available statistics impedes precise sociological analysis of the quality and quantity of European brutality, making any assessment of the random and daily acts of violence impressionistic. The picture that emerges is of corporal punishment as utterly routine, alongside racial intolerance and arbitrary violence against a Vietnamese workforce. None of this had much legal repercussion, at least for its perpetrators, but all of it served to reaffirm colonial domination.[71] Yet, as Vann makes clear, in French colonial minds Hanoi was supposed to be different. The city was often held up to contemporaries as a "model" colonial capital, whose boulevards, *beaux arts* culture, and refined European taste supposedly made it an island of tranquility amid a sea of rural hardship, piracy, and feuding warlords. The demographic reality belies this image: Hanoi remained at least 90 percent *indigène*, and urban violence within its supposedly tranquil confines was a daily occurrence. The city also contained numerous sites of notorious violent acts whose symbolic importance resonated—albeit in contrasting ways—in the minds of the French, Vietnamese, and Chinese communities. The locations of a spate of café bombings in 1913 or of the attempted poisoning of the city garrison retained their poignancy for Europeans for years to come. So, too, for the Vietnamese did the public execution grounds in which large numbers of the country's early nationalists met their end. The colonial Hanoi that Vann describes was one in which French and Vietnamese colonial minds would always remain completely at odds.

Joshua Cole's expert treatment of the intercommunal violence that erupted in the Algerian city of Constantine in August 1934 also links issues of colonial mind-set with those of urban space. He suggests that "colonial spaces" should be seen as, in some ways, "exceptional spaces" in which violence played a central part.[72] The point is proven by Cole's investigation of the findings of the Algerian government's commission of inquiry into Constantine's 1934 riots. The commission took 126 depositions and reports in the four months to October 1934 in its attempt to attribute responsibility for the killing of twenty-four Jews and four Muslims during the two days of disorder. Far from illuminating the deeper causes of this intercommunal friction, the resultant official report rehearsed a number of stereotypes and clichés regarding Jewish and Muslim character traits and the role of Jews in the local economy, in local politics, and in local culture. This inquest—a devastating example of an official colonial mind at work—articulated a vision of urban space in which *indigènes*, *Israélites*, and settlers only emerged insofar as they conformed to the bureaucratic characterization of a city demarcated into separate *quartiers*, within which particular communities could be expected to behave in certain ways. In this reading of events, the Jews of Constantine were an essentially tribal community within the city and thus, perversely, were responsible for their own persecution.

Cole's argument goes further. He also reinterprets the anti-Semitic violence of August 1934 and, in particular, the prominent role of local Algerian Muslims within it, in light of the complex identity politics of interwar Algeria in which categories of citizen and subject were more highly politicized than ever. Much as local Jews strove to capitalize on their status as citizens of the republic, Muslim community leaders wrestled with the contradictions of constitutional and legal provisions that enfranchised a narrow Muslim elite while still excluding the majority of their co-religionists. Cole's conclusion tells us a good deal about the sometimes dreadful consequences of how colonial minds worked. His chapter illuminates the devastating consequences of the ways in which the French authorities enshrined ethno-religious difference in differential legal rights and limited access to the privileges of citizenship. Appreciating the resentments fired by each of these discriminatory practices is critical in understanding what, superficially at least, has usually been interpreted as an explosion of endemic intercommunal violence—something emotive and visceral rather than highly politicized. Far from it: Constantine's deadly riots in August 1934 demonstrated that colonial constructions of difference—in housing, in law, in citizenship rights—complicated supposedly binary oppositions between European, Jewish, and Muslim populations, making the frictions between them less ethnically or religiously derived and more the product of Algeria's stumbling progress toward mass politics.

Samuel Kalman's chapter retains the focus on interwar Algeria but investigates a different community of colonial minds, those of the pieds-noirs settlers of the immediate prewar years, most notably in Oran, the most settler-dominated city in the colony. In his reassessment of *colon* support for the French ultrarightist movement, the Croix de Feu and its post-1937 incarnation as the Parti Social Français (PSF), Kalman uncovers the specifically colonial factors that underpinned European support for this quasi-fascistic group. His chapter dissects the public discourse of local PSF leaders, their violently anti-Semitic rhetoric in particular, and contextualizes this language of violence by revisiting some of the ultrarightists' most notorious practices. In doing so his essay places the exploitative nature of Algerian intercommunal relations, the de facto segregation in the urban space of Algeria's major cities, as well as rising settler fears of Algerian integral nationalism at the heart of the Croix de Feu/PSF appeal.

As Kalman demonstrates both here and elsewhere, the language of hatred and the political violence it posited were instrumental in extreme rightist action and integral to the collective identity of ultrarightist supporters, especially within the settler *quartiers* of Algeria's major towns. For all their odious invective the ultrarightists in France were significantly less violent than their counterparts in Algeria.[73] For, as Kalman argues, the glorification of violence in the febrile atmosphere of interwar Algeria was also symptomatic of something more, something attributable to distinctly colonial minds. Echoes of the demographic insecurity that nurtured the virulent racism apparent in Algeria's settler culture during the interwar years were, for instance, to be found in the continuing appeal of triumphalist Algerianist writings, typified by the work of Robert Randau, as well as in the persistent use of crude racial stereotypes in the settler press.[74] Kalman picks up these cultural undercurrents and concludes that an underlying anxiety pervaded the minds of those settlers drawn to the ultraright. Despite the virulence of their language and the violence of their activities, a sense of vulnerability about the irresistible force of Algerian Muslim nationalism characterized their outlook. Put simply, behind the extreme right's discourse of colonial domination—racial and political—lay an abiding fear in the settler mind, that of being swamped by the Muslim majority.

A different form of violence in Algeria, this time French-directed, is central to my essay, the last in this first section. It revisits the colossal state retribution meted out in the immediate aftermath of the May 1945 rebellion in the Constantine region of eastern Algeria.[75] Official blindness to the fatal weakness of the colonial state, part rhetoric, part self-deception, is fundamental to an understanding of what followed the initial revolts in and around the towns of Sétif and Guelma. The colonial authorities' refusal to admit either the extent of Algerian loathing for them or the possibility of their overthrow by revolution from below tells us much about the "colonial minds" that directed the officially sanctioned killings over the summer of 1945. The state violence occasioned by the uprising represented far more than a simple restoration of colonial order. Echoing William Gallois's chapter on the early colonial period, I argue that colonial rule created the socioeconomic circumstances in which an essentialized view of undifferentiated *indigènes*, or Muslim Algerians, as inferior, savage, and inherently prone to violence became intrinsic to the actions of security forces and settler vigilantes.

As evidence accumulated of the savagery of the killings and sexual violence in Sétif, Guelma, and, especially, the smaller settlement of Périgotville, so the tendency among an enraged settler community to ascribe collective guilt, to impugn the entire Muslim population as inherently vicious, increased.[76] There are parallels here with the ways in which European colonial populations in other empires chose to read other episodes of collective violence, and, again, Ann Stoler's work is particularly useful. In her analysis of Dutch responses to 1920s outbreaks of worker unrest in Java's plantation belt Stoler discerns a distinct interpretive pattern to colonial readings of dissent: "Here it is not violence per se that justified armed police, intelligence networks, a penal code, and physical force, but violence of a particular sort, stripped of its validity and exposed as the response of irrational and rapacious elements. It had to be shown as something outside rationality: as an unreasonable response according to the canons of Western thought."[77] Security force analyses of the Algerian situation depicted violent indigenous protest in the same way. Intelligence assessment disconnected the practice of violence by colonial subjects from socioeconomic conditions or political grievances, denying its perpetrators any voice by insisting that the killing of Europeans marked an atavistic return to the savagery inherent to Algerian identity.[78] As James McDougall notes, this insistence on inherent Algerian savagery was integral to French colonial thinking and made recourse to violence against colonial subjects seem logically imperative.[79]

In its scale, its severity, and its target selection the French repression let loose on eastern Algeria from May to August 1945 combined all that was worst about colonialism—intercommunal mistrust, socioeconomic discrimination, cultural supremacy, and security force banality toward acts of extreme violence perpetrated against a subject population.[80] My essay suggests that this consensus about the need for overwhelming retributive violence ignored the tangible socioeconomic crisis that was integral to the original outbreaks. By obscuring the very real material hardships occasioned by food shortages and a breakdown in eastern Algeria's foodstuff distribution networks in the latter stages of World War II, the colonial authorities achieved two objectives. First, they absolved themselves of blame for Algerian radicalization. Second, they negated rational explanations for popular participation in attacks on European settlers. As I contend, the Sétif uprising demonstrated the capacity of political parties, religious groups, and Muslim cultural associations to harness popular anger over long-standing economic hardship and cultural marginalization to nationalist political ends, something that the colonial minds of French officialdom in Algiers and Paris were reluctant to concede. Little wonder, then, that after Sétif there was no going back, that colonial and nationalist minds were closed to the possibility of compromise.

Volume 2's second section, "Colonial Minds and Empire Soldiers," also comprises six chapters. Collectively, they focus squarely on questions of attitude, perception, and stereotyping in the characterization and treatment of distinct strata of colonial society, including French colonial troops, Muslim populations, and African women in mixed-race relationships. The prevalence of eugenicist ideas about what was socially, racially, and sexually acceptable and what, in turn, was morally reprehensible is evident within several of the colonial minds analyzed here. So, too, was an awareness that while "acceptability" was relative, its boundaries determined by local circumstance, colonists and officials nonetheless defined their normative standards against certain benchmarks of public behavior that required the preservation of French dignity and prestige at all costs.[81] Predominantly, these were men of influence bound up in the codes of masculinity that Robert Nye has identified as integral to the ethics of French professional elites during the Belle Epoque and afterward.[82] Nowhere more so than in the arena of interracial sex, a subject whose symbolic importance, whether in terms of punitive regulation, boundaries transgressed, or bitter proof of masculine colonial power, makes it central to any consideration of colonial minds.[83] Contrary to what we—with twenty-first-century minds—might consider the worst sexual transgressions, "scandalous" behavior among serving imperial officials signified actions that undermined French colonial standing rather more than activities that might, in hindsight, be considered cruel, criminal, or morally reprehensible.[84] Owen White's chapter touches on all of this section's central themes: colonial minds, bodies, and power relationships. His chapter makes extensive use of diaries and private letters to shed new light on four interracial relationships that took place in different parts of French West Africa during the 1890s and 1900s. The sensitivity of his account challenges us to rethink ideas of colonial iniquity and sexual exploitation by confronting deceptively difficult questions. Were loving relationships between French men and African women either possible or sustainable in a colonial context? Were such unions inherently exploitative? If we know something of the answers in relation to African women, albeit inevitably too little, we know less about the Frenchmen involved, whose intimate thoughts have tended to become lost in sensationalist or recriminatory depictions of interracial colonial sex.[85]

White's examination is of the most personal aspect of the colonial mind, perhaps the most impervious to dispassionate analysis. As he suggests, it is easy to find reference to such relationships, many of them depicted in exoticized, Orientalist language. It remains much harder to establish what such unions meant, especially to the two people involved. At one extreme there were undoubtedly numerous cases of clear sexual exploitation, often implicating those in high authority. To take but one example, Governor-General of French West Africa François Clozel, while on tour in northern Côte d'Ivoire, ordered daily "requisitions" of African women for him and his retinue, something that disgusted anthropologist Maurice Delafosse and others who witnessed it. Martin Klein has also demonstrated that the French Sudan of the 1890s was a colony run by and for the French Army, and a place where local women were often treated as part of the spoils of conquest, as de facto sex slaves.[86] Here the violent and exploitative nature of interracial sex conformed closely to the stereotypical, two-dimensional characterization of white men using powerless black women. Moreover it is apparent that any interracial relationship typically involved the removal of indigenous women or girls from their familiar spaces and local cultural environments to European ones. These new locations and spaces became charged with colonial meaning as a consequence. Nonetheless, in uncovering the more intimate reaches of the French colonial mind, White's essay points the way to a subtler, more multifaceted approach to interracial relationships, and so to the most intimate dimensions of colonial thinking, in the early years of French dominion in West Africa.

J. Kim Munholland's essay revisits a well-known colonial military career, that of Ernest Psichari. Often depicted in heroic terms, Psichari, in the twenty years before he died on the Western Front, followed a distinct, but not unusual, political trajectory. It began with his upbringing in a secular, republican, liberal family and ended in espousal of ardent nationalism and high Catholicism. The path that connected these two contrasting outlooks was his protracted colonial military service. Even as a republican Dreyfusard, Psichari was ardently nationalist, but from a colonial viewpoint he increasingly perceived metropolitan bourgeois society as decadent and spiritually empty. Munholland shows that Psichari was increasingly driven by fear of the power of radical Islam to overturn French imperial achievements. His vision grew more millenarian and racially exclusive as a result. Psichari's remedy to what he articulated as an impending "clash of civilizations" was a more vigorous, Catholic-tinged pursuit of the civilizing mission. As Munholland makes plain, the development of Psichari's colonial mind suggests that we need to rethink the categories of republican, nationalist, imperialist, Left, and Right, rejecting any simplistic antagonism between them.

Joe Lunn's consideration of colonial minds and African military bodies focuses upon the enormous numbers of young West African men conscripted into the French Army to help fight the Great War. At one level the massive recourse to African military manpower was rooted in fears of France's worsening demographic disparity next to Germany. At another level the placement of armed colonial units in the front line was a logical next step for French military thinkers long accustomed, like their British counterparts, to the exploitation of African labor for porterage and colonial campaigning.[87] But as Lunn illustrates, only by considering the assumptions of those army officers in charge of the process can one appreciate the form that this conscription eventually took.[88] As Richard Fogarty, another outstanding scholar of colonial soldiery in World War I, points out, the enforced recruitment of empire troops offers the starkest evidence of the contradictions inherent in a "republican imperialism" that sought to reconcile universalist ideas with the entrenched racial hierarchies of colonialism. By identifying whiteness with authority, maturity, and competence, the French military necessarily invested nonwhiteness with the opposite traits: indiscipline, immaturity, and lesser intellectual capacity.[89] The one quality supposedly left to the empire's "martial races" was their unquestioned capacity to fight. It was from this first principle that the concept of a *force noire* arose. The idea was initially propounded by a small coterie of career officers in the Sudanese units of the colonial army. They drew upon their own observations of West Africa's "warrior races" and their reading of the hierarchies that they claimed to exist between them.[90] Ardent proponents of the prevailing martial race theories of the day, these officers insisted that West Africans would make redoubtable infantry and outstanding assault troops.[91] Crude racism also underpinned their arguments: certain Africans were allegedly attuned to particular military tasks because they were accustomed to being beasts of burden, to endurance. Others were supposedly equipped with "lesser" nervous systems, making them more tolerant of pain and suffering. And according to General Charles Mangin, the foremost architect of the *force noire* scheme, West African soldiery had no conception of scientific progress, a contention repeatedly used to justify differential treatment of colonial troops in Europe. Tracing the development of the *force noire* from initial conception to ultimate deployment, Lunn demonstrates that for many of the 140,000 soldiers involved, the working of the French colonial military mind had devastating consequences.

Where Joe Lunn's essay indicts French military officials for their attitudes and behavior prior to and during World War I, Martin Alexander's contribution does much the same by focusing on the fate of West African troops in the Battle of France during May–June 1940. Alexander notes the relative lack of interest, whether official, historical, or popular, in the actions of colonial troops during this brief but bloody campaign next to their participation in the protracted trench warfare of 1914–18. With the notable exceptions of historians Myron Echenberg, Nancy Lawler, and, more recently, Raffael Scheck, African losses in the summer of 1940 remain little studied.[92] Yet, as Gregory Mann has suggested, the *tirailleurs'* contribution to the defense of France in both world wars did more than anything else to change the ways in which colonial obligation, whether that of rulers to ruled, or of subjects to the mother country, was articulated in twentieth-century France. Indeed, the discourse of colonial sacrifice and reciprocal duties still inflects contemporary thinking about the rights of France's African immigrant communities today.[93] This marks something of an advance on the racist caricatures so convincingly exposed by William Cohen's work on French attitudes to black Africans before the twentieth century, and demonstrates once more the formative influence of wartime experience on French attitudes, both public and private.[94] Martin Alexander's essay builds on this, discerning a peculiarly colonial mixture of officer paternalism and abiding infantilization of African soldiers, with clear echoes of the characterization of colonial troops evident in World War I.[95] Alexander examines the recruitment, training, and eventual deployment of colonial army divisions in the Battle of France, all factors immensely revealing of the persistent tropes that marked out French military thinking about the utility and purpose of colonial soldiers. Alexander shows how little military minds had altered in the twenty years from 1919 to 1939. By focusing on particular units through a series of four detailed—and heart-rending—battle case studies in which colonial infantry found themselves pitched into the battle for France from first encounters to final surrender, Alexander shows that senior military commanders remained in thrall to stereotypes familiar from the earlier Franco-German conflict. Colonial units were, once more, expected to play an assault role to which they were quite unsuited in the face of markedly superior German equipment. In describing the inevitable, tragic outcome, Alexander brings us face to face with the consequences of false assumptions in the French military mind.

The final two essays in this volume investigate lesser-known elements of the violence of Algeria's decolonization. Their perspectives on colonial minds are unusual. The historical and present-day focus on extreme acts of violence perpetrated on colonial or occupied populations perhaps obscures the more pervasive, indeed omnipresent experience of psychological terror and routine acts of lesser violence against civilian populations that were a more or less daily occurrence. Such was certainly the case in late colonial Algeria, the focal point of Neil MacMaster's essay. His is a study both of colonial and anticolonial minds as well as of the victims of the uncompromising thinking among the strategists of the Algerian War. MacMaster argues convincingly that the quotidian terror meted out by both sides was just as central to colonial rule—and to revolutionary movements' efforts to overthrow it—as the more spectacular killings of which more is now being written.[96]

The most salient—and damning—point here is that both sides, the colonial state and its anticolonial opponents, were utterly intolerant of *attentisme*, of civilians who sought, quite understandably, to straddle the political fence. Neither side forgave the noncommittal, making it impossible for civilians to shield themselves from the conflict by avoiding taking sides.[97] This intolerance developed into a full-blown strategy of compliance terrorism.[98] It was particularly effective as practiced through the Front de Libération Nationale's collection of prohibitions—bans on smoking, drinking, fraternization, as well as its ruthless punishment of any cooperation with the colonial state. Focusing on the FLN's smoking ban and efforts made by French military and civil authorities to countermand it, MacMaster provides a revealing point of entry into the social reality of the Algerian War and the mind-sets of those who fought it. His conclusion is clear: we should read the Algerian conflict as more of a civil war than is widely assumed.

Mathilde von Bülow surveys another facet of the Algerian War in the final essay in this closing section. Her chapter examines a particular facet of the internationalization of the conflict by discussing French police and intelligence service monitoring of FLN activists and Algerian immigrant workers in Paris, northeastern France, and West Germany from 1957 to 1962. In its account of arbitrary arrests, expulsions, detentions without trial, and even summary killings, von Bülow's essay describes the working of security service minds driven toward increasingly extreme acts of violence. The catalyst here was the reorganization and relocation to Cologne in West Germany of the FLN's former covert network in mainland France.⁹⁹ Using an array of recently declassified French and West German state documents, the essay traces the blurring of distinctions between terror and counterterror as the fight against the FLN's covert apparatus in Western Europe became more desperate. It also reveals how the violence perpetrated by the French security services escalated beyond the control of politicians, civilian officials, and diplomats. It is a frightening insight into the workings of security service minds as they struggled to counteract the growing successes of the FLN as a revolutionary organization committed to the overthrow of French colonial rule.

Robert Aldrich surveys the issues raised across the two volumes in a reflective conclusion, a chapter in its own right, which discusses how we might usefully understand concepts of a "colonial mind." He examines the long-term shifts in historical approaches to France's troubling colonial past, reminding us in doing so that any academic analysis of colonial minds must acknowledge factors liable to shape the interpretations of those doing the analyzing. Aldrich therefore evaluates the development of a French "national memory" of empire, relating this to changing historical readings of French colonialism. He discusses the phenomenon of "postcolonial forgetting" or the "occultation" of colonial misdoings. Evidence of such forgetting extended beyond France to many of its former colonial territories where a number of single-party states, themselves rooted in erstwhile anticolonial nationalist movements, have been proscriptive and highly selective in their representation of the colonial past.

Matters began to change in the 1980s as interest in problems of collective memory grew dramatically, not least in French scholarship where Annalist and structuralist, often Marxist, approaches to history had, by then, lost their avant garde luster. Yet the colonies remained strangely absent from this process, initially at least.¹⁰⁰ As Aldrich suggests, something akin to a "thirty-year rule" seemed to apply to the study of colonial memory. A certain inverse equation was also at work here: space only opened up for the empire to command public attention as debates over Nazi occupation and Vichy collaboration slowed. Media interest was stirred by the impending thirtieth anniversary of Algerian independence in 1992, but extraneous events in former colonial dependencies were perhaps more significant. New Caledonia's 1980s *évènements* compelled recollection of the Algerian War. So, too, did

Algeria's tragic descent into bloody civil war after the annulment of the Front Islamique du Salut (FIS) electoral triumph in 1991.[101] The trial of Maurice Papon and media reexamination of torture cases in Algeria added momentum to the study of colonial memories and representations of empire in France.[102] It is this increasing memorialization, itself deeply politicized, that leads Aldrich to pose the critical question: who is the proper "guardian," if any, of colonial memory?

It bears emphasis, of course, that the sum total of the essays in both volumes might be dismissed as nothing more than the ruminations of the scholastic postcolonial mind, as the thoughts and ideas of rarefied academics—predominantly white, predominantly "Anglo-Saxon" (to use the French phrase)—attuned to the specialist debates that hold sway in the early twenty-first century and writing in an international climate in which accusations of a revival of Western colonialism, albeit in new guises, are commonplace. This may be true. But the fact that perspectives on empire and colonialism change over time is surely to be applauded. If these essays contribute to that process, they have done their job.

Notes

1. Alan K. Henrikson, "The Geographical 'Mental Maps' of American Foreign Policy Makers," *International Political Science Review* 1:4 (1980), 496–530; Henrikson, "Mental Maps," in *Explaining the History of American Foreign Relations*, ed. Michael J. Hogan and Thomas G. Paterson (Cambridge: Cambridge University Press, 1991).

2. Thomas W. Smith, *History and International Relations*, Routledge Advances in International Relations and Politics, vol. 9 (London: Routledge, 1999), 188; Philip E. Tetlock, "Theory-Driven Reasoning about Plausible Pasts and Probable Futures in World Politics: Are We Prisoners of Our Preconceptions?" *American Journal of Political Science* 43:2 (1999), 338; Richard Heuer, *The Psychology of Intelligence Analysis* (Washington DC: Center for Study of Intelligence, CIA, 1999); all cited in Milo Jones, "History in Foreign Affairs, 1965–2000," BSIS *Journal of International Studies* 1 (2004), 36–40. See also Yaacov Y. I. Vertzberger, *The World in Their Minds: Information Processing, Cognition and Perception in Foreign Policy Decisionmaking* (Stanford CA: Stanford University Press, 1990). The latest work to integrate all three approaches is Stephen Casey and Jonathan Wright, eds., *Mental Maps of the World War Era* (Basingstoke UK: Palgrave Macmillan, 2008).

Introduction

3. For consideration of this phenomenon at the extreme, violent end of this spectrum of behavior, see Kathleen E. Taylor, "Intergroup atrocities in war: a neuroscientific perspective," in *Medicine, Conflict and Survival* 22 (2006), 230–44.

4. Edgar Schein, *Organizational Culture and Leadership*, 2nd ed. (San Francisco: Jossey-Bass, 1992), 36; for parallels with lack of doctrinal innovation in the interwar French Army, see Barry Posen, *The Sources of Military Doctrine: France, Britain, and Germany between the World Wars* (Ithaca NY: Cornell University Press, 1984).

5. Johannes Fabian, *Out of Our Minds: Reason and Madness in the Exploration of Central Africa* (Berkeley: University of California Press, 2000); Nicola J. Cooper, *France in Indochina: Colonial Encounters* (Oxford: Berg, 2001).

6. Jock McCulloch, *Psychiatry and the "African Colonial Mind"* (Cambridge: Cambridge University Press, 1995); Jonathan Sadowsky, *Imperial Bedlam: Institutions of Madness in Colonial South-West Nigeria* (Berkeley: University of California Press, 1999); Lynette Jackson, *Surfacing Up: Psychiatry and Social Order in Colonial Zimbabwe, 1908–1968* (Ithaca NY: Cornell University Press, 2005); Richard C. Keller, *Colonial Madness: Psychiatry in French North Africa* (Chicago: University of Chicago Press, 2007).

7. Ann Laura Stoler, "Imperial Debris: Reflections on Ruins and Ruination," *Cultural Anthropology* 23:2 (2008), 193. I am very grateful to Ann Stoler for sharing with me her insights regarding forms, practices, and legacies of colonial coercion.

8. Benjamin Claude Brower, *A Desert Named Peace: The Violence of France's Empire in the Algerian Sahara, 1844–1902* (New York: Columbia University Press, 2009), part 1; Marnia Lazreg, *Torture and the Twilight of Empire: From Algiers to Baghdad* (Princeton NJ: Princeton University Press, 2008), especially chapter 7, "Conscience, Imperial Identity, and Torture," and chapter 10, "Moralizing Torture."

9. Brower, *Desert Named Peace*, 6–21.

10. Raphaëlle Branche, "Si tu veux la paix, contrôle la guerre: Les Conventions de Genève dans la guerre d'Algérie," in *L'idée de paix en France et ses représentations au XXe siècle*, ed. Robert Vandenbussche and Alain-René Michel (Lille, France: CRHEN-O, 2001), 385–92.

11. Raphaëlle Branche and Jim House, "Silences on State Violence during the Algerian War of Independence: France and Algeria, 1962–2007," in *Shadows of War: A Social History of Silence in the Twentieth Century*, ed. Efrat ben-Zeev, Ruth Ginio, and Jay Winter (Cambridge: Cambridge University Press, 2010), 115–16.

12. Matthew Connelly, *A Diplomatic Revolution: Algeria's Fight for Independence and the Origins of the Post–Cold War Era* (Oxford: Oxford University Press, 2002), part 3.

13. Two highly polemicized examples covering the nineteenth and twentieth centuries are Olivier Le Cour Grandmaison, *Coloniser, Exterminer: Sur la guerre et l'Etat colonial* (Paris: Fayard, 2005); Yves Benot, *Massacres coloniaux, 1944–1950: La IVe République et la mise au pas des colonies françaises* (Paris: Editions la Découverte, 2005).

14. We await a detailed academic study devoted to Cao Bang, the worst French loss of the Indochina War before the siege of Dien Bien Phu, but we now have an outstanding treatment of Palestro: Raphaëlle Branche, *L'embuscade de Palestro, Algérie 1956* (Paris: Armand Colin, 2010).

15. Herman Lebovics, *Imperialism and the Corruption of Democracies* (Durham NC: Duke University Press, 2006), 14–21.

16. Caroline Ford, "Violence and the Sacred in Nineteenth-Century France," *French Historical Studies* 21:1 (1998), 101–6.

17. For discussions of interwar extremist violence on left and right, see Allen Douglas, "Violence and Fascism: The Case of the Faisceau," *Journal of Contemporary History* 19:4 (1984), 669–87; David Berry, *A History of the French Anarchist Movement, 1917–1945* (London: AK Press, 2002), chapter 7, and Berry, "'Fascism or Revolution!' Anarchism and Antifascism in France, 1933–39," *Contemporary European History* 8:1 (1999), 51–71; Samuel Kalman, "Faisceau Visions of Physical and Moral Transformation and the Cult of Youth in Inter-War France," *European History Quarterly* 33:3 (2003), 343–66; Georges Vidal, "Violence et politique dans la France des années 1930: Le cas de l'autodéfense communiste," *Revue Historique* 308:4 (2008), 901–22.

18. For British Empire examples of this male socialization to colonial violence in practice, see Keith Breckenridge, "The Allure of Violence: Men, Race and Masculinity on the South African Goldmines, 1900–1950," *Journal of Southern African Studies* 24:4 (1998), 669–93, and especially 667–77. But, for another South African case study in which white women played a central role in collective violence in the colonial workplace, see Jeremy Krickler, "Women, Violence, and the Rand Revolt of 1922," *Journal of Southern African Studies* 22:3 (1996), 349–72. As Elizabeth Collingham notes, "British sensitivity to the slightest hint of a challenge to their dignity or authority meant that they frequently met any act which suggested insolence with physical violence." See Collingham, *Imperial Bodies: The Physical Experience of the Raj, 1800–1947* (Oxford, 2001), 142. The most insightful treatment of interracial violence in the British Empire is now Martin J. Wiener, *An Empire*

on Trial: Race, Murder and Justice under British Rule, 1870–1935 (Cambridge: Cambridge University Press, 2009).

19. See, for instance, the literature on forced labor in Francophone black Africa during the early twentieth century, such as Bouboucar Fall, *Le travail forcé en Afrique occidentale française (1900–1946)* (Paris: Karthala, 1993); Dennis D. Cordell and Joel W. Gregory, "Labour Reservoirs and Population: French Colonial Strategies in Koudougou, Upper Volta, 1914 to 1939," *Journal of African History* 23 (1982), 205–24; Richard L. Roberts, *Two Worlds of Cotton: Colonialism and the Regional Economy in the French Soudan, 1800–1946* (Stanford CA: Stanford University Press, 1996); Jean Filipovich, "Destined to Fail: Forced Settlement at the *Office du Niger*, 1926–45," *Journal of African History* 42:2 (2001), 239–60; Ibra Sene, "Colonisation française et main d'oeuvre carcérale au Sénégal: De l'emploi des détenus des camps pénaux sur les chantiers des travaux routiers (1927–1940)," *French Colonial History* 5 (2004), 153–71.

20. Bourdieu's early fieldwork resulted in the publication of his first book, *Sociologie de l'Algérie*, by Presses Universitaires de France in 1958.

21. Peter Jackson, "Pierre Bourdieu," in *Critical Theorists and International Relations*, ed. Nick Vaughan Williams and Jenny Edkins (London: Routledge, 2009), 98.

22. Jackson, "Pierre Bourdieu," 99; see also Jackson, "Pierre Bourdieu, the 'Cultural Turn' and the Practice of International History," *Review of International Studies* 34:1 (2008), 155–81.

23. Van Nguyen-Marshall, *In Search of Moral Authority: The Discourse on Poverty, Poor Relief, and Charity in French Colonial Vietnam* (New York: Peter Lang, 2008), 33–34, 133–34; see also Nguyen-Marshall, "The Moral Economy of Colonialism: Subsistence and Famine Relief in French Indo-China, 1906–1917," *International History Review* 27:2 (2005), 237–58.

24. Martin J. Murray, "'White Gold' or 'White Blood'?: The Rubber Plantations of Colonial Indochina, 1910–40," *Journal of Peasant Studies* 19:3–4 (1992), 42–63; Pierre Brocheux, "Le prolétariat des plantations d'hévéas au Vietnam méridional: Aspects sociaux et politiques (1927–1937)," *Le Mouvement Social* 90:1 (1975), 55–86. For a parallel case in West Africa, see Emily Lynn Osborn, "'Rubber Fever,' Commerce and French Colonial Rule in Upper Guinée, 1890–1913," *Journal of African History* 45:3 (2004), 445–65.

25. Marie-Paule Ha, "From 'Nos Ancêtres les Gaulois' to 'leur Culture Ancestrale': Symbolic Violence and the Politics of Colonial Schooling in Indochina," *French Colonial History* 3 (2003), 101–17; Gail Kelly, "Colonialism, Indigenous Society, and School Practices: French West Africa and Indochina, 1918–1938," in *Education and the Colonial Experience* (New Brunswick:

Transaction Books, 1984), 9–32. See also Fanny Colonna's now classic volume, *Instituteurs algériens 1883–1939* (Paris: Presses de la FNSP, 1975).

26. David Sciulli, "Response to Senechal-Courage and Care in 'Blackian' Social Theory: A Word in Praise of Senechal de la Roche," *Sociological Forum* 11:1 (1996), 130.

27. H. L. Wesseling's *Imperialism and Colonialism: Essays on the History of European Expansion* (Westport CT: Greenwood Press, 1997), chapters 1–2 on colonial wars are useful here. My thanks to the University of Nebraska Press readers for pointing this reference out to me.

28. Regarding multidisciplinary approaches to the relationship between violence and social order, see Stathis N. Kalyvas, Ian Shapiro, and Tarek Masoud, "Introduction: Integrating the Study of Order, Conflict, and Violence," in *Order, Conflict, and Violence*, ed. Kalyvas, Shapiro, and Masoud (Cambridge: Cambridge University Press, 2008), 1–3, 10–12.

29. Charles Tilly, "Repression, Mobilization, and Explanation," in *Repression and Mobilization*, ed. Christian Davenport, Hank Johnston, and Carol Mueller (Minneapolis: University of Minnesota Press, 2005), 211–14.

30. For details of Le Bon's impact in Third Republic France, see Susanna I. Barrows, *Distorting Mirrors: Visions of the Crowd in Late Nineteenth-Century France* (New Haven CT: Yale University Press, 1981); Robert Allen Nye, *The Origins of Crowd Psychology: Gustave Le Bon and the Crisis of Mass Democracy in the Third Republic* (London: Sage, 1975). For expressions of the collective violence as social protest view, see Charles Tilly, Louise Tilly, and Richard Tilly, *The Rebellious Century, 1830–1930* (Cambridge MA: Harvard University Press, 1975).

31. Roberta Senechal de la Roche, "Collective Violence as Social Control," *Sociological Forum* 11:1 (1996), 105–16. Regarding the related concept of "partisanship" as an explanatory tool for collective violence in divided societies, see Senechal de la Roche, "Why Is Collective Violence Collective?" *Sociological Theory* 19:2 (2001), 126–44.

32. Marc Howard Ross, "A Cross-Cultural Theory of Political Conflict and Violence," *Political Psychology* 7:3 (1986), 428–31.

33. Jeff Goodwin, *No Other Way Out. States and Revolutionary Movements, 1945–1991* (Cambridge: Cambridge University Press, 2001), especially chapter 7 on "persistent insurgency."

34. This argument concurs with Kathleen A. Mohoney-Norris, "Political Repression: Threat Perception and Transnational Solidarity Groups," in *Paths to State Repression: Human Rights Violations and Contentious Politics*, ed. Christian Davenport (Oxford: Rowman and Littlefield, 2000), 72.

35. Senechal de la Roche, "Collective Violence as Social Control," 98–99.

36. Albert Memmi, *The Colonizer and the Colonized* (reprint, Boston: Beacon, 1991); originally published in French as *Portrait du colonisé—portrait du colonisateur* with a preface by Jean-Paul Sartre in 1957, the book did not appear in English translation until 1965.

37. Lawrence R. Schehr, "Albert Memmi's Tricultural *Tikkun*: Renewal and Transformation through Writing," *French Forum* 28:3 (2003), 60–61. I am grateful to Ruth Ginio for her advice on this point.

38. The phrasing borrows from Kalyvas, Shapiro, and Masoud, *Order, Conflict, and Violence*, 3.

39. Ann Laura Stoler, "Racial Histories and Their Regimes of Truth," *Political Power and Social Theory* 11 (1997), 181–83.

40. Ricardo Roque, "The Razor's Edge: Portuguese Imperial Vulnerability in Colonial Moxico, Angola," *International Journal of African Historical Studies* 36:1 (2003), 107–9; see also the landmark article by Bruce Berman and John Lonsdale, "Coping with the Contradictions: The Development of the Colonial State, 1895–1914," *Journal of African History* 20:4 (1979), 487–505.

41. Jack Goody, "Establishing Control: Violence along the Black Volta at the Beginning of Colonial Rule," *Cahier d'Études Africaines* 38:150/1 (1998), 227–34.

42. Matthew Hughes, "The Banality of Brutality: British Armed Forces and the Repression of the Arab Revolt in Palestine, 1936–39," *English Historical Review* 124:507 (2009), 314–29.

43. David Killingray, "The 'Rod of Empire': The Debate over Corporal Punishment in the British African Colonial Forces, 1888–1946," *Journal of African History* 35:2 (1994), 201–4.

44. For affirmation that colonial violence was common in other empires and inherent to them, see the following examples drawn from British India: Rana P. Behal, "Power Structure, Discipline, and Labour in Assam Tea Plantations under Colonial Rule," *International Review of Social History* 51 (2006), supplement, 143–72; David Arnold, "Industrial Violence in Colonial India," *Comparative Studies in Society and History* 22:2 (1980), 234–55; Arnold, "The Armed Police and Colonial Rule in South India, 1914–1947," *Modern Asian Studies* 11:1 (1977), 101–25; Subho Basu, "Strikes and 'Communal' Riots in Calcutta in the 1890s: Industrial Workers, Bhadralok Nationalist Leadership and the Colonial State," *Modern Asian Studies* 32:4 (1998), 949–83; Jordanna Bailkin, "The Boot and the Spleen: When Was Murder Possible in British India?" *Comparative Studies of Society and History* 48:2 (2006), 462–94.

45. Karma Nabulsi, "Traditions of Justice in War: The Modern Debate

in Historical Perspective," in *Order, Conflict, and Violence,* ed. Stathis N. Kalyvas, Ian Shapiro, and Tarek Masoud (Cambridge: Cambridge University Press, 2008).

46. Martin Thomas, "France Accused: French North Africa before the United Nations, 1952–1962," *Contemporary European History* 10:1 (2001), 91–121; P. E. Hemming, "Macmillan and the End of the British Empire in Africa," in *Harold Macmillan and Britain's World Role,* ed. Richard Aldous and Sabine Lee (Basingstoke: Palgrave-Macmillan, 1995), 112.

47. Take, for example, the adaptation of paramilitary gendarmerie policing in nineteenth-century France to the French North African territories and the adoption of colonial-style identity checks and restrictions on freedom of movement in mainland immigration control during the interwar years. See, respectively, Clive Emsley, *Gendarmes and the State in Nineteenth-Century Europe* (Oxford: Oxford University Press, 1999; reprint, 2002), especially chapter 7; and Clifford Rosenberg, *Policing Paris: The Origins of Modern Immigration Control between the Wars* (Ithaca NY: Cornell University Press, 2006). Regarding the links between colonial urban planning, social control, and political surveillance, see Janet L. Abu-Lughod, *Rabat: Urban Apartheid in Morocco* (Princeton NJ: Princeton University Press, 1980); David Prochaska, *Making Algeria French: Colonialism in Bône, 1870–1920* (Cambridge: Cambridge University Press, 1990); Gwendolyn Wright, *The Politics of Design in French Colonial Urbanism* (Chicago: University of Chicago Press, 1991); Zeynep Çelik, *Urban Forms and Colonial Confrontations: Algiers under French Rule* (Berkeley: University of California Press, 1997).

48. William Hoisington Jr., "In Search of a Native Elite: Casablanca and French Urban Policy, 1914–24," *Maghreb Review* 12:5–6 (1987), 160–65; Nicola Cooper, "Urban Planning and Architecture in Colonial Indochina," *French Cultural Studies* 11:1 (2000), 75–99.

49. Sophie Leclercq, "Le colonialisme mis à nu: Quand les surréalistes démythifiaient la France coloniale (1919–1962)," *Revue Historique* 310:2 (2008), 315–24; Claude Liauzu, *Histoire de l'anticolonialisme en France du XVie siècle à nos jours* (Paris: Armand Colin, 2007), 138–56, 160–74.

50. Gary Wilder, *The French Imperial Nation-State: Negritude and Colonial Humanism between the Two World Wars* (Chicago: University of Chicago Press, 2005), 126; Alice L. Conklin, "'Democracy' Rediscovered: Civilization through Association in French West Africa (1914–1930)," *Cahiers d'Etudes Africaines* 145:37 (1997), 59–84; Benoît de l'Estoile, "Rationalizing Colonial Domination: Anthropology and Native Policy in French-Ruled Africa," in *Empires, Nations, and Natives: Anthropology and State-Making,* ed. Benoît de l'Estoile, Federico Neiburg, and Lygia Sigaud

(Durham NC: Duke University Press, 2005), 44–47; Byron D. Cannon, "Irreconciliability of Reconciliation: Employment of Algerian Veterans under the *Plan Jonnart*, 1919–1926," 24:1–2 (1999), 42–50.

51. M. P. M. Finch, "*Outre-Mer* and *Métropole*: French Officers' Reflections on the Use of the Tank in the 1920s," *War in History* 15:3 (2008), 303–8; David Killingray, "'A Swift Agent of Government': Air Power in British Colonial Africa, 1916–1939," *Journal of African History* 25:4 (1984), 429–44; Sebastian Balfour, *Deadly Embrace: Morocco and the Road to the Spanish Civil War* (Oxford: Oxford University Press, 2002), chapters 4–5; Michael Paris, "The First Air Wars: North Africa and the Balkans, 1911–13," *Journal of Contemporary History* 26:1 (1991), 97–109.

52. Edward M. Spiers, "The Use of the Dum Dum Bullet in Colonial Warfare," *Journal of Imperial and Commonwealth History* 4:1 (1975), 3–14.

53. Priya Satia, "The Defense of Inhumanity: Air Control and the British Idea of Arabia," *American Historical Review* 111:1 (2006), 26–32, 40; Phillip S. Meilinger, "The Historiography of Airpower: Theory and Doctrine," *Journal of Military History* 64:2 (2000), 471–72; Charles Townshend, "Civilisation and 'Frightfulness': Air Control in the Middle East between the Wars," in *Warfare, Diplomacy and Politics: Essays in Honour of A. J. P. Taylor*, ed. Chris Wrigley (London: Hamish Hamilton, 1986), 142–62.

54. Zara Steiner, "On Writing International History: Chaps, Maps, and Much More," *International Affairs* 73 (1997), 536.

55. Herman Lebovics, *True France: The Wars over Cultural Identity, 1900–1945* (Ithaca NY: Cornell University Press, 1992), xii–xiv; James E. Genova, *Colonial Ambivalence, Cultural Authenticity, and the Limits of Mimicry in French-Ruled West Africa, 1914–1956* (New York: Peter Lang, 2004), 146–68; Mary Dewhurst Lewis, *The Boundaries of the Republic: Migrant Rights and the Limits of Universalism in France, 1918–1940* (Stanford CA: Stanford University Press, 2007), 188–215.

56. Stovall makes equally plain that popular belief in clearer racial differentiation in France also had its wartime antecedents; see his "The Color Line behind the Lines: Racial Violence in France during the First World War," *American Historical Review* 103:3 (1998), 739–69.

57. Tyler Stovall, "National Identity and Shifting Imperial Frontiers: Whiteness and the Exclusion of Colonial Labor after World War I," *Representations* 84 (Autumn 2003), 52–72, quotes at 52–53.

58. See Kathleen Keller, "On the Fringes of the 'Civilizing Mission': 'Suspicious' Frenchmen and Unofficial Discourses of French Colonialism in AOF (1918–1939)," *French Colonial History* 9 (2008), 103–29; and Keller, "Colonial Suspects: Suspicious Persons and Police Surveillance in French West Africa, 1914–1945," PhD diss., Rutgers University, 2007.

59. Ministère des Affaires Etrangères archive (MAE), Paris, Série K: Afrique, sous-série: Défense Nationale, vol. 31, EMA (État-Major d'Armée) 2e Bureau to Sous-direction d'Afrique, "A/S Contre-espionnage en Tunisie," 5 July 1932; Juliette Bessis, *La Méditerranée fasciste: La Tunisie et l'Italie mussolinienne* (reprint, Paris: Karthala, 2000). For Franco-Italian tensions in Tunisia in the pre-1914 period, see Mark I. Choate, "Identity Politics and Political Perception in the European Settlement of Tunisia: The French Colony versus the Italian Colony," *French Colonial History* 8 (2007), 97–109.

60. For detailed analysis of the part played by a reactionary colonial administration in triggering conflict—in this case, the start of the first Indochina War—see Stein Tønnesson, *Vietnam 1946: How the War Began* (Berkeley: University of California Press, 2010).

61. The now-classic study of the internationalization of France's severest colonial conflict is Connelly's *Diplomatic Revolution* (note 12). For the colonial roots of at least some postcolonial violence in Africa, although not in former French territories, see Jeremy M. Weinstein, *Inside Rebellion: The Politics of Insurgent Violence* (Cambridge: Cambridge University Press, 2007).

62. For an unsurpassed global analysis, see Orde Arne Westad, *The Global Cold War: Third World Interventions and the Making of Our Times* (Cambridge: Cambridge University Press).

63. For numerous insights here, see Frederick Cooper, *Colonialism in Question: Theory, Knowledge, History* (Berkeley: University of California Press, 2005), 204–30 *passim*.

64. Gil Merom, *How Democracies Lose Small Wars: State, Society, and the Failures of France in Algeria, Israel in Lebanon, and the United States in Vietnam* (Cambridge: Cambridge University Press, 2003), chapters 7 and 8.

65. Building on George Armstrong Kelly's *Lost Soldiers: The French Army and Empire in Crisis, 1947–1962* (Cambridge MA: Harvard University Press, 1965), Martin Alexander traces this warped military logic and the alienation that underpinned it with forensic clarity in his "Seeking France's 'Lost Soldiers': Reflections on the French Military Crisis in Algeria," in *Crisis and Renewal in France, 1918–1962*, ed. Kenneth Mouré and Martin S. Alexander (Oxford: Berghahn, 2002), 242–59. The definitive study of extreme military violence in the Algerian War is Raphaëlle Branche, *La torture et l'armée pendant la Guerre d'Algérie: 1954–1962* (Paris: Gallimard, 2002). See also Lazreg, *Torture and the Twilight*.

66. Brower, *Desert named Peace*, parts 1–3.

67. In this context, see Cheryl B. Welch, "Colonial Violence and the Rhetoric of Evasion: Tocqueville on Algeria," *Political Theory* 31:2 (2003), 235–64. For a very different interpretation of Tocqueville's views on Algerian

conquest, see Mourad Ali-Khodja, "Tocqueville orientaliste? Jalons pour une reinterpretation de ses écrits politiques et de son engagement en faveur de la colonisation française en Algérie," *French Colonial History* 7:1 (2006), 77–96.

68. See F. Buret and M. A. Legrand, *Les Troupes coloniales: Maladies du soldat aux pays chauds* (Paris: Ballière, 1897); Michael Osborne, *Nature, the Exotic, and the Science of French Colonialism* (Bloomington: Indiana University Press, 1994).

69. This view is also central to a seminal article by Ann Stoler, "Perceptions of Protest: Defining the Dangerous in Colonial Sumatra," *American Ethnologist* 12:4 (1985), 642–58.

70. Milton Osborne, "From Conviction to Anxiety: Reassessing the French Self-Image in Vietnam," Flinders University Asian Studies lecture 7, 1976, 1–27.

71. Vann's argument parallels that of Micheline Lessard regarding the growth of racially derived economic nationalism in northern Vietnam; see her "'Organisons Nous!' Racial Antagonism and Vietnamese Economic Nationalism in the Early Twentieth Century," *French Colonial History* 8:1 (2007), 171–202.

72. In this sense, Cole's argument builds on the pioneering work of Janet Abu-Lughod regarding colonial urban segregation and the "dual city" phenomenon; see, in particular, Abu-Lughod, *Rabat*.

73. See his "*Le Combat par tous les moyens*: Colonial Violence and the Extreme Right in 1930s Oran," *French Historical Studies* 34:1 (2011), 125–53.

74. Peter Dunwoodie, *Writing French Algeria* (Oxford: Clarendon Press, 1998), 148–49; David Prochaska, "History as Literature, Literature as History: Cagayous of Algiers," *American Historical Review* 101:3 (1996), 671–711.

75. My focus here is on issues of political economy and peasant hunger, contrary to much recent work on Sétif, which is principally concerned with the intercommunal tensions behind the violence. This includes the most recent, excellent additions to the literature, Jean-Louis Planche, *Sétif 1945: Histoire d'un massacre annoncé* (Paris: Perrin, 2006) and Jean-Pierre Peyroulou, *Guelma, 1945: Une subversion française dans l'Algérie coloniale* (Paris: Editions la Découverte, 2009). The scale of French repression is still bitterly disputed. Conservative French estimates count between 3,000 and 7,000 victims; Algerian government figures up to 40,000 killed.

76. Jean-Pierre Peyroulou, "La milice, le commissaire, et le témoin: Le récit de la répression de mai 1945 à Guelma," *Bulletin de l'Institut d'Histoire*

du Temps Présent 83 (premier semestre, 2004), 12–19; Marcel Reggui, *Les Massacres de Guelma: Algérie, mai 1945: Une enquête inedite sur la furie des milices colonials* (Paris: Editions La Découverte, 2006).

77. Ann Laura Stoler, *Capitalism and Confrontation in Sumatra's Plantation Belt, 1870–1979* (New Haven CT: Yale University Press, 1985), 48.

78. Similar stereotypes re-emerged in Western readings of civil conflict in 1990s Algeria; see Yacine, "Genealogy of Violence," 23–24.

79. James McDougall, "Savage Wars? Codes of Violence in Algeria, 1830s–1990s," *Third World Quarterly* 26:1 (2005), 120–22.

80. For analysis of collective race killing in another colonial location dominated by acute racial discrimination and postwar economic disruption, see Jeremy Krikler's discussion of collective violence in the 1922 Rand Revolt in South Africa: "The Inner Mechanics of a South African Racial Massacre," *Historical Journal* 42:4 (1999), 1051–75.

81. As Emmanuelle Saada points out, colonial law provided legal frameworks designed to uphold the prestige of the colonial state and the dignity, or standing, of French officials; see Saada, "The Empire of Law: Dignity, Prestige, and the 'Colonial Situation,'" *French Politics, Culture, and Society* 20:2 (2002), 98–120, especially 98–105.

82. Robert Nye, "Medicine and Science as Masculine 'Fields of Honor,'" *Osiris* 12:1 (1997), 60–79.

83. Sexuality and empire remains a burgeoning field of inquiry. Seminal works include Ann Laura Stoler, *Carnal Knowledge and Imperial Power: Race and the Intimate in Colonial Rule* (Berkeley: University of California Press, 2002); Luise White, *The Comforts of Home: Prostitution in Colonial Nairobi*, 2nd ed. (Chicago: University of Chicago Press, 1990); Owen White, *Children of the French Empire: Miscegenation and Colonial Society in French West Africa, 1895–1960* (Oxford: Oxford University Press, 1999); David M. Pomfret, "Raising Eurasia: Race, Class and Age in French and British Colonies," *Comparative Studies in Society and History* 51:2 (2009), 314–43; Robert Aldrich, *Colonialism and Homosexuality* (London: Routledge, 2002); and Christelle Taraud, *La Prostitution coloniale: Algérie, Tunisie, Maroc (1830–1962)* Paris: Payot, 2003); Taraud, "Urbanisme, hygiénisme, et prostitution à Casablanca dans les années 1920," *French Colonial History* 7 (2006), 97–108.

84. See, for example, Erdmute Alber, "Motorization and Colonial Rule: Two Scandals in Dahomey, 1916," *Journal of African Cultural Studies* 15:1 (2002), 79–92.

85. For a useful case study on African women, see Jeremy Rich, "'Une Babylone Noire': Interracial Unions in Colonial Libreville, c. 1860–1914," *French Colonial History* 4 (2003), 145–70.

86. Martin Klein, *Slavery and Colonial Rule in French West Africa* (Cambridge: Cambridge University Press, 1998), chapter 5.

87. David Killingray, "Labour Exploitation for Military Campaigns in British Colonial Africa 1870–1945," *Journal of Contemporary History* 24:3 (1989), 483–89.

88. Lunn's focus on the quasi-intellectual roots of martial race theory departs from the bulk of work on French responses to the *tirailleurs*, which concentrates on stereotyping and popular attitude. As examples: Annabelle Melzer, "Spectacles and Sexualities: The *mise en scène* of the *Tirailleur Sénégalais* on the Western Front, 1914–1920*,*" in *Borderlines: Gender and Identities in War and Peace, 1870–1930*, ed. Billie Melman (London: Routledge, 1998), 213–44; Christian Koller, "Race and Gender Stereotypes in the Discussion on Colonial Troops: A Franco-German Comparison, 1914–1923," in *Home/Front: The Military, War and Gender in Twentieth-Century Germany*, ed. Karen Hagemann and Stefanie Schüler-Springorum (Oxford: Berg, 2002), 134–57; Nicole M. Zehfuss, "From Stereotype to Individual: World War I Experiences with *Tirailleurs Sénégalais*," *French Colonial History* 6:1 (2005), 137–58.

89. Richard S. Fogarty, *Race and War in France: Colonial Subjects in the French Army, 1914–1918* (Baltimore: Johns Hopkins University Press, 2008), 130–31, 270–71.

90. Éric Deroo and Antoine Champeaux, *La Force noire, gloire et infortune d'une légende coloniale* (Paris: Tallandier, 2006).

91. Fogarty, *Race and War*, 85–87; Joe Lunn, "'Les Races Guerrières': Racial Preconceptions in the French Military about West African Soldiers during the First World War," *Journal of Contemporary History* 34:4 (1999), 517–36.

92. Myron Echenberg, *Colonial Conscripts: The Tirailleurs Sénégalais in French West Africa, 1857–1960* (Portsmouth NH: Heinemann, 1990); Nancy E. Lawler, *Soldiers of Misfortune: Ivoirien Tirailleurs of World War II* (Athens: Ohio University Press, 1992); Raffael Scheck, *Hitler's African Victims: The German Army Massacres of Black French Soldiers in 1940* (Cambridge: Cambridge University Press, 2006).

93. Gregory Mann, "Immigrants and Arguments in France and West Africa," *Comparative Studies in Society and History* 45:2 (2003), 363–67, 373–74.

94. William B. Cohen, *The French Encounter with Africans: White Responses to Blacks, 1530–1800* (Bloomington: Indiana University Press, 1980), 62–63.

95. Officers' paternalist attitudes to their colonial troops are also discussed in Zehfuss, "From Stereotype to Individual," 140–46.

96. MacMaster's argument here echoes that of James C. Scott, whose conceptualization of forms of peasant resistance to colonial rule stresses quotidian, semiclandestine forms of resistance—what he terms "infrapolitics"—over more blatant actions. See Scott, *Domination and the Arts of Resistance: Hidden Transcripts* (New Haven CT: Yale University Press, 1990), 183–97.

97. Neil MacMaster shows elsewhere how Algerian women, in particular, suffered from such "for or against us" zero-sum logic. See his *Burning the Veil: The Algerian War and the "Emancipation" of Muslim Women, 1954–62* (Manchester: Manchester University Press, 2009), chapters 4–9.

98. The term was popularized by Martha Crenshaw Hutchinson in her book *Revolutionary Terrorism: The FLN in Algeria, 1954–1962* (Stanford CA: Hoover Institution Press, 1978).

99. Details of this relocation were first described in print by one of its key participants: Ali Haroun, *La 7e Wilaya: La Guerre du FLN en France 1954–1962* (Paris: Editions du Seuil, 1986).

100. It has often been noted that with the exception of a single chapter by French historian Charles-Robert Ageron, Pierre Nora's influential multivolume collection on French historical memory neglected the colonial empire. See Ageron, "L'Exposition Coloniale de 1931: Mythe républicain ou mythe impérial?" in *Les lieux de mémoire*, vol. 1: *La République*, ed. Pierre Nora (Paris: Gallimard, 1984). For critiques of this omission, see Daniel J. Sherman, "The Arts and Sciences of Colonialism," *French Historical Studies* 23:4 (2000), 708; Eric Jennings, "Remembering 'Other' Losses: The *Temple du Souvenir Indochinois* of Nogent-sur-Marne," *History and Memory* 15:1 (2003), 7; both cited in Gregory Mann, "Locating Colonial Histories: Between France and West Africa," *American Historical Review* 110:2 (2005), note 15.

101. For discussion of this, see Hugh Roberts, *The Battlefield: Algeria, 1988–2002: Studies in a Broken Polity* (London: Verso, 2003); David L. Schalk, "Of Memories and Monuments: Paris and Algeria, Fréjus and Indochina," *Historical Reflections* 28:2 (2002), 241–53.

102. William B. Cohen, "The Sudden Memory of Torture: The Algerian War in French Discourse, 2000–2001," *French Politics, Culture and Society* 19:3 (2001), 82–94; Raphaëlle Branche, "La mémoire dans tous ses états: Désirs et verities, volontés d'oublis: la torture pendant la guerre d'Algérie," *Cahiers Français* 303 (September 2001), 70–76.

THE FRENCH COLONIAL MIND

VOLUME 2

PART 1

*Cultures of Violence
in the Empire*

1

Dahra and the History of Violence in Early Colonial Algeria

WILLIAM GALLOIS

On 17 June 1845 Colonel Jean Jacques Pélissier directed one of the most notorious atrocities of the early Algerian colony. As part of General Thomas Bugeaud's push to pacify the Kabyle, Pélissier had been assigned the task of subduing the Ouled Riah, but at Dahra he faced a dilemma for the tribe had ensconced themselves in a complex of caves. Such tactics were familiar to Pélissier, for the Kabyles stood little chance of fighting off the French on open ground. Consequently, just as they had done under Ottoman rule, the Ouled Riah had turned to the caves as a last redoubt. The tribe had, however, made a fatal error in their belief that the caves constituted a place of safety, for after a short period of spasmodic fighting and failed negotiations, Pélissier's men threw burning bundles of twigs into the caverns. Twelve hours later, once the flames and smoke had dispersed, Pélissier ordered his men to carefully enter the caves to ascertain whether the Ouled Riah were subdued and in a position to make a pact with the French Army. Six hundred bodies were dragged from the caves, of which fifty to a hundred showed signs of life.

Although news of events at Dahra reached the French press only through a leak from within the Ministry of War, the massacre quickly acquired a scandalous reputation across Europe, where it was seen as representative of the relative inhumanity of French imperialism. The *Belfast News-Letter*, for instance, reported on "the abominable atrocity committed by the French at Dahra, in Algeria, when a mass of miserable human beings, 800 in number, men, women, and children, were deliberately broiled to death. . . . The French have committed many a villainous act in that unhappy colony, but they all sink into insignificance when compared with this black and dastardly deed."[1]

The initial, popular revulsion at Pélissier's actions was, however, countered over a period of time by a series of defenses of the morality of his behavior. The colonel would eventually find himself cast as a form of "modern Hamlet": a man faced with a terrible choice, who had acted selflessly for the greater good. He also found himself described as a heroic exponent of a new style of warfare in the Maghreb, and far from endangering his career, Dahra arguably enhanced Pélissier's prestige, for he became the governor-general of Algeria only three years later.

Pélissier's actions were in fact relatively mundane in the context of the history of the early colony, and the emblematic, almost legendary status of the massacre at Dahra arose largely from press coverage of the affair. Readings of Dahra are nonetheless vital for they tell us much about the culture of violence created by the French Army in Algeria. The severity, specificities, and contours of that culture—and of the colonial minds that created and perpetuated it—remain under-analyzed in current literatures, so this chapter aims to use Dahra as a means of revisiting what became known as the "système Pélissier," looking especially at nineteenth-century accounts of the moral world in which the actions of the French Army were interpreted. Dahra's importance arose partly from its emblematic qualities, but also because once the events became public knowledge, the resulting scandal forced key actors such as Pélissier and Bugeaud to articulate an ethical defense of the new forms of violence used in Algeria.

The "colonial military mind" revealed at Dahra might be seen as a corruption of the ostensibly progressive ideas of empire used to justify the original conquest, ideas that were subsumed within the violence of the conquest and the insistence on total Algerian submission. Was it perhaps the case that the horrific character of war in the conquest of Algeria destabilized colonial minds? While such views can be supported with reference to popular revulsion at the news of Dahra, and the explorations of guilt we find in the writings of those who directed the massacre, it seems more likely that a "colonial military mind" quickly developed that justified any violence perpetrated against Algerians. Such harm was rationalized in two connected observations: that the peoples of Algeria were of a lesser order than Europeans, and that any means could be countenanced to pacify the colony.[2]

The logical connection of these two claims can be found even in the writings of "liberal" theorists of empire, as Jennifer Pitts observes so astutely in the case of Tocqueville.[3] While Tocqueville's view of the Algerian colony shifted from an initial stress on assimilation, through a determined defense of violent submission, to a seemingly more tempered account of the need to contain the excesses of the army, Pitts notes that each of these stances was founded on the idea that the need for national glory superseded any Algerian rights. The blunt reality of this argument was that it was ultimately expressed through violence, for as Tocqueville remarked, "In the interest of France's glory and reputation in Europe, the French must accept the violence and expense necessary to establish a permanent French presence in North Africa."[4]

Hamdan Khodja and the New Culture of Violence in Algeria

One of the main reasons why we might think that a new culture of violence developed in the early colony is that this claim is made by one of our best sources: Hamdan Khodja's *Le Miroir*. This was the only detailed reading of the invasion and occupation written by an Algerian, a notable who had served under the Ottomans and who had initially been willing to work with the French, but who quickly became disillusioned with the character of Algiers' new foreign rulers. This dismay was of a moral character, and his book's title pointed to the great gap that he perceived between the image of the occupation that France presented to itself, to Algerians, and to the world, and the cruel realities of this new colonial society.

Khodja argued that the actions of the conquerors "ran contrary to French principles of liberalism and therefore against the French state itself which, in principle, they symbolized."[5] He asked his readers to acknowledge that the meaning of the early colonial enterprise was to be found more in violence than in the idea of a liberal empire. France's failure to acknowledge this fact arose from an unwillingness to see that the symbolic value of violence lay less in "its immediate effectiveness or its relation to the Algerian past" than in the manner in which it represented "the dawn of a renaissance, the eruption of the future" into the Algerian present. Khodja appreciated that a structuring of human relations took place in the early colony that would create what he called a long-lasting "colonial night."[6] He adjudged that what he saw in the early colony was the permanent reordering of a moral world in which Algerians would be brutally subjugated, and not a brief moment of militarized violence that would precede some more humane future. One reason why he was able to make such claims was his intimate knowledge of Ottoman rule, which allowed him to compare the behavior of Algeria's old and new imperial rulers. While the Ottomans had been "despots," their "iniquity" had extended only as far as the imposition of harsh taxes, unlike the "forced exile, pillage and massacres" that accompanied French "progress."[7]

Khodja identified a new and distinct culture of violence that was centered on the "razzia," a term that arguably was incorporated into the French language more than any other Arabic word. Bugeaud defended the razzia as a strategy from which "we owe all our progress,"[8] but what we learn from Khodja is the novel way in which this local expression was recast by the French. Taking an existing word that referred to raids on cattle and possessions, Bugeaud reimagined the *razzia* as a form of destruction of habitats in which crops, livestock, and people were destroyed. The razzia came to describe a novel form of massacre, yet in a moral sense it rested on the belief that it borrowed from local forms of violence.

Khodja stood as a witness to the exterminatory[9] policies of the French in their appropriation of the idea of the razzia: to "the theatre of horrors" that they had staged in Algiers, to the "shameful massacre" of men, women, and children by Count Bertrand Clauzel's forces at Blida, where breast-feeding children had been sliced apart, and to the more general "yoke of extermination and war crimes." Yet Khodja was able to see beyond such atrocities to observe that the true danger for Algerians lay in the fact that such discrete acts together constituted the formation of a broader policy environment in which "extermination" came to be seen as a natural feature of liberal empire. In fact, Khodja noted, there were but two "solutions" to France's Algerian problem: "to fight to the point of either exterminating, subjugating or exiling Algerians, or the abandonment of the colony."[10]

In stressing this element of choice and the structuring of political possibilities and their human consequences, Khodja displayed a remarkable insight into the way in which an avowedly exterminatory politics came into being. While it was not the case that politicians in France had originally planned that their invasion of Algeria would entail the slaughter of the native population, they maneuvered themselves into a decision-making process whereby extermination moved from being a theoretical possibility, and one policy option among many, to becoming a practical and logical means of resolving "the Algerian problem."[11]

In 1838 the deputy Amédée Desjobert had called for honesty in admitting that France wanted to exterminate Algerians, observing that this was a predictable outcome in colonial situations, and, indeed, that it needed to be acknowledged that an exterminatory "système" had already been established in Algeria.[12] Although the Commission on Africa of that same year rejected extermination as a policy option (primarily on the grounds of cost rather than morality), we are only beginning to understand the annihilatory consequences of French policies in Algeria. Le Cour Grandmaison's work is of critical importance in this regard, while *The Administration of Sickness* describes the "either/or" logic of a colonial humanitarian ethics, which was solely centered on questions of beneficence and maleficence. In this moral system, the French argued that Algerians deserved to be punished if they rejected the goods of French civilization, while violence was instinctively understood as a mode of communication with local peoples.[13] This came in part from a willful misinterpretation of the modes of behavior of local cultures, but it also expressed a strategy on the part of the French to locate an ethical justification for killing as a form of intercultural dialogue.

Taussig, Terror, and the Space of Death

An additional form of contextualization of the violence of Pélissier and of the French across the early colony can be found in the work of Michael Taussig. He identifies a distinct "space of death" in nineteenth-century colonies that was predicated on the production of distinct forms of terror:

> which as well as being a physiological state is also a social fact and a cultural construction whose baroque dimensions allow it to serve

as the mediator *par excellence* of colonial hegemony. The space of death is one of the crucial spaces where Indian, African and white gave birth to this new world.[14]

Taussig provides not only theoretical forms with which we might compare massacres but also a determination to abandon "the standard rational explanations of the culture of terror. . . . For behind the search for profits, the need to control labor, the need to assuage frustration, and so on, lie intricately construed long-standing cultural logics of meaning—structures of feeling—whose basis lies in a symbolic world and not in one of rationalism."[15]

This symbolic world lies absent in existing writing on Algeria, but it would seem apparent that French perceptions of the distinct forms of violence in Algerian culture played a formative role in their development of strategies that aped such practices. That such forms of ritualized violence may have been mythic was unimportant, for in Taussig's schema it was their capacity to induce a sense of terror in Europeans that served as the justificatory basis for forms of behavior that would not have been sanctioned in European theaters of war. At Dahra what we see are the consequences of the "construction of colonial reality" identified by Taussig.

The centuries-old reputation of the Barbary Coast for extreme forms of violence and enslavement provided a moral backdrop for France's construction of a distinct form of "colonial reality" well understood by Khodja. As would be the case at Dahra, French soldiers were obsessed with the idea that their capture would lead to torture, decapitation, and the most horrendous atrocities, and it was in this world of terror that any sense of proportionality or distinction between combatants and civilians was definitively lost in the French Army. The ritualized slaughter of a French sentry might serve as the justification for the defensive massacre of hundreds of villagers. This was fully understandable within the logic of this world of colonial violence, and any sense that isolated attacks on French posts were nothing more than understandable and legitimate forms of resistance to foreign invaders was completely forgotten in the strangeness of this barren and inhospitable environment, in which local languages, climate, culture, mores, and diseases were so poorly understood.

Captain Blanc

Having contextualized Dahra within a broader culture of violence, let us consider the shifting manner in which the massacre was interpreted in the nineteenth century, especially in *Les Grottes du Dahara: Récit historique*, a book written by an anonymous soldier, "Un ancien Capitaine de Zouaves," in 1864. The book was composed from notes taken at the time of the events at Dahra, and its author, a Captain Blanc of the Premier Zouaves, conceived it as a contribution to debates about Pélissier in the year of his death. The book's value derives partly from the fact that the author not only had been at Dahra but had also fought in other campaigns in the Kabyle that preceded and followed it.

Blanc argued that Dahra needed to be compared with earlier French engagements with difficult tribes in the region, for the later standoff with the Ouled Riah was explicitly compared with the army's dealings with the Sbéah in 1843. On that occasion the French commanding officer was Louis-Eugène Cavaignac, who had tired of chasing a headstrong tribe in and around the hills, to the point that he was "determined to finish things with this faithless and pitiless enemy."[16] A wearingly familiar game of hide-and-seek culminated with the Sbéah retreating to a set of caverns, which Cavaignac proceeded to besiege. After a set of abortive negotiations, the Sbéah held a white flag outside the cave, and a Captain Jouvencourt took a group of men to the cave entrance. Cavaignac had warned his compatriot against such a course of action for he knew the Sbéah to be "murderous," as was proven when the French intermediary and his men were shot at close range.[17] An enraged Cavaignac then ordered his men to cut branches from trees, to bundle the branches together, and to light them and throw them into the caves. Blanc then went on to describe the culminating moments of this encounter:

> The smoke entered the caves and soon after we began to hear desperate cries from inside. A small number of Arabs fled, moving around the flames and demanding pardon. Given that the murder of the brave and generous Jouvencourt was all too recent, with the bodies of our comrades lying there before us, the colonel could have been merciless, but he resolved not to fire on these miserable

specimens and ordered that the fires be put out. Those who were in the caves then exited, with the exception of fifty or so who had been asphyxiated, and the colonel offered them the peace they now requested. They offered solemn promises that they would end their brigandage, though we would later see how little their word was worth. (p. 6)

This tale is of great importance in coming to understand Dahra, for it explains how many of the tropes of engagement with Kabyle tribes had already been established before the Ouled Riah fled into their own caverns in 1845. It was already known that these barbarous people had long relied on the caves as a means of avoiding justice, that they would use underhand tricks in order to try to fight off the French, and there was a casual acceptance of the tactic of burning and smoking them out of such redoubts. The killing of fifty of the Sbéah was barely worth mentioning next to the horror of the death of Jouvencourt and his colleagues, while Blanc made it plain that the locals were indeed lucky that Cavaignac had chosen to exercise restraint in not truly punishing them.

In a narratological sense there is something suspicious about the manner in which accounts such as this one so closely mirror events at Dahra, for there was an obvious implication that Pélissier's decision to smoke out the Ouled Riah had just precedents and that extra levels of violence might well be necessary and deserved following the behavior of the Sbéah (Blanc noted that the caves of the Ouled Riah were "similar to those of the Sbéah"; p. 9). In this exemplary moral case, Blanc wrote as though Cavaignac had actually behaved in a rather liberal and humane fashion, as though the bodies of the fifty dead locals (presumably including women and children as well as those who were notionally combatants) did not exist, as indeed they do not appear at all in this passage, in marked contrast to the descriptions of the French corpses.

Blanc then went on to offer further contextualization for events at Dahra, detailing a series of bloody incidents in the region in 1845. These included what Blanc described as "one of those atrocities which we know one must not flaunt before the arabophiles" where two French soldiers were captured by the Kabyles and burned alive in full view of their comrades. "Reprisals were quick to follow", noted Blanc, "for a few days afterwards fifteen or so Arabs fell into our hands and our exasperated men executed them on the spot" (p. 7). The burning of French troops was therefore incontrovertibly beyond the pale, when only months before it had been presented as a banal feature of conflict when Algerians were the victims (p. 9).

In describing events at Dahra, Blanc stressed the limited choices that were open to Pélissier. Given the dangers to the French that were inherent in attacking the fortified caves with their narrow entrances, Blanc claimed that the only real option open to Pélissier had been to lay siege to the caves. This course of action—which Blanc insisted was the path that the French commander had taken—was, however, problematic, for the Ouled Riah were well stocked with food and water, and a long siege might have proven difficult in terms of "the plans of the commander in chief" (p. 9). In other words, Pélissier understood that if he was to achieve the wider set of goals that Bugeaud had assigned him, he had needed to find another means of ending the standoff.

Although somewhat laboring the point, it is significant that in Blanc's text this new option was actually seen merely as a slight variant on the peaceful siege of the caves, for in terms of moral categorization, Blanc was determined to show that Pélissier's actions were driven by prudence. This new choice was in fact a threat put to the Ouled Riah that "they would be burned if they did not accept the conditions they were being offered" (p. 9). Blanc implied that Pélissier menaced the tribe in this way—with accompanying visible preparations of the materials for starting a fire—simply as a negotiating tactic, yet given the well-known predilection of the French Army for using fire as a weapon, this was scarcely credible. The colonel was "exasperated" by the Kabyles who, he insisted, "reveled in the impunity which their caves offered them" and who "responded to the French exhortations with insults and exchanges of fire" (p. 9). This claim that the tribe felt safe in their caves was obviously not true, and it is important to note that an apparently cruel and ignorant foe were already beginning to be blamed for bringing their own deaths upon themselves, as though there was a moral equivalence between exasperating a French officer and burning scores of innocents alive.

It was at this point that the French troops began to burn and smoke people from the caves, and as in many accounts of these events by participants, Blanc used conditional language as a grammatical means of distancing himself from the immorality of an event that he notionally assures us was both moral and humane (for example, "Le nombre de fagots fut augmenté," p. 10). He also claimed that the French troops had been ready to extinguish the flames at the first sign of submission, thus extending the idea that the tribe—and their leaders especially—were at fault. It was in fact these "fanatical" chiefs who then chose to fire on their own people who were attempting to flee from the caves.

Once the fires went out, Blanc was quick to switch to the subject of medicalization and care, claiming that Pélissier "rapidly organized a system to help the hundred and fifty to two hundred survivors, most of whom were returned to life" (p. 10). The miraculous implications here stand in contrast to the ways in which Blanc as a writer tended to occlude the reality of the massacre as a means of evading or sublimating any sense of guilt (Pélissier was to write of the "providential luck" that some survived in the caverns).[18] Blanc admitted that they found the bodies of men, women, and children in the caves, but their deaths were neither mourned nor accorded any kind of emotion or meaning, unlike the much smaller number of survivors whose significance in the story of Dahra was writ large.

Pélissier's own account of the events at Dahra—in a letter to Bugeaud of 22 June 1845—employed many of the rhetorical strategies that we find in Blanc's later work. He, too, stressed his "exasperation" with the tactics of the Ouled Riah, and his evasion of direct language to describe the starting of the fires is still more striking than we find in Blanc, for he remarks, "At three o'clock, fires started all around" (A trois heures, l'incendie commença sur tous les points).[19] Throughout the letter Pélissier was understandably determined to stress the morality of his actions, though he was often blind as to the ways in which his words might be interpreted in a much less sympathetic way than he imagined. For instance, in describing the way in which the tribe fired on some of those who sought to escape the cave, Pélissier stressed "the cruelty of firing on women," seemingly oblivious of the comparison that might be made with the much larger number of women he was at that very point putting to death (p. 180).

It is of broader significance that in his letter to Bugeaud, Pélissier felt not only a need to offer moral justification for what had happened at Dahra but also a sense of being haunted by events there. As he said, "These were the kind of operations which one undertakes when one is forced to do so, but which one prays to God one never needs to undertake again" (p. 190). While Pélissier surely wrote with sincerity, his notion that such events were somehow forced upon him ought to be questioned, and we should remember that Dahra was but one massacre in a long-standing campaign replete with such actions, in which Pélissier had often been and would often be involved. Pélissier could not avoid writing of the "horrible" sights that greeted them in the caves, but this was forcefully undermined by his assertion that the deaths of the tribe were a "terrible lesson which they had brought upon themselves with their obstinacy" (p. 181).

General Thomas Bugeaud

The role that Bugeaud played in events at Dahra is somewhat disputed, but fortunately there exist sets of correspondence between Bugeaud and Minister of War Nicolas Soult on the affair. The chief uncertainty with regard to Bugeaud seemed to be the extent to which his orders to Pélissier had specifically countenanced and imagined the use of an assault of fire and smoke in advance of the event, and precisely when such orders had become public knowledge. General Victor Derrécagaix claimed that it was only in 1850 that Pélissier revealed the existence of a memo from Bugeaud "which covered him completely" (in other words, which specifically ordered an assault of the kind that Pélissier had mounted), while Commandant Grandin and others insisted that Bugeaud quickly took responsibility for the events at Dahra, absolving Pélissier of personal guilt for the massacre.[20]

Many contemporary accounts of Dahra certainly regarded Pélissier's defense that he was following Bugeaud's orders as being of doubtful veracity, but this line of argument seems a futile one, for it was predicated on the humanitarian implication that Dahra was somehow an aberration. It thereby implied that Bugeaud had behaved honorably in defending the actions of his men after the fact, though it should not be thought that the French could have planned such an atrocity. Such a view seems delusional for it was quite clear that events at Dahra were part of a broader, collective *système* theorized by Bugeaud and others, and there seemed little reason for believing that there was anything especially unusual about Pélissier's actions. What were extraordinary in this instance were the debates stirred by the incident in metropolitan France because details of this particular massacre happened to have been leaked.

Bugeaud was, after all, a man who, according to Eugène Bodichon, "strutted around, proud in his role as the exterminator of the Arabs. He was unremitting and wholly committed to burning their harvests, killing their animals, cutting down their trees, driven to use every scourge of war."[21] If anything, it was Pélissier who most closely followed a military code of honor in not implicating his superiors, for on 11 June 1845 Bugeaud had issued an order to Pélissier which read: "If those rogues retreat to their caverns, you should imitate what Cavaignac did to the Sbéahs and smoke them out like foxes."[22]

In his private correspondence with Soult, Bugeaud vigorously defended both Pélissier's actions and the principles of warfare on which they were based, determined that Soult should not be able to make a scapegoat of his colonel or impose restrictions on the conduct of campaigning in the colony. On 25 June, Bugeaud repeated his subordinate's claim that it was the Ouled Riah who had "forced" Pélissier toward "such extremely rigorous action," insisting that his colonel had acted with "all possible moderation and patience" (p. 182). Far from seeming to be on the defensive, Bugeaud impressed upon Soult the fact that "the repercussions of this example would be felt terribly across the mountains and would therefore have a salutary effect," for within a few days all resistance would be quelled in the region of Dahra (p. 182).

Under pressure from newspapers and the Chamber of Deputies, Soult wrote back to Bugeaud demanding more information about events at Dahra and explaining, "Public feeling about the destruction of the Ouled-Riah is running so high that if the new explanations I am asking of you do not offer me the means to calm sentiment towards colonel Pélissier, it may be that I will have to recall the officer to France and to discipline him" (p. 184).

This was not, however, a dispute that Bugeaud was prepared to lose, in part because of the broader principles involved with regard to control of the army in Algeria. On 14 July he forced Soult's hand in declaring that he took "full responsibility for this act" and also offering a more detailed account of what he saw as the morality of the massacre (p. 185). In doing so he offered a series of important clarifications regarding the ethics of the decision-making processes taken at Dahra.

First, there was Bugeaud's account of why simply blockading the Ouled Riah in their hiding place and laying siege to them had been an unrealistic strategy. Given that, as we know, the tribe had taken cattle and provisions in with them, Bugeaud explained that it would have taken much longer than a fortnight to starve them from their quarters, "and Colonel Pélissier did not have two weeks to devote to this operation for he needed to then meet up with Colonel Saint-Arnaud to ensure the submission of the lower Dahra region. Their two columns of troops were to march alongside each other," and "neither of them could therefore have tarried long without harming the progress of the other division" (p. 185). This operational argument was promoted to the colonial public in the *Moniteur Algérien* of 22 July, which contended that "the delay of a blockade would have endangered the success of the operation in which the columns of Saint Arnaud and l'Admirault were equally engaged with that of Pélissier."[23]

Second, in his correspondence with the minister, Bugeaud became increasingly blunt in accounting for the massacre at Dahra, eventually admitting that the Ouled Riah had been killed to set an example and to serve a wider goal. He asked Soult if he truly understood "just how important it was for [colonial] politics and for humanity that the confidence in the safety of the caves for these and other tribes be utterly destroyed."[24] Set against such higher priorities, all that rendered Dahra exceptional was the number of Algerians killed, and Bugeaud reminded Soult that when Cavaignac had killed "only fifty" in 1844, "there had been little fuss" (p. 186). The problem with that assault on the Sbéah was actually that "the effect produced [asphyxiation] had been attributed to the shallow depth of the cavern and locals had not lost their sense that such places offered a means of resisting the French" (p. 187). Again, resorting to conditional language, Bugeaud went on to say that "what was needed was a more powerful example, related to a better known set of caves, in order to destroy a belief that lay at the very heart of all revolts in the past and which had contributed powerfully to this most recent insurrection," for "without the option of the perceived absolute safety of these retreats, many tribes would not have taken part in the recent revolt" (p. 187). In response to Soult's fear that such an incident would intensify the hatred of the Ouled Riah toward the French, Bugeaud reiterated that "more than a hundred cases had taught him that the submission of local tribes was only true and enduring when such tribes had suffered terrible war crimes" (p. 187).

So, if we are to believe Bugeaud's rationalization of events at Dahra, what took place there was significantly worse than had been described in the French press. Where such papers concentrated on the immediate horror of the massacre in the caves, not even they would have gone as far as Bugeaud privately did in justifying the attack on the grounds that it was a premeditated, calculated, and strategic strike against France's enemies. Such events were "cruel" but "indispensible," and they "would in time prove to be as advantageous to those who had been defeated as to their victors" (p. 188). Such sentiments, of course, viewed morality as a self-regulating realm in which the idea that ethics related to dialogue between peoples—in this case the dead, defeated bodies in the caves and their victorious interlocutors—did not occur to Bugeaud, who saw violence as a powerful and instructive mode of conversation with Algerians.

Colonel Jean Jacques Pélissier

Bugeaud was to remark, "There was nothing to add to this letter," reinforcing the impression of his operating in a hermetic moral realm driven by its own logic, and in political terms he was quite right (p. 189). Soult calmed the opposition, once he was sure his own position had not been endangered by the actions of Bugeaud and Pélissier. What Blanc described as "the hatred of a certain party, journalistic rhetoric and the affronted sensibilities of a portion of the bourgeoisie" began to wane.[25] In many ways this in fact served to confirm the unexceptional character of events at Dahra, for this was no Dreyfus affair, but merely a brief scandal related to a fairly typical colonial atrocity. As Edward Behr noted:

> The Army in Algeria quickly learned its lesson: barely two months later, Saint-Arnaud suffocated fifteen hundred Moslems in another

cave, carefully left no survivors to tell the story, and in a confidential message reported to Bugeaud: "No one went into the cave; not a soul . . . but myself." Following Bugeaud's advice, the Government agreed that French newspapers should not have access to "too precise details, evidently easy to justify, but concerning which there is no advantage in informing a European public."[26]

In reading literatures on Dahra after the event what is most striking is the backlash against earlier criticisms of Pélissier's cruelty and the great number of reasons that were essayed in defense of his actions. The very fact that there was such a plethora of explanations is suggestive of a certain desperate anxiety among his supporters to identify what might be perceived to be legitimate explanations for Pélissier's actions, explanations that might, in turn, have assuaged the sense of moral uncertainty surrounding Dahra.

General Derrécagaix, for instance, offered two, wholly different rationalizations of the events. The first was a repetition of Bugeaud's argument that all means can be justly used in war, but the second rationalization was that it had generally not been noticed that "the deaths of the Kabyles in the Dahra caves were essentially caused by an unforeseen accident," which was that the wind had unexpectedly accelerated the fires in the caves, panicking the tribe, who then shot wildly at each other.[27] It would seem hard to find an explanation of disquiet more telling than Derrécagaix's assignation of blame for the massacre to nature rather than man.

For Marshal Canrobert, Pélissier had made only one mistake at Dahra, which was "to have made too much fuss about the incident."[28] Pélissier "had not been able to resist the temptation to adopt a literary tone in his report, with its eloquent, realist descriptions, which had described much too realistically the suffering of the Arabs."[29] Canrobert's remarks also hint at the aforementioned sense of Pélissier being haunted by the massacre, with his need to offer at least some justice to the dead through a memorialization in writing. The literary tone on which Canrobert remarked was, after all, a mode of writing that attended to and explored the specificities of human suffering, as opposed to the prosaic qualities of the official report that baldly enumerated facts and outcomes. Pélissier's openness contrasted with the suppressed descriptive urge that we find in an 1843 letter on extermination from a fellow soldier, Montagnac, who wrote, "If I let my verve for extermination carry me away, I could fill four pages for you on the subject."[30]

Writing in 1860, Pierre Marbaud blamed "fussy and jealous politicians" and those who wished to abandon Algeria for the excoriation of Pélissier, suggesting that the colonel would be better reclaimed as a hero. He was, after all, a man who at Dahra had accomplished "one of those supreme necessities on which often depend the honor and well-being of an army and a country."[31] Marbaud went on to repeat the literary analogy suggested by Canrobert, claiming that Pélissier should have been admired as a kind of modern Hamlet who had had to wrestle with a testing moral conundrum and who had emerged a hero borne down by his own remorse at the tragic choice he had had to make.[32]

There were, additionally, a whole series of other explanations offered up for Pélissier's behavior, which drew on some aspect of life in the colony at that time, but which stretched facts so far that they ought to be considered as forms of conspiracy theory. First, there was the idea, advanced by Grandin, that the press had turned against Bugeaud and Pélissier because of the support they were offering the Jesuits to establish themselves in Algeria.[33] Second, there was Arsène Berteuil's notion that the destruction at the caves had struck at the heart of an Islamist revolt that was centered on Dahra.[34] The interesting generic point about such explanations is that they resort to the idea of the hidden conspiracy in part—from our perspective—because they were unable to offer any kind of rational account of the massacre.

In blaming the vengeful "dandies" of the press Blanc also deployed a literary metaphor, speaking of the "theatrical bombast" of such articles.[35] In an even more extreme fashion than Bugeaud, he focused relentlessly on contrasting the innocence of the French and the guilt of the Algerians for the massacre, expressing a frustration with those who could not see that the "common good" had, in fact, been enhanced by what had taken place there, for the "savage men" who had "treacherously murdered" the "young, brave Jouvencourt as he undertook a humanitarian act," who "had burned soldiers alive" and committed various other atrocities, had now been eliminated (pp. 10–11). The contraditions in Blanc's account were, of course, rife: the loading of blame for all recent atrocities onto one particular tribe, his evasion of the fact that civilians were in the caves as well as those men who had allegedly shot Jouvencourt, his rejection of any sense of proportionality, and his unwillingness to countenance the idea that Algerians could constitute a defending army that might use lethal force. He tellingly remarked, "Can the blood of the brutish Kabyles really be as precious as the blood of French soldiers?" (p. 11).

Blanc concluded, "The terribly cruel acts of the Ouled-Riah were not designed to stir generosity towards them, yet it was clear that Pélissier would never have taken such an extreme course of action if circumstances had not forced him to; circumstances ultimately forced upon us by our enemy themselves" (p. 11), so twenty years after the events at Dahra Algerians were now more clearly blamed for their own demise than had been the case at the time of the massacre. Bugeaud had himself proudly argued that the massacre at Dahra was a planned assault, but as events there became historicized, a more heroic narrative emerged, with even fewer connections to the specificities of the Dahra campaign.

Blanc's memoirs also confirm the unexceptional nature of events at Dahra. The use of fire as a weapon of intimidation and destruction continued unabated, with Blanc boasting that he took part in the burning of twenty-nine villages with Colonel Bourbaki in 1851. He took particular pleasure in recounting the fate of the Béni-Koufi tribe, who, like the Ouled Riah, believed themselves to have "found shelter from our fire in three large villages sited at the base of a narrow ravine," yet the villagers had not imagined that the French would be able to shell them down the ravine, burning them from their villages (pp. 12–13). The cumulative effect of such assaults was that "the Arabs, beaten back by the force of our arms, day by day began to appreciate the gifts of our paternalistic domination" (p. 16). Like most authors, Blanc could not resist this direct linking of brutal violence with humanitarianism. "And if ever wild ideas of insurrection came into their minds, they had only to think of the name of the marshal who now governed over them in Algeria, M. le maréchal Pélissier" (p. 16).

Far from Pélissier suffering in his career after Dahra, the massacre provided a rapid means of ascent for him. He soon became Maréchal

Pélissier, then governor-general of Algeria, from 1848 to 1854, and later the Duc de Malakoff. He raised his own standard as governor-general bearing the message, in Arabic, "Peace to those who submit, the sand for the unsubdued ones." Yet in spite of Blanc's claims about the strategic success of Dahra and subsequent campaigns of terror, there is actually remarkably little evidence that such actions diminished revolts in the Kabyle. It was, in fact, only a few months after events at Dahra that Bou-Maza, the clerical leader who had been the putative target of the French, went back on the attack against the army of Africa.[36]

Given that on their arrival in Algeria the French invaders constantly sought to contrast their own civility with the brutal oppression of Ottoman rule in the Maghreb, it seems apt to return to the history of the tribes of the Kabyle under that earlier empire. What even sources sympathetic to Pélissier and France admit is that groups such as the Ouled Riah had a long history of resisting central government control, of refusing to pay taxes, and of retreating to caves when pursued by their imperial foes. As Derrécagaix wrote, "their Turkish or Arab masters had never dared wholly to constrain them, which had given them a great sense of confidence."[37] It was this sense of confidence in the limits of their masters' behavior that was to be cruelly exposed by the French.

Conclusion

In his memoirs of 1887 General Cluseret wrote of "the système Pélissier which had been inaugurated in the caves at Dahra."[38] While in one sense it was true that Pélissier's actions there systematized a method of pacification that had gone largely unreported before that time, it is important to see that the reason why this "système" had such emblematic qualities was that it was so broadly representative of an eliminationist culture before and after Dahra.

A distinct culture of violence had developed in Algeria in which the occasional realities and the constant fears of fantastic violence perpetrated against French soldiers had generated a "space of terror" in which the results and the morality of France's retributive violence were rendered banal. Interlocking justifications were capable of explaining and justifying all forms of violence up to and including genocide.[39] France massacred because this was a form of conflict appropriate to the locale;

it systematically eliminated tribes in order to send a message to other Algerians; and it saw violence as an inevitable consequence of any Algerian rejection of other modes of dialogue.

We should not underestimate the powerful political and strategic effects of the horrible violence that was written on the bodies of French soldiers who were captured, tortured, and mutilated in this conflict. Such atrocities confirmed the fears of Europeans who for centuries had believed that unique forms of savagery were practiced by the inhabitants of "the Barbary Coast," and the sight of the butchered bodies of fallen comrades understandably created a culture of fear of the kind described by Taussig. Where there must be more historical debate, though, is with regard to the use of this knowledge, for it may have been one thing for ordinary soldiers to massacre and pillage as a form of revenge, but it was quite another for their superiors to channel such behavior into a specific military and political strategy. The interplay between indigenous violence and both uncoordinated and strategic colonial violence in response awaits analysis.

While there are inherent problems in relying on French sources to describe their own culture of violence, we are lucky that we are also able to call on Hamdan Khodja as a guide to the terrible novelty of this culture in the Maghreb. We are also fortunate that French writers were so attendant to exploring the morality of the actions of the army in Africa. This generalized anxiety as to the ethics of French violence is wholly understandable when the brute realities of events such as Dahra are confronted, yet it was also apparent that a moral culture developed that excused and even at times celebrated the fantastic violence perpetrated by the French army.

Both the strangeness and the scale of French violence have been flattened and underestimated in historical literatures, in part because the expectations and tropes of the genre of the history of war often tended to occlude the specific horrors and scope of violence (most especially in the massive body of histories of this conflict written in the nineteenth century, which have gone on to become important sources for subsequent generations of historians). Since it goes without saying that wars and invasions are political events framed around death and brutality, there has seemed little need to ascribe any uniqueness or particularity to the horrors of the Algerian example. In a sense, this critical assumption borrows from the writings of men like Bugeaud and Blanc, who constantly sought to compare the morality of war in Algeria with equally bloody moments from the history of conflict in modern Europe, yet such borrowing easily slides into an elision of the realities of the Algerian situation.

The parallel existence of a distinct culture of violence and an accompanying set of moral justifications in the early colony matters both for our understanding of structures that shaped Algeria into the twentieth century and for the way in which we view the nineteenth-century colony. Should we, for instance, persist with the idea that the "victoire des colons" in 1870 brought with it new levels of brutality toward Algerians, or might we admit that its sublimation of violence into rhetoric and apartheid social structures brought less harm and pain to Algerians than had been perpetrated in the "years of the army"? After all, local populations, which had fallen markedly between 1830 and 1870, began to rise again under the colony's new civilian rulers.

While the moral of the story of Dahra was somewhat confused for French audiences, since so many different justifications were offered for Pélissier's actions, it was surely received in a less ambiguous way by local populations. Unlike the legislative repression of the later colonial period, Dahra and the time of army rule brought organized violence and slaughter to Algerians.

The provision of moral justifications for such brutality was central to the colonial mission, and it was the logic of the "colonial military mind" that imagined and made Algeria. Violence was seen not merely as being a means to an end, but as a powerful form of communication and an end in itself. As Tocqueville commented, "in order for us to colonize to any extent, we must necessarily use not only violent measures, but visibly iniquitous ones."[40] Dahra did not therefore express the worst excesses of French imperialism, but the dominant strategy and ethos of the army in the early history of the Algerian colony.

Notes

1. *Belfast News-Letter*, 29 July 1845.
2. Although undiscussed in this essay, one of the most original and illuminating readings of the events at Dahra comes in the Algerian novelist Assia

Djebar's *L'Amour: La fantasia* (Paris: Albin Michel, 1985). As well as describing the massacre, along with other moments in the modern history of Algeria, the novel explores the capacities of history, literature, and autobiography to understand the self and the national self, most especially the often hidden story of the lives of Algerian women.

3. Alexis de Tocqueville, *Writings on Empire and Slavery*, ed. and intro. Jennifer Pitts (Baltimore: Johns Hopkins University Press, 2000).

4. Tocqueville, *Writings on Empire and Slavery*, xxi.

5. Hamdan Khodja, *Le Miroir: Aperçu historique et statistique sur la Régence d'Alger* (Paris: Sindbad, 1985), 25. All translations are by the author unless otherwise noted.

6. Khodja, *Le Miroir*, 32.

7. Khodja, *Le Miroir*, 214–15.

8. H.-A. L. d'Ideville, *Memoirs of Marshal Bugeaud: From His Private Correspondence and Original Documents, 1784–1849*, 2 vols. (London: Hurst and Blackett, 1884), 92.

9. The terms "exterminatory" and "extermination" have become deeply controversial in French colonial history. In essence, two opposing positions exist: one that insists "extermination" meant something close to the modern idea of the planned mass killing of civilians; the other that contends its true meaning in the nineteenth century was less programmatic and more indicative of "uncivilized" forms of warfare. This controversy centers on the work of Olivier Le Cour Grandmaison, most especially, *Coloniser, Exterminer: Sur la guerre et l'état colonial* (Paris: Fayard, 2005), which argues for the first of these two positions. A good guide to criticisms of Le Cour Grandmaison's work can be found in Emmanuelle Saada, "Coloniser, Exterminer: Sur la guerre et l'état colonial," *Critique internationale* 32:3 (2006), 211–16. Such discussions are additionally complicated in that they also feed into debates taking place in contemporary France with regard to the nature of the colonial legacy and also to more general discussions of the intentionality of planned violence in European empires, as seen in Mike Davis, *Late Victorian Holocausts: El Niño Famines and the Making of the Third World* (London: Verso, 2005). This essay is broadly allied to the positions of Le Cour Grandmaison and Davis in that it alleges that specifically new forms of violence originated in Algeria, but it is important to clarify that the essay is describing a new culture of violence that emerged at a very specific historical moment in a particular place. The article is emphatically not attempting to make connections between this violence and later forms of modern mass killing.

10. Khodja, *Le Miroir*, 38, 155, 211, 27.

11. Jacques L. Kob, *L'Algérie: Un moyen pratique pour faire un pas en*

avant (Paris: Sandoz and Fischbacher, 1880), 3. In fact, the idea that "Algeria" was a problem that needed to be "solved" was a constant theme in French texts from the 1830s to the 1890s.

12. A. Desjobert, *L'Algérie en 1838* (Paris: P. Dufart, 1838), 85–86.

13. Le Cour Grandmaison, *Coloniser, Exterminer*; William Gallois, *The Administration of Sickness: Medicine and Ethics in Colonial Algeria* (London: Palgrave Macmillan, 2008).

14. Michael Taussig, "Culture of Terror—Space of Death: Roger Casement's Putumayo Report and the Explanation of Torture," in *Violence in War and Peace*, ed. Nancy Scheper-Hughes and Philippe Bourgois (Oxford: Blackwell, 2004), 39–53, especially 39–40.

15. Taussig, "Culture of Terror," 41.

16. Un ancien capitaine de Zouaves, *Les Grottes de Dahara: Récit historique* (Paris: M. Blot, 1864), 5. This essay is exclusively concerned with a specific culture of violence in the Algerian colony, but it should of course be noted that when Cavaignac left Algeria, his career continued to be marked by extreme forms of violence as he "pacified" the streets of Paris in the June Rising of 1848. The dialogue between metropolitan massacres (including those of the earlier revolutionary periods) and colonial killing is an important theme in much recent work, including David El Kenz, ed., *Le massacre, objet d'histoire* (Paris: Gallimard, 2005); Bertrand Taithe, "The Red Cross Flag in the Franco-Prussian War: Civilians, Humanitarians and War in the 'Modern Age,'" in *War, Medicine and Modernity*, ed. Roger Cooter, Mark Harrison, and Steve Sturdy (Stroud: Sutton, 1998), 22–47; and Alain Corbin, Jean-Jacques Courtine, and Georges Vigarello, eds., *Histoire du Corps*, 2 vols. (Paris: Éditions du Seuil, 2005), 2:215–73.

17. Capitaine de Zouaves, *Les Grottes de Dahara*, 5–6; subsequent page citations are given in the text.

18. Général Derrécagaix, *Le Maréchal Pélissier, Duc de Malakoff* (Paris: Librairie Militaire R. Chapelot, 1911), 181.

19. Derrécagaix, *Le Maréchal Pélissier*, 180; subsequent page citations are given in the text.

20. Derrécagaix, *Le Maréchal Pélissier*, 192; Commandant Grandin, *Le Maréchal Pélissier, duc de Malakoff* (Abbeville: C. Paillart, 1898), 64.

21. Eugène Bodichon, *Considérations sur l'Algérie* (Paris: Schneider and Legrand, 1845), 35. See also Desjobert, *L'Algérie en 1838*, 56.

22. Derrécagaix, *Le Maréchal Pélissier*, 174; subsequent page citations are given in the text.

23. Julie de Marguerittes, *Italy and the War of 1859* (Philadelphia: George G. Evans, 1859), 130.

24. Derrécagaix, *Le Maréchal Pélissier*, 186; subsequent page citations are given in the text.

25. Un ancien Capitaine, *Les Grottes*, 10.

26. Edward Behr, *The Algerian Problem* (London: Hodder and Stoughton, 1961), 23.

27. Derrécagaix, *Le Maréchal Pélissier*, 183, 189.

28. Derrécagaix, *Le Maréchal Pélissier*, 190.

29. Derrécagaix, *Le Maréchal Pélissier*, 190.

30. Le Cour Grandmaison, *Coloniser, Exterminer*, 117.

31. P. Marbaud, *Coup d'œil sur l'Algérie pendant la crise de 1859–1860 et réflexions sur le décret relatif à la vente des terres domaniales* (Constantine: V. Guende, 1860), 5–7.

32. Marbaud, *Le Maréchal Pélissier*, 6–7.

33. Grandin, *Le Maréchal Pélissier*, 67.

34. Arsène Berteuil, *L'Algérie française: Histoires, mœurs, coutûmes, industrie, agriculture* (Paris: E. Dentu, 1856), 297.

35. Un ancien Capitaine, *Les Grottes*, 10; subsequent page citations are given in the text.

36. Derrécagaix, *Le Maréchal Pélissier*, 194–95.

37. Derrécagaix, *Le Maréchal Pélissier*, 174.

38. G. Cluseret, *Mémoires du général Cluseret* (Paris: Lévy, 1887), 196.

39. The use of the term "genocide" is evidently as problematic as the earlier discussed use of the terms "exterminatory" and "extermination." The literature in this field is considerable, though the particular use of the term in this essay draws from one very specific, anthropological strand of such discussions. In contradistinction to Bauman's claim that genocide was a product of European modernity, many anthropologists have sought to describe specific forms of earlier mass killing that they argue merit such description. Scheper-Hughes, for instance, has argued for the existence of a "genocide continuum" that included "small wars and invisible genocides" in the past, while Kuper has claimed that the "genocidal massacre" formed a specific subset of this continuum, and that this was especially evident in the French invasion of Algeria: Nancy Scheper-Hughes, "Coming to Our Senses: Anthropology and Genocide," in *Annihilating Difference: The Anthropology of Genocide*, ed. Alexander Laban Hinton (Berkeley: University of California Press, 2002), 348–81; and Leo Kuper, "Genocide: Its Political Use in the Twentieth Century, in *Genocide: An Anthropological Reader*, ed. Alexander Laban Hinton (Oxford: Blackwell, 2002), 48–73.

40. Tocqueville, *Writings on Empire and Slavery*, xxiv.

2

Losing Their Mind and Their Nation?

Mimicry, Scandal, and Colonial Violence in the Voulet-Chanoine Affair

BERTRAND TAITHE

This chapter explores afresh the story of the "infernal *colonne*" led by two French colonial army officers, Voulet and Chanoine, across West Africa in 1898–1899.[1] Accumulating some eight hundred slaves along their way, this roving column behaved increasingly brutally, revealing much about the forms of violence that marked colonial conquest. Ever since their deaths on 15 and 16 July 1899, respectively, Captains Voulet and Chanoine have left a controversial imprint on colonial memory. If we add to these two names that of their French victim, Colonel Klobb, whom they murdered on 14 July when he attempted to arrest them, one arrives at a complex colonial triptych. Voulet and Chanoine were to be arrested by Klobb to answer for a long trail of devastation that stretched from the outpost of Say, a border town of French colonial Soudan, to the environs of the sultanate of Zinder.[2] Ultimately, both captains were killed by their own soldiers soon after Klobb's murder on 14 July. Their crimes and grizzly fate illustrate contradictions central to republican colonialism at the end of the nineteenth century. As an event the "Voulet-Chanoine Affair," including the crimes committed before 14 July 1899, has variously been portrayed as a *fait-divers*, an incident symptomatic of a complex and menacing pathology of empire, or as a window upon widespread but hidden practices. For the Parisian authorities it was a scandal at a moment when the French army could least afford it.

The scandal arose not only from the mutiny of French officers against their superiors but also from how these men allegedly justified their acts. Hours after killing Colonel Klobb, Paul Voulet reportedly declared: "I do not regret anything that I have done, I am an outlaw, I renounce my family, my country, I am no longer French, I am a black chieftain. . . . What I have just done is nothing more than a coup. If I were in Paris I would be the master of France." Turning to his second in command, Captain Julien Chanoine, Voulet continued, "as a matter of fact, you were even more compromised than I was. I have read the papers of the Colonel, they were accusing you even more than us all [*nous tous*]." Chanoine then responded in a "failing yet cavernous voice": "I am going to the bush, I am following you, long live freedom! [Moi je prends la brousse, je te suis, vive la liberté!]"[3]

Written by Joalland, then lieutenant of artillery and fourth in command in the Voulet expedition, this central section of the survivors' account has shaped the way the Voulet-Chanoine story has been told ever since. The anecdote was then reported to the two consecutive inquests that took place between 1900 and 1902. Written conveniently by survivors attempting to salvage their honor (although one should note the *nous tous* that is the singular admission that crimes had been more widely shared than is otherwise admitted), it made Voulet and to a lesser extent Chanoine entirely culpable for Klobb's murder. By association, it assigned full responsibility for every other crime to the commanding officers. Conveniently, it also left room for a postdiagnostic of insanity, which the only doctor of the mission, Dr. Henric, never seemed to have noticed prior to the events. Beyond homicide, and at the origin of this internecine killing, the manifestations of this madness were dual: the renunciation of French identity and civilized deportment; and its flip side, the "naturalization" of the war chieftains into native warlords. They had gone native. By a swift rhetorical device, Joalland and every single French writer, commentator, or filmmaker thereafter excised Voulet and Chanoine from the *geste Coloniale*.[4] Their story became an African story framed and told according to African narrative tropes infused with irrationality. Did they not choose to have Griots singing their praise, comparing them to the African king Samori Touré?[5]

African scholars beg to differ from this Conradian analysis. So, too, this chapter considers the Franco-African "affair" in its context of the Dreyfus affair and the various ways in which it has been interpreted before concluding with an alternative postcolonial reading of the events that takes into account how it has been remembered by Africans themselves. Four aspects of this story are examined: First the scandal itself. It highlights the tensions arising from colonial violence in late nineteenth-century France and, in particular, in the work of Paul Vigné d'Octon and Georges Clemenceau.[6] Second I reflect on how this violence unfolded, and third I move on to how it was explained, taking note of how a psychiatric perspective on the colonial mind evolved to cover the acts committed by the mission. Fourth I consider how the narration of this story over time reflects the variable threshold of cruelty associated with the civilizing mission.

The Scandal

The Voulet-Chanoine Affair was protracted and not easy to conceal. The main protagonists were public figures in colonial circles. Voulet had been hailed a modern hero for his conquest of the Mosse and his energetic intervention in the affairs of the Naba speakers of Ouagadougou.[7] He had written authoritative accounts that were published in various periodicals including the *Revue Générale des Sciences Pures et Appliquées*.[8] His profile was that of a scholarly man of action. His subordinate and perennial associate, Julien Chanoine, had been an assiduous correspondent of the Société de Géographie.[9] Chanoine was the son of an influential general who briefly became minister of war in 1898 before he resigned over the Dreyfus affair. He was known largely thanks to his father's political connections, but his own exploits in the Gurunsi region south of Ouagadougou were also well publicized.[10]

The last expedition they led, which was launched using Comité de l'Afrique Française and Ministry of Colonies funds in April 1898, coincided with several other initiatives that taken together became a larger plan for a three-pronged attack on the "kingdom" of Rabah of Burnu (Rabah Zubayr or Rabih Fold Allah), near Lake Chad.[11] The mission had other secret, more ambitious though vaguer aims. Voulet was originally under instruction to push beyond Chad toward the Nile to meet Marchand's roving *colonne* and hopefully create the trans-African colonial landmass dreamed of by Ministers Gabriel Hanotaux and Théophile Delcassé.[12]

By 1898 the principal West African states to the west of Chad were either defeated, in severe decline, or facing takeover. The greatest opponent of France in the region, Samori Touré, was on the run but was captured in 1898. The king of Dahomey had been deposed, the sultanate of Sokoto in what is now northern Nigeria was in decline, and the minor sultanate of Zinder was unlikely to defend itself against a well-armed and disciplined colonial force.[13] The military colony of Soudan, east of Senegal and north of Dahomey, stood at the pre-Saharan frontier of France's growing West African Empire. Traversing the Sahara, the Lamy and Foureau mission was due to meet Voulet and Chanoine in the city of Zinder.[14] From Zinder they would march against Rabah, linking up with yet another mission coming from French Congo.

Yet, less than a year after the finances for the Voulet-Chanoine mission were secured, a Paris government telegram to Dakar requested the governor-general to send someone to investigate the mission's high-profile leaders, placing them under arrest if need be. The man sent after Voulet was the commander of Timbuktu, Lieutenant-Colonel Klobb. Departing a full eight months after Voulet, his small and mobile unit nevertheless managed to catch up with Voulet in what would prove a fatal encounter on 14 July 1899. Klobb, as we have seen, was murdered by Voulet, who, allegedly at least, proclaimed himself an African chieftain, as did his associate Chanoine. Both men would soon discover how fragile self-appointed monarchies tend to be. Their Senegalese soldiers, by then in open revolt, shot Chanoine a day later. When Voulet returned to camp in the early hours of the following morning, he too was killed by a sentry. Subordinate officers Pallier and Joalland then assumed command of the mission with the support of their African noncommissioned officers.[15] As a reward for these troops, the new mission leaders led their force to Zinder to pillage the city. The French then deposed and executed the sultan of Zinder in conformity with Voulet's instructions before splitting into three forces: a large column composed of irregulars, rebellious soldiers, and a substantial group of women and children walking back to French Soudan; a small garrison awaiting the Foureau-Lamy expedition; and a fast-moving and relatively small unit led by the second-in-command, Captain Joalland, and Klobb's assistant, Lieutenant Meynier. This smaller unit advanced toward Lake Chad following the spirit if not the letter of the original instructions given to Voulet.

What had gone wrong, and how did the Voulet expedition become scandalous? First of all, the Parisian political context is central. This mission, directed and financed from Paris, was linked to the political climate of the Fashoda climbdown and the last throes of the Dreyfus affair.[16] There were many who doubted the reliability of the army in the republican polity. Their fears were compounded by the hyper-nationalistic welcome given to returning Commandant Marchand. For some on the far right, Marchand represented a model leader for France who might inherit the populist support of General Boulanger. In Marchand the anti-republicans saw a providential man apt to seize power from the corrupt republic. Voulet and Chanoine seemed to be made of the same stuff. Far from being lost in Africa, the mission leaders were in regular correspondence with Paris, using a secret code specific to them to send telegrams direct to the minister of colonies and to the pro-colonial press. This tenuous linkage was maintained until the *colonne* reached the borders of French Soudan, then set precariously at Say.

The mission was extremely large by West African standards. It had a cavalry of irregular Hausas, which, with the addition of captives, seems to have grown in size as it proceeded. It had a field gun with smokeless shells and rapid-fire weapons. Walking in the middle of the long procession of porters was an entire herd of animals, which served as load carriers and as a meat reserve. Beyond the tirailleur units recruited in Bambara and Mosse territory, the so-called *races guerrières* of Soudan described by Joe Lunn, one finds what Joalland described as the "impedimenta": the women and children in tow who met the domestic requirements of a West African force on the march.[17] By the time that the force reached Zinder, this part of the mission had grown to about eight hundred women and children, most of them captives. Revealingly Voulet referred to this segment of the mission as his "horde." All in all, about eighteen hundred men and women marched under the French flag, but regular soldiers made up only a small fraction.

The number of load carriers, fixed at about eight hundred by Chanoine at the end of his muscular recruitment drive in Mosse territory was, in fact, never static. A high mortality rate, which reached nearly 20 percent at the outset, combined with desertions and executions, depleted the ranks. New captives were constantly brought in to plug the gaps. Such a large column also exacted terrible demands on the land it traversed. Voulet estimated the mission's daily water needs at forty tons. Satisfying this most basic requirement in the Sahel presented a major challenge. Following its original guidance the mission soon found out that it could not reconnoiter the official June 1898 borders established between French and British colonial territory. This artificial borderline had drawn a neat semicircle north of Sokoto, but this left the French without sufficient water supplies.[18] Voulet decided, as a result, to limit his communications with Paris and contravene his written orders by crossing into the north of British-claimed Sokoto territory following the itineraries of earlier French travelers, Cazemajou and, in part, Parfait-Louis Monteil.[19] Going south before going east, Voulet's mission met increasing resistance after traversing the Soudan-Dahomey border. This was partly a result of the constant politico-military tension in this notoriously unstable region, which since the late fifteenth century and the collapse of the Songhai imperium had never experienced a hegemonic power and was exhausted by constant wars.[20] But the further the mission went east the more the mission faced the consequences of repeated droughts, which ravaged the whole West African continental landmass in the 1890s.

The Road to Atrocity

The list of Voulet and Chanoine's crimes began in earnest in Sansané Haoussa, a small village on the Niger. It was here that the *colonne* reunited when the group that had sailed down the river met with the porters recruited (often violently) by Chanoine in the Mosse region. Reaching this village was something of an achievement since the river had never been navigated by such a large expedition. In Sansané Voulet and Chanoine massacred a number of women and children, all of them slaves. The alleged uncooperativeness of the villagers was cited as explanation for these killings. Similar massacres were perpetrated after the forcible seizure of any fortified Tata (fortress) or following any resistance. Voulet and Chanoine have left a number of texts that reveal how their colonial minds justified such cold-blooded killing. Chanoine placed their mission in the context of an African and Muslim political system based on fear and duplicity:

> We, the civilized, in our immense pride, believe all the blacks prostrated before us in deep admiration and we think that they take us for gods or supernatural beings; that's what comes from the stories of travelers who have not travelled much and who tell lies or who have not seen or understood or who think that they will seem more interesting if they write that they were taken for gods or wizards. Hence all these sentimental theories which go so well with the government's miserly policies and which make so many of our enterprises fail from lack of weapons and ammunitions.
>
> In reality, most blacks are not much impressed by our science, it is God's will; but what they are surprised by is our immense naivety and our imperturbable trust in their lies ... this great parenthesis brings me to my conclusion: when one fools the chief one despises him, in Muslim land submission is made of fear; one does not fear those one despises and as one hates the master, the cursed Christian, one is always near revolt, whether openly or not.[21]

According to this logic fear would build respect and respect loyalty.

Voulet agreed. The reports he filed from January to April 1899 repeatedly referred to the need to rule without fear of opposition, stating even that "the locals are only just beginning to take us seriously."[22] Both officers sought to earn admiration and prestige through a mixture of fear and rewards intended to secure devotion and loyalty.[23] This accorded with French respect for the immense dedication of the soldiers of the Muslim kingdoms they had defeated. El-Hajj Umar Tall and Samori were widely seen as bloodthirsty brutes whose soldiers were willing to die for them nonetheless. Voulet and Chanoine's perspective on colonial war was the direct continuation of Bugeaud's and Faidherbe's guidelines on expeditionary *colonnes* and a strategy adapted to local warfare.[24] They had not gone native; rather, they were applying to the letter a philosophy of colonial war based on mimicry of local warfare and adaptation to local conditions. Chanoine, who has left the most extensive documents on the matter, was like many others in French Soudan and saw no harm in aping their former enemies.

Added to this philosophy were the constraints of limited means and urgent political imperatives. Furthermore, Voulet and Chanoine were adapting their practices to the rhetorical moral constraints of their age. Voulet thus insisted that a humanitarian war had to be short and brutal in order to impose a durable peace and cooperation at minimal cost. The high levels and methods of conquest violence were designed to shock. In a sense Voulet exemplified what Foucault described as the embodiment of sovereign power when he chose to exhibit bodies on trees, heads on sticks, or piles of corpses half-eaten by wild animals left at the entrance of the abandoned villages.[25] Village burnings, which according to Voulet and Chanoine's diaries were often accidental in the early days, became systematic and were used as beacons by the commanders of the various parts of the mission (it had become so large that it was in effect split into three to four sections).

Moreover, some of the column's soldiers had previously served with Samori. Voulet and Chanoine assumed that these men could relate to empire building, raids, and extreme violence. Through bloody example, power could be displayed brutally but infrequently. Since neither man believed in the innate qualities of their African subjects, they understood African politics as being of a primitive monarchical type. Within this economy of violence Voulet and Chanoine sought to compete with the loyalty and respect granted to their enemies, local chieftains, and Tuaregs:

> The black population will never become ours until they are certain they have been freed forever from their savage oppressors. This deliverance can only come from the power of our weapons. A fighting spirit [esprit de lutte] is no longer in their soul, which has been shaped to accept all tyrannies. Never will the Songhai emerge by themselves from the most servile submission to combat their masters (the Tuaregs).[26]

These lines, written by Chanoine as he was crossing the Mosse territory on his way to Say in late 1898, articulated two central concerns shared by many officers in Soudan: French methods of war had to be decisive to win over the local people, and African subjects had to be coerced brutally into supporting the French so that their eventual moral renewal would follow from utter subjection.[27] Pallier's report, endorsed by all the members of the mission in August 1899, associated Voulet and Chanoine's methods closely:

> A number of women and children were massacred on his [Voulet's] order [in Birnin Konni] but, except for Chanoine, our attitude at the Sansané Haoussa massacre had made our feelings clear; during subsequent meals our freezing cold attitude had irritated Voulet, who complained about us to Chanoine, who responded: "you are wrong to tell them off, they are not used to it, they'll understand when we are attacked that these people are hostile, [then] they will come round."

Pallier then argued that "his usual theory was that by taking terrifying measures one would deter resistance and prevent even more bloodshed."[28] Although Pallier and his colleagues were at pains to distance themselves from Voulet and Chanoine, this is not borne out by the evidence. Pallier, like Joalland and the other officers and NCOs talked of the "moral sufferings we had to endure." He nevertheless defended or qualified some of the practices attributed to his superiors. For instance, in other passages of the report, Pallier did not condemn the mission's brutal practices: "Tirailleurs had orders to bring back the hand not of the porters but of enemies killed in their raids, in order to check their stories because they habitually exaggerated their successes enormously."[29] Clearly, Voulet and Chanoine sought absolute victory and total submission. They understood any attempt to temporize or negotiate as tantamount to rebellion. This explains, but does not justify, their extreme brutality toward villages that reluctantly surrendered a portion of what the conquerors demanded. The best-known example was the destruction of Birnin Konni during which several thousand people were massacred after the capture of the fortified city.

While there is wide-ranging evidence from diverse sources indicating that imperial conquest was brutal, the reality of its violence was always minimized or censored in the French media and in much subsequent historiography. A good example of this self-censorship lies in the disparity between the original manuscript and the printed memoirs of Sergeant Ernest Bolis, who served in the French foreign legion between 1889 and 1905. Bolis's manuscript account relates without compunction that wounded prisoners were scalped and beheaded. The memoir version comments negatively on the scalping, and the wounded are described as already dead. He makes no mention of the beheading.[30] His manuscript also describes the beheading of men and the crushing of women's heads under elephants' feet during the Tonkin campaign of 1892–93.[31] Both are excised from the printed version. Similar editing out is to be found in published accounts for which we have a draft text. In the public domain the conquest was narrated in gallant terms, as a test of the French race and the gentlemanly qualities of its officers and soldiers. In an international system in which colonialism played a central part, unexpurgated accounts were always liable to enter the public arena, threatening to become a source of anti-French propaganda. It took extraordinary acts to go beyond acceptable norms of *à la guerre comme à la guerre*.

What distinguished the Voulet mission was its relentlessness and duration. Even though people fled before it, the long list of raided villages included towns of between three and ten thousand inhabitants. In every case "all the villages, all evacuated were burnt, the few individuals we met were taken prisoner." Guides who lost their bearings or refused to show the way were executed. In the village of Tibiri, Voulet executed those of the chief's female dependents who had fled. On 1 July, in the village of Karankalgo, Chanoine had 150 women and children massacred in reprisal for the village's attempt to defend itself. In other instances captives were used as spies. Chanoine wrote a short note to Voulet on 1 April 1899: "you have entire families captive; send the father [as a spy] and promise to free the rest of the family on his return as a reward; then you will need to send two from each to check the results."[32] Increasingly the *colonne* raided with the express purpose of sustaining itself economically by gathering slaves. Yet the large number of captives became one of the column's logistical nightmares. Unable to provision them, the *colonne* diverted further, conducting ever more raids and gathering yet more slaves in the process. Slaves were also the principal victims of its violence.

The account of events at Sansané Haoussa reflected the economic reality of slavery, highlighting Voulet's targeting of slaves in his reprisals: "The women were not all old said [the chief] many had only had one child . . . and one man was a freeman from Sansané Haoussa. The tirailleurs skewered them with their bayonets until they had all fallen then they cut their throats." These orders emanated from Mamadou Koulibaly, Voulet's interpreter.[33] A report from a Lieutenant Salaman, filed in May 1899, described his visit to the village in these terms: "On 15th February, I arrived in Sansané Haoussa where I found the remains of about one hundred beheaded bodies—1300 meters from the village, 300 meters from the river—the ground was covered with the bones scattered and torn by the hyenas, a blood trail thirty meters [long] and a meter across was still visible. A communal grave contained the bodies of the freemen (forty I was told) buried on the chief's orders. I could not find out the reasons for *these rigorous measures*."[34] The "rigorous measures" described were, in fact, exaggerated since the freemen were not killed by Voulet, and it appears that, in the early massacres at least, he took care to select slaves as victims, regarding them in the same way as he regarded the punitive destruction of other assets. Indeed, most claims registered against the expedition by village chiefs along the Niger were primarily for compensation for lost income.

The captives' role within the mission's hierarchy was complex. Many of the slaves were female, and sexual appetites played a role in the mission's internal violence and disciplinary breaches. Conquest army officers promoted the values of hyper-masculinity and homosocial loyalties.[35] In the words of André Mévil in an 1899 article published in *l'éclair* and subsequently reprinted in nationalist magazines, Soudan "was a tough school where the more robust constitutions are forged. A great people needs schools like these."[36] The army was not composed of warrior monks, and masculinity was displayed by constituting a family *à la mode du pays*, in this case composed of sexual slaves. Both Voulet and Chanoine took "wives," as did their officers.[37] The officer in Say who was a friend of Pallier asked him in a letter whether he had managed to "break in" his new companion.[38] French NCOs had their own spouses selected among the captives whom they guarded jealously. Sexual tensions between the soldiers and the NCOs resulted in at least two executions of serving tirailleurs after the racial divide between white officers and black troops was traversed by competition over access to women.[39] In a sense the sexual dynamics of the mission reveal it as a microcosm of colonialism.[40] Far from monolithic, the *colonne* replicated the traits of imperial hierarchy in a highly hostile environment.

Recording Violence and Atrocity

To the latent or open hostility they met after the crossing of the Niger, Voulet responded with extreme brutality and crossed some threshold that defined his *colonne*'s behavior as intolerable. When does violence become an atrocity? None of Voulet's techniques were new. Only two years earlier he had burned part of Ouagadougou in reprisal actions that won universal approval from the Paris media and military hierarchy. By 1899, in contrast, the military had a weakened political position in Paris, and the sensationalist press had a growing appetite for leaked reports of colonial violence. Occasionally images came out too. A set of pictures exposing the summary execution of unarmed enemies and including a photograph of a pile of heads artistically arranged had been publicized, controversially to be sure, in *L'Illustration* in April 1891 to the great embarrassment of the French government.[41] Johannes Barbier, a Lyonnais photographer had brought back these grim mementos and had them published. But the officer responsible had only to respond to a meek enquiry letter, and the story was duly buried. Within Soudan, censorship was then applied more consistently and efficiently. Increasingly dual standards became part of the colonial way of fighting and ruling. In spite of a strident antislavery campaign in Europe, taking captives was deemed part of African warfare French style. One of the most renowned colonizers of Soudan, Archinard, had been involved in public distributions of captives to the troops. The killing of uncooperative porters was reprehensible but also relatively commonplace, as was the very public style of their execution. The *colonne* dispatched to the Kong against Samori two years before Voulet's arrival was a case in point.[42] While this was well known to the few people genuinely concerned or interested in Soudanese affairs, few of these incidents had become well known in France before the end of the 1890s. Journalists were seldom allowed access to information, let alone to details, and civilians were not welcome as eyewitnesses.

Yet the context was fast changing. First, the civilizing mission was now central to the army's last-ditch attempt to promote its mode of governance and maintain its last "private" colony in Soudan.[43] The colony's governor favored a more developmental model of colonial pacification, akin to the Gallieni doctrine practiced in Madagascar. For instance, Colonel de Trentinian was keen to promote mechanized modes of transport to replace human portage. The first phase of a railroad line was built, admittedly with forced labor but also employing wage laborers. Grand development schemes of *mise en valeur* were elaborated for a colony that was still in the making. The pro-colonial lobby led by Paul Leroy-Beaulieu, Auguste Terrier, and their associates of the Comité de l'Afrique Française promoted French pacification of these new territories and dreamed of a fertile Niger valley that they portrayed as the "French Nile."[44] Voulet's methods were thus already at odds with the dreams of his supporters, but his practices had a track record in delivering cheap and rapid conquests. Nonetheless, from the date of its departure from France to that of the dispatch requesting Voulet's arrest, the mission's political support in Paris melted away. Chanoine's father had resigned in unusual circumstances that infuriated his parliamentary colleagues and ended a long list of anti-Dreyfusard war ministers. African policy faced more critical scrutiny, and Fashoda demonstrated the weakness of the colonial master plan defended by Gabriel Hanotaux.[45] Finally, the Dreyfus affair stirred lively interest in the rights of individual citizen and their defense.[46] Perhaps more importantly, it undermined the moral high ground previously used to protect military ventures from unwelcome scrutiny.

For their part Voulet and Chanoine made several errors of judgment. First, they alienated their Soudanese army colleagues, Klobb among them. Trading on the autonomy accorded by their original instructions from Paris, they were tactless and arrogant in their dealings with administrators who struggled to satisfy their disproportionate demands. The resident in Say was especially aggrieved, having been working with only a handful of soldiers and two French associates to parley his neighbors into quietly accepting French overrule.[47] Here, as in many other areas of the empire, French control was wafer thin, and Voulet's demands stretched the limited authority his peers had imposed over the newly conquered territory. The only reports favorable to Voulet came from Dahomey, where the mission's methods seemed in keeping within this recently and violently conquered colony, a fact confirmed when the Voulet *colonne* "pacified" Dahomey's rebellious northern regions. Due to poor communications between Soudan and Dahomey, Voulet and Chanoine's friends in this latter colony failed to provide sufficient evidence in time to clear their name in the spring of 1899.[48] Until its arrival at Say the mission was careful to feed pro-colonial media in France, but its reports became less frequent in the spring 1899, and the silence allowed their opponents to become more vocal.[49] More importantly the mission was divided, riddled with tensions among Frenchmen, among Frenchmen and Africans, and among Africans themselves.

A disgruntled Lieutenant Péteau was the whistleblower who brought the mission to the attention of the Paris press. Péteau was a colonial officer who had seen most service in Tonkin rather than Africa. Increasingly uneasy with the mission's leadership, he was dismissed over a personality clash.[50] Sent back to Say, the lieutenant realized that his career was at risk and that he might even face a court-martial. To avoid the censorship applied to all official correspondence, he wrote denunciatory letters to his fiancée describing Voulet's acts of violence in emotional terms.[51] His fiancée passed on the letter to her parliamentary deputy, who leaked it to Paul Vigné d'Octon, the most notorious critic of colonial violence in the National Assembly. Vigné then wrote it up in Clemenceau's newspaper.[52] Embarrassed, the minister of colonies reacted feverishly, sending two partially contradictory telegrams requesting a full enquiry and Voulet's arrest. Aware that Péteau's dismissal might provoke a scandal, Voulet and Chanoine attempted to respond, but much of their crucial correspondence sent en route never reached its destination and was discovered only after their deaths.

Without the intervention of the whistleblower Péteau, it seems unlikely that the column's excesses would ever have reached the media or the archives. Those men closest to the earliest abuses, such as the murders committed immediately on the colony's borders, were reluctant to commit witness testimony to paper, a typical response being, "I will be happy to make some things known to you that I do not want to write down."[53] It took Voulet's conflict with the administrators in

Say to trigger an official record of his actions, sent as a confidential report to Kayes, the capital of French Soudan.[54] Yet in Kayes this highly critical report remained buried until Péteau leaked information to the press. Similarly, it is unclear that the Crave report following a visit on the tracks of the *colonne* in February 1899 would have come about had Voulet survived and succeeded in his mission. In fact, the administrative process worked in contrary fashion. When Paris sent a telegram asking for an officer to be sent after Voulet, the administration opened a file intended to prove that it knew of Voulet's activities and was building up a case against him. On 28 April 1899 de Trentinian wrote in the margins of a report: "the Voulet mission horrors, who can tell me more about them? Send to bureau politique."[55]

The wider context of international rivalry also bears emphasis. A German colonial officer had recently been tried for sadistic behavior in Togo,[56] and events in German Southwest Africa had tarnished Germany's colonial reputation still further. Rumors of atrocities in Congo abounded, the echo of which can be found in Joseph Conrad's *Heart of Darkness* published in early 1899: a novel whose plot strikingly resembles the Voulet-Chanoine Affair. The French press was re-examining its attitudes to the military and in the wake of the Dreyfus affair had become more open to antimilitaristic viewpoints. When news of Klobb's death reached Paris in late July 1899, Alfred Dreyfus faced a military court for the second time in Rennes in a famously flawed trial. Indeed, Julien Chanoine's father was appearing as a witness for the anti-Dreyfusard legal team when the rumor spread that his son had murdered a superior officer and might have become a renegade warlord rampaging Africa. The anti-Dreyfusard press leapt to Chanoine's defense, claiming that he was victim of scurrilous accusations, orchestrated by Jews, Freemasons, and other army haters, intended to discredit his father.[57] Until October 1899 the French government had to assume in contingency plans that the mission might have turned into a private army that had to be contained or even militarily defeated.[58] Only in October did confirmed and certain news of the deaths of Voulet and Chanoine bring an end to this excruciating embarrassment on the international stage.[59] The event required explanation nevertheless, and the only valid explanation seemed to be insanity.

Psychiatric Stories

Remarkably, considering that it was generally assumed that Voulet and Chanoine had succumbed to depression or to a form of mania, there is no medical case to investigate. Henric, the doctor who traveled with them and survived the mission, seems to have made few diagnoses. Neither in his field reports nor in the inquest did he produce any evidence of the men's insanity. Rather, the diagnosis of psychiatric disorder was one imposed by "common sense," and all military authorities rallied to it as a convenient way out. For the nationalists, the officers' loss of moral fiber was insanity indeed. It resembled the wanderlust afflicting monomaniacs. Friends, associates, colleagues, and even enemies of Voulet and Chanoine chose to blame their insanity on Africa. Their form of madness even had a name: Soudanite.[60] In many ways this myth has stuck to the Voulet-Chanoine legend. Yet from a medical viewpoint it is a myth since Soudanite was not a genuine pathology prior to the affair, but a loose term coined to describe the social tensions dividing the region's colonists. As the first French female visitor to Soudan expressed it:

> The soldiers call *Soudanite* a disease, which consists of avenging one's ennui by being malicious, impatient, quarrelsome. Every year—it is forbidden to duel on the front—comrades, divided by this so-called *Soudanite* take the boat back ready to cut each other's throat on their return to France. Sea air and the joy of their return cure them. When they arrive in Bordeaux and have their last meal together the enemies have forgotten to meet on the field! One might think that this is specific to the officers. Not at all. Not only are civilians equally prone to it but even simple privates! The Captain commanding the *cercle* of Bakel told me that in his fort he had seven soldiers from various arms and occupying different roles and that these seven men who were close friends initially had ended up living separately and not communicating except when on duty. "Yes Madam they were cooking seven separate meals eaten at seven separate tables!" . . . I am inclined to think that *Soudanite* reigns in Kayes, and once again, I can explain it without excusing it: "We are bored!"[61]

In its original form, then, Soudanite connoted the social divisions and bickering, the jealousy and petty squabbles of an isolated society remote from the metropolis. A few years later the "disease" re-appeared, in light of the Voulet-Chanoine Affair, but this time in more terrible guise:

> fever, dysentery, anaemia; for them, absinth and deadly spirits, the despair of interminable isolation, agony or the disorder of the senses and brain. They are not obsessed with ranks like their officers; they are not savages like their indigenous comrades; but the excess of suffering and the feeling that so much pain heroically withstood are of no use to the motherland fill them with a dark anger. They grow accustomed to slaughter. Human life loses its worth in their eyes.[62]

The left-wing author of these lines added that when transposed to France, this colonial disease lent itself to violence against workers, as in the famous repression of strikers at Fourmies on 1 May 1891.[63] For Vigné d'Octon, Voulet's and Chanoine's Soudanite was a consequence of the bloodlust of uncontrolled African sensuality—a theme he had already developed in his autobiographical novels.[64] For others, like the official who published his denunciation of the Soudan administration under the pseudonym Jean Rode in *La Revue Blanche*, Soudanite was the product of a specific promotion-obsessed and hysterically violent military culture.[65] In this light Soudanite was the systemic insanity of the military in colonial context rather than the individual neurosis of individuals. Thus the so-called diagnostic reveals absolutely nothing of Voulet's or Chanoine's psyche but is more explicitly indicative of the "psychological turn" in French politics at the turn of the century.

Furthermore it was the parallel between Klobb's killing and a coup d'état that won most attention. Voulet seemed the counterrevolutionary type, the authoritarian military disconnected from the republican polity. There were several ironies here. For one, Voulet was the product of Parisian colonial plotting rather than the infamous Soudanese empire builders. For another, it was Chanoine's father who had attempted to block re-examination of the Dreyfus case in the name of discipline, of law and order. Klobb's murder was thus seen as indicative of an army at odds with the nation and sensitive to, if not yet conquered by, ultranationalistic arguments. The same year Paul Déroulède romantically attempted a coup at Félix Faure's funeral. Ultimately the Voulet-Chanoine Affair contributed to the end of the military colony of Soudan in 1899.[66] Crucially, this diagnosis of military dysfunction was deployed to explain Klobb's death rather than the acts committed along the way and for which all the French officers of the mission had to answer. The rebellion against Klobb hid the original criminal case against them: the atrocities committed along their journey that were not so easily reducible to a *coup de sang*.

Conclusion

Whether psychotic or neurotic, the actions of Voulet and Chanoine are still seen as singular excesses. Even critics of colonialism have largely explained the mission's violence by stressing the absolute agency of two delusional men. There is a gap between the now commonplace denunciation of colonialism as a system based on violence, as a third totalitarianism of the West in Hannah Arendt's phrase, and the detailed understanding of the individual cases of violence. Marc Ferro, Catherine Coquery-Vidrovitch, and a multitude of scholars have denounced the violence as part of a broader historiographical trend, labeled *la repentance*, which conflicted with recent attempts to sanitize the colonial past.[67] Among the plethora of terrible events that took place over the colonial era, incidents such as the Voulet-Chanoine Affair merely demarcated the outer limits of violent norms.

This chapter, which set aside as incidental and ahistorical the madness theory, has sought to set the story more squarely within other reflections on violence and politics in colonial conflict. The Voulet-Chanoine scandal was a product of French politics rather than a revelation of French practices in Africa. What the Voulet-Chanoine Affair says most convincingly about the French colonial mind is that it was fundamentally unstable, divided between ancient modes of production of space, of people (captives) and modern projections of power and republican values promoted by anti-republican soldiers. The affair revealed a divided nation lancing its boils abroad and channeling its inner violence through the greatest military expansion of its history. In Mosse territory as elsewhere in the new colony, violence was accepted practice, and instances of "exemplary" punishments abound. Anthropologists such as Jean-Pierre Olivier de Sardan have argued that this era marked a radical break for the people of the Niger River.[68] Others saw in it the continuity of centuries of violent rulers sometimes backed by terrifying divinities. In this account the notions of masculinity embodied by hard men conformed to a mythology linked to the Songhai kingdom much admired by Voulet and Chanoine.[69] Paul Stoller suggests that the violence corresponded to forms of monarchy in the fifteenth-century Songhai kingdom led by the empire builder Sonni Ali Ber. Songhai kings could be transposed to Voulet and Chanoine (themselves almost one entity), while Voulet and Chanoine's soldiers routinely compared them to Samori. From this game of mirror violence emerged new mimicries, which expose the dreadful symmetry of the Voulet-Chanoine story.[70]

How conscious were Voulet and Chanoine of what they were doing? About as conscious as educated soldiers could be in their context of an anthropological and geographical void. They had read the racialist anthropologist Broca and combined this knowledge with older forms of imperial fantasies. They traveled with copies of Julius Caesar's *Gallic Wars* as well as older travel accounts such as that by Mongo Park, who detailed the past glories of Songhai civilization. They thought they knew something profound about the African mind-set and had adapted theirs to counteract and challenge their African foes. In this they were not deviant in the least from mainstream colonial thinking. They embodied a form of violence that is always found in the confrontation between the self-appointed civilized and so-called barbarians; one that always reflects badly on the barbarians since it is because of them that the "civilized" claim to outdo the barbarians in brutality. The tragic ironies of the Voulet-Chanoine Affair have universal meanings precisely because they have been and are endlessly reiterated in every colonial and neocolonial war since.

Notes

Bertrand Taithe has published a monograph on the Voulet Chanoine affair for Oxford University Press. Thanks are due to colleagues in Manchester, the London IHR, and Hull University who responded to this paper and to colleagues in Exeter who gave helpful feedback. In particular many thanks to Martin Thomas for his help and support in this project.

1. A *colonne* was a French colonial war formation that temporarily combined resources from the cavalry, infantry, and artillery. The *colonnes* were set up to be mobile and yet have considerable firepower. Developed in Algeria under General Bugeaud, the *colonnes* were in continuous use throughout the expansion of the empire. In order to make clear that I am referring to this specific arrangement I have chosen to use the French term.

2. French Sudan (henceforth Soudan) was a territory distinct from what is now called Sudan (which was then known as British Sudan). It covered the territories of present-day Burkina Faso, Niger, and Mali. At the onset of the story none of these territories were yet fully controlled by the French military, and many wars were fought in the 1890s in order to control them. For details, see, for instance, Lieutenant Gatelet, *Histoire de la conquête du Soudan Français (1878–1899)* (Paris: Berger Levrault, 1901).

3. General Joalland, *Le Drame de Dankori: Mission Voulet-Chanoine, Mission Joalland-Meynier* (Paris: Argo, 1930), 84–85. This is the text that was read in the Chamber of Deputies by Minister of Colonies Decrais on 30 November 1900. All translations are by the author unless otherwise noted. Also see later accounts such as General Octave Meynier, *Mission Joalland-Meynier* (Paris: Collection les grandes missions coloniales, 1947). Also Arsène Klobb, *Dernier carnet de route au Soudan Français* (Paris: Flammarion, 1905); *Documents pour servir à l'histoire de l'Afrique Occidentale française de 1895 à 1899, correspondance du capitaine Chanoine pendant l'expédition du Mossi et du Gourounsi—correspondance de la mission Afrique Centrale—Annexe rapports officiels du Lt Gouveneur du Soudan*, Jules Chanoine, ed., n.d., n.p. On the Voulet mission see the account of Muriel Mathieu, *La Mission Afrique Centrale* (Paris : L'Harmattan, 1995), originally a 1975 University of Toulouse doctoral thesis.

4. See, for instance, Antoine Tshitongu Kongolo, "L'étonnante aventure de Blackland," in Jules Verne, *L'étonnante Aventure de la Mission Barsac*, 2 vols. (Paris: Harmattan, 2005).

5. Jean-Pierre Olivier de Sardan, *Concepts et conceptions Songhay-Zarma* (Nubia, 1982), 224–30.

6. Paul Vigné d'Octon had served as a medical officer in the navy and had experienced some of the atrocities of the conquest. On his return he launched a successful literary and political career, making him the most constant critique of colonial policies if not colonialism in general. Hélia Vigné D'Octon, *La Vie et l'oeuvre de Paul Vigné D'Octon* (Montpellier: Imp de Causse, n.d.,

c. 1950), 53. Vigné d'Octon is now most famous for his denunciation of colonial exploitation in colonial Tunisia, published under the title *La sueur du burnou* (1911), which is still in print (Paris: Les Nuits Rouges, 2001).

7. In fact, Voulet's clumsy interventions created a dynastic problem that took a generation to appease. Jeanne-Marie Kambou-Ferrand, *Peuples Voltaiques et Conquête coloniale, 1885–1914, Burkina Fasso* (Paris: L'Harmattan, 1993), 353–80; Yenouyaba Georges Madiega and Oumarou Naro, eds., *Burkina Faso, cent ans d'histoire, 1895–1995* (Paris: Karthala, 2003); Samuel Salo, "Le Moog-Naaba Wogbo de Ouagadougou (1850–1904)," in Madiega and Naro, *Burkina Faso*, 631–57.

8. Lieutenant Voulet, "La Jonction du Soudan et du Dahomey, 1896–7," *Revue Générale des Sciences Pures et Appliquées* 8 (1897), 893–902; Ned Noll, "Le Mossi, la Mission du Lieutenant Voulet," *A Travers le Monde* A3 (1897), 257–60.

9. The Société de Géographie found it difficult to refer back to the events. See Baron Hulot, "Rapport sur les progrès de la géographie en 1899," *Bulletin de la Société de Géographie* 1, 1 semestre (1900), 202–5.

10. See, for instance, "Missions Politiques et Militaires: Les Français au Gourounsi," *A Travers le Monde* A4 (1898), 21–23.

11. The French financial control office, the Cour des comptes, later queried the financing of the mission in 1902: Centre des Archives d'Outre-Mer (hereafter CAOM), Missions, 11, 7 January 1902. *Question Diplomatiques et Coloniales*, "L'expansion française vers le Tchad," vol. 8, 15 December 1899, 169–72.

12. The earlier drafts of the instructions were much clearer in that particular direction; see CAOM, Afrique III, 37, 32, "Projet d'instruction," approved by Delcassé.

13. For a narrative see Michael Crowder, *West Africa under Colonial Rule* (London: Hutchinson, 1968), 100–111.

14. Foureau, *D'Alger au Congo par le Tchad* (Masson, 1902; reprint, Paris: L'Harmattan, 1990).

15. The position of Pallier and Joalland was a pragmatic one since they had authority only through the colonial army itself. Henri Brunschwig, *Noirs et Blancs dans l'Afrique Noire Française ou comment le colonisé devint colonisateur, 1870–1914* (Paris: Flammarion, 1974).

16. J. F. V. Keiger, "Omdurman, Fashoda and Franco-British Relations," in *Sudan: The Conquest Reappraised*, ed. Edward M. Spiers (London: Frank Cass, 1998), 162–76; "Le Livre Jaune sur Fachoda," *Questions Diplomatiques et Coloniales* 5 (1898), 273; see also M. J. L. de Lamessan, "L'évacuation de Fachoda: Ses véritables causes," *Questions Diplomatiques et Coloniales* 5 (1898), 321–30.

17. Myron Echenberg, *Colonial Conscripts: The Tirailleurs Sénégalais in French West Africa, 1857–1960* (Portsmouth NH: Heinemann, 1991); Lieutenant Gatelet, *Histoire de la conquête du Soudan Français, 1878–1899* (Paris: Berger Levrault, 1901), 2–10; Joe Lunn, "'Les Races guerrières': Racial Preconceptions in the French Military about West African Soldiers during the First World War," *Journal of Contemporary History* 34:4 (1999), 517–36; Charles Mangin, *La Force Noire* (Paris, 1910); Éric Deroo and Antoine Champeaux, *La Force noire: Gloire et infortune d'une légende coloniale* (Paris: Tallandier, 2006); J. Malcolm Thompson, "Colonial Policy and the Family Life of Black Troops in French West Africa, 1817–1904," *International Journal of African Historical Studies* 23:3 (1990) 423–53.

18. Lieutenant Colonel Monteil, *Les Conventions Franco-Anglaises des 14 juin 1898 et 21 mars 1899* (Paris: Plon Nourrit, 1899), 12.

19. Cazemajou was murdered in Zinder; Monteil survived and brought back a detailed itinerary; see Lieutenant Colonel Parfait-Louis Monteil, *De Saint Louis à Tripoli par le lac Tchad voyage au travers du Soudan et du Sahara pendant les années 1890–91–92* (Paris: Felix Alcan, 1894). Monteil had chosen to visit Sokoto. Since then Sokoto had been claimed by the British even though it is unclear that the sultan fully appreciated that situation until 1901. See H. A. S. Johnston, *The Fulani Empire of Sokoto* (Oxford: Oxford University Press, 1967), 240–41.

20. Idrissa Kimba, *Guerres et sociétés: Les populations du Niger occidental au XiXe siècle et leurs réactions face à la colonisation*, Etudes Nigériennes 46 (Niamey: Institut de recherches en sciences humaines, 1981), 78–79.

21. Chanoine, *Documents*, 290–91.

22. CAOM, Afrique III, 37, 1. Voulet to Ministre des colonies, Sansanne Hawsa, January 1899.

23. CAOM Afrique III, 37, 29, Voulet to Ministre, 9 July 1898.

24. Parfait-Louis Monteil, *Vade Mecum de l'officier d'infanterie de marine* (Paris: L. Baudoin et Cie, 1884) 162; Voulet had publicized his organizational skills and had published on the best means of setting up a colonne. Voulet, "La Jonction du Soudan," 895–96.

25. See Michel Foucault, *Discipline and Punish* (1977; new ed., London: Penguin, 1991) intro. and chap. 1.

26. Capitaine Chanoine, "Mission Voulet-Chanoine, de Dienné à Sansanné-Haoussa," *Bulletin de la Société de Géographie de France* 20 (1899), 234.

27. As Alice Conklin points out, the concept itself was recent: see Conklin, *A Mission to Civilize: The Republican Idea of Empire in France and West Africa, 1895–1930* (Stanford CA: Stanford University Press, 1997), chap. 1.

28. CAOM, Mission 110, Rapport Pallier, 15 August 1899.
29. CAOM, Mission 110, Rapport Pallier, 15 August 1899.
30. Sergent Ernest Bolis, *Mes Campagnes en Afrique et en Asie, 1889–1899*, ed. Claude Gassmann (Strasbourg: Gassmann, 2001), 5–7, 32–33.
31. Bolis, *Mes Campagnes*, 46.
32. CAOM, Mission 110, Papiers Voulet, Chanoine to Voulet, 1 April 1899.
33. CAOM, Mission 110, Rapport politique de Say, March 1899. The role of the interpreter is always crucial in episodes such as this one. It reflects a power relation well studied in Emily Lynn Osborne, "Circle of Iron: African Colonial Employees and the Interpretation of Colonial Rule in French West Africa," *Journal of African History* 44:1 (2003), 29–50.
34. CAOM, Mission 110, Rapport du Ltnt d'artillerie de Marine Salaman au Lt Gal, flotille du Niger, lettre T 106, Segou, 8 May 1899.
35. See Robert Aldrich, "Colonial Masculinities," in *French Masculinities: History, Culture, and Politics*, ed. Christopher E. Forth and Bertrand Taithe (Basingstoke: Palgrave Macmillan, 2007).
36. Mévil, reprinted in *Question Diplomatiques et Coloniales* 8 (1 September 1899), 110.
37. The surviving evidence is obviously more discreet on the matter, but the archives contain a few letters that cast a faint light on the domestic arrangement of the mission Voulet: CAOM, Mission 110, Rapport Joalland, Mafoita, 25 July 1899.
38. CAOM, Mission 110, Letter to Pallier from Captain Angeli in Dosso, no date, February 1899.
39. CAOM, Mission 49, 350 Conclusions rapport Laborie.
40. For a controversial discussion of what sexual tensions entail see Greg Thomas, *The Sexual Demon of Colonial Power* (Bloomington: Indiana University Press, 2007). The theme is, of course, central in Franz Fanon's *Black Skin, White Mask*. See also Ann Laura Stoler, *Carnal Knowledge and Imperial Power* (Berkeley: University of California Press, 2002).
41. The event took place in Bakel in April 1897. CAOM, Soudan II, 2, Report from Ambassador Waddington; Report from de Lamothe on the events; notes sent to Captain Roix.
42. The campaign was highly controversial because of its cost and lack of success. As a result, Monteil lost all the credit he had accumulated during his travels to Chad a few years earlier. Lt Col. Parfait-Louis Monteil, *Une page d'histoire coloniale, la Colonne de Kong* (Paris: Henri Charles Lavauzelle, 1904). See the Archives Missionnaires d'Afrique, diaire de Ségou.
43. For a detailed account of civil-military relations in Soudan see A. S. Kanya Forstner, *The Conquest of the Western Sudan: A Study in French Mili-*

tary Imperialism (Cambridge: Cambridge University Press, 1969), 245–62; see also Richard L. Roberts, *Warriors, Merchants and Slaves: The State and the Economy in the Middle Niger Valley, 1700–1914* (Stanford CA: Stanford University Press, 1987), 152–64.

44. Paul Leroy-Beaulieu, *Le Sahara, Le Soudan et les Chemins de Fer Transsahariens* (Paris: Guillaumin, 1904); Finn Fuglestad, *A History of Niger, 1850–1960* (Cambridge: Cambridge University Press, 1983), 49–51; Robert Cornevin, préface to Maurice Delafosse, *Haut Sénégal-Niger* (1908; reprint, Paris: Maisonneuve et Larose, 1972), 6–8.

45. Roger Glenn Brown, *Fashoda Reconsidered: The Impact of Domestic Politics on French Policy in Africa, 1893–1898* (Baltimore: Johns Hopkins University Press, 1970); Marc Michel, *La Mission Marchand, 1895–1899* (Paris: Mouton, 1972); Gabriel Hanotaux, *Le Partage de l'Afrique: Fachoda* (Paris: Flammarion, 1909); Guy de la Batut, *Fachoda ou le renversement des alliances* (Paris: Gallimard, 1932), 195–96; Paul Webster, *Fachoda: La bataille pour le Nil* (Paris: Edition du Felin, 2001).

46. See, inter alia, William D. Irvine, *Between Justice and Politics: The Ligue des Droits de l'Homme, 1898–1945* (Stanford CA: Stanford University Press, 2007).

47. CAOM, Mission 110, exchange of letters with Delaunay, 31 January 1899.

48. CAOM, Afrique III, 38bis, 22 November 1899, report from Dahomey, Ltnt Viola and Cornu.

49. Chanoine, "Mission Voulet-Chanoine," 221–35, 79–84.

50. CAOM, Afrique III, 37, 89, Kiladi, 2 February 1899, to General de Trentinian.

51. The fragments of the final report on the mission led by Commandant Laborie in 1899–1900 showed that Péteau had himself masterminded two massacres: CAOM, Mission 49, 149 Rapport du ministre Doumergue.

52. Of course, the issue is not whether Clemenceau should be regarded as a genuine anticolonialist; see Jean-Pierre Biondi, *Les Anti-colonialistes (1881–1962)* (Paris: Robert Laffont, 1993), 27.

53. CAOM, Afrique III, 38, 75 bis, report of Cmmdt Crave, December 1898.

54. CAOM, Afrique III, 38, 9, rapport du chef de bataillon Crave.

55. CAOM, Afrique III, 38, 75bis, report Grandeyere & Crave.

56. L. H. Gann and Peter Duigan, *The Rules of German Africa, 1884–1914* (Stanford CA: Stanford University Press, 1977); Dennis Laumann, "A Historiography of German Togoland, or the Rise and Fall of a 'Model Colony,'" *History in Africa* 30:2 (2003), 195–211; Kenneth Mackenzie, "Some

British Reactions to German Colonial Methods, 1885–1907," *Historical Journal* 17:1 (1974), 165–75.

57. *Le Petit Journal*, 6 October 1899.

58. CAOM, Afrique III, 38, 65. Doubt persisted until the receipt of Pallier's full account on 14 October 1899.

59. CAOM, Afrique III, 38, 15, note ministère des affaires étrangères, 26 August 1899.

60. Variants were then developed; see Dr. Marie, "La folie à la légion étrangèr," *Revue blanche* 26 (1902), 401–20; Dr. Louis Catrin, *Aliénation mentale dans l'armée* (Paris: Rueff, 1901); Marius Antoine Cavasse, "Les dégénérés dans l'armée coloniale," Thèse de la faculté de médecine, Bordeaux, 1903. See also Jean-Marie Lundy, "Mémoire de criminologie appliqué à l'expertise medicale: Le Traitement pénal dans l'armée Française sous la troisième république," Thèse de doctorat, Université René Descartes, Droit Medical, 1987, 34.

61. Raymonde Bonnetain, *Une Française au Soudan, sur la route de Tombouctou, du Sénégal au Niger* (Paris, 1894), 160.

62. Urbain Gohier, preface to Paul Vigné d'Octon, *La Gloire du Sabre*, 4th ed. (Paris: Flammarion, 1900), vii.

63. Odile Roynette-Gland, "L'armée dans la bataille sociale: Maintien de l'ordre et grèves ouvrières dans le Nord de la France (1871–1906)," *Le Mouvement social* 179 (April–June 1997), 33–58.

64. Paul Vigné D'Octon, *Chair noire, preface de Leon Cladel* (Paris: Alphonse Lemerre, 1889). His foremost success was *Terre de Mort, Soudan, Dahomey* (Paris: Alphonse Lemerre, 1892), a novel that traced the sexual and physical decay of the colonial officer in the outposts of Africa. See Jennifer Yee, "Malaria and the Femme Fatale: Sex and Death in French Colonial Africa," *Literature and Medicine* 21:2 (2002), 201–15.

65. Jean Rode was, in fact, a civilian administrator named Eugène Bouton, as revealed by Vigné D'Octon in the parliamentary debate of 30 November 1900 on the Voulet-Chanoine Affair. His article had been published in the fall of 1899: "Un regard sur le Soudan," *La Revue Blanche* 20 (1899), 321–30.

66. "La dislocation du Soudan Français," *Questions Diplomatiques et Coloniales* 8:1 (October 1899), 137–38.

67. Marc Ferro, ed., *Le livre noir du colonialisme, xvie–xxie siècle: De l'extermination à la repentance* (Paris: Robert Laffont, 2003); Dimitri Nicolaidis, *Oublier nos crimes: L'amnésie nationale, une spécificité française?* (Paris: Autrement, 1994); Pascal Blanchard, Nicolas Bancel, and Sandrine Lemaire, *La Fracture Coloniale* (Paris: Découverte, 2005); Nicolas Bancel, Pascal Blanchard, and Françoise Vergès, *La République coloniale* (Paris: Pluriel, 2003).

68. J-P. Olivier de Sardan, *Les Societes Songhay-Zarma (Niger-Mali): Chefs, guerriers, esclaves, paysans* (Paris: Karthala, 1984), 152–55.

69. Jean Rouch, *La réligion et la magie Songhay: Anthropologie Sociale* (Brussels: Université de Bruxelles, 1989, 72–73; Dongo was notorious for his violence, notably the killing of entire villages; his role was to be the God of Thunder. On healing see Rouch, *La réligion et la magie Songhay*, 306, and Rouch, *Les Hommes et les dieux du fleuve, essai ethnographique sur les populations songhay du moyen Niger, 1941–1983* (Paris: Artcom, 1997).

70. Paul Stoller, *Embodying Colonial Memories: Spirit Possession, Power and the Hauka in West Africa* (London: Routledge, 1995); also see Adeline Masquelier, "Road Mythographies: Space, Mobility and the Historical Imagination in Postcolonial Niger," *American Ethnologist* 29:4 (2002), 829–56, at 830.

3

Fear and Loathing in French Hanoi

*Colonial White Images and
Imaginings of "Native" Violence*

MICHAEL G. VANN

As Michael Taussig has so persuasively argued, violence was central to the colonial encounter.[1] For three generations, from the French conquest to the Vietminh liberation, racialized physical violence saturated every aspect of life in colonial Hanoi. This colonial city, capital of France's Southeast Asian possessions, was born in violence, nurtured in violence, came of age in violence, and died in violence. Violence was so omnipresent that it became a central feature of white identity. The relationship of colonial whiteness with violence was paradoxical, demonstrating a combination of power and vulnerability. On the one hand, white privilege was built upon the bloodshed of conquest, the brutal crushing of revolts, and the repression of daily life. White violence constituted the colonial situation. On the other hand, whites, as a tiny minority surrounded by a hostile majority, were in constant danger. The threat of native violence, under the guise of rebellion, political struggle, or criminality, weighed heavy on the settlers' minds. The contradiction of white power and white vulnerability elevated cases of violence to a frequently irrational level of importance and symbolism. Racial violence thus became a central feature of life in French Hanoi. While to many historians the argument that colonialism was violent may seem an obvious statement, it is a thesis that must be rearticulated and fully explored to create the most accurate portrait of the colonial encounter. Despite its repeal, the law of 23 February 2005 indicates that there is a strong tendency within France toward a historical revisionism that would deny the brutal, unsavory, and exploitative details of France's imperial past. Thus, we not only need to recognize the violence of colonialism but must also show how violence was at the heart of empire.

Unfortunately the limited archival record makes a comprehensive social history of violence in colonial Hanoi impossible. The dearth of police records and court proceedings forces the researcher to turn to other, more innovative sources. Fortunately, thanks to the central role violence played in the colonial encounter, a wide variety of texts, ranging from political reports to memoirs, contain tales, descriptions, and vignettes covering everything from daily, almost mundane, brutalities to extraordinary and shocking outbursts of rage. While the available sources are insufficient for a sociology of violence, they do permit a cultural inquiry into the role of violence in the making of the white colonial mind. An exploration of the meaning, perception, and interpretation of such behavior is revealing. As in case studies by Dane Kennedy, Amirah Inglis, Pamela Scully, and Vron Ware of interracial rape or suspected rape in colonial Africa or the American South, the white response to these acts far outweighed their actual significance.[2] In other words, even if the higher level of violence in Hanoi than in Paris cannot be proved to be statistically significant, the understanding of such violence in the context of colonial tension — Milton Osborne's "background anxiety" — provides crucial insights into the formation and maintenance of colonial whiteness.[3]

Colonial ideology encouraged violence. Colonialism's racial hierarchies gave individual whites tremendous power over nonwhites. These power relationships included the political, economic, and physical control of the native population. Granting such power to the settlers without a meaningful system of restraint encouraged the likelihood that the colonized would be physically abused. The racial inequality of colonialism lifted the social constraints that kept violence in check in the home country, allowing the colonial white to strike, lash out, or shoot with relative impunity.[4] Colonial racism dehumanized the *indigènes*, rendering them a classic "Other" to such an extent that violent acts against nonwhites were less significant, relatively inconsequential, in the eyes of the colonial white. As violence is an act of physical domination with powerful psychological implications, the beating of a native humiliated and degraded the victim. David Spurr has shown how this debasement of the colonized signaled their inferiority and the colonizer's superiority.[5] The ideology of empire also helped to place the blame for white-on-nonwhite violence upon the native victim. Pointing to the *indigènes*' psychology (which included lower intelligence, moral flaws, and dishonesty), the colonial mind saw the native and his insolent behavior as provoking harsh responses from the colonial white.[6] In this perspective colonial violence was understood as a common frustration felt by settlers who had to deal with problematic natives.[7]

The colony's political context cast all aspects of violence in a dramatically different light than violence in the home country. Prior to the First World War and the arrival of significant numbers of nonwhites, cases of interracial violence were practically unheard of in France (obviously because there were very few nonwhites around).[8] Inter-ethnic violence between French and immigrant workers—most notably Italian, Polish, and Spanish—was common but did not entail the same racial dynamics as violence between white colonizers and colonized Asians, Africans, Arabs, or Polynesians.[9] Because it is part of a larger political conflict, interracial violence, in either the colonial or postcolonial context, is invested with much greater meaning than intraracial violence. As Hannah Arendt observed, "Violence in interracial struggle is always murderous, but it is not 'irrational'; it is the logical and rational consequence of racism."[10] As every white man or woman was a representative of a ruling racial elite and every nonwhite man or woman was a member of the conquered race, any act of physical interracial violence was part of the larger political conflict. Every time a white man beat a servant, he was reinforcing white supremacy. Any time a nonwhite committed a crime against a white, the colonial community saw this as an affront to the colonial order of things. As this political constellation of powers was both unimaginable in France and dramatically different than the situation in pre-French Vietnam, the uniqueness of colonial violence is apparent.

The spectacle of violence in Hanoi was unlike violence in the rest of the colony. As the incompletely pacified countryside had been subject to a variety of revolts and rebellions of differing severity since the dawn of French rule, the white colonials grew accustomed to the idea of a dangerous rural Indochine. If the French considered disorder to be endemic to the Tonkinese hinterland, the cities of Hanoi, Haiphong, and Saigon were considered to be islands of safety and order for the settler community. In the colonial imagination Hanoi was different. With its stately streets and impressive beaux arts buildings embodying the power, orderliness, and stability of French colonial rule, Hanoi was more than a political capital, it was an imperial symbol. Through the built environment and social space, the city conveyed the idea that the French intervention was a crusade for civilization. Hanoi's legal status as French territory, and not a protectorate like the rest of Tonkin, reinforced the idea that the city was a distinct entity from the rest of Indochine. The capital's special legal status implied that it was under tighter surveillance, better policed, and therefore more orderly than its surroundings, which were beset with piracy, warlordism, and rebellion. Thus instances of native disorder and violence within the city limits, whether criminal, political, or personal, were an unbearable affront to the colonial order.

Unfortunately for the colonials, the idea that Hanoi was a world apart was an illusion. With Vietnamese and Chinese comprising over 90 percent of the population, the white minority was too small to assure the calm and tranquility it so desired. Nonetheless, the official and popular minds of French colonialism believed Hanoi to be uniquely impervious to regional chaos. It came as a profound shock when the specter of anti-French violence reared its ugly head in the heart of French Hanoi. Vietnamese terrorism, while very limited in scale, had the double impact of poisoning Franco-Vietnamese relations and increasing white solidarity. Attempted coups and deadly bombs reminded the colonials that they were a racially distinct ruling class that owed its position to the use of organized force and violence. The message was particularly shocking to the recently arrived bureaucrats who had not lived through the conquest and pacification. Faced with violent acts of real or perceived revolt, both the civilian community and the state reacted with anger, quickly seeking to reestablish order. Interpreting native violence in the capital as a mockery of all that the French civilizing mission stood for, those who would transgress the colonial order of things suffered the colonial whites' brutal and often excessive revenge.

The physical confines of life in the city also made violence more apparent. With the white and nonwhite communities living in such close contact, the colonial urban experience gave a certain transparency to acts of violence, this despite attempts to erect a system of urban apartheid within Hanoi. Thus violent acts, ranging from the assassination of administrators and the execution of rebels to the beating of servants and the murder of employers, could not hide in the anonymity of the provincial hinterland. Rather, they were open to scrutiny in the heart of the city. Even if the acts occurred behind closed doors, the gossip network assured that the residents of Hanoi would know where the events occurred. The familiarity of place that comes with urban living gave a certain concreteness to the news of acts of violence that reports of revolts or massacres in the far-off highlands or distant small villages lacked. Long after the event in question, urban memories preserved violent incidents, making them part of Hanoi's psychocultural geography. Thus the blood from the 1913 café bombing may have been washed away, but the site retained significance in the minds of white colonials for years to come. For the Vietnamese, the same was true for the location of the public execution of the 1908 coup plotters.[11] In a city saturated with symbolism for both the French and Vietnamese, the sites of violence played a crucial role in a mental map of empire.

Paradoxically, in light of what I have just argued, violence in Hanoi cast doubt upon the solidity of French rule. Native-on-white violence shook the white colonial's faith in the order and power of French rule. How could a settler feel safe in a colony where one could be killed in the very seat of white power? Conversely, white-on-native violence disillusioned the Vietnamese. What were the colonized to make of the colonizer's talk of a civilizing mission when the individuals who represented "civilization" were prone to hitting the natives on the head for not pulling a *pousse-pousse* fast enough? Violence in the city thus undermined the colonial state's justifications for its presence. Furthermore, the ability of native offenders to get away with violent crimes in Hanoi caused the colonial state to lose face in the eyes of the colonized population. The location of many violent acts in the suburbs and the *quartier indigène* highlighted the areas of the city that were poorly policed or barely under control.[12]

Seen in its totality, colonial violence was dialectical: native-on-white violence was the antithesis to the thesis of white-on-native violence. The nature, intensity, and form of native violence corresponded to the various manifestations of white supremacy in Hanoi. Both sides of the city's racial equation interpreted instances of native-on-white violence as carrying significance greater than the specific details of the case at hand. For the colonized, native violence symbolized the fight against the many injustices of the colonial order. Frantz Fanon has described native violence as an almost purifying act, a way for the colonized male to reassert his agency as a man.[13] For the colonizers, native violence raised the specter of a criminal and illegitimate revolt against the sociopolitical arrangements that maintained white supremacy. In this tense atmosphere, the hysterical fears of the white community frequently blew relatively minor infractions out of proportion, and the rare cases of organized rebellion produced a mob mentality among the Europeans of Hanoi.

Demographic realities determined that white reaction to native violence in Hanoi would be a different phenomenon than in the countryside. The high concentration of French civilians, civil servants, and soldiers within Hanoi's small city limits assured that news of native violence would quickly spread. With both the informal gossip network and the vitriolic local press spreading the word of native affronts to the colonial order, incidents could quickly snowball, producing mob hysteria. The political gatherings in the formal dining halls of the white quarter's hotels in 1908 and 1909 show the lynch-mob mentality that could overcome the white community.

As a means of coping with this polarized situation, the French state sought to delegitimize and silence the political aspect of native-on-white violence. Eager to keep the colony from spinning out of control and descending into a race war, the French administration actively depoliticized and criminalized native violence. By declaring violent thefts, kidnappings, and murders to be motivated by greed and not political agency, the state portrayed such events as the product of inherent violent behavior and not symptoms of a diseased colonial society. In his essay "The Prose of Counter-Insurgency," Ranajit Guha considers similar patterns under the British Raj. He describes the rhetoric of British administrators who invalidated the motivations, tactics, and aims of

Indian rebels. Instead of rational political actors, the colonial authorities recast them as religious fanatics who used riotous behavior to achieve wild demands.[14] The French version of this process presented Vietnamese rebels as violent criminals. Such a move was a double-edged sword. It discredited the rebels and provided a justification for the extension of French control. The state's early attempts to attribute the 1929 murder of Alfred François Bazin to a business rivalry, thus denying its political content, illustrate this process at work. As Bazin worked as a laborer "recruiter" who sent impoverished Tonkinese villagers to the rubber plantations in southern Vietnam and as his assassins left a tract accusing him of various crimes against the Vietnamese people, this narrative did not last. This initial denial of political motivation soon gave way to a wide-ranging press debate about nationalism, communism, and violent state tactics in the colony. The murder and subsequent wave of repression pushed the colony into the high tension and violence of the 1930s, including the Yen Bey mutiny and the Nghe An Soviet.[15]

This is not to say that there was no violent criminal activity in Hanoi. On the contrary the city's white population was far more likely to fall victim to armed robbery or murder than to be the target of political assassination. Travel outside of Hanoi remained dangerous throughout the colonial era; even the short jaunt between Hanoi and the port city of Haiphong could prove dangerous, as a certain M. Jobard discovered in an ill-fated 1906 trip. While he was using Paul Doumer's new road system, bandits attacked and robbed him.[16] Highwaymen, pirates, and rebels harassed, robbed, abducted, and killed white voyagers who strayed from the security of the French cities.[17] Yet one could find danger within Hanoi's immediate vicinity. Pirates ravaged the rivers and canals surrounding Hanoi. Making use of higher water levels, they were especially troublesome during the rainy season. Pillaging villages and making off with livestock were the typical method of operation, but on occasion they undertook more daring crimes. For example, on the night of 5 December 1898 an audacious band attacked Hanoi itself. French police and soldiers responded in force, killing four, wounding six, and taking seventy-one prisoners.[18]

An especially worrisome aspect of colonial life was the presence of native servants within the home. Servant thefts were common in Hanoi.

The local press carried regular reports on items missing from white homes or suspicious natives found with European objects (evidently they were suspicious only because of their possession of objects of value such as jewelry).[19] Generally these crimes were quiet, discrete, and non-violent; such as the ruse known as "theft by amnesia," where domestic servants would hide an item inside the home for several months, waiting until the object was forgotten about before actually making off with it.[20] Unfortunately some robberies also included bloodshed. For example, when M. Massotte, a Hanoi entrepreneur, awoke to find one of his domestic servants in his bedroom, the startled boy tried to kill his employer.[21] A more serious case was the murder of the widow Beljonne on 19 November 1906. Sometime during the night two of her domestics killed her in a villa on rue Carreau, supposedly in one of the safest neighborhoods in the city.[22] During the chaos of 1945, when two domestics poisoned their employers, Jean Dol recorded it as an event symbolizing the wartime breakdown of the colonial order.[23] Tellingly neither the archival records nor the press from the period considered the possibility that the white employers may have abused their servants or otherwise provoked crimes of retribution. On the contrary the press, official reports, and memoirs cast whites as innocent victims of "audacious" crimes. That these incidents occurred in the homes of the white colonials caused tremendous anxiety in the minds of the French. The question "where could one be safe if not in one's bed?" inflamed the paranoia of Hanoi's white community. White suspicion of their servants actually increased the racial distance between colonizer and colonized; this despite the fact that servant and master lived together under the same roof in fairly intimate contact. While servants were a necessary risk of the colonial lifestyle, the colonial could never completely relax with the native Other in his home. One always had to be on guard for possible treachery. Here again, we see the underlying fear and vulnerability that belied colonial whiteness' facade of power.

To the white colonial, native violence affirmed what many suspected; that the native people were of a different, and probably inferior, moral character.[24] A common consensus among both administrators and civilians held that due to their shortcomings the *indigènes* should be judged by a separate code of values. One long-term Hanoi resident recorded the following in his memoirs: "In all seriousness, our magistrates now have to administer an oath to the Annamites who swear to tell the whole truth and nothing but the truth. Those who know the native mentality could die laughing."[25] This quote displays the contemptuous attitude held toward the Vietnamese, a perspective that failed to consider why *indigènes* might mislead the French authorities or employers—if indeed they did perjure themselves as was assumed. With the "Asiatic mind" considered inherently deceitful, administrators deemed European laws inappropriate for these uncivilized people. This idea was part of the move from assimilation and toward association in colonial theory and practice, seen in the larger reordering of the interwar French empire as described by Alice Conklin.[26]

Hanoi, with its unique status as French territory, complicated this issue. In 1891 Mayor Beauchamps pondered the conflict between French and *indigène* law codes within his city. Noting the insolence of Vietnamese toward figures of French authority, he suggested that French laws were too lenient for the native mind to comprehend. He argued that the application of French laws assumed a moral outlook that the Vietnamese lacked.[27] To further complicate matters, the coexistence of French and Vietnamese within Hanoi produced a dangerous deculturization of the natives. A 1905 political report stated the following:

> The Résident Supérieur au Tonkin notes, however, that these attacks against French denote a more and more troubling attitude in the native population immediately around the Europeans, either employees or domestic servants. It is thought that, faced with the audacity of these crimes, it is permitted to think that our French laws are not always of sufficient character to rapidly and severely repress criminality in the eyes of the natives.
>
> This attitude is most noticeable in the large cities or the centers inhabited by Europeans and natives more or less perverted by their time in the city. The majority of the population in the countryside remains honest, hard working, and respectful of authority.[28]

This text provides an enlightening view of the colonial mind at work. While Hanoi's urban social environment and general contact with Europeans were factors in the production of native criminals, this author argues for harsher punishment of native offenders. Rather than trying to respond to the causes of criminality and violence, the colonial state was in favor of responding with greater force and violence. The justification for this escalation was that the native only understood force, not reason. As another civil servant reported:

> At the same time that there have been audacious attempts at jail breaks, it should be noted that there is an augmentation of native criminality in the cities, that this all might be attributed to the ineffectiveness of our penal laws when applied to individuals of a mentality so different from our own.[29]

The conclusion is clear: native violence could be met only with state violence, and this state violence was to be more intense than that used in France. To put it in vulgar terms, the uncivilized only understood brutality.

Political violence committed by natives upon white bodies shook the colonial order to its foundations. Obviously, just what was and what was not political within the colonial context is a thorny question. However, it is possible to recognize what was an overtly political act; for example, assassinations and bomb throwing. Events such as the 1908 poisoning of the Hanoi garrison, the 1913 bombing of the Hanoi-Hotel café, and the 1929 Bazin murder cast a long shadow of fear in the tense white community. While these dramatic events were rare, they were frequently blown out of proportion by the French collective hysteria. As Stoler notes regarding the Dutch of Sumatra's plantation belt, "the persistence of fear ... was not a measure of the actual frequency and severity of assaults on whites."[30] Dane Kennedy has found an irrational longevity in incidents of black-on-white violence in Kenya and Rhodesia.[31] Such acts brought the latent anxiety of colonial life to the forefront.

Two attacks galvanized colonial popular opinion against the *indigènes*. The first was the now infamous attempt to poison the Hanoi garrison on the night of 27 June 1908. A collection of Vietnamese soldiers, servants, and cooks hatched the plot in an Old Quarter boarding house. Several of the plotters had ties to Phan Boi Chau, a rising nationalist leader living in South China, and De Tham, an aging pirate-cum-nationalist hero who had been a thorn in the side of the French for several decades. The plan was complex. As cooks in the citadel poisoned the food for a large officers' banquet and cohort soldiers either destroyed or seized French weapons, several bands of irregulars, including a team lead by De Tham himself, would take up positions around the city.[32] The attack on the city, by what was officially termed *"misérables,"* was to include the disabling of the electric and water plants, the disruption of telephone lines within Hanoi and the cutting of Hanoi's telegraph link to the outside world, the pillaging of arms depots, and the seizing of control of French cannons on the Pont Doumer and the route de Sontay. With Hanoi plunged into darkness, the state's command and control structure in chaos, and the city's defenses destroyed, some two to three hundred rebels would swarm into the city. In confidential reports the French administration admitted that it feared a general massacre of white civilians, a situation made worse by the rebels' ability to use the cannons to repel provincial troops trying to rescue French Hanoi.[33] Investigators produced a document attributed to the pen of Phan Boi Chau stating "that it would have been an indescribable joy for us to put to death all the French and the voluntary slaves of the French that we found [in Hanoi]."[34] Unfortunately for the conspirators, the plan failed miserably. The poison did not kill a single French soldier; instead, several hundred reported gastrointestinal discomfort (nothing new for the colonial troops). Failing to receive the signal to attack, the irregulars retreated and then vanished into the countryside. Most damaging of all, the French obtained useful confessions from nervous Catholic members of the plot.[35]

Despite the incident's inconsequential military impact, it did produce other, more serious repercussions. A wave of hysteria and self-righteous indignation overtook Hanoi's French population.[36] The plot soon achieved mythic importance in the minds of the colonials, who decades later repeated their belief that "the massacre of all of the French in Tonkin" was the conspirators' goal.[37] Such a brazen act of anti-French violence in the heart of this white island of safety infuriated the colonials. Their wrath was directed at two targets. First they screamed for vengeance, demanding serious repression of the Vietnamese. Second they voiced their anger and frustration with the French administration, whom they accused of codling the natives. In the following months at large gatherings—often resembling lynch mobs—prominent members of the colonial community publicly attacked the French colonial state.[38]

The white response to native political violence can be considered in two categories: official reaction and popular reaction. With the state's desire to keep the colony under control, the official reaction to political violence was typically measured and calculating. If the popular response of the white community was to scream for blood, the official response of the French administration, albeit shocked and angered, was more philosophical. In his annual report on the situation in Tonkin, the Hanoi Resident shook his head in paternal dismay at the unintended consequences of French colonial tutelage:

> The bourgeoisie of the big cities have become critical and lost all respect for Europeans; their children know French, read newspapers, cite Voltaire, Jean Jacques Rousseau, and interpret them in their own fashion; to the detriment of other skills, activism has developed simple memorization amongst the native students who are hardly capable of reasoning, of penetrating the spirit which inspired these orators and writers, of seizing in all their nuances the concepts, so different from those they are brought up with, they have generally just set foot in the world of letters and are taking in the most diverse sociological ideas with the greatest carelessness: it is these semischolars, concerned with pride and conceit, from which statements of loyalty imperfectly conceal hostile sentiments which they profess for the nation which has given them the benefits of instruction and of Western civilization.[39]

We must note the obvious hostility toward the policy of *assimilation* apparent in this quote. This attitude manifested itself in a policy of retrenchment and retraction. High-ranking officials in both Paris and Hanoi decided to reverse the few concessions made to the Vietnamese.[40] Previously, a 1905 report questioned the effectiveness of French laws in maintaining control over the *indigènes*, noting that the cities were becoming particularly dangerous:

It is believed that in the face of the audacity which forebodes criminality, it is permitted to think that our French laws are not always sufficient to give the repression of criminality the character of speed and severity that is must always have in the eyes of the natives. This state of spirit is most notable in the large cities or urban centers inhabited by Europeans and natives more or less perverted by time spent in the city. The mass of the population of the countryside seems honest, hard working, and respectful of authority.[41]

This text reveals the ambiguous results of colonial urbanism. While the cities were a central symbol of France's colonial mission, the creation of *indigènes déracinés*—who were not of their "true" culture nor of the modern French culture—cast doubt on the success of France's work.

This should not be taken to mean that the state was lenient, soft, or indulgent. Acts of terrorism resulted in waves of arrests, detentions, executions, and deportations.[42] Use of the extra-legal Commission Criminelle ensured that large numbers of suspects would be drawn into the French judiciary and penal systems. Convened by special decree on 28 June 1908, this body was infamous for the secrecy, swiftness, and severity with which it dispatched the alleged plotters.[43] Officially the commission was only used in extreme conditions, such as in 1908, 1913, and 1930, when the normal methods of state repression proved insufficient to deal with the threat of native revolt; however, its investigations could linger for years, as the police hunted down suspects and extracted further confessions.[44] Hard-liners and the military hailed the Commission Criminelle's work, and very few of the colonials questioned, still less opposed, this expansion of the colonial state's already authoritarian powers.[45] The Hanoi branch of the Ligue Française pour la Défense des Droits de l'Homme et du Citoyen, which served as defense counsel for the accused 1908 plotters, was one of the few organizations to challenge the French administration (a job taken up by the French Communist Party in the interwar years).[46]

The *Sûreté*, the semisecret political police, were the main form of French response to Vietnamese rebellion. With its central office in Hanoi, the Sûreté was an impressive secret police bureaucracy charged with keeping an eye on anticolonial and Communist conspiracies. In

1935 Andrée Viollis recorded her amazement at the Sûreté's beehive of activity: "Twenty thousand political dossiers and in them fifty thousand files classified in a perfect order in a vast library by the hard-working employees are as numerous as they are zealous."[47] More recently Charles Fourniau has chronicled the brutal pacification of Annam and Tonkin; Patrice Morlat has written a detailed history of the methods of colonial repression in Vietnam that describes the impressive energy and resources that went into maintaining French rule in Asia; and Yves Benôt has recorded the history of the massacres during Vietnam's war for national liberation.[48]

The colonial regime tried and sentenced suspects with great speed. Several individuals received death sentences, with the penalty carried out as a public spectacle.[49] The administration used the public executions to serve dual purposes. On the one hand the events served as a catharsis for the white community. If the colonials screamed for blood, their governors would give them blood in the hope that they would be satiated and then calm down. Executions in Hanoi were thus a form of collective therapy whereby the whites could reestablish their position of dominance through the spilling of Vietnamese blood.[50] On the other hand the administration wanted to use the long tradition of public state violence in Vietnam to communicate with the natives in the strongest possible terms. The administration took an essentialist position regarding the need to make a strong impression on the Vietnamese, following a commonly held belief that the only thing the *indigènes* understood was force and violence.[51] To display the fate of the rebels to as many natives as possible, one of the convicted conspirators was sent to Haiphong, where an elaborate ceremony took place. As part of a colonial bastardization of an indigenous practice, the plotter was marched about the city in a five-kilometer procession, compelled to watch several rituals, and then dispatched with a blow from a traditional weapon.[52]

French vengeance was not limited to Hanoi. Troops went into the Tonkinese highlands in search of De Tham and his allies. Ironically the administration had previously tried to work a deal with the former pirate by buying him off with promises of a small private fiefdom in Yên-Thê.[53] Now, embarrassed by his betrayal, the French state felt compelled to chase him down. The military campaign got off to a less than impressive start. The year 1909 was marred by the "cruel losses of officers, *sous-officiers*, European soldiers, and *tirailleurs indigènes*" due to both fighting and disease.[54] De Tham appeared unstoppable, regularly outwitting his hunters. The colonial community in Hanoi was incredulous when he managed to kidnap a M. Voisin, a member of the team trying to track him down.[55] While De Tham no longer threatened Hanoi, his presence and the perceived danger to the white community undermined attempts at "normalization" of colonial life. A satirical play, performed in the monumental Municipal Theater in 1912, mocked the administration's impotence by portraying De Tham as spending his time drinking and carousing with white women in Paris and in Hanoi. The played also utilized numerous racist stereotypes of the Vietnamese to ridicule De Tham.[56] Due to the failures of the hunt, the active official search for De Tham was abandoned in favor of a standing bounty on the pirate's head. On 11 February 1913 a group of Chinese with unclear ties to the French administration lured De Tham into a trap with promises of guns and ammunition and killed him while he slept.[57] The rebel leader and two of his chiefs were decapitated and their heads paraded around Tonkin. The news was cause for celebration in Hanoi.[58] In honor of the death of their mortal enemy, a white entrepreneur issued commemorative postcards with graphic photographs of the heads.

The wave of repression stymied but did not stop anticolonial action. Indeed the second major attack occurred on 26 April 1913, when Vietnamese terrorists threw a bomb onto the terrace of the Hanoi Hotel, a popular meeting place for officers, civil servants, and white civilians. An eyewitness recorded the following description:

> Last night at the Hanoi Hotel in Hanoi, I was quietly sipping my drink, when an explosion shook the air, projecting debris into my glass and releasing a cloud of smoke. A bomb had been thrown onto the terrace. Two old friends from the regiment, Commanders Chapuis and Montgrand, were covered in a sea of blood which flowed onto the sidewalk.[59]

When the smoke cleared, Montgrand, Chapuis, and an unnamed *indigène* lay dead, while a dozen Europeans and Vietnamese were wounded.⁶⁰ The perpetrators managed to flee in the ensuing chaos. As the hour of the attack, seven in the evening, was the time of the traditional *apéritif*, and the location, rue Paul-Bert, was the center of white civilian Hanoi, there can be no doubt that the objective was to create fear in the general colonial community. Our eyewitness recorded the following:

> Unique reaction of a young woman seated near the table of Commanders Théry and Montgrand, and whose drink had been contaminated by debris from the walls and other debris:
> "Damn country [*Sale pays*]! One can't even drink an absinthe in peace. Boy! Give me another absinthe."
> And very calmly she continued.⁶¹

As an official report put it, "the goal was to strike at the spirits [of the whites] and perhaps to provoke irreparable incidents between the *indigène* and European populations."⁶² Indeed, such a violation of one of the most important white rituals in the very heart of *la ville européenne* was a shocking affront to the colonial social order. The attack reinforced racial solidarity among the French population and increased the social distance between white and nonwhite. Official documents describe this polarization at the funeral of the fallen colonial officers:

> the admirable calm, the perfect *sang-froid*, the spirit of solidarity, and the confidence in the Government given to us by the French of Hanoi and Tonkin have not ceased to strike us and move us as admirable. On the tragic night of 26 April, the European population gave a preview of the sentiments of bravery and of discipline which has since not dissipated. Containing their indignation over the abominable crime, they have kept a noble and virile attitude in front of the native population. All the French, men and women, of Hanoi and the surrounding area, despite the new menaces which threatened them, gathered around the Chief of the Colony at the funerals of Commanders Chapuis and Montgrand, and gave their moving characters' highest significance to this large demonstration.⁶³

Anti-French violence was thus critical in reminding the colonizers of the need for racial solidarity.

Despite the colonial state's actions the white civilian population demanded more protection. In the press and in public meetings advocates of a hard-line policy vis-à-vis native political violence won many supporters. Following the 1908 and 1913 terrorist attacks, men such as Henri de Monpezat held boisterous meetings in Hanoi's elegant cafés. There the white colonials gave hysterical and inflammatory speeches, claiming that the French administration was not only putting them at risk but was betraying them by negotiating with rebels such as De Tham.[64] Local papers called for more public executions in prominent sections of the city. When native political violence drove the French of Hanoi into states of mass hysteria and collective racial anxiety, white colonials saw themselves as combatants in a racial war. Louis Bonnafort quipped, "Civilians—why speak of civilians, since we are all soldiers."[65] In these heated times, vigilantism reared its ugly head. Following the 1913 blast, a group of *"indigènophobes"* took it upon themselves to seek vengeance, if not justice. Governor-General Albert Sarraut reacted angrily but did his best to calm both whites and nonwhites alike.[66] In short, whites interpreted native political violence as an attack on all Europeans and responded with an unspecified fear and loathing for all natives.

Hanoi's most serious cases of native political violence occurred in the confused and chaotic times following the Japanese Army's shattering of the colonial order of things. Indeed, after the Japanese coup against the incumbent French colonial administration on 9 March 1945, with the colonial order turned upside down, French Hanoi descended into a charivari of racial conflict. Those who survived or avoided the Japanese coup de force and detention in makeshift prison camps faced another danger. Venting their anger at decades of colonial rule, rebellious Vietnamese transformed Hanoi into a festival of the oppressed. Eager to exploit the chaos for their own purposes, the Japanese occupiers did little to restrain the rowdy native crowds. Almost daily, but in an arbitrary and random manner, bands of radical students and political activists dragged French civil servants from their offices, beat them, forced them to wear humiliating placards, and paraded them around the streets of

Hanoi. White civilians became so fearful of being poisoned by their servants that vendors began to stock a large selection of purgatives. To make matters even more bewildering to the whites who had once ruled Hanoi, Vietnamese resistance organizations set up their own *milice* patrols. Jean Dol described his vexation at the petty harassment by Vietminh officials, as well as the threats he received from nationalist youth.[67]

As the first salvo in Vietnam's long war of national liberation, the Battle of Hanoi, December 1946 to January 1947, was a fitting end to the illusion of calm and safety that was French Hanoi. The battle illustrates the contradictory ways in which colonizer and colonized interpreted native-on-white violence. To the French the event was a symbol of the barbarity of the colonized, while to the Vietnamese it was an honorable struggle to liberate their capital.[68] The French press presented the battle as an act of treachery. Both reflecting and further enflaming white hysteria, European journalists spoke of "Asiatic cruelty" and "sadism."[69] In a fit of hyperbole designed to resonate in the hearts of Frenchmen, a journalist went so far as to invoke the image of the St. Bartholomew massacre.[70] Using the city as a metaphor for French civilians, the French press accused the Vietminh of trying to kill French Hanoi.[71] From this perspective, the battle was a violent act designed to eliminate the civilizing work of the French. By focusing on the violence of the urban guerrilla revolt, this "prose of counter-insurgency" silenced the Vietnamese nationalist discourse. Rather than considering the Vietminh as heroically resisting foreign domination (something the French refused to do after 1941), the battle was cast as bloodthirsty and irrational native violence.

The course of the battle demonstrated colonial Hanoi's racial geography of violence in the city. The fighting began as a general insurrection and raged throughout the city for a few days but was soon confined to the *quartier indigène*.[72] Once the Vietminh forces were surrounded in the native quarter, the French Army adopted brutal house-to-house fighting tactics. The end result was tremendous destruction in the Old Quarter, while the *quartier européen* escaped with less severe damage.[73] That the anti-French forces were unable to hold the white neighborhoods attests to the fact that this section of the society was more or less alien to them. The wide streets made the insurgents vulnerable to attack and allowed for the deployment of French armored vehicles. The open space between structures prevented quick escape, trapping many Vietminh units in French buildings. Conversely the Vietminh successfully utilized the familiar geography of the thirty-six Streets, holding the French at bay for several weeks. The Battle of Hanoi demonstrated, in an urban setting, that guerrilla fighters need to be of the physical and cultural environment that is serving as the battlefield. Like Mao's "fish in the sea of peasants," Hanoi's fighters used the native quarter to their advantage. Hiding in the small streets, moving from house to house with ease, and firing from balconies or around corners, the very structure of Old Hanoi became a weapon in the struggle against the French.

In conclusion, to understand the experience of daily life in colonial Hanoi, to map the colonial mind, one must understand the central role of the image of native violence in the mind of French colonials. Despite their impressive power over the colonized nonwhite population, the white residents of Hanoi obsessed over the threat of native violence against white bodies. This obsession was far out of proportion to the actual threat posed to the white colonials. Nonetheless, the anxiety of the white community became a central feature of colonial whiteness. This racialized fear of the Vietnamese points to a key paradox of colonial white identity; despite their power, they were constantly afraid. This combination of power and fear, strength and vulnerability, was at the heart of the colonial experience in Hanoi.

Notes

1. Michael Taussig, *Shamanism, Colonialism, and the Wild Man: A Study in Terror and Healing* (Chicago: University of Chicago Press, 1987). Taussig combines history, anthropology, and personal reflections in his complex and stimulating exploration of colonial violence and the native response in South America's Putamayo rubber region.

2. Dane Kennedy, *Islands of White: Settler Society and Culture in Kenya and Southern Rhodesia, 1890–1939* (Durham NC: Duke University Press, 1987), 128–47; Amirah Inglis, *The White Women's Protection Ordinance: Sexual Anxiety and Politics in Papua* (New York: St. Martin's Press, 1975); Pamela Scully, "Rape, Race, and Colonial Culture: The Sexual Politics of Identity in the Nineteenth-Century Cape Colony, South Africa," *American Historical Review* 100:2 (April 1995), 335–59; Vron Ware, *Beyond the Pale: White Women, Racism and History* (London: Verso, 1992).

3. Milton Osborne, "From Conviction to Anxiety: Reassessing the French Self-Image in Viet-Nam," Flinders University Asian Studies lecture 7, 1976; and Osborne, *Fear and Fascination in the Tropics: A Reader's Guide to French Fiction on Indochina* (Madison: University of Wisconsin Press, 1986). These relatively neglected articles have had a profound impact on my research on French and white identity in the colonial encounter. Osborne is to be commended as a pioneer in the exploration of colonial whiteness.

4. The horrors of the Belgian Congo are the quintessential illustration of the unleashing of social restraints on violence: see Adam Hochschild, *King Leopold's Ghost: A Story of Greed, Terror, and Heroism in Colonial Africa* (Boston: Houghton Mifflin, 1998).

5. On debasement as a process of colonization, see David Spurr, *The Rhetoric of Empire: Colonial Discourse in Journalism, Travel Writing, and Imperial Administration* (Durham NC: Duke University Press, 1993): 76–91. Frederick Douglass witnessed the corrupting and debasing effects of racial violence. He records how one of his owners, a woman living in Baltimore who had never had a slave before, was divested of her good qualities by her introduction to the cruel realities of slave owning. Frederick Douglass, *Narrative of the Life of Frederick Douglass, an American Slave, Written by Himself* (New York: Signet, 1968): 52–53.

6. See Syed Hussein Alatas, *The Myth of the Lazy Native: A Study of the Image of Malays, Filipinos and Javanese from the 16th to the 20th Century and Its Function in the Ideology of Colonial Capitalism* (London: Frank Cass, 1977), for a discussion of this process in colonial Southeast Asia.

7. Eugène Pujarniscle, *Philoxène ou de la littérature coloniale* (Paris: Librarie de Paris, 1931), 85–89.

8. John Horne, "Immigrant Workers in France during World War One," *French Historical Studies* 24:1 (1985), 57–88; Tyler Stovall, "Colour-Blind France? Colonial Workers during the First World War," *Race and Class* 35:2 (1993), 33–55; Stovall, "The Color Line behind the Lines: Racial Violence in France during the Great War," *American Historical Review* 103:3 (June 1998), 739–69.

9. Charles Tilly, *The Contentious French* (Cambridge MA: Harvard University Press, 1986); Eugen Weber, *France: Fin de Siècle* (Cambridge MA: Harvard University Press, 1986), 130–42. Like the rest of Western Europe, postcolonial France's struggle with multiculturalism has resulted in an interracial violence and the militant xenophobia of the Front National; see Maxim Silverman, *Deconstructing the Nation: Immigration, Racism, and Citizenship in Modern France* (New York: Routledge, 1992); Roger Brubaker, *Citizenship and Nationhood in France and Germany* (Cambridge MA: Harvard University

Press, 1992); Emmanuel Todd, *La nouvelle France* (Paris: Seuil, 1987); Todd, *Le destin des immigrés: Assimilation et ségrégation dans les démocraties occidentales* (Paris: Seuil, 1994).

10. Hannah Arendt, *On Violence* (New York: Harcourt, Brace, and World, 1969), 76.

11. Centre des Archives d'Outre-Mer (hereafter CAOM), 9 PA 2 dossier 1, Papiers Albert Sarraut: Pham-Boi-Chau, "Histoire des Héros de la ville de Hanoi," 1908.

12. CAOM, Papiers Marius Moutet 28 PA carton 7, dossier 167, sous-dossier 5; M. H. Virgitti and B. Joyeux, *Le péril vénérien dans la zone suburbaine de Hanoi* (Hanoi: IDEO, 1937).

13. Frantz Fanon, *The Wretched of the Earth* (New York: Grove Press, 1963), 35–106.

14. Ranajit Guha, "The Prose of Counter-Insurgency," in *Selected Subaltern Studies*, ed. Ranajit Guha and Gayatri Chakravorty Spivak (New York: Oxford University Press, 1988), 45–88.

15. See Michael G. Vann, "White Blood on Rue Hue: The Murder of 'le négrier' Bazin," *Proceedings of the Western Society for French History* (2006); and William J. Duiker, *The Rise of Nationalism in Vietnam, 1900–1941* (Ithaca NY: Cornell University Press, 1976), 160–61. Ann Laura Stoler notes that the Dutch rubber companies in Sumatra made an effort to depoliticize coolie violence in order to limit state and army intervention in their lands; Stoler, *Capitalism and Confrontation in Sumatra's Plantation Belt, 1870–1979* (Ann Arbor: University of Michigan Press, 1984), 50–53. Considering Balzac's work, Louis Chevalier links crime with popular revolt; Chevalier, *Laboring Classes and Dangerous Classes in Paris during the First Half of the Nineteenth Century* (Princeton NJ: Princeton University Press, 1973), 78.

16. CAOM, AF, carton 9, dossier 54, "Rapport général bimestriel-14 septembre," 1906.

17. CAOM, AF, carton 9, dossier 54, "Situation politique et économique du Tonkin," 1906.

18. Louis Bonnafort, *Trente ans de Tonkin* (Paris: Eugène Figuière, 1924), 123, 149.

19. See the "Echos du Tonkin" section of *L'Indo-Chine Française*, a Hanoi periodical that came out twice a week.

20. S. Abbatucci, "L'Habitation coloniale et le mode rationnel d'existence aux colonies," in Fédération Française de l'Enseignement Ménager, *La vie aux colonies: Préparation de la femme a la vie coloniale* (Paris: Larousse Editeurs, 1938), 78.

21. CAOM, AF, carton 9, dossier 51, "Rapport sur la situation politique et économique de l'Indochine," 1905.

22. CAOM, GGI, dossier 4664, "Justice, affaires divers: Assassinat de Madame Vve. Beljonne," 1906. Back in France, the national and provincial press did much to sensationalize similar violent crimes and foster a sense of anxiety; see Weber, *France*, 42. The case of the Papin sisters, servants who murdered their employers, provides an example of similar fears about servants back in the home country; see Janet Flanner, *Paris Was Yesterday, 1925–1939* (New York: Viking Press, 1972), 98–104; and Eugen Weber, *The Hollow Years: France in the 1930s* (New York: W. W. Norton, 1994), 129.

23. Jean Dol, "Pages de carnet: Hanoï 1945," *Ecrits de Paris: Revue des Questions Actuelles*, July 1957, 81.

24. M. le Dr. Roux, "Intelligence et moralité de l'Annamite Tonkinois," *Bulletin de la Société de Géographie et d'Études Coloniales de Marseille*, 1906, 190–91; Pujarniscle, *Philoxène*, 81; "De la mentalité et de la criminalité chez les annamites," *La revue Indochinoise*, 7 October 1901, 897–900.

25. Bonnafort, *Trente ans*, 139. All translations are by the author unless otherwise noted.

26. Alice L. Conklin, *A Mission to Civilize: The Republican Idea of Empire in France and West Africa, 1895–1930* (Stanford CA: Stanford University Press, 1997), 1–10.

27. Hanoi National Archives, MdH, dossier 35, "Rapport sur le fonctionnement de la Municipalité de Hanoi," 1891.

28. CAOM, AF, carton 9, dossier 51, "Rapport sur la situation politique et économique de l'Indochine," 1905.

29. CAOM, AF, carton 9, dossier 54, "Situation politique et économique du Tonkin," 1906.

30. Stoler, *Capitalism and Confrontation*, 150.

31. Kennedy, *Islands of White*, 128–47.

32. CAOM, 9 PA 2 dossier 1, Papiers Sarraut: Pham-Boi-Chau, "Histoire des Héros de la ville de Hanoi," 1908; and *Les armées française d'outre-mer: L'Armée française en Indochine* (Paris: Imprimerie Nationale, 1932), 262.

33. CAOM, GGI, dossier 64179, "Tonkin," 1908.

34. CAOM, 9 PA 2, dossier 1, Papiers Sarraut: Pham-Boi-Chau, "Histoire des Héros de la ville de Hanoi," 1908, 5–6.

35. David Marr, *Vietnamese Anti-Colonialism: 1885–1925* (Berkeley: University of California Press, 1971), 193–94; CAOM, GGI, dossier 64179, "Tonkin," 1908.

36. *Les armées française d'outre-mer*, 262; Marr, *Vietnamese Anti-Colonialism*, 208–9.

37. Claude Bourrin, *Choses et gens en Indochine: A Hanoi avant-guerre au Vieux-Colombier en guerre contre l'Allemange, 1908–1916* (Hanoi: IDEO, 1941), 202.

38. CAOM, GGI, dossier 19211, "Réunion publique tenue à Hanoï (Hôtel Métropole) le 6 juillet 1909," 1909.

39. CAOM, GGI, dossier 64179, "Tonkin: Rapport Politique Générale pour l'année 1908," 1908.

40. It is useful to place this rise in racial tensions and violence in comparison with the wartime racial violence in France; see Stovall, "Color Line."

41. CAOM, AF, carton 9 dossier 51, "Rapport sur la situation politique et économique de l'Indochine," 1905.

42. CAOM, Papiers Sarraut, 9 PA 2, dossier 2, 1913. That the colonial prison system, including the infamous Poulo Condore Island, was one of the most fertile areas for Communist Party recruitment remains one of the great ironies of the French colonial empire. See Peter Zinoman, "The History of the Modern Prison and the Case of Indochina," in *Crime and Criminality in Indonesia, the Philippines and Colonial Vietnam*, ed. Vince Rafeal (Ithaca NY: Southeast Asia Program Publications, 1999); Zinoman, *The Colonial Bastille* (Berkeley: University of California Press, 2001), for a study of the Indochinese prison system, as well as David Arnold, "The Colonial Prison: Power, Knowledge, and Penology in Nineteenth-Century India," in *Subaltern Studies VIII: Essays in Honour of Ranajit Guha*, ed. David Arnold and David Hardiman (Delhi: Oxford University Press, 1994), 148–87, for a discussion of prisons under the Raj.

43. CAOM, GGI, dossier 64179, "Tonkin," 1908.

44. CAOM, GGI, dossier 50673, "Commission criminelle. Procédures Arrêt Pourvoir. Affair Hanoi-Hôtel," 1913/1919; GGI, dossier 50763: "Commission Criminelle. Procédure. Arrêt. Pourvoir. Affaire bombe 'Hanoi-Hôtel'," 1913–19; GGI, dossier 53430, "Commission Criminelle de Hanoi. Rapport, corréspondances," 1930–31; GGI, dossier 53455, "Commission Criminelle siégéant à Hanoi. Rapport au Gouverneur Général," 1931.

45. *Les armées française d'outre-mer*, 262.

46. J. Gounelle, *Ligue Française pour la Défense des Droits de l'Homme et du Citoyen, Section d'Hanoi Son Oeuvre au Tonkin durant ces trois dernières années, 1910–1911–1912* (Hanoi: Imprimerie Tonkinoise, 1913).

47. Andrée Viollis, *Indochine S.O.S.* (Paris: Gallimard, 1935), 127.

48. Charles Fourniau, *Annam-tonkin 1885–1896: Lettrés et paysans vietnamiens face à la conquête coloniale* (Paris: L'Harmattan, 1989); Patrice Morlat, *La Répression colonial au Vietnam (1908–1940)* (Paris: L'Harmattan, 1990); Yves Benôt, *Massacres coloniaux 1944–1950: La IVe République et la mise au pas des colonies françaises* (Paris: Éditions la Découverte, 1995), 69–113.

49. Brieux, *Voyage aux Indes et en Indo-Chine: Simples Notes d'un Touriste* (Paris: Librairie Ch. Delagrave, 1910), 36.

50. See Michel Foucault, *Discipline and Punish: The Birth of the Prison* (New York: Vintage Books, 1979), 14; William J. Harris, "Etiquette, Lynching, and Racial Boundaries in Southern History: A Mississippi Example," *American Historical Review* 100:2 (1995), 387–411.

51. Paul Bonnetain, *L'Extrême-orient* (Paris: Maison Quantin, 1887), 299–301.

52. Brieux, *Voyage aux Indes*, 36.

53. Brieux, *Voyage aux Indes*, 144–47; Jean Ajalbert, "Le Dé-Tham, la piraterie et les complots," *Les Nauges sur l'Indochine* (Paris: Louis-Michaud, 1912), 119–23.

54. Bourrin, *Choses et gens en Indochine*, 202.

55. CAOM, GGI, dossier 19211, "Réunion publique tenue à Hanoï (Hôtel Métropole) le 6 juillet 1909," 1909.

56. Trois Margouillats Tonkinois, *Hanoi-Sur-Scène* (Hanoi: Imp. de l'Avenir du Tonkin, 1912).

57. Bourrin, *Choses et gens en Indochine*, 203.

58. CAOM, GGI, dossier 64187, "Tonkin: Rapport Politique Premier Trimestre 1913," 1913.

59. Bonnafort, *Trente ans*, 319–20.

60. Obviously the dead Vietnamese man did have a name. The point here is that in French accounts of the event, the white deaths eclipsed the native fatality.

61. Bonnafort, *Trente ans*, 320.

62. As if the brutal French conquest, excessive tax system, and daily indignations of colonial rule had not already provoked such irreparably damaging incidents; CAOM, Papiers Albert Sarraut, 9 PA, dossier 2, "Procès verbaux des séances du Conseil du Protectorat et rapports au Conseil du Protectorats du 11 septembre 1913," 1913.

63. CAOM, Papiers Sarraut, 9 PA, dossier 2, "Rapport de GGI Sarraut au Ministre les Colonies," 1913, 45–46.

64. CAOM, GGI dossier 19211, "Réunion publique tenue à Hanoï (Hôtel Métropole)," 1909.

65. Bonnafort, *Trente ans*, 164–65.

66. CAOM, Papiers Sarraut, 9 PA 2, dossier 7, "Lettre de Albert Sarraut à Guèsde," 1913.

67. Dol, "Pages de Carnet," 73, 77, 80–81.

68. Stein Tønnesson, *1946 Déclenchement de la guerre d'Indochine: Les vêpres tonkinoise du 19 décembre* (Paris: Harmattan, 1987), 167–78.

69. CAOM, AGEFOM, carton 167 dossier 20, Paul Bastid, "L'Indochine sévère: Hanoï et le Tonkin," 1949.

70. CAOM, AGEFOM, carton 272, dossier 452, André Blanchet, "Le Saint-Berthelemy des français."

71. CAOM, AGEFOM, carton 236, dossier 294, Paul Munier, "La Capitale assassinée," 1947.

72. CAOM, AGEFOM, carton 269, dossier 441. Considered alongside the revolt and repression of the Commune, the similarities between the social geography of Paris 1871 and Hanoi 1946 are telling. In both cases the oppressed—in one situation the Parisian working class; in the other case the Vietnamese militants—took over a Haussmanized city as a whole but were quickly dislodged from those areas that were alien to them—the wealthier *arrondisements* and the *quartier blanc*, respectively—and forced back into their own neighborhoods, where the repressive violence of the state was the most excessive. See Jacques Rougerie, *Paris insurgé: La Commune de 1871* (Paris: Gallimard, 1995); Kristin Ross, *The Emergence of Social Space: Rimbaud and the Paris Commune* (Minneapolis: University of Minnesota Press, 1988), Stewart Edwards, ed., *The Communards of Paris, 1871* (Ithaca NY: Cornell University Press, 1973).

73. CAOM, AGEFOM, carton 236, dossier 294.

4

Anti-Semitism and the Colonial Situation in Interwar Algeria

The Anti-Jewish Riots in Constantine, August 1934

JOSHUA COLE

In August 1934 the city of Constantine in Algeria became the site of the worst episode of anti-Semitic violence to occur on French territory during peacetime in the modern period.[1] This violence broke out as French Algeria was drawn into the turmoil that beset France in the decade before the Second World War. For several years Constantine—like other Algerian cities—had been unsettled by conflicts that pit the colonial republican establishment against an array of newer political formations, including an association of elected Muslim officials, a resurgent group of right-wing anti-Semites in the middle-class Croix de Feu, and the Communist Party.[2] These tensions all came to the surface following a banal incident at a mosque on 3 August 1934, when a Jewish man insulted several Muslim men as they prepared for their prayers. In the weekend of rioting that followed, twenty-eight people were killed—twenty-five Jews and three Muslims.[3]

In the aftermath of the rioting in Constantine the city's residents and the colonial authorities sought to determine its consequences in a secondary struggle about its meaning. Was it a momentary aberration or the result of long-nurtured grievances? How had the anger of the rioting crowds come to focus on the Jews of Constantine? Was it their perceived place within the middle-class settler political establishment? Were Jews targeted because of the role that some Jewish individuals in the city played within the town's commercial or political elite? Had the Muslim population of the city come under the influence of European anti-Semitism? Were they acting under the influence of newer militant ideologies such as Communism or pan-Islamic nationalism? Or had Constantine's Jews somehow come to stand for everything that colonial subjects in Algeria had come to resent about the French empire, that is, the way that the settler-dominated elite continually worked to reinforce the exclusion of Muslim Algerians from political participation and economic opportunity?

Historians who have discussed the riots in Constantine have usually been divided between those who saw the riots as an anomalous local event and those who sought to classify the violence as a "classic pogrom," in which a vulnerable Jewish population was victimized by a majority population motivated by hatred and abetted by the passivity of local authorities.[4] More recently a few scholars have suggested that the riots in Constantine might best be understood in the context of evolving relationships between settlers, Jews, and Muslims in French Algeria that had been recast by the experience of colonialism.[5] The present study seeks to develop this latter argument further, without denying the riot's origins in the particular local circumstances of interwar Constantine.

In the most immediate sense the violence in 1934 in Constantine emerged from a dynamic in local politics that was introduced by the French colonial regime's attempt to offer a limited form of political citizenship to Algeria's Muslim colonial subjects in the years after World War 1. The effect of these reforms was to exacerbate local tendencies to think of political and social interests in ethno-religious terms and to make conflict between groups conceived in these terms more likely. The government's official reports in the aftermath of the riots nevertheless attributed the violence to the atavistic hatreds between Muslims and Jews that were allegedly a permanent part of the social landscape in North Africa. From the perspective of the colonial state, such an interpretation had the political advantage of obscuring the complexities of local politics under the colonial situation. Blaming two apparently homogeneous and irreconcilable ethno-religious groups—"Muslims" and "Jews"—served to divert attention from the failures of the local French authorities and acted as a justification for the continued concentration of power in their hands. It also obscured the extent to which anti-Semitism was built into the political process in Algeria and minimized evidence that some anti-Semites among the settler population may have sought to provoke the spread of violence after it began.

Anti-Semitism and the Colonial Situation in Algeria

Constantine was the largest city in eastern Algeria, with a very old and vibrant Jewish quarter, a Muslim population known for its devotion to traditional religious practices, and a French settler population that was not as large as its counterparts in other Algerian cities. As of the 1931 census, the population was just over 101,000. As the region's commercial center for textiles and grains, and as the administrative capital of the department, Constantine had undergone especially rapid population growth during the First World War and the 1920s, increasing by over 50 percent from a population of 65,000 in 1911.[6] During these years, the absolute numbers of Jews in the city increased slowly, and the percentage of Jews within the total population actually fell slightly.

According to the categories commonly in use by the colonial administration, 12 percent of the population was *israélite* (Jewish) in 1931, 36 percent was *européenne* (European), and 51 percent was *indigène* (native). As Phyllis Cohen Albert has pointed out, the term *israélite* was adopted by French Jews in the nineteenth century as a way to counter the increasingly ethnic or national uses of *juif* with a term that was more closely associated with confessional behavior.[7] The use of *israélite* by the Algerian census under the Third Republic clearly reflected a similar desire to find a term for assimilated Jews that would allow their distinctive presence within the population to be noted, without implying any form of difference that might contradict the universalist promise of citizenship embodied in republican doctrine. The label *européenne*, on the other hand, was used in the Algerian census until 1926 and widely in many official documents for much longer as a thinly disguised racial term whose primary function was to distinguish the French, Alsatian, Spanish, Italian, and Maltese settler population of Algeria from the *indigènes* of Algeria. Because of the Third Republic's inconsistent citizenship laws, this "European" population also included Constantine's 12,058 native (i.e., North African) Jews, who were enumerated as a separate subcategory in the census until 1936.[8]

The use of these three terms had a long history.[9] When Algeria was annexed to France by the Royal Ordonnance of 24 February 1834, the populations of the region were a heterogeneous group, divided into intersecting categories that included Arabs, Ottomans, Berbers, Muslims, Jews, town dwellers, and inhabitants of the countryside, as well as complex relations of kinship. The French military amalgamated these peoples together indiscriminately into a group henceforth labeled *indigène* (indigenous, native born). The Ordonnance of 1834 claimed a form of French nationality for this amalgamation but denied Algerians the full rights of citizenship. The juridical status of this new category *indigène* was inferior to that of other French citizens, and the conquered peoples of Algeria came to occupy an intermediary position, somewhere between "foreign" and "French." Within this intermediary space, they lived in accordance with Islamic or Jewish laws regarding marriage and inheritance, but this very "privilege" also became a justification for excluding them from the full rights enjoyed by citizens under the French civil code.[10] During the Second Empire, the Sénatus-consulte of 1865 reaffirmed the distinction between the nationality and citizenship of Algerian Jews and Muslims, even as it granted a limited right for certain *indigènes* to become "naturalized" citizens, so long as they surrendered their rights to live in accordance with Jewish or Islamic customary laws.

The Crémieux decree of 1870 granted citizenship to Algeria's Jews, removing them from the population labeled *indigène*. At the same time, the Third Republic codified the inferior juridical status of the remaining (largely Muslim) subject population in the 1881 Code de l'indigénat, creating a list of crimes specific to this portion of the Algerian population. This severe code prohibited colonial subjects from meeting in groups or traveling without official permission and punished "disrespectful" acts with sanctions that included the sequestration of property, imprisonment, and fines.[11] The Third Republic's legislation thus created a situation where the majority of Algerians were technically "French" but also "native" without citizenship and subject to a harsh juridical regime, while another "native" group—Algeria's Jews—became French citizens with the same rights as all other non-"native" French people. Many of Algeria's Jews accepted this opportunity for civic belonging by embracing the republican doctrine of assimilation offered to them as citizens.

In contrast, as Muslim elites began to organize themselves and call for reform of the Republic's treatment of its colonial subjects, very few opted for the onerous naturalization process that seemed to demand a repudiation of their religious beliefs. Instead, organized political activity by Muslim colonial subjects in Algeria increasingly focused on a call for a form of full citizenship that would preserve the personal legal status granted to them as Muslims. Both Algerian Jews and Muslims faced continued discrimination in many aspects of their lives, but the rigorous exclusion of Muslims from political life meant that the gap between the two groups, measured in terms of economic opportunity, cultural capital, and political voice, had widened considerably by the interwar years.

Anti-Semitism among the settler population in Algeria had been widespread since the last decades of the nineteenth century.[12] In cities such as Oran, Algiers, and Constantine, where many of Algeria's Jews resided, settler anti-Semitism was largely associated with the calendar of municipal elections. Nowhere numerous enough to form a majority, Algeria's urban Jewish electorate during the Third Republic was at times large enough to affect the outcome of municipal elections. The stakes of these mayoral contests were high, because they determined which political clans would divide the bountiful spoils and patronage that came with local dominance. Coalitions that lost to a group allied with local Jewish leaders were often tempted to base their subsequent campaigns on populist anti-Semitic demagoguery. During the Dreyfus affair of the 1890s, anti-Jewish unrest in Oran, Algiers, and Constantine led to violence that resulted in several deaths. The long-serving mayor of Constantine, Émile Morinaud, came to power in 1898 with just such an opportunist and vitriolic anti-Semitic message at the height of the Dreyfus affair.[13] Once Morinaud was in office, Jews were fired from jobs with the municipality, turned away from the local hospital, and struck from the welfare lists. The city government even considered excluding Jews from public schools.[14] These policies did not prevent Morinaud from consolidating his power some time later in an alliance with members of the same Jewish political leadership that he had earlier attacked.[15] Morinaud was still in office in 1934 when the August riots broke out, and the events of that month coincided with the dissolution of his alliance with Jewish elected officials. Many of Constantine's Jews later came to blame him for the event.

What made the 1934 riot unusual was not the expression of a vicious anti-Semitism, but rather the fact that so many Muslim Algerians—that is, so many of Algeria's excluded colonial subjects—participated in the violence. During the notorious wave of anti-Semitic violence in Algiers in the 1890s, there were cases of Muslim colonial subjects being observed among the crowds attacking Jews, but the historical evidence indicates that these crowds were not spontaneously generated, but organized and paid for by settler political groups that sought to profit from the instability caused by the violence.[16] In Constantine during the summer of 1921 a wave of anti-Semitic provocation by local French journalists provoked street battles between young Jewish men and anti-Semites among the settler population, but there is no evidence that the Muslim colonial subjects of Constantine were anything more than passive spectators to this confrontation.[17] And although one can point to a renewal of anti-Semitic agitation among certain elements of the settler population in the early 1930s, the riots of August 1934 occurred well before the peak of this agitation in 1935–1936, during the electoral campaign that brought the Popular Front to power and made Léon Blum the first Jewish prime minister of France. In other words, the decades before this event saw relatively frequent outbreaks of tension between settler anti-Semites and Jews in Algeria, but there is little evidence that such tensions were inevitably linked with widespread expressions of anti-Semitism by the large majority of Muslim colonial subjects who allegedly had reason to resent their Jewish neighbors for having benefited from French colonialism.

In August 1934, on the other hand, attempts by European anti-Semites to instigate a response among Constantine's colonial subjects seem to have worked. Why then, and not before or later, when expressions of European anti-Semitism were even stronger? Presumed bitterness among Algeria's Muslim colonial subjects about the success of Algeria's Jews in accommodating themselves to the French colonial system only goes so far in explaining this specific outbreak of violence, since the relatively frequent agitation by European anti-Semites in Algeria so rarely led to the large-scale involvement of Muslim colonial subjects. On the other hand, there is considerable evidence that political reforms after World War I reinforced a tendency of all parties in Algeria to conceive of organized political activities largely in ethno-religious terms, thereby straining relations between individuals who also thought of themselves in this way and increasing the possibility that local disagreements might lead to broader collective confrontations.

This appears to be what happened in Constantine: the local Jewish leadership responded to the provocations of settler anti-Semites in the postwar years with a combination of public claims about their place in the polity and the cautious cultivation of alliances with local representatives of the colonial government. At times of crisis, when settler anti-Semites stepped up their efforts to demonize the Jewish population of the city, the political strategies of Jewish elected officials were accompanied by a more aggressive posture of self-defense on the part of certain Jewish men within the city, which over time evolved into informal neighborhood networks led by young men willing to defend their homes and associations with their fists and, eventually, with more lethal weapons. This more aggressive posture of self-defense was in no way dictated or controlled by the individuals who made up the political leadership of the Jewish population, but it became increasingly difficult for others in Constantine to distinguish between the actions of individuals or small groups and the defense of the various communities in the city as a whole, and there may have been some who perceived a political incentive in avoiding such distinctions, both within the settler population and among the population of colonial subjects in Constantine. These circumstances made it more likely that momentary misunderstandings or altercations between individuals would escalate into more violent conflict between groups defined in ethno-religious terms.

The most significant of the post–World War 1 reforms that contributed to the exacerbation of ethno-religious conflict in Algeria was the law of 4 February 1919, known as the Jonnart Law. This law granted a limited form of citizenship for 425,000 of Algeria's colonial subjects (43 percent of the adult male population), allowing them to vote, in a separate electoral college, for their own candidates in local elections.[18] In its insistence on a separate electoral college, the Jonnart Law maintained the previous legal distinction between French citizens and colonial subjects, and the law's provisions limited the number of seats set aside for Muslim representatives to one third of the total, thus guaranteeing that no elected assembly would ever face the possibility of a Muslim majority.

Given this inescapably communitarian departure point, it was almost inevitable that the dynamics of the political process would be shaped by the common perceptions of racial difference that permeated public discourse in France during this period. Such a dynamic had already been implicit in the process by which Algeria's Jews were collectively granted the rights of citizens in 1870—the Jonnart Law merely pursued this logic further, by granting a limited number of Algeria's previously excluded colonial subjects the right to participate in politics, but only as "Muslims."[19]

The political reforms of February 1919 thus created overnight a new political space for a cohort of Muslim elected officials who sought to define the boundaries and aspirations of a new and as yet untested political constituency. In his study of political life in Algiers, the Algerian capital, Mahfoud Kaddache suggested that these first Muslim elected officials were quite cautious in the support that they offered for their constituency.[20] Nevertheless, the possibility of a new assertiveness on the part of Muslim Algerians who had previously been effectively excluded from the political system was deeply disturbing to the members of the settler establishment in Algiers, Oran, and Constantine.[21]

This colonial establishment, which had dominated Algerian politics with no significant competition during the prewar decades, also faced a new boldness on the part of Jewish elected officials who felt, as did many Muslim Algerians, that their participation in the war effort should be rewarded by recognition of their place within the polity. Several Jewish elected officials in Constantine were veterans of the French military, and their actions in the postwar period demonstrated a desire to place themselves and the civic organizations that they represented more clearly at the center of public life in the city. This assertiveness undoubtedly strained their relations with some of their allies on the municipal council, most notably with Mayor Émile Morinaud, who since 1908 had maintained close relations with Elie Narboni, the president of the Jewish Consistoire in Constantine. During the 1920s Morinaud did not back away from his Jewish allies, in spite of the fact that many of his ostensible supporters among the settler population were known to harbor anti-Semitic views.

Unfortunately for the social peace of the region, however, this self-assertion on the part of some Jewish officials within municipal governance coincided with the French Parliament's debate and eventual passage of the law of 29 July 1920, which reestablished many of the disciplinary powers associated with the harshly punitive Code de l'indigénat. The 1920 law was clearly an attempt to appease the most powerful representatives of the colony's settler elite, as it reestablished the terms of a prewar penal code that gave local administrators and the police the right to punish summarily any colonial subject found guilty of violating the code's list of crimes, which included mundane acts of disrespect toward French authority, public statements critical of the government, and violations of the laws regarding permission to travel.[22] The months before and after the passage of this law in 1920 thus witnessed a potentially toxic mix of increasing visibility for both Muslim and Jewish elected officials, increasing defensiveness on the part of a fearful colonial establishment, and a reassertion of the colonial government's right to apply the harshest forms of legal coercion against a subject population with few rights or protections under law. Unfortunately, and perhaps predictably, this context led to several localized incidents of tension or minor violence, especially between Jews and anti-Semites in the settler population. A few isolated incidents of violence between Muslims and Jews did occur in the immediate postwar period, but they appear to have been exceptional and did not lead to widespread conflict.[23]

Throughout the 1920s, Jewish civic leaders in Constantine reacted to the very present threat of settler anti-Semitism by embracing a more visible role in patriotic associations, in public welfare organizations, and in promoting educational institutions for Jewish children. Jewish leaders in Constantine had long been concerned about two issues: the poor quality of the available housing in the Jewish quarter and the inadequacy of primary instruction in both religious and academic subject matter for Jewish children from the many poorer families in the community. Taking advantage of the opportunities offered by Parliament's passage of the Ribot and Loucheur laws in 1922 and 1928, each designed to increase the availability of low-cost housing, Jewish elected officials in Constantine sought to encourage the movement of poorer Jewish families from the *hara* into new subsidized buildings (*habitations bon marché* or HBM). The Office Public des HBM in Constantine was directed by two prominent leaders within the Jewish community: Henri Lellouche, a member of the departmental assembly, and Maurice Laloum, a municipal councilor. Many Jewish families were initially reluctant to leave the older neighborhood in the center of town for the HBM, but by December 1930 the demands for places in the newly constructed apartments far outstripped the supply, with more than four hundred applications for sixty-three apartments.[24] During these same years, Rabbi Maurice Eisenbeth and Émile Barkatz, who had succeeded Elie Narboni as the president of the Jewish Consistoire in Constantine, founded a new departmental federation of Jewish religious associations. One of the federation's initial projects was to support the work of a newly founded Hebrew school in Constantine, the École Etz Haïm, which aimed to encourage both religious teaching and an awareness of Jewish history in the region.[25]

In the eyes of the Jewish leadership in Constantine there was no contradiction between the explicitly Jewish mission of the École Etz Haïm and the assimilationist housing program that aimed to break the isolation of Constantine's Jews in the traditional Jewish quarter. The Jewish leadership in Constantine cautiously but resolutely embraced a modernist vision of Jewish identity that strongly identified with the protections offered to Jews by the republican state and saw no inconsistency in their self-awareness as a Jewish minority and their place as citizens in the French nation.[26] Nevertheless, this renewed civic activity on the part of Constantine's Jews took place against the background of an increasingly intense expression of anti-Semitism elsewhere in France and Europe, and inevitably this widely held French antipathy toward Jews had an echo in Constantine among the settler population.[27] The response among the local Jewish community in Constantine during these years was similar to their reaction at the turn of the century or in the immediate postwar years of the early 1920s. Jewish elected officials cautiously cultivated alliances with members of the republican settler establishment and attempted to maintain good relations with the prefect. Other groups of Jewish men with a more activist inclination organized themselves more informally with the physical defense of their communities, their streets, and their homes.

During these years, however, several new developments made the

Jews of Constantine even more vulnerable than in the immediate postwar years. First, Algeria was not immune to the global economic crisis brought about by the Depression, and by 1930 the numbers of unemployed in the city's poorer neighborhoods was growing rapidly.[28] Second, the dominance of the Radical Republicans over the political life of the settler population had been threatened by the increased importance on the one hand of the Communist Party and the corresponding rise of a more strident form of right-wing political activism in the Croix de Feu. The Communists appeared poised to divide the settler population by attracting a significant number of working-class votes, and the party's embrace of an anticolonial position in the 1920s caused many in the administration to fear the spread of a new militancy among Algeria's colonial subjects.[29] The Croix de Feu, on the other hand, presented itself as an authoritarian veteran's organization that sought broad support among Constantine's settler middle class.[30] The increasing importance of the Croix de Feu, whose local chapter became increasingly anti-Semitic during this period, eventually forced mayor and deputy Émile Morinaud to choose between two increasingly incompatible wings within his coalition—that is, between the group of Jewish elected officials close to Elie Narboni and Émile Barkatz that had supported him in the municipal council for nearly three decades, and the growing portion of the settler electorate who vocally embraced anti-Semitic views. The riots of August 1934, among other things, marked the moment when Morinaud's rupture with his former Jewish allies became unavoidable, and he returned to the aggressive and opportunistic anti-Semitism that had been his stock in trade at the beginning of his political career in the 1890s.

In the early 1930s the city's majority population of colonial subjects had also been more effectively brought into the political life of the region by the rise to prominence of a new cohort of Muslim politicians based in Constantine. Most notable among them was Mohamed-Salah Bendjelloul, a medical doctor who served on the municipal and departmental councils and who in 1932 became the president of the Fédération des élus musulmans de Constantine (FEC), an association that brought together elected Muslim officials from throughout the department.[31] Under his leadership the federation set about the task of unifying the loose affiliation of Muslim elected officials around a program aimed both at the educated Muslim elite and the larger body of colonial subjects who had thus far been completely excluded from the political process. For members of the relatively small Muslim middle class, Bendjelloul advocated equal pay for Muslim functionaries in civil service and for Muslims serving in the military, an abrogation of the Code de l'indigénat, and an end to police surveillance and special tribunals, as well as the right to vote for their own parliamentary representatives.[32] For the much larger mass of colonial subjects, Bendjelloul outlined a more populist program aimed at establishing easier forms of credit for rural farmers, an end to the harsh collective punishments meted out to villages for violations of the forest code, tax reforms, and improvements in housing for the poor.

In advocating such a program, which was in many ways compatible with the modernizing rhetoric of the Third Republic, Bendjelloul occupied a transitional space between the Muslim elites of the prewar generation, some of whom allowed themselves to be co-opted by the French administration, and the more overtly nationalist figures, such as Messali Hadj, who succeeded him later in the 1930s and in the post–World War II years.[33] Bendjelloul was outspoken in his support for full citizenship rights for Algeria's colonial subjects, and he also called upon the republic to preserve their special legal status as Muslims. He never resorted to nationalist rhetoric, and his most visible goal before 1934 was, in fact, to become more of an insider: in the early 1930s he attracted a name for himself by a very public campaign to gain a seat as a representative of Algeria's Muslims on the Commission interministérielle des affaires musulmans (CIAM), a government body that had authority over Muslim affairs in France and the colonies.[34] This commission, which oversaw matters relating to the practice of Islam and the organization of mosques, as well as Islamic education and the Arabic press, had been created in 1911 but had never actively sought input from independent representatives of France's Muslim colonial subjects. On 16 May 1934, only six weeks before the outbreak of anti-Semitic violence of 3–5 August, Bendjelloul's year-long campaign culminated when he spoke at an outdoor public meeting before at least four thousand of his supporters, demanding that he be seated as a member of the CIAM, and that the Muslim population recognize the members of the FEC as their representatives.[35]

Even as Constantine was becoming known as a center of more effective political organization on the part of Algerian colonial subjects in the early 1930s, the city was also increasingly associated with a movement for Islamic renewal led by Abd al-Hamid Ben Badis, a native of the city from a prominent Muslim family. Ben Badis and the Islamic scholars associated in Algeria with his *salafiyya* movement sought a return to the original precepts of the Islamic tradition, a position that put them into opposition with the French administration, as well as with other Algerian religious leaders associated with local shrines and confraternities. Their emphasis on religion, cultural separatism, and the use of Arabic also put them into potential conflict with leaders such as Bendjelloul, who publicly endorsed a moderate assimilationist program, and who sought alliances with politicians in Paris. Ben Badis's organization, the Association of Algerian Muslim Scholars, played an important role in the development of a revitalized sense of North African culture that rejected French influences and recast the predominant sense of what an authentic Muslim culture in Algeria might be. They published a newspaper, *Ech-Chihab* (the Meteor), and encouraged efforts to improve Islamic education, to provide instruction in classical Arabic, and to produce new forms of writing about the history of North Africa and Algeria in particular.[36] Ben Badis and Bendjelloul did not always get along, but it is significant that the two appeared together on the podium during the public meeting of 16 May 1934 in Constantine, the meeting that consecrated Bendjelloul in the eyes of his supporters as their only legitimate representative. This meeting was the last large political gathering of Muslim colonial subjects in the city before the riots of August 1934.

There is no evidence that Abd al-Hamid Ben Badis harbored anti-Semitic views. Bendjelloul's relationship with anti-Semitism is more complex, however, and between the riots of August 1934 and the electoral victory of the Popular Front in 1936 he may have sought support from or responded to overtures from anti-Semitic right-wing settlers from the local section of the Croix de Feu. After the riots, Bendjelloul sought to gain political advantage from the anger among his constituencies at the city's Jewish population, and he was openly supportive of a boycott of Jewish businesses that took place in the weeks after the violence. From the available evidence in the colonial archives, however, Bendjelloul did not appear to resort to anti-Semitism in his public pronouncements between his accession to the presidency of the FEC in 1932 and the riots of August 1934. During this period he worked above all to consolidate his position as the leading secular politician who might give voice to Algeria's Muslim majority within the terms set up by the Jonnart Law. Nevertheless, Bendjelloul's mobilization of an explicitly "Muslim" electorate in Constantine may have contributed to the development of antagonistic feelings between Muslims and Jews in Constantine, since the Jewish political establishment had been allied for so long with the very same settler elites who were Bendjelloul's primary opponents in the local assemblies. This situation created the potential for a kind of structural antagonism between the two political groups, and in the aftermath of the riot it became clear that there was a great deal of mistrust and suspicion on both sides separating Bendjelloul and the members of his *fédération* from the Jewish elected officials on the town council.

Taken together, these political tensions appear to have led to a new pattern of confrontations between Muslims and Jews in Constantine. In a letter of 9 August 1930 to the prefect of Constantine, the governor-general in Algiers listed thirty-one incidents in which Jews had attacked Muslims in Constantine over the previous year and a half. Most of the incidents were minor, involving petty disputes on the street that escalated quickly from insults to blows, but without serious injury. A few, however, involved serious beatings. Most of the victims were Muslim colonial subjects, some quite young, who were quickly overwhelmed by groups of Jewish men or teenagers who were quick to assume the worst when an altercation broke out. Most regrettably, one of the victims was Abd al-Ḥamid Ben Badis himself, the prominent Islamic cleric, who was attacked as he returned home one evening with a companion, though it does not appear that his attackers knew who he was.[37] Some of this belligerence on the part of certain Jewish men in the town appears to have had its origins in a perception that the police did not do enough to defend them against the provocations of settler anti-Semitism. In subsequent months the police responded by arresting some of the more outspoken and aggressive local Jewish figures who were active in street-level community self-defense activities.[38] Finding themselves isolated within the city and unsure of the protection that they could expect from an increasingly hostile police force, the Jewish leadership of Constantine wrote a petition to Mayor Émile Morinaud and the prefect in June 1932, calling for the replacement of Police Commissioner René Miquel. The petition met with no response. During the increasingly frequent moments when the provocations of settler anti-Semites led to outbursts of momentary violence between individuals on the street, the police responded by shutting down the Jewish quarter and controlling circulation on the streets of the old city.[39] In August 1934, however, this strategy was either not implemented, or it failed.

The Riots of August 1934

The immediate cause of the violence on the weekend of 3–5 August 1934 was a banal incident similar to the many others that had occurred in the city since the late 1920s.[40] On a Friday evening, 3 August, a Jewish tailor and member of a local Zouave regiment, Elie Khalifa, became embroiled in an altercation with several men as he returned to his home after a few drinks in a café. The men were washing themselves as they prepared for their prayers in the mosque opposite Khalifa's apartment, and Khalifa first confronted them through an open window that was separated from the street by an iron grill. According to Khalifa's later testimony, he was insulted by their visible nakedness, and he cursed them, their religious leaders, and their religion. Several of the men inside the room later claimed that he also spat or urinated on the wall of the mosque before retreating to his apartment. Incensed by Khalifa's words and by his profanation of their sacred space, a small group of angry men soon gathered in front of the mosque, while Khalifa returned to his apartment. One of the men who had been bathing in the chamber on the alley, Ahmed ben Salah Bach-Mohaden Bendjelloul, attempted to calm the growing crowd and was soon joined by the muphti of Constantine, Mouloud Benelmouhoub. Their efforts at first seemed successful, but by 9:30 p.m. a new group had gathered in front of Khalifa's building, and somebody in the crowd threw a stone at Khalifa's window. Khalifa's wife suddenly appeared, shouted a few curses at the crowd down below, and precipitously closed the shutters. The crowd—now approaching fifty people—began to shout and throw more stones at the apartment. The muphti again came out of the mosque and tried once more to quiet the crowd, and three police agents, who attempted to enter the building to speak to Khalifa, joined him. Eventually, the police and the muphti managed to disperse the people who had gathered before Khalifa's house.

Sometime between 10:00 and 11:00 p.m., however, a much larger crowd of nearly two thousand people, armed with clubs, sticks, knives and stones, came through the rue Vieux-Sidi-Moussa, the rue Bleue, and the rue Combes to the place des Galettes and the small place in front of the mosque. The crowd's intention was ostensibly to enter the Jewish quarter by moving down the rue de France, but they found their way blocked by the police, who were soon supported by the two regular evening patrols of Tirailleurs Algériens. The situation deteriorated rapidly as members of the crowd seized and beat several unfortunate passersby, and debris rained down on the demonstrators' heads from the apartments above. Shots were fired on the place des Galettes—apparently coming from inside the besieged apartment buildings. A man in the crowd—later identified in police reports as an "*indigène*"—was shot in the stomach. The muphti continued to try to calm the angry demonstrators, and he was also joined by the city's most well-known Muslim notable, Mohamed Salah Bendjelloul.

The police chief for Constantine, René Miquel, was in Algiers when the trouble started, and Émile Morinaud, the mayor of Constantine, was also away from the city, as was Jean-Marie Laban, the departmental prefect. In Miquel's absence Commissioner Fusero, normally the station chief of the second arrondissement, assumed control of the city's police forces. When he heard of the growing disturbance on the place des Galettes, Fusero went to see for himself, accompanied by several police agents. Finding his forces quickly overwhelmed, Fusero managed to get word out asking for reinforcements, and soon a squad of twenty-five soldiers from the Third Zouaves arrived, along with the secretary-general of the prefecture, Landel, and the director of the prefecture's office of departmental security, Henri Coquelin. After an hour or so of struggle, the police, soldiers, and civil authorities, acting alongside Bendjelloul and the muphti, managed to clear the place des Galettes of demonstrators, but outbreaks of violence continued in the surrounding neighborhoods throughout the rest of the night. Not until an additional squad of Zouaves had arrived after midnight, along with a detachment of gendarmes, did the troops succeed in clearing the public spaces of the central city. In the course of the fighting, three police agents were injured—two of them Jewish—and twelve injured demonstrators were taken to the police commissariat of the second arrondissement. The man who had been shot in the stomach, apparently a participant in the demonstration, was hospitalized in serious condition, his intestine perforated in fifteen places. This man died on Monday, 6 August. A Jewish man who had been beaten on 3 August was taken to the clinic with a broken arm, broken ribs, and contusions on his head. Six storefronts of Jewish-owned jewelry stores had their windows broken that Friday evening. Meanwhile, groups of Jewish men began to organize the defense of their neighborhood, causing tension with the gendarmes and troops who were manning the police barricades in the narrow streets of the Jewish quarter.

The next morning, Saturday, 4 August, a flurry of meetings took place, bringing together members of the local political establishment with the police and military authorities. Henri Lellouche, a Jewish member of the *conseil général*, made the rounds of the city's synagogues and called for the Jewish population to remain calm and avoid any provocation. At 9:30 a.m. Lellouche and other Jewish elected officials went in the company of Rabbi Halimi to the city hall, where the secretary-general of the prefecture informed them that the department's Muslim elected officials wanted to meet with the leaders of the Jewish community in his office at 11:30 a.m. During the meeting, the assembled figures, self-consciously representing the constituencies reserved for them under the colonial political system, pledged to cooperate in spreading a message of calm and social peace. Both Bendjelloul and Ben Badis attended, and they announced a public meeting for the following morning, to take place at the same outdoor amphitheatre used by Bendjelloul six weeks earlier when he demanded to be seated on the government's interministerial commission for Muslim affairs. The prefect, obviously wishing to avoid any public gathering by colonial subjects that could be associated with a political message, refused to give permission for such a meeting. The prohibition came too late, however, as it had already been announced in the streets.

On the morning of Sunday, 5 August, therefore, a crowd of nearly a thousand interested followers began to gather at the appointed site, known as Les Pins, a sort of natural outdoor amphitheatre on the outskirts of Constantine. When an emissary from Bendjelloul arrived and announced that he would not be speaking, the crowd began to walk back into town. As they did so, two individuals ran toward them, shouting that Bendjelloul had been assassinated. This rumor was soon disproved by the appearance of Bendjelloul himself on the streets, but his presence had little effect. Shots were again fired on Muslims in the Jewish business quarter, and for several hours. By midday the police effectively lost control of the city. The crowds ransacked dozens of Jewish-owned businesses, pulling their goods out into the street and setting the buildings on fire. At least two homes were invaded by members of the crowd, and the families hiding inside were discovered and murdered, including their children. The victims were beaten and stabbed. Several had their throats cut. The violence was not limited to Constantine—later that day and on 6 August, Jews and Jewish-owned businesses were attacked in as many as five nearby towns. In all, twenty-eight people died—twenty-five Jews and three Muslims.

Talking about the Riots: The Reports

Talking about the violence of 3–5 August 1934 in Constantine is as hard for historians writing today as it was for contemporaries of the event in the 1930s. There are the usual problems of sources. It is difficult to discern what happened on Friday evening at the mosque, and how this event became the flash point for Sunday's riot. The individual accounts are necessarily fragmentary and partial, and some questions are difficult to answer definitively. Were the demonstrators fired upon before they began to attack individual homes? Did the police and soldiers stand by while rioters ransacked the Jewish business district? Were the local sections of the Croix de Feu involved? Did Bendjelloul incite the crowd or try to stop it? Were those who spread the rumors of Bendjelloul's assassination acting intentionally as provocateurs? The French language press contributed to the atmosphere of dread and horror by publishing lurid photographs of the bodies of the murdered families in the morgue. Individuals close to the events endeavored to speak for both the perpetrators and the victims, with predictably confusing results. Both the colonial administration and the Muslim political establishment tried to attribute the outbreak of violence to unusual local circumstances and had no incentive to push for explanations that might call into question the delicate balance of municipal politics in the colonial situation. Jewish political leaders, shocked at the inability or unwillingness of the authorities to confront the crowd, openly suspected collusion between known anti-Semites in the administration and Muslim political elites, particularly Mohamed Salah Bendjelloul.

The official reports do little to clarify the situation. The mayor, the prefect, the police chief, and the general in charge of the local garrison were clearly under pressure to justify their own responses to a violent event that none had foreseen nor been able to control. A flurry of correspondence flew from all levels of the colonial administration in an effort to reassure the governor-general, the Parisian government, and the public at large that the situation remained under control. In the background of every report one can sense the fear engendered by this violence, a fear that what was most significant was not the fact that Muslims had attacked Jews, but that Algerians had proved themselves capable of violent and organized collective action, and that their target next time might not be the Jews of Constantine, but the colonial order itself.

On 8 August the victims were buried in a collective ceremony attended by many leaders of the Jewish community as well as officials from the municipal and prefectural administration and the local military and police leadership. Bendjelloul and the Muslim elected officials of the FEC agreed to stay away in order to avoid any incident, but they published a letter in the local press denouncing both the violence and those who sought to use the situation for political ends. On 10 August the governor-general announced the creation of the *commission d'enquête administrative*, which undertook the task of taking depositions from witnesses and local notables and synthesizing the reports that came from the various offices of the colonial administration. Working separately from the criminal investigation undertaken by the police into the deaths of those murdered on 5 August, the investigating commission limited its work to the origins of the violence, as well as an evaluation of the local authorities' handling of the incident. The commission submitted its report to the governor-general on 7 October, after having taken depositions from 126 witnesses and officials.[41] Meanwhile, journalists covering the trials of the 210 individuals arrested during the violence reported a steady stream of convictions for looting, theft, or receiving stolen goods (sentences averaged two to three years), and carrying prohibited weapons (two to six months). Minors were sentenced to three years of detention in a juvenile *maison de correction*. More sensational news reports followed the arrests on 14, 16, 20, and 30 August of several young men for the murders of the Attali and Halimi families and for several other Jewish victims of violence. All of those charged had confessed under interrogation, but several attempted to recant these confessions in court.

The report reveals a great deal about the administration's attitude toward the non-European populations of the city and the spaces that they inhabited. The Jews and Muslims of Constantine appear in these pages as two different hostile communities whose mutual antipathy is unrelated to the French colonial presence. The "Arab town," with its "narrow streets and tortuous alleys," was juxtaposed to the "Ghetto"—a multitude of "little streets, hardly larger than that of the Arab quarter," constituting the "sensitive nerve [*point névralgique*] where the first incident broke out, and where the struggle was the most intense on Sunday morning."[42] Elsewhere, in describing the topography of the city, the report managed to mention the Remblai, a neighborhood where the poorest Muslims lived, in connection with the difficulties that the French had in conquering the city in 1836–37, as if the urban landscape were permanently inscribed with resistance to French rule. Only later do the authors admit that the Remblai was a relatively new neighborhood, a product of the colonial situation where recent migrants from an increasingly impoverished countryside made their homes. The inhabitants of this quarter were nevertheless described as a "lazy and primitive proletariat, with a rude and aggressive temperament" constituting a "permanent danger" for the city.[43]

The report's section entitled "Renseignements démographiques" completed the picture of an irrevocably divided population. As was customary in Algeria, the census contained three categories: *européenne*, *israélite*, and *indigène*. Although the city had grown by half between 1911 and 1930, to about a hundred thousand total inhabitants, Constantine remained about one-third European, slightly less than one-sixth

Jewish, and a little more than one-half "Native."[44] The report seemed to acknowledge the peculiarity of treating Jews and Europeans separately in the census but justified the practice with what was essentially a political explanation:

> Following the Crémieux decree (24 October 1870), the Israélites are French citizens, but whereas those who are of French origin are voluntarily independent, and disperse their votes, the [Algerian] Israélites form a strongly disciplined collectivity, obeying orders from above, and constituting a powerful electoral mass; hence the tendency on the part of elected officials to cultivate them and privilege them, at times to the detriment of the indigenous who are far from having the same electoral importance.[45]

Of course, the Jews of Constantine were not a "powerful electoral mass." They were at most 15 percent of the electorate, capable of occasionally picking the winner in a close election, and at times therefore a part of a governing coalition. They were in no way in control of municipal politics in the city, which had been the personal fiefdom of a virulently anti-Semitic mayor, Émile Morinaud, since 1899. The report implied that Constantine's Jews had not lived up to their end of the bargain contained in the Republic's offer of citizenship to Jews in France, a bargain summed up most famously in Clermont-Tonnerre's speech to the National Assembly in 1789, that the French state "must refuse everything to the Jews as a nation and accord everything to Jews as individuals."[46] Of course, as Joshua Schreier recently demonstrated, the Crémieux decree had actually done the opposite—offered citizenship to Jews collectively, even as the Republic continued to deny citizenship to Muslims.[47] It is hard not to read the official report's confusion about Jewish citizenship and Jewish political behavior as a reminder of the "indigenous" origins of Algerian Jews and their essentially North African personality.

Rather than acknowledging that the atmosphere of tension between *israélites* and *indigènes* might have something to do with the political arrangements made by the colonial regime, the report preferred references to an atavistic anti-Semitism on the part of the Muslim population, who were inflamed by the ability of Jews to manipulate the colonial order to their benefit. The resentment arose, the report said, because Constantine's Jews had been too successful in winning for themselves the jobs of public functionaries, especially in the justice system, the police force, and the post office. The report also cited the role played by Jews in banking and moneylending, especially to Muslims, "whose lack of thrift and ignorance in these matters is well-known."[48]

The official report preferred to recycle anti-Semitic clichés about the undue political influence wielded by Constantine's Jews, mixed with a few accurate though unexamined propositions about the defensive political behavior of the Jewish electorate under the colonial system. Such conclusions, delivered indirectly in the descriptive sections of the report, allowed the colonial administration to blame both sides in an apparently age-old communitarian conflict without admitting or accepting any responsibility for a situation in which communitarian identities had become the only acceptable vehicles for political mobilization. Shortcomings in the colonial regime's policies toward the city's Muslim population were blamed on the Jewish political establishment, while the lurid descriptions of the violence were used to justify a hardening of the colonial state's security apparatus and an increased level of surveillance and manipulation of both Jewish and Muslim political activity, even of those Muslim elected officials such as Bendjelloul, who never ceased to proclaim their essential loyalty to the regime.

Presented as a synthesis of the reports produced by the prefect, the police, and the military, the commission's report contained little that might be called "testimony." In fact, the report's very structure seemed to militate against the relevance of any individual voices from the city's various populations. The only individuals who emerged as distinct voices in the official account were public officials—the police agents directing the attempts to maintain public order on the streets, the officials of the prefecture, and the military decision makers who organized the defense of the city by calling in reinforcements of *Tirailleurs Sénégalais* from nearby garrisons. What emerges most clearly from the commission's synthesis of these reports is a vision of urban space permeated with interlocking civil and military jurisdictions, a kind of bureaucratic topography in which the city was rendered visible to the administration only through its own institutions, and the population was only visible in so far as its members conformed to the categories of *indigènes*, *israélites*, and *européens*. Those spaces that had been appropriated by others for their own uses—the Remblai or Les Pins—and those that were vestiges of a precolonial order—the "Ghetto"—were the grains of sand in this well-oiled mechanism, spaces that did not conform to the colonial administration's normative distinctions of public and private, urban and rural, "European" and "Indigenous."

Both Mohamed Salah Bendjelloul and Henri Lellouche, a Jewish municipal councilor, attempted to influence the outcome of the commission's report by submitting their own documentation concerning the events of 3–5 August 1934. Lellouche's report, which was also published in two installments in the Jewish periodical *Le Reveil Juif*, was a bitter denunciation of the mayor's and the prefecture's mismanagement of the crisis, containing a blunt accusation that the violence had been organized from the outset by cynical Muslim politicians who sought to use anti-Semitism as a rallying point for their own political ambitions. Regarded by officials as more evidence of a tendency among Jewish political leaders to speak to their own constituency before addressing the wider world, Lellouche found himself isolated on the city council, and for the next two years he was the target of increasingly vicious anti-Semitic attacks from his former allies on the council, including Mayor Morinaud.

Bendjelloul's strategy was quite different. Publicly, he and his Muslim colleagues on the municipal council deplored the violence of 5 August with a campaign of posters placed on the walls of the city in both French and Arabic. At the same time, he prepared a careful dossier of dozens of personal testimonies from witnesses to the events and submitted it directly to the commission. Bendjelloul's dossier did not seek to synthesize these individual testimonies into a coherent narrative. Most were quite short—several paragraphs at most, typed carefully in French on individual sheets under a heading that included the relevant incident being described and the name, age, and address of the witness. No less than sixteen Muslim witnesses described the initial encounter at the Sidi Lakhdar Mosque. These witnesses reported Khalifa's insults in detail, his acts—spitting, urinating, and provocatively displaying his penis. It did not seem to matter if the accounts did not exactly correspond to one another; their cumulative effect was to outweigh the account given by Khalifa himself, who portrayed himself as equally outraged at the men's nakedness and their nonchalant display of their bodies in front of his family. Bendjelloul's chosen strategy—to give individual voices to Muslims on the streets on the weekend of 3–5 August—thus dovetailed perfectly with the administration's desire to portray the Jews of Constantine as an essentially tribal community within the city and thus responsible for their own persecution. In the end this strategy succeeded; Bendjelloul was able to ride the wave of discontent among his Muslim supporters to a seat on the *délégations financières* in January 1935, a position that made him the most important Muslim elected official in Algeria during the years of the Popular Front.

Bendjelloul was not responsible for the anti-Semitic violence in Constantine in August 1934, but he did little in its aftermath to disassociate himself from expressions of anti-Semitic anger among certain elements of the Algerian Muslim population. Émile Morinaud may have attempted to incite some form of violence on the weekend of 3–5 August, but he probably did not anticipate the horrific results of his provocations, if they did indeed take place, as many members of Constantine's Jewish population later came to believe.[49] It is also likely that the shots fired from Jewish residences inflamed members of the crowd on both 3 and 5 August. The initial passivity on the part of the mayor's aides, the police, and the military may also have contributed to the loss of control that led to the deaths of the Halimi and Attali families. There is, in other words, plenty of blame to go around, making the task of assigning responsibility among the Muslim, Jewish, and European communities of Constantine a futile one. I suggest that the important historical question lies elsewhere: what constellation of circumstances makes it appear that the only way to understand this event is to attribute responsibility to individuals who are conceived of primarily as members of one of these three groups, which are themselves portrayed as ahistorically irreconcilable bodies juxtaposed in one city? Why should such a tripartite vision of this event, which is a product of the colonial situation itself, impose itself as the only possible way of telling this story?

There is a tendency in the historical literature to explain the eruption of violence in this region during these years—especially the anti-Semitic riots in Constantine in 1934—as a result of a breakdown, that is, of a failure to reform the colonial system in Algeria. It may be, however, that the opposite is the case: the violence of the 1930s resulted not from the failure of reform but rather from its success. The electoral reforms passed after World War I created a dynamic by which a new generation of Muslim political leaders were faced with a dilemma: their participation in local politics depended on their willingness to embrace the racialized categories that lay behind the creation of a separate electoral college for Muslim voters and special seats set aside on municipal councils for Muslim officials. It was this embrace of a racial dynamic in local politics—emanating from the republic itself—that exacerbated tensions at the local level, creating a political crisis in the cities and towns of eastern Algeria, and that reached a murderous climax in August 1934 in Constantine. This violence was the logical endpoint of a series of confrontations that emerged from the politics of the colonial situation itself: on these summer days in Constantine the contingencies of local social and political life—the inevitable conflicts between individuals in public spaces, the machinations of unscrupulous or cynical politicians—came together with the reformist logic of a colonial system that could not dispense with its reliance on exclusion.

Historian Clifford Rosenberg has suggested that historians discussing the way racial categories were used by the French state in the interwar period can be divided into two camps: those, like Gérard Noiriel, who have emphasized the Third Republic's capacity for generating new categories of exclusion that led the way toward Vichy's brutal policies; and those, like Patrick Weil, who emphasized that these new categories also functioned to protect certain vulnerable groups—especially new arrivals such as migrant laborers or refugees—by extending the rule of republican law to encompass and address the particular needs of these people. Rosenberg's work on the policing of immigrant labor during this period tries to bridge the gap between these two positions by arguing that "both liberal protections and new forms of inequality must be considered together."[50] Certain moments of violence, such as the riots in Constantine, might be seen as the point where these opposing practices and policies converge as different groups, in this case the Muslims and

Jews of Constantine, found that the very terms of their inclusion—the Crémieux decree, the Jonnart Law—drove them into conflict with one another, producing both surprising opportunities for political mobilization and murderous consequences for the victims of August 1934.

Notes

The author would like to acknowledge several colleagues whose help has made this essay possible. At the very outset, conversations with Malika Rahal helped me organize my time in the archives. Daho Djerbal welcomed me warmly to Algiers in 2006 and has been an invaluable guide to work on Constantine ever since. Ethan Katz on more than one occasion has pushed me to clarify my argument and has generously shared his research with me. Matti Bunzl, Geoff Eley, Miranda Johnson, Mary Lewis, Maud Mandel, Todd Shepard, Miranda Spieler, Judith Surkis, Martin Thomas, and Gary Wilder offered helpful criticisms when I presented this material at conferences at the University of Exeter, the University of Michigan, the Society for French Historical Studies, and the Association of Jewish Studies.

1. The archival documentation resulting from the official government commission appointed to investigate the origins of the violence, including the final report, is preserved in four cartons at the Centre d'Archives d'Outre-Mer (CAOM) in Aix-en-Provence: 9 H 52, 9 H 53, 9 H 54, 9 H 55. All translations are by the author unless otherwise noted.

2. On politics in Algeria during the interwar years, see Mahfoud Kaddache, *La Vie politique à Alger de 1919–1939* (Alger: Société nationale d'édition et diffusion, 1970); Jean-Louis Planche, "Antifascisme et Anticolonialisme à Alger à l'époque du Front Populaire et du Congrès Musulman, 1934–1939," Thèse de 3e cycle, Université de Paris VII, 1980; Emmanuel Sivan, *Communisme et nationalisme en Algérie 1920–1962* (Paris: Fondation nationale des sciences politiques, 1976); Jean Leca, *L'Algérie Politique: Institutions et Régime*, Cahiers de la Fondation nationale des sciences politiques (Paris: Presses de la Fondation Nationale des Sciences Politiques, 1975). For an indispensable look at local politics before World War I, see David Prochaska, *Making Algeria French: Colonialism in Bône, 1870–1920* (Cambridge: Cambridge University Press, 2004).

3. The official government report after the riot gave a figure of twenty-six deaths, twenty-three *israélites* and three *indigènes*. These numbers were revised several times after the initial press accounts. Many of the reports submitted by members of the Jewish community in Constantine in the aftermath

of the violence include an individual who died in violence in the nearby town of Hamma and an additional victim who died later of his injuries, thus giving a figure of twenty-five Jewish victims (fourteen men, six women, and five children).

Some sources cite a figure of only two *indigène* deaths, and it is possible that they do not include either the death of Belkacem Boutarane, aged thirty, who died on 23 August of a bullet wound to the stomach received in Constantine on the night of 3–4 August, or Athmane Saidi, aged twelve, who died on 7 August in the hospital in Constantine after receiving a bullet wound to the abdomen that same day during unrest in Aïn Beïda, a nearby market town and agricultural settlement. The third *indigène* death is an unidentified eighteen-year-old boy, found on the rue Clemenceau near the Medersa in Constantine on 5 August. See CAOM 9 H 52, "Emeutes du 3 au 5 août 1934, Etat nominatif des blessés indigènes admis en traitement à l'hôpital civil de Constantine," and "Lists des Victimes du 5 Août avec indication du lieu où elles ont été tuées."

4. The best and most helpful of historical analyses that emphasize the local and contingent causes of the riots in Constantine remains Charles-Robert Ageron, "Une émeute antijuive à Constantine (aout 1934)," *Revue de l'Occident Musulman et de la Méditerranée*, no. 13–14 (1973), 23–40. Perhaps the best indication of the fact that the riots in Constantine are held by some to be an event of purely local significance is the fact it was possible for a historian to write an entire book about anti-Semitism in France in the 1930s without mentioning the riots at Constantine at all: see Ralph Schor, *L'Antisémitsme en France pendant les années trente: Prélude à Vichy* (Paris: Editions Complexe, 1992).

For analyses of the event that seek to establish its status as a "pogrom" comparable to attacks on Jews in Eastern Europe, see Yves-Claude Aouate, "Constantine 1934: Un pogrome 'classique,'" *Nouveaux cahiers—Alliance israélite universelle* 68 (1982), 49–56; Richard Ayoun, "À propos du pogrom de Constantine (août 1934)," *Revue des Études juives* 154 (1–3, January–September 1985), 181–86; and Robert Attal, *Les Émeutes de Constantine, 5 août 1934* (Paris: Editions Romillat, 2002). Attal, the son of a victim of the riots, also published an unusual anonymous document, evidently written by an eyewitness to the event: see Robert Attal, "Un témoignage inédit sur le pogrom de Constantine (1934)," *Revue des Études juives* 148 (1–2, January–June, 1989), 121–42. For an account that emphasizes the role of "European" anti-Semites in shaping the reactions to the event in Algeria, see Emmanuel Debono, "Antisémites européennes en Algérie après le pogrom de Constantine (1934–1939)," *Revue d'histoire de la Shoah* 187 (2007), 305–28.

Cultures of Violence in the Empire

5. In this connection see especially Geneviève Dermenjian, "Le Malaise colonial de l'Algérie des années trente au miroir du pogrom de Constantine (août 1934)," paper given at a conference, "Juifs en terre d'islam et dans les Balkans, XIXe–XXe siècle," Ecole française d'Athènes, 2–4 April 2000; and Roschdi Ali Younsi, "Colonial Triangle: Competing Loyalties within the Jewish Community of Algeria, 1842–1943," unpublished PhD diss., University of Chicago, 2003, especially chap. 3, "Behind the Disputed Pogrom of Constantine, 1934–1935," 142–92. For a penetrating analysis of the reactions to the riots in Constantine among Jews and Muslims in France, see also Ethan B. Katz, "Jews and Muslims in the Shadow of Marianne: Conflicting Identities and Republican Culture in France (1914–1975)," unpublished PhD diss., University of Wisconsin, 2009, especially chap. 2, "Negotiating the Boundaries of France: Jews and Muslims amidst Crisis and Opportunity in the 1930s," 106–73.

6. This population increase appears to have had two components: a 29 percent increase in the number of colonial subjects during the decade of the war and a nearly 50 percent increase in the "European" population in the five years that separated the census of 1921 from 1926.

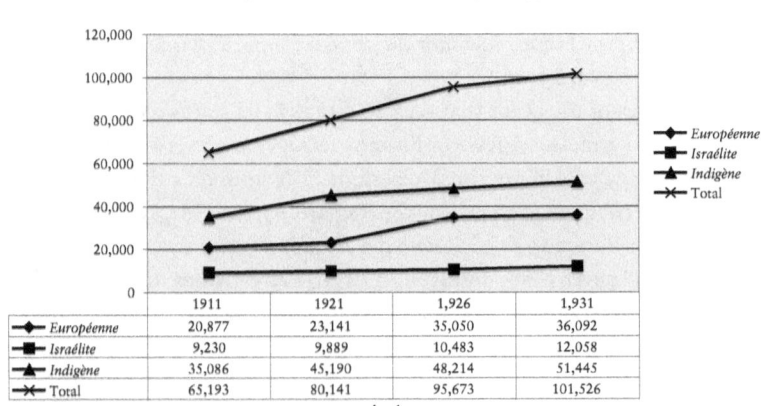

Population of Constantine, 1911-1931

	1911	1921	1,926	1,931
Européenne	20,877	23,141	35,050	36,092
Israélite	9,230	9,889	10,483	12,058
Indigène	35,086	45,190	48,214	51,445
Total	65,193	80,141	95,673	101,526

Année

Source: CAOM 9 H 52. "Commune de Constantine, Etat numérique de la population de la commune pour les annees 1911, 1921, 1926, 1931," 11 September 1934. Note: the figures for the total population have been adjusted to correct errors of addition in the original document.

7. See Phyllis Cohen Albert, "Israelite and Jew: How Did Nineteenth-Century French Jews Understand Assimilation?" in *The Jews in Nineteenth-Century Europe*, ed. Jonathan Frankel and Steven J. Zipperstein (Cambridge: Cambridge University Press, 1992), 88–109. See also the discussion of this issue in Katz, "Jews and Muslims," 27.

8. For the Algerian censuses of 1926, 1931, and 1936, see *Tableau general des communes de l'Algérie, Situation au 7 Mars 1926* (Algiers: Émile Pfister, 1927); *Répertoire statistique des Communes de l'Algérie, Mars 1932* (Algiers: Victor Heintz, 1932); and *Répertoire statistique des Communes de l'Algérie, Décembre 1936* (Algiers: Victor Heintz, 1937).

9. On the evolution of census categories in Algeria, see Kamel Kateb, *Européens, "Indigènes" et juifs en Algérie (1830–1962): Représentations et réalités des populations* (Paris: Institut national d'études démographiques, 2001).

10. The process by which this "customary" law became codified during the colonial period made it possible for the French authorities to interpret local customs in ways that benefited their own interests. See Katherine Hoffman, "Berber Law by French Means: Customary Courts in the Moroccan Hinterlands, 1930–1956," *Comparative Studies in Society and History* 52:4 (2010): 851–80.

11. On the inferior legal status of Muslims in Algeria and the "native code," see Patrick Weil, *How to Be French: Nationality in the Making since 1789* (Durham NC: Duke University Press, 2008), 214–16.

12. On the crisis of anti-Semitism in Algeria in the 1890s, see Geneviève Dermenjian, *La Crise anti-juive oranaise 1895–1905: L'antisémitisme dans l'Algérie coloniale* (Paris: L'Harmattan, 1986); Stephen Wilson, *Ideology and Experience: Antisemitism in France at the Time of the Dreyfus Affair* (Rutherford [NJ]: Fairleigh Dickinson University Press, 1982).

13. Emile Morinaud, *Mes Mémoires: Première campagne contre le décret Crémieux* (Alger: Baconnier, 1941).

14. Wilson, *Ideology and Experience*, 233.

15. Carol Iancu, "The Jews of France and Algeria at the Time of the Dreyfus Affair," *Studia Hebraica* 7:7 (2007), 51–66.

16. Geneviève Dermenjian, *La Crise anti-juive oranaise 1895–1905: L'Antisémitisme dans l'Algérie coloniale* (Paris: L'Harmattan, 1986), 79–80.

17. Isolated moments of violence between Muslims, Jews, and settler groups are reported for the years 1920–1921 in CAOM 11 H 47. The most significant episode of violence between settler anti-Semites and Jews during the immediate postwar period occurred in Constantine in June 1921, following several months of anti-Semitic articles in a local paper, *La Tribune*. Valuable

firsthand reports from this event are found in the archives of the Alliance israélite universelle (AIU) in Paris, Carton Algérie 1C.

18. Among those who qualified for the right to vote under the Jonnart Law were veterans, landowners and business proprietors, civil servants, recipients of French decorations such as the *légion d'honneur*, elementary school graduates, and members of chambers of commerce and agriculture. See Ageron, *Les Algériens musulmans et la France*, 2: 1203–24.

19. On the circumstances surrounding the Crémieux decree and debates about Jewish citizenship in the nineteenth century, see Joshua Schreier, "Napoleon's Long Shadow: Morality, Civilization, and Jews in France and Algeria, 1808–1870," *French Historical Studies* 30 (Winter 2007), 77–104. On the importance of settler anti-Semitism in Algeria in establishing fears of Jewish conspiracies in France and Jewish voting habits after the Crémieux decree, see Lisa Leff, *Sacred Bonds of Solidarity: The Rise of Jewish Internationalism in Nineteenth-Century France* (Stanford CA: Stanford University Press, 2006), especially chap. 6, "The Myth of Jewish Power," 200–228.

20. Kaddache, *La Vie politique à Alger*, 38–41, 53.

21. A report from June 1920 from Constantine's police chief, René Miquel, explicitly stated that "the law of February 1919 seems to have compromised the work of colonization in Algeria." CAOM 9 H 53, Extrait du Rapport mensuel du Commissariat Central du mois de Juin, 1920.

22. Emile Morinaud, mayor of Constantine, deputy in Parliament, and president of the departmental assembly (*conseil général*) of Constantine, called for the reestablishment of the Code de l'indigénat in terms that directly tied these powers to the uncertainty caused by the participation of Muslim colonial subjects in local political life: "The elections have awakened among the indigenous hatreds and a clannish tribalism [*les haines et l'esprit de çoff*]." See Kaddache, *La Vie politique à Alger*, 39.

23. On 17 July 1920, only three days before the passage of the law on the *indigénat*, an incident of anti-Semitic violence took place in Sétif, a military garrison and market town about a hundred kilometers east of Constantine. Following the death of a Muslim man who had been a veteran of the French army (identified in reports only as "ex-militaire Debbah"), several Jewish shops were pillaged by Algerian colonial subjects. See CAOM 11 H 47, Sous-Préfecture de Sétif, Rapport Mensuel de l'administrateur-détaché à la sous-préfecture de Sétif sur la surveillance et l'administration des indigènes des communes de plein exercice de l'arrondissement, mois de Juillet 1920. The following month the administrator in Perigotville, a smaller colonial settlement about twenty kilometers north of Sétif, reported that because of anti-Jewish sentiments expressed by the local population of dayworkers in the

commune of Takitount, he had asked Jewish merchants to refrain from presenting their wares in the markets of small country villages. See CAOM 11 H 47, Département de Constantine, Arrondissement de Sétif, Commune Mixte de Takitount, Rapport Mensuel sur les faits ou circonstances de nature à appeler l'attention de l'Administration, mois d'Août 1920. In Constantine the police report for July 1920 indicated that following the incident in Sétif there was a "rumor of probable brawls between natives [*indigènes*] and Jews [*israélites*] that circulated in town with a certain persistence." The rumors predicted that the fights would occur after afternoon prayers at the central mosque, and several Jewish shopkeepers closed their stores out of fear. No such trouble occurred. See CAOM 9 H 53, Extrait du Rapport mensuel du Commissariat Central du Mois de Juillet 1920. Other reports of tension between Jews and Muslims in Algeria that were apparently related to the political reforms came from Tlemcen in western Algeria in April 1919. See CAOM 11 H 46, Gouverneur Général d'Algérie, Direction des Affaires Indigènes, Rapport mensuel sur la situation politique et administrative des indigènes pendant le mois d'avril 1919. All of these incidents stand as a reminder that Algeria was an exception to the waning of anti-Semitism in France during World War I and its immediate aftermath pointed to by Michael R. Marrus and Robert O. Paxton. See Marrus and Paxton, *Vichy France and the Jews* (New York: Basic Books, 1981), 31–32.

24. Eisenbeth, *Le Judaïsme nord-Africaine*, 99–105.

25. Eisenbeth, *Le Judaïsme nord-Africaine*, 50–55.

26. In this sense, the Jews of Constantine faced a challenge similar to those of Jews elsewhere in France, as they attempted to understand the significance of the Third Republic's offer of citizenship for their continued sense of Jewish identity and feelings of solidarity with Jews elsewhere in the world. On this challenge, see Paula Hyman, *From Dreyfus to Vichy: The Remaking of French Jewry, 1906–1939* (New York: Columbia University Press, 1979).

27. Historians remain divided as to the main causes of renewed French anti-Semitism during the 1930s. Some, such as Jacob Katz and Pierre Birnbaum, see the virulence of French anti-Semitism during the decade prior to the Second World War as a long-simmering reaction to the successes of Jewish assimilation in France over many decades. See Jacob Katz, *From Prejudice to Destruction: Anti-Semitism, 1700–1933* (Cambridge MA: Harvard University Press, 1980); Pierre Birnbaum, *Anti-Semitism in France: A Political History from Léon Blum to the Present* (Oxford: B. Blackwell, 1992). Gérard Noiriel contends on the other hand that anti-Semitism in France became most virulent at moments when it was conflated with xenophobia. See Noiriel, *Le Creuset français: Histoire de l'immigration, XIXe–XXe siècle* (Paris: Seuil,

1988), 337–38; Noiriel, *Immigration, Antisémitisme et Racisme en France, XIXe–XXe Siècle: Discours Publics, Humiliations Privées* (Paris: Fayard, 2007), 677–79. Others such as Vicki Caron and Ralph Schor emphasize conjunctural factors such as the economic crisis of the Depression and the influx of Jewish refugees from Central and Eastern Europe after 1933 as factors that engendered a virulent anti-Semitic response in particular from elements within the middle class who connected Jews to a threatening vision of a capitalist society committed to free markets. See Vicki Caron, "The Antisemitic Revival in France in the 1930s: The Socioeconomic Dimension Reconsidered," *Journal of Modern History* 70:1 (March 1998), 24–73; Caron, *Uneasy Asylum: France and the Jewish Refugee Crisis, 1933–1942* (Stanford CA: Stanford University Press, 1999); Ralph Schor, *L'Antisémitisme en France Pendant Les Années Trente: Prélude à Vichy* (Bruxelles: Ed. Complexe, 1992). A few historians, including Eugen Weber and Stephen Schuker, have emphasized the involvement of Jews in left-wing politics during these years as a contributing factor in the spread of anti-Semitism. See Stephen A. Schuker, "Origins of the 'Jewish Problem' in the Later Third Republic," in *The Jews in Modern France*, ed. Frances Malino and Bernard Wasserstein (Hanover NH: University Press of New England, 1985), 103–4; Eugen Weber, *The Hollow Years: France in the 1930s* (New York: Norton, 1994). Most of these books treat Algerian anti-Semitism as a special case, if they treat it at all.

28. On the effects of the economic crisis on labor patterns in the Constantine region, see Johan H. Meuleman, *Le Constantinois entre les deux guerres mondiales: L'évolution économique et sociale de la population rurale* (Assen, Netherlands: Van Gorcum, 1985), 177–91.

29. The colonial administration followed with growing alarm the French Communist Party's increased interest in Algeria in the second half of the 1920s, noting that the party's papers, including *L'Humanité* and *La Lutte sociale*, were calling for a revision of the Code de l'indigénat, suppression of the laws restricting movement, and the granting of rights of association to Algeria's colonial subjects. The police were particularly concerned that the anticolonial position of the Third International would facilitate a convergence between militants within the labor movement and pan-Arab nationalists. There is little evidence that such a convergence was taking place in the late 1920s, but the fear generated a great deal of surveillance of the various movements. See, for example, CAOM 11 H 47, Rapport sur la situation politique des indigènes de l'Algérie au 1er Juillet 1927. On the perceived danger posed by communism to colonial Algeria see CAOM 93 B3 404, Propagande communiste chez les indigènes.

30. The Constantine section of the Croix de Feu was founded in May

1930, and by March 1932 the section had 1,400 members. For the police reports on the Croix de Feu's activities during these early years see CAOM 93 B3 522, 1930–1935; and CAOM 93 B3 707, 1930–1935, Croix de Feu.

31. The first federation of Muslim elected officials in Algeria began meeting in the spring of 1928, but divisions among the leadership eventually led to the creation of separate federations for each Algerian department. See CAOM 11 H 47 (47/1), GGA, Direction des Affaires Indigènes, "Rapport sur la situation politique et administrative des indigènes d lAlgérie au 1er mai 1928." The FEC met for the first time on 29 June 1930 at the Cinema Nunez, with five hundred people in attendance. Bendjelloul emerged as a contender for leadership following his election to the Conseil général (departmental assembly) in October 1931. On the founding of the FEC, see CAOM 93 B3 277.

32. On 17 April 1931 a senatorial commission headed by the former governor-general of Algeria, Maurice Viollette, passed through Constantine, where it met with members of the FEC. Although this meeting occurred the year before Bendjelloul assumed control, the document that the FEC presented to Viollette contains a good summary of the main points on the Federation's agenda. See CAOM 9 H 45, "Note sur les réformes désirées par la Fédération des élus des indigènes du département de Constantine présentée à la Commission sénatoriale de l'Algérie présidée par M. Maurice Viollette lors de son passage à Constantine," 17 April 1931.

33. On the early history of Algerian nationalism, see Mahfoud Kaddache, *Histoire du nationalisme algérien*, 2 vols. (Paris: Paris-Méditerranée, 2003); Benjamin Stora, *Les Sources du nationalisme algérien* (Paris: L'Harmattan, 1989); André Nouschi, *La Naissance du nationalisme algérien* (Paris: Minuit, 1962). In spite of the importance of Messali Hadj's movement for the later history of nationalism in Algeria, most of his initial support in the late 1920s and early 1930s came from Algerian laborers working in metropolitan France. He did not have a wide base of support in Algeria until the founding of the Parti du Peuple Algérien (PPA) in 1937.

34. The most significant of these campaigns began on 27 May 1933 with a lecture before four hundred followers in Batna, a city to the south of Constantine. His tour through the department continued with speeches in Constantine (two hundred followers), Souk-Ahras (1 June, "one thousand listeners"), Djidjelli (2 June, "400 *indigènes*"), Bougie (also 2 June), Saint-Arnaud (4 June, "300 *indigènes*") and Sétif (4 June). Eventually his run of speaking engagements included stopovers in Canrobert, Aïn-Beïda, Sédrata, Montesquieu, Bône, El-Kseur, Sidi-Aich, Akbou, Bordj Bou Arréridj, and Chateaudun du Rhumel. See CAOM, GGA 3 CAB 40. On the activities of CIAM, see Pascal le Pautremat, *La Politique musulmane de la France au XXe siècle* (Paris: Maisonneuve et La rose, 2003), 39–73.

35. For the prefecture's records on the public meeting held by Bendjelloul and Abd al-Hamid Ben Badis on 16 May 1934, see CAOM, 93 B3 277, 93 B3 707, and 9 H 53.

36. On the ʾUlamaʿ and their relation to the nationalist movement, see Ali Merad, *Le Réformisme musulman en Algérie de 1925 à 1940: Essai d'histoire réligieuse et sociale* (Paris: Mouton, 1967); and James McDougall, *History and the Culture of Nationalism in Algeria*, Cambridge Middle East studies 24 (Cambridge: Cambridge University Press, 2006).

37. For the police and prefecture's correspondence on incidents between Jews and Muslims in Constantine in 1929–30, see CAOM 93 6740. It is possible, even probable, that the police records of these incidents are selective both in the choice of incidents that are recorded and in their assignation of responsibility in the incidents they describe. The records available in the archives were assembled under the authority of Police Commissioner René Miquel, who took office in 1930 as the situation began to deteriorate. Miquel was well known for his support for the anti-Semitic and xenophobic right wing in the city, and he later boasted about his efforts to increase the "French element" among the police force and to lessen their reliance on Jewish and Muslim officers.

38. In January 1932 a prolonged controversy erupted when the police arrested Ruben Aouizerat—also known as "Cabassou"—following a brawl that occurred in the rue de France. Aouizerat was known informally as "the Prefect of the rue de France," and the police reports also mention him as an important figure in organizing Jewish voters during municipal elections. After the brawl in January 1932 Aouizerat was charged with "rebellion" and imprisoned, and the affair became linked in the minds of the local Jewish leadership with the firing of several Jewish police officers by Commissioner René Miquel later that spring. The reports on the Aouizerat affair and the ensuing letter from the Jewish leadership to Morinaud are in CAOM 9 H 53.

39. For example, a brawl that followed a water polo match between a Jewish team and a "European" team led to a week of brawls and inflammatory rumors in May 1933. Reports on the violence of May 1933 are in CAOM 9 H 53.

40. In what follows, I have largely relied on the archival evidence in CAOM 9 H 52, 9 H 53, 9 H 54, and 9 H 55 in reconstructing the major events of 3–5 August 1934.

41. CAOM 9 H 53, Commission d'enquête administrative sur les événements qui se sont déroulés du 3 au 8 août 1934, Rapport de la commission (henceforth Rapport de la commission). The commission interviewed and took depositions from 126 people, including 30 officials in civil government, 43 members of the military, and 55 "local personalities and diverse witnesses."

42. Rapport de la commission, 3.

43. "Au Sud-Ouest et à l'Ouest, le Plateau du Koudiat, les avenues Bienfait et du 11 novembre ouvrent l'accès direct de la campagne par des routes à forte déclivité, tandis qu'à proximité du pont de Sidi Rached s'érige le "Remblai" où grouillent 2 à 3,000 indigènes misérables. Cette topographie si spéciale évoque les difficultés qu'ont recontrées nos troupes d'Afrique pour s'emparer de Constantine." Rapport de la commission, 2. For the reference to recent Remblai arrivals, see p. 6.

44. For the history of these census categories in Algeria, see Kamel Kateb, *Européens, "Indigènes, et Juifs en Algérie (1830–1962): Réprésentations et réalités des populations* (Paris: INED, 2001).

45. "Par suite du décret Crémieux (24 octobre 1870), les israélites sont citoyens français, mais tandis que les Français d'origine sont volontiers indépendants et dispersent leurs bulletins de vote, les israélites forment une collectivité fortement disciplinée, obéissant à des mots d'ordre, et constituent une masse électorale puissante; d'où la tendance, de la part des élus, des les ménager et de les favoriser, parfois même au détriment des indigènes qui sont loin d'avoir la même importance électorale." Rapport de la commission, 5.

46. Clermont-Tonnerre's full speech is on the web. See Clermont-Tonnerre, "Speech on Religious Minorities and Questionable Professions," 23 December 1789, http://chnm.gmu.edu/revolution/d/284/.

47. Joshua Schreier, "Napoleon's Long Shadow: Morality, Civilization, and Jews in France and Algeria, 1808–1870," *French Historical Studies* 30:1 (Winter 2007), 77–103.

48. Rapport de la commission, 6.

49. The Archives de l'Alliance israélite universelle (AIU) in Paris contains a typewritten report dated 21 November 1934 from Maurice Eisenbeth, the grand rabbin of Constantine, accusing Morinaud of planning to provoke the violence of 5 August the day before in order to compromise the Muslim political leadership, especially Bendjelloul, while simultaneously delivering a painful lesson to his own Jewish allies on the municipal council. See AIU Algérie 1C. A copy of the same report is in the Archives de la Consistoire de Paris, Carton B 130. I would like to thank Ethan Katz for drawing this report to my attention.

50. Clifford D. Rosenberg, *Policing Paris: The Origins of Modern Immigration Control between the Wars* (Ithaca NY: Cornell University Press, 2006), 77.

5

Fascism and Algérianité

The Croix de Feu and the Indigenous Question in 1930s Algeria

SAMUEL KALMAN

In Algerian novelist Robert Randau's 1926 work *Les Colons*, one of the central characters proclaims: "I am an African. I am the law. I am neither a lazy Arab nor a Maltese dog. I am a *colon*."[1] Randau's contention that the *pieds-noirs*, the European settlers, constituted a new racial synthesis represented the culmination of a pervasive theme in the European literature of the Maghreb. Termed the Algérianiste movement, these authors followed the dictum of Louis Bertrand, that only the vigor and will of the Africanized European "barbarians" could regenerate a decadent France.[2] Such a vision naturally excluded inferior *indigènes*, lazy criminals who practiced primitive customs inferior to French civilization. When Musette's Cagayous proclaims "Algériens nous sommes!" he specifically excludes Muslims in violent terms: "An Arab tried to run off with a roll of fabric and a blue coat. I gave the bastard a punch in the head that laid him out, and if they hadn't dragged me off him, I would've smacked off his mustache and his big mouth too."[3]

Despite their violent and xenophobic discourse these authors reflected everyday relations between European settlers and Algerian Muslims and an idealized vision of Algeria shared by many pieds-noirs, particularly those identified with the political center and right wing. As Azzedine Haddour notes, the creators of Algérianité proffered a staunchly mythological framework, obscuring the genuine history and culture of French

Algeria. Bertrand, for example, sought to justify European dominance, proclaiming the eternal Gallic presence in the Maghreb, a literary counterpart to the Warnier Law, the 1873 act that enabled the seizure of vast tracts of Algerian land. Similarly Haddour notes that Cagayous's machismo and frivolity hide a more sinister agenda: "The myth of the Mediterranean joviality of the Cagayous is a way of exorcizing the history of colonial exploitation and racism . . . it wards off the fear of what was repressed, it is the forgetting of guilt."[4] Most importantly, the Algérianité expounded by Randau, Bertrand, and Musette provided the basis for a distinct Algerian identity that both incorporated French politics and mores yet simultaneously demanded the formation of a uniquely Algerian national construct. As Jonathan Gosnell observes, "*Algérianité* was a proclamation of their imagined and strongly felt identity, the recognition of a distinct colonial consciousness."[5]

Neither was this merely a literary sojourn, the fanciful creation of a few isolated intellectuals. Xenophobia frequently devolved into both symbolic and physical violence. As many historians note, the doctrine of the pieds-noirs was frequently mobilized to justify the seizure of land from Arabs and Berbers and their utter exclusion from the European-dominated social and political sphere.[6] Thus the *sénatus-consultes* of 1863 and 1865, and the 1873 Warnier Law, deprived the colonized of land and citizenship, only obtainable through a renunciation of Koranic law, unthinkable for a devoutly Muslim population. The latter became mere subjects, with no political representation or legal standing, subject to special "Arab" taxes and the repressive Code de l'indigénat.[7] For as Neil MacMaster writes: "imperial propaganda, even when not grossly racist but anodyne and paternalist, created the opinion among even the poorest of French that they were inherently superior to the benighted Arab."[8] No area of colonial life remained unaffected by this racial inequality. Even the civil service entrance requirements for the lowliest positions in government service were rigged to prevent all but the most servile *indigènes*, the so-called *beni oui-ouis*, from actually sitting the exams. This was done despite frequent calls to at least provide Arabs and Berbers with a token representation within the colonial bureaucracy.[9] These attitudes further provided the justification for physical attacks against Muslims from both the authorities and the general public, including cases of armed assault and police brutality.[10]

Colonial historians readily discuss the Algérianiste mentality and everyday xenophobia in the imperial setting, yet most do so in the context of the pre-1914 period or under the short-lived North African Vichy regime during the Second World War. Explanations for the persistence of such attitudes during the interwar era, and pied-noir intransigence during the murderous civil war from 1954 until 1962, rarely include such themes. Authors variously blame the unwillingness of the European settlers to discuss reform, French determination to resist decolonization, and even economic malaise.[11] Although all of these factors were critical to the escalating resentment of the Muslim population and concomitant resistance to the colonial governing structure, they must be wedded to another significant factor: the implantation of extreme right-wing attitudes in Algeria, the interwar descendant of Algérianité.

As Alice Conklin notes, there occurred a constant "cross-fertilization of ideas, habits, and trends between the Republic and the empire."[12] One of the most prominent such migrations was fascism, which proved to be a tremendous success in 1930s Algeria. In this climate Gallic extreme right-wing leagues struck a chord with pieds-noirs increasingly worried about the revolutionary potential of Muslims and disgusted by the "weak and corrupt" French government, which they perceived as favorable to indigenous rights and freedoms, and particularly eager to grant additional privileges to war veterans in order to pacify the local population.[13] Their local membership adopted the Algérianiste mantra, that the *colons* were inherently superior to the Muslim population, and thus supported the denial of rights and freedoms for non-Europeans.[14] None better positioned itself as a defender of l'Algérie française than the Croix de Feu (CDF), the most prominent such league, with over one million members by 1938. With the authorization of metropolitan leader Colonel de la Rocque, the Algerian sections initiated a recruitment campaign that attracted 26,000 *colons* by 1939, a figure comparable to the metropolitan membership rate.[15] The group drove right-wing politics in the department of Constantine from 1934 onward and gained an equally substantial membership base in Oran, where it joined Mayor Gabriel Lambert's Rassemblement national d'action sociale, which dominated local politics during the Popular Front era. Following their 1936 transformation into the "parliamentary" Parti social français (PSF), after the Popular Front government banned the leagues, they added a daily newspaper (*La Flamme*) and sent Constantine Lycée professor Stanislas Devaud to the Chamber of Deputies, while gaining the allegiance of a host of mayors and local officials in all three Algerian departments. All of these efforts concentrated upon defending French colonial superiority in Algeria, while simultaneously deflecting the threat represented by Muslims, purportedly whipped into a nationalist and revolutionary frenzy by Communist agitators and Islamic propaganda.[16]

Curiously CDF/PSF propagandists originally rejected this line of thinking, instead claiming that Muslims were welcome in both the group and colony. Initially opposed to the idea, local partisans actively recruited Muslims from 1935 onward. Police in the *communes mixtes* of Bordj-bou-Arrèridj, El Biar, and Oujda reported that CDF/PSF members used various tactics, including anti-Semitism and cash payments, to bring local Arabs into the fold. Disdained until very recently, Algerian youth were mobilized by group activists against the Left (and particularly the newly enshrined Popular Front) in Bordj-bou-Arrèridj during 1934 departmental and 1935 municipal elections, and on 14 July 1935 a gathering of Croix de Feu and Volontaires nationaux solicited Muslim agricultural workers in the fight against socialism.[17]

In each case candidates and speakers used anti-Semitic themes to buttress their arguments and appeal to the *indigènes*. This argument frequently appeared during electoral campaigns, expounded by a variety of CDF/PSF personnel. During the 1935 electoral contest in Bordj-Bou-Arrèridj, the mayor of Ouled Eanêche, a group sympathizer, employed a local Arab notable named Bouhadjar to mobilize the Muslim vote through anti-Semitic rhetoric, urging electors to cast their ballot in favor of the mayor and his friends, all Croix de Feu members, as they opposed the Jews.[18] The August 1934 Constantine pogrom, in which rioting Muslims killed twenty-five Jews and ransacked houses and businesses, also contributed significantly, for the Croix de Feu press blamed the disturbance on the 1870 Crémieux decree, which granted French citizenship to Algerian Jews, permitting them to vote and granting them legal equality. Claims that Muslims were justified in attacking them proved very popular with Algerians, and the group further labeled Jews as the progenitors of international finance and republican-socialist ideology, held responsible for the second-class status of Arabs and Berbers in Algeria.[19]

War veterans proved particularly susceptible to group appeals. From 1932 onward, CDF/PSF leadership and rank and file continuously praised those who paid the "blood tax" for France. Members of this veterans' association claimed no distinction based on race or religion, and early meetings often included testimonials from Muslim officers.[20] Due to their loyal service to France, in 1935 the group's Paris-based leadership officially invited Muslim *ancien combattants* to apply for membership. Local support for this endeavor was decidedly mixed, however, with certain sections rejecting the notion, while others embraced the concept of Arab or Berber confreres. Thus the El-Biar CDF/PSF denounced the practice, and in Boufarik a local luminary angrily demanded: "The *indigènes* can only be signed up with the utmost scrutiny, and even then it is preferable to admit only the most prominent Muslims." In sharp contrast to more skeptical responses, the Oujda CDF/PSF promptly dispatched a retired army captain, Bel Habich, to offer support for higher army pensions, compensation payments, and other benefits in return for membership.[21] However, few joined in most towns and communes, with the exception of Algiers, where four hundred veterans signed on, primarily due to the promised perks.[22]

Women from the CDF/PSF Service Social also used home visits as membership drives, promising a variety of charitable goods and services, along with the threat of a boycott should business owners and their employees refuse to comply.[23] For those who could not afford the annual dues, the group agreed to waive all fees, particularly in the case of unemployed workers. Where economic arguments failed, group leaders appealed to the idea of "reconciliation," believing that the group's social Catholic discourse proved equally appealing to followers of Islam. Thus one Muslim speaker at a March 1937 meeting in Bône claimed: "Our leader is no false prophet. He knows you and speaks your language. He wants what is best for you." The group's mantra of *travail-famille-patrie*, he opined, embraced all Algerians, regardless of religion or race.[24] Parti social français candidates additionally sought Muslim votes in municipal and departmental campaigns, including Stanislas Devaud, whose public meetings led police to worry that his presentation might incite violence against local Jews.²⁵ The group enjoyed considerable success in this regard, both encouraging municipal campaigns by non-European members and harnessing local Arab votes in support of CDF/PSF candidates. During the July 1935 municipal elections in Maison-Carré, two retired army officers—Said Greffon and Amar Akli—actively worked to sway Muslim electors in favor of the group's slate of municipal councilors. During the same campaign, the Medjana-Blondel section colluded with supporters of Dr. Mohamed Bendjelloul, the leader of the assimilationist Fédération des elus musulmans (FEM) to successfully elect candidates in Bordj-Bou-Arréridj.²⁶

Yet such sporadic attempts to attract Muslims yielded little, for the indigenous population continued to mistrust the extreme Right. As Mahfoud Kaddache writes, the doctrinal vision of the CDF/PSF and like-minded organizations "remained fascinated with the political myth of the French empire," a fact not lost on leading Muslim intellectuals. For example, Messali Hadj, founder of the nationalist Étoile nord-africaine (and later the Parti du Peuple Algérien), frequently lambasted La Rocque and the CDF/PSF in speeches and editorials, and Algerian membership stalled accordingly.²⁷ Outside major urban centers the group's numbers were far from impressive.²⁸ In the department of Algiers, the section in Maison-Carré reported in June 1935 that only 2 of its 130 members were non-European, both ex-army officers, while the Affreville CDF/PSF also listed 2 Muslims out of 110 members, along with another 2 in Aumale.²⁹ The Constantine sections, recruiting in the group's Algerian organizational stronghold, also failed to convince non-Europeans for the most part, with the exceptions of Khenchela (21 of 59 members) and Batna (7 of 90 members), two *communes mixtes* in the south. However, in the first case the individuals concerned were associates of Bendjelloul, including three municipal councilors and the *administrateur adjoint* of the commune, and sought an alliance with anti-Republican forces in order to further a reformist agenda, rather than proffering genuine support for the CDF/PSF program.³⁰ As in Algiers, cities in Constantine also reported few members, and only two Arabs ever ascended into the leadership ranks: a M. Medjamel in 1937 acted as a *délégué de la propagande* in Bône, and a M. Meneroud functioned as president of the Constantine Volontaires nationaux in 1934.³¹ Nonetheless, this certainly trumped the participation rate in the department of Oran, where rabidly anti-Muslim sentiment among the European population, along with the ascendancy of the rival Parti populaire français after 1936, effectively prevented any sizable Muslim membership.

Due to the relative paucity of recruitment, local leaders attempted to forge links with prominent Arab individuals and organizations, hoping to draw their followers to the CDF/PSF. Thus in 1935 President Faucon of the Algiers Croix de Feu initiated contact with Mohamed Benhoura, editor of the newspaper *La Justice* and later president of the Association des 'Ulama', Abd al Hamid Ben Badis's reformist-Islamist brotherhood, to become the head of a new Section Indigène.[32] This represented a seemingly bizarre choice, given the movement's belief that Algerian national identity could be reconstructed only on the basis of Islamic principles. Although not hypernationalist in the manner of Hadj and the Étoile nord-africaine/Parti du Peuple Algérien (ENA/PPA), as the 'Ulama' were willing to find accommodation with colonial authorities on certain issues, their reformism nonetheless rejected any similar secular movements, chiding fellow *Salafist* voices such as Lamine Lamoudi, Ferhat Abbas, and Rabeh Zenati. Thus a partnership with the Christian and un-Islamic Croix de Feu was out of the question.[33] However, if the effort ultimately faltered, in no small measure because of the CDF/PSF's commitment to l'Algérie française, the enthusiastic response in elite Muslim circles nonetheless convinced the group's leadership to redouble their efforts. Stanislas Devaud was subsequently dispatched in April 1935 to meet with Bendjelloul, a leading voice in the campaign to grant assimilation to Algerians. Through the Fédération des elus indigènes and its newspaper, *La Voix indigène*, he commanded the loyalty of a large section of the Arab intellectual elite.[34]

Bendjelloul agreed to support Croix de Feu–sponsored candidates in 1935 local elections, principally in response to the perceived support of the league for the aims of FEM. By July CDF/PSF and the FEM partisans collaborated in Sétif, Batna, Blida, and several other large districts, and the Muslim leader privately praised the group's anti-Semitic campaign in Constantine, while publicly telling the *Dépêche Algérienne* in October 1935 that "genuine sympathy has been forged between the Croix de Feu and Muslims."[35] The local police, and French observers such as Ligue des droits de l'homme stalwart Victor Basch, also noted a more sinister rationale for the alliance: that FEM supporters consistently lauded CDF/PSF anti-Semitism. Various Muslim intellectuals perceived the group as a useful bulwark against Jewish influence in large urban centers, particularly enthused about the group's rejection of the Crémieux decree.[36]

Bendjelloul and others were initially swayed by the rhetoric of the CDF/PSF. From 1932 onward, group officials consistently praised Algerian Muslims. That year Constantine section president Paul Levas wrote that the CDF/PSF aimed to replicate the camaraderie of the front, where no divisions existed on the basis of race or religion. He welcomed European and Muslim alike, speaking of common goals and aspirations.[37] Such sentiments reemerged in print and in speeches by group luminaries across Algeria. Bendjelloul and various 'Ulamaʿ leaders believed members like Marcel Ribère, the PSF *délégué de la propagande*, who loudly proclaimed at a November 1937 meeting: "we dream of an Algeria where we can live within a fusion of races and religions under the tricolor flag."[38] Yet by 1936 both the 'Ulamaʿ and the Fédération des elus musulmans denounced the CDF/PSF in no uncertain terms. The group's seeming espousal of the Muslim cause in Algeria masked a far different reality: that the CDF/PSF were ardent defenders of l'Algérie française and colonization, fiercely opposed to any extension of rights and freedoms to Algerians.

To begin with, the vaunted collaboration between *français* and *indigène* could only be achieved under the rubric of Christian civilization. The group frequently contrasted the "good Arabs," who recognized the benefits of French dominance, with "a minority of citizens more or less developed, very ambitious, very unruly, jealous of French prerogatives, and eager for power and status."[39] Thus in September 1938 a cartoon in *La Flamme*, the group's daily newspaper in Algeria, portrayed an Arab tribesman, an *évolué* intellectual, a pied-noir, and Colonel de la Rocque joining hands in unison under a French banner, with a Muslim and European woman holding children together in the background. Yet the accompanying caption made clear the limits to any collaboration: Arabs and Berbers would have to share the French vision of Algeria as a colony, rallying to the *tricolore* and accepting their reduced socioeconomic status. For the CDF/PSF defended Christian civilization and the French Empire, rather than the hopes and needs of the Islamic and non-European *indigènes*.⁴⁰ As the group's Algerian leader Alfred Debay made clear, Muslims had to join their European brethren in respecting la France civilisatrice. His discourse echoed the common Algérianiste notion that North Africa had been a chaotic mess before the French arrival, mired in civil war, its people starving due to inefficient agriculture. Originally expounded by Louis Bertrand, the notion of Latinité—that North Africa's dormant Roman-European roots and prosperity were restored by European conquest—became a popular theme in 1930s parlance. According to one author in the Sidi-Bel-Abbès daily *L'Algérien*, the Gallic moment replaced misery and strife with civility, well-being, and economic efficiency. This notion was hardly exclusive to the pieds-noirs. Pierre Bordès, the *colon*-friendly governor-general of Algeria from 1927 to 1930 ended his tenure by declaring that pre-1830 Algeria symbolized "anarchy, ignorance, and misery in regions abandoned to wasteland."⁴¹ To Debay, a simple palliative existed for these symptoms: the acceptance of French rule. This involved a common effort to live with one another and an end to parasitism, a direct reference to high non-European unemployment during the economic slump of the 1930s and the necessary welfare and charity to provide for starving *indigènes* during times of widespread famine. Charles X may have invaded Algeria due to the insulting behavior of Hussein Dey and the vicious activities of Mediterranean pirates, he declared, but the true French mission of the *colons*—to repel savagery in North Africa—remained a priority over a century later.⁴²

However, certain CDF/PSF members charged that a minority of extremists obfuscated the wishes of the silent Muslim majority. Determined to win Algerian independence and replace French rule with an Islamic state, allied with international communism, and inspired by Nazi Germany, local provocateurs simply awaited their chance to drive the pieds-noirs into the Mediterranean Sea.⁴³ At an October 1937 meeting in Bône one speaker referred to the combination of left-wing and nationalist forces, singling out Messali Hadj and the PPA as the worst offenders. One month later Debay berated the colonial administration, accusing them of ignoring the threat of foreign provocateurs and rebellious Muslims in equal measure. Addressing a crowd in Bougie, he begged his *frères indigènes* to eschew violent nationalism in favor of the CDF/PSF doctrine of reconciliation.⁴⁴

These concerns mirrored another common Algérianiste trope; namely that non-Europeans were instinctively Jihadists, perfidious Muslims out to eliminate the presence of infidels in Algeria. Writing in the *Dépêche Algérienne* in 1935, one author summed up the fears of every pied-noir, bluntly stating, "we are living on a volcano where the Arab, knife in his teeth, stokes the fire."⁴⁵ Yet such responses also reacted to heightened agitation in both the countryside and the urban Bidonvilles, where increasingly impoverished Muslims demanded bread and liberty. Rioting became a constant feature of Algerian life by the mid-1930s. Following the 6 February imbroglio in France, when extreme-rightist leagues came perilously close to breaching the Chamber of Deputies, imitators emerged in Algiers, and the Casbah remained under police siege for days. That August the Constantine anti-Semitic riots further unnerved Europeans, and in the aftermath of renewed disturbances in Sétif in February 1935 the European inhabitants of Guelma forged emergency procedures in preparation for a bloody uprising, while those living in the tiny *commune mixte* of Canrobert demanded guns in order to better defend themselves.⁴⁶

By the mid-1930s dozens of Muslim activist associations emerged, ranging from the religious (the reformist ʾUlamaʿ, for example) to the political (the separatist ENA/PPA). Previously confined to *évolués* like the Young Algerians and Ferhat Abbas, dissent now tilted toward nationalism and the revolutionary left. The heavy-handed response of the French authorities only aggravated the situation. By the 1930s even reformist voices chafed at official attitudes toward Muslim associations. From the movement's founding in 1931, Ben-Badis and the ʾUlamaʿ had explicitly rejected attacks against the *colons* in favor of, in the words of James McDougall, "resurrecting Muslim Algeria from decadence and defeat, a partnership that idealized France, whose immense power and resources were to be employed for the improvement of Algerians."⁴⁷ Yet by 1936 persistent French legal feints engendered broad support for the organization from both the Arab intellectual elite and the working masses. As a result, Ben-Badis took tentative steps toward nationalism, foreshadowing the association's post-1945 programmatic shift: "The

Muslim Algerian nation has been created and exists in the same manner as other previously existing nations of the earth. This nation is not France and does not wish to be France." Although far from the unified and cohesive movement of the Algerian War era, the mere threat of organized indigenous reprisals created widespread panic among the European population and the Algerian government, which welcomed the Mediterranean High Committee in 1935, created to investigate the new radicalism and recommend palliatives.[48]

Staunchly anti-Communist like their metropolitan brethren, the Algerian CDF/PSF claimed that revolutionary forces had infiltrated the Muslim population throughout the colony. Speaking at an October 1935 rally in Arba, one local member referred to the *péril indigène*, a Communist-led plot to take control through a general strike, removing the French root and branch from the very land that they rendered *assainies*.[49] One CDF/PSF newspaper columnist blamed the Congrès musulman, the supposed provider of support for Communist candidates through its extensive press network. Taking this theme to its logical conclusion, the first annual North African Congress of the PSF tendered a final motion that specifically addressed presumed left-wing participation in the nationalist movement, proclaiming that the group "denounces the renewed agitation of Marxist agents, Communists, and Pan-Islamists who imperil the admirable oeuvre of colonization and civilization, realized on this African soil by the tenacious labor and creative genius of the French people."[50] Various group polemicists further reminded their audience that such revolts pitted six million Arabs against fewer than one million Frenchmen.[51]

The personification of this threat was variously portrayed as the 'Ulama' or the Étoile nord-africaine, led by the mercurial Messali Hadj, whose secular nationalism rejected the Islamist formula in favor of the slogan "neither assimilation nor separation, but emancipation." Courted by the group just years earlier, the purportedly nationalist 'Ulama' were deemed a threat to the public welfare by Debay in a May 1938 newspaper column, the declared enemy of l'Algérie française. His confreres heartily agreed, claiming that their ultra-orthodox Islamic views had little to do with religion, instead forming a tool to build a nationalist consciousness, initiating the complete removal of the

French colonial presence. One author further claimed that the schools run by Ben-Badis's organization taught only the Qur'an and Muslim supremacy: propaganda rather than education. Thus despite the incompatibility of such a depiction with the reformist agenda of the 'Ulama', commentators charged the movement with allying itself with a variety of partners, from the Communists to assimilationist Muslims, in order to seize political power, and were deemed fanatical in its pursuit by CDF/PSF commentators.[52] One of the most commonly mentioned co-conspirators was the Étoile nord-africaine. Despite the fact that Messali Hadj was no Communist, having rejected the Popular Front and abandoned the PCF in disgust by the 1930s, the CDF/PSF accused the ENA of practicing leftist terrorism.[53] They provided a training ground for revolutionaries, demanding the vote and equal rights for Muslims and the nationalization of industry and the banks, as a prelude to the seizure of power. In tandem with Moscow the ENA, and its successor, the Parti du Peuple Algérien, were cast as traitors, out to dismantle the French empire and diminish Gallic power.[54]

Such tough talk was accompanied by physical violence directed by settlers and security forces against Algerians, particularly in smaller *communes*, where the "indigenous threat" appeared overwhelming due to the demographic imbalance in favor of the Arab population.[55] Urbanization provided one of the central tropes of interwar Algerian life, and by the 1930s a veritable rural exodus occurred with stunning alacrity. By 1936 the largest nine cities claimed over 14 percent of the population, and the vast majority of Europeans lived in urban centers. Of the 112,000 inhabitants of Algiers in 1926, only 45,000 were identified as Muslims. The Algerian urban population grew by leaps and bounds, as the *fellahs* abandoned the *bled* in search of employment opportunities in the newly industrialized cities, although only in 1948 did they become the outright majority. In the countryside, however, only 197,500 Europeans remained in 1936, out of a total population of 946,000, facing millions of repressed and impoverished Arabs and Berbers.[56]

In the resulting climate of fear *indigènes* stood accused of nationalism and Communism in equal measure, each one a potential insurgent against the rural European population. Blaming left-wing agitators, CDF/PSF luminaries attempted to counter revolutionary propaganda by mobilizing Muslims in the service of l'Algérie française. In May 1935, during the heated electoral campaign in Bordj-Bou-Arrèridj, a Volontaire national and brother-in-law of the mayor, Henri Akefane, rounded up Arab youths for this purpose, and mere weeks later during a Bastille Day rally CDF speakers invoked the group's "alliance" with Bendjelloul and the reformists, demanding that local Algerians descend upon the town to trounce Popular Front sympathizers.[57] The 1936 banning of the Croix de Feu by the socialist-led government and subsequent transformation into the parliamentary PSF did little to stem the violence. On 29 June 1936 the Algerian section of the Ligue internationale contre l'anitisémitisme reported the beating of indigenous news vendors selling the LICA's *Droit de Vivre* and other left-wing newspapers. The perpetrators were a group of Volontaires nationaux in Constantine, anxious to strike a blow against hated sympathizers of the Popular Front, as part of a general campaign waged against the Left in the aftermath of their electoral triumph.[58]

Various CDF/PSF commentators blamed the governor-general and local authorities in Algeria for the rebellious mentality of the *indigènes*. Here the group's analysis criticized the economic dominance of the pieds-noirs, who by the interwar era controlled over 2.5 million hectares of land, leaving uneducated and unskilled Arabs to fend for themselves in the *communes mixtes* or *casbahs*.[59] Although the Algerian economy boomed in the 1920s, with Algeria becoming the largest trading partner of metropolitan France and a major global supplier of wine, agricultural produce, and minerals, its effects were limited to European businessmen and laborers. While the industrialized pieds-noirs brandished tractors, automobiles, and factories, the rural Muslim population relied upon animals and plows, and their urban and unskilled brethren often suffered unemployment due to a lack of familiarity with complex tools and machines.[60] Forced to work seasonally, and earning vastly lower wages than their European counterparts, Arabs and Berbers often existed in utter poverty, a fact trumpeted by European commentators as proof of their backwardness. As novelist Jules Roy bluntly stated: "It must be understood as a natural law that Arabs are servants, the French are masters, and all is well because the French belong to an entrepreneurial but generous race while the Arabs always depend on someone else."[61]

Worse still, the global recession arrived in North Africa from 1930 onward, buffeting the Muslim population, always the first victims in times of economic uncertainty. Textile, mining, and agricultural production plummeted, while credit-dependent farms and urban businesses faced bankruptcy. Although the local and colonial governments formulated plans to alleviate the disastrous effects of unemployment and famine on Algerian communities, they took action only in 1934, and even then corruption and fraud reduced the available credits to a miniscule amount. Dependent upon charity to survive, Arabs and Berbers proved increasingly susceptible to the appeals of nationalism and Communism, and worried pieds-noirs blamed the Depression, along with governmental inaction, for the atmosphere of uncertainty and rebellion.[62]

Solutions to the plight of the *indigènes* abounded in the Algerian press and political sphere, from controls on population growth to the exportation of excess labor variously to France or Nigeria, and the CDF/PSF joined the growing litany of voices. Writing in *La Flamme* in February 1937, Jacques Labruyère protested the fact that Muslims lived in unhygienic shacks with no stable income. The resulting exodus to urban centers, with concomitant unemployment, literally spawned revolt against the French presence in Algeria, driven first and foremost by the relative prosperity of the *colons*. Other group authors concurred, variously blaming usurers (usually Jews), unemployment, and poverty for the rise of Communist and nationalist agitators.[63] Alfred Debay went further, demanding that the *colons* actually provide steady wages and proper employment conditions, even granting land to loyal Arabs: "Each *fellah*'s family should have a house and *lapin de terre* from which to draw at least what is necessary for his subsistence."[64] This comprised the "special duty" of the pieds-noirs toward *indigènes*; how could they be loyal to France while leading lives of desperation and starvation? Rather than apathy and exploitation, Stanislas Devaud told the PSF 1937 National Congress, the government must act to stem the tide of refugees to urban ghettos and redistribute land.[65] In his report on Muslim *anciens combattants* at the 1938 Congress, the group's directeur générale de propagande, Marcel Rédares, went even further, demanding legislation to prevent further European encroachment in the *communes mixtes* of southern Algeria. Not only would land seizures become illegal, but every community would receive a hospital, a school, and French economic assistance to revitalize local business and agriculture.⁶⁶ In his closing address Colonel de la Rocque added the need for French employers to pay a living wage to Muslims. By respecting indigenous labor, employers—dubbed the "qualified representatives of our civilization"—prevented revolutionary activity and aided race relations in Algeria.⁶⁷

Yet once again the group's spirited defense of the *indigène* as a crucial component of the *famille française* served to obfuscate far less benevolent plans. During his speech to the 1938 PSF Congress La Rocque specifically rejected the notion that Muslims could be equals within l'Algérie francaise. Although they deserved better treatment, he stated, the notion of assimilation, or even a specifically Muslim electoral college and bill of rights was absurd.⁶⁸ Devaud likewise derided an extension of political and social policies to include Muslims. Had not the 1865 Senatus Consulte declared that any Arab could become a French citizen if they renounced the Personal Statute, which granted the right to accept Qurʾanic law rather than the *code civil*? Echoing a centuries-old European critique of Islamic practice and recent proclamations by leading *colons* such as Paul Cuttoli, the radical senator and mayor of Philippeville, he decried the acceptance of polygamy and prepubescent marriage, along with Islamic restrictions on divorce and intermarriage, as tenets incompatible with French civilization. Even the renunciation of the statute changed little, for the pieds-noirs would never allow an Arabic mayor or governor to rule Algeria. Seemingly barbaric Muslim rituals and purported misogyny thus trumped any genuine prospects for assimilation.⁶⁹

CDF/PSF refusals to recognize indigenous claims for rights and citizenship culminated in the group's bitter struggle against the Popular Front's 1936 colonial reform, known in common parlance as the Blum-Viollette bill. The proposal represented yet another attempt to confront the thorny issue of Muslim nationalism, for few were interested in renouncing Islamic law, the cornerstone of their faith, in order to obtain citizenship. Yet the non-European population increasingly rejected the inequality that characterized Algerian political and socioeconomic life. Although far from universally rich and powerful, every pied-noir, regardless of nationality or occupation, enjoyed tremendous privileges.

Living in respectable housing segregated from urban slums or country hovels, enjoying a virtual monopoly on skilled and well-paying employment, and benefiting from the rights and freedoms denied their Muslim neighbors, European superiority was omnipresent. Yet such a scenario, in which a humble dockworker wielded far greater power than his metropolitan brethren could imagine, naturally engendered even greater distrust and hostility among the Arab and Berber communities. As Pierre Bourdieu writes, "Political life and political conscience [became] Manichean in form."[70] Hence following the military service of thousands of Algerian soldiers during the Great War, the Clemenceau ministry tendered the Jonnart Law, which created a special Muslim electoral college of 421,000 members and granted less restrictive conditions for citizenship to various categories of Arabs, including war veterans and the educated elite.[71] Given a more visible role in the political process, the authorities reasoned, the *indigènes* would naturally support continued colonial rule.

Despite the fact that fewer than four hundred Muslims actually applied for citizenship, while the repressive Code de l'indigénat remained untouched, the furious pieds-noirs lambasted Jonnart and vowed to prevent the "Arabization" of Algeria by French authorities. Worse still, the French government alone rendered the decision, without consulting the Algerian Délégations financières. Hence any renewed attempt to curb the repression of non-Europeans in North Africa received only obloquy from irate settlers.[72] The introduction of a second enfranchisement bill in 1936 thus represented a bold riposte, particularly given its author: none other than the hated Maurice Viollette. A former governor-general, he was nicknamed "Viollette l'arabe" because he warned the pieds-noirs in 1927 that their failure to properly address Muslim grievances hastened the destruction of colonial Algeria. However, his proposed law granted citizenship solely to 25,000 so-called *évolués*, the intellectual, French-educated, and mostly antinationalist elite, without the renunciation of the personal statute. The bill only applied to ex-officers, soldiers who received the Croix de Guerre or a similar military medal, university graduates, members of the Chambers of Commerce and Agriculture, representatives on the Conseils généraux and Delegations financières, and union leaders. Nonetheless, the *colons* unanimously rejected the plan, and emotions ran so high that Algeria's two hundred mayors resigned in March 1938 in protest. They particularly chafed at the provision for the continued practice of Qurʾanic law. How could any citizen reject French jurisprudence in favor of Islamic superstition, yet still gain legal recognition? One senator went even further, claiming that Blum-Viollette symbolized "the beginning of a civil war," as Arabs would subsequently demand full political and legal equality.[73]

Naturally both the metropolitan and Algerian sections of the CDF/PSF virulently opposed the Blum-Viollette bill. La Rocque and the Paris-based leadership decried the projected law as a recipe for Islamic domination in North Africa. In March 1938 the group's French newspaper, the *Petit Journal*, characterized Blum and Viollette as "the champions of racial hatred, the Soviets, and their religious allies the ʾUlamaʿ." How could a true citizen follow Qurʾanic precepts and ignore French legislation? Did the new law recognize the legality of practices like polygamy and prepubescent marriage? The CDF/PSF might approve economic reforms—a minimum wage for Arab workers, for example—but nothing more. Legal rights could be acquired only after a painfully slow civilizing process, La Rocque frequently argued, involving education, proper hygiene, and the abandonment of barbaric traditions.[74]

Algerian CDF/PSF members brandished an even harsher critique of Blum-Viollette, often tinged with outright xenophobia. An anonymous contributor to *La Flamme* in February 1938 used pidgin French to insult both Viollette and lampoon uneducated Arabs: "L'Endigen's tous dis freres!/Li Endigen's de mon couer!/Li Arab's race soperieure, et les colons exploitateurs!/Tous li Francais a la mer!/Et Ferhat Abbas emp'rur."[75] Devaud similarly derided the plan, not least because the Arabic elite did not really exist: "If you continue to practice . . . polygamy, the repudiation of women, forced marriages, and the deprivation of young girls, you might become 'intellectuals,' but you will never be 'evolved' in the sense of that other word you often use."[76] Others noted that the Blum-Viollette plan only accentuated indigenous problems rather than resolving them, for it envisioned citizenship only for a few educated civil servants and politicians, leaving out the Muslim masses, those most in need of assistance. Articles in *La Flamme* invariably condemned the proposed law on the grounds that it angered the Fellahs, driving them into the arms of

Messali Hadj, Ben-Badis, and the now-demonized Mohamed Bendjelloul.⁷⁷ Only nationalist and Communist insurgents, the authors declared, benefited from the provisions contained in the Blum-Viollette bill. Given this fact, in combination with the socialist beliefs of Blum and his ministry, more than one CDF/PSF member wondered aloud about the ultimate aim of the legislation and its potentially revolutionary consequences.⁷⁸

Naturally, the group tendered a counterproposal, introduced by Devaud in the Chamber of Deputies on 11 February 1938.⁷⁹ The draft was based upon the recommendations of Augustin Iba-Zizen, a Berber attorney from Tizi-Ouzou who directed the PSF Commission des Affaires Indigènes.⁸⁰ From 1935 onward Iba-Zizen directed recruitment efforts aimed at Arabs, warning audiences of the dangers of Communist revolution and preaching the gospel of slow assimilation. A true *évolué*, he constantly praised French civilization as superior and berated nationalists like Messali Hadj, who he termed "mauvais bergers solde a l'étranger."⁸¹ Although not exclusively composed of Arabs and Berbers, his audiences were often Muslims, as the group's European leadership assumed that such gatherings would be more receptive to the CDF/PSF message when delivered by one of their own.⁸²

In keeping with CDF/PSF doublespeak, the *contre-projet* was declared a boon for all Arabs, going far beyond Blum-Viollette, which only served the elite. For example, instead of enfranchising intellectuals, Iba-Zizen and Devaud included those who received the baccalaureate or a professional degree/certification. But there was a catch: citizenship would only be conferred if the candidate renounced the personal statute, echoing the Senatus-Consulte. Given that few Arabs had previously agreed to abandon Koranic law, it was highly unlikely that the PSF *contre-projet* would make any difference.⁸³ Iba-Zizen attempted to rationalize the project for Europeans and Arabs alike in a November 1938 report, arguing that it negated sterile debates about assimilation by insisting upon the renunciation of the Personal Statute. Genuine progress could only be made once the *indigène* abandoned fanaticism, laziness, and nationalism. To be sure, Europeans must raise wages, expand education, and provide stable employment—even a Crédit Agricole for small farmers. Yet if the *indigène* rejected the PSF proposal, he could expect little from justly angry pieds-noirs.⁸⁴

Iba-Zizen's rhetoric perfectly represents the duplicitous discourse of the CDF/PSF. They publicly preached the gospel of assimilation, that Muslims could be transformed into Frenchmen, albeit only in the long term, and were welcome to join the group and (by extension) France. Yet their real goal remained association, the notion that French institutions and culture would always be superior, and hence colonial domination symbolized a permanent condition.[85] Like the pieds-noirs whose cause they staunchly defended, the CDF/PSF rejected the notion of a *mission civilisatrice* in Algeria, because it implied an unacceptable racial fusion as the ultimate imperial goal, or at the very least provided the tools (education, steady employment and higher wages, the vote) with which the *indigènes* could foment rebellion. Albert Memmi has stated that "the colonizer constructs his own self-image," and the colony thus represented a phantasmatic construct in support of European political, economic, and social dominance.[86] Race became the central trope in colonial life, and particularly in Algeria, a genuine colony fused politically and economically with metropolitan France rather than a mere protectorate. This explains the insistence of various CDF/PSF commentators that the *indigènes* were at once racially unfit and a potentially revolutionary force. The discourse of La Rocque or Devaud concerning the Projet Blum-Viollette in no way differed from the xenophobic Algerianité proffered by Louis Lecoq and Robert Randau at the time of the Jonnart Law.

The group by no means parroted French colonial discourse, instead adopting the mantra of l'Algérie française: that the pieds-noirs proved superior to their metropolitan brethren and were better equipped to deal with the *indigènes*. The governor-general and his staff and indeed the Republic itself neither understood the racial realities of colonial life nor possessed the will to fight for the survival of French Algeria. As Emmanuel Sivan notes: "the *algérianiste* trend rejected the idea of racial harmony, in a North Africa destined to be subjected to Latin influence . . . [it] associated Roman conquest and French penetration—by the sword and the plow—and forged a mythology of the *colon* which became that of a new nation."[87] Given the immense power wielded by the pieds-noirs, from their absolute control of municipal politics to the European near-monopoly of industrial and agrarian production, they routinely rejected France from the 1890s onward, berating politicians in Parisian offices who could never understand the realities of colonial life. Although they required metropolitan funding and military support, the settlers ignored republican imperial discourse in favor of Algérianité and the purported superiority of local institutions and sociopolitical norms. Exponents of a Manichean doctrine, which contrasted the barbaric "other" with true Frenchmen, the extreme right-wing leagues were perfectly situated to adopt the demonization of "perfidious" Muslims and corrupt deputies alike.[88] As a major political movement with thousands of members, the CDF/PSF—alongside numerous other such groups—provided a bulwark for pieds-noirs identity, dedicated to the maintenance of French Algeria, whose continued existence provided the spark for nationalist movements in the coming decades. Their rejection of any genuine reforms aimed at the Muslim population, culminating in the group's unanimous drubbing of the Blum-Viollette bill, furthered a tradition dating from the separatist rhetoric of Max Régis and Edouard Drumont in 1898 onward, encouraging the settler intransigence that culminated in the 1954–62 Algerian War.

Notes

The author wishes to thank the Social Sciences and Humanities Research Council of Canada for funding the research presented in this chapter.

1. Robert Randau, *Les Colons* (Paris, 1926), 311. All translations are by the author unless otherwise noted.
2. Louis Bertrand, *Le Sang des Races* (Paris, 1921), x–xi, 89–90. This work was originally published in 1898. The new elite was deemed European rather than French due to the presence of sizable Italian, Spanish, and Maltese populations in Algeria, living alongside their Gallic brethren and distinguished from Muslim or Berber inhabitants by their common heritage.
3. Musette, *Cagayous: Ses meilleures histoires* (Paris, 1931), 103-4.
4. Azzedine Haddour, "Algeria and Its History: Colonial Myths and the Forging and Deconstructing of Identity in *Pied-Noir* Literature," in *French and Algerian Identities from Colonial Times to the Present*, ed. Alec G. Hargreaves and Michael J. Hefferman (Lewiston NY: E. Mellen Press, 1993), 80–82; Azzedine Haddour, *Colonial Myths: History and Narrative* (Manchester: Manchester University Press, 2000), 130.

5. Jonathan K. Gosnell, *The Politics of Frenchness in Colonial Algeria, 1930–1954* (Rochester NY: University of Rochester Press, 2002), 186–90.

6. Martin Thomas, *The French Empire between the Wars: Imperialism, Politics and Society* (Manchester: Manchester University Press, 2005), 138–40; Gosnell, *Politics of Frenchness*, 186–212; Haddour, "Algeria and Its History," 80–82.

7. Patricia M. E. Lorcin, *Imperial Identities: Stereotyping, Prejudice, and Race in Colonial Algeria* (London: I. B. Tauris, 1999), 186; Neil MacMaster, *Colonial Migrants and Racism: Algerians in France, 1900–1962* (New York: St. Martin's Press, 1997), 6–7, 122; John Ruedy, *Modern Algeria: The Birth and Development of a Nation* (Bloomington: Indiana University Press, 1992), 74–76, 81, 89–90; Bruno Etienne, *Les Problèmes juridiques des minorités européenes au Maghreb* (Paris, 1988), 21.

8. MacMaster, *Colonial Migrants and Racism*, 122.

9. Thomas, *French Empire between the Wars*, 72.

10. On civilian attacks, see Jean-Pierre Peyroulou, *Guelma 1945: Une subversion française dans l'Algérie coloniale* (Paris, 2009), 66–69. On the issue of police brutality, see GGA 3CAB/95, Oran/1 juillet 1936; Préfet to Governor General Le Beau; Institut d'histoire sociale/Archives Charles Dumas I, "Rapport sur la situation politique à Sidi-Bel-Abbès" (1937); IHS/Dumas III, Governor General Le Beau to Minister of the Interior Marx Dormoy, Paris/9 mars 1937.

11. See, variously, Ruedy, *Modern Algeria*; Daniel Lefeuvre, *Chère Algérie* (Paris, 2005); Matthew Connelly, *A Diplomatic Revolution: Algeria's Fight for Independence and the Origins of the Post–Cold War Era* (Oxford: Oxford University Press, 2002); Jeannine Verdès-Leroux, *Les Français d'Algérie de 1830 à aujourd'hui* (Paris, 2001); James Le Sueur, *Uncivil War: Intellectuals and Identity Politics during the Decolonization of Algeria* (Philadelphia: University of Pennsylvania Press, 2001); Charles-Robert Ageron, *Histoire de l'Algérie contemporaine* (Paris, 1999); Anne-Marie Duranton-Crabol, *Le Temps de l'OAS* (Paris, 1995); Daniel Leconte, *Les Pieds-Noirs: Histoire et portraites d'une communauté* (Paris, 1980).

12. Alice L. Conklin, *A Mission to Civilize: The Republican Idea of Empire in France and West Africa, 1895–1930* (Stanford CA: Stanford University Press, 1997), 253.

13. Leconte, *Les Pieds-Noirs*, 101. This charge is often denied by pied-noir historians and memoirists, who tend to overlook any such agenda. See Eric Savarèse, *L'Invention des Pieds-Noirs* (Paris, 2002).

14. Gosnell, *Politics of Frenchness*, 186–212; Haddour, "Algeria and Its Myths," 78–83.

15. This figure is mentioned in Jacques Cantier, *L'Algérie sous le régime de Vichy* (Paris, 2002), 230–31. Although no precise number of CDF/PSF members is discussed in the archives of the governor-general or police services, various documents provide partial listings by section. See, for example, Centre des Archives d'Outre-Mer (CAOM), Aix-en-Provence, Oran //70, "Croix de Feu et Briscards," 1939, and Constantine B/3/707, Préfet de Constantine to Gouverneur Général d'Algérie, "Activité des sections de Croix de Feu depuis le 1er janvier 1934," 3 August 1935.

16. As Martin Thomas writes: "Signing up for the PSF in France could be a gesture of protest against Popular Front social and industrial reform. In Algeria, it was an affirmation that the Muslim population should be kept in their place." See Thomas, *French Empire between the Wars*, 303.

17. CAOM, Constantine B/3/323, Bordj-Bou-Arrèridj, Administrateur de la Commune Mixte to Sous-préfet, 12 July 1935; Alger 1 K/26, Commissaire de Police to Préfet, 25 June 1935; GGA 3CAB/47, Contrôleur Civil/Chef de la Région d'Oujda to Résident General, 1935.

18. CAOM, Constantine B/3/323, Administrateur de la Commune Mixte de Bordj-Bou-Arrèridj to Sous-préfet, 12 juillet 1935.

19. Ruedy, *Modern Algeria*, 140; CAOM, GGA 3CAB/47, "Notes sur le mouvement Croix de Feu parmi les indigènes," 1935. The group's judgment was no mere propaganda exercise, for the Algerian sections of the CDF/PSF were notoriously anti-Semitic, and anti-Jewish newspaper articles, speeches, and violence appeared regularly.

20. CAOM, Alger 1K/26, Sureté Départementale d'Alger, note de 25 novembre 1935; Constantine B/3/522, Commissaire de Police d'Aïn-Beïda, 28 May 1934; Constantine B/3/635, Sureté Départementale de Constantine, note de 14 septembre 1936; Constantine B/3/707, Tract: "Communication du Président du Comite Départementale," 1932.

21. CAOM, Alger 1K/26, Commissaire de Police d'El Biar to Préfet, 25 June 1935; Alger F/405, Commissaire de police de Boufarik to Préfet, 25 October 1935; GGA 3CAB/47, Chef de la Région d'Oujda to Résident général, 1935.

22. CAOM, GGA 3CAB/47, "Notes sur le mouvement Croix de Feu parmi les indigènes," 1935.

23. CAOM, GGA 3CAB/47, "Notes sur le mouvement Croix de Feu parmi les indigènes," 1935.

24. CAOM, Constantine B/3/635, Commissariat spécial de Bône, "Rapport—Parti social français," 8 March 1937.

25. CAOM, Constantine B/3/323, Administrateur de la commune mixte de Biban to Sous-préfet, 4 July 1935; Alger 1K/26, Préfet to GGA, July 1935; Constantine B/3/522, Commissaire de Police de Batna to Sous-préfet, 30 April 1936.

26. CAOM, Alger 1K/26, Préfet d'Alger to Gouverneur général d'Algérie, juillet 1935; Constantine B/3/323, Administrateur de la commune mixte de Biban to sous-préfet, "Activités des Croix de Feu," 4 juillet 1935.

27. Mahfoud Kaddache, *Histoire du nationalisme algérien* (Paris, 2003), 380–84, 512.

28. The top figure was twenty-one recruits in Khenchela. Rarely did the drives reach double digits. See, for example, CAOM, Alger 1K/26, Administrateur de la Commune Mixte de Bou-Saada to Préfet, 27 June 1935, Commissaire de Police de Maison-Carré, "Rapport de quinzaine," 29 June 1935 and Commissaire de Police d'Affreville to Préfet, 29 June 1935; Constantine B/3/522, Commissaire de Batna to Sous-préfet, "Assemblée Générale de la section des Croix de Feu, Briscards, et Volontaires Nationaux," 17 June 1934; Constantine B/3/323, Commissaire de Police de Batna to Sous-préfet, 30 June 1935, Commissaire de Police de M'Sila to Sous-préfet, 1 juillet 1935, and Commissaire de Police de Khenchela to Préfet, 9 July 1936; Constantine B/3/635, "Liste nominative des principaux dirigeants des différentes sections du Parti social français dans le Département de Constantine," 1937.

29. CAOM, Alger 1K/26, Commissaire de Police de Maison-Carré, "Rapport de quinzaine," 29 June 1935; Alger 1K/26, Commissaire de Police (Affreville) to Préfet, 29 June 1935; Alger 1K/75, Gouverneur général d'Algérie to Préfet/Alger, 5 February 1937.

30. CAOM, Constantine B/3/323, Commissaire de police de Khenchela to Préfet, "Activités des Croix de Feu," 9 July 1936; Constantine B/3/323, Commissaire de Police de Batna to Sous-préfet, 30 June 1935.

31. On Medjamel, see CAOM, Constantine B/3/635, "Liste nominative des principaux dirigeants des différentes sections de Parti social français dans le Département de Constantine"; Constantine B/3/522, Sureté départementale de Constantine, 11 June 1934. In addition, a French citizen named Caid Allahoum Fadi is listed as a member in M'Sila.

32. CAOM, GGA 3CAB/47, Sureté Départementale D'Alger, "Rapport," 11 January 1935.

33. On Ben Badis and the ʾUlamaʿ, see James McDougall, *History and the Culture of Nationalism in Algeria* (Cambridge: Cambridge University Press, 2006), 12–15, 64–66, 74–76, 82–86.

34. Ruedy, *Modern Algeria*, 133.

35. CAOM, Constantine B/3/323, Sureté Départementale de Constantine, "Surveillance politique des indigènes," 29 April 1935; Sous-préfet de Sétif to Préfet, 19 July 1935; Sureté Départementale de Constantine, notes dated 7 and 10 October 1935; Constantine B/3/707, Préfet de Constantine to Gouverneur général d'Algérie, "Activité des sections de Croix De Feu depuis 1er

janvier 1935," 3 August 1935; GGA 3CAB/47, "Notes sur le mouvement Croix de Feu parmi les indigènes," 1935. The CDF/PSF subsequently attempted to expand the alliance with the FEM to include the ʾUlamaʿ through their contact with Benhoura.

36. CAOM, GGA/3CAB 47, "Notes sur le mouvement Croix de Feu parmi les indigènes," 1935; Constantine B/3/323, Sureté départementale de Constantine, report of 10 octobre 1935; Victor Basch, "Impressions d'Algérie," *Les Cahiers des droits de l'homme*, 15 January 1937, 38.

37. CAOM, Constantine B/3/707, Tract: "Communication du Président du Comité départemental," 1932.

38. "La Réunion de la Salle Mazella," *La Flamme*, 23 November 1937. For similar pronouncements, see also CAOM, Alger 1K/26, Sûreté departmentale d'Alger, "Réunion Croix de Feu et Volontaires nationaux," 25 November 1935.

39. "L'Imbroglio de la politique musulmane en Algérie," *La Flamme*, 15 February 1937.

40. "France," *La Flamme*, 30 September 1938.

41. On Bertrand and Latinité, see Patricia M. E. Lorcin, *Imperial Identities: Stereotyping, Prejudice, and Race in Colonial Algeria* (London: I. B. Tauris, 1999), 196–97, 201–4. *L'Algérien* quote taken from Kaddache, *Histoire du nationalisme*, 227. Bordès quoted in Yaël Simpson Fletcher, "Irresistible Seductions: Gendered Representations of Colonial Algeria," in *Domesticating the Empire: Race, Gender, and Family Life in French and Dutch Colonialism*, ed. Julia Clancy-Smith and Frances Gouda (Charlottesville: University Press of Virginia, 1998), 195.

42. Alfred Debay, "Afrique du nord: Terre de l'union," *La Flamme*, 7 December 1937; Alfred Debay, "Conserver ou maintenir?" *La Flamme*, 18 February 1938. On the slump and the resulting immiseration and starvation, see Lefeuvre, *Chère Algérie*, 12.

43. Jacques Dupoux and Jacques Allain, "Le PSF et l'idée impériale," *La Flamme*, 7 April 1939; CAOM, Constantine B/3/635, Commissariat Spéciale de Bône, "Parti social français: Préparation pour la campagne électorale," 2 October 1937.

44. CAOM, Constantine B/3/635, Commissariat spéciale de Bône, Rapport: "Parti social français: Préparation de la campagne électorale," 2 October 1937; Constantine B/3/635, Commissaire de police de Bougie to Préfet, 6 November 1937.

45. Quoted in Kaddache, *Histoire du nationalisme*, 348.

46. Kaddache, *Histoire du nationalisme*, 265, 344.

47. McDougall, *History and the Culture of Nationalism*, 76.

48. Thomas, *French Empire between the Wars*, 251–52, 260–68; Lefeuvre, *Chère Algérie*, 14. Ben-Badis quoted in Kaddache, *Histoire du nationalisme* 12.

49. CAOM, Alger 1K/26, Commissaire de Police de l'Arba to Préfet, 18 October 1935.

50. Testis, "Les Elections municipales indigènes d'Alger," *La Flamme*, 16 July 1937; "Motion finale," *La Flamme*, 28 October 1938.

51. CAOM, Oran //70, Commissaire de Police du 1er Arrt. de la ville de Mostaganem to Commissaire Central, 13 December 1936; Ruedy, *Modern Algeria*, 121.

52. A. Debay, "L'Algérie française ne doit pas périr," *La Flamme*, 6 May 1938; "Les Oulémas: Agents du Panislamisme," *La Flamme*, 15 February 1937; "L'enseignement 'moderne' des Oulemas est simplement réactionnaire et nationaliste," *La Flamme*, 17 June 1938; Testis, "La Tyrannie par la terreur," *La Flamme*, 5 March 1938.

53. On Hadj and the ENA, see Thomas, *French Empire between the Wars*, 259–65; and Kaddache, *Histoire du nationalisme*, 301–2, 330–31, 438–53.

54. "Le Noyautage des organisations musulmanes," *La Flamme*, 1 February 1938; "Socialistes et communistes sont les promoteurs de l'agitation antifrançaise en Afrique du Nord," *La Flamme*, 3 October 1937; Testis, "Moscou contre Chekib Arslan," *La Flamme*, 22 January 1938.

55. Samuel Kalman, "*Le Combat par tous les moyens*: Colonial Violence and the Extreme Right in 1930s Oran," *French Historical Studies* 33 (2011), 127–54.

56. Lefeuvre, *Chère Algérie*, 72–75; Ruedy, *Modern Algeria*, 94; Jacques Berque, *French North Africa: The Maghrib between Two World Wars* (London, Faber, 1967), 209; David Prochaska, *Making Algeria French: Colonialism in Bône, 1870–1920* (Cambridge: Cambridge University Press, 1990), 11.

57. CAOM, Constantine B/3/323, Administrateur de la Commune Mixte de Bordj-Bou-Arrèridj to Sous-préfet, 12 July 1935.

58. Institut d'histoire social/Archives Charles Dumas I, "Premiers éléments d'enquête de la section constantinoise de la LICA sur les graves incidents des 24-27-28-29-30 juin et 1er juillet 1936." On the group's anti–Popular Front campaign in Algeria, see IHS/ACD III, Gouverneur général d'Algérie to Président du Conseil, 30 June 1936.

59. Lefeuvre, *Chère Algérie*, 62, 71; Thomas, *French Empire between the Wars*, 68, 253. These facts were not lost on the governor-general's office or the metropolitan government, whose Haut Comité Méditerranéen in 1937 stated that "la cadence de la progression de la natalité est telle que dans l'avenir proche la marge des possibilités offertes par l'Algérie à l'économie indigène sera dépassée."

60. Jacques Marseille, *Empire colonial et capitalisme français* (Paris, 1984), 59–60, 75–77; Lefeuvre, *Chère Algérie*, 22, 55, 181–82; Berque, *French North Africa*, 40–43.

61. Roy quoted in Jacques Cantier, *L'Algérie sous le régime de Vichy*, 17.

62. Lefeuvre, *Chère Algérie*, 43–53; Kaddache, *Histoire du nationalisme*, 256–59; Pierre Mannoni, *Les Français d'Algérie: Vie, moeurs, mentalité* (Paris, 1993), 131–40.

63. Jacques Labruyère, "Des maisons pour les indigènes," *La Flamme*, 1 February 1937; "La Problème indigène," *La Flamme*, 1 February 1937; CAOM, Alger F/405, Commissaire de Police d'Affreville to Préfet, 20 October 1936.

64. Alfred Debay, "De la terre et du travail pour nos populations indigènes," *La Flamme*, 5 March 1938. CDF/PSF leaders viewed such policies as an extension of leader Colonel de la Rocque's policy of *service social* and the "equality of souls," a social Catholic platform that focused on helping *les humbles*.

65. CAOM, Constantine B/3/327, Report of the Sureté départementale de Constantine, 6 July 1936; "Le PSF et les problèmes algériens," *La Flamme*, 15 January 1937. The group's report at the 1938 National Congress revisited the same themes and solutions. See Constantine B/3/635, Report of the Police Spéciale de Constantine, 23 October 1938.

66. CAOM, Constantine B/3/635, Police spéciale départementale de Constantine, "Congrès du PSF," 23 octobre 1938.

67. "Le Triomphal meeting du clôture," *La Flamme*, 28 October 1938.

68. "Le Triomphal meeting du clôture."

69. "Le PSF et les problèmes algériens," *La Flamme*, 15 January 1937. On the Sénatus Consulte, see MacMaster, *Colonial Migrants*, 27–29. For a discussion of European attitudes toward Muslim religious practices and treatment of women, see Julia Clancy-Smith, "Islam, Gender, and Identities in the Making of French Algeria, 1830–1962," in Clancy-Smith and Gouda, *Domesticating the Empire*, 163, 173; and Jeanne Bowlan, "Polygamists Need Not Apply: Becoming a French Citizen in Colonial Algeria, 1918–1938," *Proceedings of the Annual Meeting of the Western Society for French History* 24 (1997), 111–13.

70. Pierre Bourdieu, *The Algerians* (Boston, Beacon Press, 1961), 132. On racial and socioeconomic segregation, see Prochaska, *Making Algeria French*, 153–79. The non-European population had resented their second-class status for some time, particularly in light of the 1870 Crémieux decree, granting French citizenship to Algerian Jews, most of whom were far from Europeanized. See Emanuel Sivan, "Stéréotypes antijuifs dans la mentalité Pied-noir,"

Les Relations entre Juifs et musulmans en Afrique du nord, XIXe–XXe siècles: Actes du Colloque international de l'institut d'histoire des pays d'outre-mer (Paris, 1980), 166.

71. Jacques Cantier, "Les Gouverneurs Viollette et Bordes et la politique algérienne de la France à la fin des années vingt," *Revue française de l'histoire d'outre-mer* 84 (1997), 24–25; Thomas, *French Empire between the Wars*, 69–73, 247–48.

72. Thomas, *French Empire between the Wars*, 71–73; Mannoni, *Les Français d'Algérie*, 129. See also the relevant sections in Jacques Bouvaresse, *Un parlement colonial: Les délégations financières algériennes, 1898–1945* (Mont Saint-Aignon: Publications des Universités de Rouen et du Havre, 2008).

73. Thomas, *French Empire between the Wars*, 297–302; Malcolm Richardson, "Algeria and the Popular Front: Radicals, Socialists, and the Blum-Viollette Project," *Proceedings of the Annual Meeting of the Western Society for French History* 5 (1977), 356. That the provision against the practice of Qurʾanic law had protected the pieds-noirs by preserving their monopoly on citizenship was never discussed. It is also worth noting that the actual interest of the Popular Front government in colonial reform was miniscule at best. Few ministers actively opposed imperialism, and no voice advocated a major role in government for the *indigènes* (including Blum and Viollette).

74. Pierre Apestuguy, "La Présence de M. Viollette dans le gouvernement menace directement l'Algérie," *Petit Journal*, 15 March 1938. For a more comprehensive discussion of the metropolitan CDF/PSF reaction, see Pierre Machefer, "Autour du problème algérien en 1936–1938: La Doctrine algérienne du PSF: Le PSF et le projet Blum-Viollette," *Revue d'histoire moderne et contemporaine* 10 (1963), 147–56.

75. "Sidi Viollette," *La Flamme*, 18 February 1938.

76. Stanislas Devaud, "Frères indigènes d'Algérie," *Dépêche de Constantine*, 31 January 1937.

77. "Monsieur Sarraut: Nous vous prenons au mot," *La Flamme*, 5 February 1938; Jacques Dupoux and Jacques Allain, "Le PSF et l'idée impériale," *La Flamme*, 7 April 1939. Following the rupture between Bendjelloul and the CDF/PSF, the group turned on Muslim politicians, arguing for a vast conspiracy between Bendjelloul and the Congrès Musulman, Ben-Badis and the Oulémas, Hadj and the ENA/PPA, Bernard Lecache and the Ligue internationale contre l'antisémitisme, and the Communist Party. Examples of this thesis appear in almost every issue of *La Flamme* during 1937–39, mainly in the press roundup columns by Testis.

78. See, for example, "Réunion du PSF," *La Flamme*, 29 January 1937.

79. Counterproposals were tendered by Parti populaire français leader Jacques Doriot and Jeunesses patriotes head Pierre Taittinger, among others.

80. La Rocque announced the commission in June 1937: CAOM, Alger 1 K/75, Sûreté Départmentale d'Alger report, 2 July 1937; "Les Affaires indigènes d'Algérie au PSF," *Le Journal*, 5 June 1937.

81. CAOM, Constantine B/3/635, Commissaire de Police de Sétif to Sous-préfet, 2 November 1936; Alger 1K/75, Commissaire Centrale de Police a Blida to Préfet, 1 June 1938.

82. See, for example, CAOM, Constantine B/3/707, Commissaire de police to Sous-Préfet, 10 April 1936. The report describes a meeting in Bougie addressed by Iba-Zizen, to which eight hundred *indigènes* were sent special invitations.

83. CAOM, GGA 3CAB/89, PSF Contre-projet, 11 February 1938; Augustin Iba-Zizen, "La Citoyenneté intégrale doit être conférée office à certains catégories d'indigènes," *La Flamme*, 12 February 1938; "Le Contre-projet présenté par le groupe parlementaire PSF," *La Flamme*, 18 February 1938.

84. The commission's report appears in its entirety in *La Flamme*, 11 November 1938.

85. I use the terms "assimilation" and "association" in the manner of Alice Conklin here, referring to the "refined" versions of Raymond Betts's definitions, mobilized by the pieds-noirs during the interwar era. The new definitions were much harsher than the nineteenth-century originals, precluding any real advancement for indigenous peoples in North Africa, or anywhere else in the French empire for that matter. See Raymond F. Betts, *Assimilation and Association in French Colonial Theory, 1890–1914* (New York: Columbia University Press, 1961), 8–9; Conklin, *A Mission to Civilize*, 210–11.

86. "Mechanisms of Oppression: Interview with Albert Memmi," in *Race, Discourse, and Power in France*, ed. Maxim Silverstein (Aldershot: Ashgate, 1991), 30; Jean-François Guilhaume, *Les Mythes fondateurs de l'Algérie française* (Paris, 1992), 223–29; Lorcin, *Imperial Identities*, 212. On the construction of phantasmatic colonial identities, see Panivong Norindr, *Phantasmatic Indochina: French Colonial Ideology in Architecture, Film, and Literature* (Durham: University of North Carolina Press, 1996).

87. Haddour, "Algeria and Its History," 83; Gosnell, *Politics of Frenchness*, 186–90; Emanuel Sivan, "Colonialism and Popular Culture in Algeria," *Journal of Contemporary History* 14 (1979), 32. For an example of *Algérianité* and North African Arabs, see Louis Bertrand, *Le Sang des races* (Paris, 1921), 238.

88. Thomas, *French Empire between the Wars*, 138–40. Thomas notes that "the idealization of the settler farmer as the embodiment of virile, patriotic dynamism echoes the ultra-rightism of French leagues such as the Croix de Feu."

6

Colonial Minds and Colonial Violence

*The Sétif Uprising and the
Savage Economics of Colonialism*

MARTIN THOMAS

This chapter revisits the tragic history of the rebellion that erupted across northeastern Algeria in May 1945. It does not rehearse the now familiar debates over the motivations behind the extreme violence of the so-called Sétif uprising, nor its precise timing at the close of World War II.[1] Nor does it dwell at length on the mechanics of state-sanctioned repression that would see thousands of Algerians die during four months of bloody retribution. Suffice to say that the counterviolence sanctioned by the French state in eastern Algeria over the summer of 1945 probably exceeded the total deaths—both the court-ordered executions and the extrajudicial killings—carried out during the *épuration* in post-Liberation France.[2] The staggering magnitude of the 1945 violence in colonial Algeria has rightly drawn historical attention, but with neither definitive agreement over total Algerian fatalities nor over the uprising's status as precursor or, perhaps, first act of the Algerian War of Independence, the account on Sétif can hardly be considered settled.[3] The grotesque irony of its contemporaneousness with France's anticollaborationist purge surely merits further examination. So, too, do the rebellion's religious constructions, its gender dynamics, and the social backgrounds and political affiliations of the security forces and vigilantes that repressed it.[4] All are critical questions. But my aim here is more modest: to consider one facet of the uprising's prehistory that, it seems to me, remains poorly understood: its roots among eastern Algeria's peasants, sharecroppers (*khammès*), and farm laborers. This chapter tries to rectify this lack of information by focusing on questions of political economy. The purpose is to shed light on the chronic food supply crisis that gripped much of Algeria over the winter and spring of 1944–45. If this illuminates the revolt's socioeconomic impulsions, something else emerges regarding the institutional workings of colonial minds in crisis conditions.

The characters involved here were for the most part senior colonial officials, whether working in eastern Algeria's prefectural administration in Constantine, in the Algiers colonial government-general, or within their parent government agency in Paris: the Ministry of Interior. It is thus a partial history—an account based on the interrogation of written colonial archives alone. But it is self-consciously so. The constructed nature of the archival record, the acute one-sidedness of the materials involved, is integral to the argument advanced. For this is a study of the normative standards prevalent among colonial bureaucrats and leading French politicians as revealed by their evaluation of the information provided to them about a particular colonial situation, one that they imagined and dealt with in particularly colonial ways. That the 1945 rebellion—often ascribed the shorthand appellation "Sétif"—was proof of acute political and social upheaval in Algeria may appear self-evident; that it was also the product of profound economic crisis less so. Was this how it appeared to French colonial decision makers at the time? Were Algerians' political grievances and social conditions interwoven with their underlying economic causes? Did it make sense to view matters this way? If not, why not? As we shall see, the answer lies in the particular reading of economic indicators and popular responses to material hardship in the Algerian countryside during the final months of the Second World War. It is a story of colonial minds sometimes lacking sufficient information to make informed decisions, but more often denying the validity of evidence presented to them because it conflicted with their underlying assumptions about the attitudes and behavior of Algerian colonial subjects. In rejecting evidence that conflicted with their presumptions about Algeria and its people, French officials offered terrible proof of the tenacity of a mental universe constructed upon colonialist ideas of superiority and difference.

The colonial Algeria to emerge from World War II remained a contradiction. It was constitutionally tied to the *métropole*, on paper at least, and the restoration of republican democracy in postwar France would reaffirm Algeria's status as a core element of the French polity. What was new in the emergent Fourth Republic was the mounting interest in translating Algeria's theoretical integration with France into reality through economic modernization and wider access to citizenship. Both acquired fresh impetus as schemes for the new French Union and Algerian Statute took shape in 1945–47. Whether we regard such measures merely as elaborate subterfuge, disguising continued imperial domination, or as a genuine attempt to break down the colonial divides between rulers and ruled, the outcome would ultimately prove disappointing to all sides.[5]

France's postwar colonial supremacy would perpetuate the differential treatment of subject populations, whether on the basis of economic stratification, communal affiliation, language, religion, or an amalgam of cultural differences.[6] Acute inequalities, particularly, as we shall see, in a postwar environment marked by economic deprivation and political uncertainty, created a climate of fearful anticipation among colonial bureaucrats and security force analysts, especially the Arabic-reading specialists tied to local, prefectural administrations.[7] Their anxiety was reflected in closer surveillance of those colonial subjects and groups thought most likely to threaten French power.[8] Security assessments of indigenous opinion also veered toward "moral panic" as signs of colonial breakdown proliferated in early 1945, shaping the forms of state repression pursued after the initial explosion of Algerian political violence in May.[9] But the concern here is less with the extreme reactions that made overwhelming state violence possible than with how a key contributor to rebellion—foodstuff shortage—was read, or misread, by official colonial minds.

Political Economy and Colonial Violence

Was Sétif a rebellion driven by the threat of mass starvation? If not, then what drove popular participation in what were primarily rural uprisings among farm workers, sharecroppers, and other food producers? Clues may lie in the peculiar structure of the agricultural economy of eastern

Algeria and its particular situation in early 1945 when problems of foodstuff supply and distribution, linked to wartime disruptions, became acute. Manus Midlarsky's correlation of mass political violence in Latin America with iniquitous land distribution and, more precisely, with acute land scarcity and oligarchic control of the agricultural market lends itself to eastern Algeria in spring 1945, where a combination of incipient famine conditions and preferential treatment of settler farmers provoked intense hostility among Muslim farmworkers and smallholders.[10] There is also an analogy to be drawn here with Chris Allen's analysis of the interconnectedness of economic iniquity, political violence, and state collapse in postcolonial Africa, the argument being that violence becomes endemic once the socially marginalized are given room to express extreme opposition by the implosion of state power.[11]

Lest we be tempted to adopt these economically determinist models outright, however, it is worth bearing in mind Mahmood Mamdani's warning about the inadequacy of political economy as a framework to explain colonial social divisions and political violence. Assigning identities and collective behaviors to discrete groups on the basis of their lowly economic status—as agricultural workers or tenant farmers, for instance—ignores multitiered colonial legal systems that tied material discrimination to a distinct communal identity; in the Algerian case, as Muslim colonial subjects with limited civil rights under French law.[12] The Sétif example suggests that socioeconomic discrimination and, more particularly, unequal access to scarce resources, cannot be neatly differentiated from communal discrimination as catalysts to killing.[13] Quite the reverse: the two processes overlapped, contributing to nationalist mobilization in support of political violence. Here Elizabeth Thompson's reconceptualization of civic rights, responsibilities, and gender roles within mandate Syria and Lebanon is particularly revealing. Syrians and Lebanese experienced famine both as a weapon of war from 1915 to 1918 and as a searing collective memory thereafter.[14] In Algeria, too, famines were as integral to the lived experience of colonial conquest as state control over food supply became to French strategies of domination thereafter.[15] The lesson of both examples was much the same. Chronic food shortage lends itself to intense politicization whenever state action—or inaction—is identified as the cause of the social crises to which famine gives rise.

Where does this leave us? Political economy may not entirely explain Algerians' turn to violence in 1945, but it seems reasonable to postulate that economic concerns were critical motivating factors nonetheless. Jeremy Weinstein's research on the form and extent of violence in civil wars in postcolonial Africa hinges on the proposition that insurgents' actions and state coercion in response to them are closely linked to levels of resource availability in the affected locality. On the one hand an abundance of natural resources may discourage popular involvement in rebellion, encouraging those committed to overthrowing the state to employ higher levels of violence in order to reshape civilian loyalties. On the other hand chronic shortages of natural resources may render civilians more inclined to support an insurgency that is, in turn, less likely to employ indiscriminate violence in order to compel popular compliance with its dictates.[16] The central point here is that the availability of essential commodities affects not only political choices but also the levels of political violence linked to those choices. Such was the case in eastern Algeria during early 1945, a period in which shortages of basic foodstuffs escalated into a crisis of survival.

The Economics of Hatred?

From February 1945 onward, prefecture staff and gendarmerie units reported signs of worsening hardship and incipient famine among the Muslim population. It soon became apparent that the Algiers government relief efforts and, in particular, the rural rationing scheme administered at the commune level by the government's Sociétés indigènes de prévoyance, could not cope with the scale of the colony's food supply crisis.[17] Algeria's developing famine, much like its deadlier wartime equivalents in British-ruled Bengal and French-ruled northern Vietnam during 1943–45, exposed the bankruptcy of European claims to colonial benevolence, laying bare the hopeless inadequacy of colonial states under the stresses of global war.[18] In the Algerian case the colonial authorities alone could never resolve the bureaucratic, monetary, and supply challenges inherent in famine relief. For one thing food distribution was a multi-agency problem. Securing adequate foodstuffs, whether through purchase, requisition, or charitable donation from allied states, necessitated coordination between six ministries in Paris: Interior, Foreign

Affairs, Finance, Agriculture, Labor, and National Economy, not to mention the active engagement of the colonial authorities on the ground. For another thing neither France nor Algeria could overcome the crisis without foreign support. By the start of April 1945 Algeria relied entirely on imported wheat to supply the country's bread requirements. The logistics of vessel availability within the allied shipping pool of friendly merchant fleets thus assumed a critical importance. By 24 May only 61,074 tons of the colony's estimated basic two-month requirement for 119,000 tons of wheat had been delivered.[19]

Chronic foodstuff shortages, a mounting supply crisis, and the prospect of a dismal harvest in July–August 1945 clearly bore upon Algerian colonial subjects' lives, but French readings of the food crisis and its possible connection with the May uprising reveal more about the official "colonial mind." While the archival record frequently lacks precise information about the material impact of the food crisis on families and communities, it overflows with predictions, prejudices, and assumptions made about local Algerian responses, whether psychological, physical, or political, to severe deprivation. Supply difficulties also registered as both symptom and cause of bitter divisions within French officialdom as arguments intensified in early 1945 between administrative agencies in Paris and Algiers over their relative culpability for the lack of available foodstuffs.[20]

These splits tell us a good deal about bad governance and bureaucratic confusion in the immediate aftermath of Liberation. Yet, while they reveal abundant evidence of jurisdictional rivalry, there is little indication that those involved looked upon Algeria's subject population in conflicting ways. Far from it: the one constant in this bureaucratic infighting was the shared presumption that Algerians' preoccupation with securing enough food to eat was proof of their political immaturity. Simply put, much official reportage ran thus: rather than attributing their hardship to any deeper political wrongs, Algeria's colonial subjects simply complained about the most glaring manifestations of misrule, namely, the authorities' inability to provide adequate relief through emergency foodstuff distribution. The lesson underlying such reportage was reassuringly simple. Satisfy their most basic needs, and Algeria's peasantry would rediscover their sullen indifference to high politics. Neither the 'ulama's radical ascetic purity nor nationalist incantation would register the same impact once bellies were full. Apprised of this apparently straightforward correlation between cause and effect, Governor Yves Chataigneau seized on the advice of the colonial administration's economic committee (Comité supérieur économique) on 31 March, establishing local scrutiny committees (Comités de vigilance économique) to monitor grain distribution and, if necessary, overrule the communal authorities whenever abuses were uncovered.[21] Here, too, it seemed, all was not well within the colonial bureaucracy. Before looking in detail at official views of the Algerian supply crisis, it is worth dwelling on these inter-agency disputes because they reveal how little Paris politicians and senior officials actually understood the severity of the problem on the eve of Sétif.

On 31 January Interior Minister Adrien Tixier fired off a letter to the head of the Ministry's Algeria subdivision. It made uncomfortable reading for its recipient, Émile Laffon. Tixier had the sharp tongue characteristic of a no-nonsense socialist trade unionist and former ex-servicemen's association organizer. He had cemented his reputation among the new republican political elite through his robust, if sometimes indelicate, defense of Free France as head of the Gaullist diplomatic mission to Washington. As interior minister over the winter of 1944–45 he headed a department in the throes of a post-Liberation purge of former Vichy sympathizers. Laffon's Algeria subdivision had suffered especially heavily, many of its staff having transferred from the Algiers government bureaucracy where, it was widely held, support for Vichy ran deep. As a result, before the provisional government's transfer from Algiers to Paris in July 1944, its Commissariat of the Interior had accrued administrative responsibility at the expense of the Vichy-tarnished Algiers colonial government. The net result was to make it harder still for the depleted Interior Ministry Algeria subdivision to prepare policy advice for Tixier once the provisional government was installed in Paris. Having watched his deputy summarily dismissed, Laffon also saw his clerical staff depleted. With few experienced backroom staff still in situ the subdivision failed to keep Tixier abreast of developments in Algeria.[22] The minister was thus unable to brief the newly created interministerial committee on North Africa, which was scheduled to meet once a month from the end of January 1945 onward. The failure of the Interior Ministry to keep on top of its traditional Algeria brief was especially embarrassing because the new committee was the creature of de Gaulle's prime ministerial office, where the committee secretariat was based.[23] Lacking verifiable factual information from subdivision staff, Tixier and Laffon filled the gaps with guesswork, thereby exposing how easily ingrained prejudice could take the place of more rational, dispassionate analysis.

At no stage before 8 May did Tixier feel he was kept adequately informed of the Algerian supply crisis or of the colony's affairs more generally. Despite the interior minister's increasingly urgent demands for more comprehensive briefing papers on local Algerian affairs in April and early May, he remained poorly apprised of socioeconomic conditions in the colony—its rural interior above all.[24] Indeed, on 7 May Pierre Vrolyk, principal adviser in the Algeria subdivision, conceded that "confusion reigned" among Paris officials in the four main government agencies with responsibility for the formulation of economic policy in Algeria.[25] Preoccupied with resolving these jurisdictional clashes, the Interior Ministry's Algeria specialists had lost sight of events on the ground. It took the violence of 8 May to stir the Algeria subdivision into submitting its first complete survey of the Algerian situation later that month.[26] To summarize, throughout the early months of the Algerian foodstuff crisis, and even on the very eve of the Sétif and Guelma outbreaks, the ministry most directly responsible for ameliorating the supply problem knew precious little about its escalation or its likely impact.

Lack of good economic intelligence did not mean, however, that bureaucrats or their political masters were reluctant to voice an opinion about what was happening in Algeria. Substantial economic information was sometimes available but was eclipsed by more sensational and apparently urgent political intelligence drawn principally from police and military sources. Security analysis of mounting Algerian political opposition in early 1945 had no time for dry economic data, still less for the structural problems of Algeria's agricultural sector to which such material pointed. As we shall see, political intelligence gatherers in Constantine and Algiers and their ministerial masters in Paris were instead preoccupied with evidence of a dangerous new alignment among Algeria's foremost nationalist parties and the colony's leading Islamic cultural association. Before discussing these internal political shifts, a little contextual background about the process of state intelligence gathering in eastern Algeria is essential, specifically in regard to the creation of new administrative agencies and police networks dedicated to the surveillance and control of Muslim colonial subjects in the Constantine prefecture.

Stung by its failure to anticipate the anti-Semitic riots in Constantine town in late August 1934 (discussed in Joshua Cole's chapter), Georges Le Beau's Algiers government overhauled its intelligence-gathering procedures during the following year, focusing in particular on the analysis of public opinion by district and prefectural authorities.[27] Where previously the native affairs service and district administrators' reports were distilled by subprefects into periodic reviews of local sentiment, systematic intelligence collation by dedicated Arabic-speaking staff attached to the prefecture became the norm.[28] The outcome, by the time the Popular Front began its abortive reform program in mid-1936, was the crystallization of a more professional—and sedition-oriented—political intelligence office, the Information Analysis Center (Centre d'information et d'études—CIE), that filtered human intelligence from informants and police interviews, "open source" intelligence from press and other media, and sensitive information from gendarmerie posts and police stations, mayors, and other local officials into a blended mix of predictive net assessment. Generously funded and already deeply embedded within the colony's bureaucratic apparatus by 1938, CIE offices were at the cutting edge of Algeria's "intelligence state."[29] And by March 1945 the Constantine CIE exemplified official fears of incipient rebellion.[30]

If bureaucratic anxiety about popular insurrection was already widespread, it nonetheless intensified owing to the convergence of views in incoming intelligence reports during early 1945. In the five months preceding the May 1945 disorders the Algiers government-general, the Paris Interior Ministry, the War Ministry, and General de Gaulle's prime minister's office received a steady stream of alarming political intelligence from four principal sources: the Constantine prefect André Lestrade-Carbonnel and the CIE attached to his prefecture; the officers of the secret police, the Renseignements Généraux (RG), posted in Algiers and Constantine; the Africa Section of the XIXth Army's Corps headquarters in the Algerian capital; and the Algeria gendarmerie command. These four offices within the state apparatus were most directly involved in amassing, processing, and analyzing information about sources of internal opposition, changes in public opinion, and threats to colonial authority before and after Sétif. None contained economic specialists, and with the sole exception of the CIE, all were primarily concerned with direct threats to state security rather than with longer-term trends in Algerian society. Colonial power in eastern Algeria would stand or fall on the quality of source information, the efficiency with which intelligence was relayed to decision makers, and the accuracy of their predictions.[31]

By April 1945 the bulk of the information received by these groups pointed in the same direction. It indicated that the three political groups with greatest leverage over Algeria's Muslim population were working in greater unison, notably in the Algiers and Constantine departments.[32] The Association of Reformist 'Ulamaʿ, the Amis du Manifeste et de la Liberté (AML), and, first and foremost, the Parti du Peuple Algérien (PPA) faced constant state surveillance, albeit of differing quality and intensity. The PPA was subject to a government ban; its senior figures, led by the charismatic Messali Hadj, were in detention, most under house arrest. Already driven underground, the PPA, it was thought, had devised alternative methods to advance its cause of integral nationalism.[33] Less uncompromisingly nationalist, and with fewer connections to the Algerian immigrant community in mainland France, the AML led by Ferhat Abbas was emerging as a major political force owing to its sponsorship of the 1943 "Manifesto," a document that rallied Algerians to claim enfranchisement, citizenship, and civil rights broadly equivalent to those of the settler population.[34] Outside Algiers, the AML's power base was eastern Algeria, the home region of Abbas, who was born in the coastal *wilaya* (department) of Jijel and practiced as a pharmacist in Sétif.[35] Last of the three groups was the Association of Reformist 'Ulamaʿ. Dedicated to the purification of Algerian Islam, and since 1941 under the spiritual leadership of another Constantinois, Sheikh Taleb Bachir Ben Saadi, better known as Bashir Brahimi, the Muslim teachers, or 'Ulamaʿ, of this religious-cultural organization enjoyed unrivalled respect among the faithful.[36] Nominally apolitical, their defense of the cultural integrity of Algerian Islam rejected French colonialism in all its forms, whether political, economic, religious, or linguistic in favor of the rediscovery of Algeria's authentically Muslim spiritual—and national—identity.³⁷ As James McDougall has demonstrated, the cultural nationalism of the ʾUlamaʿ was resilient, defiant, and utterly incorruptible.³⁸

In late January 1945 the Algiers government's Muslim affairs service directed by Jacques Berque received a number of agents' reports indicating that the ʾUlamaʿ had entered a formal working alliance with the two main nationalist parties. ʾUlamaʿ, PPA, and AML organizers henceforth coordinated their activities through a six-member "Central Commission" in Algiers and three subordinate commissions at the departmental level in which ʾUlamaʿ leader Bachir Brahimi played the pivotal role. ʾUlamaʿ involvement gave religious sanction to nationalist militancy, precluding any cooperation with the European population.³⁹ The strategy could succeed only if colonial officials were, in turn, prevented from sowing division among the differing shades of nationalist opinion. From the PPA's more hard-line perspective, it was vital that the nonviolent AML be radicalized. PPA activists duly infiltrated AML ranks while their party bosses appealed to Ferhat Abbas not to undermine the struggle for independence by accepting other, lesser concessions.⁴⁰ Despite the AML's abiding commitment to nonviolent reformism, PPA-led demonstrations over the spring of 1945 helped persuade AML activists that an open breach with their more radical brethren would be divisive and, in the short term at least, counterproductive.⁴¹

Read by French security analysts in Constantine, Algiers, and Paris, PPA stratagems were a plot to undermine the emerging scheme to reintegrate Algeria into France's new Republic through economic modernization, the reorganization of local government, and limited enfranchisement of the "moderate" Algerian Muslim elite. The natural political home of such moderates was the AML and, to a lesser extent, the AML's more conservative forebear, Dr. Mohamed Salah Bendjelloul's Federation of Elected Muslims. PPA success in subverting such groups thereby acquired greater significance. What made things worse was that the Association of Reformist ʾUlamaʿ seemed complicit in the process. It has long been understood that ʾUlamaʿ calls to ascetic devotion and rejection of alien colonial culture complemented the PPA's integral nationalism; indeed this had informed the prewar decision to outlaw the association in 1935. The full implications of the Vichy authorities' decision to revoke this ban in 1941 only became apparent in the changed political climate created by the presence of Allied Forces in French North Africa from November 1942 and the subsequent consolidation of de Gaulle's provisional government in Algiers during 1944.[42]

By March 1945 'Ulamaʿ pronouncements, mosque speeches, and Qurʾanic Free Schools reiterated a simple message: Muslim self-respect precluded cooperation with the colonial authorities. This insistence on Islamic authenticity and cultural rediscovery was especially appealing to the young. In their devotional ethos, their nationalist chants and hymns, their parades and paramilitary styling, the Federation of Muslim Scouts (Fédération des scouts musulmans Algériens, FSMA), to which thousands of adolescent adherents flocked over the winter of 1944–45, threatened to become a vanguard of nationalist protest.[43] The colonial minds at work in the offices of the Constantine CIE, the Algiers government, and the Interior Ministry's Algeria subdivision attached particular cultural meaning to these organizational changes. By the spring of 1945 ministers, policy advisers, and security force analysts concurred that PPA-directed protest might escalate into something more as young FMSA zealots spurred on by 'Ulamaʿ teachings urged the crowd toward communal rebellion in the language of religious war.[44]

The cumulative result of these gathering threat perceptions was that by March 1945 the Constantine prefecture had been identified as epicenter of a tripartite menace to French rule in Algeria. Put another way, while there was certainly debate among the Paris political elite over Algerian policy options, there was significant disparity between the quality and quantity of information on political matters relative to economic. It bears emphasis, for instance, that the interministerial committee on North Africa (Comité de l'Afrique du Nord) mentioned above only came into its own after Sétif, not before. Run by Colonel Henri Spillman, who served as its secretary, this advisory committee in early 1945 was still picking up the reins of its Third Republic predecessor, the Mediterranean High Committee (Haut Comité Méditerranéen), as the foremost permanent ministerial advisory group on policy in the Maghreb. By the early summer the Comité de l'Afrique du Nord acted as a government think tank on North African affairs, on security questions above all. In his role as committee secretary Spillman established himself as principal counselor on Algerian matters to de Gaulle's prime minister's office in the aftermath of the uprising.⁴⁵ His committee secretariat acted as a clearinghouse for de Gaulle's office, analyzing and summarizing the incoming and outgoing telegrams from the Interior and War Ministries and the Algiers government in the immediate aftermath of Sétif.⁴⁶

The first major report prepared at Spillman's behest for the North Africa Committee and de Gaulle's personal cabinet reviewed the situation across the Maghreb in the weeks after Sétif. Its watchword was "malaise"—economic, social, and political. The three French North African territories were certainly in crisis, but according to this analysis, the core problem was reducible to three causes. Lack of grain supplies and the consequent food supply crisis headed the list, with the prospect of malnourishment, if not full-blown famine, looming largest in colonial subjects' minds. Pan-Arab propaganda, much of it indirectly sponsored by Britain, the principal external backer of the Arab League, drew its lifeblood from the discontents produced by lack of adequate food. Perhaps inevitably in a report of this type, the Vichy heritage was also blamed for the crisis. The ignoble Vichy past was personified in the many colonial administrators still in office who were accused of sitting idle during the preceding years of wartime misrule in the Maghreb. Their lack of initiative, of patriotic vigor, was allegedly still manifest in lax administration, the consequences of which became tragically apparent on 8 May. If the structural causes of eastern Algeria's problems were threefold, so, too, were the solutions. Indeed, the remedy for French North Africa as a whole lay in resolving the region's supply crisis, confronting Anglo-American tolerance of the Arab League's pan-Arabism, and purging the Maghreb administrations of their Vichyite dead wood.⁴⁷

Officials' propensity to draw remarkably sweeping conclusions from limited information found its echo in the local appreciations of the foodstuff crisis compiled by the security forces in situ. Responsible for policing the transportation and distribution of emergency relief, gendarmerie commanders in Algeria were closest to the worsening foodstuff crisis. Along with the Interior Ministry's Algeria subdivision, the colony's gendarmerie command generated most correspondence on the subject. At one level this pointed to a lack of consensus over the origins and likely consequences of food shortages. At another, deeper level, though, gendarmerie officers, much like the Interior Ministry bureaucrats who applied Algeria's communally differentiated rationing system, never questioned the principle that Algerian colonial subjects' basic needs should be subordinated to those of the Europeans living among them. Perhaps this was only to be expected. It was, after all, a colonial situation. More revealing, and more shocking, were the calculations made—and very deliberately so—about how much the Muslim population could tolerate—physiologically, mentally, and socially—before adverse political consequences ensued.

Reviewing local trends in the month of April 1945, Algeria gendarmerie commander general Ferdinand Taillardat acknowledged that popular hunger was increasingly widespread, but he dismissed this as the original cause of the increasingly rebellious atmosphere in the colony.[48] Admittedly Taillardat's second-in-command, Lieutenant-Colonel Roubaud, was less sure. The more junior officer had watched the food crisis develop over the spring, deputizing for Taillardat during the latter's absence from Algeria in February and March. Roubaud singled out the lack of grain deliveries as the predominant Muslim concern. Moreover, the crisis was national. While Sétif in the east figured among the towns worst affected by shortages of grain and meat, several *douars* in the *communes mixtes* of Lower Kabylia had been without cereal supplies for months. The poorest Algerians in the Mascara region in the far northwest of the colony were reportedly surviving on grass and roots, and the population of Batna, a key eastern market center, was on the verge of famine.[49]

The imminent demobilization and repatriation from France of Algerian servicemen and former prisoners of war also threatened to catalyze the colony's discontents. Both the War Ministry's Muslim affairs service and Marcel Michel's North African affairs service (Service central des affaires nord-africaines, SCANA) within the Interior Ministry worried that these soldiers posed a significant threat to public order in Algeria. Many former servicemen nursed grievances over the discriminatory treatment meted out to them while in uniform. The widespread use of North African conscripts and prisoner returnees as labor battalions, often working alongside Wehrmacht POWs in mending roads and restoring basic utilities in liberated France, antagonized them still more, not least as the German prisoners were generally better fed and better paid than the colonials working alongside them.⁵⁰ Former POWs had been exposed to the full force of Nazi propaganda and had been alienated from a France that allegedly neglected them both during the long years of captivity and the weeks and months during which they languished in holding camps awaiting repatriation. Mixed among them was a "floating population" of unemployed war workers, dislodged immigrants, deserters, and POW stragglers. According to the SCANA, these were irredeemable malcontents bound to stir things up on returning to hungry relatives and friends in Algeria. Another call on the overstretched shipping pool, it was anticipated that this combustible mix of aggrieved ex-servicemen, embittered POWs, and rootless workers would be repatriated to Algiers at a rate of two hundred per day from June 1945 onward. Neither the colonial government, nor the army garrison, nor local police captains had sufficient resources to screen the new arrivals to separate out potential troublemakers as both the Foreign Ministry and the Ministry of Prisoners of War and Refugees recommended.⁵¹

Constantine prefecture staff shared Roubaud's concern. In its monthly survey of "native" opinion, filed on 21 April 1945, the prefecture's information analysis center, still at the heart of local government, noted that the local Muslim population was already suffering acute hardship worsened by persistent drought and lack of grain supplies. The probability of a renewed locust infestation in the summer ahead added to their foreboding. The sole beneficiaries were PPA and AML activists for whom arid farming conditions in rural *douars* and market towns blighted by the cereals shortage made fertile ground for the recruitment of new members.⁵² It was noteworthy in this connection that from March 1945 onward the AML made its greatest inroads in Constantine's *communes mixtes* where the socioeconomic iniquity and differential rights between Europeans and Muslims were most acute. This was a trend noticed by the Constantine CIE but not counteracted by any positive administrative steps either to improve conditions for hungry rural families or to make less obvious the preferential rationing system then in force.⁵³ As the CIE's Constantine secretary warned, what made the situation politically explosive was the widespread conviction that the administration did not care about its colonial subjects' plight. What began as whispered conversations, café rumor, and persistent complaints about inadequate relief measures and priority foodstuff distribution to the settler population had morphed into a "collective psychosis," an absolute conviction among eastern Algeria's hard-pressed agricultural communities that only the overthrow of French rule could end their misery. This line of deduction was impervious to reason, or to official denials. Only a massive increase in emergency grain distribution—tangible evidence of French goodwill and administrative wherewithal—stood any chance of reversing the rapid decline in intercommunal relations.[54]

No such outcome was in prospect, at least not in the short term. With little merchant shipping unilaterally at French disposal, the provisional government faced inevitable delays and endless bureaucratic infighting over the release of additional vessels from the inter-Allied shipping pool.[55] Urgent supply demands in France and the other North African territories compounded the problem. Moreover, Governor Chataigneau was less concerned about the situation in the east of the colony than that in and around its two largest cities, Algiers and Oran. Advised in the second week of May that two American steamers, the *Ingersoll* and *Fort Lennox*, each carrying 8,500 tons of wheat, would be ten days late in reaching Algiers and Mers el-Kébir (port of Oran), he ordered the diversion to Algiers of a French vessel, the *Ville de Bastia*, then heading for the eastern port of Philippeville.[56] While this focus on the urban areas of highest population density was understandable, it nonetheless pointed to the governor's skepticism about the severity of Constantine's food crisis. Summarizing the supply situation and the progress of army sweep operations north of Sétif and Guelma in a telegram to the Interior Ministry on 24 May, Chataigneau dismissed out of hand any suggestion that hunger had helped trigger the recent violence:

> The order that has been restored thanks to the measures taken risks being compromised by tendentious press campaigns focusing on the inadequacy of food supply to the rural population even though it has come to light during searches made in the worst affected areas that stocks were not so low as to justify revolt.[57]

Whatever the governor's opinion, bald facts suggested other conclusions entirely. On the very day that Chataigneau's above message came in, Pierre Vrolyk, head of the Interior Ministry's Algeria subdivision and a former subprefect in Algeria, was trying to make sense of the figures supplied by the Algiers government, the three prefectures, and commune officials regarding what remained of government wheat stockpiles in the colony. Not one to exaggerate, Vrolyk was extremely worried by what his calculations indicated.[58] Two weeks after the Sétif uprising, the Algeria subdivision felt compelled to revise its estimates of Algeria's minimum monthly requirement for imported wheat upward from 59,000 to 66,000 tons. The decision was taken because of reports from native affairs bureaus in the colony's army-administered southern territories indicating "almost complete harvest failure in the pre-Saharan region." Even on the most optimistic reading of available stockpile figures, it appeared that the colony's grain consumption amounted to no more than 1,400 tons per day. Existing government policy was predicated on a minimum figure of 2,200 tons per day. The shortfall suggested that on average Algeria's population was receiving no more than 190 grams each day per person, well short of the 300 grams of wheat flour promised by the colonial government. Since city populations and European settlers appeared to have received the designated 300 grams per day, the implication of Vrolyk's figures was that a significant proportion of Algeria's peasantry had received far less; indeed, in many cases, nothing at all.[59] Furthermore, rural families tended to rely more exclusively on a cereal-based diet for carbohydrate than their urban counterparts, whose weekly protein intake was also generally higher. Giving the lie to Chataigneau's earlier dismissiveness, officials within the economic department of his own administration conceded on 12 June that their monthly figures for grain distribution in 1944–45 indicated that the colony's rural population had survived on less than 150 grams of flour per day: barely half of the officially sanctioned minimum.[60]

Even though this report was meant to stir Chataigneau's Algiers bureaucracy and the Interior Ministry into greater action, its presumptions about the acceptable disbursement of resources said much about the "colonial mind" of both. The cold arithmetic of the government-general's rationing policy divided the colony's population into five groups.

First were the 715,000 authorized wheat producers, farmers—some European, some Muslim—who were permitted to conserve a personal supply of eighteen kilograms of grain before surrendering any surplus to the government-regulated market in wheat and barley. Second were the estimated 2,145,000 agricultural laborers and their families who worked for the wheat producers and who were expected to satisfy at least part of their foodstuff requirements directly from their employers. The third category was also the largest: the 4.5 million sharecroppers and landless peasants who were registered as eligible for emergency relief supplies from the administration's Sociétés indigènes de prévoyance. The central finding of the Algiers economic department's June 1945 report was that few among this group ever received their designated monthly allowance of 7.5 kilograms of flour. The fourth and fifth categories, 2.3 million urban consumers, a high proportion of them Europeans, and Algeria's military garrison of Armée d'Afrique units and gendarmerie, were also the best provisioned. With few exceptions the *boulangeries* of the coastal cities had been able to distribute the requisite bread allowances as envisaged.

These five categories were as much about the socioeconomic disparities of class and the primordial requirements of urban security for the colonial state as they were about the more obvious hierarchy of ethnicity. Certainly Muslim colonial subjects languished at the bottom of the rationing pile while European urban communities stood at the top. But a closer dissection of the ration categories indicates that Algerian farmworkers and, above all, day laborers and sharecroppers received less government support than smallholders and other local landowners.[61] The point bears emphasis on two counts. Rationing policy reveals that not only did the colonial state discriminate against the poorest among the Muslim peasantry economically, but in doing so it also discounted them as a coherent political force. Yet, around Guelma, for instance, anger among Algerian farmworkers over rising land prices, the marginalization of Algerian smallholders from the most fertile wheat-growing area of the Seybouse plain, and the lack of credit facilities for small-time cultivators had simmered on since the early 1930s.[62] None of these problems had been squarely addressed by local or national authorities in the intervening years. The centrality of rural communities, and young day laborers, to the violence in Sétif and Guelma's rural hinterlands suggested that this was a fatal mistake.

A month after Sétif an interministerial committee convened at the Ministry of National Economy to discuss U.S. rejection of the ministry's request for 2.7 million tons in food aid supplies for French North Africa. If past experience offered any guide to future distribution policy, Algeria's coastal cities would continue to receive the bulk of the grain imported to the colony from North America and elsewhere. While talks continued in Washington over a reduced figure, the committee sought to identify possible economies in the existing supply figures. As we have seen, these posited a 300-gram daily grain allowance for Algeria's urban population, and only 250 grams for rural dwellers. Much was made of the fact that although their ration was 50 grams greater, town dwellers received it as finished bread whereas rural families received their 250 grams as flour, from which larger loaves could be made. Questionable in terms of basic dietary statistics, this presumption also ignored the most fundamental tenets of existing government policy: 300 grams was already designated a bare minimum necessary for survival. To make matters worse, the ministers in session at the Ministry of National Economy were evidently unaware that a large proportion of the rural population was unable to get to the widely scattered relief centers to obtain their allotted ration.[63] The inadequacies of the Interior Ministry's collection of economic data were thus to be found in the poor distribution of basic information between departments and in the facile disregard of the foremost supply problems confronting Algeria's rural poor. In reading between the lines of relief policy planning such as this, it seems clear that the colonial state's emergency measures bypassed a significant proportion of the poorest in the countryside, most often by accident, but sometimes by design.

Peasant resentment at this manifest discrimination had occasionally exploded into violence in the days before Sétif. On the morning of 1 May, for example, a crowd estimated by police at five hundred gathered outside the subprefecture in Orléansville to protest the inadequacy of emergency relief distribution and the iniquity of flour rationing. In the early afternoon the protesters tried to storm two *boulangeries* in the town. A gendarmerie detachment called out to disperse them was unable to do so unassisted and, by three in the afternoon had called out the local garrison of *Tirailleurs Sénégalais* to assist the process. Preliminary police reports on those detained suggested that many of the demonstrators were peasant sharecroppers who had come into Orléansville convinced that the town's settlers were being provisioned to the exclusion of its rural hinterland.[64] If the differential ration system for urban and rural populations lent substance to peasant complaints, why did the colonial administration and the Paris government continue with it? The answer lay in a damaging combination of the inadequate information mentioned above and discriminatory official presumptions about the political marginality of landless agricultural workers. The former sustained the widely held belief that the rural poor were not faring as badly as appeared; the latter nourished political complacency about those at the bottom of Algeria's socioeconomic strata.

Throughout the summer, the Algiers government and the Interior Ministry's Algeria section still predicated regional grain distribution on the assumption that Algeria's smallholders, sharecroppers, and day laborers had managed to hoard substantial quantities of wheat and other cereals for use in times of shortage. The calculation that hidden stockpiles of grain made the food shortage in the Algerian interior less chronic than might first appear recurred time after time in prefecture correspondence and police and gendarmerie reports. Hoarding occupied that middle ground in a black market economy in which lines were often blurred between what was technically illegal and what was merely prudent. Recent French wartime experience probably played a part here, too, reflected in a tendency to displace the lessons of metropolitan occupation to colonial Algeria. Didn't everyone put aside what they could to cope with harder times ahead? And no one was about to admit the fact to their neighbors, let alone to policemen, tax collectors, or official statisticians. Certain that it was taking place, and yet rarely able to confirm it, the police and, more often, the gendarmerie intensified their efforts to prevent illicit stockpiling as shortages deepened and food prices soared over the spring of 1945.[65] Hoarders were increasingly criminalized, portrayed not as cautious farmers who had squirreled away the odd sack of grain but as gluttonous enemies of the community happily living off the fat of the land while those around them went hungry. Much was made in gendarmerie correspondence of searches of smallholder properties that revealed the existence of hoarded grain, flour, or other foodstuffs. Although such occasions were few and far between, they were cited as definitive proof of the perceived reality: that the outward poverty of the Algerian countryside concealed hidden plenty. Put crudely, several rural gendarmerie posts suggested that claims of famine were an elaborate ruse, affirmation of wily peasant duplicity and their tendency to incessant complaint.

The most significant dissenting voice, which rejected the pervasive official depiction of Algeria's foodstuff crisis as a short-term, oftentimes exaggerated problem, was that of Jacques Berque, director of Muslim affairs in the Algiers government. Berque was an intellectual, a pied-noir sociologist, and a graduate of Algiers University. Still only thirty-five years old, he had returned to Algeria in 1944 after a decade as an army agronomic specialist for the French protectorate administration in Morocco. His understanding of rural economics combined with his anthropological sensitivity to the crosscurrents of Algerian society and Islamic culture left him out of place in the authoritarian, urban environs of Algeria's central administration. Berque's was a more enlightened, better-apprised colonial mind, subtler and less willing to rush to judgment than most of his colleagues. This perhaps explains why his presence was not felt at the height of the Sétif crisis in May 1945. Indeed, it was not until 29 June that Berque set out his views unequivocally in a fourteen-page analysis, "Algerian Muslim Society in 1945," sent to the Interior Ministry.[66] Drawing on local historical precedents and packed with hard economic data, it pulled no punches. Algerian society was in turmoil; urbanization, unemployment, and rural poverty were running out of control. At its core lay the peasantry, drawn into a French-controlled wage economy over preceding decades yet denied resources in land to survive unaided. If the most striking urban evidence of these long-term processes was the growth of shantytowns on the margins of the coastal cities, the impact on rural society was registered in socioeconomic terms as loss of cultivatable land, income, and status. Compelled, for the most part, to work as sharecroppers, as day laborers, or, if they were lucky, as smallholders scratching a livelihood as independent farmers, Algeria's rural workers formed a vast underclass, increasingly alienated from all forms of French authority by the iniquities of the colonial market and the state's preferential treatment of their European neighbors. Their antagonism to colonial authority had been brought into sharper relief by the vicissitudes of the war in general and the experience of chronic shortages in particular. Socially and politically, the food crisis marked a tipping point.

Admittedly Berque's statistics pointed to 180,000 *fellah* cultivators who each owned between thirty and a hundred hectares of land. Set against this, 434,000 Algerians possessed less than ten hectares, 600,000 had access to plots only as sharecroppers, and 760,000 owned nothing at all, relying on day laboring to make ends meet.[67] These smallholders, sharecroppers, and farm laborers were the agriculturalists hardest hit by the 1945 food crisis. Their situation was worsened by widespread crop failure, livestock losses, and the continuing difficulties, from transporting goods to acquiring sufficient fuel, occasioned by wartime economic disruption. At the same time, rural communities had rediscovered in the ʾUlamaʿ their sense of self: their multiple identity as Algerians, as Muslims, and as a marginalized majority of colonial subjects with lesser rights than their European neighbors. This mounting sense of injustice led to changes in forms of religious practice. The veneration of local saints and marabouts, as disparate as it was doctrinally loose, was losing ground to the stricter devotional discipline of the ʾUlamaʿ, a puritanical force that lent itself to political mobilization. Sétif, then, was rooted in two converging strands of cultural renaissance and economic change: in the permeation of avowedly Islamic nationalism through the countryside, and in a growing class consciousness that tied the reassertion of Algeria's authentic national identity to the overthrow of an oppressive European overclass.[68]

Berque's analysis was, by some margin, the most prescient of the memoranda circulating in French government circles in the aftermath of Sétif. Not surprisingly, it put him at odds with his boss, Yves Chataigneau. In his self-justificatory memorandum of 11 May, the Algiers governor took a sideswipe at those who criticized his administration for its desultory management of Algeria's foodstuff supply crisis. Far from being driven to rebel by hunger in their bellies, the uprising's organizers acted cynically, knowing that the administration would quickly remedy

Algeria's economic crisis as soon as the end of hostilities in Europe released additional funds and shipping, making supply distribution easier.[69] Chataigneau's robust defense of his administration was taken up by another plain-speaking official with little time for Muslim grievances: Maurice Papon. Papon was saved from the rolling purge of former Vichy administrators, and over the coming fifteen years his career in local government centered on North Africa, where he achieved preeminence through rigid enforcement of discriminatory communal policing.[70] Appointed deputy-director of the Interior Ministry's Algeria subdivision in October 1945, Papon personified the post-Sétif turn toward heightened authoritarian control in Algeria. His first task in his new job was to identify the security apparatus needed to achieve it.[71]

Papon began his work by touring those regions worst affected by the May violence. His findings formed the basis for a series of recommendations on the improvement of state security through administrative restructuring. On arrival in Algiers, he was briefed by an old acquaintance, Algiers government secretary-general Pierre-René Gazagne, and the long-serving police chief Bringard. Papon then set off for the Constantine *département* where he spent most of his time in the company of another new appointee, the prefect René Petitbon. Like Chataigneau, Gazagne's reputation was inextricably bound up with coercive policing and, thus, with Sétif. It was Gazagne, for instance, who took the key decision in late April to exile Messali Hadj to the French Congo.[72] Bringard, meanwhile, had been immersed in the labyrinthine politics of the capital's policing since his days as deputy director of the Algiers *Sûreté* under Admiral Darlan. And the newcomer Petitbon would come to wider public attention when he submitted official figures in November 1945 claiming that only 1,145 Algerians had died throughout eastern Algeria as a result of state repression.[73]

Each of Papon's new colleagues shared his predilection for a rapid overhaul of security practices. Gazagne pressed for reform of the Interior Ministry's Algeria subdivision, radical restructuring of Algerian local government, and more frequent personnel transfers to ensure that district officers did not become isolated or complaisant as a result of prolonged service in a single commune (something that had occurred by force of circumstance during the war years). Bringard wanted regional

RG offices better integrated with central police headquarters to speed up transmission of police intelligence to government decision makers. Petitbon, too, favored tighter security and advocated the deployment of four motorized riot police (Compagnies Républicaines de Sécurité—CRS) squadrons in Sétif, Guelma, Bougie, and Constantine. To each of these demands, Papon's report gave a warm welcome. Limiting his focus to remedial security measures, Papon said nothing about the factors that made such repressive mechanisms necessary. It was enough to know that the subject population could be kept in its place. With his accent on surveillance and coercion, Papon showed no interest in the origins of popular dissent, only in its restriction. That the subject population would remain unremittingly hostile was taken as a given, a problem to be contained rather than addressed.[74]

Only after the additional security precautions recommended by Papon and the XIXth Army Command were being implemented over the winter of 1945–46 did the Interior Ministry and the Algiers government at last concentrate squarely on the root economic causes of Muslim alienation.[75] Tixier warned Prime Minister Félix Gouin in February 1946 that Algeria's intercommunal "malaise" would endure as long as rural poverty, devastating livestock losses, and cereals shortages remained open to exploitation by nationalist groups in Algeria and Communists in France. He warned that any political benefits expected to accrue from the imminent general amnesty for those detained after Sétif would be quickly undone.[76] From Algiers, Gazagne sent details on 6 February of increased welfare spending, more efficient distribution of emergency relief, and the opening of 157 shelters for the unemployed in Constantine department alone.[77]

Conclusion

Did the political amnesties and social reforms pursued during 1946–47 signify a changing of colonial minds, an acceptance of the views laid out by Jacques Berque in the immediate aftermath of Sétif? The answer is probably not. The operating assumption remained that social policy should elevate the living standards of colonial subjects without disrupting the constitutional structures and socioeconomic hierarchies that placed the settler population above them. Insofar as a common "official mind" persisted, it remained as colonial as before. But this has also been a story of information misread, misused, and, on occasion, crowded out. That the intelligence gathered by policemen, local officials, gendarmes, and military officers was partial and predisposed to focus on immediate signs of political dissent is not in doubt. But that such material overshadowed the more prosaic, yet oftentimes more revealing economic information about food shortages in eastern Algeria deserves closer attention—more so in light of the fact that those bureaucrats most concerned by the mounting evidence of chronic hardship and rural hunger were, in turn, eclipsed by security-minded personnel such as Maurice Papon and René Petitbon with the ear of Governor Chataigneau in Algiers and the de Gaulle provisional government in Paris. Figures such as Pierre Vrolyk of the Interior Ministry and Jacques Berque of the Algiers native affairs service were not at the heart of the colonial decision-making process either before or straight after Sétif. Theirs were the more rational colonial minds, the more inclined to read incipient famine and the disintegration of the agricultural economy as deeper structural causes of political unrest.

Perhaps, then, this is also a story of how differing types of political intelligence tend to be read in times of crisis—tragic certainly, but otherwise sadly unremarkable. Here, too, the colonial aspect to this particular crisis—a violent breakdown of order and a brief attempted rebellion—bears emphasis. The first priority of any central authority faced with armed insurgency is to restore order. But the first priority of a colonial state was at once more and less: to restore a particular form of social order based on communal hierarchy and differential rights, but without necessarily addressing the fundamental causes of the original outbreaks once such order was restored. In other words the first and ultimate priority of colonial rule was colonial control itself. Political intelligence served this purpose and was integral to French governmental action in the summer of 1945. The economic reportage and evidence of a food crisis addressed in this chapter was less easily assimilated by colonial minds preoccupied with the restoration of order. Why? Because the economic information pointed in an unacceptable direction: to an agricultural economy that was profoundly dysfunctional, dreadfully iniquitous, and ultimately unsustainable. It was not a message that resonated with political leaders and colonial authorities determined to reimpose the hierarchies of colonial rule with an iron fist as quickly and spectacularly as possible in the summer of 1945.

Notes

Research for this chapter was supported by the UK Economic and Social Research Council and a Leverhulme Trust Major Research Fellowship. Parts of this chapter draw on two articles: "Colonial Violence in Algeria and the Distorted Logic of State Retribution: The Sétif Uprising of 1945," *Journal of Military History* 75:1 (2011), 523–56, and "Intelligence and the Transition to the Algerian Police State: Reassessing French Colonial Security after the Sétif Uprising, 1945," *Intelligence and National Security* 26 (2011).

1. The fullest accounts are now Jean-Louis Planche, *Sétif 1945: Histoire d'un massacre annoncé* (Paris: Perrin, 2006), and Jean-Pierre Peyroulou, *Guelma, 1945: Une subversion française dans l'Algérie coloniale* (Paris: Editions la Découverte, 2009). We also have Marcel Reggui's heartrending personal indictment of settler retribution against his family in Guelma, the other town at the heart of the rebellion, *Les Massacres de Guelma: Algérie, mai 1945: Une enquête inedite sur la furie des milice colonials* (Paris: Éditions la Découverte, 2006). The issue of timing and the connection with the end of World War II is central to Annie Rey-Goldseiguer, *Aux origines de la guerre d'Algérie 1940–1945: De Mers-el-Kébir aux massacres du nord-constantinois* (Paris: Éditions la Découverte, 2002), part 3. Understandably, questions of leadership and inspiration figure large among historians of Algerian nationalism and the origins of the Front de Libération Nationale (FLN). See Mohammed Harbi, *Aux origines du FLN: Populisme révolutionnaire en Algérie* (Paris: Christian Bourgeois, 1975); Mahfoud Kaddache, *Il y a trente ans, le 8 mai 1945* (Paris: Éditions du centenaire, 1975); Benyoucef Ben Khedda, *Les Origines du 1er Novembre 1954* (Algiers: Éditions Dahlab, 1989); Jean-Charles Jauffret, ed., *La Guerre d'Algérie par les documents*, vol. 1: *L'Avertisssement, 1943–1946* (Vincennes: Service Historique de l'Armée de Terre, 1990); Gilbert Meynier, *Histoire Intérieure du FLN* (Paris: Fayard, 2002). Useful short introductions to the events of the uprising are Charles-Robert Ageron, "Les troubles du Nord-Constantinois en mai 1945: Une tentative insurrectionnelle?" *Vingtième Siècle* 4 (October 1984), 23–38; and Anthony Clayton, "The Sétif Uprising of May 1945," *Small Wars and Insurgencies* 3:1 (1992), 1–21.

2. Marcel Baudot, "L'épuration: Bilan chiffré," *Bulletin de l'IHTP* 27 (Sep-

tember 1986), 37–53; Henry Rousso, "L'épuration en France: Une histoire inachevée," *Vingtième Siècle* 33:1 (1992), 81–82. Based on a composite regional assessment, Baudot suggested a figure of 7,306 executions. Other close analyses put the figure at between 8,000 and 9,000 deaths. There is no agreement over the numbers of Algerians killed in 1945 with French and Algerian official figures, then and since, ranging from 1,500 to 40,000. It seems highly probable, however, that the total number exceeds the *épuration* estimates.

3. Imprecision regarding the number of violent deaths after Sétif is matched by that regarding the War of Independence between 1954 and 1962; see Guy Pervillé, "La guerre d'Algérie: Combien de morts?" in *La Guerre d'Algérie 1954–2004, la fin de l'amnésie*, ed. Mohammed Harbi and Benjamin Stora (Paris: Robert Laffont, 2004), 477–93, at 488.

4. Jean-Pierre Peyroulou has gone furthest in exploring the latter question. See Peyroulou, *Guelma, 1945*; and Peyroulou, "Rétablir et maintenir l'ordre colonial: La police française et les Algériens en Algérie française de 1945 à 1962," in Harbi and Stora, *La Guerre d'Algérie*, 99–101, 107–13.

5. Todd Shepard, *Inventing Decolonization: The Algerian War and the Remaking of France* (Ithaca NY: Cornell University Press, 2006), 39–43; Andrew Shennan, *Rethinking France: Plans for Renewal, 1940–1946* (Oxford: Oxford University Press, 1991), chap. 7; James I. Lewis, "French Politics and the Algerian Statute of 1947," *Maghreb Review* 17 (1992), 147–72.

6. Hendrik Spruyt, *Ending Empire: Contested Sovereignty and Territorial Partition* (Ithaca NY: Cornell University Press, 2005), 89–90, 94–97; Martin Shipway, *The Road to War: France and Vietnam, 1944–1947* (Oxford: Berghahn, 1996), 87–104; Martin Thomas, "The Colonial Policies of the Mouvement Republicain Populaire, 1944–54: From Reform to Reaction," *English Historical Review* 118:476 (2003), 380–87.

7. Centre des Archives d'Outre-Mer (hereafter CAOM), Gouvernement-Général de l'Algérie (GGA), 9H/44, CIE political intelligence summary: "Note sur la situation générale en Constantine," 23 April 1945; no. 3305/EMA, "Rapport mensuel de l'OFF/AN.M. de la sub-division de Sétif," 30 April 1945.

8. The security service analyses discussed here reflect other, long-standing transnational fears about challenges to predominant whiteness in colonial societies; see Marilyn Lake and Henry Reynolds, *Drawing the Global Colour Line: White Men's Countries and the International Challenge of Racial Equality* (Cambridge: Cambridge University Press, 2008), 1–5, 350–52.

9. Jock McCulloch, *Black Peril, White Virtue: Sexual Crime in Southern Rhodesia, 1902–1935* (Oxford: James Currey, 2000), 9. Following McCulloch's typology of "black peril" in colonial Rhodesia, at its broadest, "moral panic" connotes official and settler fears about colonial subjects transgressing

the racial, sexual, and political boundaries of colonial rule. For an example of such political intelligence reportage, see CAOM, Constantine departmental archives, B/3/19, no. 112/4, "Rapport de l'Adjudant-chef LUCAS, Commandant la Section [Gendarmerie] de Constantine sur l'état d'esprit des populations dans le Centre de Chateaudun-du-Rhumel," 26 July 1944.

10. Manus I. Midlarsky, "Rulers and the Ruled: Patterned Inequality and the Onset of Mass Political Violence," *American Political Science Review* 82:2 (1988), 493–96.

11. Chris Allen, "Warfare, Endemic Violence and State Collapse in Africa," *Review of African Political Economy* 26:81 (1999), 367–84.

12. Mahmood Mamdani, "Beyond Settler and Native as Political Identities: Overcoming the Political Legacy of Colonialism," *Comparative Studies in Society and History* 43:4 (2001), 651–64. For analogous discussion of these "plural" legal systems in French West Africa, see Lauren Benton, "Colonial Law and Cultural Difference: Jurisdictional Politics and the Formation of the Colonial State," *Comparative Studies in Society and History* 41:3 (1999), 563–65, 583–86. For a classic political economy-based analysis of colonial political violence, see Nii-K. Plange, "The Colonial State in Northern Ghana: The Political Economy of Pacification," *Review of African Political Economy* 31 (December 1984), 29–43.

13. Peter Uvin suggests that postcolonial Burundi and Rwanda illustrate these contributory factors working separately; see Uvin, "Ethnicity and Power in Burundi and Rwanda: Different Paths to Mass Violence," *Comparative Politics* 31:3 (1999), 253.

14. Elizabeth Thompson, *Colonial Citizens: Republican Rights, Paternal Privilege, and Gender in French Syria and Lebanon* (New York: Columbia University Press, 2000), 19–30.

15. Benjamin Claude Brower, *A Desert Named Peace: The Violence of France's Empire in the Algerian Sahara, 1844–1902* (New York: Columbia University Press, 2009), 103–7.

16. See Jeremy M. Weinstein, *Inside Rebellion: The Politics of Insurgent Violence* (Cambridge: Cambridge University Press, 2007), 12–16, 20–23, 169–70, 329–30.

17. Archives Nationales (AN), Paris, F/1a/3296, Dossier V-B-8/5, CAB/057/45, Chef du Cabinet Maisonneuve to Pierre Vrolyk, "Fonds communs des Sociétés de prévoyance," 5 June 1945.

18. For multiple perspectives on the wartime famines in Bengal and Tonkin, see Paul R. Greenough, "Indian Famines and Peasant Victims: The Case of Bengal in 1943–44," *Modern Asian Studies* 14:2 (1980), 205–35; Partha Chatterjee, "The Colonial State and Peasant Resistance in Bengal,

1920–1947," *Past and Present* 110 (February 1986), 169–204; Lance Brennan, "Government Famine Relief in Bengal, 1943," *Journal of Asian Studies* 47:3 (1988), 541–66; Bùi Minh Dũng, "Japan's Role in the Vietnamese Starvation of 1944–45," *Modern Asian Studies* 29:3 (1995), 573–618; and especially, Sugata Bose, "Starvation amidst Plenty: The Making of Famine in Bengal, Honan and Tonkin, 1942–45," *Modern Asian Studies* 24:4 (1990), 699–727.

19. AN, F/1a/3296, Governor Chataigneau telegram 851 to Sous-Direction de l'Algérie, 24 May 1945. All tonnage figures are for metric tons.

20. AN, F/1a/3296, CAB 5941/5, Interior Minister Adrien Tixier memo for Ministry of Supply, "Ravitaillement en blé de l'Algérie," 1 May 1945.

21. AN, F/1a/3296, *Journal Officiel de l'Algérie*, "Note sur la création en Algérie de Comités de vigilance économique," 3 April 1945.

22. AN, F/1a/3293, Dossier VI-B-I, Interior Minister Adrien Tixier to M. Laffon, Sous-Direction de l'Algérie, 31 January 1945. Physically ailing, Tixier nonetheless cut a striking figure, notable for his limping gait (he had lost his left leg in August 1914). He died on 18 February 1946. The minister's criticisms evidently did Laffon's career little harm. He soon went on to greater things as head of the French occupation administration in West Germany.

23. AN, F/1a/3293, Dossier VI-B-I, Tixier to Governor Chataigneau, Algiers, 21 January 1945.

24. AN, F/1a/3293, Dossier VI-B-I, Tixier to Emile Laffon and Pierre Vrolyk, Sous-Direction de l'Algérie, comments on "Rapport général sur les problèmes actuels en Algérie," 24 May 1945.

25. AN, F/1a/3294, Dossier VI-B-4, Interior Ministry Cabinet memo, "Étude sur les organismes chargés de représenter les intérêts algériens à Paris," 7 May 1945. Vrolyk identified the four key agencies as follows: Office du Gouvernement Général de l'Algérie; Office algérien d'Action économique et touristique; Délégation de la Direction Générale de l'Économie algerien; Mission d'assistance aux prisonniers et réfugiés algériens. Vrolyk's proposals to streamline these organizations, which were affiliated with the Algiers government, the Interior Ministry, and the Ministry of Prisoners of War and Refugees, were rejected by the agencies involved.

26. AN, F/1a/3293, Dossier VI-B-I, Tixier to Emile Laffon and Pierre Vrolyk, Sous-Direction de l'Algérie, comments on "Rapport général sur les problèmes actuels en Algérie," 24 May 1945.

27. This overhaul extended to the protectorate administration in French Morocco as well; see Service Historique de l'armée, Vincennes (SHA), Moscow, Carton 286/D428, no. 1780, Direction des affaires indigènes (Rabat), "A/S des incidents de Constantine et de leur répercussion possible au Maroc,"

23 August 1934. See also Planche, *Sétif 1945*, 33–34, who dates the overhaul to December 1934.

28. CAOM, GGA, Alger/41/1, no. 2281/NA, Governor General Naegelen to Algeria Prefects, "Rôle et attributions des SLNA départementaux," 29 August 1950, which summarizes the history of the Services des Liaisons Nord-Africains (SLNA) and its CIE antecedent.

29. CAOM, GGA, Alger/41/1, no. 13/CIE, Direction Générale des Affaires indigènes et des Territoires du Sud, "Note relative au fonctionnement du CIE," Algiers, 28 July 1936; no. 900 Direction Générale des Affaires Indigènes, Sous-direction des affaires indigènes, 2e Bureau, Administration générale, Governor General to Algiers Prefect, "Centre d'Information et d'études: Délégation de crédits provisionnels," 22 February 1938.

30. See AN, F60/871, sous-dossier Comité de l'Afrique du Nord, for the series of Constantine CIE reports relayed to the Interior Ministry and the Paris provisional government's North Africa committee in 1945. The CIE's early development is also discussed in Joshua Cole's chapter in this volume.

31. Correspondence files of these sources are available in Centre des Archives d'Outre-Mer (CAOM), Gouvernement-Général de l'Algérie, Cabinet civil du gouverneur général Yves Chataigneau, sous-série 8CAB, especially 8CAB 88 and 8CAB 118; CAOM, Fonds de la prefecture de Constantine, série B3, Cabinet du Préfet files; AN, Secrétariat-Général du Gouvernement et Services du Premier Ministre, files F60/871—F60/874; AN, Ministère de l'Intérieur, Cabinet du Ministre files, F/1a/3292—F/1a/3298; and Service Historique de la Gendarmerie Nationale (SHGN), Commandement Général de la Gendarmerie en Afrique du Nord, Corréspondance Algérie, R/2, Cartons 140–144. The following authors consulted these records extensively: Benoît Haberbusch, *La Gendarmerie en Algérie (1939–1945)* (Vincennes: SHGN, 2004); Planche, *Sétif 1945*.

32. AN, F60/871, no. 1345/CAB/C, and no. 1395/CAB/C, two reports sent by Algiers Prefect report to Governor Chataigneau, each with the same title: "A/S collusion entre le P.P.A. et les 'Amis du Manifeste,'" 21 March and 7 April 1945; no. 1485/CAB/C, further Algiers Prefect report, "A/S collusion entre le P.P.A. et les 'Amis du Manifeste,'" 1 May 1945.

33. AN, F60/871, Direction des RG, Section Empire, "Activité dans la clandestinité du Parti du Peuple Algérien," 16 July 1945. See especially Annex I, "Tableau déscriptif de l'organisation et de l'activité du PPA en France," describing the client groups and front organizations through which the PPA operated in the aftermath of the Sétif repression.

34. AN, F60/871, no. 1114, Algiers Prefecture Police des RG, "Rapport: Activité des Amis du Manifeste et de la Liberté," 3 March 1945.

35. AN, F60/871, no. 847/ Centre d'Information et d'études (CIE) Algiers renseignement, "Activité des Amis du Manifeste et de la Liberté," 17 April 1945.

36. For background to ʾUlamaʿ activity and debate during and after Sétif, see al-Semmari, "The Role of the ʾUlamaʿ in the Algerian *Revolution*," 83–102; James McDougall, "S'écrire un destin: L'Association des ʾUlamaʿ dans la révolution algérienne," *Bulletin de l'IHTP* 83:1 (2004), 38–51.

37. AN, F/1a/3293, Jacques Berque, Directeur des Affaires Musulmanes, note, "La Société Musulmane Algérienne en 1945," 29 June 1945.

38. James McDougall, *History and the Culture of Nationalism in Algeria* (Cambridge: Cambridge University Press, 2006), especially chaps. 2 and 3.

39. AN, F/1a/3295, Algiers Government, Cabinet, memo to Interior Ministry, "A/S du cheikh BRAHIMI Bashir et l'Association des Oulémas," 5 June 1945. The Interior Ministry's Algeria Subdirectorate circulated an abridged version of this report on 11 June, which formed the basis for the provisional government's approval of Chataigneau's earlier decision to order the Algiers judicial authorities to arrest senior ʾUlamaʿ leaders on 27 May 1945.

40. AN, F60/871, Constantine prefecture, CIE, "Rapport mensuel d'information sur l'activité indigène, Département de Constantine, période du 22 mars au 21 avril 1945," 21 April 1945.

41. CAOM, GGA, 9H/44, no. 4853, Commissariat de Police de Sétif, "Conférence organisée à Sétif le 29 avril 1945 par les Amis de la Manifeste et de la Liberté," 30 April 1945.

42. AN, F/1a/3295, Algiers Government, Cabinet, memo to Interior Ministry, "A/S du cheikh BRAHIMI Bashir et l'Association des Oulémas," 5 June 1945.

43. AN, F/1a/3295, Interior Ministry, Sous-Direction de l'Algérie, "Note d'information, Objet: Scoutisme musulman," 15 August 1945 (the FSMA resembled its Syrian cousin, the Steel Shirts, an obvious role model and still a bête noir among French Muslim affairs specialists); Mahfoud Kaddache, "'Les soldats de l'avenir': Les Scouts musulmans algériens (1930–1962)," in *De l'Indochine à l'Algérie: La jeunesse en mouvements des deux côtés du miroir colonial 1940–1962*, ed. Nicolas Bancel, Daniel Denis, and Youssef Fates (Paris: Éditions la découverte, 2003), 70–71.

44. Jean-Jacques Gauthé, "Les Scouts musulmans algériens vus par les services de renseignements français (1945–1962)," in Bancel, Denis, and Fates, *De l'Indochine à l'Algérie*, 84.

45. As examples, see AN, F60/871, Comité de l'Afrique du Nord Secretariat, "Note à l'attention du Général de Gaulle: Situation en Algérie," 6 October 1945; "Note au sujet de l'activité du Parti Communiste Algérien," n.d. November 1945.

46. AN, F60/872, Lieutenant-Colonel Spillman memo, "Extrait des télégrammes envoyés par le Cabinet Militaire du Gouverneur Général de l'Algérie au Ministère de l'Intérieur," 18 May 1945.

47. AN, F60/872, no. 3278/DIR, Cabinet du Général de Gaulle, "Rapport dirigé par M. Juge et concernant la situation actuelle en Afrique du Nord," 25 May 1945.

48. SHGN, C142, no. 950/2, CGG-AFN, General Taillardat, synthèse mensuelle, mois d'avril 1945, 1 May 1945. Membership of the North African committee included representatives from the Ministries of Interior, National Economy, and Foreign Affairs, as well as from the three French North African administrations.

49. SHGN, Commandement Général de la Gendarmerie en Afrique du Nord, Corréspondance Algérie, C141, no. 406/2, CGG-AFN, Lieutenant-Colonel Roubaud, synthèse mensuelle, mois de février 1945, 1 March 1945; C142, no. 745/2, Lieutenant-Colonel Roubaud, synthèse mensuelle, mois de mars 1945, 3 April 1945. The other towns listed as chronically short of grain in February were Algiers, Blida, and Sfax [in Tunisia], to which Oran, Mascara, and Orléansville were added in March.

50. AN, F/1a/3297, Dossier VI-B-13, EMGG, Services des affaires musulmanes, Bulletin de renseignements, 20 January 1945.

51. AN, F/1a/3297, Dossier VI-B-13-2, Interior Ministry, Cabinet note, "Repatriement en Algérie de prisonniers de guerre nord-africains," 10 June 1945.

52. AN, F60/871, Constantine préfecture, Centre d'Information et d'études, "Rapport mensuel d'information sur l'activité indigène dans le Département de Constantine, période du 22 mars au 21 avril 1945," 21 April 1945.

53. AN, F60/871, Constantine préfecture, Centre d'information et d'études, "Rapport mensuel d'information sur l'activité indigène dans le Département de Constantine, période du 22 avril au 21 mai 1945," 21 May 1945.

54. AN, F60/871, Constantine préfecture, Centre d'Information et d'études, "Rapport mensuel d'information sur l'activité indigène dans le Département de Constantine, période du 22 mars au 21 avril 1945," 21 April 1945.

55. AN, F/1a/3296, Dossier VI-8-4-1, Ministère des Travaux Publics et des Transports, Cabinet note, 18 May 1945.

56. AN, F/1a/3296, Dossier V-B-8/5, Ministry of Public Works and Transport, ministerial cabinet note for Ministry of National Economy, 18 May 1945.

57. AN, F/1a/3296, Dossier VI-8-4-1, tel. 851, Chataigneau to Sous-Direction de l'Algérie, 24 May 1945 (second part of message, sent at 9:30 a.m.). Chataigneau was here referring to press criticism of poor organization of the

Sociétés indigènes de prévoyance, see AN, F/1a/3296, Chataigneau letter to Sous-Direction de l'Algérie, 29 May 1945.

58. It is worth recording that Vrolyk was widely considered to hold particular insight into Algerian opinion, partly because of his extensive experience in Algerian local government, partly because he had a Muslim grandmother. He was also rumored to have performed the *hajj* to Mecca.

59. AN, F/1a/3296, Dossier VI-8-4-1, EL/CB, Interior, Direction générale de l'Administration régionale, départementale et communale note, "Situation du ravitaillement en blé en Algérie à compter du 1er Avril 1945," 24 May 1945.

60. AN, F/1a/3296, Dossier VI-8-4-1, no. 3959/DF/PIII, Délégation de la Direction générale des affaires économiques, "Rapport sur le ravitaillement de l'Algérie en blé pour la campagne 1944–45," 12 June 1945.

61. AN, F/1a/3296, Dossier VI-8-4-1, no. 3959/DF/PIII, Délégation de la Direction générale des affaires économiques, "Rapport sur le ravitaillement de l'Algérie en blé pour la campagne 1944–45," 12 June 1945. Two other points are worth noting here. Algeria's population was estimated to be rising by four hundred per day by this point, and the feedstuff requirements of the colony's livestock population were discounted in official figures. Both would be factored into the long-term agricultural modernization scheme, the Balensi Plan, devised by the colonial government's Comité supérieur économique a month before Sétif.

62. Peyroulou, *Guelma, 1945*, 80–81, 99–101; Daniel Lefeuvre, "Les trois replis de l'Algérie française," in *Des hommes et des femmes en guerre d'Algérie*, ed. Jean-Charles Jauffret (Paris: Autrement, 2003), 61–62.

63. AN, F/1a/3296, Dossier VI-8-4-1, Interior Ministry Cabinet report, "Compte-rendu de la conférence ayant eu lieu le 8 juin 1945 au Ministère de l'Économie Nationale sous la présidence de M. Cusin: Réapprovisionnement en céreales de l'Afrique du Nord, campagne 1945–46."

64. AN, F60/872, Algiers procurer-general to Ministry of Justice, 1 May 1945.

65. SHGN, Corréspondance Algérie, C142, no. 745/2, CGG-AFN, Lieutenant-Colonel Roubaud, synthèse mensuelle, mois de mars 1945, 3 April 1945, p. 22.

66. AN, F/1a/3293, Dossier VI-B-1, Jacques Berque memo to Algeria subdivision, "La Société musulmane algérienne en 1945," 29 June 1945.

67. "La Société musulmane algérienne en 1945," 3–4.

68. "La Société musulmane algérienne en 1945," 1, 6–7.

69. AN, F60/872, no. 911/CPD, Yves Chataigneau to Minister of Interior/Cabinet Politique, 11 May 1945.

70. Jim House and Neil MacMaster, *Paris 1961: Algerians, State Terror and Memory* (Oxford: Oxford University Press, 2006), 35–37.

71. AN, F/1a/3293, Sous-dossier: "Visite en Algérie de M. Papon."

72. AN, F/1a/3295, Note for the Governor-General, "Objet: Transfert de MESSALI d'El Goléa à Brazzaville," n.d. May 1945. On arrival at El Goléa on 30 April, Messali Hadj was immediately notified that he would be transferred to the French Congo the following day. Angered that they had not been informed in advance of this transfer, the authorities in French Equatorial Africa charged the costs of Messali's imprisonment to the Algiers government. A pied-noir, Gazagne had spent the mid-1930s as deputy commander of the Paris police Service de surveillance, protection, et d'assistance aux indigènes nord-africains (SAINA). Aside from this police background, he also shared Papon's anti-Semitism and his connections to the Vichy administration in South Western France; see House and MacMaster, *Paris 1961*, 35.

73. Best known in France for his connections with the resistance against Admiral Darlan's Vichyite administration ousted by the U.S. invasion in November 1942. Petitbon remained in his post at the Constantine prefecture until 1952. Petitbon worked with General Duval in determining the Muslim death figures in the department, which were subdivided as follows: 173 killed by the gendarmerie, 133 by the police, 114 by vigilantes, and 755 in the course of army operations. Figures cited in "Principe de dénégation et bilan de la répression," *El Moudjahid*, 8 May 2006.

74. AN, F/1a/3293, Dossier VI-B-1, Sous-direction de l'Algérie, "Compte-rendu de la visite d'information de Monsieur Papon en Algérie," n.d. (probably early November) 1945.

75. It is interesting to note that the writer Albert Camus was one of the first to state publicly that the Sétif uprising might be the product of economic discrimination and call for the need for social reform rather than Muslim communal animosity toward the French; see John P. Chesson, "Colonialism and Violence: Camus and Sartre on the Algerian War, 1945–58," *Maghreb Review*, 15:1–2 (1990), 17.

76. AN, F/1a/3293, Dossier VI-B-1, Interior Minister, projet de letter (draft memo) to Prime Minister's Office, n.d. February 1946.

77. AN, F/1a/3293, Dossier VI-B-II: Rapports généraux du Gouverneur Général de l'Algérie sur la situation générale ou politique, tel. 895, Secretaire Gazagne to Office Algérie, Paris, 6 February 1946.

PART 2

*Colonial Minds and
Empire Soldiers*

7

Conquest and Cohabitation

French Men's Relations with West African Women in the 1890s and 1900s

OWEN WHITE

If there was an "official mind" of French imperialism it was often shaped in relation to unofficial practices, such as the cohabiting unions that countless French men across the empire entered into with local women.[1] It is now commonplace to observe that imperial minds had bodily desires; that they acted upon them, and that imperial policymakers took a more than passing interest in the outcome.[2] But as historians of empire have made "the intimate" a topic of inquiry, the encounters that took place between individuals in private tend to remain inscrutable, due to the challenge of finding "intimate" sources. For this reason, while the choices made by the men involved in cohabiting unions may have been subject to official or unofficial judgment (and sometimes still are, under the eye of modern-day historians), it has generally proven difficult to say what these men's relationships meant to them, and still less what the relationships meant to their female consorts. This essay represents an effort to gain access into the men's lived experience of cohabiting unions, and in doing so to cast some sliver of light on the intimate workings of "colonial minds."

For Frantz Fanon, writing in *Black Skin, White Masks* in 1952, relationships between colonizing Europeans and local women could be analyzed straightforwardly. "The white man," Fanon wrote, "can allow himself the luxury of sleeping with many women," and "especially in colonies," because "he is the master." Fanon dismissed the claim made by the psychologist Octave Mannoni that when Joseph-Simon Gallieni's troops "pacified" Madagascar in the 1890s, the "more or less temporary" marriages they made at the same time with Malagasy women "presented no difficulties at all," because Malagasy sex life was open, easy, and "unmarred by complexes." Fanon disagreed, or rather found Mannoni's judgment irrelevant: what did it matter if Malagasy society was sexually accommodating? In a situation where male entitlement was magnified by a sense of racial superiority, "when a soldier of the conquering army went to bed with a young Malagasy girl, there was undoubtedly no tendency on his part to respect her entity as another person."[3] These conquerors would scarcely have taken "no" for an answer.

For Fanon, these relationships—the word is almost too delicate for his argument—represented another category of the violence of imperial conquest. But the men involved had minds as well as bodies; orders to carry out, but also individual consciences that could be troubled. In the minds of at least some French men, attempting to explain their actions either to others or to themselves, they were not simply conquerors, of territory or of women. The unequal power relations that Fanon identified allowed French men to initiate relationships in ways that would not have been true in France. But for many, making their way in an unfamiliar environment, emotional vulnerability was a counterpart to their power.

This essay looks at relationships between French men and "colonized" women in a particular region in a particular time, namely French West Africa in the 1890s and 1900s. The period was one of transitions, as, from 1895, a civilian government-general for the French West African federation gradually established its authority, while the military influence that had accompanied the conquest and ensuing "pacification" progressively waned.[4] (Madagascar underwent its own move toward civilian rule under Gallieni's governorship between 1896 and 1905.) During this time, particularly in the regions into which the French had recently expanded, relationships between French men and African women were still more the norm than the exception they would later become.

While it is easy enough to find references to the fact that such relationships took place—as well as the circumstantial evidence represented by *métis* (mixed-race) children—it is much harder to get any sense of what they meant for the individuals involved. Africanists have recently begun the difficult but important task of considering the implications of such relationships for African women.[5] The focus of this essay is more on French men, as a handful of sources—private letters, unpublished diaries—that are more intimate than official documents or the standard soldier's or administrator's memoir offer us the possibility of gaining access to the private thoughts of a few individuals.

Most of the sources that inform the case studies here are of a particular type.[6] They are not *merely* private letters or diaries: they are intimate letters written to intimates, usually men—a male friend, a male cousin—or a diary whose author had not just the inclination but also the time to reflect on his relationships with women. In the letters especially the candor is intermittent, and there is a tendency, in view of the subject matter, for a certain male bravado occasionally to appear. In spite of such limitations, the group of men whose relationships feature in this essay should probably be considered more self-reflective than many of their peers: their correspondence or their diaries, after all, were full enough and interesting enough to be worth keeping. While the self-selected nature of the sample should caution us against broad generalizations, the sources presented here do allow us to consider how some French men perceived the emotional and social content of their relations with West African women. At the outset these men were sexually eager yet at the same time frequently unsure of themselves, and their relationships had the capacity to change them in ways they did not expect.

The types of relationships French men had with West African women varied widely in the decades either side of 1900. They ranged from casual connections that might, and often did, involve some form of coercion, through longer-term unions that might last weeks, months, or even years, to a few permanent unions of full legal standing.[7] The full variety of relationships was practiced in both the military and the civil authority, and it was not uncommon for officers or officials individually to experience this variety, by engaging in both casual and longer-term connections in the course of their time in West Africa.[8]

The French administrator in West Africa, no less than the officer in the colonial army, inhabited a resolutely masculine world in the 1890s and 1900s.⁹ From around 1905 one can detect a very gradual increase in the number of French women accompanying their husbands to West Africa, but beyond a handful of urban centers this presence, as well as the transplanted French family life it connoted (however imprecisely, given the difficult environment and short-term nature of many postings), was to remain rare until after World War I. For the most part French men's intimate interactions with West African women evolved with little if any metropolitan oversight and few consistent and public voices of opposition from within the French community in West Africa: to be sure, Catholic missionaries were frustrated or dismayed by some of the conduct they witnessed or learned about, but only rarely did they voice their displeasure outside of internal documents.[10]

All the same, it is true that French men were closely observing and passing judgment on the choices and proclivities of their compatriots—if not exactly "policing" each other, then at least keeping watch. To take one example, the administrator Albert Nebout, a leading figure in the establishment of French rule in Côte d'Ivoire in the 1890s and 1900s, wrote to an old school friend in 1905 about the behavior of that territory's governor, François-Joseph Clozel, during an administrative tour of the northern part of the colony. "The tour would have been agreeable," Nebout wrote, "but for the daily recruitment of women, for Clozel and his retinue." European traders in some of the towns they passed through, he noted, were fully aware of these "extra-administrative requisitions." Nebout's judgment on his senior colleague was harsh; he and his friend Maurice Delafosse, then an administrator in northern Côte d'Ivoire, were "disgusted," he wrote, while a captain with whom they were traveling "could not conceal his surprise."[11] In a later letter, Nebout speculated that what he called Clozel's "vices" may even have cost him the job of governor-general of French West Africa in 1908, besides jeopardizing his health.[12]

Nebout seems to have felt secure in condemning the promiscuity he witnessed among his peers, albeit only in a private letter; he himself was in a conventionally monogamous relationship. Yet his own choices were similarly subject to the judgment of those around him. Nebout was a rarity among French administrators, being married under French law to a West African woman, a Baule named Ago. They married in 1895 and remained wed until her premature death in 1919, at which time she and their six children were living in France.[13] But Nebout never reached the rank that his experience and competence as an administrator seem on the surface to have merited. Instead, he was marginalized in Côte d'Ivoire after 1908 in the administration of Gabriel Angoulvant, who had a pronounced dislike for so-called *indigénophiles*.[14] Nothing could make one seem more of an *indigénophile* than marriage to an indigenous woman, and in the long run it may have been Nebout's choices that held back his career more than those of Clozel, who eventually did become governor-general.[15]

In Albert Nebout and Ago one has a rare example of a stable and apparently loving relationship involving a French man and a West African woman. The beginnings of the relationship, however, were much like the vast majority of others that went beyond a single night. Nebout told his school friend in 1895 that "one must ... resign oneself to local unions" due to the difficulty of resisting one's natural impulses and the fact that one could not bring French women to such an "unhealthy" country.[16] Thus "resigned" to a union with a local woman, in the course of his duties as an administrator in Toumodi, in Baule country in central Côte d'Ivoire, he noticed a young girl—we rarely find out how young in such accounts, and Nebout's is no exception—and he used an African intermediary to request that she become his wife. He chose to ignore the parents' visible lack of enthusiasm for the arrangement, and he offered a bride-price. That same evening, in Nebout's telling, a very nervous Ago sat trembling in his bedroom, with an oddly fixed smile on her face.

From these unpromising beginnings Nebout and Ago were able to fashion a relationship that went beyond the short-term needs of its initiator and the unequal power relations that brought it about. Other French men, however, would perhaps not have extended to their young spouse the same courtesy Nebout wrote that he offered on their first evening together: he confided in his friend that in the end three months would pass before he and Ago consummated their union. And Nebout later found out that his African intermediary had told Ago that Nebout would have her father killed if she did not smile for him.[17] As considerate as he portrayed himself in his correspondence, at no point was Nebout fully aware of (or concerned to recognize) the power he held and the way this set the contours of his initial interactions with Ago and her kin. The indications are that Ago's family was socially well placed, but on the evidence of Nebout's correspondence her connections do not seem to have given her any protection when faced with the demands of this representative of French authority.[18]

Rather than Nebout and Ago's example of long-term marriage, the more common forms of relationship involving French men and West African women were short-term unions, often marked with local rites and referred to—in a phrase that concealed a myriad of French presumptions about the nature and history of local marriage practices—as *mariages à la mode du pays* (marriages according to the customs of the country).[19] In the Soudan in the 1880s and 1890s, for example, such relationships were widely practiced by colonial officers. One French woman traveler observed in 1894 that these unions were actively encouraged at the highest levels, "where they preach by example."[20] Almost until the beginning of the twentieth century the Soudan was, in historian Martin Klein's words, "run by and for the army." Klein shows how some French officers regarded African women, often women of slave status, as being among the spoils of conquest. They allowed the African *tirailleurs* under their command to capture wives and chose women, sometimes multiple women, for their own desires and comfort.[21] Such evidence helps to reinforce Fanon's image of the colonial army as a violent and unpredictable force that treated women in the manner of stereotypical conquerors.

It is clear that in some degree this image is valid, relating as it does to an army bent on demonstrating its power and its prowess not long after an emasculating defeat (in 1870–71) on a European battlefield, if not continuing to refine techniques of violence that had already been tested in venues like Algeria. Historians have identified a "crisis of masculinity" in fin-de-siècle France, a world beset with social and cultural fears that found expression in a host of bodily metaphors.[22] The prevailing historical image of colonial officers in the Soudan comes close to situating them as the answer to these fears. They sometimes appear to inhabit a place unburdened by any sort of anxiety or self-reflection.

Officers are required to command and be ready to use violence, and a great deal of both took place in the colonial army during the period of expansion; the peoples of the Soudan and elsewhere in West Africa suffered greatly in consequence.[23] There is room, however, to add some nuance to our image of the officer corps in West Africa, and in particular its relations with African women, for what was expected of them as soldiers—as well as the armed conflict in which they uniformly hoped to participate and "prove" themselves—did not make their personal lives any less complicated or free of ambivalence. I illustrate this point through two case studies. The first concerns Émile Dussaulx, an officer in the *infanterie de marine* whose personal correspondence during his time in the Soudan between 1894 and 1898 was recently published.[24] The second case, which I treat at greater length, draws on the unpublished diary of Robert Altmayer, a lieutenant in the colonial cavalry in Timbuktu between 1901 and 1903.

Émile Dussaulx participated in two unions with West African women, one in each of his tours of duty. During his first tour he served, contrary to what he had expected, as an administrator in the *cercle* (administrative district) of Kouroussa, in the east of what is now Guinea. At first he wrote to his cousin—also a soldier—that he was in no way attracted to the local women.[25] But as he became acquainted with compatriots who had formed cohabiting unions, he eventually overcame his "repugnance" sufficiently to enter one himself with a fourteen-year-old Somono.[26] Dussaulx described the young woman, whom he referred to as Mama, as a worthy and attractive *compagne d'exil* (companion during exile). He obliged his cousin with a brief evaluation of their first night together, as well as the mechanics of their sexual interaction: it had been excellent, he said, but he had found it "impossible to operate face to face!" As if to reassure his cousin that his relationship with an "othered" partner did not also involve othered sexual practices, however, he hastily added: "No orientalism, though."[27]

The six-month union between Dussaulx and Mama, as Dussaulx described it in his letters, rested on a rather material exchange of favors, with Mama's principal interest presented as the gifts he could offer her.[28] But almost in spite of himself, the relationship seems to have begun to mean more to Dussaulx than a purely material, or physical, exchange. Dussaulx expressed his yearning for France in letters and poetry during their relationship, but when he did return, taking the waters at Vichy after falling ill, he wrote to his cousin that he now pined for his *beau Niger*, and he confided that he and his recuperating fellow officers missed their *moussos* (African women). Worse, he added, "with bitterness [we] note the profound decrepitude of the white-skinned fair sex."[29] Perhaps Dussaulx and his comrades were bemoaning a problem particular to the town of Vichy, yet the real point of interest in this case is the way the French men saw African women as the mark of their sense of *dépaysement* or cultural disorientation: the way, in effect, that these women induced ambivalence in the minds of the conquerors.

On his second tour of duty, garrisoned at Goumbou in what is now Mali, Dussaulx sought perhaps to lessen this sense of patriotic or racial alienation by treating his new consort, Fatma Hély, as if she were something like a normal member of his family. He sent pictures of her to his sisters and brother in Lorraine, and one of the sisters then forwarded a photo to Dussaulx's cousin, with the note that it depicted *"la belle* Fatma, our dear sister-in-law."[30] The note may have been written with tongue in cheek but is no less striking in the acceptance it appears to show for the arrangement Dussaulx had made. The relationship did not last long and ended with regrets and embarrassment for Dussaulx, arising mainly from his failure to deliver on promises he had made to Fatma regarding certain gifts: he felt he had not kept his side of their bargain, though this failure had no personal consequences beyond a guilty conscience.[31]

Civilian rule was slow to take root in the Soudan, but by 1899, shortly after Dussaulx's departure, the military's preeminence there was at an end.[32] But the attachment to cohabiting unions of officers in the Soudan appears to have continued unabated into the new century. One of the best sources for this is the private diary of a young officer stationed in Timbuktu between 1901 and 1903, which survives in the army archives at Vincennes.[33] The officer in question, Lieutenant Robert Altmayer, provides us with perhaps the most intimate insight we have into what cohabiting unions could mean to their French protagonists. His diary therefore merits extended attention.

Robert Altmayer arrived in Timbuktu in June 1901, a month before his twenty-sixth birthday. Born in Bordeaux, he came from a military family; by 1901 his father was a colonel, and his younger brother René was also an officer. (Both Robert and René, like their father, would eventually rise to the rank of general.) In Timbuktu Robert commanded the fourth platoon of the second squadron of the Soudanese *spahis*, the word *spahi* designating a member of the colonial cavalry in North and West Africa. In his platoon Altmayer had under him two noncommissioned officers—one French, one African—and thirty-two African cavalrymen drawn from a variety of different ethnic groups.[34]

Altmayer was stationed at Fort Hugueny, the smaller of the two French fortresses in Timbuktu. The relatively heavy military presence in Timbuktu in 1901—the town and its hinterland would remain under military rule until 1912[35]—protected both French interests and, or so the argument went, the local inhabitants from hostile nomads, particularly Tuareg raiding parties. Timbuktu was also a base for the extension of French power further into the southern fringes of the Sahara. That, in any case, was what Altmayer desperately hoped. At a time of relative peace in Europe, the colonial army had become a key avenue for combat experience and promotion.[36] But as Altmayer ruefully put it in his diary, "with typical luck, I am arriving in Timbuktu at a time when, unless something unexpected occurs, absolutely nothing will happen."[37]

So it was to prove during his two-year tour of duty. In peaceful times, colonial officers could expect to find themselves laying telegraph lines or making maps. Altmayer was assigned the latter task, but while this kept him occupied, a career as a topographer was hardly what he had envisaged for his time in Africa. During Midnight Mass on Christmas Eve in 1901 Altmayer found himself studying the commemorative plaques on the wall of the mission chapel that honored the men who had died to make Timbuktu French. He thought of these men on his way back to barracks and concluded his diary entry with the words: "Happy time when the *spahis* of Timbuktu were always in the bush—lucky cavaliers killed in the charge!"[38] To his intense disappointment, an expedition to secure for France a mountainous region northeast of Timbuktu, where the Soudan met southern Algeria, did not come to pass during his tour.[39] Some colonial officers were apt to claim that to learn about war one had to go to the colonies, rather than the École de Guerre.[40] But Altmayer spent twenty-one months in Timbuktu before he received any kind of instruction of a military nature, leading him to wonder whether, in career terms, he had been wasting his time in the Soudan.[41]

His frustration must have been widely shared among his peers. In Altmayer's Timbuktu, one has a clear image of young French officers with a lot of pent-up energy and not much to do. In the past overeager officers with dreams of conquest had caused problems in the Timbuktu region. But the bloody mayhem of the 1899 Voulet-Chanoine expedition ensured that by the time Altmayer arrived, officers in the Soudan were subject to far greater civilian oversight.[42] And although within the terms of French colonialism the Timbuktu region still effectively represented a frontier society, the frontier had few directions left in which to expand.

In consequence, most French officers were bored by life in Timbuktu. Local women were perceived to offer one kind of diversion. Hunting was another. Some officers liked to tame wild animals; one of Altmayer's peers tamed a leopard, or rather thought he had, until it mauled a young girl.[43] Altmayer himself kept an ostrich, a monkey, some goats, and poultry, and he developed strong attachments to his horses. Cards provided another distraction. A great deal of money changed hands in games of baccarat or poker that could go on all night; Altmayer's account books that accompany his diary show that a significant proportion of his monthly salary of 570 francs was sometimes needed to cover his gambling debts.[44] Near the end of Altmayer's time in Timbuktu a few extreme cases of debt prompted the regional commandant to ban games played for money on military property.[45]

Altmayer certainly participated in this culture of drinking, gambling, and endless talk in the mess. But he also frequently became irritated with the company of his fellow officers and tired of debating the rumors that appeared, mutated, and disappeared at regular intervals. Altmayer found that reading offered one way of escaping his miniaturized social world, or in some cases perhaps making sense of it; books he read, such as Machiavelli's *The Prince* or the collection of Theodore Roosevelt's speeches and essays called *The Strenuous Life*, may have spoken to his current situation in different ways. In the course of his time in Timbuktu he read a broad mixture of mostly recent novels and nonfiction, the authors ranging across the political spectrum from Édouard Drumont to Émile Zola and Anatole France. Altmayer's enthusiasm for Émile Faguet's *Le libéralisme* (1902) helps us (along with the dislike for Freemasons and "antimilitarists" that he avows in his diary) to locate him politically as a conservative liberal, who believed the powers of the state should be strictly curtailed.[46] But all the same, reading in Timbuktu was something of a challenge. This Altmayer partly put down to a self-diagnosed case of anemia. "I am becoming a complete idiot," reads one entry. "I can no longer understand abstract ideas and my brain is so anemic that I no longer even have the urge to read."[47]

Amid the frustrations Altmayer experienced in Timbuktu—his stalling career, the pettiness of his fellow officers, the difficulty of staying mentally sharp—his diary shows that the cohabiting union in which he was involved for twenty-one months mostly represented a welcome source of comfort and connection. Altmayer's tender record of this union, it should be said, stands in contrast to his description of some of his fellow officers' relationships with African women. Rather like Albert Nebout, Altmayer registered disgust at the actions of certain of his peers, such as the officer who forcibly took a woman as his consort and publicly beat a blacksmith whom he suspected of opposing their union.[48] With similar distaste, Altmayer recorded the actions of an officer who abandoned a young woman in a town far from her home, leaving her only fifteen francs to make her way; described in the diary as barely more than a child, she was four months pregnant.[49] In the Soudan of the time, Altmayer observed, one's actions were determined more by one's individual conscience than out of concern for the judgment of one's family or community.[50] Altmayer's comments nonetheless suggest that some members of the army in the Soudan enjoyed certain standards of honor in relation to African women, however vague these standards were.

Altmayer initially showed no interest in finding a local woman as his temporary consort; in the early part of his diary, indeed, he is more often concerned with the memory of two French women, whom he refers to only as "G" and "B." But surrounded by officers who showed no hesitation in contracting cohabiting unions, he eventually overcame any ambivalence and engaged an African intermediary to seek out a suitable light-skinned woman from among the nomadic peoples who lived around Timbuktu. The first attempt to find such a woman ended with the candidate running away in fear. In December 1901, though, Altmayer succeeded in finding a woman who met his requirements.

Her name, as Altmayer transcribed it, was Koudiedia, from an Arabic-speaking nomadic people known to the French as Kountas.[51] Altmayer paid a bride-price of 150 francs to her parents and guaranteed the well-being of the young woman. (The diary does not reveal her age.) Altmayer describes her as "pretty—yes pretty—with a Semitic profile," and he adds that she is "the whitest and least ugly of all the women I have seen in a year, including the European women in Kayes [then the capital of the French Soudan], and not to mention the Sister Superior in Ségou."[52] Though the diary does not explicitly address this point, Koudiedia seems to have joined Altmayer in his lodgings at Fort Hugueny.[53] Altmayer celebrated his consummation of their match with a sheep barbecue (*méchoui*) for his fellow officers and then lost his pay playing baccarat.[54]

Racial ideas obviously entered Altmayer's assertion that he would have found it impossible to embrace a black African woman—an attitude that many of his comrades did not share—though Altmayer's aversion arose in part, he said, from his dislike of the smell of the shea butter (*karité*) that they used on their bodies, while his attraction to Koudiedia was increased by the possibility that she might help him learn some Arabic.[55] The latter interest progressed at least as far that after a few months he could hold "fairly long" conversations with her.[56] And notwithstanding a few "infidelities" that Altmayer notes in passing,[57] his diary is striking in part for the depth and apparent sincerity of the respect he developed for Koudiedia, her family, and their religion. He often compares her favorably with French women; she has "very delicate thoughts just like a European," and he states that her knowledge of her religion outstrips that of French women of comparable status.[58] In fact, he finds her thought processes to be so similar to those of Europeans that he declares, "Arabs are white, not black."[59]

Of course, these loaded statements manifest racial thinking, but nonetheless they suggest that Altmayer, to use Fanon's words but to run against his argument, was capable of respecting Koudiedia's "entity as another person," and that their relationship forced him to challenge some of his preconceptions. When their son, Robert-Omar, was born, Altmayer resolved that the boy should grow up in the nomadic society of his mother, reasoning that if the boy would not follow his father's Catholicism, he would at least believe in a single God among people of deep faith. (Like other French Catholics with experience of Islam in or around the Sahara—Charles de Foucauld and Ernest Psichari are two of the more prominent examples—Altmayer was much impressed by the professions of faith he witnessed among Muslims.)[60] Altmayer's planning turned out to be as premature as the child himself. The boy died within twenty-four hours of his birth, and the Catholic missionaries who buried him in a grave marked with a wooden cross perhaps never learned of the plans that Altmayer, who was a fairly regular visitor to the mission, had made to allow his son to grow up a Muslim.[61]

Koudiedia returned to her family's encampment to the northeast of Timbuktu just before Altmayer left the town at the end of his tour of duty in September 1903. The diary provides indications that the family had, within Koudiedia's lifetime, been relatively wealthy but fell on hard times as a result of Tuareg raids and disease among their livestock. These hardships had led the family to relocate to the Timbuktu region around 1899, and very likely produced the circumstances in which Koudiedia entered her relationship with Altmayer.[62] Throughout the time of their union she regularly visited her family in the desert outside Timbuktu, sometimes accompanied by Altmayer, with whom her father seems to have been on good terms, and to whom he occasionally communicated "bush rumors."[63] It is not clear whether the family gained any kind of material advantage from her union, or whether it cost them anything in terms of status. At the time of Altmayer's departure, though, he reports that they had plans to return with their herds to the region where they had lived before their fortunes declined, which had long been the family's wish.[64] Perhaps their circumstances had recovered since 1901, and if so, perhaps Altmayer played some role in this. His personal account books show that just before he left he gave Koudiedia 125 francs, almost as much as the initial bride-price he had paid her family, as well as supplying her with various provisions. (To put the sum of 125 francs in perspective—Altmayer's, if not hers—it could be noted that two months previously he recorded a loss of 153 francs playing poker.)[65]

There are clues in the diary that Koudiedia felt some unease that the relationship was alienating her from her own culture: on one occasion, for example, she described for Altmayer the content of a dream her mother had in which Koudiedia no longer liked "Arab cuisine."[66]

But whatever the unknown costs of the relationship, there is not much reason to doubt Altmayer's diary assertion that it ended on good terms, with tears on both sides. If Altmayer had entered the union with some uncertainty, he left with no doubt as to its value, as well as the rectitude of his own conduct within it. His comparative underemployment in Timbuktu had also, perhaps, both allowed and encouraged him emotionally to invest something in the relationship. His final judgment was that "I made her happy—and I will only keep good memories of her."[67]

By the time Altmayer left Timbuktu in 1903, cohabiting unions were still commonly practiced by both French soldiers and administrators in West Africa. There also remained a general sense among representatives of French authority that the official line was tacitly supportive of such relationships, on the basis that they offered a degree of stability in colonialists' lives and were a way of protecting against ills such as venereal diseases and (though this was usually only voiced by implication) homosexual activity. One administrator in Senegal noted that he and fellow district administrators had received from official sources a book written in 1902 by Dr. Louis Joseph Barot, in which could be found the statement that a "temporary union with a well-chosen native woman" was an acceptable line of conduct for representatives of French authority in Africa. For him this represented official approbation for cohabiting unions.[68]

Yet this same administrator, Marius Leclerc, in a letter that survives in the archives of the Masonic organization the Grand Orient de France, gives us some indication of a less tolerant official attitude to temporary unions by around 1905. Leclerc was writing to the Masons in October of that year because his actions with an African woman had gotten him in trouble with the administration, and he wanted help getting his career back on track. As Leclerc described it, he had been accused of the kidnapping and rape of a young woman in the administrative district of Louga, in Senegal.[69] An enquiry, he said, found against the allegations, concluding that he had simply made a *mariage à la mode du pays*. Even so, Leclerc was transferred to a less desirable post in Guinea, and the governor-general of French West Africa, Ernest Roume, compounded Leclerc's outrage by demoting him.

The governor-general's objections to Leclerc's behavior fell roughly in two categories. First, Roume seems to have thought that a temporary union might entangle an administrator in local politics or compromise his authority through cultural missteps.[70] For these reasons the governor-general disliked the fact that Leclerc had used a local chief to make the marriage arrangements, and also that he had not asked the permission of the young woman's mother. Second, Leclerc's actions went against the grain of official policy, since the young woman in question was a captive, while Roume was working toward the abolition of slavery in French West Africa; in fact, he would pass a decree to that effect in December 1905.[71] Leclerc argued that in marrying the young woman he had also liberated her, but Roume was not interested in freeing slaves in this piecemeal way.[72] Leclerc's justifications therefore cut little ice with the governor-general: this kind of behavior may have been tolerable in the early days of expansion, but not as an increasingly legalistic and scandal-averse government-general sought to assert its authority. (Roume met with Leclerc in June 1905 at a moment of particular scrutiny of colonial practices; at the time, the famed explorer Pierre Savorgnan de Brazza was on a well-publicized mission to gather evidence of abuses in the French Congo.)[73] Perhaps Roume saw *mariages à la mode du pays* as exploitative; even Leclerc admitted that they were an exercise in bad faith, in the sense that the European did not consider the marriage to be a *real* marriage.[74]

Over the coming years administrators used to the old ways—the *vieux africains* or "old Africa hands," as they liked to call themselves—would criticize the "bureaucratization" of empire and the end of the "pioneering spirit" of the early days of expansion. The colonial mind retained its interest in *métissage* (miscegenation), for reasons prurient or practical, yet cohabiting unions declined progressively, albeit without ever disappearing entirely. The decline was especially marked after World War I as the administration overcame much of its ambivalence toward temporary unions, the more single-mindedly to promote a more "respectable" empire—meaning, in practice, an empire that valorized French bourgeois domestic life as the norm for colonialists' comfort.[75]

There is likewise, of course, the possibility of a simultaneously hardening attitude toward temporary unions among Africans. In 1913, for example, the administrator Maurice Prouteaux completed a systematic tour of the *canton* (administrative district) of Noolou in the northwest of Côte d'Ivoire. The principal objective of this exercise was to record the names of the district's inhabitants to facilitate taxing them. As he toured the district, Prouteaux noticed that it was rare to see female adolescents in the villages he visited. Instead, on the day of the census, it appeared that they were all at the villagers' plantations. If heads of household provided the names of their adolescent daughters, Prouteaux observed, they commonly insisted that they were twelve years old.

Since children became taxable at the age of ten, to claim they were twelve would have had no implications in terms of reducing a community's tax burden. The best explanation Prouteaux could come up with for the "dissimulation" he perceived was that "these people fear having to satisfy a *droit de jambage*"—an allusion to the purported pre-Revolutionary practice in which a lord had the right to deflower newlywed brides on his domain.[76] Prouteaux wrote that he did not notice the same fear among the inhabitants of smaller villages that, to his knowledge, he was the first French administrator to visit.[77] Apparently, one learned through experience to be wary of representatives of French power and the forms of tribute they might command. We cannot say if the villagers Prouteaux met were aware that French law at the time recognized an age of consent of thirteen. But when they said their teenage daughters were twelve they seem to have done so advisedly and in the knowledge that French exactions could hardly be consigned to the realm of *ancien régime* practices.

Prouteaux's observations should remind us that for African women the stakes were much higher than for the French men with whom they became involved, sometimes against their will. At the same time, the case studies presented in this essay from a particular region and time in the history of French colonization should be enough to demonstrate that in the men's minds there could be some degree of meaningful interaction even during relatively brief unions between French men and "colonized" women. Some cohabiting unions clearly became more than "an emotionally unfettered convenience" even for quite conservative French men.[78] Robert Altmayer was still thinking about Koudiedia in 1941, when in enforced idleness during the Nazi Occupation he made notes for a possible book about the Soudan and the time he had spent there. By now a general and very much a member of the French establishment, he had not changed his views on the moral acceptability of the unions in which he and many of his comrades had participated.[79]

France's failure to respect the entity of other peoples, to paraphrase Fanon, left little space for these fleeting moments of connection to alter the way different cultures interacted. But, as has been observed for a different and earlier French colonial context, there was room for "both exploitation and love."[80] In the self-judgment of colonialists, some part of the colonial mind, as on a phrenological skull, was quartered off for intimacy.

Notes

1. Ronald Robinson and John Gallagher coined the idea of the "official mind" of empire in *Africa and the Victorians: The Official Mind of Imperialism* (London: Macmillan, 1961). Christopher M. Andrew used the phrase "unofficial mind" to refer particularly to the workings of the French *parti colonial* in his article "The French Colonialist Movement during the Third Republic: The Unofficial Mind of Imperialism," *Transactions of the Royal Historical Society* 25:1 (1976), 143–66, but the concept might be expanded into other areas of French imperial practice. The notion of an "unconscious" mind of empire has also surfaced, for example, in Elizabeth Ezra, *The Colonial Unconscious: Race and Culture in Interwar France* (Ithaca NY: Cornell University Press, 2000).

2. Attention to "intimacy" in colonial contexts owes much to the influential work of Ann Laura Stoler; see especially Stoler, *Carnal Knowledge and Imperial Power: Race and the Intimate in Colonial Rule* (Berkeley: University of California Press, 2002). For a recent contribution to this line of inquiry see Durba Ghosh, *Sex and the Family in Colonial India: The Making of Empire* (Cambridge: Cambridge University Press, 2006).

3. Frantz Fanon, *Black Skin, White Masks* (1952; English ed., trans. Charles Lam Markmann, New York: Grove Press, 1967), 46; O. Mannoni, *Prospero and Caliban: The Psychology of Colonialism* (1950, English ed., trans. Pamela Powesland, New York: Praeger, 1956), 112–14. For an analysis of Fanon's use of Mannoni's work, see Christopher Lane, "Psychoanalysis and Colonialism Redux: Why Mannoni's 'Prospero Complex' Still Haunts Us," *Journal of Modern Literature* 25:3–4 (2002), 127–49.

4. For an account of this process see Alice L. Conklin, *A Mission to Civilize: The Republican Idea of Empire in France and West Africa, 1895–1930* (Stanford CA: Stanford University Press, 1997), 23–37. The French West

African federation eventually covered the area now occupied by the states of Senegal, Mauritania, Mali, Burkina Faso, Niger, Benin, Côte d'Ivoire, and Guinea.

5. See, e.g., Rachel Jean-Baptiste, "Une Ville Libre? Marriage, Divorce, and Sexuality in Colonial Libreville, Gabon, 1840–1960," PhD diss., Stanford University, 2005; Jeremy Rich, "'Une Babylone Noire': Interracial Unions in Colonial Libreville, c. 1860–1914," *French Colonial History* 4 (2003), 145–70. See also Jeanne-Marie Kambou-Ferrand, "Souffre, gémis, mais marche! Regard d'une paysanne lobi sur sa vie au temps colonial," in *La Haute-Volta coloniale: Témoignages, recherches, regards*, ed. Gabriel Massa and Y. Georges Madiéga (Paris: Karthala, 1995), 147–56.

6. I did not use any of these sources in my book: Owen White, *Children of the French Empire: Miscegenation and Colonial Society in French West Africa, 1895–1960* (Oxford: Oxford University Press, 1999).

7. In an attempt to avoid terminological Eurocentricity I prefer here to use the terms "union" or "cohabiting union" rather than "concubinage." The latter word, with an etymology that connotes "lying together," is defined in the *Oxford English Dictionary* (2nd ed., 1989) as implying cohabitation without legal marriage. Yet, in African eyes, some of the arrangements I describe were legally valid. For similar reasons I have generally preferred the vaguer "consort" to either "concubine" or "wife." I have chosen not to focus on casual liaisons in this piece or the related question of prostitution, though it might be argued that the latter phenomenon should not be disconnected from discussion of longer-term unions. It would require a separate chapter to do justice to these topics, however, and they do not lend themselves readily to exploring the theme of intimacy that I wish to develop here. No historian of the period covered in this essay has yet written about prostitution in any part of the former French West Africa in the manner of Luise White's pathbreaking *The Comforts of Home: Prostitution in Colonial Nairobi* (Chicago: University of Chicago Press, 1990).

8. For a case study of such relationships in the administrative district of Ségou in the French Soudan, see Francis Simonis, "Splendeurs et misères des moussos: Les compagnes africaines des Européens du cercle de Ségou au Mali (1890–1962)," in *Histoire africaine du XXe siècle: Sociétés—villes—cultures*, ed. Catherine Coquéry-Vidrovitch (Paris: L'Harmattan, 1993), 207–22. For a brief study of miscegenation as a theme in colonial fiction at the time under consideration see Jennifer Yee, "Neither Flesh nor Fowl: 'Métissage' in *fin-de-siècle* French Colonial Fiction," *L'Esprit Créateur* 38:1 (Spring 1998), 46–56.

9. See Emmanuelle Sibeud, "'Science de l'homme' coloniale ou science de 'l'homme colonial'? Rapports de genres et ethnographie coloniale en Afrique

française au début du XXe siècle," in *Histoire des femmes en situation coloniale: Afrique et Asie, XXe siècle*, ed. Anne Hugon (Paris: Karthala, 2004), 187.

10. See Simonis, "Splendeurs et misères," 211; Guy Dervil, *Trois Grands Africains: Dans l'intimité de Lyautey, Laperrine, Foucauld. Souvenirs personnels* (Paris: J. Susse, ca. 1945), 34.

11. Albert Nebout, *Passions Africaines* (Geneva: Editions Eboris, 1995), 255, letter from June 1905. Two of Nebout's descendants oversaw the publication of this collection of his correspondence. All translations are by the author unless otherwise noted.

12. Nebout, *Passions Africaines*, 266, letter from May 1908. The job of governor-general was given instead to William Ponty, about whom Nebout wrote, "his reputation as a reveler [*noceur*] was well founded" (264). By 1908 Clozel had married a French woman, who accompanied him to Côte d'Ivoire, though Nebout wrote disparagingly of her, too (260).

13. Nebout, *Passions Africaines*, 331. It is not clear from the letters if the regularization of their union under French law took place in 1895 or later. Other administrators who married West Africans under French law include François de Coutouly, who served in several West African territories; see Emmanuelle Sibeud, *Une science impériale pour l'Afrique? La construction des savoirs africanistes en France 1878–1930* (Paris: Editions EHESS, 2002), 286–87; O. White, *Children of the French Empire*, 137. Regarding Henri d'Arboussier, who married a descendant of Umar Tal in the French Soudan and later became governor of New Caledonia, see William B. Cohen, "The French Governors," in *African Proconsuls: European Governors in Africa*, ed. L. H. Gann and P. Duignan (New York: Free Press, 1978), 44. Perhaps the best-known example of a French man who married a West African woman under French law was the sometime Catholic missionary Auguste Dupuis; on Dupuis see Owen White, "The Decivilizing Mission: Auguste Dupuis-Yakouba and French Timbuktu," *French Historical Studies* 27:3 (2004), 541–68.

14. For much the same reason Angoulvant disliked Maurice Delafosse, whose temporary union (and its abrupt ending) with a Baule woman is well documented; see Louise Delafosse, *Maurice Delafosse: Le berrichon conquis par l'Afrique* (Paris: Société française d'histoire d'outre-mer, 1976), 163–64, 216, 271–72.

15. The careers of de Coutouly and d'Arboussier (note 13) similarly did not develop as might have been expected. Clozel finally became governor-general in 1915, after Ponty's death.

16. Nebout, *Passions Africaines*, 189.

17. Nebout, *Passions Africaines*, 189–92. Nebout also records that he had an African consort before Ago, but she died during childbirth.

18. According to the editors of Nebout's correspondence (p. 5), Ago was a cousin of Félix Houphouët-Boigny. What we know of the latter's chiefly lineage allows us to surmise a relatively elevated social status for Ago's family.

19. See O. White, *Children of the French Empire*, 9, 19–21.

20. Madame Paul Bonnetain, *Une française au Soudan: Sur la route de Tombouctou du Sénégal au Niger* (Paris: Librairies-Imprimeries Réunies, 1894), 173.

21. Martin Klein, *Slavery and Colonial Rule in French West Africa* (Cambridge: Cambridge University Press, 1998), 77, 82–84. See also Simonis, "Splendeurs et misères," 210–11; and J. Malcolm Thompson, "Colonial Policy and the Family Life of Black Troops in French West Africa, 1817–1904," *International Journal of African Historical Studies* 23:3 (1990), 438–40. Thompson quotes from Gallieni's account of the "distribution" of women during the early part of his career in the Soudan around 1886.

22. On body imagery and masculinity in *fin-de-siècle* France see Christopher E. Forth, *The Dreyfus Affair and the Crisis of French Manhood* (Baltimore: Johns Hopkins University Press, 2004); Robert A. Nye, *Masculinity and Male Codes of Honor in Modern France* (New York: Oxford University Press, 1993); also Bertrand Taithe, *Defeated Flesh: Welfare, Warfare, and the Making of Modern France* (Manchester: Manchester University Press, 1999).

23. See, for example, Bertrand Taithe's chapter in this volume.

24. Émile Dussaulx, *Journal du Soudan (1894–1898)*, ed. Sophie Dulucq (Paris: L'Harmattan, 2000). Two other sources that use correspondence from officers in the Soudan, though more heavily mediated by their editors than Dulucq's volume, are Fabrice Métayer, "Des Français à la conquête de l'Afrique occidentale: Le regard d'Henri Gaden à travers sa correspondance 1894–1899," Mémoire de maîtrise, Université de Provence-Aix-Marseille I, 2002; and François Descostes, *Au Soudan (1890–1891): Souvenirs d'un tirailleur sénégalais d'après sa correspondance intime* (Paris: Librairie Picard, 1893), which despite its title edits the correspondence of an officer named Anselme Orsat.

25. Dussaulx, *Journal du Soudan*, 51.

26. Dussaulx, *Journal du Soudan*, 99–100. Dussaulx mentions in passing several other examples of such unions (235, 261, 275). The Somono are a Mande-speaking people who have traditionally made their living by fishing the river Niger. See David C. Conrad, "Somono Identity in History and Tradition," in *Somono Bala of the Upper Niger*, ed. Conrad (Leiden: Brill, 2002), 1–2.

27. Dussaulx, *Journal du Soudan*, 166–67. On the then-widespread view of sodomy as an "oriental" practice, see Robert Aldrich, *Colonialism and Homosexuality* (London: Routledge, 2003), 63.

28. Dussaulx, *Journal du Soudan*, 196–97. The women involved in such relationships were stereotypically seen by French observers (and participants) as covetous (see O. White, *Children of the French Empire*, 22), though from the woman's point of view it was important to try to ensure that the union involved some transfer of property in her or her family's favor in addition to the initial payment of a bride-price.

29. Dussaulx, *Journal du Soudan*, 211, 213–15. The generic colonial term *mousso* was a Gallicized rendering of the Bambara word for "woman" or "wife" (*muso*). On colonial officers in Vichy, see Eric T. Jennings, *Curing the Colonizers: Hydrotherapy, Climatology, and French Colonial Spas* (Durham NC: Duke University Press, 2006), 190–92.

30. Dussaulx, *Journal du Soudan*, 265, 269–70; the picture referred to follows p. 258. Fatma Hély is described as a *maure* (moor), "of noble race," and a "desert girl"; more precisely the text points to her coming from the tribal confederation known as the Awlad Embarek (Dussaulx renders it variously as M'Baruk and Embaruk). For another description of "moors" in the Goumbou region shortly after Dussaulx was there, see Lieutenant Gaston Lautour, *Journal d'un spahi au Soudan 1897–1899* (Paris: Perrin et Compagnie, 1909), 108–12.

31. Dussaulx, *Journal du Soudan*, 299–300. This second relationship lasted no more than four months, from April to July 1897.

32. A. S. Kanya-Forstner, *The Conquest of the Western Sudan: A Study in French Military Imperialism* (Cambridge: Cambridge University Press, 1969); see 224–33, 255–62.

33. Service Historique de la Défense-Terre, Vincennes, 1K 161, carton 1 (henceforth Altmayer). Altmayer's papers were donated to the archive at Vincennes by his son. The diary is in five separate *carnets*, of which the second, third, and fourth cover Altmayer's time in Timbuktu. The variable legibility of Altmayer's handwriting and his frequent use of abbreviations make this a challenging source.

34. All details from Altmayer, carnets de notes diverses.

35. See Captain L. Marc-Schrader, "Quand j'étais maire de Tombouctou," *Le Tour du Monde* (1913), 405, 430.

36. For a useful overview of the activities and outlook of the colonial army in this period, see Douglas Porch, *The March to the Marne: The French Army, 1871–1914* (Cambridge: Cambridge University Press, 1981), 134–68.

37. Altmayer, diary, carnet 2, entry from June 1901 (no exact date).

38. Altmayer, carnet 2, 25 December 1901.

39. Altmayer, various entries, e.g., carnet 3, 26 October 1902. The expedition was canceled at the last moment due to a lack of funds and reinvented

as a much more limited reconnaissance mission, on which Altmayer served as topographer. The area, which Altmayer referred to as Adrar, was finally taken in 1904–5 by Lieutenant-Colonel Henri Laperrine; see Douglas Porch, *The Conquest of the Sahara* (London: Jonathan Cape, 1985), 270–72.

40. Porch, *March to the Marne*, 154.

41. Altmayer, carnet 4, 9 March and 1 April 1903.

42. On Voulet and Chanoine, see Porch, *Conquest of the Sahara*, 181–97, and Taithe in this volume.

43. Altmayer, carnet 3, 5 May 1902.

44. See Altmayer, carnet 2, 2 September 1901; also Altmayer's three *carnets de dépenses* in the same carton.

45. Altmayer, carnet 4, 9 August 1903.

46. For the various books mentioned here (and over a dozen others), see Altmayer, notes at back of carnets 2, 4, and 5. He read Drumont's *Les héros et les pitres* (Heroes and Clowns), Zola's novel *Vérité*, and Anatole France's *Monsieur Bergeret à Paris*, which he admired in spite of it being "the purest Dreyfusism."

47. Altmayer, carnet 2, 20 April 1902. I have not here explored the mental condition known as "Soudanite," to which officers in the Soudan, Altmayer included, attributed a wide range of antisocial symptoms; but for a sense of how the dimensions of this disorder were understood, see Louis Huot and Paul Voivenel, *Le Cafard* (Paris: Bernard Grasset, 1918), esp. 101–74.

48. Altmayer, carnet 2, 21 September 1901.

49. Altmayer, carnet 2, 17 March 1902.

50. Altmayer, carnet 2, 17 March 1902.

51. The woman's name is also rendered in the diary as Koudeida and Koudièdia, though most often simply as "K." The Kountas (or Kuntas) in the nineteenth century have been characterized as "a large confederation with a reputation for trade and scholarship"; Timothy Cleaveland, *Becoming Wal ta: A History of Saharan Social Formation and Transformation* (Portsmouth NH: Heinemann, 2002), 45.

52. Altmayer, carnet 2, 16 December 1901; for the bride-price, see his personal account books in the same carton.

53. In this sense the cohabitation of officers with local women suggests strong similarities to the contemporaneous practice of "barracks concubinage" among the Dutch in the East Indies, on which see Hanneke Ming, "Barracks-Concubinage in the Indies, 1887–1920," *Indonesia* 35 (April 1983), esp. 65–71. In January 1903 Colonel Dagneaud, the officer in charge of Timbuktu's other fort, Fort Bonnier, banned women from the post during the daytime. This restriction was not extended during Altmayer's time to the

spahis at Fort Hugueny, and moreover Dagneaud's objections do not seem to have extended to cohabiting unions; though rumors circulating at the time of the ban labeled him homosexual, Dagneaud later pulled rank and took a fellow officer's consort for himself, breaking his own rules and dismaying his subordinates in the process (Altmayer, carnet 4, 1 January 1903; 12 August 1903). On living arrangements for African soldiers and their wives, see Thompson, "Colonial Policy and the Family Life of Black Troops," 437, 448.

54. Émile Dussaulx, "following Arab custom," marked the consummation of his union with Fatma Hély by displaying her bloodied chemise at the entrance to her family's camp (*Journal du Soudan*, 269); Altmayer does not mention doing the same.

55. Altmayer, carnet 2, 16 December 1901. In an earlier part of the diary (carnet 1, 19 April 1901) Altmayer compares African women's cleanliness favorably to that of women from Lorraine.

56. Altmayer, carnet 2, 17 March 1902. Altmayer had previously received some instruction in the language from the *qadi* (judge), Ahmad Baba bin Abu'l-'Abbas; see Altmayer, carnet 2, 16 October 1901; 16 December 1901.

57. Altmayer, carnet 3, 1 August 1902; carnet 4, 12 January and 8 February 1903.

58. Altmayer, carnet 4, 7 April 1903; carnet 3, 8 August 1902; 15 August 1902.

59. Altmayer, carnet 2, 24 April 1902; also see carnet 3, 14 August 1902.

60. See Altmayer, carnet 4, 1 January 1903.

61. The boy was about seven weeks premature. Altmayer gives a long account of his birth and death in carnet 3, 8 August 1902. See also Archives of the Société des Missionnaires d'Afrique, Rome (the society commonly known at the time as the White Fathers), diary of the mission at Timbuktu, entry from 9 August 1902. For more on the White Fathers' mission in Timbuktu see O. White, "Decivilizing Mission," 542–53.

62. Altmayer, carnet 3, 30 June 1902. On the impact of cattle disease on marriage patterns in 1890s Kenya see L. White, *Comforts of Home*, 32.

63. Altmayer, carnet 3, 23 June 1902; 19 October 1902.

64. Altmayer, carnet 4, 30 August 1903.

65. Altmayer, carnet de dépenses, November 1902 to September 1903.

66. Altmayer, carnet 4, 6 June 1903. In a few entries Altmayer records his own dreams.

67. Altmayer, carnet 4, 30 and 31 August 1903.

68. Archives of the Grand Orient de France, Paris (henceforth GODF), 1829, dossier 2, Marius Leclerc, administrateur des colonies, commandant de la région du Fouta Djallon to Grand Orient de France, 24 October 1905.

The book by Barot was his *Guide pratique de l'Européen dans l'Afrique occidentale* (Paris: Flammarion, 1902), 328–31; see also White, *Children of the French Empire*, 13–14, 51–52.

69. Leclerc claimed that the source of the accusation was a *métis* notable, Justin Devès, whose motive was to prevent Leclerc from exposing his involvement in corruption. On Justin Devès (and allegations of impropriety) see David Robinson, *Paths of Accommodation: Muslim Societies and French Colonial Authorities in Senegal and Mauritania, 1880–1920* (Athens: Ohio University Press, 2000), 110–11.

70. This reasoning bears some resemblance to part of the logic of the British colonial secretary Lord Crewe's Circular of 1909, which argued that for a British colonial administrator to take part in "arrangements of concubinage" with local women risked "lowering himself in the eyes of the natives" and "diminishing his authority." The circular threatened punishment for administrators who continued to involve themselves in such activity. See Ronald Hyam, "Concubinage and the Colonial Service: The Crewe Circular (1909)," *Journal of Imperial and Commonwealth History* 14 (1986), 170–86.

71. Klein, *Slavery and Colonial Rule*, 134–37; Conklin, *Mission to Civilize*, 98. On Freemasons and slavery in French West Africa, as well as Leclerc's Masonic affiliation, see Owen White, "Networking: Freemasons and the Colonial State in French West Africa, 1895–1914," *French History* 19:1 (2005), 102–4.

72. Roume may also have had in mind a brewing scandal in the Futa Jallon region of Guinea that involved an administrator named Hubert, who had taken five local women as his consorts and forced local people to subsidize his extravagant way of life. If Roume was already aware of the extent of the problems in Futa Jallon, however, it would seem somewhat surprising that this was the very area to which Leclerc was reassigned. On this scandal see Emily Lynn Osborn, "Interpreting Colonial Power in French Guinea: The Boubou Penda-Ernest Noirot Affair of 1905," in *Intermediaries, Interpreters, and Clerks: African Employees in the Making of Colonial Africa*, ed. Benjamin N. Lawrance, Emily Lynn Osborn, and Richard L. Roberts (Madison: University of Wisconsin Press, 2006), 56–76; also Klein, *Slavery and Colonial Rule*, 148–50.

73. See the firsthand account of Félicien Challaye, "Au Congo français," in Challaye, *Un livre noir du colonialisme: Souvenirs sur la colonisation* (1935; reprint, Paris: Les Nuits Rouges, 1998), 58–71.

74. GODF 1829, dossier 2, Leclerc to GODF, 24 October 1905. I have not been able to locate a personnel file for Leclerc to learn more about this case.

75. On French West Africa see O. White, *Children of the French Em-*

pire, 23–32, and Alice L. Conklin, "Redefining 'Frenchness': Citizenship, Race Regeneration, and Imperial Motherhood in France and West Africa, 1914–1940," in *Domesticating the Empire: Race, Gender, and Family Life in French and Dutch Colonialism*, ed. Julia Clancy-Smith and Frances Gouda (Charlottesville: University Press of Virginia, 1998), 69–71, 76–82. For a similar pattern in other contexts, see Stoler, *Carnal Knowledge and Imperial Power*, 55–57.

76. Whether the *droit de jambage* (alternately *droit de cuissage* or *droit du seigneur*) was ever or anywhere practiced is strongly disputed by historians. See Alain Boureau, *The Lord's First Night: The Myth of the Droit de Cuissage* (Chicago: University of Chicago Press, 1998).

77. Maurice Prouteaux, "Rapport sur une tournée effectuée dans le canton de Noolou (Côte d'Ivoire) (1913)," in *Le commandant en tournée: Une administration au contact des populations en Afrique Noire coloniale*, ed. Francis Simonis (Paris: Editions Seli Arslan, 2005), 116–19. *Cantons* were administrative units that made up the larger *cercles*. Prouteaux does not say if Muslims were more likely than what he calls "fétichistes" to deflect attention from their daughters; he does, however, observe that "fétichistes" were in the majority in this canton. On Prouteaux's career see Sibeud, *Une science impériale pour l'Afrique?*, 310–11. Prouteaux's comments are all the more notable for the fact that he had served in Côte d'Ivoire since 1904 and would therefore have been aware of the types of practice that might occur. For more on apparent African resistance to temporary unions around this time, see O. White, *Children of the French Empire*, 19–23.

78. The phrase is Stoler's; see *Carnal Knowledge and Imperial Power*, 51.

79. Altmayer, "Notes et études sur le Niger et le Soudan en 1900, rédigées en septembre–octobre 1941." Altmayer commanded the French Xth Army during the defeat to Germany in 1940.

80. Carolyn Podruchny, *Making the Voyageur World: Travelers and Traders in the North American Fur Trade* (Lincoln: University of Nebraska Press, 2006), 11. Matt Matsuda draws some broader connections between love and empire in his *Empire of Love: Histories of France and the Pacific* (New York: Oxford University Press, 2005).

8

The French Colonial Mind and the Challenge of Islam
The Case of Ernest Psichari

KIM MUNHOLLAND

Among the young French intellectuals of the post-Dreyfus years who rebelled against the secular, scientific, and pacifist values of their fathers' generation, none was more uncompromising than Ernest Psichari. A number of accounts, notably that of Agathon (pseudonym for Henri Massis and Alfred de Tarde), prominently feature Ernest Psichari's trajectory from his early secular skepticism and materialism toward the Catholic Church by way of the colonial army.[1] His evolution was typical of a new generation, seen in the experiences of Psichari's friends, Jacques Maritain and Charles Péguy, who embraced a taste for action, celebrated an ardent nationalism under the influence of Maurice Barrès, and searched for spiritual meaning by returning to the Catholic faith.

What distinguishes Psichari's rebellion is that he escaped the confines of republicanism as well as the intellectual atmosphere of Paris by choosing a career in the colonial army. His experiences in the Congo and the desert of Mauritania would convince Psichari that the republic's secular civilizing mission would be inadequate without the church, which provided a spiritual dimension to offset the appeal of Islam in Africa. In going beyond the intellectual confines of Paris, Psichari brought a colonial dimension to this generational rebellion. Most writers on Psichari have cast his African epiphany in personal terms. This essay argues that his moment in the desert and the encounter with Islam reinforced his critique of contemporary France and provided an authoritarian, military, and ardently Catholic map of France's civilizing mission. Although other right-wing intellectuals came to see the importance of the empire as a source of renewal for a decadent France, Psichari used Catholicism as the necessary means to combat the strength of Islam.

The Young Psichari

Grandson on his mother's side of the philologist and biblical scholar Ernest Renan, Psichari has left a series of writings that chronicle a personal, spiritual quest that led first toward a military career in the French colonies and then brought him to the Catholic Church on the eve of the First World War when he entered the Third Order of St. Dominic.[2] Within nine months of Psichari's admission to the Dominican Order, war broke out in Europe, and the young Catholic officer, serving at his colonial army garrison in Cherbourg, went to the front to lead his men in the cause of France. On 22 August 1914, he fell in battle, one of the first casualties of that deadly conflict. Like his friend Charles Péguy, who also had followed a course from republican secularism and pacifism to an ardent French nationalism and who also would be killed in battle, in September 1914, Ernest Psichari became a symbol and martyr for this staunchly nationalistic and intellectually conservative generation's sacrifice.[3]

As a young lycée student, Ernest Psichari adhered to the values of his father's generation. In religious matters he was a skeptic and anticlerical. At the end of the 1890s he became engaged in the great French cause célèbre, the defense of Captain Dreyfus and republican justice in opposition to the military's condemnation of the Jewish officer wrongfully accused of treason. In a lengthy letter to his father, Ernest Psichari deplored the way that "Catholicism and clericalism, anti-Semitism and narrow ideas have invaded France." The lycée student was among those who were active in condemning the forces of reaction, seen in the French Army and the Catholic Church. Yet even in this early, Dreyfusard phase of Ernest's life, he greatly admired France, a France, as he put it, "that surpassed all other nations with its beautiful and great ideas."[4] While Ernest Psichari, at least in his early writings from the Dreyfusard years, had very little to say about France's colonial role, the seeds of his later, ardent nationalism were already present at the time of Dreyfus. The colonial role would follow when he discovered his true France in the Congo and then in the desert of Mauritania, proclaiming that one could serve France, but not the France that had been deformed by the arid debates of the Dreyfusards and their antimilitary republicanism.[5]

Within eight years, the intellectual climate began to change in Paris. No longer was the Psichari household home to the impassioned debates of the Dreyfusard generation. Instead, it had become a gathering place for Ernest Psichari's new friends, Henri Massis, Jacques and Raïssa Maritain, and Charles Péguy, whose publication *Cahiers de la Quinzaine* was a vehicle for the new thinking that gave voice to a younger generation of nationalists and spiritual seekers. Ernest Psichari represented those who preferred action to reason, spiritual values to scientific ones, and a militant nationalism to pacifism and the universal, humanistic beliefs of their fathers. Enlistment in the colonial army enabled Psichari to put into practice the active life admired by Agathon's new generation, and he welcomed the opportunity to become part of France's colonial adventure, at least in military terms. Like others before him, such as Lyautey, Psichari turned to the empire to escape the confines of republican France, but in so doing he would discover France's colonial mission and confront the challenge that other cultures presented in that context. Psichari went to the empire without any fixed ideas about France's civilizing mission abroad but to escape from the confines of Parisian intellectual life and to find a military career of order and authority. At this point he had not yet formulated his view of France's colonial role. If, as yet, he had no clearly discernible "colonial mind," this would take shape once he gained direct experience of empire.

Military Service and the Emergence of a Colonial Mind

What had happened in the space of eight very short but important years? The changes can be found in a personal and intellectual crisis that Psichari had experienced when he was just eighteen. The break came when he was spurned in a love affair. He had become enamored of the elder sister of his friend Jacques Maritain, but she was seven years his senior. Her decision to marry someone else plunged Ernest into despair. He left home and spent several months wandering the streets of Paris in search of menial employment, staying in cheap, rundown hotels, often in the company of prostitutes. He twice attempted suicide and was stopped only by the intervention of a friend. He then decided to bury himself in the army. As he put it in one of his diary entries, the army offered order against disorder, but he worried how his family with its strong antimilitary traditions would react to his decision.[6]

After his initial year of obligatory military service, he decided to enlist in the colonial army. Ernest Psichari's enlistment dismayed his family, as he had feared, and it caught his friends by surprise. Even his superiors were astonished that the grandson of Ernest Renan should embark upon a military career. He informed his parents and his commanding officer that a desire for action and his distaste for Paris and a life as a bureaucrat inspired his decision.[7] He wanted to go on campaign, to seek action, which led him to choose service in the colonial army. In his letters to his mother and to Mme. Jules Favre, who even more than his mother became confidante to his innermost thoughts, he spoke of his spiritual dissatisfaction and his rejection of the skepticism and materialism of metropolitan France. The army appeared to be order against what he perceived as the disorder, the intellectual questioning, the decadence and the spiritual emptiness of his time.[8] This essay examines the way in which Psichari's encounter with Africa and Islam powerfully influenced his conversion to Christianity and the Catholic Church, a personal conversion for him but one that he also made in the name of France's civilizing mission and its true identity. In this way Psichari created a mental map of the French empire that differed from the secular, materialistic vision of the republican-sponsored civilizing mission.[9]

Psichari's first assignment as a colonial soldier was in the French Congo, where he participated in a military exploration sponsored by the Geographic Society of Paris that was led by Psichari's mentor, Major Lenfant, to the region (later, a colony) then known as Ubangi-Shari south of Lake Chad. Here Psichari had contacts with native soldiers, porters, and the local population, of whom many had not seen a white person before. Psichari found the region physically attractive, but he was not impressed with the absence of a true religion among the practitioners of animism. Although now very much engaged in his military career and a life of action rather than contemplation, Psichari maintained his intellectual activity. He began his writing career with a series of journal entries that would be published after his death as *Carnets de Route*. These reflections served as the basis for his first autobiographical novella, *Terres de Soleil et de Sommeil*, in which he explored his contact with Africa and also extolled the military life, its action, and its discipline.

Like other colonial soldiers Psichari considered the colonial experience to have been an opportunity for renewal, a school for those who, like himself, were fleeing what they considered to be the narrow confines and rigid expectations of life in France. Beyond the personal, the colonial experience was an opportunity to reinvigorate a decadent metropolitan France, a renewal of the French race and a France that in gendered and racist terms seemingly had lost its (male) vitality. In Psichari's mind Africa was seen as a space that would restore moral force to Western man.[10] Psichari, then, would rediscover and remake himself through a sense of strength and domination, but he also would find the source for a national revival and spiritual renewal in Africa. He would argue that Africa was essential for France. In Africa a French soldier was able to maintain the virtues that had been lost in Europe.[11] During the exploration of the Congo he would experience his first cultural encounter with Islam. In his initial contact Psichari was in the role of the outsider, the scientific observer and analyst, very much in the tradition of his father the philologist or of his grandfather Renan's historical, scientific approach to religion. His was an intellectual exercise in understanding a foreign culture. A more profound, personal, and emotional engagement with Islam would follow in which he would see in Islam a powerful source of resistance to France's civilizing mission.

At first Psichari considered the Congo to be a land without any spiritual meaning, whose inhabitants lived "absolutely without religion," but a prolonged stay of ten months at Binder provided an opportunity for him to gain a favorable impression of Islam. He engaged in conversations with his fellow soldiers from Senegal concerning their faith, although he did not believe that they were very deeply religious. At this point Psichari shared the views of other French Islamists that Islam in sub-Saharan Africa was less sophisticated and less devout than the Islam preached and practiced in the north.[12] In his account of these early encounters in *Terres de Soleil et de Sommeil* Psichari reflected the influence of Renan, whose works he had read, including his grandfather's critical account of Islam in his essay "Mahomet et les origines de l'Islam" in *Études d'histoire réligieuse*, in which Renan argued that Islam had missed the turn toward modernity.[13] Nevertheless, Psichari was greatly impressed with the calm and peace that Islam seemed to give its practitioners. He much admired the broad knowledge of an Islamic cleric at Binder, who enjoyed a great influence in the region. Not only was he conversant with the subtleties of the Qurʾan, but he also had "a perfect knowledge of Christianity."[14] Islam was a true civilization, although Psichari, reflecting Renan's assessment, looked to the Islam of the past and its glories, not the Islam of his own day. His initial appreciation of Islam was more aesthetic, an admiration for an influence that had shaped the culture of central African cities. In this initial encounter Psichari was less concerned with Islam's religious or spiritual message than its aesthetic and cultural impact. However, toward the end of his first African tour of duty, Psichari encountered a Marabout at Carnot, and he began to consider what attitude France should adopt in response to the spread of Islam among Africans. Although he was sensitive to the Islamist revival sweeping through West Africa in the late nineteenth century, at this point he believed that Islam was not dangerous nor a threat to France's colonial domination, but it could become so in the future.[15] On his second trip to Africa and his encounter with *Islam maure*, Psichari's reaction would be quite different.

Psichari's first African tour satisfied his taste for the authority that the military provided. The army was the instrument of France's domination, and he gloried in this manifestation of French power and achievement. France had demonstrated its vitality by imposing its will overseas, having lost nothing of its martial traditions, despite the pacifist sentiments of his father's generation.[16] He had come to fulfill himself as a military crusader and looked upon colonial service as a form of crusade on behalf of French civilization and its traditions. He extolled the military life and reveled in the exhilaration that it provided. His military experience was chronicled in another book, begun while he was in the Congo and published on his return, *L'Appel des Armes*, which enjoyed a tremendous popular success, including praise from General Lyautey. For Psichari the sword was the instrument of French glory and the colonies the place where France would be renewed and reinvigorated.

In the Congo Psichari had found a passion for writing, beginning first with his diary, later published as his *Carnets de route*, in which he recorded his reflections and thoughts, evidence of his personal voyage of discovery, followed by the appearance of his novel of colonial military life, *L'Appel des Armes* in which the hero, Maxence, a thinly disguised Psichari, rebels against the conventional life of metropolitan France to pursue a more challenging and risky adventure in the colonial army. At this point Maxence still had not defined his new life, and it meant separating himself from an "intellectualism that had failed." The path ahead was uncertain, but Maxence/Psichari's quest for order and authority had begun. The lure of military service and the empire in Africa offered adventure and risk.[17] His spiritual quest had not yet begun. In a reply to a letter from Maritain, who hoped that he would return from his solitary adventures believing in God, Psichari readily admitted that he found the church's values superior to those of the positivists and rationalists of the day. While he was attracted to the house, he informed his good friend, he was not yet ready to enter.[18] That would come on his second tour in Africa in the deserts of Mauritania, where a more profound encounter with Islam would be the precipitating event.

Upon his return to France from his fifteen months in the Congo in 1908, Psichari was admitted to the officer training school at Versailles. He would spend a year gaining his commission as a lieutenant in the colonial artillery. During this time he engaged in conversations with his friends Henri Massis, Jacques Maritain, and Charles Péguy. They also attended the lectures of Henri Bergson at the Collège de France and were impressed with the philosopher's critique of scientific rationalism. Their discussions often focused upon religion and the vital contribution that Catholicism played in French culture. Maritain pressed Psichari to make a commitment to the church, but Psichari still hesitated to make his formal conversion, despite his admiration for the church and its spiritual message.

Psichari's Second Encounter with Africa

After graduating from officer training, Psichari returned to Africa, this time going to Mauritania, where in the solitude of the desert he would encounter a particularly fervent Islam. In his novella *Le Voyage du Cen-*

turion, which was based upon his experiences in Mauritania, Psichari wrote of the powerful appeal that Islam had for those French who had lost their faith.[19] A sense of Islam's impact upon Psichari may be found in a letter that Ernest wrote to his sister, Henriette, at the end of his time in Mauritania. "You cannot imagine," he wrote, "what it is to live three years in a country where everyone prays."[20] In his *L'Appel des Armes* the protagonist, Maurice Vincent, cried out when confronted by Muslims at prayer, "Me too, my dear children, I have my prayers and I have my good God." Later he expressed his shame over his own "race," which had become incapable of such adoration. In the face of this religious conviction, Vincent expressed his humiliation at being on Muslim territory, and he deplored the irreligious attitude of the West. Here the encounter with Islam reminded him of the lack of spirituality in his own cultural heritage and decisively influenced the way he assessed the limitations of the republican ethos at home; and he would soon challenge that republican ethos in its imperial setting. In this way Psichari brought to the empire, as had other colonial soldiers, "their own metropolitan preoccupations and political battles."[21]

The danger of irreligion was a threat to the France that he had discovered in Mauritania.[22] His response to such Islamic fervor brought Psichari to the brink of embracing an ardent Catholicism, and it was in the course of his experience in Mauritania that his break with the ideas and ideals of his father and his father's generation became even more apparent. His encounter with Islam challenged his own culture and the materialism that had come to dominate the republican ethos of France. He would conclude that only by returning to the traditions of the past, particularly in religion, could France be saved and find the strength to confront the challenge posed by Islam. Simple military strength and physical domination were not enough. The colonial experience itself had configured Psichari's map of empire as part of his map of a true France that had been lost under the republic. He now wrote of a France that was "military and Christian" at home and abroad.[23]

During this second voyage to Africa, Psichari embarked upon a serious, scholarly study of Islam and its manifestation in the desert. In his pursuit of an understanding of Islam, Psichari began to learn Arabic. The Moors of Mauritania impressed him in a way that the people of

Congo had not. They were a nomadic people divided into two groups, the religious Marabout and the Warriors, and the Marabout scholars possessed a sophisticated philosophic tradition, thus refuting Renan's judgment that fanaticism had stifled Islam's intellectual development.[24] Psichari once more engaged in conversations with the Muslims serving the French forces. While he previously had had contact with the Muslim Senegalese *tirailleurs* on duty with the colonial army, he had considered them to be superficial in their religious commitment and overall cultural sophistication. But he was greatly impressed by three guides, who came from among the political and religious elite of Mauritania. With them a discussion of religious questions could take place on an equal basis. Mohammed Fadel and two other guides, identified only as Ahmed and Sidïa, provided him with an understanding of the depth and strength of the Muslim faith among the Moors of Mauritania.[25] Psichari's language skills enabled him to have a far deeper discussion of religion than had been possible during his first expedition in the upper Congo, and he was impressed with the power of Islam. Psichari's encounter with Islam in Mauritania produced his own map of empire and held a lesson for metropolitan France as well. If only his countrymen could see Islam, he wrote, they would understand what the French owed to Christian thought.[26]

Psichari greatly admired the Islamic culture of Sheik Mohammed Fadel, whose spirituality turned the colonial officer toward religious contemplation and an assessment of France's religious heritage.[27] Psichari established a strong and respectful relationship with Fadel in the course of conversations about Islam and Christianity. They exchanged texts from the two religions as the starting point for their dialogue. Fadel, Psichari noted, was more open and less prejudiced against Christianity than other Muslims with whom he had contact. Yet Fadel made no concessions to the French or their civilization, and from these conversations Psichari concluded that Islam represented an alien culture. Each held to his convictions: "He remained a Moor, I remained French."[28]

For Psichari the possibility of Muslim assimilation or even accommodation under a republican colonial ethos appeared to be another mistaken idea.[29] French techniques of pacification in which accommodation was sought with moderate Islamists, such as Sidiyya Baba, to bring order and stability against a more radical, fundamentalist Islam preached by Ma' al 'Aynayn was no more than a temporary political solution that did not resolve the underlying issue of religious and cultural difference. In adopting this position, Psichari considered himself to be at odds with French Islamic specialists, who believed that favoring the more quiescent version of Islam practiced by traditional Islamic elites would undermine and check the more radical movements within Islam.[30] In the desert Psichari discovered what would later be described as a clash of civilizations. Psichari realized that not only he personally but also France as a nation needed a spiritual strength to match the fervor of Islam. Under the secular republic this force was missing. The belief that accommodation with moderate Islam would establish a French claim to be a "Muslim power" in its imperial mission was an error. In Psichari's eyes French strength derived from its role as a Christian power, and efforts to cast France as a Muslim power betrayed his conception of true France. Psichari concluded that France as an imperial nation could prevail by becoming the France that he admired: the France of St. Louis, Joan of Arc, Bossuet, and Pascal, a France "that is above all military and Christian." As Psichari saw it, the health of France and, therefore, "that of the world and civilization itself" depended upon the spiritual and intellectual renewal advocated by the generation that came of age in France at the beginning of the twentieth century.[31] This would be the civilization of a France that held to its religious traditions that the secular republican rationalists had dismissed in the name of scientific progress and a materialistic civilization.

The decisive revelation came during a visit in the company of his Muslim companions to Port Étienne, where an electric generator had been constructed to power a radio station that could reach all of French West Africa.[32] Psichari thought that this technical achievement would impress the nomads of the desert, and he pointed to this accomplishment as a sign of French power and authority. He turned to one of his Muslim companions, Sidïa, noting the folly of Africans resisting a people as rich and powerful as the French. Sidïa replied in a way that stunned Psichari: "You French, you have the realm of the earth, but we, the Moors, we have the realm of heaven."[33] Psichari's encounter with Islam thus challenged his own culture and its scientific, material values.

Ironically, Psichari had invoked a scientific, technological achievement, much prized in the republican ideology of progress and its civilizing mission, to convince his Muslim companions of the strength and accomplishments of French civilization. At this moment Psichari realized that neither military dominance nor material progress were enough to establish French claims to superiority. Even more, Sidïa's comment meant that the policy of mutual accommodation with the Sidiyya, in which the French exercised political and military control and left the realm of Islam to the Muslims, gave only short-term temporal advantages to the French imperial authorities. In the long run it was the spiritual world that would endure and have an impact, particularly with the emergence of a more militant Islam following World War I that would challenge the policy of accommodation. While this encounter in the desert brought Psichari to his own personal conversion, it was one in which he also embraced Catholicism in the name of France and its civilizing mission in Africa.

The importance of Psichari's confrontation with Sidïa may be seen in the reference made to it in all of his communications from Mauritania back home to Maritain, Massis, and Barrès, as well as to Monsigneur Jalabert in Dakar. Psichari thus provided a personal and a religious map of empire and of France that was at odds with the secular accommodations of the republican map of empire. The stress upon the church's role in advancing the French colonial project was not, though, to be construed as a call for a crusade. "We no longer have the spirit of the Crusades," he wrote, but France would only prevail in Africa insofar as "the strength of our faith can gain the respect of the Muslim population." France would have a successful imperial policy when, showing respect for the beliefs of the Muslims, "we remain fervently attached to our own."[34] Psichari was calling neither for a religious conversion nor the triumph of secular modernity, but for a policy of association in which an ardent French faith in Christianity would impress religious Muslims.

What the French had, Psichari believed, was the civilization of Christendom, and this tradition was necessary if France were to prevail spiritually as well as militarily in Africa. Earlier he had written that in Africa France was "indeed alone in our pride and our domination."[35] France could secure its domain in Africa by compelling the Moors to respect the religion of France. In a crucial passage of his letter to Monseigneur Jalabert he wrote, "During the six years I have known the African Muslims, I have realized the folly of certain moderns who want to separate the French race from the religion which has made it what it is, and whence comes all its greatness."[36] Only by returning to the spiritual tradition of the church could France prevail. Psichari's conversion, which followed, was at once personal but also made in the name of imperial France. In response to Sidïa's challenge to the French colonial regime Psichari sent Msgr. Jalabert a contribution for the construction of a cathedral at Dakar, which would be an assertion of French spiritual power and civilization against Islam's challenge and would, as he put it in a letter to Massis, "modify the strange idea that the Muslims have of us."[37]

Reflections on Islam

Ernest Psichari's experience may be found in his last published work of fiction, the autobiographical novella *Le Voyage du Centurion*, which appeared after his death. In this autobiographical novella the protagonist, Maxence, observes that the so-called educators and masters of French literature, such as Maxence's own father, had forgotten the existence of a soul, of the human capacity for belief, love, and hope.[38] Through Maxence, Ernest Psichari thanked Africa for having saved him from "a detestable life."[39] Above all he rejected everything that was "modern." The army and the church represented French traditions that were eternal in opposition to the forces of change and progress. "Progress is one form of Americanism," he has his protagonist of *L'Appel des Armes* complain, "and Americanism disgusted him."[40] In another passage he had two generations confronting one another: "By a kind of transmutation of values, it was the father who represented the present and the son who represented the past, the son who turned toward history and the father who appealed to the future" in the name of progress rather than tradition.[41]

The strength of the Christian faith confronted by the Muslim challenge appears in an unpublished work, *Nuit d'Afrique*, a play in verse that most critics agree is best left unpublished. Nevertheless this sketch outlines Psichari's uncompromising attitude toward Islam and its relationship to Christianity. In the play the Moors hold captive one of the two main characters, Fortis. If he converts to Islam, his life will be spared, but if he refuses, he will die. Although he has been an agnostic up to this point, Fortis chooses to die with a prayer on his lips. Here, presumably, is Psichari embracing Christianity in the face of another civilization. Moreover, this is religion tied to France, as Fortis realizes that if he accepted the Koran, he would renounce his own country. In the *Voyage du Centurion* the protagonist, Maxence, experiences the same "national" and religious evolution.[42]

Rejecting both his father's and grandfather Renan's scientific materialism, Psichari was almost ready to enter the church. Struggling with his own conscience and knowing the pain that his conversion would cause his father and his mother as well, Psichari hesitated until the eve of his return to France at the end of 1912. In August he wrote to Mme. Favre that tradition rather than dogma attracted him to the church, and in a letter to Maritain two months earlier he admitted that he still lacked faith and divine grace.[43] Then, on the eve of his return he wrote to Maritain that his days of meditation in the desert had brought him to God.[44] In the crucial first weeks of 1913 he would find the faith and divine grace that would bring him fully into the church.

And he did convert. He decided to take up the faith that his father and his grandfather had abandoned. On 4 February 1913 Psichari read his confession of faith in a small chapel in the Maritain household where he received the benediction of the priest present. He also received absolution and was assured that his Greek Orthodox baptism was valid, something that he had questioned during his time in Africa. The following Saturday he became confirmed by Monsigneur Gibier, the bishop of Versailles. The next day he took his first communion. Father Clérissac, a Dominican who had been a major guiding spirit for Psichari, said mass, and Jacques Maritain assisted. That afternoon under a brilliant sky they made a pilgrimage to Chartres.[45] Ernest Psichari's conversion to the Catholic faith was complete and wholehearted. His religious odyssey would continue, culminating in his initiation into the Dominican Order. The discipline and asceticism of the Dominicans appealed to Psichari, and his decision to enter the Dominican Order marked a decisive turn toward the church and a step beyond his earlier commitment to the traditions of the army. His African experience had made Psichari a military and a religious crusader. Whether he would have left the army for his religious vocation cannot be known. For the moment he intended to continue active military service as a lay member of the Dominican Order, expecting to be sent to Morocco in October of 1914 while he prepared for a further advancement in the Dominican Order. He was, though, strongly committed to a French colonial mission strengthened by a religion strong enough to confront Islam. In a late letter to the Abbé Georges Tournebise, Psichari spoke of the need for priests overseas in the service of France.[46]

He then completed his work on *Voyage du Centurion*, which he regarded as a kind of repentance for his previous work, *L'Appel des Armes*, which he considered not sufficiently devout since it was written before his religious conversion. The book won critical acclaim, particularly among those close to the anti-republican, nationalist *Action Française* and its editor, Charles Maurras. A number of Catholic writers also praised it. This would be his final work of fiction (*Les Voix qui crient dans le desert*, his diary account of his experience in Mauritania, would appear in 1920), and he would never make the next step in his religious vocation. Whatever the future might have held, Ernest Psichari had completed his pilgrimage toward an absolute devotion to France's military and religious heritage. He would give his life in the service of this national devotion.

Conclusion

Little remembered today, Psichari's writings and life have left a legacy that has been variously interpreted. On one level Psichari's experience in Africa and his call for an active Catholic Church role in the advancement of the French imperial project would seemingly confirm J. P. Daughton's argument that an instrumental, if often fraught, accommodation between republicanism and Catholic missionaries who found common, national cause in advancing the civilizing mission of France came to mutually reinforce France's civilizing mission in the empire. That the confessional issue was less divisive in the empire could be seen when General Gouraud went to Dakar in 1935 to represent France at the dedication of the Dakar Cathedral. Gouraud cited three examples of ways in which such divisions over confessional matters were set aside, including a full citation of Psichari's letter to Monsigneur Jalabert, cited above, in which Psichari had insisted upon the need for a powerful Catholic presence and a cathedral in Dakar to confirm the spiritual strength of France as a way to impress the Muslims.[47] Psichari wished to restore the Catholic Church for France, for its true civilization, and for its place in the world as a colonizing power. His ardent nationalism, along with the writings of Péguy, had an impact upon the young Charles de Gaulle, but Vichy and Henri Massis also praised his call for a return to traditional values and identified his search for order, authority, and hierarchy with Vichy's own National Revolution in the tropics.[48] However, it is in his critique of modernity and purely material progress divorced from spiritual values, as seen in the Third Republic's ideology, that his views represented, perhaps more than any other of the "Agathon generation," a conservative, religiously inspired critique of a republican assumption that modernization (to cite a recent formulation) in the form of "science, technology, urbanization and education would 'disenchant' the charmed world of believers."[49] For Psichari the spiritual strength of the church, not material progress, was essential to counter what he perceived to be the persistent force of Islam's challenge to France's true civilizing mission.

Notes

1. The young generation has been described in several texts, among them Agathon (pseudonym for Henri Massis and Alfred de Tarde), *Les jeunes gens d'aujourd'hui* (Paris: Plon-Nourrit, 1913); Richard Griffiths, *The Reactionary Revolution: The Catholic Revival in French Literature, 1870–1914* (London: Constable, 1966); Robert Wohl, *The Generation of 1914* (Cambridge MA: Harvard University Press, 1979); and Ronald Thomas Sussex, *The Sacrificed Generation: Studies of Charles Péguy, Ernest Psichari, and Alain-Fournier* (Townsville: James Cook University of North Queensland, 1980). Important works on Ernest Psichari include a recent study based upon new archival sources, Frédérique Neau-Dufour, *Ernest Psichari: L'ordere et l'errance* (Paris: Les Éditions du Cerf, 2001); Wallace Fowlie, *Ernest Psichari: A Study in Religious Conversion* (New York: Longmans, 1939); Eugen Weber, "Psichari and God," *Yale French Studies* 12 (Fall–Winter 1953), 19–53; Alec G. Hargreaves, *The Colonial Experience in French Fiction: A Study of Pierre Loti, Ernest Psichari and Pierre Mille* (London: Macmillan, 1981); Henri Massis, *La vie d'Ernest Psichari* (Paris: Librairie de l'art catholique, 1916); Massis, *Notre ami Psichari* (Paris: Flammarion, 136); Henri Daniel-Rops, *Psichari*

(1942; revised ed., Paris: Plon, 1947); A.-M. Goichon, *Ernest Psichari d'après des documents inédits* (1925; reprint, Paris: Louis Conard, 1946); Paul Pédech, *Ernest Psichari ou les chemins de l'ordre* (Paris: Tequi, 1988); and Paul M. Cohen, *Piety and Politics: Catholic Revival and the Generation of 1905–1914 in France* (New York: Garland, 1987).

2. Massis, *Notre ami Psichari*, 230.

3. Sussex, *Sacrificed Generation*.

4. Letter from Ernest Psichari to his father, 13 July 1898, in *Oeuvres complètes de Ernest Psichari* (Paris: Conard, 1948), 3: 110–13. All translations are by the author unless otherwise noted.

5. Ernest Psichari, *L'Appel des Armes*, in *Oeuvres complètes*, 2:151.

6. Henriette Psichari, *Ernest Psichari, mon frère* (Paris: Plon, 1933), 107. In his analysis of Psichari, Hargreaves considers his writings to be the outpourings of a social maladjustment and emotional extremism more than a reflection of the young generation's new thinking. See Hargreaves, *Colonial Experience in French Fiction*, 89.

7. Letter from Ernest Psichari to his father, 2 February 1904, *Lettres du Centurion*, in *Oeuvres complètes*, 3:125–27.

8. Henriette Psichari, introduction to *Oeuvres complètes*, 1:15, 17.

9. In a recent reconsideration of the conflict between church and state in the French Empire, J. P. Daughton notes the way in which conflicting values of republicanism and clericalism became two strands within the civilizing mission overseas; see J. P. Daughton, *An Empire Divided: Religion, Republicanism, and the Making of French Colonialism, 1880–1914* (New York: Oxford University Press, 2006), 9.

10. Neau-Dufour, *Ernest Psichari*, 169.

11. E. Psichari, *L'Appel des Armes*, in *Oeuvres complètes*, 2:140.

12. Christopher Harrison, *France and Islam in West Africa, 1860–1960* (Cambridge: Cambridge University Press, 1988), 2; David Robinson, *Paths of Accommodation: Muslim Societies and French Colonial Authorities in Senegal and Mauritania, 1880–1920* (Athens: Ohio University Press, 2000), 95. Robinson notes the distinction between *Islam noir* and *Islam maure*. The latter is what Psichari would encounter on his second tour in Mauritania.

13. Cited by Marie-Hélène Ryckmans, "L'Islam et la conversion de Psichari," part 1, *Les Lettres Romanes* 12:4 (1958), 397.

14. Ernest Psichari, *Carnets de Route* in *Oeuvres complètes*, 1:37.

15. Ryckmans, "L'Islam et la conversion de Psichari," 400–401.

16. Hargreaves, *Colonial Experience in French Fiction*, 94–95.

17. E. Psichari, *L'Appel des Armes*, in *Oeuvres complètes*, 2:32.

18. Letter from Ernest Psichari to Jacques Maritain, 6 August 1908, in *Oeuvres complètes*, 3:130; and H. Psichari, *Ernest Psichari, mon frère*, 129.

19. Ernest Psichari, *Les Voix qui crient dans le desert*, in *Oeuvres complètes*, 2:193; and in *Le Voyage*, cited in Neau-Dufour, *Ernest Psichari*, 216.

20. H. Psichari, *Ernest Psichari, mon frère*, cited in Ryckmans, "L'Islam et la conversion de Psichari," 402.

21. Harrison, *France and Islam*, 4.

22. E. Psichari *Les Voix*, in *Oeuvres complètes*, 2:193.

23. E. Psichari, *Les Voix*, in *Oeuvres complètes*, 2:235.

24. Ernest Renan, *Averroès et averroïsme* (Paris: Calmann-Lévy, 4th ed.): 4–5; cited in E. Psichari, *Les Voix*, in *Oeuvres complètes*, 2:409.

25. Sidïa was one of the Sidiyya coalition that under the leadership of Sidiyya Baba had chosen to cooperate with French forces during Colonel Gouraud's pacification of Adrar in 1908–9. In turn the French favored the moderate Sidiyya Baba as an alternative to the fundamentalist opponent of French penetration in the Sahara, Ma' al 'Aynayn. Sidiyya Baba's accommodation with the French earned him the sobriquet "the Marabout of the Whites." See Robinson, *Paths of Accommodation*, 92–93, 184. Marie-Hélène Ryckmans, "L'Islam et la conversion de Psichari," part 2, *Les Lettres Romanes* 13:1 (1959), 20–21.

26. E. Psichari, *Les Voix*, in *Oeuvres complètes*, 2:245.

27. Colonel Gouraud, who conducted the military pacification of Adrar, identified Sheik Mohammed Fadel as one of the more celebrated of the nomadic Marabout scholars from the region. Colonel Gouraud, *La Pacification de la Mauritanie: Journal des marches et operations de la colonne de l'Adrar* (Paris: Comité de l'Afrique française, 1910), 277.

28. E. Psichari, *Les Voix*, in *Oeuvres complètes*, 2:205.

29. Recent scholarship prefers "accommodation" to describe the complexity of arrangements between colonizers and colonized during the process of pacification, avoiding the ideological implications of "collaboration." See David Robinson and Jean-Louis Triaud, eds., *Le Temps des marabout: Itineraries et stratégies islamiques en Afrique occidentale française* (Paris: Karthala, 1997), 13–14, cited in Ruth Ginio, *French Colonialism Unmasked: The Vichy Years in French West Africa* (Lincoln: University of Nebraska Press, 2006), 139–40.

30. Sean Hanretta, *Islam and Social Change in French West Africa: History of a Emancipatory Community* (New York: Cambridge University Press, 2009), 140. Cooperation—or accommodation—with local elites had become a tried technique of colonial military pacification. In an earlier context see J. Kim Munholland, "'Collaboration Strategy' and the French Pacification of Tonkin, 1885-1897," *Historical Journal* 24:3 (1981), 629-50.

31. E. Psichari, *Les Voix*, in *Oeuvres complètes*, 2:235–36, 242.

32. Hargreaves notes that this episode appears in five places in Psichari's work, three times in his letters, once in *Les Voix*, and once in *Le Voyage du Centurion*. See Hargreaves, *Colonial Experience in French Fiction*, 101.

33. Letter from Ernest Psichari to Maurice Barrès, 15 June 1912, in *Oeuvres complètes*, 3:229, cited by H. Psichari, introduction to *Oeuvres complètes*, 1:15. Several writers have noted the exchange with Sidïa as the decisive moment that brought Psichari's conversion to Catholicism. See Hargreaves, *Colonial Experience in French Fiction*, 101, and Ryckmans, part 2, "L'Islam et la conversion de Psichari," 39–41.

34. E. Psichari, *Les Voix* in *Oeuvres complètes*, 2:318–19.

35. Ernest Psichari, *Terres de Soleil et de Sommeil*, in *Oeuvres complètes*, 1:270; Neau-Dufour, *Ernest Psichari*, 216.

36. Letter from Ernest Psichari to Monsigneur Jalabert, bishop of Senegambia in Dakar, [ca. 30 septembre] 1912, *Oeuvres complètes*, 3:233, cited in Weber, "Psichari and God," 24; see also Neau-Dufour, *Ernest Psichari*, 216–17, 225–27. In his letter to Monseigneur Jalabert, Psichari noted that he sent the donation as a member of the Eastern Church since his conversion to Catholicism had not yet occurred. On the impact of Islam on Psichari's conversion, Ryckmans, "L'Islam et la conversion de Psichari," part 1, 389–413, and part 2, 19–44.

37. Letter from Ernest Psichari to Monsigneur Jalabert, *Oeuvres complètes*, 3:233. As Hargreaves notes, Psichari saw in Sidïa's comment a threat to the colonial regime. Hargreaves, *Colonial Experience in French Fiction*, 102.

38. Cited in Peyrade, *Psichari: Maître de grandeur*, 24.

39. Ernest Psichari, *Voyage du Centurion* in *Oeuvres complètes*, 3:42.

40. E. Psichari, *L'Appel des Armes*, in *Oeuvres complètes*, 2:25.

41. E. Psichari, *L'Appel des Armes*, in *Oeuvres complètes*, 2:93.

42. Neau-Dufour, *Ernest Psichari*, 200–201.

43. Letters from Ernest Psichari to Mme. Jules Favre, 26 August 1912, and Jacques Maritain, 15 June 1912, in *Lettres*, in *Oeuvres complètes*, 3:230–31, 224–27, cited in Weber, "Psichari and God," 24–25.

44. Letter from Ernest Psichari to Jacques Maritain, December 1912, in *Lettres*, in *Oeuvres complètes*, 3:239.

45. Pédech, *Ernest Psichari*, 162–64.

46. E. Psichari, *Lettres du Centurion* in *Oeuvres complètes* 3:302.

47. Henri-Joseph Gouraud, *Mauritanie, Adrar: Souvenirs d'un Africain* (Paris: Plon, 1945), 323–25.

48. Psichari as well as Péguy was one of those "myriad of forces from previous decades" that helped shape Vichy's colonial vision. See Eric Jen-

nings, *Vichy in the Tropics: Pétain's National Revolution in Madagascar, Guadeloupe, and Indochina, 1940–1945* (Stanford CA: Stanford University Press, 2001), 23. In 1943 Henri Massis commended Psichari as a guide out of uncertainty and doubt enabling the resurrection of "notre armée, notre marine, notre Empire, notre Patrie meme." Henri Massis, "Psichari: Conférence donnée au Prytanée le 28 janvier 1943" (Le Pryttanée-Valence, 1943), 47.

49. See the assessment of Mark Lilla, "The Politics of God," *New York Times Magazine*, 19 August 2007, section 6, p. 50.

9

French Race Theory, the Parisian Society of Anthropology, and the Debate over *la Force Noire*, 1909–1912

JOE LUNN

After three years of often acrimonious public debate, on 7 February 1912 France initiated a policy of compulsory military recruitment in West Africa designed to create *la force noire* for eventual use in Europe should the need arise. During the next four decades about 725,000 West Africans were conscripted into the French Army as a result of this policy, most of whom served as combatants on the Western Front during two world wars. This temporary enforced migration of Africans to Europe has never been surpassed in scale, while the unintended effects of this unprecedented cross-cultural encounter ranged far beyond the outcome on the battlefields. This essay examines one critical aspect of this unique policy: the fashion in which a small coterie of prewar military advocates drew upon and appropriated social science theory to help sanction the implementation of the recruitment program. In so doing it also affords an opportunity to examine the racial preconceptions underpinning the creation of *la force noire* and the consequences these ideas—perpetuated in French military doctrine over more than forty years—had for the individual soldiers affected.

This analysis addresses three principle themes: (1) the arguments advanced by prewar proponents of undertaking expanded recruitment in West Africa, which laid the foundations for the subsequent military deployment of these soldiers; (2) the debate between 1909 and 1912 in metropolitan France about the advisability of implementing such a policy, with emphasis on the Société d'anthropologie de Paris and the intellectual validation advocates sought to obtain for their ideas from it; and (3) the consequences for African soldiers of the application of race theory to them during two world wars. In so doing I hope not only to shed new light on French military views of Africans at the beginning of the twentieth century but also to exemplify the very real human consequences of the interplay between theory and practice.

La Force Noire *and the Origins of the French Recruitment Policy*

The origins of the French recruitment policy in West Africa during the twentieth century were rooted in the particular exigencies of France's military situation prior to 1914. Having suffered defeat, occupation, and the loss of Alsace-Lorraine to Germany in 1871, the French, despite public avowals of *revanche* as the sacred aim of national policy, had seen their military position vis-à-vis their former foe progressively deteriorate. This was due to the ever increasing demographic disparity existing between France, with a stagnant prewar population of 39 million, and Germany, with a growing population of 64 million and, hence, the discrepancy in the size of the armies the two countries could mobilize in the event of war. As a result reliance on domestic conscription (especially for only a two-year term of service after 1905) was increasingly viewed as an inadequate guarantee of national security amid an atmosphere of escalating international tensions. Under these circumstances France sought to enhance its military strength on the eve of the First World War: conscription was introduced in Algeria in 1912, and a year later the size of the peacetime army was significantly increased with the adoption of a three-year service law.[1]

It was within this general context that the idea of augmenting French strength through the extensive recruitment of West Africans was advanced.[2] This proposal represented a dramatic departure from the previous use of African troops by all other colonial powers; the scheme aimed at transforming a small, mercenary army designed for duty in Africa into a much larger force intended for eventual use in Europe. Although such ideas remained anathema to other European powers, the efficacy of this proposal was nevertheless widely debated in France on the eve of the war.³ As discussed, the outcome of the metropolitan discourse on this proposal not only exemplified the primacy of defense considerations over all other matters but also affords telling insights into the French image of Africans during the first decade of the twentieth century.

The idea of undertaking extensive recruitment in sub-Saharan Africa was initially propagated by a small coterie of "Soudanese" officers in the French Colonial Army. Citing their experiences there during the conquest, and during the military administration of Afrique Occidentale Française (AOF) thereafter, these officers—including Generals Louis Archinard, Henri de Lacroix, Charles Perreaux, and Marie Audéoud—contended that one solution to the shortage of French effectives lay in making use of colonial troops for service overseas.[4] The most visible and ardent exponent of this doctrine after 1910 was, however, Lieutenant Colonel (later General) Charles Mangin. Born in Lorraine of a military family—two of his brothers were killed in colonial service—he was Catholic (during an era of post-Dreyfus republican anticlerical sentiment) and a social conservative. As a career colonial officer and *Commandant supérieur des troupes* du Groupe de l'Afrique Occidentale Française between 1907 and 1911, he was also uniquely placed to argue in favor of the efficacy of adopting such a policy.[5] In 1910, at the official behest of the Governor-General William Ponty of French West Africa, he conducted an extensive tour of the colonies to determine the feasibility of undertaking expanded recruitment and concluded, not surprisingly, that such a policy was possible and would permit the creation of a reserve of 40,000 additional soldiers, raised in increments over four years of 10,000 annually.[6] Concurrently a publicity campaign was launched in metropolitan France in which Mangin's proposals appeared in two articles published in the *Revue de Paris* in 1909; these were followed the next year by the book *La Force Noire*, which elaborated upon his earlier ideas and crystallized in the popular imagination the arguments in favor of the use of African troops.[7] In these works, as well as in a series of other reports presented to a more restricted audience of French military and government officials and other African "specialists," Mangin advanced a series of points designed to demonstrate the desirability of implementing a program of colonial conscription.

Mangin argued that the long-term strategic solution to the growing demographic imbalance between France and Germany lay in the creation of a large African reserve for use in the event of a European war: "If the struggle is prolonged, our African troops would constitute an almost indefinite reserve—the source of which is beyond the reach of the enemy. And they would allow us to continue fighting until we obtain a first victory, and once victory is with us, we can pursue it until our final triumph."[8] The efficacy of this proposal was based on three military premises: that West Africa contained sufficient numbers of young men to create such a reservoir, that military recruitment among them was feasible, and that such troops, once they were raised, would make good soldiers.

Mangin advanced support for the first proposition by employing a combination of historical and demographic arguments. Citing often inflated military estimates of the size of the West African armies during the conquest, Mangin contended that collectively more than 300,000 soldiers had been under arms.[9] Furthermore, estimating the population of French West Africa at 10,000,000 and comparing recruitment levels there to the numbers drafted annually in metropolitan France—an industrial rather than an agrarian society as existed in AOF—he contended that an annual contingent of 55,000 ought to be available.[10] Based on these calculations, Mangin concluded that the human reservoir that could be tapped in West Africa was certainly sufficient to sustain expanded recruitment of 7,500 per year.[11]

Mangin also contended that recruitment would be welcomed by West Africans, and they would make excellent soldiers. He based these premises on a series of racist theories consistent with the widely held belief in biological determinism of the age, but where appropriate Mangin also employed cultural relativism to buttress his case. Invoking Herbert Spencer—"the philosopher," in Mangin's view, "who had conducted the most profound study of the organization of human societies and their development in history"—he embraced the Englishman's theoretical construct of "progressive evolution" and dichotomy between as yet "primitive" but "militant" societies and their more highly evolved "industrial" counterparts.[12] Referring to the "warrior instincts that remain extremely powerful in primitive races," Mangin asserted that once Africans were made aware of the benefits of French military service—including the right to bear arms once again after the European conquest—recruits for the army would be plentiful.[13]

Mangin also asserted that from a military standpoint Africans were endowed with a series of natural attributes that made them outstanding soldiers. Their unique qualities included (1) an ability—due to "severe selection" of high infant mortality rates—to live in harsher climates than other races; (2) the capacity to carry heavy loads great distances owing to centuries of porterage and migration; (3) a nervous system that was less developed than that of Europeans and thus gave them greater resistance to pain and hence more willingness to shed blood in battle; (4) the patriarchal nature of African societies, which—echoing the Spencerian paradigm about militant primitive societies—endowed them with a sense of discipline and hierarchy that was readily transferable to military life in general and their French officers in particular; and (5) a final selectionist argument, that their natural inclination was to be excellent soldiers, gained from Africa having been for centuries a "vast battlefield."[14] Collectively, he argued, these factors not only contributed to making Africans ideal soldiers but, considering the character of European warfare, rendered them especially valuable to be used as "shock troops." In his words, "The black troops . . . have precisely those qualities that are demanded in the long struggles in modern war: rusticity, endurance, tenacity, the instinct for combat, the absence of nervousness, and an incomparable power of shock. Their arrival on the battlefield would have a considerable moral effect on the adversary."[15] Thus were the hereditary traits of Africans to be utilized against Germans.

Though arguing that all West Africans possessed these particular attributes, Mangin contended that the comparative military value of various African groups was further delineated by an internal racial hierarchy. Drawing on the conceptual framework provided by Spencer's *Principles of Sociology*, Mangin also incorporated the racial psychology of his friend and intellectual mentor Gustave Le Bon, who argued in favor of a link between the alleged psychological unity of races and their inherited genetic structure.[16] In addition, he cited the recent field studies conducted by his compatriot in AOF, the colonial administrator and ethnographer Maurice Delafosse, to support his proposal, based on a hierarchical ranking of racial groups.[17] These ranged from those "races" that constituted a "superior element" among West Africans, through a series of lesser peoples that were reckoned as progressively more "backward," to the "coastal" inhabitants in the colonies that he characterized as the "least advanced" of all. Those races at the upper end of this scale were distinguished, in Mangin's eyes (as well as in the estimation of other French military officers serving in the Western Sudan), not only by their "courage" and "warrior qualities" but also by their "intelligence" and their relatively high degree of "civilization."[18] Those at the lower end lacked these latter two attributes. Even though fearless fighters, they were, he claimed, bereft of notions of "progress," which he viewed as accounting for the retarded and in some cases "anarchistic" nature of their societies. His scheme roughly resembled a Spencerian evolutionary ranking of biological and social "progress."

Mangin's martial hierarchy, therefore, was not based exclusively on the "primitive" character of the populations involved (indeed, he excluded the inhabitants of Afrique Equatoriale Française from consideration precisely for this reason).[19] Rather, by applying a set of subjective criteria as an index of the degree of "civilization" among African groups, Mangin contended that the best soldiers came from what might be called the most "advanced" of West Africa's "primitive" races. Excepting Maures and Tuaregs, which, though of superior racial stock, were excluded from the projected recruitment scheme because they were reckoned to be too "individualistic" to submit to military discipline, Mangin categorized the racial and martial hierarchy in West Africa (see table).[20]

The classification system Mangin outlined not only reflects contemporary assumptions about the racial superiority of "whites" over "blacks" but also illustrates, in its ranking of West Africans, a series of other European prejudices.[21] Assessments of the comparative degree of "civilization" among African groups relied upon a set of subjective value judgments about the relative merit of their respective cultures and customs, and they also generally corresponded to the size, and hence the military strength, of the precolonial African kingdoms. This, in turn, bore a close correlation to the extent of resistance (or in some cases, such as among the Bambara, support) they had offered to the French during the conquest.

Répartition numérique par races des populations de l'A.O.F.

Races		Families	Population par famille	Observations
Arabe-Berbère	398,959	Arabe	6,134	
		Maure (et leurs anciens esclaves noirs)	280,062	Musulmans
		Touareg (et leurs anciens esclaves noirs)	112,403	
Peuhl	1,671,649	Peuhl	1,288,499	
		Rimaibés (anc. escla. noirs)	103,302	
		Toucouleurs	211,487	Musulmans
		Khassonkés (Métis)	45,817	
		Ouassoulonkés (Métis)	21,864	
		Laobé	680	
Mandingue	3,971,060	Malinké	1,127,421	
		Bambara	872,934	
		Saracolé	315,518	Musulmans
		Sénégalaise	661,105	tièdes pour
		Sénoufo	349,058	la moitié
		Nigérienne	11,031	fétichistes
		Soussou	323,945	pour l'autre
		Nord-Forestière	307,048	
Voltaïque	2,553,005	Mossis	1,751,667	
		Bariba	230,578	
		Gourounsi	82,095	Fétichistes
		Lobi	77,616	
		Bobo	290,302	
		Habbé	120,717	
Centre-Africaine	875,307	Sonraï	318,712	
		Nagot	77,980	Musulmans
		Dazza	168,668	
		Haoussa	309,917	
Achanti	724,758	Agni	323,137	
		Achanti	3,679	Fétichistes
		Oué (sous-tribu Achanti)	397,942	
Côtière	575,259	Casamance	87,987	
		Guinée	88,405	Fétichistes
		Côte d'Ivoire	398,867	
Total	10,769,637	Total	10,769,637	
Population non recensée		Territoire nouvellement acquis dans la Komadougou (Zinder) environ	200,000	Musulmans
		Forêt de la Côte d'Ivoire D'après M. le gouverneur Clozel, environ	1,200,000	Fétichistes
		Mauritanie. A ajouter d'après les chiffres de l'annuaire 1910	375,000	Musulmans
		Evaluation totale pour l'A.O.F.	12,544,637	

Source: Mangin, 'L'Utilisation des Troupes Noires', op. cit., 85.

In contemplating recruitment in the colonies, Mangin placed a premium on attracting those groups deemed to be of the greatest military value to the French. Thus, in the case of Senegal, for example, he explicitly stressed the need for the "Tukulor" and the "Mande" (including the Wolof, the Serer, and the Lebu) to be strongly represented in the African contingents on the assumption that these races produced the best soldiers.[22]

Finally, drawing upon the terminology of race psychology, Mangin claimed that African troops were especially easy to train. Since the "thought" processes of recruits were "very little used" before entering the army, it was possible to "reach [their] unconscious practically without passing through the conscious." Hence, by means of learning through "imitation" and "suggestion," many Africans became excellent shots and with proper instruction demonstrated an aptitude for maneuver required of foot soldiers and also of mastering all the diverse skills necessary for the functioning of a "modern" army.[23] As such, he concluded, these disciplined, brave, and congenial *grands enfants*—a well-worn analogy used since the Comte de Buffon in the eighteenth century and tirelessly propagated by the proponents of *la force noire*—would undoubtedly comport themselves in combat in a manner befitting the proudest traditions of the French army: "In future battles, these primitives, for whom life counts so little and whose young blood flows so ardently, as if avid to be shed, will certainly attain the old 'French fury,' and will reinvigorate it if necessary."[24] Far from harboring any moral compunctions about the ethics of recruiting Africans to fight in Europe, Mangin paradoxically contended that the constitution of *la force noire* represented just recompense for the blood and energy France had expended during the long and difficult struggle to establish *la paix française* and to abolish slavery in Africa.[25] As he put it,

> The organization of black troops represents the civilization of Africa regenerated. It is the climax of our work. When a nation has started such a chapter in the history of the human race, that nation is entitled to finish it. This nation has the right to call upon all of its children for its defense, even upon its adoptive children, without any distinction of race.[26]

In this sense African recruitment represented one of the most significant achievements of France's "civilizing mission" because as a consequence all Africa would be uplifted.

The Parisian Society of Anthropology and the Metropolitan Debate on African Recruitment

Mangin's proposals engendered a heated debate in French society, the tenor of which, although usually cloaked in the parlance of military efficacy, graphically illustrates the image Africans evoked in the metropolitan mind. Between 1909 and 1911, over 4,300 articles appeared in more than five hundred French newspapers and journals responding in one way or the other to the subject of *la force noire*.[27] Presenting widely divergent views on the relative merits of undertaking recruitment in Africa, the arguments the antagonists employed (or frequently neglected to employ) were nevertheless framed within the context of a series of collective assumptions about Africans that were deeply ingrained in French thought.

Central to the French outlook was a long-standing and nearly universal belief in the inferiority of Africans and the corresponding superiority of Europeans and their civilization. This prejudice dated from the onset of the transatlantic slave trade and was later systematized by Enlightenment thinkers, who posited the existence of a universal "chain of being" among peoples based on their presumed degree of cultural advancement.[28] By the beginning of the twentieth century, however, these negative preconceptions were accentuated by two comparatively recent, and indeed interrelated, developments: the ascendancy of biological determinism as the prevailing paradigm within the European scientific community and the onset of colonialism.

During the last half of the nineteenth century, racial rather than cultural differentiation gradually became accepted as the essential arbiter of human evolution. In the seemingly immutable progressive hierarchy believed to exist among the races, Africans were almost invariably relegated to the lowest stratum. Corroboration for this view was provided by the "findings" of physical anthropologists, who, in their attempts to classify the hereditary characteristics of various peoples, stressed the innate "primitiveness" of Africans, which was reflected in their less developed mental faculties and in a series of other "animal-like" physical attributes.[29]

This derogatory, pseudoscientific image of Africans became suffused during the 1890s with the legacy of the French conquest. In justifying colonial expansion and glorifying the exploits of the military, the French depicted Africans in a light that reinforced preexisting metropolitan prejudices. Though viewed as resisting the French with the appropriate "savage ferocity," Africans were presented as being fundamentally flawed by their barbarity and brutality—traits that were exemplified in a catalogue of crimes ranging from slave trading to human sacrifice and cannibalism. The upshot was that by the first decade of the twentieth century, French stereotypes about Africans—which were sanctioned by the scientific community and disseminated in the mass press, popular literature, and colonial exhibitions—were perhaps more negatively value laden than at any other time in the past.[30]

It was against this backdrop that the metropolitan debate over West African recruitment took place. Those publicly endorsing Mangin's ideas included numerous "Sudanese" officers in the Colonial Army; Governor-General William Ponty of West Africa; the Comité de l'Afrique Française; most of the "Group colonial" in the Chamber of Deputies; and several prominent generals in the French High Command. Arrayed against these protagonists were a series of other Colonial Army officers; members of the Socialist Party in Parliament; most of the metropolitan High Command; and the *Union coloniale*, which represented the business interests of the major French import-export firms in the overseas territories.[31]

Though encompassing a diverse collection of soldiers, scholars, politicians, businessmen, and colonial administrators (who also occasionally held common professional allegiances), these disputants were nevertheless drawn from among those claiming expertise in some facet of the recruitment question. The nature of the debate in which they engaged—as well as the assumptions about Africans implicit in their arguments—was exemplified in a wide variety of forums, ranging from the Chamber of Deputies to the High Command of the French Army. But the views of the scientific community about Africans are perhaps best illustrated by the reaction of the Anthropological Society of Paris to Mangin's recruitment proposal.

Following in the footsteps of General Louis Faidherbe, the soldier-scholar who was the first governor of Senegal as well as president of the Société d'Anthropologie de Paris in 1874, Mangin presented his arguments in favor of *la force noire* before the society's members on 2 March 1911.[32] Accompanied by an entourage of five generals and other high-ranking military officers, half a dozen army medical doctors, and a handful of colonial administrators, Mangin's coterie was intended to impress the members of the society, but its composition also illustrates the range of professional backgrounds of those claiming particular knowledge in this aspect of African affairs.[33] In so doing, Mangin and his military and administrative associates also exemplified Robert A. Nye's formulation of "the process by which a well-defined interest group appropriates social-science theory for internal rationalization and external ideologization."[34]

In the ensuing discussion a majority of members voiced their support for Mangin's ideas. The president of the society, Dr. Charles Henri Weisgerber, an Alsacian and the author of *Les Blancs d'Afrique*, was cited by Mangin as an authority on the African past during his presentation. Summarizing the points in Mangin's thesis, Weisgerber afterward concurred that "accounts of the campaigns in Africa" made it clear that the continent was a source "for obtaining peerless soldiers," provided they were well led. Though cautioning French officers to be aware of the differences between peoples as diverse as the Bambara and the Tukulor, Weisgerber concluded that expanded recruitment in Africa would eventually redound to the economic benefit of the colonizers when veterans returned to their villages; hence, it would be "in the interest of humanity and civilization."[35]

Dr. Georges Papillault, assistant director of the anthropological laboratory at the École des Hautes Études and a self-proclaimed "sociobiologist" specializing in, among other things, the anatomy of Africans, concurred with Mangin's characterization of colonial troops as "disciplined, devoted to their officers, [and] stoic in the face of danger." Although originally harboring reservations akin to those voiced by the political Left (discussed below) about introducing "African mercenaries" similar to those employed in ancient Greece and Rome into metropolitan France, Papillault's concerns were overcome by Mangin's reassurance that *la force noire* would only be deployed in France in the event of war. He concluded by expressing the hope that the soldiers' collaboration in the defense of French civilization might help raise their "savage consciousness" to a new, but as yet unknowable "level."[36]

Dr. Deyrolle, principal physician of the First Regiment of Zouaves, lauded Mangin's "powerful military conception" and disputed the characterization of African recruits as potential mercenaries, while reiterating the loyalty they felt for their French officers. Deyrolle's primary concern related to "biology applied to anthropology": how would the various African "races" react to one another and their new surroundings once they were removed from their natural habitat? This "purely scientific" question, he argued, required additional study, and he called upon the members of the society to continue discussion of this subject at future meetings in order to lend their expertise to the realization of Mangin's project.[37]

Though expressing a minority view, opposition to Mangin's proposals was also voiced at the meeting. While concurring with the racial and martial ranking of West Africans that Mangin presented and acknowledging his statement of the ease by which they could be recruited, various counterarguments focused on the dire consequences of pursuing such a policy, contending that the use of "black troops" constituted "more of a peril than an advantage." Specifically, Professor Sigismond Zaborowski-Moindron of the École d'Anthropologie and a past president of the society as well as the author of *Disparité et avenir des races humaines*, among other works, called attention to the adverse effects that the deployment of African soldiers in Algeria would have on the "stability" of the French regime there. He also emphasized the inherent dangers of introducing Africans into the nation's army because of the "assimilation" that would inevitably take place between them and French soldiers and children, along with the moral destructiveness of relying on "mercenaries" when the principle of obligatory military service was the accepted standard among "all civilized nations."[38]

The meeting's discussion was concluded by Léonce Manouvrier, secretary-general of the society between 1902 and 1914 and the director of the anthropological laboratory at the École des Haute Études. A craniologist in the tradition of Paul Broca, Manouvrier believed in the evolution of the human brain and, hence, in the "progressive" development of civilizations linked to racial typologies. Dismissing the suggestion to continue discussion of Mangin's proposal at a subsequent meeting, he thanked Mangin for his presentation, which, in his eyes, was "perfectly anthropological, since it concerned above all the question of the physiological and psychological aptitudes of the African races." But, he continued, subsequent discussion about "the possible use of African troops in a Europe[an] war" would depart from the domain of science into "questions of legitimacy, opportunity, and the advantages or disadvantages of such a deployment, and hence, leave the realm of anthropology and enter into areas of law, the military art, and politics." As such, he felt that an additional session devoted to the subject of *la force noire* would take the anthropologists beyond their purview, and he recommended that further discussion of the topic cease with the evening's presentation, which it did.[39]

The most striking aspect of Mangin' s presentation before the Société d'Anthropologie is that, aside from largely political concerns voiced by some members about the introduction of African troops into Algeria or France, the core of his thesis—his evolutionary categorization of the hierarchy among African races, as well as his characterization of their comparative primitiveness, their less highly developed mental and physiological faculties, and their still-savage consciousness—went unchallenged. Indeed, the tenor of the reaction to these anthropological assumptions—derived from Spencer, Le Bon, and Charles Letourneau (general secretary of the Society of Anthropology from 1886 to 1902)—suggests that far from being considered controversial, they carried broad currency. What is indisputable, however, is that none of the members of the Société d'Anthropologie de Paris were prepared to dispute the most basic premise of Mangin's argument: the fiction that Africa consisted of warrior races that would be easy to recruit in the event of a war. Indeed, this racial stereotype came to constitute the cornerstone of French tactical doctrine, as well as future national defense policy, when the expanded recruitment program in Africa was eventually implemented.

Concerns similar to those raised by some of the anthropologists were echoed in political and military forums. In the Chamber of Deputies opposition to recruiting Africans for service overseas was voiced in February 1910 by the leader of the Socialist Party, Jean Jaurès. Declining to restrict his remarks to the specifics of the government's proposal allocating funds to garrison a battalion of Senegalese *tirailleurs* outside of AOF in Algeria, Jaurès seized the opportunity to raise a series of fundamental objections to the entire recruitment scheme. Apart from arguing against uprooting Africans from their natural milieu and arousing Arab anger against the French, Jaurès stressed two major objections to the policy. First, consistent with his calls for a sweeping reorganization of the military to create a democratic citizen's army, he asserted that efforts to supplement French strength through recourse to African troops constituted nothing less than an "act of despair, which demonstrates that the present system is finished." Second, the presence of African "mercenaries" in France would constitute a veritable "Praetorian Guard" in the hands of "capital" and pose a mortal threat to the "proletariat." Although the motion carried by a substantial margin, Jaurès's intervention illustrates the magnitude of the concerns aroused by the prospect of African troops on French soil among a significant portion of the population.[40]

Finally, the desirability of recruiting Africans was also debated within the highest echelons of the French Army. This discourse hinged on a series of military considerations that were cited as evidence of the Africans' comparative worth as soldiers. In addition to General Archinard, Mangin's assessment of the fighting capabilities of Africans was enthusiastically endorsed by some of the foremost military theoreticians in France, including General Henri Bonnal, director of the École de Guerre Supérieure between 1889 and 1902 (when he was ousted in the republican purges of the anti-Dreyfusards); General M. L. de Gamiers de Garets, former member of the Conseil Supérieur de la Guerre; General Henri de Lacroix, former generalissimo of the French Army; and Bonnal's successor at the École de Guerre Supérieure, General Hippolyte Langlois. Support for African deployment in Europe was predicated on the soldiers' alleged value as "shock troops," a valuation that Langlois summarized when he asserted that the "warrior qualities" of the "black race" were "hereditary" and that, in the prevailing conditions of "modern" warfare, "their cold blooded and fatalistic temperament [would] render them terrible in the attack."[41]

Ironically, the most prominent critics of Mangin's proposals included fellow officers serving in the Colonial Army, primarily in North Africa. These included General Louis de Torcy, the former commander of the French forces in Madagascar; General Charles Moinier, the commandant of the expeditionary corps in Morocco; Archinard's old nemesis, General Hubert Lyautey; and General Louis Franchet d'Esperey. Reservations voiced by them and echoed by others raised the following negative considerations: greater African susceptibility to diseases in colder climates, as well as the danger that they would spread tropical contagions; increased costs, owing to the need to seclude African troops in "isolated" training camps; and, despite taking such precautions, the specter of "permanent contacts" between Africans and the "white population" if the former were garrisoned in France. More to the point, the military opponents of *la force noire* also argued that African soldiers suffered from a series of fundamental technical shortcomings because of their less developed mental faculties, which limited their military utility: they were mediocre marksmen, lacked fire discipline, and were incapable of maneuvering effectively. In an implicit critique of their mental aptitudes, Moinier concluded that Africans were simply "not capable of adapting themselves with the same facility [as Europeans or North Africans] to the necessities of modern warfare."[42]

These counterarguments against creating *la force noire* initially proved persuasive. The army general staff, which held ultimate authority to decide this question, was imbued with the belief that the next war would be short. Accordingly, it declined to endorse the more grandiose plans for African recruitment and sanctioned such plans—exemplified by the so-called Plan Ponty of 1912, which called for 20,000 extra soldiers—only on a limited and experimental basis. In short, prior to the First World War, the creation of a large African reserve for eventual use in Europe remained nothing more than a possible contingency plan. Nevertheless, the idea of West Africa as a "land of warriors" who could be utilized in the defense of France in the event of a national emergency had been sown.

The Human Consequences of the Application of Race Theory

Within four years of the conclusion of the metropolitan debate over undertaking expanded African recruitment, the outbreak of war in Europe and the staggering losses suffered by the French Army between 1914 and 1916 led to a reassessment of Mangin's prewar proposal. No longer representing a disagreeable potential strategic alternative, African troops were now deployed in large numbers on the Western Front after 1916, amounting to 140,000 combatants by war's end.[43]

French tactical doctrine about how best to use Senegalese troops (as West African soldiers were collectively called) in the fighting initially mirrored many of the prewar arguments about the comparative capabilities of Africans as combatants. Eventually, however, these opposing views about Senegalese aptitudes became reconciled in French military doctrine. Principles governing the tactical use of Africans were codified in the "Notice sur les Sénégalais et leur emploi au combat" issued during the last year of the conflict, which, with minor revisions, became the mainstay of military thinking thereafter.[44]

Accepting the martial ranking of African races first delineated by Mangin, the "Notice" enumerated the specific military attributes of each group. Infantry battalions comprised of Wolofs, Serers, "Tukulors," and Bambaras—all deemed "warrior races"—for example, were considered to be among the very "best" combat formations, and colonial officers frequently explicitly asked for them as replacements.[45]

African combat characteristics were discussed in detail in the "Notice," and a series of tactical recommendations concerning their use were also made. Though possessing "[highly] developed warrior instincts," defensive operations frequently posed difficulties for Africans because of their "unskillful" use of terrain. Offensive actions were, however, a different matter. "Brave" and "impetuous" in attack, the Senegalese were said to pursue assaults to the very "limit of their endurance," if these developed favorably. Hence, by the final year of the war, when African battalions were dispatched from the Colonial Army to metropolitan formations for the first time and Senegalese casualties reached their peak, French tactical doctrine embraced the notion that the Senegalese were useful primarily as "shock troops" in assaults, but recommended that European units be placed both behind them and at their sides to fulfill this role properly.[46]

African soldiers paid a very high price during the First World War for this mixing of pseudoscientific racial assumptions with tactical doctrine.

Indeed, during the last two and a half years of the conflict, when Africans first appeared in large numbers on the Western Front, Senegalese casualties were approximately twice as high as those suffered by French infantry combatants. Yet beyond these excessive losses, those soldiers recruited from "races" deemed by the French to be especially "warlike" were most prominent in the assault battalions that bore the heaviest casualties. In terms of what this portended for the soldiers, it is probable that a Wolof, a "Tukulor," or a Bambara recruited as a *tirailleur* between 1915 and 1917, for example, was about three times as likely to die in combat as his French counterpart, while absolute losses were on the order of two and a half to one.[47]

Disproportionate though the African loss of life was between 1916 and 1918, the importance of their contribution to the French war effort was indisputable, and thereafter they became a linchpin of imperial, as well as continental, policy considerations. By a decree of 30 July 1919 recruitment was instituted on a regular basis in AOF for terms of three years; indeed, by 1923 African recruits were inducted for terms of service that were twice as long as French recruits. In this context Africans provided garrison troops not only in Europe (most sensationally during the French occupation of the Rhineland in 1919) but also throughout much of the French Empire during the interwar period.[48]

A second massive mobilization took place between 1939 and 1945, when more than 200,000 soldiers were forcibly recruited to serve France. Although there are discrepancies in the records owing to the confusion of the Third Republic's collapse, as many as 63,300 fought against the Germans in 1940, while between 10,000 and 24,000 were listed as killed or missing in action. Thereafter, the balance of African recruits either served the Vichy regime in AOF until its collapse in November 1942 or fought with the Free French, constituting virtually all of their meager forces in the summer of 1940 (when five battalions of *Tirailleurs Sénégalais* in Afrique Equatoriale Française joined de Gaulle), two-thirds of Free French operational strength (along with North Africans) in July 1943, and 20 percent of the troops liberating southern France in August and September 1944.[49] No matter in which French army they fought, the conditions of service of West Africans—including the classification of the soldiers' military aptitudes by race, their separation in isolated formations prior to sometimes being "mixed" with European units in combat, and their continued aggressive use as assault troops—reflected institutionalized ethnomilitary doctrines formalized by the Armée Coloniale after the First World War, which persisted throughout the Second.[50]

Worse yet were the race theories of their Nazi adversaries, who espoused the dogma of Aryan supremacy developed by, among others, fin de siècle French anthropologists such as Georges Vacher de Lapouge. Although largely ignored in his own country, Vacher de Lapouge had a marked influence on his German protégé Hans Günter, chief Nazi race theorist, who linked Africans with Jews as being genetically related. Such pseudoscience fed Nazi propaganda, which fueled racial hostility among German troops in 1940 and, in Raffael Scheck's analysis, led to the massacres of African troops after combat, which he estimated at 3,000 murdered, as well as to their comparative maltreatment in German prisoner of war camps.[51]

Indeed, fragmentary though the evidence is, it suggests that measured by any comparable standard African losses compared to those of their French counterparts may have been proportionately even higher than during the First World War. Comparative casualty rates during the Second World War may be calculated as follows. Accepting the lowest casualty estimates and excluding those likely massacred among combatants in May–June 1940, African losses totaled about 11.1 percent of those engaged (i.e., approximately 7,000 combatants killed out of 63,300 fighting). French losses amounted to about 4.1 percent, or 90,000 out of 2,200,000 combatants. Among those mobilized during the war, African losses likely constituted about 12.5 percent of all servicemen, or 25,000 out of 200,000. Conversely, French losses were not more than 3.1 percent, reckoned at 200,000 out of 6,000,000 mobilized in 1940 and 400,000 among the Free French by September 1944, when France was liberated. Finally, African losses due to massacre after capture (estimated at 3,000), as well as in German POW camps (where they may have numbered nearly half of the 16,000 imprisoned compared to losses of about 1.6 percent among French prisoners) were certainly much higher than those of their French counterparts. In short, in all instances during the Second World War—whether comparing the numbers of killed and missing during combat, casualties among all those mobilized, or mortality rates after surrender in Germans hands—African losses were invariably more than two and a half times greater than those of their French counterparts and, in some instances—such as rates of survival after combat—much higher still.[52] Nor did these racial stereotypes about Africans in the French Army dating from the beginning of the twentieth century, which were amplified and distorted by Nazi Germany, cease after the conclusion of hostilities. Instead, in the Armée Coloniale they persisted until the eve of African independence in the 1950s.[53]

In all, some 725,000 West Africans served in the French Army between 1912 and 1956, while at least 60,000 likely lost their lives, largely during the two global conflicts.[54] It is from this perspective that the relationship between the theory of racial classification and the practice of troop deployment according to ethnic criteria comes clearly into focus. The prewar debate, with its seemingly objective scientific underpinnings, became reified during the first half of the twentieth century into a policy that carried dire consequences for African soldiers.

Notes

Earlier versions of this paper were presented at the International Society for the History, Philosophy, and Social Studies of Biology conference, Vienna, 10 July 2003 and at "Encountering Modern French History: A Conference Honoring the Contributions of William B. Cohen," Bloomington, Indiana, 6 December 2003.

1. Jules Maurin and Jean-Charles Jauffret, "L'Appel aux Armes, 1872–1914," in *Histoire Militaire de la France*, ed. Guy Pedroncini, vol. 3, 1871–1940 (Paris: Presses Universitaires de France, 1992), 80–97; Gilbert Meynier, *L'Algérie révélée: La guerre de 1914–1918 et le premier quart du XXe siècle* (Genève: Librairie Droz, 1981), 88–114; Gerd Krumeich, *Armaments and Politics in France on the Eve of the First World War* (Oxford: Berg, 1985); Hubert Tison, *La Loi de trios ans et l'opinion publique française* (Paris: D.E.S, 1966); Catherine Faure, "La Préparation de la 'loi de trois ans' (1913) à travers cinq grands quotidiens de la presse parisienne," *Guerres Mondiales et Conflits Contemporaines* 184 (1996), 51–67.

2. More extensive recruitment of North Africans was also debated as a remedy to this problem and eventually promulgated during the prewar period. See Jean-Charles Jauffret, "Les Armes de la plus grande France," in Pedroncini, *Histoire Militaire de la France*, 43–69. The recruitment of Viet-

namese was also proposed but deferred until 1915. See Mireille Le Van Ho, "Le Général Pennequin et le projet d'Armée Jaune (1911–1915)," *Revue Française d'Histoire d'Outre-Mer* 75 (1988), 145–67.

3. On the prewar French debate over *la force noire*, see *Les Troupes Noires (Le Parlement. Rapports. Commissions. Séances. L 'Opinion Militaire et Coloniale. La Presse. Les Conférences. Conférénces. Documents. Conclusion.)* (Paris: Edition du Journal "L'Armée Coloniale," 1911). See also Marc Michel, "Colonisation et défense nationale: Le général Mangin et la force noire," *Guerres Mondiales et Conflits Contemporains* 37 (1987), 27–44; and Michel, "Un mythe: La 'Force Noire' avant 1914," *Relations Internationales* 1 (1974), 83–90.

4. Archinard commanded French forces during the conquest of the Western Sudan and wrote the preface to Charles Mangin's *La Force Noire*; de Lacroix, Perreaux, and Audéoud, commanders of French troops in AOF between 1899 and 1907, collectively undertook the first studies of the military resources in the colonies and advocated expanded local recruitment to create a reserve force for external use outside AOF if the need arose.

5. On Mangin's background see Louis-Eugène Mangin, *Le Général Mangin* (Paris: Éditions F. Lanore, 1986).

6. Charles Mangin à Gouverneur-Général, 2 November 1910, Archives Nationales du Sénégal (hereafter ANS), Affaires militaires, 4 D 31. Mangin's estimates of the numbers of additional soldiers that could be raised in AOF varied considerably: in *la force noire* he called for 7,000 to 7,500 extra men to be recruited annually; in his address before the Société d'Anthropologie de Paris on 2 March 1911, he contended that 40,000 African "volunteers" were available for military service per year (see notes 9, 10, and 11 below).

7. Charles Mangin, "Troupes Noires," *Revue de Paris* 94 (Juillet-Août 1909), 61–80, 384–98; Mangin, *La Force Noire* (Paris: Hachette, 1910).

8. Mangin, *La Force Noire*, 343. All translations are by the author unless otherwise noted.

9. Mangin, *La Force Noire*, 262–68.

10. Mangin, *La Force Noire*, 276. On recruitment levels in pre-industrial agrarian societies, which very seldom exceeded 3 percent of the total population, see Gwyne Dyer, *War* (New York: Crown, 1985), 44.

11. Mangin, *La Force Noire*, 288–89.

12. Mangin, *La Force Noire*, 347; Herbert Spencer, *Principles of Sociology* (New York: D. Appleton, 1898). Also see Naoimi Beck, "The Diffusion of Spencerism and Its Political Interpretations in France and Italy," in *Herbert Spencer: The Intellectual Legacy*, ed. Greta Jones and Robert Peel (London: Galton Institute, 2003), 37–60.

13. Mangin à Gouverneur Général, 2 November 1910, ANS: 4 D 31; Mangin, *La Force Noire*, 228, 289.

14. Charles Mangin. "L'Utilisation des Troupes Noires," *Bulletins et Mémoires de la Société d'Anthropologie de Paris* 2 (1911), 89; Mangin, *La Force Noire*, 225–28, 247–52. Regarding African nervous systems, Mangin was reiterating the claims of Charles Letourneau, secretary-general of the Paris Society of Anthropology from 1886 to 1902, who, in *La Sociologie d'après l'ethnologie* (Paris: C. Reinwald, 1880), asserted that the ill-developed condition of the "nervous centers" was "inherent in every inferior race of men" (555).

15. Mangin, *La Force Noire*, 343. For the value of Africans as "shock troops," see also, 257–58.

16. On Mangin's relationship with Le Bon, see the introduction to *Le Déséquilibre du monde* (Paris: Ernest Flammarion, 1923), which the author dedicates to "my disciple," Charles Mangin. On Le Bon's ideas—including national traits, racial superiority, herd behavior, and crowd psychology—see Gustave Le Bon, *L'Homme et les Sociétés: Leurs Origines et Leur Histoire* (Paris: J. Rothschild, 1881); and Le Bon, *Psychologie des Foules* (Paris: Alca, 1896). See also Robert A. Nye, *The Origins of Crowd Psychology: Gustave Le Bon and the Crisis of Mass Democracy in the Third Republic* (London: Sage, 1975).

17. On Mangin's racial hierarchy, which is derived from Delafosse's "comprehensive work," see Maurice Delafosse, *Haut-Sènègal-Niger (Soudan Français): Le Pays, les Peuples, les Langues, l'Histoire, les Civilisations* (Paris: Emile Larose, 1912), vol. 1, 106–351. On Delafosse, see Jean-Loup Amselle and Emmanuelle Sibeud, eds., *Maurice Delafosse: Entre orientalisme et ethnographie: L'itinéraire d'une africaniste (1870–1926)* (Paris: Maisonneuve and Larose, 1998).

18. On ethnic military stereotypes propagated in the French Colonial Army, see Lieutenant Éugene Mage, *Voyage au Soudan occidental, 1863–66* (Paris: Hachette, 1872); Commandant Joseph-Simon Gallieni, *Voyage au Soudan Français, 1879–81* (Paris: Hachette, 1885); and Lieutenant Colonel Albert Ernest Augustin Baratier, *A travers l'Afrique* (Paris: A. Fayard, 1910).

19. Mangin. "L'Utilisation des Troupes Noires," 81.

20. Mangin. "L'Utilisation des Troupes Noires," 85.

21. It should be stressed that these implicit prejudices were by no means uniquely French. Similar classification systems were also used by other European powers in their recruitment of colonial troops. See, for instance, A. H. M. Kirk-Green, "'Damnosa Hereditas': Ethnic Ranking and the Martial Races Imperative in Africa," *Ethnic and Racial Studies* 11 (1980), 393–414;

J. Bayo Adekson, "Ethnicity and Army Recruitment in Colonial Plural Societies," *Ethnic and Racial Studies* 11 (1979), 151–65; Timothy H. Parsons, "'Wakamba Warriors Are Soldiers of the Queen': The Evolution of the Kamba as a Martial Race, 1890–1970," *Ethnohistory* 46 (1999), 671–701; Risto Marjomaa, "The Martial Spirit: Yao Soldiers in British Service in Nyasaland (Malawi), 1895–1939," *Journal of African History* 44 (2003), 413–32; and Hal Brands, "Wartime Recruiting Practices, Martial Identity and Post–World War II Demobilization in Colonial Kenya," *Journal of African History* 46 (2005), 103–26. The converse was also true: racial categorizations were also used to stigmatize African Americans, for instance, as distinctly unwarlike. See *The Use of Negro Manpower in War* (Carlisle PA: U.S. Army War College, 1925), which stigmatized African Americans as a "subspecies of the human population" who were "cowards and poor technicians and fighters, lacking initiative and resourcefulness."

22. Mangin à Gouverneur Général, 2 November 1910, ANS: Affaires militaires: 4 D 31.

23. Mangin, "L'Utilisation des Troupes Noires," 90–91; Mangin, *La Force Noire*, 236–39.

24. Mangin, *La Force Noire*, 258, 332. On childlike stereotypes of African soldiers, which persisted into the post–World War II era, see Myron Echenberg, *Colonial Conscripts: The Tirailleur Sénégalais in French West Africa, 1857–1960* (Portsmouth NH: Heinemann; London: James Currey, 1991); and Brett A. Berliner, *Ambivalent Desire: The Exotic Black Other in Jazz-Age France* (Amherst: University of Massachusetts Press, 2002).

25. Mangin, *La Force Noire*, 228.

26. Mangin, *La Force Noire*, 350.

27. On the debate in the French press, see *Les Troupes Noires* (Paris: Édition du Journal *L'Armée Coloniale*, 1911).

28. William B. Cohen, *The French Encounter with Africans: White Responses to Blacks, 1530–1880* (Bloomington: Indiana University Press, 1980), 35–100. Also see Sue Peabody, *"There Are No Slaves in France:" The Political Culture of Race and Slavery in the Ancien Régime* (Oxford: Oxford University Press, 1996).

29. George L. Mosse, *Toward the Final Solution: A History of European Racism* (London: Dent, 1978); William B. Cohen, "French Racism and Its African Impact," in *Double Impact: France and West Africa in the Age of Imperialism*, ed. G. Wesley Johnson (Westport CT: Greenwood Press, 1985), 305–18; and Sue Peabody and Tyler Stovall, eds., *The Color of Liberty: Histories of Race in France* (Durham NC: Duke University Press, 2003).

30. William H. Schneider, *An Empire for the Masses: The French Popular*

Image of Africa, 1870–1900 (Westport CT: Greenwood Press, 1982), 152–211; Véronique Campion-Vincet, "L'image du Dahomey dans la presse française (1890–1895): Les sacrifices humains," *Cahiers d'Études Africaines* 25 (1967), 27–58; William B. Cohen, "Literature and Race: Nineteenth Century French Fiction, Blacks and Africa, 1800–1880," *Race and Class* 16 (1974), 181–205; Thomas August, *The Selling of Empire: British and French Imperialist Propaganda, 1890–1940* (Westport CT: Greenwood Press, 1982).

31. On French factions see Michel, "Une mythe"; Marc Michel, *L'Appel à l'Afrique: Contributions et reactions à l'effort de guerre en A.O.F. (1914–1919)* (Paris: Publications de la Sorbonne, 1982), 2–39; Charles J. Balesi, *From Adversaries to Comrades-in-Arms: West Africa and the French Military, 1885–1918* (Waltham MA: Crossroads Press, 1979), 149–211.

32. On the Société d'Anthropologie de Paris during this period, see Jennifer Michael Hecht, *The End of Soul: Scientific Modernity, Atheism, and Anthropology in France* (New York: Columbia University Press, 2003); Claude Blanckaert, ed., *Les politiques de l'anthropologie* (Paris: l'Harmattan, 2001); Jean-Claude Wartelle, "La Société d'Anthropologie de Paris de 1859 á 1920," *Revue d'Histoire des Sciences Humaines* 10:1 (2004), 125–71; Elizabeth A. Williams, "The Science of Man: Anthropological Thought and Institutions in Nineteenth Century France," PhD diss., Indiana University, 1983; and Joy Harvey, "Races Specified, Evolution Transformed: The Social Context of Scientific Debates Originating in the Société de Anthropologie de Paris, 1859–1902," PhD diss., Harvard University, 1983.

33. The composition of late nineteenth- and early twentieth-century French learned societies reflected this diversity. French medical doctors, for instance, accounted for 51 percent of the 1,100 members of the Société de Anthropologie de Paris in 1909. On the contribution of French military doctors to anthropological theories from 1830 to 1920, see Michael A. Osborne and Richard Fogarty, "Views from the Periphery: Discourses of Race and Place in French Military Medicine," *History and Philosophy of the Life Sciences* 25:1 (2003), 363–89.

34. Nye, *Origins of Crowd Psychology*, 126.

35. Dr. Henri Weisgerber, *Les Blancs d'Afrique* (Paris: O. Dion, 1910). The discussion of Mangin's proposals by the anthropologists was published following his article. See Mangin, "L'Utilisation des Troupes Noires," 95–100. For Weisgerber's comments, see 95–96.

36. Mangin, "L'Utilisation des Troupes Noires," 96–97. Also see Georges Papillault, "La forme du thorax chez des Hovas et chez des Nigres Africains et Malagaches: Contribution à l'étude de l'indice thoracique," *Revue de l'École d'Anthropologie de Paris* 16:2 (1906), 63–68; and Papillault, "Galton

et la bio-sociologie," *Revue Anthropologique* 21:2 (1911), 56–65. On Papillault, who was one of three candidates for election to a chair at the *Collège de France* in 1929, see Laurent Mucchielli and Jacqueline Pleut-Despatin, "Halbwachs au Collège de France," *Revue d'Histoire des Sciences Humaines* 1:1 (1999), 179–88; and Benoît de l'Estoile, "From the Colonial Exhibition to the Museum of Man: An Alternative Genealogy of French Anthropology," *Social Anthropology* 11:3 (2003), 341–61.

37. Mangin, "L'Utilisation des Troupes Noires," 98–99. For a survey of the treatment of racial differences by French anthropologists, see the articles in Claude Blankaert, ed., *Des sciences contre l'homme*, vol. 1: *Classe, hiérarchiser, exclure* (Paris: Éditions Autrement, 1993).

38. Mangin, "L'Utilisation des Troupes Noires," 97–98. In addition to Zaborowski-Moindron, *Disparité et avenir des races humaine* (Vincennes: A. Levy et frère, 1893), also see, among his other works, Zaborowski-Moindron, *Les Peuples aryennes d'Asie et d'Europe, leurs origines en Europe, la civilisation protoaryenne* (Paris: O. Doin, 1908).

39. Mangin, "L'Utilisation des Troupes Noires," 99–100. Also see Léonce Manouvrier, *Recherches d'anatomie comparative et d'anatomie philosophique* (Paris: Meulan, 1882). On Manouvrier see Jennifer Hecht, "A Vigilant Anthropology: Léonce Manouvrier and the Disappearing Numbers," *Journal of the History of Behavioral Sciences* 33:3 (1997), 221–40.

40. *Journal Officiel de la République Française, Débats de la Chambre*, 28 February 1910, 962–65; Jean Jaurès, *L'Armée nouvelle: L'organisation Socialiste de la France* (Paris: l'Humanité, 1915), 522, 543.

41. Hyppolyte Langlois, *Temps*, 12 November 1909.

42. Cited in Captain Rachou, *Le Mirage des armées indigènes* (Angoulême: 1911), 65. See also General de Torcy, "La Question des troupes noires en Algérie," *Bulletin de la Reunion d'Études Algériennes* (Paris: 1911), 4–28.

43. Pre-June 1916 French losses amounted to 62 percent of the wartime total. On Africans and the First World War, see Joe Lunn, *Memoirs of the Maelstrom: A Senegalese History of the First World War* (Portsmouth NH: Heinemann; Oxford: James Currey; Cape Town: David Philip, 1999), and Michel, *L'Appel à l'Afrique*.

44. Centre militaire d'information et de documentation sur l'Outre-Mer, Versailles: "Notice sur les Sénégalais et leur emploi au combat" (no date, but written between May 1917 and September 1918). For favorable reactions to the "Notice" from French officers who commanded Senegalese combat units in 1918, see Archives de la Guerre, Service Historique de l'Armée, Château de Vincennes (hereafter AG): GQG: 16 N 2094.

45. For examples, see AG: 6 N 2094, AG: 24 N 3027, and AG 26 N 870.

Race Theory, Anthropology, and *la Force Noire*

On racial preconceptions and French military organization, also see Lunn, *Memoirs of the Maelstrom*, 120–56; and Richard S. Fogarty, *Race and War: Colonial Subjects in the French Army, 1914–1918* (Baltimore: Johns Hopkins University Press, 2008), 55–168.

46. Centre militaire d'information, "Notice sur les Sénégalais."

47. On West African losses, see Rapport Marin, *Journaux Officiels: Documents Parlementaires*, 1920, vol. 2, annexe 633, 76; on French losses, see Rapport Marin, *Journaux Officiels*, 44, 66, 74. For more detailed discussion of comparative casualty rates, see Joe Lunn, "'Les Races Guerrières': Racial Preconceptions in the French Military about West African Soldiers during the First World War," *Journal of Contemporary History* 34:4 (1999), 517–36. For a different interpretation, see Michel, *L'Appel à l'Afrique*, 405–8. Also see Christian Koller, *"Von Wilden aller Rassen niedergemetzeld": Die Diskussion um die Verwendung von Kolonialtruppen in Europa zwischen Rassismus, Kolonial-und Militärpolitik (1814–1930)* (Stuttgart: Franz Steiner, 2001), 100.

48. On the provisions of the 1919 decree and postwar terms of service see, respectively, *Journal Officiel: Débats*, 1919, 632; and Echenberg, *Colonial Conscripts*, 47–86. On the use of Africans as troops of occupation in the Rhineland, see Keith Nelson, "The 'Black Horror on the Rhine': Race as a Factor in Post–World War I Diplomacy," *Journal of Modern History* 42 (1970), 606–27; Sally Marks, "Black Watch on the Rhine: A Study in Propaganda, Prejudice and Prurience," *European Studies Review* 13 (1983), 297–334; Ruth Harris, "The 'Child of the Barbarian': Rape, Race and Nationalism in France during the First World War," *Past and Present* 123 (1993), 170–206; Sandra Maß, "Das Trauma des Weißen Mannes: Afrikanische Kolonialsoldaten in propagandistischen Texten, 1914–1923," *L'Homme: Zeitschrift für feministische Geschichtswissenschaft* 12:1 (2001), 11–33; Hans-Jürgen Lüsebrink, "'Tirailleurs Sénégalais' und 'Schwarze Schande': Verlaufsformen und Konsequenzen einer deutschfranzösischen Auseinandersetzung (1910–1926)"; and Joachim Schultz, "Die 'Utschebebbes' am Rhein—Zur Darstellung schwarzern Soldaten während der französischen Rheinlandbesetzung (1918–1930)," in *"Tirailleurs Sénégalais": Zur Bildlichen und Literarischen Darstellung Afrikanischer Soldaten im dienste Frankreichs—Présentations Littéraires et Figuratives de Soldats Africains au Service de la France*, ed. János Riesz and Joachim Schultz (Frankfurt am Main: Peter Lang, 1989), 57–100; and Jean-Yves Le Naour, *La honte noire: L'Allemagne et les troupes coloniales françaises 1914–1945* (Paris: Hachette Littérature, 2003).

49. On Africans and World War II, see Echenberg, *Colonial Conscripts*; Nancy Lawler, *Soldiers of Misfortune: Ivorian Tirailleurs of World War II* (Athens: Ohio University Press, 2002); Bakari Kamian, *Des tranchées de*

Verdun à l'église Saint-Bernard: 80,000 combattants maliens au secours de la France (1914–18 et 1939–45) (Paris: Éditions Karthala, 2001); Gregory Mann, *Native Sons: West African Veterans and France in the Twentieth Century* (Durham NC: Duke University Press, 2006); and Raffael Scheck, *Hitler's African Victims: The German Army Massacres of Black French Soldiers in 1940* (Cambridge: Cambridge University Press, 2006). Echenberg's estimate of 200,000 recruits is also cited by Mann, *Native Sons*, 88 and 232 n. 73, respectively). On the range cited for West African casualties in 1940, see, in ascending order, Echenberg, *Colonial Conscripts*, 88 (10,000), Scheck, *Hitler's African Victims*, 58 (17,000), and Kamian, *Des tranchées de Verdun*, 343 (24,271), which is also cited by Mann, *Native Sons*, 18, who views Echenberg's estimate as "both arbitrary and low" (231 n. 68). On the African composition of the Free French forces, see Jean-Pierre Azéma and François Bédarida, eds., *La France des années noires*, vol. 1: *De la défaite à Vichy* (Paris: Éditions du Seuil) 81, 213, and Mann, *Native Sons*, 19.

50. On the contents of French instruction manuals for officers and NCOs and their continued ranking—largely undifferentiated during forty years from Mangin's original categorization in 1910—of the particular martial qualities (or lack thereof) of specific West African "races," see Marc Michel, "Les Peuples et l'histoire de l'Afrique noire dans les manuels d'instructions militaire entre les deux guerres," *Histoire d'Outre-Mer: Mélanges en l'honneur de Jean-Louis Meige*, vol. 2 (Aix-en-Provence: Publications de l'Université de Provence, 1992), 313–27. On the tactical "mixing" of some African units with French ones during combat, see Echenberg, *Colonial Conscripts*, 91.

51. See Georges Vacher de Lapouge, *L'Aryen: Son role social* (Paris: A. Fontemoing, 1899). On Lapouge's influence on and patronage of Hans Günter, chief Nazi race theorist, see Jennifer Michael Hecht, "Vacher de Lapouge and the Rise of Nazi Science," *Journal of the History of Ideas* 61:2 (2000), 285–304. On Günter's work contributing to Nazi propaganda, which in turn influenced German soldiers' attitudes toward Africans and was a contributing factor in their massacre in 1940, see Scheck, *Hitler's African Victims*, 102. On the massacre of African soldiers and their abuse in German POW camps, see Scheck, *Hitler's African Victims*, 17–74; and David Killingray, "Africans and African Americans in Enemy Hands," in *Prisoners of War and Their Captors in World War II*, ed. Bob Moore and Kent Fedorowich (Oxford: Berg, 1996), 181–204; Martin Thomas, "The Vichy Government and French Colonial Prisoners of War, 1940–1944," *French Historical Studies* 25:4 (2002), 657–92.

52. On the range of casualty estimates for the First World War, as well as comparative casualty rates among combatants, which between 1916 and

1918 were on the order of two-to-one, see Lunn, *Memoirs of the Maelstrom*, 140–47. On African fatalities as a percentage of combatants and those mobilized, see, respectively, Echenberg, "'Morts pour la France': The African Soldier in France during the Second World War," *Journal of African History* 26:3 (1985), 364–65, and Scheck, *Hitler's African Victims*, 17. On the massacre of Africans and their POW losses, which are disputed, see Scheck, *Hitler's African Victims*, 41–60; and Killingray, "Africans and African Americans in Enemy Hands," 181–90. On French fatalities, see *Les Grandes Unités Françaises (GUF)*, vol. 5, part 2, Service Historique de l'Armée de Terre (Paris: Imprimerie Nationale, 1975); Gerhard L. Weinberg, *A World at War: A Global History of World War II* (Cambridge: Cambridge University Press, 1994); Eugenia C. Kiesling, *Arming against Hitler: France and the Limits of Military Planning* (Lawrence: University Press of Kansas, 1996); Pierre Gascar, *Histoire de la captivité des Française en Allemagne (1939–1945)* (Paris: Gallimard, 1967); and Yves Durand, *Les prisonniers de guerre dans les stalags, les oflags et les kommandos, 1939–1945* (Paris: Hachette, 1994). See also Martin Alexander's essay in this volume.

53. See Michel, "Les Peuples et l'histoire de l'Afrique noire dans les manuels d'instructions militaire entre les deux guerres," 323–24.

54. This mobilization figure is derived from Echenberg's "rough estimates." His calculations are as follows: 1912–1913: 16,315; 1914–1918: 175,000; 1919–1929: 165,767; 1929–1938: approximately 120,000 (at 12,000 recruits per year); 1939–1945: more than 200,000; 1946–1956: approximately 50,000 (at least 4,000 recruits per year). See Myron Echenberg, *Colonial Conscripts*, 7–64, and 108–22; Echenberg, "Paying the Blood Tax: Military Conscription in French West Africa, 1914–1929," *Canadian Journal of African Studies* 9:2 (1975), 171–92; and Echenberg, "Morts pour la France," 363–65. The mortality estimate is based on approximately 30,000 African dead for the First World War, at least 25,000 for the Second World War, as well as losses during conflicts in Morocco, Indochina, and Algeria and from other causes—primarily disease—while on garrison duty in Africa, Asia, and Europe.

10

Colonial Minds Confounded: French Colonial Troops in the Battle of France, 1940

MARTIN S. ALEXANDER

People say some Senegalese have been massacred on the road from Chères. Is it true ? [. . .] a nun, her white habit spotted with blood, grabbed hold of me: "Over there", she said, "to the left". In the distance, near a ditch, we made out a yellowing mass, frightful-looking, the sunlight glistening here and there on patches of red. It was a shocking sight: a misshapen pile of black and khaki, a bloody pulp. Faces half torn off, skulls smashed in—soft brain tissue here, a crushed hand there, detached from its arm. Ten meters away a pulped head, the helmet stove in. By my feet a clenched-up body, arms outstretched, hands clasped together in entreaty. The victors of this unimaginable battle had, the following day, burst into the Château du Plantin where the Senegalese detachment was hiding and screamed: "Where are the Blacks?" Surrounded, hunted down, their hands up, this band of humanity had been shoved towards the highway to Chères, a kilometer away. There, in a roadside field, an order was barked out to the French: "Get over there. Lie down. Look away." Another rang out towards the Senegalese: "On our signal, Go. You'll be free." There was a tank either side of the road. On a whistle-blast the Senegalese scattered. But machineguns then raked the ground, and grenades finished off the job. So none could escape the panzers crushed the dead bodies, the dying, the wounded and those taken unawares. Harrying those who were fleeing, the mechanical killing machines ploughed them into the ground. At the site of the massacre, in a nondescript and nameless ditch, we laid out the human remains.

FRANÇOISE-MARIE MEIFREDY,
Missions sans frontières

Colonial Minds Confounded

Postscript as Prologue: Chasselay, near Lyon (21 June 1940)

The atrocity recounted here by Françoise Meifredy, a volunteer auxiliary nurse, is probably the most familiar episode concerning French colonial troops in 1940.[1] It is certainly among the most infamous. Recently scholars, with Nancy Ellen Lawler, Raffael Scheck, and Julien Fargettas to the fore, have provided overdue attention to the troops from the French Empire as victims of war crimes such as Chasselay. The focus on victimhood and the human sufferings of colonial soldiers after capitulation has, however, deflected our gaze from French colonial soldiers as combatants—and prominent as well as highly capable ones, albeit in a losing cause.

This chapter concentrates on the battlefront experiences of France's West African troops in 1940. In doing so it holds up a mirror to attitudes in "colonial minds" on both sides of the Franco-German conflict that began in September 1939. A series of combat case studies illustrates how the understanding of colonial-metropolitan relationships by both nations' political-military elites was so prejudiced that French astonishment was surpassed only by German anger in the face of the remarkable sacrifices of the colonial troops.

The men from the French Empire bulked large in the composition of the French Army that fought against Hitler's two-stage offensive into Western Europe, code-named "Case Yellow" (10 May 1940) and "Case Red" (5 June 1940), with many thousands losing their lives in the Battle of France.[2] Despite this, however, the overseas troops have little visibility in the historiography of 1940.[3] Chasselay is absent from the index of Sir Alistair Horne's well-known and still-reprinted book *To Lose a Battle*.[4] So are Airaines and Le Quesnoy in the department of the Somme, sites of other massacres. Missing from Horne's index are the words "war crimes," "atrocities," "massacres," "Senegalese," even "colonial troops." Another standard work, *Why France Collapsed* by Guy Chapman, pays French colonial and North African formations scarcely greater attention. It, too, severely neglects their training, equipment, experiences of battle, and retreat, failing to assess their combat effectiveness.

Here, therefore, by an examination of engagements fought by units of the 1st, 5th, and 7th Colonial Divisions in 1940, pointers are offered about the quantity, quality, and significance of the French overseas forces. This chapter also aims to raise, if not definitively answer, questions about these troops' discipline, their conduct in the face of air attacks and armored breakthroughs, their fighting prowess, and the responses by friends and foes to them. It moves us toward an enriched sense of the relationships between the French "colonial mind" and military affairs in the decisive crisis of the Third Republic, the regime that had overseen France's greatest colonial expansion.

There is a temptation toward a simplifying and stereotyped dichotomy, wherein the soldiers from the empire are either corps d'élite or cannon fodder. Taking that route leads to an interpretative cul-de-sac, obscuring the roles of the colonial forces and their varied battlefield experiences. A Manichean presentation of them as heroic supermen or victims is unconvincing. In practice French colonial forces were diverse in their nature and their experiences—experiences ranging from arrival and deployment in September 1939 to enduring the freezing winter of the "Phony War" to both creditable combat records and victimhood in 1940. One chapter cannot do justice to the variety within their histories. What follows strives, nonetheless, to delineate some elements for a richer interpretation of what was, by any reckoning, the remarkable odyssey of the men from Overseas France.[5]

Prewar: French Colonial Forces in the Late 1930s

French propaganda during World War I cultivated a notion of West Africans as innately warlike, as natural soldiers—*les races guerrières*.[6] Rather conveniently in a conflict whose battlefields saw the defensive assume a murderous tactical primacy, the West Africans were considered particularly suitable for employment in initial assault waves. They certainly paid a high price for this theory. Between 30,000 and 31,000 died out of the 192,000 Senegalese Tirailleurs who served on the Western Front and in Turkey, Togoland, and Cameroon.[7] In the 1930s, with the rise of a new challenge to French security from Hitler's Reich, "strength through Empire" became a key part of French defense calculations and war planning, as Marc Michel and others have shown.[8] In French eyes, as Martin Thomas has pithily summarized things:

Colonial Minds Confounded

Total war was not global war. Rather the totality of metropolitan and imperial resources was required to defeat Germany. In the words of Deputy Chief of Staff General Alphonse Georges, "the colonies would be defended on the Rhine." Britain's blue-water imperialism did not resonate in France where imperial power denoted the capacity to deploy colonial resources in defense of the home country.[9]

Examining the first of what are a number of "received" images—that of the necessary but unreliable colonials—the presence of the broader "ambivalence" discerned by Robert J. Young in the eve-of-war Third Republic is notable. Coexisting in an unstable equilibrium, in Young's persuasive account, was evidence of a resurgent self-confidence (boosted by the opening of staff talks with Britain and a recovery of foreign exchange reserves after spring 1939), with recurrent shivers of self-doubt.[10] The latter were most notable when leaders and newspaper editorialists pondered French prospects in another big war. Had the country sufficient stamina, resolve, and energy to endure another round in what Finance Minister (and from 21 March to 16 June 1940, Prime Minister) Paul Reynaud called "the Franco-German duel"?[11]

Reflecting this ambivalence in the French political and public mood were the colonial troops—their morale, dependability, and combat capabilities.[12] To be sure, politicians as well as military chiefs paid public homage to imperial resources. These were, it was often proclaimed, a key to the defense of metropolitan France. After all, the overseas formations more closely attained wartime establishment strengths than the twenty standing "Active type" infantry divisions of the peacetime metropolitan army.

For optimists what mattered was that over a third of the colonial army troop strength was long-service career professionals (*engagés volontaires*). This helped them undergo realistic and demanding peacetime training, often using live ammunition. It bred confidence that the imperial forces would, in war, prove tough and capable. For example, the four North African infantry divisions based in metropolitan France before the 1939 mobilization were, in the words of the historian of the French Army, Henry Dutailly, "more deployable than French units, and able to take a part in providing [frontier mobilization] *couverture* in the shortest time delays."[13]

Alongside such paeans, however, were sources of anxiety. Thus appeals multiplied before 1939 to improve "the living conditions and career prospects offered to the native troops." These, however, were consistently ignored.[14] Just a week into the French Second Army Group's plodding advance into the Saar in mid-September 1939—an unsuccessful bid to draw German units that were attacking Poland back to the Western Front—the French high command betrayed ambivalence about the steadiness of their colonial troops. The "delicate position" of the 4th Colonial Infantry Division (DIC—Division d'Infanterie Coloniale) under General Joseph-Maurice de Bazelaire de Ruppière concerned General Maurice Gamelin, the army generalissimo. On 16 September 1939 Gamelin instructed General Georges, now commanding the North-East theater of operations, to exercise caution in the introduction of the West Africans to the frontline's rigors and risks. 'It would not do," emphasized Gamelin, "for it to be our Senegalese troops who first experience the shock of [. . .] tanks and low-flying aircraft."[15] One may wonder whether this signified payback time given the fact that, in one historian's words, "for the army general staff, the North African and colonial formations remained, whatever their military qualities, merely a back-up army."[16]

Yet, to a significant degree, concern for colonial units in the test of battle masked wider weaknesses in the French Army. These were the fruits of successive governments' prewar policies—military as well as colonial. In 1936, fully three years before World War II, General Gaston Billotte, then inspector of colonial forces, warned after touring French West African depots that the pay structure and promotion obstacles above the senior NCOs and junior officer ranks militated against enlisting well-educated Africans. The army attracted few *indigènes* with ambition, initiative, and command potential. "If a military career is lucrative enough to appeal to the average native," reported Billotte, "it is noticeable, in contrast, that it does not tempt the educated indigenous young who are happier [. . .] in local administration." A dearth of promotion opportunities for the Senegalese created "major drawbacks for the training of leadership cadres."[17]

African recruits were neither expected nor encouraged to demonstrate leadership or initiative. Low expectations and low aspirations were, in turn, reflected in very modest prospects.[18] Illustrative of the problem, a Muslim sergeant major in French North Africa earned only half the rate of pay of a white equivalent. In West Africa a rank-and-file railway worker earned as much as an African sergeant major.[19] In 1937 General Georges warned that the "truly irritating pay inequalities that divide French and native non-commissioned officers of identical rank, seniority and family situation is a thing that may be dangerously exploited against us."[20]

French prejudices and a tendency to patronize their "colonial children," then, excluded West Africans from leadership. However, it was an unavoidable acknowledgment of real physical pathologies that prompted the French authorities to withdraw the colonial divisions from northern France in winter, the troops from the tropics being unsuited to extreme cold and snow. Quartered in the warmer climes of the French Midi between December 1939 and March 1940, the men from Senegal, Côte d'Ivoire, Guinea, and Madagascar avoided the rigors of one of Northern Europe's three coldest winters of the twentieth century. This decision of the high command so early in World War II reflected a willingness to learn from experience in 1914–18 when frostbite, tuberculosis, and other illnesses took a heavy toll among colonial divisions left freezing on the Western Front in the 1914–15 winter. It was in subsequent years that the practice of *hivernage* had been adopted—wintering the colonials in camps around Fréjus, Cahors, Toulon, and Marseilles.[21]

With lessons learned, *hivernage* was reintroduced in 1939–40—though without matching provision for the North African Tirailleurs. These men languished in subzero temperatures on the Franco-German frontier. Their fingers frozen, they had to entrench in iron-hard ground or try to build strongpoints with concrete that crystallized as it was poured.[22] Visiting Toulon for Christmas leave in December 1939, Captain Daniel Barlone of the 2nd North African Division noted in his diary:

> The only infantry to be seen are the Senegalese. They are trained carefully in order to get them used to wear[ing] the heavy soldiers'

boots. [. . .] These excellent fighters, who have shown fine courage and physical resistance in our colonies, can be used in Europe only during the fine season, because they succumb rapidly to the cold weather. During the winter they return to garrisons in the south of France.[23]

The English playwright and novelist Somerset Maugham, with a house at nearby Cap Ferrat, went so far as to regard the presence of the West African soldiers as a kind of bellwether of French security, telling guests "there was no danger, until the Senegalese troops from the colonial infantry base at Fréjus began appearing on the roads."[24]

Pre-battle: The Deployment and State-of-Readiness of Colonial Troops, 1939–40

A brief overview of the development of the Third Republic's overseas forces in 1939–40 is all that can be accommodated here. But with its context, we should better appreciate the military roles assigned colonial forces by the high command, and the images French people had constructed of the colonial soldiers.[25]

The first point is that the number of colonial formations and the number of colonial troops comprising them expanded at the end of the 1930s and in the war's early months. Besides the four North African infantry divisions already stationed in peacetime France, and other large formations that were retained in Morocco, Algeria, and Tunisia, three more reservist North African divisions, the 5th, 6th, and 7th, were formed in metropolitan France during the phony war of 1939–40.[26] La Coloniale also expanded as war approached, there being 21,760 colonial *indigènes* serving in France in January 1939 compared with 12,351 four years earlier—an increase of 9,409 and worth almost another infantry division (what one of General Gamelin's staff referred to as "the project tending to 'blacken' the colonial divisions and which constituted the beginning of the utilization of the demographic resources of our Africa").[27] This marked a success for Gamelin's pressure at defense planning meetings to expand military recruitment from overseas resources, after Germany had annexed Austria in March 1938.[28] Meanwhile the North African troops in the métropole during this period altered little: 36,927 in 1935, rising to 37,188 in 1939, because strong forces were kept in French North Africa to parry the threat of fascist Italy (which had troop contingents in the Balearic Islands and in 1938–39 reinforced its colony of Libya to menace the flank of Tunisia).[29]

When war had threatened before 1914—and during World War I—the value of overseas troops was proclaimed by a chorus of French voices. The loudest advocate had been General Charles Mangin. This officer had articulated the cause in several articles and a book entitled *La Force Noire* (Hachette, 1910). He had then gone on to command a colonial corps during some of the fiercest fighting on the Western Front at Verdun in October 1916 and later.[30] Mangin's political and spiritual successor as the evangelist of imperial forces during the interwar decades was Georges Mandel—a vigorous Germanophobe who had been political secretary to Georges "Tiger" Clemenceau, French prime minister once again in 1917–20.[31] Holding high office in his turn as minister of the colonies and then minister of the interior in several successive governments from 1938 to June 1940, Mandel pledged the empire as a "reservoir" of soldiers. He promoted a discourse that was centered on rescue and replenishment—the cohorts of colonials to fill the shortfall between Germany's mobilized resources and the lesser forces that metropolitan France could field in another grim war of attrition.

On this point Mandel enjoyed the full support of General Maxime Weygand, the commander-in-chief of the army in 1931–35 and recalled to resume that role in the crisis of May 1940.[32] Indeed there was probably no more public a preacher of the argument that Hitler would be opposed, and by implication defeated, not by a mere 39 million *gens de la métropole* but by the deep human reservoirs in "Greater France." As noted by Britain's military attaché in Paris, Colonel William Fraser, in December 1938 as prospects for lasting peace faded: "the manpower of her African Empire [. . .] inspires General Weygand in his public utterances to refer to France and French Africa as one country with a population of 110 million, and to urge his countrymen [sic] to realize and make use of this fact."[33] Some French officers were troubled by possible fallout from bragging of this sort. "Let's note in passing," wrote Major Jacques Minart of Gamelin's staff, "the poisonous consequences of the repeated affirmation [. . .] that France constituted an Empire of

110 million people.... This theme, exploited too often for insufficiently objective ends by certain military chiefs or politicians, led the Nation to believe too much that its civilizing mission gave it the right to entrust the métropole's defense to its children from overseas."[34]

The next point to be made is that formations from "overseas France" were neither regarded as an elite force nor as supermen—shock troops marching in to save the Motherland. It is not in doubt that the colonial troops, especially some of the North and West African units, enjoyed thoroughly merited respect among French commanders. They had proven reputations for élan and bravura, particularly on the offensive. Yet there was no operational logic to dictate they be retained in reserve to play the role of latter-day "imperial guard," in the multiple senses of this originally Napoleonic term.

Evidence from 1914–18 and 1940 demonstrates incontrovertibly that the colonial divisions were not held back till the attrition of industrialized combat had left the enemy ripe for a culminating blow. Yet neither was there a cynical expenditure of the colonials' lives by the French high command as cannon fodder. The troops of the empire were supplements, not substitutes, for young, white Frenchmen-in-uniform.

French "Overseas" Troops, 1939–1940: A Brief Typology

The French Army of 1939–40 was no monolith. It comprised some 116,000 career soldiers and officers, also about three times that number of active-service conscripts and several hundred thousand older reservists whose compulsory service had occurred between 1921 and 1935.[35] This diversity inevitably meant an uneven quality prevailed among French units. The army had both horsed and mechanized cavalry, armored divisions, motorcycle reconnaissance squadrons, infantry and artillery regiments, engineer battalions, signals troops, and motor and horsed transport detachments, along with field kitchens and medical, veterinary, and quartermaster services. Such diversity also characterized the colonial forces.

Who, then, were the overseas troops, and how may we delineate their types of formations? Troops from Algeria, Morocco, and Tunisia, along with those raised in West Africa, Equatorial Africa, Madagascar, and Indochina, were, in the popular imagery and semiofficial films and utterances, described as "colonial" (albeit those from Algeria were not so in French constitutional statute). Taken together, the overseas divisions and other higher formations (such as the Spahi cavalry independent brigades from North Africa) formed by April 1940 about one-fifth of the French Army's formations on a war footing.

Administratively the imperial forces in 1940 were split into two categories. First there were the units of the Armée d'Afrique. These comprised the seven North African infantry divisions in France already mentioned, consisting of regiments raised from European and Muslim personnel in Algeria and Tunisia, plus the 1st Moroccan Division (with the 2nd and 3rd Moroccan divisions remaining in North Africa, classed as *divisions de protection*).[36] In addition to these units were a number of independent regiments of Moroccan riflemen (Régiments de Tirailleurs Marocains or RTM). The latter were incorporated into "metropolitan" formations, as exemplified by the 8th RTM, which served alongside two metropolitan French infantry regiments in General Marcel Baudouin's 13th Infantry Division, and the 3rd RTM, which with two other metropolitan regiments constituted General Jean Vernillat's 43rd Infantry Division.[37]

The second types of units were those of the Armée Coloniale. These were heavily though not solely recruited in French West Africa, chiefly in the colonies of Senegal and Ivory Coast. They constituted eight colonial infantry divisions (DICs) in 1940. Two were concentrated into the Colonial Corps, initially led by General Henry Freydenberg, a "nice friendly old gentleman who gave me a feeling of quiet efficiency" (in the words of a senior British officer in France, General Sir Alan Brooke), and from 5 June 1940 by General Emile-Jean Carlès.[38] The remaining colonial divisions were distributed among the other French armies on the northeast theater of operations, facing Germany. It is on these troops of La Coloniale, somewhat imprecisely called Tirailleurs Sénégalais, that the remainder of this chapter concentrates. They were the colonial army proper, the World War II equivalents of those used as shock troops in 1914–18. Such focus is appropriate because, first, little attention has been paid until recently to France's sub-Saharan African troops in World War II. Second, these were the majority of the overseas divisions in metropolitan France until in June 1940 additional and weaker North

African formations, the DIAS (Divisions d'Infanterie d'Afrique) were rushed across the Mediterranean to partly compensate Allied losses suffered in the May 1940 operations.[39]

In the colonial formations, as in metropolitan ones, an uneven quantity and quality of weapons and equipment exacerbated the variable quality of the manpower. But the army's trainers did not doubt the dedication of those with whom they worked, as Colonel Frémanger, commandant of the Center for Motorization of Colonial Troops, recorded in his annual report on morale and material in September 1938. "The tank officers," he stated, "having a sufficient quantity of old but hard wearing equipment at their disposal, give everything of themselves to educate and train their subordinates and get remarkable results."[40] Certainly there was no neglecting the coming forms of modern war, with air attacks bound to add a terrifying dimension to the more traditional artillery and infantry engagements. Frémanger's colleague Colonel Ouvrard reported on 30 September 1938 on the training of native colonial troops. He remarked on exercises conducted by the 4th Regiment of Senegalese Tirailleurs with mechanized vehicles, signals, artillery, and airpower that had been "to the utmost degree instructive for the command cadres." The different phases of a battle had been studied "and attention tirelessly drawn to anti-aircraft defense (low-flying aircraft) and to antitank defense, the importance of defiles, woods and positions."[41] When the Senegalese left their winter quarters for northeast France in March 1940, top priority was accorded to weapons training, tactical exercises, and familiarization with new technologies such as antiaircraft range finders and wireless sets. Noted the war diary of General Charles Roucaud's 1st Colonial Division: "The particular character of this 'phony war' has nevertheless permitted the 1st DIC to acquire excellent cohesion and train in perfect peace and quiet. Against this, the men and even sections of the leadership cadres betray a surprise they do not disguise in the face of this form of war in which one does not do any fighting. The wake-up will be hard."[42] Thanks to the impressive progress and consolidation of the instruction taught to French colonial regiments since 1938, it would be the destiny of many a Wehrmacht assault formation to experience a "hard wake-up" in 1940 and learn how misleading was Nazi propaganda about African troops.

Combat Case Study 1: The 33rd RICMS from Amiens to the Oise

During the Dunkirk evacuation (completed by 4 June 1940) the French sought to establish a new defensive line on the Somme and Aisne Rivers. This was their last serious hope to halt the Blitzkrieg and mire Hitler's dream of decisive victory in a stalemate that would accord with Allied grand strategy. A serious problem from the outset was the Wehrmacht's seizure of bridgeheads on the south bank of the Somme at Abbeville, Amiens, and Péronne. These breached the integrity of what was rapidly termed the "Weygand Line."

Among the earliest of the new formations rushing north to form General Aubert Frère's new VIIth Army and try to restore the integrity of the Weygand Line was the 7th Colonial Infantry Division commanded by General Louis-Émile Noiret. Its leading elements deployed on 20 May 1940 around Oeilly, south of Amiens. As its infantry regiments arrived over the following three days, the 7th DIC was ordered to expel the Germans who had seized the Amiens suburbs on the south bank of the River Somme.

To execute this order its troops attacked northward along two axes at 17h00 on 24 May. The more westerly striking force comprised infantry of the 33rd Mixed Senegalese Regiment (RICMS-Régiment d'Infanterie Coloniale Mixte Sénégalais), led by Lieutenant-Colonel Chapon, supported by a troop of S35 Somua tanks. On the right, further east, the assault was led by the 7th DIC's motorized reconnaissance battalion in coordination with the 2nd Colonial Infantry Regiment, a "European" unit of General de Bazelaire's 4th DIC. The 33rd RICMS was pounded by a Luftwaffe attack from around sixty aircraft that flew "with impunity at low altitude," dive-bombing and machine-gunning the troops for many hours, but the Tirailleurs' morale held firm. The "only desire of the soldiers was to avenge the spectacle of death and frightful woundings" to which they had been party. On 26 and 27 May the 33rd RICMS "grappled vigorously with the enemy, repelling him at several points" during bitter combat in the southern outskirts of Amiens. Numerous gallantry citations in this action attested to the "fighting spirit" demonstrated by the Senegalese.[43]

The attack by the 33rd RICMS was not, however, ultimately crowned by success. On the left "the Senegalese Tirailleurs of Chapon's detachment barely got out of their start lines." Some were cut down, and others forced to the ground by fire from enemy detachments at Charmilles Farm north of Dury and in the village of Saleux, just southwest of the outskirts of Amiens. The Senegalese made a second assault soon after darkness fell at 22h00, but with no better results. During 25 and 26 May, to comply with orders from General Charles Grandsard, commander of the Xth Corps, the 7th DIC remained on the defensive and improved its positions. At 16h00 on 26 May corps headquarters summoned General Noiret and told him to try again to seize the villages of Saleux and Salouel the next day.

The mission was entrusted once more to the 33rd RICMS. This time, on 27 May, the infantry assault went in with the support of eight modern and very capable Somua tanks armed with 47mm turret cannons and two companies of the 19th Battletank Battalion's older D2 mediums (seventeen tanks). Clanking forward from 10h00 the tanks "advanced without difficulty," nosing into the outer Amiens suburbs. The accompanying colonial infantry, however, came under enemy fire as soon as they moved off. As a result, in the west and center they made little progress. More encouragingly, French fighter aircraft beat off an attempted attack on the infantry by numerous Luftwaffe bombers.[44] The French assault to the east fared better. It secured the high ground of the ridge at Hill 102 between 11h00 and 13h00, together with the ridge north of Charmilles Farm. Unfortunately the advance was not reinforced. The 1st Battalion/7th Infantry Regiment (European troops) mistook some French D2 tanks returning to their own lines for German panzers and simply sat tight when they should have pressed forward.

On the 7th Division's right, de Bazelaire's adjoining 4th DIC progressed well, capturing the railway station at Longueau. They also secured the southern bank of the Somme as far as Blangy and Trouville. At 16h00 its units received new orders from corps headquarters to prepare defensive positions, taking special precautions against German endeavors to infiltrate French lines with infantry or armor. The Somua squadron remained to support Noiret's troops, while the eleven still serviceable D2 tanks regrouped (six having been knocked out in the earlier battle).[45]

On 28 May further heavy fighting occurred as 7th DIC and German spearheads contested control of the hamlets and farms immediately west of the Amiens outskirts. The front then stabilized, while the Germans concentrated on the battle at Dunkerque and the French hastened to improve their new Somme-Aisne line. It was only a month earlier, on 26 April 1940, that the 54th, 58th, 60th, and 62nd Senegalese Tirailleurs battalions had arrived to convert the hitherto "white" 33rd and 57th Colonial Regiments into RICMS. The transformation was complete barely three weeks before the formations went into action. Yet neither war diaries nor field orders suggest any disorder or disorganization in the 33rd or 57th RICMS. Furthermore the 4th Colonial Division underwent similar reorganization, gaining the 24th Senegalese Tirailleurs Regiment on 7 April 1940 and the 16th Senegalese Tirailleurs Regiment on 9 April while shedding one of its two "European" infantry regiments, the 4th RIC, on 16 April. It seems not in doubt that the colonial formations were adaptable, professional, and pugnacious.

As May 1940 closed, the Germans were focusing on the defeat of the Allied pockets around Calais and Dunkerque, and the French colonial troops joined other divisions along the hastily constituted Somme-Aisne line in urgent toil against the clock. Many of the men formed working parties, the soldiers helping the French army engineer companies, the *corps du génie militaire*, improvise a checkerboard of fieldworks against the next Wehrmacht assault. Fresh divisions arrived almost daily between 28 May and 4 June from general reserve, along with others switched by rail and road from Alsace-Lorraine, the Jura, the Alps, and the depots of the interior.

On 30 May the 7th DIC was relieved by the 16th Infantry Division and withdrawn into the VIIth Army reserve. It subsequently redeployed along the River Oise between Ribécourt and Pont-L'Eveque to establish an antitank barrage. Meanwhile it detached some men for working parties ordered to make the Carlepont Forest a bastion impenetrable to infantry and tanks. Noiret's division was now unusually strong, having gained the 4th RIC on 2 June and thus now comprising two European regiments (4th and 7th RICS) along with its two Senegalese mixed regiments (33rd and 57th RICMS).

When the battle resumed on 5 June most of the French army fought far more effectively. Tactics were much improved on the shallow linear deployments that had typified French defensive endeavors in mid-May. Now strongpoints and "hedgehogs" confronted the Germans. These were arranged in interlocking checkerboard layouts that made lethal killing zones out of the open ground in between. The modified dispositions were the handiwork of Weygand—appointed by Prime Minister Paul Reynaud on 20 May to replace Gamelin as generalissimo—and Frère, the new commander of the VIIth Army. Troops of either the 33rd RICMS or a sister unit defending the "Weygand hedgehogs" caught the eye of the Reuters journalist Gordon Waterfield. He and other war correspondents were traveling in the new frontline zone, northwest of Soissons, on 4 June. "Every 500 yards near the front line we passed barricades across the roads, built of huge blocks of stone, old Fords, ploughshares and anything that there was to hand."[46] With barricaded and sandbagged villages and farms, along with machine-gun nests and infantry bastions (*points d'appui*) sited in woods to a depth of eight to twelve miles, supported by freshly laid minefields, the German assaults would be channeled to run into the toughest French positions.

In such defenses behind the Aisne, in early June 1940 Noiret's colonial troops rejoined the battle. The 33rd RICMS came under fire beginning at 20h00 on 6 June as the 29th Alpine Division was pressed back from Roye and Champien following forty-eight hours of exceptionally heavy attack. The "European" 4th Colonial Infantry Regiment (RIC)—hitherto the 7th DIC reserve—was committed, one of its battalions supporting the hard-pressed neighboring 23rd Infantry Division of General Joseph Jeannel. Another of the colonial regiment's "European" battalions, Major Paing's IInd/4th RIC, meanwhile repulsed a German assault toward Salency, east of Noyon.

For the men of 7th DIC the hardest fighting occurred on 9, 10, and 11 June, when they bore the brunt of the onslaught by the German Xth Corps (Generalleutnant Christian Hansen) and XXXIXth Motorized Corps (Lieutenant General Rudolf Schmidt). Though heavily outnumbered and outgunned, Noiret's soldiers—African, Malagasy, and European—gave no ground. Their steadfast defense permitted orderly withdrawals by the 3rd Light Division and the 23rd Infantry Division, each badly mauled in the preceding days.

However, the 7th DIC's positions now formed an exposed salient that jutted into ground controlled by the Germans. Consequently, retreating on 9 June and finding the road bridge over the Oise blown up at Verberie, elements of the 4th and 7th RICs, along with part of the mixed European/Malagasy 32ndArtillery Regiment, had to abandon their vehicles and use the rail crossing. Further east the Senegalese Tirailleurs of the 33rd and 57th RICMS crossed the Oise unimpeded, although the divisional artillery transport was hampered when the Luftwaffe demolished the road bridge at Pont-Ste. Maxence.

Falling back toward Paris by late afternoon of 10 June, the 9th and 10th Companies of the 33rd RICMS were without promised motor transport. Withdrawing on foot, they were overtaken by their pursuers and engaged at 07h00 on 11 June in the village of Rully. However, launching a series of storming breakouts toward Baron that punched southward through the encircling enemy, the Senegalese "so greatly distinguished themselves that the Germans sullied their name by speaking of their 'savagery' in the course of the action."[47]

Combat Case Study 2: The 5th Colonial Division on the Lower Somme

On the River Somme's western reaches Weygand's hedgehog villages were outflanked and bypassed by the daring advance of the "Phantom Division," 7th Panzer, led by one of Germany's most charismatic Second World War commanders, Major General Erwin Rommel. The tanks and their mechanized grenadiers, supported by soldiers of four German infantry divisions (the 2nd, 6th, 27th, and 46th), achieved devastatingly deep and rapid inroads. South and southwest of Hangest-sur-Somme they punched through the French lines just as the 3rd Light Cavalry Division of General Robert-Marie Petiet was relieved by General Félix-Pierre Séchet's 5th Colonial Division (5th DIC). The latter had just come into line, having been assigned to General Marcel Ihler's IXth Corps. Two companies of Senegalese, before they could even occupy the outposts and strongpoints vacated by the cavalry on 5 June, were caught "on the hop, right in the middle of their movement" by Rommel's assault.[48]

Yet even in these catastrophic circumstances the Germans encountered formidable opposition. An account from the Pomeranian infantry regiment that made the assault crossing described the battle on the Somme at Condé-Folie:

> The locality [proved] a particularly difficult point to reduce. There our troops again met stiff resistance, the enemy fighting with ferocity. The Blacks in particular utilized every opportunity to stage a defense to the bitter end. [. . .] Many comrades-in-arms met their deaths there, but we had to take the place[. . . .] These were difficult hours: the enemy defended every house, and every window and skylight was spitting fire at us. To break this resistance, once-and-for-all, we then brought flame-throwers into action before our fusiliers bravely plunged with grenades and bayonets into hand-to-hand combat, thus to subdue this important position.[49]

Striving to break out toward Montagne-Fayel, eight kilometers to the southwest, other German assault troops were held up in further "heavy fighting against strong enemy forces." The most obdurate resistance was offered by the Senegalese of the 53rd RICMS. These troops had dug into cleverly camouflaged positions on wooded slopes near Quesnoy-sur-Airaines. Supported by "large numbers of field and anti-tank guns," the West Africans "defended themselves desperately," one battalion having "installed itself very skillfully" in the walled grounds of the Château du Quesnoy.[50]

Rommel's men also met fierce opposition from parts of the 3rd Light Cavalry Division—the formation that the 5th Colonial Division had been moving up to relieve. A particularly heavy toll was taken of the Germans by Captain d'Ornano's 25mm guns of the French cavalry's antitank squadron.[51] With the Wehrmacht pouring south of the lower Somme, however, neither the gallantry of these antitank gunners nor the courage of the Senegalese at Quesnoy could stop over two hundred panzers and four infantry divisions. Nevertheless, the African soldiers' pugnacity shocked the Germans and helped other French units escape. The 53rd RICMS was all but annihilated at Airaines, suffering nearly 90 percent casualties. This remarkable, dreadful statistic may have charted the bloodiest sacrifice of any French regiment in 1940, when even the

29th Alpine Division's losses in its diehard defense of the hedgehog villages between Roye and the River Somme over four days of unforgiving combat from 5 to 8 June, often house-to-house, did not exceed 60 percent of its infantry.

By nightfall on 7 June, at the conclusion of two days of unrelenting battle, all but a few small groups of the 53rd RICMS had been overrun or forced to withdraw, losing contact with the 13th Division to their right.[52] About fifty Senegalese soldiers who surrendered were then murdered. These included Captain Charles N'Tchoréré, commanding officer of 7th Company/53rd RICMS. A German drew his revolver and shot him dead for claiming his right to remain with the captured European officers rather than obey instructions to muster with African rank-and-file POWs.[53]

Combat Case Study 3: The 33rd RICMS at Orléans

From the area around Noyon, the 7th Colonial Division fought with bravery and skill against the June offensive of the Germans, Case Red.[54] The 33rd RICMS fell back only when instructed—and in impeccable order—at times withdrawing by train, at times on military trucks, but often on their own feet. By the middle of the month the men were part of the flow of troops making for the south bank of the Loire. There the 57th RICMS, along with 17th Senegalese Tirailleurs Battalion, defended the river crossing at Châteauneuf.

As the 33rd RICMS under Lieutenant-Colonel Chapon fell back around the outskirts of Paris on 10–11 June 1940, its 9th Company found itself "very hard pressed by the enemy." Nevertheless it smashed an escape route for itself, through the village of Rully (p. 2). Over the next two days the Senegalese clung unflinchingly to their positions under a "systematic and simultaneous" bombardment by German aviation and artillery. Senegalese morale "soared" after putting up such a successful fight, with "many Tirailleurs pleading to be allowed to go over to the attack." German prisoners captured during this bitter action "were strongly impressed by the ardor of our native troops (p. 2)." Instead of counterattacking, however, the 33rd RICMS was instructed on 12 June to fall back again. Making a forced march between 22h00 that day and 10h00 on the morning of 14 June, the men withdrew through Claye-

Souilly to Servon. It was a remarkable feat of endurance—a retreat on foot of 105 kilometers, completed in thirty-six hours (p. 2).

During the afternoon of 14 June, shortly after the Wehrmacht entered Paris, the 33rd RICMS was again ordered to pull back. This time the men were given motor transport to Moigny, south of the capital. There, on 15 June, they boarded trains that took them into the country below Châteauneuf-sur-Loire. Disembarking at Aubraies, the 1st Battalion of 33rd Regiment under Major Schneider—about two hundred soldiers—was commandeered by Colonel de Froissard-Broissia, the chief of staff to the XXVth Corps. Despite holding a job that would usually have stamped him as a "paper pusher," the colonel still had an instinct for battle. With fine tactical acumen he rapidly assembled an ad hoc force to secure the Loire bridges in Orléans—crossings abandoned by units previously allotted to their defense.

Deploying the Senegalese alongside detachments of the 8th Moroccan Regiment and the 60th Infantry (both part of the 13th Division), de Froissard-Broissia's battlegroup disregarded "serious losses" from *Minenwerfers* (mine launchers) and defended the Orléans-Sandillon road defiantly. The "Germans were not expecting resistance of this kind," and from mid-afternoon on 16 June to mid-afternoon on the 17th the Senegalese had everything thrown at them (p. 2). Unable to capture the key bridges at Orléans, the Germans lost the opportunity to envelop the left flank of the Seventh DIC. They also failed to trap the survivors of the 11th Infantry Division, 29th Alpine Division, and 47th Infantry Division—formations that escaped south across the Loire at Jargeau and Gien because the colonials and their comrades kept open the escape routes.

Meanwhile, in Orléans, Schneider's 1st Battalion/33rd RICMS put up an aggressive defense of the rail bridge in the southeast of the city, with support from survivors of the 8th Moroccan Regiment. Discovering the bridge in enemy hands, the battle group retook it in a counterattack and held it for the next twenty-three hours, until nightfall on 17 June, denying passage to an impatient Wehrmacht spearhead.

Falling back again on 18 June, the 33rd RICMS fought a further rearguard action, this time led by its IIIrd Battalion. The engagement stopped the Germans completely, despite "strong pressure from a powerful column of tanks and motorized troops" that inflicted heavy casualties on the colonial soldiers at Nouan-les-Fuzelier and Salbris. Finally the 33rd's survivors withdrew south over the Cher, some swimming the river under enemy fire and others crossing on makeshift rafts (p. 3).

The last action for the 33rd RICMS occurred on the evening of 24 June at Champagne-Mouton. There "once again they inflicted serious losses on the enemy." In total the regiment lost 42 officers, 183 NCOs, and 1,500 other ranks killed and wounded by enemy fire. Along with its parent formation, Noiret's 7th Colonial Division, it had withstood the exhausting summer heat and dust, plus a dearth of fresh rations—trials that, in the words of the 33rd RICMS commander, "tested human capacities to the utmost limit" (p. 3). Maintaining exemplary spirit, discipline, and combat effectiveness, the remainder of the 7th DIC fell back, successively crossing the rivers Cher, Indre, and Creuse. The division's survivors had reached the Vienne, north of Angoulême, when the Armistice took effect on 25 June. Of the 7th Colonial Division as a whole it may be said, as of the 33rd RICMS, that it "had never withdrawn except when ordered to." The troops "held onto their flag, their weapons and, to the end, their will to win (p. 3)."

Combat Case Study 4: The 14th Senegalese Tirailleurs on the Meuse

The 14th RTS (Régiment de Tirailleurs Sénégalais) led by Colonel Montangerand was one of the three infantry regiments of General Charles Roucaud's 1st Colonial Division. When battle commenced in mid-May 1940, it was stationed in support of fortress garrison troops of the Montmédy sector at the westernmost limit of the Maginot Line. The regiment was soon redeployed west, as the French high command reacted to the breach of the Meuse between Sedan and Mouzon on 14 and 15 May. Rapidly the leading elements of 14th RTS were rushed into action to improvise a defense on the southeast flank of the German mechanized thrust over the Meuse between Pont-Maugis and Mouzon, immediately upriver of Sedan. Falling back here to Laneuville-sur-Meuse was a machine-gun detachment from the support company of the 120th Infantry Regiment, part of General Joseph-Antoine Baudet's 71st Infantry Division that had just been severely mauled by the panzers. The machine-gunners' commander, Lieutenant Paul-André Lesort, noted the next day, 16 May, what a stirring sight the advancing African soldiers presented to his own tired, hungry troops:

> Late in the evening before [15 May], in the twilight gloom, our path at last crossed that of a detachment moving forward into the line: Senegalese Tirailleurs, a small force in number of one or two sections, in approach-march formation, the infantrymen deployed on either side of the road. As we passed them I questioned one of their NCOs, who knew nothing. The big Black lads marched at a calm measure, loping forward with long, supple strides. Toward the rear a Tirailleur was holding a rabbit or hare at arm's length by its feet and with a laugh, his white teeth flashing, he held it out to one of our men—though I don't know what he was able to do with it, the night being a bit short to cook up a stew.[55]

On the northern edge of the Dieulet Forest, just south of Pouilly-sur-Meuse and Beaumont-en-Argonne, the Senegalese repelled the German assaults, notably on 23 May. As the 9th Company's commander, Captain Jarty, recorded: "Under a violent bombardment the Tirailleurs have been splendid and all the groups that were attacked responded by putting up magnificent resistance. No man gave any ground."[56]

On 13 June the 1st Colonial Division was assigned to reinforce the Colonial Corps, now under General Carlès and dangerously dispersed between Ste.-Ménéhould and Vitry-le-François. The moment the 1st DIC was relieved by the 3rd Colonial Division, at 15h00, it was instructed to proceed to the south of the Hesse forest and rendezvous with motor transport. Reaching the embarkation zone involved a daylight redeployment for some of the divisional units, but a move happily shielded by nightfall for others. This could easily have turned into a disaster, had the maneuver attracted attention from the skies. Fortunately the Luftwaffe failed to detect the switch, the Germans missing the inviting target presented by "this river of humanity" as the 1st DIC's troops, artillery, and service units traveled undisturbed to muster points around the village of Parois.[57]

Such ease of movement did not, however, last long. So bad was congestion on the roads that by the evening of 13 June the transport companies had managed to deliver only the 1st Battalion of Lieutenant-Colonel Cantagrel's 3rd Colonial Infantry Regiment (3rd RIC) to the concentration zone southwest of Bar-le-Duc. For now this battalion and the motorized squadron of the 71st GRDI (Groupe de Reconnaissance de Division d'Infanterie, the divisional reconnaissance battalion), were the only troops available to the divisional commander, General Roucaud, to set up a northwesterly facing defense from Vitry-le-François to Ramerupt-sur-Aube.

The arrival of the rest of the division took all night, and much of the day of 14 June as well. The 3rd RIC's remaining two battalions were the first of the follow-on elements to appear and were deployed between Bar-le-Duc and Combles. Next were the transportable detachments of the 1st Colonial Artillery Regiment, and then the 14th RTS. Last to arrive, in the evening of 14 June, was Colonel Mazayer's 12th Senegalese Tirailleurs Regiment (12th RTS). This regiment had made the move on foot in two columns, one using the Bar-le-Duc to Ligny road, the other marching via Resson. By nightfall on 14 June Roucaud had disposed his units facing west-southwest. To constitute a forward defense position he deployed the 3rd RIC on the right, toward Haironville; from that village the line was extended by the 14th RTS to Lavincourt, with the reconnaissance troopers of the 71st GRDI posted at Stainville to cover the divisional left. Meanwhile Mazayer's 12th RTS, sheltering in the Bois de Chêne after its exhausting approach march, was kept in reserve.[58]

Unfortunately for the French the oncoming German armies were not moving south along one axis—the Marne valley—but along two. The second line of advance followed the western edges of the Argonne and was directed at first toward Bar-le-Duc, before bending along the Ornain valley toward Ligny-en-Barrois. Its spearhead was Schmidt's XXXIXth Motorized Corps (1st and 2nd Panzer Divisions and 29th Motorized Division), the most westerly column of the army group of General Gerd von Rundstedt.

This powerful, agile German force fell upon the 1st Colonial Division's right flank. Simultaneously elements of Schmidt's corps collided with two of the 1st DIC's artillery groups and the divisional reserve, Colonel Mazayer's 12th RTS. Most of the staff and the commander of

1st Artillery Regiment, Lieutenant-Colonel Fadi, were captured in their headquarters; the divisional infantry commander, Colonel Baudin, escaped by sheer luck. Though taken unawares, the French artillerymen "work[ed] wonders, firing in antitank mode" over open sights. One gun of the 6th Field Battery single-handedly knocked out fifteen German armored vehicles.

The men of the 12th RTS and 3rd Colonial Regiment displayed "prodigious acts of heroism" that day. Heavy casualties among the German attackers dissuaded them from interfering with the French withdrawal that was ordered that evening. "In a fierce display of willpower," and at a heavy cost, Roucaud's division extricated itself "from a truly desperate situation."[59] Disengaging toward the south, with the 14th RTS as rear guard, the retreat was executed in good order. Though the troops were weakened by their fatigue and the losses they had now suffered, morale remained excellent as they made good their escape. Resuming its march, the 1st DIC reached the River Meuse during the night of 16–17 June and set up a defense of crossing points from Bazoilles-sur-Meuse southward to Bourmont.

The battle that Roucaud's division had withstood on 15 June, and the following two nights of forced marches, had "tested it sternly."[60] The 1st Battalion/12th RTS had been all but annihilated defending the farm in the Bois du Chêne. Numerous Senegalese straggled behind the division, "deadbeat with fatigue, depleting the combat strength. The columns experienced "sporadic attacks by [German] armor" and "some dive-bombing" as they withdrew. No sustained fighting occurred, but "all manner of convoys and the bottlenecks caused by the presence of countless fleeing refugees troubled the division's march most seriously and made its retreat so agonizing."[61]

At dawn on 17 June the 1st Colonial Division was again ready to give battle, now facing west. Its right flank, to the north, was to be protected by General Marcel Aublet's 36th Infantry Division. Screening the south was the 71st GRDI (Roucaud's divisional reconnaissance battalion) and an ad hoc battle group led by General Édouard-Octave Brussaux, the military governor of Metz, placed under Roucaud's command. Some of the infantry had covered eighty-five kilometers in the previous twenty-four hours.

The 14th Senegalese had undergone their own odyssey immediately after the action against Schmidt's panzers. Captain Jarty's 9th Company was repeatedly engaged by German tanks during its retreat, acquitting itself well and even taking some prisoners before it rejoined its comrades on 19 June. The IInd Battalion, entrusted with covering the regiment's withdrawal to Ligny-en-Barrois, went missing for four days but reappeared in good order on 20 June at Pont-sur-Madon.[62]

According to one veteran of the divisional artillery, Roucaud's units "could have made another serious effort" had they received just a day's rest now. Continuing to withdraw in the conditions of the last few days, however, "was to risk snapping even the most steely physical and moral resilience." Suddenly something close to the ultimate test occurred during the night of 17–18 June. At first the retreat continued toward Bains-les-Bains. At midnight, however, when the soldiers had already been marching for several hours, an order to about-turn arrived. They had to reoccupy the emplacements on the Meuse that they had already defended once. Some of the infantry consequently tramped sixty kilometers in fourteen hours. The effect of this was to wear out the troops—troops still ready to fight as stoutly as they had done thus far. Convinced their exhaustion had been avoidable, Roucaud found it "infinitely painful" to see the damage done his 1st Colonial Division by this needless counter-march.[63]

Back on the Meuse, several elements of the force came under strong enemy attack during 18 June. The 12th RTS, supported by the IIIrd Group/1st Colonial Artillery Regiment, successfully defended Harréville-les-Chanteurs against an armored assault. During this fierce fight the guns of the group's 8th Battery alone fired three hundred shells over open sights. That afternoon the Wehrmacht 86th Infantry Division of Major General Joachim Witthöft attempted to force the Meuse at Bourmont. This was a split-level village held by Major Voillemin's 1st Battalion/14th RTS, its defense anchored on one strongpoint in Lower Bourmont commanded by Captain Mollard, with a second in the upper village under Captain Gauthier. French mortars delivered close support, and their fire repelled an effort at 14h00 by German motorized elements to advance from St.-Thiébault on the Meuse left bank. Lower Bourmont was then pounded by artillery and *Minenwerfers* for three hours. While the French sheltered from the bombardment, a company of German infantry slipped over the river into the flanks of the defenses. Expecting the shelling to have softened up the French, the outflanking party then assaulted Lower Bourmont. Strenuous resistance, however, threw it back onto the west bank of the Meuse.

By now more German troops had crossed the river to the south. These joined the attack, sparking a "wild twenty-hour-long fight." The French struggled against their assailants in a street battle that raged all night and into the next day, 19 June, each side using hand grenades liberally in what became a "furious" close-quarters action.[64] At 08h00 two more companies joined the assault, and at midday the German commanders threw in an entire fresh battalion. Inevitably, the ammunition of the Senegalese ran low, and after more "intense pounding," their heavy weapons one by one fell silent. A runner slipped through German lines and reported to Major Voillemin that Colonel Montangerand's regimental command post had given up Nijon and ceded possession of Graffigny, the village due east of Bourmont, to the enemy. This, Voillemin realized, meant that any order to retreat would not reach him. Nor would any relief force. His mission to prevent the Germans from crossing the Meuse was now void, as the Wehrmacht was already across the river and advancing eastward. By 18h00, his troops' ammunition spent, Voillemin had no means to fight on and brought the combat to an end.

Since the previous evening the 1st/14th Senegalese battalion had lost 6 officers, 34 French NCOs and men, and 126 native troops—of which, unlike the usual ratio of about 1:3, almost as many had been killed as wounded. The Germans had suffered even more grievously, leaving 365 dead on the battlefield. Their commander was amazed to find that so small a force had resisted for so long, as he was convinced he had been facing an entire French regiment. The action "showed what the troops of the 1st DIC were still capable of." For the veterans of the divisional old comrades' association, 18 June 1940 was a date for commemorating the battle of Bourmont, not the BBC broadcast of de Gaulle in London.[65]

Conclusions

In what ways, then, should we revise our understanding of the role, and the record, of France's Senegalese troops in 1940? The archival sources show West African units fought with courage and conviction. They exhibited great military effectiveness, tactical tenacity, and readiness to give a sacrifice in blood for the distant metropolitan motherland. Despite their record on the battlefield, however, they remained distrusted by the French high command and detested by the Germans. The former never quite believed they would fight reliably. Instances when small numbers of Senegalese wavered under Luftwaffe or panzer attack were open to reading as the confirmation of prewar doubts about colonial steadiness under fire. At Cesse in the Meuse department, Auguste Camus, a factory worker, recounted that on 13 May as a German spearhead approached, "detachments of colonial infantry have just arrived in the village, and with them the looting of houses newly abandoned by their owners begins."[66] On 28 May, according to the diary of the 13th Infantry Division's commanding officer, Senegalese troops became badly rattled under an aerial bombardment.[67] It may have been stragglers from these detachments, perhaps troops of the 5th Colonial Division, whom Georges Sadoul saw pillaging Quevauvillers on 1 June en route to the rear—"ignoble scenes" evidencing "a collapse of morale" in Sadoul's mind.[68] On 4 June, making for the new frontline near Soissons, the Reuters correspondent Gordon Waterfield noticed strongpoints and barricades. These were "guarded by negro troops from Equatorial Africa, who had dealt very effectively with the Germans during the last war, but in the war of 1940 they had little chance of getting to grips with the enemy, and were frightened by the noise of the planes and the sight of the tanks."[69]

Yet if some on the Allied side sought scapegoats and repeated rumors of African indiscipline or insobriety, other French officers acknowledged the martial qualities and steadiness of soldiers from the empire. The Germans also experienced things differently—and with horrific consequences. The Wehrmacht could neither believe nor comprehend just how fiercely the French colonials fought. The tragedy of the African troops, grotesquely vilified by their enemy as "savages," is surely that their courage in battle brought down German savagery on themselves.

This, then, returns us to the question of atrocities against French colonial troops with which we began. Raffael Scheck offers a judicious and nuanced analysis of the massacres that occurred, rejecting all but a tiny number of German claims, repeatedly made to justify reprisal murders in 1940, that Senegalese soldiers had mutilated Wehrmacht personnel. Of course German fear and loathing toward France's colonial troops was deeply ingrained. In the 1914–18 war German propaganda had targeted units from French West Africa. These soldiers were represented as rapists, looters, and drunkards—archetypal "licentious soldiery." This was all the more striking when French colonial troops deployed into the Rhineland around Cologne and Mainz as part of the Allied occupation immediately after World War I—the "Black Watch on the Rhine," in the memorable phrase of Sally Marks.[70] The German discursive response, hysterically employing the racially pejorative language of a *schwarze Schmach* or *schwarze Schande*, or "Black Shame," echoed until the final withdrawal of French garrisons in June 1930.

Ten years later, in 1940, North African divisions and colonials matched or bettered metropolitan French troops for belligerence and bravery. We have scrutinized their resistance on the Somme and the Aisne, at Orléans, and on the upper Meuse at Bourmont. Their stalwart defense, and in some cases bravura counterattacks, caused shock and savagery. For twenty years the Germans had consumed a diet of propaganda about the "racial degeneracy" and military incapacity of France's imperial levies. Deaths of comrades on an unexpected scale at the hands of the despised French colonial units pushed some Germans to transgress legal codes and mete out a gruesome postcombat revenge on surrendered Senegalese, Ivoirians, and Malagasies.[71] The ferocity of the fighting at times dissolved disciplinary inhibitions. With such breakdowns, numerous bayonetings and mass shootings of French colonial troops who capitulated occurred.[72] Among the most notorious of the atrocities were those at Aubigny on 24 May, Quesnoy and Airaines on 7 and 8 June, Brillon and Bourmont on 15–16 June and 19 June, respectively (massacring men of the 12th and 14th Senegalese Tirailleurs in Roucaud's 1st DIC), and the slaughter of 25th Senegalese Tirailleurs survivors at Lentilly and Chasselay on 19–20 June.[73]

Suspected of being unreliable warriors by their own high command, the Tirailleurs' combativeness and competence was undone by the absence of these same attributes in too many of their supposed "betters," the senior French officers. The paradox about French colonial troops in 1940 is that, on both sides of the front line, it was the manufacturers of myths (French higher commanders; Nazi propagandists and indoctrinated German soldiers) who lived up to them. For France this meant defeat; for the Senegalese it often meant an atrocious death far from their West African homeland, their total losses in 1940 having been put at 35,000 (of whom 13,000 were killed).[74]

In 1940 troops from the French empire were not helpless cannon fodder; many possessed martial qualities, and demonstrated them in battle, better than those of numerous formations of metropolitan reservists. The West Africans fought more doughtily than their faint-hearted leaders predicted, but also harder than Nazi propaganda had led the Wehrmacht to expect. They performed well militarily, even when trapped in last-ditch and hopeless rear-guard actions. Their reward all too often, however, was to be butchered by frenzied German contingents who ran amok after taking heavy losses to overpower supposedly "inferior savages."

This chapter develops Joe Lunn's conclusion to *Memoirs of the Maelstrom* that for policymakers in Paris it remained the troops drawn by France from its territories in West Africa that constituted the region's most valuable resource long after 1919. And the conduct of Françoise Meifredy and her *ambulancières* of the charitable organization Amitiés Africaines, with which this chapter began, rescuing Senegalese survivors of Chasselay, suggests that at least some French civilians realized how selflessly the Africans had fought and died for France in 1940 as well as in 1914–18.

As always, further research points to complexity and ambiguity. Surviving Senegalese troops joined men who escaped from POW columns en route to Germany and others who slipped away from working parties in eastern France in 1941–42 to join the Resistance. But in many ways these African veterans remained outsiders to the Occupied French—another of the many proscribed categories under Vichy's "Dark Years," alongside Communist Party members, trade unionists, Jews, foreign immigrant workers, Spanish Republican exiles, and Italian anti-Fascist refugees.[75]

For now, we can see that French African troops earned themselves a full measure of military credit in 1940—their record being more complex and less open to caricature than would be implied by a dichotomy between corps d'élite or cannon fodder. In six desperate weeks they fought with valor, stoicism, and in places great tactical skill. Their record helps fill out a larger revisionist narrative, moreover, for so did most North African and metropolitan units that got a chance to avoid, or recover from, the shock of Blitzkrieg.[76]

There is much to Myron Echenberg's conclusion that bravery "was not sufficient by itself to defeat an opponent displaying technological and especially tactical superiority, and there was nothing objectively that African troops could have done to alter the course of events in this phase of the Second World War."[77] Yet the record of bloodying and halting the Germans so many times, of remaining battle-ready despite the grueling fatigue of retreat to the Indre and to the outskirts of Lyon, is a more remarkable testament to the colonial forces than Echenberg allows. In their courage, competence, and fighting spirit, the Tirailleurs Sénégalais shamed their own high command.[78] In their performances as soldiers, they shamed their enemies. The former were exposed as Doubting Thomas incompetents. The latter, in a bitter foretaste of the war of racial extermination soon to be unleashed in the East, were revealed to be the real savages of World War II.[79]

Notes

1. Françoise-Marie Meifredy, *Missions sans frontières* (Paris: Editions France-Empire, 1966), 18–33. All translations are by the author unless otherwise noted.

2. Benjamin Stora, "C'est eux, les Africains qui venaient de loin . . . ," *Histoire et colonies: Vers la décristallisation* (18 June 2006), available online at http://www.ldh-toulon.net/spip.php?article1353.

3. Nancy Ellen Lawler, *Soldiers of Misfortune: Ivoirien Tirailleurs of World War II* (Athens: Ohio University Press, 1992); Raffael Scheck, *Hitler's African Victims: The German Army Massacres of Black French Soldiers in 1940* (Cambridge: Cambridge University Press, 2006); Julien Fargettas, "Les massacres de mai–juin 1940," in *La Campagne de 1940*, ed. Christine Levisse-Touzé (Paris: Editions Tallandier, 2001), 448–65.

4. Alistair Horne, *To Lose a Battle: France 1940* (London: Macmillan, 1969).

5. See Scheck, *Hitler's African Victims*, 92–94.

6. Joe Lunn, "'Les races guerrières': Racial Preconceptions in the French

Military about West African Soldiers during the First World War," *Journal of Contemporary History* 34:4 (1999), 517–36.

7. Gregory Mann, *Native Sons: West African Veterans and France in the Twentieth Century* (Durham NC: Duke University Press, 2006), 17; also Anthony Clayton, *France, Soldiers and Africa* (London: Brassey's, 1988), 338–46, who records the total number of Tirailleurs killed in the 1914–18 war at 29,520, out of 161,250 recruited (340); Marc Michel, *Les Africains et la Grande Guerre: L'Appel à l'Afrique (1914–1918)* (Paris: Karthala, 2003).

8. Marc Michel, "La Puissance par L'Empire: Note sur la perception du facteur impérial dans l'élaboration de la Défense nationale (1936–1939)," *Revue Française d'Histoire d'Outre-Mer* 69:254 (1982), 35–46. Cf. Martin Thomas, *The French Empire at War, 1940–45* (Manchester: Manchester University Press, 1998), 10–14, 24–32.

9. Martin Thomas, *The French Empire between the Wars: Imperialism, Politics and Society* (Manchester: Manchester University Press, 2005), 315; see also 316–29, 334–39.

10. See Robert J. Young, *France and the Origins of the Second World War* (New York: St. Martin's Press, 1996), chaps. 1, 2, 7.

11. Service Historique de la Défense-Terre, Vincennes (hereafter SHD-T, Fonds Gamelin 1K224/9: Journal de marche (Cabinet Gamelin), 9 October 1939.

12. On the robustness or fragility of French public opinion on the eve of war, see Daniel Hucker, "French Public Attitudes towards the Prospect of War in 1938–39: 'Pacifism' or 'War Anxiety'?" *French History* 21:4 (2007), 431–49; Hucker, "Franco-British Relations and the Question of Conscription in Britain, 1938–1939," *Contemporary European History* 17:4 (2008), 437–56.

13. Henry Dutailly, *Les Problèmes de l'Armée de terre française, 1935–1939* (Paris: Imprimerie Nationale, 1980), 221.

14. Dutailly, *Les Problèmes de l'Armée*, 221.; see also Lawler, *Soldiers of Misfortune*, 24–54.

15. Cabinet Gamelin: Journal de marche, 16 September 1939, in SHD-T: 1K224/9.

16. Dutailly, *Les Problèmes de l'Armée*, 221.

17. Dutailly, *Les Problèmes de l'Armée*, 220, quoting General Billotte's 1936 Rapport on a tour of inspection in French West Africa in SHD-T: 7N3479.

18. Clayton, *France, Soldiers and Africa*, 344–50.

19. Dutailly, *Les Problèmes de l'Armée*, 221.

20. Dutailly, *Les Problèmes de l'Armée*, 221, quoting "Rapport Georges, 1937," in SHD-T: 7N 3479.

21. Clayton, *France, Soldiers and Africa*, 103, 345–47; and Ministère de la Défense: Secrétariat générale pour l'administration—Direction de la Mémoire, du Patrimoine et des Archives: Collection "Mémoire et Citoyenneté" no. 10: "Tirailleurs Sénégalais: Campagne de France (1940)," http://www.cheminsde memoire.gouv.fr/page/affichecitoyennete.php?idLang=fr&idCitoyen=22.

22. In a related observation, a French officer in the 2nd North African Division (DINA) on the French-Belgian border in midwinter noted: "10 February 1940 [. . .] 18 degrees of frost ! [. . .] The Algerian riflemen give me the impression of not being able to stand up to so rigorous a winter, and consequently their training is slowed down. One is compelled to leave these officers and men inactive." Daniel Barlone, *A French Officer's Diary (23 August 1939 to 1 October 1940)* (Cambridge: Cambridge University Press, 1942), 27. The 2nd DINA's infantry comprised a European regiment raised in North Africa (11th Zouaves) and two regiments of Algerian Tirailleurs, 13th RTA and 22nd RTA.

23. Barlone, *French Officer's Diary*, 23.

24. Ted Morgan, *Somerset Maugham* (London: Jonathan Cape, 1980), 429.

25. Joe Lunn, *Memoirs of the Maelstrom: A Senegalese Oral History of the First World War* (Portsmouth NH: Heinemann; London: James Currey, 1999); see also Claude Carlier and Guy Pédroncini, eds., *Les Troupes Coloniales dans la Grande Guerre* (Paris: Economica, 1997); and Richard S. Fogarty, *Race and War in France: Colonial Subjects in the French Army, 1914–1918* (Baltimore: Johns Hopkins University Press, 2008).

26. The National Archives: Public Record Office (hereafter TNA/PRO), London (Kew): Foreign Office General Correspondence, series FO371, 20694, C5048/122/17—"Comparison of French and German Military Strengths: Report on the French Army for 1937" by Col. F. G. Beaumont-Nesbitt, military attaché, Paris (table showing French army units, 9–10).

27. Jacques Minart, *P.C. Vincennes: Secteur 4*, 2 vols. (Paris: Berger-Levrault, 1945), 2:69.

28. Dutailly, *Les Problèmes de l'Armée*, table and text, 222–23.

29. Christine Levisse-Touzé, *L'Afrique du Nord dans la guerre 1939–1945* (Paris: Albin Michel, 1998), 48–62.

30. Marc Michel, "Colonisation et défense nationale: Le général Mangin et la Force noire," *Guerres Mondiales et Conflits Contemporains* 145 (January 1987), 27–44; Michel, *Les Africains et la Grande Guerre*; Nicole Zehfus, "From Stereotype to Individual: World War I Experiences with Tirailleurs Sénégalais," *French Colonial History* 6 (2005), 137–57. See also Joe Lunn's chapter in this volume.

Colonial Minds Confounded

31. Clemenceau had previously been the French prime minister in 1906–9.

32. Weygand had been vice-president of the Superior War Council (the army's senior policy board) and designated commander-in-chief, 1931–35, when he retired and was succeeded by Gamelin. The government recalled Weygand in August 1939 to command French forces in Syria and Lebanon, before making him generalissimo on 19 May 1940 to replace Gamelin (dismissed by Prime Minister Paul Reynaud once the magnitude of the German Army's breakthrough over the Meuse became evident).

33. TNA London, FO 371, 22915, C16018/36/17—"Appreciation of the French strategic position after Munich," (quotation, 5). Cf. Weygand's warning in an influential periodical, two years earlier, that "France with its forty million inhabitants, of whom, alas, a high proportion are elderly, cannot aspire to arm as many men as youthful Germany with its sixty millions." M. Weygand, "L'Etat militaire de la France," *Revue des Deux Mondes*, Per. 8, CVIe année, vol. 35 (15 October 1936), 721–36 (quotation, 736).

34. Minart, *P.C. Vincennes*, 2:69–70.

35. The reservist soldiers who filled out the French armies of 1939–40 not only varied in age from about twenty-four to thirty-eight, but they also had uneven levels of military training and experience because the term of conscription had been eighteen months in 1923–28 but was shortened to just twelve months during 1928–35, before being extended to two years in April 1935 and then three years in August 1936.

36. See Clayton, *France, Soldiers and Africa*, 3–28, 199–210, 220–21, 244–55, 314–21, 352–53.

37. See Clayton, *France, Soldiers and Africa*, 262–66.

38. Alex Danchev and Dan Todman, eds., *War Diaries, 1939–1945: Field Marshal Lord Alanbrooke* (London: Weidenfeld & Nicolson, 2001), 37 (6 February 1940).

39. Some DIA units had only two infantry regiments, and all had to operate with a lower establishment of permanent career officers, NCOs, artillery, and vehicles.

40. SHD-T: 9N268, Dr. 1: Ministère de la Défense Nationale et de la Guerre: Commandant Supérieur des Troupes Coloniales dans la Métropole—Centre de Motorisation des Troupes Coloniales (CMTC), No. 654-CS/B: Fascicule II (1ère partie): Le Colonel Frémanger, Commandant le CMTC: Rapport annuel 1938 "Situation matérielle et morale" (Fréjus, le 15 septembre 1938).

41. SHD-T: 9N268, Dr. 1: Ministère de la Défense Nationale et de la Guerre: Commandant Supérieur des Troupes Coloniales dans la Métropole—Centre de Motorisation des Troupes Coloniales, No. 654-CS/B:

Fascicule III (Instruction): Le Colonel Ouvrard, Commandant le Centre de Transition des Troupes Indigènes Coloniales: Rapport annuel pour l'Instruction—année 1937–1938: Section A—"Instruction de L'Armée Active—I: Officiers" (Fréjus, le 30 septembre 1938).

42. SHD-T, 32N391 Dr. 1: Journal des Marches et Opérations de la 1ère DIC, 29 août 1939–23 juin 1940, p. 10.

43. SHD-T, 32N436, Dr. 2c: 7e DIC—"Rapport du Lt.-Colonel Chapon, Commandant le 33e RICMS, sur la conduite au feu des Tirailleurs Sénégalais," 7 July 1940, p. 1.

44. SHD-T, 32N436, Dr. 3: 7e DIC—Historique: 2 septembre 1939–25 juin 1940, p. 12.

45. SHD-T, 32N436, Dr. 3: 7e DIC—Historique: 2 septembre 1939–25 juin 1940, p. 13.

46. Gordon Waterfield, *What Happened to France* (London: John Murray, 1940), 93.

47. SHD-T, 32N436, Dr. 3: 7e DIC—Historique: 2 septembre 1939–25 juin 1940, p. 29.

48. SHD-T, 32N77, Dr. 2: Extrait du Carnet de notes de Général de division Baudouin, commandant la 13e Division d'Infanterie, sur les opérations de mai et juin 1940 (19 mai–29 juin 1940), 15 [hereafter cited as Baudouin, "Carnets de notes"]. The 13th Division comprised two metropolitan French infantry units (21st and 60th Infantry Regiments) and a regiment of Moroccan Tirailleurs (8th RTM).

49. SHD-T: 9N268, Dr. 1: *Pommersche Zeitung* report (28 July 1940), reproduced in "Extrait du rapport du Lt-Colonel Polidori, Commandant le 53e Régiment d'Infanterie Coloniale Mixte Sénégalais."

50. Erwin Rommel, *The Rommel Papers*, ed. Basil H. Liddell Hart (London: Collins, 1953), 46–51.

51. See Marc-André Fabre, *Avec les Héros de 40* (Paris: Hachette, 1946), 110–12.

52. SHD-T: 32N77, Dr. 0: Chronologie de la 13e DI, reconstitué par le Capitaine de Ribou, Service Historique de l'Armée, mai 1965.

53. Scheck, *Hitler's African Victims*, 27–28. N'Tchoréré was born in Libreville in November 1896, the son of a lawyer, making his way in 1914 from Cameroon, then a German possession, to the French colony of Gabon; he joined the French army as a volunteer in 1916, serving on the Western Front before opting for a postwar career as a regular officer and serving in Morocco, Syria, Soudan, and Senegal.

54. SHD-T: 32N436, Dr. 2c: 7e DIC—Rapport du Lt.-Colonel Chapon, p. 2; subsequent page citations are listed in the text.

55. P.-A. Lesort, *Quelques jours de mai-juin 40: Mémoire, témoignage, histoire* (Paris: Editions du Seuil, 1992), 82–83.

56. SHD-T: 34N1093: (Capitaine Jarty) Journal de marche de la 9e Compagnie du 14e RTS (période du 10 mai au 21 juin 1940), 2 (23 May 1940).

57. Col. Gallim, "Le Calvaire d'une Grande Unité (La 1ère DIC du 13 au 23 juin 1940)," in *Le Souvenir Français*, no. 276 (Paris, 3e trimestre 1959), 6.

58. Gallim, "Le Calvaire d'une Grande Unité," 6.

59. SHD-T: 32N391, Dr. 0: Raymond Belly, *La 1ère Division d'Infanterie Coloniale dans la campagne de France de 1940* (Bordeaux: Taffard, 1957), 16.

60. Gallim, "La Calvaire d'une Grande Unité," 7.

61. Gallim, "Le Calvaire d'une Grande Unité," 7.

62. Belly, *La 1ère Division d'Infanterie Coloniale*, 17.

63. SHD-T, 32N391 Dr. 1: Journal des Marches et Opérations de la 1ère DIC, 29 août 1939–23 juin 1940.

64. Belly, *La 1ère Division d'Infanterie Coloniale*, 17.

65. Belly, *La 1ère Division d'Infanterie Coloniale*, 18.

66. Auguste Camus, 1940. *L'Exode. Cesse (55) — Epargnes (17)*, (entry for 13 May 1940), account from Camus's two contemporary *cahiers*, posted on the Internet by his grandson, Eric Fassi (25 January 2001) at http://perso.orange.fr/eric.fassi/exode.htm (no longer available).

67. SHD-T: 32N77, Dr. 2—13e DI: Baudouin, "Carnets de notes," 10.

68. Georges Sadoul, *Journal de guerre (2 septembre 1939–20 juillet 1940)* (Paris: Les Editeurs Français Réunis, 1977), 262.

69. Waterfield, *What Happened to France*, 94.

70. Sally Marks, "Black Watch on the Rhine: A Study in Propaganda, Prejudice and Prurience," *European Studies Review* 13:3 (July 1983), 297–334; see also Keith L. Nelson, "The 'Black Horror on the Rhine': Race as a Factor in Post–World War I Diplomacy," *Journal of Modern History* 42:4 (December 1970), 606–27; Dick van Galen Last, "'Black Shame,'" *History Today* 56:10 (2006), 14–21; Christian Koller, "Enemy Images: Race and Gender Stereotypes in the Discussion on Colonial Troops: A Franco-German Comparison, 1914–1923," in *Home Front: The Military, War and Gender in Twentieth Century Germany*, ed. Karen Hagemann and Stefanie Schüler-Springorum (Oxford: Berg, 2002); and Jean-Yves Le Nour, *La honte noire: L'Allemagne et les troupes coloniales françaises, 1914–45* (Paris: Hachette, 2004). The ambiguities of French civilian relations with colonial troops, an "encounter" noticeable in port cities, garrison towns, and zones to the rear when soldiers took leave or joined working parties, exceeds this chapter's purview, as does the deployment to France in 1917–18 of black American troops. But see Tyler Stovall, "The Color Line behind the Lines: Racial Violence in France during the Great War," *American Historical Review* 103:3 (1998),

737–69; and on soldiers' relationships with female civilians in post-1918 and post-1945 Germany, see Erika Kuhlman, "American Doughboys and German Frauleins: Sexuality, Patriarchy and Privilege in the American-Occupied Rhineland, 1918–23," *Journal of Military History* 71:4 (2007), 1077–1106; and John Willoughby, "The Sexual Behavior of American GIs during the Early Years of the Occupation of Germany," *Journal of Military History* 62:1 (1998), 155–74.

71. Scheck, *Hitler's African Victims*, 134–41.
72. Scheck, *Hitler's African Victims*, 142–44.
73. See Scheck, *Hitler's African Victims*, 53–57, for a probably comprehensive list of all the massacres in the 1940 campaign in a chronologically sequenced tabular format; see also Stora, "C'est eux, les Africains," 2–3.
74. Testimony by Général Lemoine in Carlier and Pédroncini, *Les Troupes Coloniales dans la Grande Guerre*, 197, giving a figure of 43,000 colonial troops involved in the Battle of France, of whom he says about 35,000 were West Africans. No statistics seem definitive: citing a Vichy military document from 1942, Martin Thomas (*French Empire between the Wars*, 339) suggests that the total loss of colonial troops in 1940 was 4,439 killed and 11,504 missing and presumed dead (i.e., some 16,000 killed, a figure approximately 3,000 higher than Lemoine's), the number taken prisoner being much less precisely calculated in the range from 25,000–80,000.
75. BBC Radio 4, "Why Black Soldiers in the French Army Were Denied the Glory of Liberating Paris in 1944," 6 April 2009: 20.00; and Mike Thomson, "Paris Liberation Made 'Whites Only,'" 6 April 2009, http://news.bbc.co.uk/1/hi/world/europe/7984436.stm.
76. For further evidence, see Martin S. Alexander, "After Dunkirk: The French Army's performance against 'Case Red,' 25 May to 25 June 1940," *War in History* 14:2 (2007), 219–63.
77. Myron Echenberg, *Colonial Conscripts: The Tirailleurs Sénégalais in French West Africa, 1857–1960* (Portsmouth NH: Heinemann; London: James Currcy, 1991), 92.
78. See West African excoriation of the shortcomings of Gamelin and other senior French commanders in Echenberg, *Colonial Conscripts*, 92–94.
79. See Scheck, *Hitler's African Victims*, 149–56; Christopher Browning, *Ordinary Men: Reserve Police Battalion 101 and the Final Solution in Poland* (New York: Harper & Row, 1992); Omer Bartov, *The Eastern Front, 1941–45: German Troops and the Barbarization of Warfare* (Basingstoke: Macmillan, 1985; 2nd ed., Palgrave, 2001); Bartov, *Hitler's Army: Soldiers, Nazis and War in the Third Reich* (Oxford: Oxford University Press, 1992); Charles W. Sydnor Jr., *Soldiers of Destruction: The SS Death's Head Division, 1933–1945* (Princeton NJ: Princeton University Press, 1977).

11

The "Silent Native"

Attentisme, *Being Compromised,*
and Banal Terror during the Algerian War
of Independence, 1954–1962

NEIL MACMASTER

Political scientist Stathis Kalyvas argues in his book *The Logic of Violence in Civil War* that conflict during civil wars has in most cases been about gaining information from local populations, intelligence that has been most widely accessed through informing and denunciation. The brutality of civil war has been most deadly in rural or mountainous terrain, the key locations of insurgency, typically in small communities in which violence has been *selective* or targeted at individuals who have been reported, often for personal and vindictive reasons, to one side or the other. While violence can be indiscriminate ("blind" mass killing), more "productive" is selective violence that targets individuals.[1]

Kalyvas elaborates a sophisticated model of the conditions under which individual actors were most likely to inform, usually where one side exercised dominant but incomplete control. This situation was perhaps the prevalent one throughout the rural and mountainous interior of Algeria in which a huge French military presence covered the interior with a web of army posts (*quadrillage*) while, especially after 1958, a much weakened ALN (Armée de Libération Nationale) clung to a covert existence among the peasantry through the network of the OPA (Organisation politico-administrative). Kalyvas elaborates in detail on the *intimacy* of violence, how in small-scale, face-to-face social settings the tensions and conflicts of peace-time (disputes over land, livestock, marriage arrangements, insults, and honor) that were normally mediated and settled now became the basis of denunciation that unleashed deadly force and pitted neighbor against neighbor. Most people in civil wars did not take up arms voluntarily or engage in heroic or ideologically committed resistance but sought how best to survive or protect their family and kin. But considerable difficulty was faced by individuals wishing to "keep their head down" through retaining a mask of neutrality in intimate village societies in which everyone knew each other, their detailed histories and daily moves, and in which every neighbor could be a potential informer.

Much of the debate on terrorism in the modern world has been in terms of acts of extreme *indiscriminate* violence perpetrated on civilian bystanders: in the case of the Algerian War massacres like that at Melouza or the milk-bar bombers of the Battle of Algiers. This emphasis on extreme acts has tended to obscure the significance of less violent forms of *psychological terror* that were far more omnipresent and that could assume apparently superficial forms in everyday life. Hannah Arendt noted the impact of such banal terror in permeating and atomizing civil society, a situation that was then "maintained and intensified through the ubiquity of the informer, who can be literally omnipresent because he no longer is merely a professional agent in the pay of the police but potentially every person one comes into contact with."[2] This essay sets out to examine this banal or quotidian terror, how it formed a crucial part in the strategies of the opposed French and nationalist forces, and how it was countered by the Algerian populace retreating into forms of protective resistance, of silence and *attentisme*.

The word *attentisme* was the standard term used by the army to denote the verbal mutism or resistance of the peasantry or urban masses. This word, which is not quite captured in English by "sitting on the fence" or "biding one's time," carried the meaning of a cunning and systematic refusal to reveal one's true political allegiance, so that the outwardly obtuse and ignorant peasant could as well be a friend to France as a terrorist in disguise. An army report summed up the terms widely used to describe the Algerians' attitude as "attentisme, opportunisme, mutisme, bovisme [sic]," the latter in the sense of a bovine truculence.[3] An investigation of such everyday phenomena directs attention to one of the most neglected aspects of the war, the social history of ordinary Algerian people without which it is impossible to understand the underlying dynamics of decolonization.

The French archives for the Algerian War of Independence (1954–62) contain numerous intelligence reports by officers that express a deep sense of frustration at the impenetrability or opaqueness of popular opinion, the age-old skills of the oppressed to feign incomprehension, ignorance, or rural idiocy, which became particularly dangerous under conditions of war. Officers of the Section administrative spécialisée (SAS), who were stationed in isolated rural communities to build relations with the peasantry through development projects and adjudication of local disputes (*chikâyas*), were particularly well positioned to report on the changing state of public opinion. But in their monthly reports the SAS officers constantly complained of the difficulty of obtaining information. For example, the head of the SAS in the Aumale sector noted in February 1959: "the mass of Muslims, worn down by exactions, seek escape more and more in *attentisme*. Nobody believes any more in the return of peace." In September 1959 the local bourgeoisie was reported to be avoiding engagement in conversation, "they sit on the fence and continue to make promises to both sides," while in December 1960 it was noted with some frustration that Algerians supplied officers with the information they wished to hear, with the consequence that ten SAS confronted with an identical situation could arrive at quite different interpretations of "the deeper thoughts of the population."[4] An officer of the Section administrative urbain (SAU) in Algiers expressed in his monthly reports a sense of weariness at "the population which practices the politics of sewn-up lips."[5] On occasions the army even tried to quantify the phenomenon, as did Lt.-Colonel Rafa in a report on his tour of inspection of Aumale in late 1959:

Percentage of population won over to FLN ideology — 10%
    Attentiste   70%
    Francophile   20%[6]

This has been the situation faced by many an occupying Western army, including the U.S. and British forces in contemporary Iraq and

Afghanistan, where troops making direct contact with the "natives" have felt ill at ease through an inability to communicate and to decode the values, mind-set, and intentions of the "Oriental."[7] As James Scott has shown, authoritarian and violent regimes (of slavery, serfdom, and colonialism) have faced difficulty in comprehending the "hidden transcript," the well-concealed motivations of oppressed peoples skilled in the arts of resistance.[8] However, the level of concern and urgency of the French military confronted with such *attentisme* was particularly acute since "low-grade" intelligence played a crucial role within the overall context of the doctrine of counterinsurgency (*guerre révolutionnaire*) that dominated military thinking and practice during 1956 to 1960.

The doctrine of revolutionary warfare, developed by officers after the catastrophic defeat of the French forces at Dien Bien Phu (May 1954), mirrored the Maoist theory according to which eventual victory of the guerrilla *maquis* depended crucially on establishing a support base among the populace that provided food, medicine, safe houses, intelligence, guides, and recruits to the revolutionaries. The French Army knew that the war in Algeria was not going to be won by conventional forces and superior technical firepower, and that the key to defeating the insurgents was to isolate them from the population, following the Maoist dictum of draining the lake in which the (terrorist) fish swam freely.[9] In the battle for Algerian hearts and minds the psychological warfare officers of the Fifth Bureau became obsessed with a "psephology of war," the need to gauge the state of public opinion, and with isolating and measuring the factors that determined the fluctuating conditions of support for France or the FLN (Front de Libération Nationale) rebels. Good-grade intelligence was the holy grail of counterinsurgency.

The FLN maintained a similar doctrine of "total" control of the civilian population, which it attempted to impose through a clandestine cellular network of political commissars and militants, the OPA that reached down to every small town or hamlet. Through the OPA the FLN attempted to create a virtual counterstate, with its own system of justice, welfare provision, and pensions, which in principle would enable Algerians to break all contact with the French administration. One FLN circular underlined the logic of such radical segregation: "Do not allow the French to contact the people, no matter what the motive. We must destroy in the bud any plans of the enemy and maintain a vacuum around the French administration."[10] For the FLN terror was an instrument of compliance, a means to compel Algerians not to cooperate with the colonial regime in any way but also to affirm its sole authority as the genuine voice and representative of the nation over and against other "traitorous" contenders, particularly the Messalist Mouvement National Algérien (MNA).[11]

As the war deepened the Algerian population was increasingly caught and ground between a rock and a hard place, the totalizing ambitions of the French Army and the FLN to entice or force allegiance to their own side. Mouloud Feraoun noted in his journal of Kabyle life that between the maquis and the army, "there is the population, which gets beaten up. Just like a punching ball between two boxers."[12] But this placed hundreds of thousands of Algerians in a no-win situation since an overt declaration of support for one side invariably brought the risk of punishment or assassination from the other. Inevitably individuals tried to escape this mortal dilemma by attempting, as far as possible, to conceal their position from both the French authorities and Algerian neighbors among whom there might lurk informers. Both sides were perfectly aware of this evolution, the spread of a generalized *attentisme*, and sought to counter it by a whole complex of pressure points, tactics that would "flush out" the deceitful neutral and force a public declaration or symbolic act of affiliation to one side or another. As the commander-in-chief General Allard noted, the population was caught by the OPA, "terrorized, trapped in a fine mesh net from which it cannot escape," and in reply to this, Colonel Lacheroy, the master ideologue of revolutionary warfare, stated, "It is necessary that all forms of complicity, including those of abstention and silence, be rendered impossible or treated, in the same manner as the crime of treason, by special courts."[13]

How did compliance terrorism work?[14] For the FLN two favored mechanisms of control were the call for a general strike and the monthly collection of dues. When the FLN called for a general stoppage, as during the famous weeklong strike that initiated the Battle of Algiers, or the commercial strike in Paris of 18 October 1961, this was both to demonstrate to the French the strength of its popular base and (more covertly) to locate all those individuals who might opt to disobey FLN orders by going to work, an act that would be difficult to conceal from neighborhood militants.[15] Refusal to pay dues to FLN collectors, a form of universal "taxation" that funded the nationalists, could lead to severe disciplinary action and even assassination. But my interest here is more in the deployment of mundane but nonetheless potent symbols of affiliation such as the FLN ban on smoking, alcohol, gambling, and some forms of entertainment or celebration such as dancing and feasting. Such proscriptions reflected in part the religious puritanism of the 'Ulamaʿ reformist movement that provided the dominant religious values of the nationalist movement, and also emphasized values of personal self-sacrifice and denial during the holy war of liberation.[16] Lower consumption was also used to impose economic damage on French commerce, while correspondingly increasing the saving capacity of militants, which could mean more money to go into FLN coffers.[17] But drinking alcohol and, above all, smoking constituted everyday *public* acts that could be readily monitored by militants and sympathizers in the *café maure*, bus, and street.[18] Paris police and army reports refer constantly to violent attacks and peremptory execution of miscreant Algerian workers, or internal FLN documents indicate how they were summoned before the FLN's own local justices and fined.[19]

The counterattack of the French army on such an FLN boycott represented a simple inversion, such as an enforcement of smoking. Just after the outbreak of the insurrection of 1 November 1954 the future commander Azzedine was employed in the Caterpillar factory near Algiers, where he transmitted the FLN order for a ban on smoking to his colleagues; the European management quickly called the workers to a meeting at which it berated the men for obeying "the cut-throats and looters" and ordered, "Tomorrow everyone smokes!" Azzedine had the courage to break the initiative by immediately declaring, "I have never smoked and will not start now!" This redoubtable *maquisard* was captured in July 1956 and subjected to brutal interrogation by gendarmes who wished to establish his identity: one of them offered a cigarette to the nonsmoking commander who gladly accepted it. "Had I refused he would have given me a hiding: 'You're FLN since it bans smoking!'"[20] In 1957 Captain Paul Léger formed his notorious counterinsurgency gangs, the *bleus de chauffe*, composed of former FLN toughs, to operate within the FLN fortress zone of the Casbah. One of the first tests of this unit was to challenge on their turf the young FLN militants whose job was to enforce discipline and respect for orders, and they did this by going into a *café maure* where they offered around cigarettes and turned the radio on to full volume, playing Arab music. This defiance of FLN orders created a shocked reaction inside the café, while outside on the terraces "the astonished faces of women and children leaned over the corbels overhanging the alley from which mounted long forgotten tunes." One of the Léger commandos exclaimed, "As from today the FLN no longer exists."[21]

Taken in isolation and in the context of the brutal reality of a war that saw massive violence, the low-key skirmishing between opposing sides over smoking may seem to be totally trivial. However, a closer look at what Mohand Hamoumou has called the "techniques of compromise" provides an interesting point of entry into the still little understood social reality of the war. First it can be noted that what Algerians confronted on a daily basis was the *accumulated* psychological pressure of having to negotiate a minefield of potential hazards, not to be seen smoking, or talking alone to a French officer, or being in the proximity of an SAS post, accepting a lift in an army lorry, and so on. The army specialists in psychological warfare, often using quite crude theories of behaviorism and conditioned reflexes, believed that a constant pressure should be deployed against the entire population: what Maurice Papon, a devotee of such techniques, termed a tactic of "nervous erosion".[22] Mouloud Feraoun chronicled a similar remorseless multiplication of taboos from the FLN side: "They include prohibitions of all kinds, nothing but prohibitions, dictated by the most obtuse fanaticism, the most intransigent racism, and the most authoritarian fist. In a way, this is true terrorism."[23]

The army, far from indulging in small acts of "compromise" as a kind of cat-and-mouse game in which soldiers satisfied their individual sadism, was engaged in a quite conscious and coherent strategy. The army developed a sophisticated model of "pacification," a phased program of military interventions by which control could gradually be established over large rural zones that were adjudged "rotten," in which the FLN maquis maintained an iron grip on the village or nomad population.[24] Part of this process involved building up such a level of protection and support among the peasantry that they would begin to achieve a critical mass by which they would gain confidence to openly defy the FLN, rally en bloc, and establish their own auto-defense units. Officers were keen to accelerate this process by forcing villagers out from the carapace of *attentisme* or neutrality by forcing a "choice" or dragging them into association with one side or the other.[25] One of the army's standard techniques was simply to make sure that particular individuals were seen publicly talking to or in the company of soldiers. In November 1959 the right-wing deputy, Frédéric-Dupont, conducted a parliamentary visit to Algiers, during which an admiral drove him by jeep to several villages where in each place the headman was required to accompany them in a tour. Finally, the deputy asked the reason for this and was told, "I have received orders to compromise as many as possible."[26]

The consequences of being seen with the French, even by accident, could carry fatal consequences. In one typical incident soldiers arrested a peasant who was searching for a lost cow; then they let him go. "But someone in the village saw us from far-off. He went to tell the local head of the FLN that I was giving information to the army. A friend warned me that they would come to find and kill me that night. I escaped to the army post and signed up."[27] Hamoumou notes how a lieutenant forced a village headman to provide a list of twenty-five "volunteers" to act as guards for a newly established army post, a classic instance of compromise. When one of them refused he was ordered to appear before the officer, who offered him a clear "choice" between acting as a guard or to "join up with your brothers (meaning the maquis). You have to choose."[28] The offer to Algerian men to "join the maquis" was a standard and sinister code used by the army to refer to summary execution: for example, the former SAS officer Raymond Montaner in a secret report to Maurice Papon on how to destroy the FLN in Paris suggested that suspects, instead of being interned, should be transported back to the army in Algeria, which would decide their fate "by forcing them to reveal on which side they stand, even going so far as to propose their departure for the maquis."[29]

A fascinating insight into the army tactics of compromise is provided by the journals of Mouloud Feraoun. Feraoun, as a schoolteacher in Kabylie (and later in Algiers) and a writer and intellectual of international renown, belonged precisely to the elite of highly educated and prominent Algerians that the French wished to "bring on-side." The writer was constantly being cultivated or "honored" by the French army and administration and invited to official receptions and celebrations. However, such public recognition was often, as Feraoun knew all too well, part of another agenda. When one of his books received much praise in a propagandist newspaper he detected the hand of "the army's psychological unit . . . [which] is determined not to leave me alone."[30] When General Olié, commander of the Kabyle region, made a visit to Fort National in June 1956 Feraoun was greatly relieved to know that his planned itinerary would not include an official visit to the school where he was a teacher: Feraoun would be spared the anxiety of a highly visible reception and association with the general. "I had taken advantage of this [protocol] not to put up any flags and banners . . . all I had to do was wait for a sign to go to city hall for this historic meeting." But the general ruined this arrangement by immediately striding over to the school, where the writer imagined a subtext in which he was warned not deploy his pen to record the "unbearable" reality of the war, "Of course, we are not asking you to compromise yourself—you are a family man. All we ask is that you plug your ears and close your eyes, nothing more." Several days later Feraoun "discreetly" sent a dedicated copy of his *Jours de Kabylie* to General Olié via the subprefect, who reassured him it was recognized that the writer needed to be careful. "I also believe that I am granted the same esteem, the same confidence, as well as the same distrust in the other camp. I am maintaining my balance on a very tight, thin rope. This week, for example, I have most likely given the maquis the feeling that I am leaning toward the French side. They realize, however, that in my situation I cannot avoid official receptions. . . . I have heard that Mr. H. has been killed for having accepted a subprefecture. . . . The only thing I have to do to reestablish a precarious equilibrium is to decline the next official invitation."[31]

However, Feraoun, the consummate *attentiste*, came under constant pressure from his most persistent enemy "T.", the aggressive SAS captain of Fort National, until he was forced to seek an escape from the local pressures by moving to the anonymity of the capital, Algiers, in July 1957. The source of the officer's resentment, thought Feraoun, lay precisely in his own skill as an *attentiste*: that "he was not able to use me, and not only did I get clear of him, but he now has a strong sense that I do not want to depend on him."[32] But Feraoun was not as safe in the city as he at first believed: by early 1958 he recorded that "trepidation and anxiety besieging the rural population have now reached the cities," and in February 1958 he was approached by the SAU captain, "who is a lot like 'T.'"[33] This was almost certainly Raymond Montaner, head of the SAU of Clos-Salembier, where Feraoun was a teacher, who told him that the prefect was looking for elite Algerians to stand as delegates for the municipal council. "The captain told me that he put me down as number one on the list. He added that it was the least he could do."[34] Archive sources show that the army intelligence services kept a sharp eye on the famous writer, and Montaner's successor, Captain Paris, recorded in February 1960, "Monsieur Feraoun, deeply impregnated with western culture and pure feelings, has never wished to take an official political position, despite solicitations from all sides: nonetheless, one can be certain that Monsieur Feraoun is deeply convinced of the necessity of the French presence in Algeria."[35] If Captain Paris had been privy to Feraoun's journal he would not have been so sanguine, but the writer was a marked man, and tragically he was to be brutally gunned down by the OAS, along with five colleagues, on the very eve of independence.[36]

Villagers, faced with the army drive to "pacify" and compromise entire communities, were compelled to invent subtle collective counterstrategies. One quite common tactic was for Algerians, requested or expected by the army to carry out a certain task, to intimate that a voluntary act should be reformulated as a command, an order that could not be disobeyed, and would thus keep the FLN at bay. For example, prior to the Referendum of January 1961 some Algerians, wishing to avoid having to make public their preference for one side or another, asked one commander, "to come and openly but firmly request them to attend the polls so that later they would have an alibi and also allow them to follow their own convictions without danger."[37] Sometimes the French appear not to have understood the motives for such a request,[38] and this tactic may have helped reinforce the racist and Orientalist notion, frequently expressed during the war, that Algerians liked to obey the strong hand of the master. In another, perhaps exceptional, instance village elders unable to bear any longer the combined violence of both the army and the FLN decided to rally. The ALN commander Amirouche gave a surprising assent: "Go and surrender. Say to the French that you put yourself under its protection. Like that the air-force will no longer bomb you, but you can continue to pay dues to the FLN and we can continue to remain brothers as before."[39]

Attentisme, the ruse of silence, was not only a defensive ploy against the pressure of the French Army, but also a strategy deployed against the FLN and fellow villagers. The period from 1954 to 1962 was as much one of civil war, of savage internal conflict between the FLN, MNA, and other Algerian factions, as it was a black-and-white battle between two sides over decolonization. The Algerian War, as in so many other civil or wars of occupation, provided members of local society with the opportunity to indulge in revenge and vendetta, the settling of old scores under the guise of nationalist probity or by acting as informers or armed auxiliaries (*harkis, moghaznis*) with the French Army. As anthropologists have shown, peasant societies, and in particular the societies of "honor" to be found in the Mediterranean world, are renowned for the extraordinary complexity and longevity of disputes that may divide families or "clans" against each other, conflicts relating to land, livestock, water rights, failed marriage alliances, slander, and power.[40] In Algeria such traditional forms of conflict took on an additional complexity because of the particular structures of Berber and Arab tribal society: for example, one village might be divided against another, or even internally, according to a binary system of opposing clans (*çofs*).[41]

In his journal Feraoun provides a brilliant sociopsychological dissection of the gradual descent into mutual distrust and compliance terrorism in Kabyle villages. The day-to-day socialization of peasants and shopkeepers at Fort National rested at the start of the war on a normal discourse of "gossip," "nothing special: the usual raveling and unraveling of local intrigues, spreading of anecdotes, whispers of minor scandals and small deals wrapped up," a harmless converse that came to contain a sinister potential in times of violence.[42] As informing spread, both to the army and the FLN, and locals were assassinated by one or tortured by the other, so a poisonous and Kafkaesque paranoia seeped into Kabyle society, with its inevitable and corrosive effects on human relations. "This morning, it seems that everyone has lost the desire to speak, joke, laugh, drink, come or go. It is as if each person feels trapped and sealed in an airtight bell jar. . . . any attempt at communication, even on the most ordinary and superficial level, is futile. . . . Yet, there are shadows moving about."[43] And at Béni-Douala, "there happens to be some Kabyles, shaken and afraid, who slip by quickly like ghosts."[44] The claustrophobia of the diaries becomes incessant: "An insidious and nearly invisible fear had crept in everywhere. People kept calm, but everyone knew that the police posed a threat that weighed heavily on them. . . . People no longer lingered outside. By dusk, the village streets were deserted, haunted by cries and mysterious sounds. . . . As for the noises, we never did recognize them . . . . the sound of steps, a rustling noise, and pebbles tumbling about. Wait, there is a faint knock at the door. Someone is turning the knob, whispering."[45] Was this the nocturnal visit of the FLN death squad or its French commando equivalent?

Feraoun had a disillusioned view of the extent to which the war provided an ideal opportunity for the most brutal, hooligan, or self-serving elements in local society to promote themselves as heroic nationalist fighters. "The local rebel administration set up by the maquis is almost always made up of former malcontents and 'hard heads,' and old scores are quickly settled in the name of the resistance and the fight for freedom . . . In general, the rich who made people sweat under their hats for a living are now sweating with fear. People remember that the rich treated them unscrupulously, that the father practiced usury."[46] The historian Mohand Hamoumou recounts how his father, a militant in the FLN, was arrested by the army but later freed unharmed, a fact that was sufficient to compromise him. He was in turn taken along with three cousins by an FLN escort to be assassinated, but he managed to escape and joined the *harkis* to save his life: "It was sometimes said, in a whispered voice, that they had been denounced by jealous neighbors who thus resolved their old disputes."[47] The settling of scores became so endemic that after 1957 the FLN was forced, both in Algeria and France, to impose a system of tight hierarchical control by which the designation of targets for assassination was removed from the local gunmen.[48] In April 1957 Feraoun was told by an old man how he was traveling on a bus that was stopped by the army: everyone was ordered off the bus, and a lo-

The "Silent Native"

cal informer pointed men out. "He is from our village. My God, I was afraid. He could have pointed his finger toward me. He had reasons to. Last year, his father sold me a mortgaged field. I sued him and won. And last year I beat up their shepherd when he let his herd damage my young fig trees. Yes, I beat him up. And I won my suit. That young recruit could have avenged himself using the army, and I was afraid."[49]

One begins to get a sense here of the myriad complexity of local disputes and tensions that, just beneath the surface, intermeshed with or determined the alignments of nationalist and pro-French forces. Until now most histories of the Algerian War have tended to overlook this dimension, an anthropological reading of the dynamics of civil war, and thus fail to see how individual or local group alignments operated. Which side you ended up fighting on or supporting might have had little to do with the global political or ideological divisions (nationalism versus French colonialism), but more to do with accidents of time and place, what Hamoumou calls "local contingencies."[50] As fear and suspicion deepened in Algerian peasant society, so the natural inclination was to begin to avoid the snare of the traditional locations of sociability, the *café maure* or the weekly market, where one ran the greatest risk of verbal indiscretion or being seen "in the wrong company." Feraoun describes market day as a sad business, in which, instead of the usual happy babble of activity, he sees "silent people rushing to finish their errands in order to return to their villages."[51]

The Tuesday market at Bordj Okhriss, in a zone of strong FLN activity, became a tense affair since local *maquisards* could travel more freely under the guise of legitimate traders. The army kept a special watch for the spread of nationalist propaganda and the trade in provisions that were intended to supply the local maquis. The SAS officer in his monthly reports detailed the deepening "mutual distrust" in the township, and on one market day he arrested the FLN collector A.K, who before going into the souk went to the home of the O. family to demand money, saying: "You must be crazy. I saw the rebels yesterday evening and I spoke to them about you (the O. family)—You can go back home and readily find 100 or 150,000 francs, which is nothing compared with what you own (your farm is worth 2 million)—Whatever happens FRANCE is the loser and will abandon you—You'll then see what situation you find yourself in."⁵² The previous November three men of the O. clan had been assassinated, and it can be seen why the family may have been driven toward the SAS for protection. Under the surface of local political divisions simmered tensions and recriminations that probably dated back to before the war, in this case the grievance of poor peasants or sharecroppers (*khammès*) who felt exploited by or envious of the relatively more wealthy landowners.

Public spaces became dangerous, and watching one's words became so stressful, such a minefield, that most Algerians preferred to pull back into the security of the extended family or kin group in which it was possible to unburden without danger.⁵³ Feraoun welcomed the opportunity to holiday in his home village of Tizi-Hibel, where self-censorship of speech could be momentarily placed on hold: "Once again, I was back home. They allowed me to share in the inner life of the village. I could enter into a group, a category, a clan that was hostile to the neighbors, a clan that either fights to defeat the rival or holds back and waits. Such a clan plans its vendetta or its treason, directs its propaganda prudently, consolidates its attack plans, or prepares its defense while continuing to proclaim, during its many meetings, the sacred and compulsory union that not only makes the village into one block but all of its men into one single man."⁵⁴ Feraoun had to return to his village to gain the information on local politics, on the FLN, the reactions to events, that he could no longer pick up in the frightened, suspicious and mute world of Fort National.⁵⁵

Stathis Kalyvas explores in detail how during the Greek Civil War it was possible for one village to experience massacre while a neighboring hamlet, with identical characteristics, might escape violence. In part this can be explained by the ability of villagers to put aside normal disputes and create a unified face of solidarity, preventing antagonisms descending into a vicious cycle of denunciation, killings, and counterkillings, while village leaders were able to negotiate protection for the whole community with the incumbent power.⁵⁶ Likewise, during the Algerian War traditional heads of both village councils (*djemaa*), as well as of local powerful "grandes familles," tried to negotiate the personal protection (*a na a*) of particular settlements through the customary system of lineage and quasi-feudal power.⁵⁷

The "Silent Native"

The pressures that drove individuals to seek security and support within the kin group reinforced clan solidarities at a time when it was FLN policy to try to weaken such loyalties, including regionalism, or Berber against Arab identities, in favor of an overriding allegiance to the new nation and party. However, this could be a dangerous game, and neither side was prepared to tolerate whole communities or *douars* that tried to maintain long-term neutrality as a form of defense. The ALN commander Azzedine recounts his own strategy faced with this lack of nationalism: "it sometimes happened that I located an ambush or attack on a military post close to an undecided village that until then had hesitated to make a total commitment." The French would then unleash a violent counteroperation to punish the nearest village that would be driven into the arms of the ALN.[58]

In conclusion it bears emphasis that *attentisme*, a strategy of silence, constituted a perfectly rational form of self-defense or of survival for the relatively weak and powerless when faced with the irreconcilable and totalitarian demands of the opposed sides. Such arts of resistance were certainly not invented only after the war had started, but drew on an experience honed over 130 years of colonial domination. As Jacques Berque noted of Algerian society in general: "The Muslim population maintains zones which are absolutely inviolable. It pulls back into a protective shell."[59] The European settlers invented a term for the standard forms of passive resistance or rural idiocy displayed by Algerian peasants in the face of overbearing masters: *manarf* ("I don't know").[60] The occupying military, frustrated at the inability to comprehend what the "silent native" was thinking or confronted by what he often misread as the malign cunning and deceit, if not downright treachery, of the Algerian, often responded to such "insolence" with physical assault or "extracting the truth" through torture.[61]

Lastly, silence did not end with the arrival of independence, both because the new state continued highly authoritarian forms of repression after 1962, and because the memory of individual acts of violence and treachery by Algerians remained far too sensitive and explosive to be openly aired. The bloody, and often not so heroic, acts of assassination and revenge were buried away, but this process of occultation and repression of painful memory appears to have had highly destructive long-term consequences in preparing the way, one generation later, for the unspeakable cruelty of the "second Algerian War." This collective amnesia or refusal to speak about the past may explain in part why it is that historians still face, half a century later, such difficulty in investigating the inner workings and dynamics of the war of decolonization at the local level.[62]

Notes

1. See Stathis N. Kalyvas, *The Logic of Violence in Civil War* (Cambridge: Cambridge University Press, 2006). Kalyvas applies to Algeria the term "civil war," which he defines as an "armed combat within the boundaries of a recognized sovereign entity between parties subject to a common authority at the outset of the hostilities." Understanding the Algerian conflict as both a war of decolonization and a civil war provides a better framework of analysis than the conventional approach that works on a simple, binary opposition between occupying colonial forces and indigenous nationalists. Over 200,000 Algerians fought on the French side, as opposed to 50,000 in the Armée de Libération Nationale (ALN); thousands died in various forms of internecine fighting, as between the Mouvement National Algérien (MNA) and the Front de libération nationale (FLN), while many from the same family, kin group, or village found themselves on opposing sides.

2. Hannah Arendt, *On Violence* (New York: Harcourt, Brace and World, 1970), 55; quoted by Kalyvas, *Logic*, 358.

3. Mohammed Harbi and Gilbert Meynier, eds., *Le FLN: Documents et Histoire, 1954–1962* (Paris: Fayard, 2004), 176, document from late 1960 or early 1961, Service Historique de la Défense-Terre (SHD-T), Vincennes, Carton 1H4061/5. A certain irony is added to the army's use of the term in a colonial context since *attentisme* had been used to denote passive forms of collaboration during the Nazi occupation of France.

4. Centre des Archives d'Outre-Mer (hereafter CAOM), Aix-en-Provence, 3SAS18, Echelon de liaison d'arrondissement (ELA) Aumale, reports for February and September 1959, December 1960. See also Harbi and Meynier, *Le FLN*, 169; SHD-T 1H1447/1, monthly intelligence report for Aumale, June 1956. "The most significant fact is a change in attitude among a certain number of caïds who, like the population, not only pull back into silence, but deny the state of affairs, while others even encourage the people to stay mute." All translations are by the author unless otherwise noted.

5. CAOM SAS68, intelligence report for SAU Saint-Eugene, 28 October 1958.

6. SHD-T, 1H1895/2, report of Lieutenant-Colonel Rafa, État Major, 13 October 1959.

7. Kalyvas notes that incumbent and insurgent access to information about the population is asymmetric since the latter has ready access to "inside" intelligence denied to the former; Kalyvas, *Logic*, 170.

8. James C. Scott, *Domination and the Arts of Resistance: Hidden Transcripts* (New Haven CT: Yale University Press, 1990). See p. 2 for a typical instance of such resistance in the narration by a black slave in the American South: "I had endeavoured so to conduct myself as not to become obnoxious to the white inhabitants, knowing as I did their power . . . . I wore as much as possible the aspect of slavery [and] I had never appeared to be even so intelligent as I really was."

9. On the doctrine and practice of revolutionary warfare, see Peter Paret, *French Revolutionary Warfare from Indochina to Algeria: The Analysis of a Political and Military Doctrine* (London: Pall Mall Press, 1964); Paul and Marie-Catherine Villatoux, *La République et son armée face au "péril subversif": Guerre et action psychologique, 1945–1960* (Paris: Les Indes savantes, 2005).

10. Harbi and Meynier, *Le FLN*, 64, order of commander of Mintaqa 58, spring–summer 1957.

11. On the MNA see Jacques Valette, *La guerre d'Algérie des Messalistes, 1954–1962* (Paris: L'Harmattan, 2001).

12. Mouloud Feraoun, *Journal, 1955–1962*, ed. James D. Le Sueur (Lincoln: University of Nebraska Press, 2000), 201.

13. Quoted in D. Michael Shafer, *Deadly Paradigms: The Failure of U.S. Counterinsurgency Policy* (Princeton NJ: Princeton University Press, 1988), 155–6.

14. For a definition of the term "compliance terrorism," see Martha Crenshaw Hutchinson, *Revolutionary Terrorism: The FN in Algeria, 1954–1962* (Stanford CA: Hoover Institution Press, 1978), 44–49.

15. On the strikes see Pierre Pelissier, *La Bataille d'Alger* (Paris: Perrin, 1995); Jim House and Neil MacMaster, *Paris 1961: Algerians, State Terror and Memory* (Oxford: Oxford University Press, 2006).

16. On the puritanism of the ʾUlamaʿ, which was opposed to a "decadent" Western culture that was perceived to threaten Algerian Islamic values and national identity, see Ali Merad, *Le Réformisme Musulman en Algérie de 1925 à 1940* (Paris and The Hague: Mouton, 1967); and James McDougall, *History and the Culture of Nationalism in Algeria* (Cambridge: Cambridge University Press, 2006). The links between religious orthodoxy and self-denial became particularly apparent during Ramadan, when the FLN tended

to renew its orders for a ban on the sacrifice of Aïd el kabir, on smoking and alcohol, a demand that an SAS officer described as having more impact on the population than any wave of grenade attacks: see CAOM 2SAS56, report of SAS Bas Casbah, 3 March 1959; Harbi and Meynier, Le FLN, 169, 584.

17. Harbi and Meynier, Le FLN, 112, tract of April 1956: "by boycotting tobacco and alcoholic drinks, you will make a serious blow against the colonialist economy." The Mau Mau insurrection in Nairobi during 1953–54 had deployed similar boycotts of European tobacco and beer, Asian middlemen traders, and public transport; see David Anderson, *History of the Hanged: Britain's Dirty War in Kenya and the End of the Empire* (London: Weidenfeld and Nicolson, 2005), 194–95.

18. On the writer's hiding away to smoke, his avoidance of cafés, the stories of young men assaulting smokers, while settler shopkeepers faced bankruptcy, see Feraoun, *Journal*, 15.

19. Meynier, *Histoire Intérieure*, 217; Jean-Paul Brunet, *Police contre FLN: Le Drame d'octobre 1961* (Paris: Flammarion, 1999). During the month of February 1962 the FLN system of justice in Wilaya 2 (north of the Seine) levied fines in relation to 616 cases of alcohol abuse and 68 gambling incidents; see Mohammed Harbi, ed., *Sou'al: Revue quadrimestrielle* 7 (September 1987), 36. Among the more secular leaders of the FLN the boycott of alcohol was more instrumental than a religious-moral issue. Mohammed Harbi notes how the "Stalinist" Boudaoud, head of the FLN French Federation, used an accusation of beer drinking as a form of political attack on him, even when all members of the Federal Committee consumed alcohol. The boycott existed "less to defend Islam than to bind in the militants and, on the rebound, fill the coffers." Harbi, *Une vie debout: Mémoires politiques*, vol. 1: 1945–1962 (Paris: La Découverte, 2001), 235. Meynier notes that some relaxation of the ban on tobacco began in late 1957, particularly in some areas (Wilaya 2 and 4) in which commanders, most notably Ali Kafi, were more progressive and less driven by religious puritanism; Meynier, *Histoire Intérieure*, 231–32. The football rule book for the internment camp of Paul-Cazelles stated, "All players are forbidden to smoke half an hour before the match and during half-time"; Harbi and Meynier, Le FLN, 642; SHD-T 1H1446* (files requiring a *derogation* for release to researchers are indicated with an asterisk).

20. Commander Azzedine, *On Nous Appelait Fellaghas*, reprinted in a combined volume with Jean-Claude Carrière, *C'était la guerre: Algérie 1954–1962* (Paris: Plon, 1992), 194–95, 232. Feraoun recounts how a Kabyle peasant, arrested and beaten by the police, was then offered a cigarette. "I did not take it, of course. I was glad to know that they take into account certain circumstances"; Feraoun, *Journal*, 18.

21. P.-A. Léger, *Aux Carrefours de la Guerre* (Paris: Albin Michel, 1989), 235–39.

22. House and MacMaster, *Paris 1961*, 54. The demonstration of 17 October 1961 in Paris was organized by the FLN in part as a "safety valve" to release the unbearable tensions that such a strategy had produced in the migrant worker population.

23. Feraoun, *Journal*, 53.

24. For an excellent overview of the model of pacification, see Keith Sutton, "Army Administration Tensions over Algeria's Centres de Regroupement, 1954–1962," *British Journal of Middle Eastern Studies* 26:2 (November 1999), 243–70.

25. Hamoumou, *Harkis*, 135.

26. Hamoumou, *Harkis*, 166.

27. Hamoumou, *Harkis*, 165; Caroline Brac de la Pierre records the anxiety of a domestic servant who traveled to work in an army lorry, or when her son was rushed to a French hospital, in case she was viewed as an informer through simple proximity or association; Brac de la Pierre, *Derrière les Héros: Les employées de maison musulmans en service chez les Européens à Alger pendant la guerre d'Algérie, 1954–1962* (Paris: Harmattan, 1987), 250, 252.

28. Hamoumou, *Harkis*, 167–68.

29. House and MacMaster, *Paris 1961*, 76.

30. Feraoun, *Journal*, 203.

31. Feraoun, *Journal*, 119–22. I have slightly changed the published translation, which has omitted "as well as the same distrust" (*méfiance*).

32. Feraoun, *Journal*, 237. On the cat-and-mouse battle between Feraoun and the SAS, see p. 90: "I have received a second request to attend the city council meeting. I am not going to answer this time. The captain [SAS] will be furious"; see also 129, 151, 178, 180, 182–83, 207, 215.

33. Feraoun, *Journal*, 244, 238.

34. Feraoun, *Journal*, 238–39. Raymond Montaner was soon transferred to counterinsurgency operations in Paris, where he achieved a dubious notoriety as founder and commander of the *harki* brigade that was widely accused of violence and torture: see House and MacMaster, *Paris 1961*.

35. CAOM 2SAS59, Monographie du Quartier Clos Salembier, 10 February 1960.

36. James D. Le Sueur, *Uncivil War: Intellectuals and Identity Politics during the Decolonization of Algeria* (Philadelphia: University of Pennsylvania Press, 2001), 55–56, 83–86, on the assassinations.

37. CAOM, 2SAS68, SAU Saint-Eugene, monthly report for January 1961; see also Grégor Mathias, *Les sections administratives spécialisées en Algérie: Entre ideal et réalité, 1955–1962* (Paris: L'Harmattan, 1998), 90–91.

38. For example, on the instance of an EMSI (Équipes medico-sociale itinérantes) leader who was puzzled by a refusal of Algerian women to undertake cleaning tasks unless ordered to do so, see Christiane Fournier, *Les EMSI, des filles comme ça!* (Paris: Arthème Fayard, 1959) 64.

39. Hamoumou, *Harkis*, 166. G. Mathias notes that it was a "family strategy" and insurance to make sure that it had both pro-FLN and *harkis* members; Mathias, *Sections administratives*, 137. On such "insurance" in other civil wars see Kalyvas, *Logic*, 228–29.

40. J. G. Peristiany, ed., *Honour and Shame: The Values of Mediterranean Society* (London: Weidenfeld and Nicolson, 1965); J. Davis, *People of the Mediterranean: An Essay in Comparative Social Anthropology* (London: Routlege and Kegan Paul, 1977); David G. Gilmore, ed., *Honor and Shame and the Unity of the Mediterranean* (Washington DC: American Anthropological Association, 1987). Kalyvas, *Logic of Violence*, summarizes a huge volume of research on such disputes and their translation into informing and violence under conditions of civil war.

41. See Pierre Bourdieu, *The Algerians* (Boston: Beacon Press, 1962); Ernest Gellner, *Saints of the Atlas* (London: Weidenfeld, 1969).

42. Feraoun, *Journal*, 14.

43. Feraoun, *Journal*, 11.

44. Feraoun, *Journal*, 16.

45. Feraoun, *Journal*, 21.

46. Feraoun, *Journal*, 139, 200. Kevin Toolis notes of fighters, "They were the local thugs turned community warriors"; Toolis, *Rebel Hearts: Journey's within the IRA's Soul* (New York: St. Martin's Press, 1997), 68, quoted in Kalyvas, *Logic*, 102.

47. Hamoumou, *Harkis*, 23–26.

48. Hamoumou, *Harkis*, 157; Kalyvas notes that insurgents, such as the Chinese Communist Party, were frequently compelled to adopt structures that displaced decision making on punitive violence from the local level (with risks of malicious reporting) to higher echelons; Kalyvas, *Logic*, 187–95.

49. Feraoun, *Journal*, 204.

50. Hamoumou, *Harkis*, 29. This "non-ideological" and localized contingency has been evident in many civil wars; for example, the Spanish Civil War provided a cloak for personal revenge and vendetta or the seizure of property; see Michael Richards, *A Time of Silence: Civil War and the Culture of Repression in Franco's Spain, 1936–1945* (Cambridge: Cambridge University Press, 1998); N. MacMaster, *Spanish Fighters: An Oral History of Civil War and Exile* (Basingstoke: Macmillan, 1990), 197, 204. Kalyvas is particularly rich on this aspect; Kalyvas, *Logic*, chap. 10, "Intimacy," 330–63.

51. Feraoun, *Journal*, 38.

52. CAOM, 3SAS29*, SAS report, Bordj Okriss, 21 May 1957. Names have been concealed, in respect of the archive regulation not to disclose individual identities in files under *dérogation* (indicated with an asterisk*).

53. See Feraoun, *Journal*, 140, 243, on how women have "learned from experience not to speak rashly. The cost of a hasty comment is quite costly [in FLN fines]" as in the case of Yamina, who cursed on stubbing her toe, or Fatima, who said "good day" in French to some soldiers; see Feraoun, *Journal*, 40. Sometimes the tensions became too much, the nerve snapped, and "a poor fellow ... becomes submerged in a state of lucid madness, he begins to talk and talk and talk. At the djemaâ, in the cafés—everywhere—he says exactly what he thinks about 'his brothers.'" But "one fine morning, he disappears" (243).

54. Feraoun, *Journal*, 133–34.

55. Self-censorship of speech became so ingrained that sometimes even in the family group individuals found it difficult to "let go": "you must trust no one, because words misunderstood are oftentimes words misinterpreted. . . . My poor sister, who has been deeply affected by it all, lowers her voice, asks if anyone outside can hear her, calms down, and gets up courage to speak ill of someone. Once she lashes out, just try to stop this barrage of words, suddenly accelerating like a rebellious, chaotic, and continuous cry, like an abscess that bursts, like a somber sky that suddenly purges itself in a blaze of anger"; see Feraoun, *Journal*, 242.

56. Kalyvas, *Logic*, 1–2, 294–98.

57. When such negotiation failed it could result in catastrophic violence and massacre: see the case of Abdelmadjid Ourabah and his "clients" in Harbi and Meynier, *Le FLN*, 193–84, 444–46.

58. Commandant Azzedine, *On Nous Appelait Fellaghas*, 328.

59. Berque, quoted in Benjamin Stora, *Les Sources du Nationalisme Algérien* (Paris: L'Harmattan, 1989), 50.

60. Charles-Robert Ageron, *Les Algériens Musulmans et la France* (Paris: Presses Universitaires de France, 1968), 2:995.

61. Raphaëlle Branche, *La Torture et l'Armée pendant la guerre d'Algérie, 1954–1962* (Paris: Gallimard, 2001).

62. On the problems of anthropological and oral history research on the Greek civil war, see Kalyvas, *Logic*, 403–4. Marie-Élisabeth Handman and Stanley Aschenbrenner took five and fourteen years, respectively, of patient fieldwork to try and get beneath the silence of villagers, the former with little success.

12

Exposing the "Paradoxical Citizenship"

French Authorities' Responses to the Algerian Presence in Federal Germany during the Algerian War, 1954–1962

MATHILDE VON BÜLOW

Throughout 1958 German newspapers large and small reported on the development of a new and worrisome refugee problem in the Federal Republic of Germany.[1] Refugees were hardly a recent phenomenon in the country, which had absorbed millions of ethnic Germans and Slavs displaced from their Eastern European homelands first by the Nazi terror of World War II and then by the Communist regimes that followed it. Yet there was something altogether unusual about the refugees who had begun to arrive in 1958. For one thing, they were not coming to Germany from the totalitarian and Communist East but from the liberal and democratic West. For another, these refugees were from an entirely distinctive ethnic group, since they were neither German nor Slavic in origin, but Arab and Berber. The incoming refugees were, in fact, all Algerians fleeing from an ever-intensifying "civil war" in France, where they were being subjected to tough "coercive measures" on the part of the French authorities, including "concentration camps."[2]

German newspapers were thus perfectly aware that the new influx of refugees in 1958 was closely related to Algeria's ongoing and increasingly brutal war of national liberation from France. Initially they treated this phenomenon purely from a socioeconomic and administrative perspective, expressing a strong humanitarian concern for the plight of the desperate and largely destitute individuals arriving in Germany.³ Yet in the aftermath first of the May crisis that brought down the Fourth French Republic and then of the launch by the Front de Libération Nationale (FLN) of its "second" armed front in metropolitan France on 25 August, the tone of reporting gradually began to change. By October the influential *Frankfurter Allgemeine Zeitung* (FAZ) reported that a veritable "Algerian psychosis" had come to grip some of the smaller communities along the Franco-German border, with locals fearing an "invasion of Algerians from France."⁴ One month later, the popular national tabloid *Bild* began to wonder "whether the dirty war" between France and the FLN was about to come to Germany, and Bonn's *Rheinischer Merkur* warned that if federal authorities failed to stem the surging tide of Algerian refugees, the country would soon face an "Algerian plague à la Paris and Marseille." In other words, unless the Bonn government reacted quickly, the "civil war" afflicting France would spread across the border into Germany itself.⁵

In 1958 sinister scenarios such as those depicted by the *Bild* or the *Rheinischer Merkur* appeared very real and imminent, and yet they have only received scant attention in historical research.⁶ The rising influx of Algerians into Germany can nonetheless help to shed fresh light on France's last, longest, and most brutal war of decolonization. For one thing, it demonstrates that the Algerian War cannot be understood solely within a geographically confined, "colonial" or even "national" space. This was a colonial conflict, whose course, impact, and consequences extended not merely beyond the colony (although Algeria, of course, was officially classified as an integral part of France), but even beyond the imperial metropole.⁷ The influx of Algerians into Germany at the height of that war can also offer valuable new insights into the colonialist attitudes that continued to shape and influence French policy during the era of decolonization. Indeed, the topic of transnational migration can help to elucidate further the "colonial mind" of French officialdom.

By focusing on French reactions to the growing Algerian presence in Germany during the Algerian War, this chapter seeks to illuminate the manner in which French diplomats and security officers, as well as their German counterparts, conceived not merely of the FLN but of Algerians generally. The chapter's fundamental argument is that official reactions to Algerian migration—whether in France or in Germany—came to highlight the inconsistencies and distortions that so characterized what French historian Alexis Spire has called the "paradoxical citizenship" of so-called Français Musulmans d'Algérie (FMA). This "paradoxical citizenship" was characterized by a gross divergence between legal categories and democratic principles stipulating that Algerians were full-fledged French citizens on the one hand and administrative practices and general mind-sets that continued to qualify them by the descriptor "Musulmans d'Algérie" on the other.[8]

Consequently, when it came to the treatment of Algerians based in Germany during the Algerian War, the metropolitan authorities were constantly torn between the legal and political necessity of upholding the principles of equality and unity between Algerians and French people on the one hand and their almost instinctive reactions to an ever-deteriorating security situation, both in Algeria and in France, on the other. Perhaps unsurprisingly given their different levels of involvement in the Algerian War, French diplomats were more at pains to reinforce the former precept, while security officers were much more prone to lean toward the latter attitude. As the number of Algerians on federal territory began to grow, however, particularly with the intensification of metropolitan police repression in reaction to the FLN's "second front," French security officers came to make ever more stringent and discriminatory demands of their German counterparts regarding the treatment not only of FLN "terrorists" but of Algerians generally. These demands blatantly contradicted French jurisdiction and republican rhetoric; nor could they necessarily be explained as momentary exigencies brought on by the FLN's growing challenge to French national security. Rather, they were the product of a deeply entrenched, racially motivated bias that made it difficult—even for French diplomats—to see Algerians as anything but the colonial subjects that they had been for so long.

By exposing the "paradoxical citizenship" of Algerians, and by illuminating the extent to which French attitudes and policies were shaped by modes of thought and of action that were deeply rooted in France's colonial experience, the migration of Algerians to Germany came to highlight the hypocrisy of French claims of promoting citizenship and equal rights among its colonial subjects. This, in turn, helped to discredit the illusory concept of "l'Algérie française." After all, while Bonn's reactions to Algerian migration are not at the forefront of this chapter, it nevertheless becomes clear that German officials were generally perplexed by their French counterparts' extreme and contradictory demands.[9] They, too, were torn between their obligation to act according to the law, which stated that Algerians were French, and their commonsensical recognition that Algerians were anything but French. This observation was prompted not only by the racist and discriminatory attitudes and policies of their French interlocutors but also by the fact that even most Algerians on federal territory tended to see themselves as distinct from the French—as illustrated, for instance, by their deliberate avoidance of contact with the French or German authorities. The more German officials were exposed to the problems of Algerian transnational migration, therefore, the more they came to perceive the FLN's call for an independent Algérie algérienne as the only sensible and logical solution to the Algerian War.

Colonial mind-sets and racial discrimination thus went hand in hand when one looks at the example of transnational migration during the Algerian War. To substantiate this argument, the chapter starts by chronicling French efforts to regulate the movement of Algerians into Germany, as well as their actions once there. The second part of the chapter analyzes what these efforts tell us about the French "colonial mind." Here, it is argued that French security officers, due to their traditional role as upholders of law and order, whether in France or in the colonies, were much more likely to expose and act upon their colonialist preconceptions and preoccupations than French diplomats, who, though hardly immune to racially inspired prejudice, were much more attuned to the political rationale of championing the myth of l'Algérie française. French officials, it is further argued, also appear to have been well aware of their own discriminatory attitudes toward Algerians, some even unapologetically so. Ultimately the question of Algerian migrants in Germany during the Algerian War sheds new light on one of the fundamental stumbling blocks that obstructed the process of decolonization, namely the mental and ideological clash between an old world in which colonial attitudes were the norm and a new world in which these attitudes and values were no longer accepted.

The Algerian Presence in Germany

Before embarking on a discussion of French responses to the Algerian presence in Germany, it is vital to grasp just why and how so many Algerians began to arrive in that country during the Algerian War. The main cause for this development was, of course, that conflict itself. After all, the FLN's independence struggle not only affected the 8.5 million Algerians who lived south of the Mediterranean, but also the community of 250,000 to 350,000 Algerians who lived and worked in metropolitan France. Ever since the 1920s Algerian workers in France constituted a crucible of anticolonial nationalism and a vital reservoir of financial aid and ideological inspiration for the supporters of Algerian independence.[10] Thus, it was hardly surprising that these migrants became the object of an intense and increasingly brutal rivalry between the FLN's Fédération de France, created in early 1955, and the much more established Mouvement National Algérien (MNA), which had succeeded Messali Hadj's Mouvement pour la Triomphe des Libertés Démocratiques, as both sides competed for control over this sizeable community.[11] By 1957 the rivalry between FLN and MNA had spiraled into a vicious civil war, one that would leave around 4,000 Algerian migrants dead and another 10,000 badly wounded by the time of Algeria's independence in July 1962.[12]

In addition to this "sinister fratricide," the Algerian community in France also came under increasing pressure from the police and security services, which waged their own battle against the FLN and MNA.[13] Recent works by scholars such as Linda Amiri, Jim House, and Neil MacMaster have highlighted just how ruthless and unrelenting the police crackdown on the Algerian community in France became during the Algerian War. Indeed, in their effort to contain and suppress nationalist agitation, French authorities came to rely on some of the same methods of repression and control that were deemed so effective in colonial Algeria, including curfews and travel restrictions, frequent and unprovoked searches and identity checks, mass internments, relentless interrogations, and even deportations to Algeria. The more the Algerian War escalated, the more the security and police services also resorted to brute force in their efforts to combat Algerian nationalism. As in Algeria, moreover, police repression and violence were not merely directed against nationalist militants but against Algerian society at large. The most extreme example of blatant and open police brutality occurred on 17 October 1961 as the metropolitan police moved to suppress peaceful demonstrations organized by the Fédération de France in protest against a curfew that had been imposed on Algerians living in and around Paris. Such excesses merely exacerbated the racist, discriminatory, and segregationist attitudes and policies that shaped the daily lives and experiences of Algerian migrants in metropolitan France.[14]

By 1957 the ever-intensifying pressures that Algerian migrants in France were forced to endure had prompted many to seek refuge abroad. Their motives were not always the same. Some Algerians left France in order to escape from the escalating intercommunal violence between the FLN and MNA. Others left to avoid having to pay the revolutionary tax that these movements had imposed on the Algerian community as a means of funding their diverse activities, often by forcible means.[15] Still others left in search of better employment prospects.[16] Yet many more left because, as nationalists or militant activists, they sought to evade the grasp of the French police and security services. This was particularly the case after the appointment of the former Vichy collaborator and superprefect of Constantine, Maurice Papon, to the post of police prefect in Paris in March 1958, an event that signaled a radicalization of the fight against the FLN in France.[17] By April 1958 French pressure on Algerian nationalists had become so intense that the collective leadership of the Fédération de France was forced into exile in Cologne.[18] French repression intensified further still after the opening of the FLN's "second front."[19]

Among the countries that harbored these refugees, whether willingly or not, Switzerland and Belgium emerged as popular destinations due to the fact that both were at least partially Francophone countries, which made it easier for Algerians to find shelter, work, or aid. In 1960 the Helvetic authorities estimated that between 500 and 800 Algerians resided in Switzerland. The estimates for Belgium fluctuated between 1,500 and 4,000 Algerians. By far the largest group of refugees, however, chose Germany as their destination, notwithstanding the linguistic barriers.[20] Geographical proximity, combined with the permeability of certain parts of the Franco-German and German-Belgian frontier, help to account for this phenomenon. After all, apart from Paris and Marseilles, the principal areas of Algerian migration—the industrial centers in and around Lyon, Lille, Metz, Strasbourg, and Belfort—were situated in northern and eastern regions of France, close to the German and Belgian borders.[21] German and French officials were in general agreement with the press that along this northeastern front line, the "green frontier" that ran through the Ardennes had become a particularly popular crossing point for Algerians seeking to avoid official checkpoints and police inspections.[22] Regular travel, too, had become easier for Algerians, especially after the Franco-German border agreement of 8 December 1956 eliminated the requirement for French and German nationals to carry passports and obtain visas when crossing the Franco-German frontier. Henceforth all that was required to cross the border was a valid national identity card (although long-term residence and work permits still required the possession of a passport). These more elastic regulations were particularly fortuitous for Algerians. After all, the Délégation générale du gouvernement en Algérie, which nominally remained responsible for Algerians living in metropolitan France, only rarely approved applications for passports, especially at the height of the Algerian War. Designed to restrict the free circulation of Algerians, this policy revealed the unfairness of the application of citizenship laws when it came to Français Musulmans d'Algérie. Ironically, however, the French state was undone by the contradictions of its own surveillance system. Under a 22 October 1955 decree, all Algerians living in France had become obliged to carry newly designed and standardized national identity cards, which were consequently easy to obtain.[23] Armed with this documentation, Algerian immigrants in France found the gateway to Germany open to them as never before.

The movement of Algerians into Germany was further facilitated by the special political and economic status of the Saarland, a French protectorate since the end of World War II. Only on 1 January 1957 was this Bundesland (federal state or province) politically reunited with West Germany, though it remained bound to France in a customs union until 7 July 1959. This intermediate status made the Saarland a useful transit point for Algerians seeking to travel into Germany. Economic reasons, too, motivated the migration of Algerians into the Saarland, or further still into Germany. Over five hundred Algerians had found employment in the mines and heavy industry of the Saarland while this *Land* remained under French administration. Many of these Algerians stayed in their positions even after the province's political reintegration into Germany.[24] As indicated by a rise in the number of queries at German consulates in France, other Algerians hoped to find employment in the industrial centers of the Ruhr, which during the late 1950s were experiencing their tremendous "economic miracle."[25]

One way or another, French diplomats and intelligence officers first observed a pronounced influx of Algerians into Germany during 1957.[26] Practically all of these new arrivals were young, unattached men.[27] Even so, as late as February 1958 the estimated number of Algerians residing in Germany only amounted to a few hundred.[28] By the end of the year, however, these figures had risen substantially.[29] On 2 October 1958, for instance, the interior minister of the Saarland informed officials in the Federal Ministry of the Interior that over the previous few months approximately 3,000 Algerians had arrived in that Bundesland alone, even though only about 300 had complied with federal regulations and registered with the police.[30] By March 1959 provincial police authorities in Baden-Württemberg, Berlin, Niedersachsen, Nordrhein-Westfalen, Rheinland-Pfalz, and the Saarland had registered 1,350 Algerians.[31] Two years later, the number had risen to 2,992 officially registered Algerians.[32] German authorities nevertheless believed that the total number of Algerians residing on federal territory between late 1958 and mid-1963 was actually much higher than these statistics suggested. By October 1959 the Foreign Office had collected estimates ranging from between 2,500 and 8,000 Algerians.[33] On the whole, however, official figures tended to average between 3,000 and 5,000 Algerians.[34]

Bonn's inability to compile more reliable statistics on the number of Algerian migrants rested on several factors. Germany had become an important collection and transit point for recruits intending to join the FLN or its military branch in North Africa.[35] Ironically, ever since the introduction on 19 March 1956 of a restrictive permit system for travel between Algeria and mainland France, most Algerian migrants really had little choice but to reach Germany (or another neighboring state) before they could arrange for transport to North Africa, obstacles that again highlighted the pervasive and insidious French discrimination against Algerians.[36] As a consequence many Algerians who entered Germany as tourists stayed only for relatively short durations (usually a few weeks or months), and there was a regular coming and going that became difficult for authorities to monitor. There were other reasons, too, that made it near impossible for German authorities to gauge the exact number of Algerians on their territory. Those who stayed for longer durations, for instance, often changed residence and employment on a frequent basis, making it difficult for German police and employment agencies to keep track of their numbers and whereabouts.[37] This situation was exacerbated by the fact that German police authorities fell under the auspices of the individual Bundesländer and that information regarding the movements of Algerians was rarely communicated from one Land to another.[38] More importantly still, the maintenance of accurate, up-to-date statistics and intelligence on Algerians was complicated by the fact that most of these migrants entered Germany illegally. Indeed, even those who entered the country at official border crossings often failed to register with the police; many were able to find lodging and even employment by bypassing the authorities.[39] The anonymity that this illegal existence conferred was favored particularly by members of the FLN or MNA, for it not only safeguarded their freedom of maneuver but it also protected them from pursuit by the French (and German) police.[40] Finally, even those migrants who did register with the police were not easy to monitor as a distinct group of foreigners. After all, the category "Algerian" did not yet exist as an independent nationality in international law. In theory every Algerian who moved to Germany had to be registered by the police as a *French* national. What's more, Alexis Spire makes the point that French identity cards by the 1950s no longer bore "any specific mention capable of differentiating [Français Musulmans d'Algérie] from other French citizens," except perhaps their names and places of birth.[41] Once again, the mind-set of colonial categorization created loopholes that Algerian migrants were quick to exploit.

French Reactions

This, of course, is where the troubles for French authorities began. Early on in the Algerian War French officials had begun to express fears that militant nationalists might use Germany as a refuge or an operational base beyond the reach of the French police and security services.[42] The development of Algerian transit networks during 1957 and the relocation in April 1958 of the Fédération de France's leadership to Cologne appeared to confirm these suspicions. It was from Cologne, after all, that the Fédération reached the final decision and directed the ultimate arrangements for the opening of the FLN's "second front."[43] And it was largely via Germany that the Fédération's *groupes de "choc"* acquired the arms and munitions needed to sustain that front, not to mention the ongoing struggle against the MNA.[44] Interrogations conducted by intelligence officers attached to the Paris police prefecture during 1961 established that members of these *groupes de "choc"* had even received training in the handling of weapons, terrorist tactics, urban warfare, and sabotage in Germany (though this intelligence also indicated that no Germans were involved in these training activities).[45] By mid-1958, moreover, the FLN had installed an office within the premises of the Tunisian and Moroccan embassies in Bonn. Apart from managing recruitment and transit issues, this bureau organized propaganda activities and increasingly assumed the air of a diplomatic delegation (especially after the formation in September 1958 of the Gouvernement Provisoire de la République Algérienne).[46] In light of these diverse and increasingly high-profile activities, French authorities came to the conclusion that Germany had become an important *terrain de repli* and *plaque tournante* for Algerian nationalists, as well as the *pays d'élection* in the FLN's efforts to procure military and nonmilitary supplies.[47]

Unsurprisingly these developments provoked mounting alarm in France. According to French authorities the growing Algerian presence on federal territory could only strengthen the nationalists' hand. Metropolitan police and security services worried that the continuous exodus of Algerians would undermine their efforts to combat the FLN and MNA, thus posing a significant threat to French national security and public order. After all, Algerians who fled France could no longer be exposed to the *action psychologique* or *action sociale*, through which the Interior Ministry sought to contain and counteract the spread of nationalism among the Algerian community, nor could they be subjected to the security services' severe measures of surveillance, repression, and control.⁴⁸ French military authorities, for their part, were concerned about the impact of FLN agitation on discipline and morale within the North African regiments stationed in Germany. Already in March 1956 the French military blamed "secret propaganda" by Algerian nationalists for the low levels of morale among the 13th Régiment des Tirailleurs Algériens (RTA). Thereafter, the *deuxième bureau* (military intelligence) of the Commandement en Chef des Forces françaises en Allemagne frequently noted a correlation between the appearance of Algerian migrants within the vicinity of French army bases in Germany and the rise of desertion rates at these bases.⁴⁹ French diplomats, in turn, fretted about the impact of Algerian propaganda on German opinion, which was already quite negative toward France's aims and policies in Algeria.⁵⁰ More importantly, though, French diplomats and intelligence officers were concerned that the growing mass of largely destitute, unemployed, and illegal Algerian aliens on federal territory represented an "easy prey" for the nationalist movements, especially the FLN. Their radicalization would lead to a further extension of the Algerian War on territory that the French were unable to control.⁵¹

To stifle these developments as quickly and effectively as possible, French authorities were agreed that one had to contain Algerian nationalist agitation on French territory, thus suppressing its spread into Germany altogether. Achieving this objective was easier said than done. After all, the French security and intelligence services did not know the identities of each and every member of the FLN or MNA. Nor did they always know when, where, how frequently, or by what means Algerian militants traveled to Germany, let alone whether they entered that country legally or illegally, directly or indirectly. French authorities could not even be sure that these militants possessed legitimate French identity cards, or whether they used counterfeit ones, or passports furnished by one of the Arab governments allied to the FLN.⁵² This uncertainty left only one avenue open in the struggle against the transnational spread of FLN or MNA agitation: French authorities would simply have to stem the influx of Algerians into Germany altogether, regardless of whether they were members of one of the nationalist movements, refugees seeking to escape intercommunal strife, or economic migrants with no interest in the politics of Algerian nationalism.

Yet this task, too, proved difficult. It necessitated the full cooperation of German authorities, especially the police and federal border guards. Initially Paris hoped to obtain this support through diplomatic channels. As early as January 1958 the Quai d'Orsay, acting on behalf of the French Interior Ministry, had instructed its diplomats in Bonn to approach the Foreign Office about the suppression of FLN transit networks. Thereafter the issue of Algerian refugees, migrants, and illegal aliens became a matter of frequent exchanges between French and German diplomats. By October 1958 the situation had become pressing enough from the French perspective to warrant a personal intervention by Ambassador François Seydoux with the German foreign minister, Heinrich von Brentano.[53] French pressure certainly contributed to the Federal Ministry of the Interior's decision, that same month, to convene two interministerial conferences—one at the national level, the other uniting representatives of the Bundesländer—at which the rising influx of Algerians was discussed. The new regulations devised at these conferences did not seek primarily to prevent Algerians from entering into federal territory, however. From a legal perspective, German officials felt, this was really a task for the French government.[54] Rather, Bonn's Interior Ministry sought to establish measures that would allow German authorities to exert greater control over those Algerians who had already arrived in Germany. Among other things, it was decided that temporary residence and work permits (called "tolerance papers") were to be issued to Algerians who did not possess valid French passports. Attempts were to be made to find these individuals employment in an effort to keep them out of trouble with the law and beyond the reach of the FLN. In exchange for these permits, Algerians would not only have to commit themselves to regular check-ins with local police authorities, but they would also have to promise to refrain from political activities. The Bonn authorities' new regulations thus sought to prevent Algerian nationalists from engaging in any subversive activities deemed a threat not only to law and order, whether in Germany or France, but, more broadly, to the Franco-German *rapprochement*. At the same time, however, they sought to uphold the legal precept that Algerians were French.[55]

Rigorous as they were, these measures did not go far enough to satisfy the French security and intelligence services. They could not guarantee that Algerians on federal territory would be subjected to close and constant police surveillance, and they did nothing to ensure that Algerians stopped arriving in Germany in the first place. On 18 November 1958 Jean Verdier, director of the Sûreté Nationale, and Jean-Émile Vié, head of the Renseignements Généraux, therefore decided to take up the matter of the Algerian presence in Germany directly with officials from Bonn's Interior Ministry and its subordinate security services. It was decided during this meeting to establish a permanent, top-secret, and strictly bilateral liaison service between French and German security and intelligence services relating exclusively to the Algerian question ("Operation A"). Verdier and Vié insisted that French authorities be kept informed by their German counterparts of the identities and whereabouts of all Algerians who entered, moved through, or settled in Germany. Moreover, both directors pushed for greater German collaboration in the identification and arrest of Algerian nationalists (whether FLN or MNA).[56] To assist German authorities in this task the Renseignements Généraux even communicated to the German Interior Ministry intelligence from its Fichier Z, an extensive database that listed all Algerians deemed *à surveiller, dangereux, très dangereux,* or *en réalité*.[57] Federal authorities received their first batch of 13,000 files from the Fichier Z in December 1958.[58] By the time the Algerian War ended in 1962, the number of entries communicated to the German Interior Ministry had risen to almost 30,000.[59]

French authorities' readiness to share with their German counterparts such a substantial body of sensitive and top-secret intelligence indicates just how vital the issue of the Algerian presence in Germany had become. It also illustrates a great deal about official French attitudes toward Algerians or, in this case, what might be dubbed the colonial mind of state surveillance. The fact that the Renseignements Généraux maintained such an extensive database on Algerians living in metropolitan France reveals again that Algerians—as a group—were treated very differently from *Français de souche européenne.* Indeed, the sheer size of the Fichier Z is indicative of the suspicions that the French security and police services harbored toward this community; one gains the impression that practically all Algerians of a certain age and sex were automatically deemed to be potential nationalists, subversives, or dangerous criminals.

Moreover, the fact that French intelligence was willing and even eager to share this information with a foreign power reveals just how strong the urge to dominate and contain the Algerian community was: even when they had left French sovereign territory, Parisian authorities continuously tried to control the movements and actions of these second-class citizens. Ironically, to judge from German documents, the Fichier Z was rarely helpful when it came to the identification of militant nationalists. The intelligence it provided was generally too vague to help in this process. Besides, those militants most wanted by French police were hardly likely to register with the German police; many did not even travel with legitimate identification papers that could be compared to entries from the Fichier Z.[60]

These obstacles, coupled with the ongoing spread of FLN and MNA agitation in Germany, impelled French authorities to seek even closer collaboration with their German counterparts. Throughout 1959 and 1960 Vié insisted on a series of meetings with representatives from the German security and intelligence services with a view to intensifying controls at the Franco-German border and enhancing cooperation in the matter of tracking and apprehending FLN and MNA militants.[61] Vié's aims were essentially fivefold. First, he sought to ensure that all Algerians who had no good reason for traveling to Germany were denied entry by federal border guards. Only those Algerians possessing legitimate and official invitations, such as a contract of employment or a university scholarship, were to be allowed entry into the country. Of course, the numbers of such officially sanctioned visitors were very few. In January 1960, for instance, only about one-third of the three-thousand-odd Algerians registered by the German police were in full-time employment (though it is doubtful that many of these individuals had managed to secure work prior even to entering Germany). That same year the association of German student unions (Verband deutscher Studentenschaften) estimated that fewer than thirty Algerian students had gained German scholarships.[62] Vié's stringent new criteria would therefore have barred the vast majority of Algerians from migrating to Germany. Second, Vié sought to ensure that all Algerians listed on the Fichier Z were handed over to French police, even if they had obtained a German residence or work permit.[63] Third, the intelligence director demanded that Algerians facing expulsion or deportation from Germany, either because their papers were not in order or because they had committed a crime, were placed directly into French custody, even when these individuals objected on the grounds of political persecution or fear for their personal safety. Here, Vié's demand openly contravened German laws, which stipulate that all foreign nationals claiming persecution in their home country must either be granted asylum, at least until their claims can be verified, or else be deported to a third state. Fourth, Vié wanted federal authorities to implement special surveillance measures for those Algerians residing in Germany under an assumed Arab (usually Moroccan, Tunisian, or Egyptian) identity. The names of these individuals were to be supplied by French intelligence. Finally, French security and intelligence authorities expected their German counterparts to provide them with the names, whereabouts, movements, and activities of all Algerians residing in or passing through Germany.[64]

Algerians in Germany and the French Colonial Mind

These five rather unrealistic and unworkable demands essentially summarize the French government's forceful reaction to the Algerian presence in Germany during the Algerian War. Vié's extreme requests can partly be explained by national security imperatives in the context of an ever-intensifying colonial insurgency that was threatening to spiral out of France's territorial control. Yet the stringent demands made by French authorities also highlight the extent to which official attitudes and actions toward Algerians were shaped and influenced by an enduring colonial mind-set. Vié's efforts to bar the entry of Algerians into Germany, to have them expelled and deported from that country, or to have their every move shadowed by the German police underline that this group of individuals did not benefit from the rights and civil liberties that were typically enjoyed by French citizens. Indeed, quite the reverse: the intelligence director's demands suggested that Algerians belonged to a distinct and dangerous community that had to be tightly controlled and constantly monitored, no matter where. To French intelligence and security officers, therefore, Algerians were not French nationals, let alone citizens. Rather, they were French colonial subjects, and as such they were always deemed potential anticolonial rebels, or terrorists, who had to be restrained and held in check.

This attitude of racism and discrimination was not, of course, one that French authorities should have openly professed to a foreign power. After all, according to French law and republican rhetoric, Algeria was not a colony but an integral part of France, and Algerians were not colonial subjects but French citizens. Thus, on the one hand, French authorities made stringent demands of their German counterparts aimed at curtailing the movements and activities of Algerians, while, on the other hand and often in the same breath, reminding their perplexed German counterparts that Algerians still had to be treated as French citizens.[65] This argument became particularly crucial beginning in February 1958, when the widely read and highly reputable *Frankfurter Allgemeine Zeitung* first demanded that Algerian refugees in Germany be granted political asylum, contending that Bonn was obliged to such action not only by the principles enshrined in §16.2 of the German "Basic Law" (constitution), but by being a signatory of both the 1950 European Convention on Human Rights, and the 1951 Geneva Convention relating to the Status of Refugees.[66]

The publicity that suddenly accrued to the problem of Algerian refugees prompted serious alarm in French diplomatic circles. In fact, Jean Jurgensen, the head of the Quai d'Orsay's Central European Service, noted that "Germany is the first country in which the problem of the right of asylum for members of the FLN has been posed before public opinion; the solution to this problem, and our [the French government's] reactions to it, will in some measure determine the attitude of other European countries [toward this question]."[67] By conceding the right of asylum to Algerian nationalists, German authorities would set a dangerous precedent. After all, the act of granting asylum to Algerians constituted an implicit recognition by a foreign government, not only of the oppressive nature of France's treatment of Algerians, but also of the FLN as a legitimate political movement pursuing a just cause, and consequently also of Algeria as a culturally as well as politically distinct community and nation. By exerting strong diplomatic pressure (emphasizing, in particular, how inimical such a move would be to the all-important Franco-German *rapprochement*), by stressing the fact that Algerians were French nationals and citizens (and that France was itself a signatory of the 1950 European Convention on Human Rights and the 1951 Geneva Convention relating to the Status of Refugees), and by underlining that the FLN and MNA were nothing more than criminal and terrorist organizations, the Quai d'Orsay successfully steered Bonn away from any decision to grant Algerians the status of political refugees. As French citizens, so the argument went, Algerians hardly required asylum, for they belonged to a civilized and democratic society that respected and upheld the rights and responsibilities of all of its members. Indeed, France's harsh line toward certain Algerians, so the argument continued, was driven, not by political considerations, but purely by the rationale that these individuals, by belonging to either the FLN or MNA, were dangerous criminals and terrorists. In principle, therefore, Algerians were still to be treated by German authorities as any other French citizens would be.[68]

This argument was certainly reinforced by Ambassador Seydoux in his discussions with Foreign Minister von Brentano in October 1958. Seydoux reiterated in the strongest terms that "it is essential to avoid all discrimination between French citizens of Algerian or metropolitan origin." At the same time, however, he observed that "it would be desirable, on the one hand, for the cooperation between French and German security services to be intensified, especially with regard to the search for the authors of criminal acts, and on the other hand, for no particular facilities (for example, the right of asylum) to be accorded to Algerians who found themselves in an irregular situation in Germany."[69] Such rhetoric was indeed scrupulously adhered to by the Quai d'Orsay. Legally and administratively, it enabled French consular authorities to retain a degree of authority and control over the Algerians who traveled through or settled in Germany. After all, Algerians seeking to live in German territory for longer periods theoretically had to approach French consular authorities in order to obtain the passports that were required for the processing of work and residence permits. By insisting that Algerians were French nationals, French consular authorities were also able to repatriate those Algerians who found themselves living on the margins of legality in Germany.[70] Yet politically, too, the rhetoric of Franco-Algerian equality was important, for it reinforced that all-important notion of l'Algérie française. French diplomats' warnings against discrimination, combined with their persistent indictment of the FLN as a criminal organization, served not only to underline the purported unity between Algeria and France but also to counteract the FLN's claim that Algeria was a distinct nation under foreign and colonial subjugation.

French security and intelligence officers expressed similar views in their discussions with members of the Federal Ministry of the Interior in November 1958, maintaining that "[o]f the 300,000 Algerians in metropolitan France, only a *small minority* could be considered to be terrorists," and that it was France's duty to protect all French nationals, "including the *overwhelming majority of decent Algerians*," from these criminal elements. On that occasion, Vié's superior Jean Verdier still concluded that "it was not the intention of the French government to induce the German authorities to control and monitor *all* Algerians on federal territory," but rather to draw attention "to a *small minority* of Algerians who abused German hospitality for their terrorist actions against France."[71] In other words, French authorities sought to justify their demands for tough controls and surveillance measures from their German counterparts by arguing that an uncompromising attitude toward the minority of Algerian "terrorists" was the only way to protect the majority of loyal and law-abiding French-Algerians, whether in Germany or in France.

Yet this attempt to distinguish between a minority of fanatical criminals and a majority of faithful citizens became increasingly difficult to maintain, especially after the intensification of French counterterrorist measures in reaction to the FLN's "second front." It also became impossible to reconcile with the increasingly stringent demands that French security and intelligence officers, notably Vié, came to make of their German counterparts. Indeed, the more French authorities intensified their efforts to contain and suppress Algerian nationalism, the more they blurred the distinction between the decent majority and the terrorist minority. After all, the demands made regarding the treatment of Algerians in Germany did not single out a small group of terrorists; they increasingly came to target the Algerian community at large. French officials were certainly aware of just how detrimental such policies could be in the eyes of an international audience. On the one hand, they undermined the French argument that Algerians were accorded the same rights and responsibilities as all French citizens. On the other hand, they bolstered the FLN's claims for national liberation and political independence. French authorities therefore went to considerable lengths to try to conceal from international opinion the increasingly harsh and inequitable manner in which they treated Algerian refugees in Germany (or elsewhere). As early as September 1957, for instance, when Vié ordered an intensification of border inspections for all Algerians trying to leave mainland France, he insisted that these controls had "to be exercised with judgment, avoiding vexatious measures [. . .] and with a maximum of discretion in order to prevent potentially unfavorable commentaries by foreign witnesses."[72] Similarly, during his discussions with German officials in November 1958 Verdier "insisted on the *secret* character which the cooperation between French and German [security and intelligence] services had to preserve, whatever the circumstances."[73] Even Jean Jurgensen instructed French diplomats in Bonn in July 1958 that they had to convince German authorities that the measures being demanded of them regarding the treatment of Algerians were "not at all motivated by racial discrimination or by political preoccupations, but [were necessary in order to] prevent the entry [into Germany] of a drifting population that is dangerous to public order."[74] The colonial mind of the French security establishment thus certainly persisted, but it increasingly expressed itself in euphemistic terms.

Jurgensen's instructions, as with those by Vié and Verdier, are revealing for three reasons. First, they expose just how ubiquitous and engrained French stereotypes of and prejudice against Algerians had become. These were no longer views held predominantly by colonial officers in Algeria; rather, they had come to permeate not just the metropolitan security services but even the diplomatic service. Second, these remarks further demonstrate just how difficult it had become for French authorities to conceal these biased views. After all, in the same sentence in which Jurgensen denied that French policies toward Algerians were racially or politically motivated, this senior diplomat also managed to depict Algerians—and not simply those involved with the FLN or MNA—as essentially rootless and ruthless, iniquitous and terrorist, untrustworthy and hence undeserving of the same rights and liberties as French citizens of European descent. Finally, Jurgensen's denial of racial or political motives behind French policy toward Algerians in Germany, just like

Vié and Verdier's insistence on secrecy and discretion when it came to the treatment of Algerian refugees and expatriates, indicate just how aware these senior officials were of the discriminatory nature of their directives. At the end of the day they were only paying lip service to the notion of l'Algérie française.

Some officials in metropolitan France even called for an end to this charade, which merely impeded their counterterrorist operations. An unapologetic memorandum drafted by members of Maurice Papon's personal *cabinet* and dating from mid-1958, for instance, illustrates how the police prefect and many of his subordinates were frustrated by the fact that the government refused to declare a state of emergency in the métropole as it had in Algeria. Referring to the ongoing freedom of movement of Algerians on the European continent, the memorandum noted that it was "inconceivable that in times of war an enemy can cross the border just like all inoffensive individuals." The memorandum concluded that "one must cease in times of war, as is the case now, to uphold the ridiculous taboo of civil liberties" for Algerians, and it advocated that one had to "fight the separation that exist[ed] in the struggle against the [FLN's] rebellion between Algeria and France and abolish the ridiculous principle that says that everyone makes do [*se débrouille*] with his Algerians."[75] Thus rather than continuing to uphold the myth of unity, equality, and harmony between France and Algeria or the claim that members of the FLN were common criminals who were unrepresentative of the Franco-Algerian community at large, Papon called for an open recognition of the fact that Algeria and Algerians were not only a distinct but also a hostile community. Papon's suggestions would have exposed the French colonial mind for all, and thus it comes as no surprise that they were never officially enacted. At a tactical and operational level, they would certainly have facilitated the fight against Algerian terrorism and subversion in metropolitan France. In some ways, they would also have made it easier for the French to justify their stringent demands on the treatment of Algerians in Germany. Strategically and politically, however, Papon's proposals would have undermined the entire rationale of France's counterinsurgency, which sought to maintain and reinforce the unity between Algeria and France. At a time of growing domestic and international opposition to colonialism, such openly racist and discriminatory tones would merely have doomed the French state's struggle for l'Algérie française.

Conclusion

When one considers the ambiguities and inconsistencies that characterized French attitudes toward Algerian migrants and refugees in Germany, it becomes clear that the myth of l'Algérie française was already being undercut, even while it was being rhetorically upheld. French reactions to the Algerian presence in Germany ultimately highlight one of the fundamental paradoxes of the manner in which French authorities perceived and treated Algerians: namely the gross divergence between an official rhetoric that emphasized equality before the law and inclusiveness in French society, and a practical reality of widespread discrimination, arbitrary maltreatment, and even persecution. The more the French intensified their interventions in Bonn, the more obvious this "paradoxical citizenship" became, leading one German diplomat to complain to his interlocutor from the French embassy as early as September 1958 that "while we do not doubt in any way that Algerians, legally speaking, are French citizens; *the entire world realized that, de facto, they are not French.*"[76]

What does this tell us about colonial minds on either side of the Franco-German border? For one thing, it suggests that German authorities were both very aware of the colonial nature of the Franco-Algerian relationship and increasingly ill at ease with it. For another, it indicates that irrespective of their official rhetoric, French authorities were unable to escape colonial categories in their treatment of Algerians, even when these Algerians had themselves escaped the territorial confines of French sovereignty. If anything, their colonial impulse to control and coerce only intensified as Algerians escaped their direct control. As a result French officials pushed for their German counterparts also to deny Algerians their legal rights as French citizens and to treat them as colonial subjects. By attempting to curtail Algerian movements, by sharing intelligence from the Fichier Z, by calling for the deportation of every Algerian deemed somehow suspicious—even though German police often felt that French accusations were entirely unfounded[77]—and by insisting on stringent controls and constant surveillance of Algerians residing in Germany, the behavior of French authorities betrays a deliberate attempt to impose on the German state a diluted version of the system of colonial repression and discrimination that dominated the struggle against the FLN in both Algeria and metropolitan France. What French officials seemed not to realize was that this behavior went a long way to discredit the very notion it sought to uphold, namely the idea that Algeria was French. To an international audience, in this case Germany, the inability of French authorities to practice what they preached helped to expose the colonial nature of France's grip over Algeria. Ultimately therefore, French attitudes toward the Algerian presence in Germany had a counterproductive effect: instead of containing and combating the spread of Algerian nationalism, they reinforced international awareness of Algeria's distinct national identity and therefore strengthened the FLN's claims to national independence.

Notes

1. For reasons of brevity, this article will typically refer to the Federal Republic of Germany and West Germany simply as Germany.

2. "Soziales Freiwild," *Vorwärts* (the official organ of the Social-Democratic Party), 10 October 1958; "Algerier bittet um Asyl: Aus Frankreich geflohen—Aachener Grenzbeamte beschworen—Furcht vor KZ," *Westdeutsche Allgemeine Zeitung* (Essen), 26 June 1958. All translations from French or German are by the author.

3. See, for example: "Algerier flüchten in die Bundesrepublik," *Frankfurter Allgemeine Zeitung* (hereafter FAZ), 25 February 1958; "Wie steht es mit dem Asylrecht?" *Die Welt* (Hamburg), 21 March 1958; "Algerier suchen in der Bundesrepublik Zuflucht," *Neue-Rhein-Zeitung* (Essen), 1 March 1958.

4. "Algerier in Lörrach: Die 'Badische Zeitung' in Freiburg untersuchte die Gerüchte über eine angebliche Invasion von Algeriern aus Frankreich über den Rhein," FAZ, 6 October 1958. See also "Algerische Invasion? Die Ausstrahlung des französisch-algerischen Konfliktes auf die Bundesrepublik," *Rheinischer Merkur* (Bonn), 31 January 1958; "Algerier flüchten über den Rhein: 2000 algerische Flüchtlinge in der BR—ohne Arbeitsgenehmigung," *Generalanzeiger* (Bonn), 4–5 October 1958.

5. "Algerische Aktivität," *Rheinischer Merkur*, 14 November 1958. The *Bild* (Hamburg) is cited in Archives du Ministère des Affaires Étrangères (hereafter MAE), Paris, Mission de Liaison pour les Affaires algériennes (here-

after MLA/2), télégramme no. 2662/65 de l'ambassade de France à Bonn, 7 November 1958.

6. The subject is touched upon loosely in Jean-Paul Cahn and Klaus-Jürgen Müller, *La République fédérale d'Allemagne et la Guerre d'Algérie (1954–1962): Perception, implication et retombées diplomatiques* (Paris: Le Félin, 2003); Jean L. Doneux and Hugues Le Paige, *Le Front du Nord: Les Belges dans la guerre d'Algérie, 1954–1962* (Bruxelles: Politique & Histoire, 1992); Marc Perrenoud, "La Suisse et les accords d'Evian: La politique de la Confédération à la fin de la guerre d'Algérie (1959–1962)," *Politorbis: Revue trimestrielle de la politique étrangère* 31:2 (2002), 8–38.

7. In their recent and excellent study of police brutality in Paris during October 1961 and that event's lasting memory, Neil MacMaster and Jim House point out just how unusual it was for a colonial conflict to invade—quite literally—the space of the imperial metropole. Jim House and Neil MacMaster, *Paris 1961: Algerians, State Terror and Post-Colonial Memories* (Oxford: Oxford University Press, 2006), 5, 15, 25.

8. Alexis Spire, *Étrangers à la carte: L'administration de l'immigration en France (1945–1975)* (Paris: Grasset, 2005), 195; Spire, "Semblables et pourtant différents: La citoyenneté paradoxale des 'Français Musulmans d'Algérie' en Métropole," *Genèses* 53 (December 2003): 48–68. See also Todd Shepard's chapter in the first volume of this collection.

9. For French and particularly German reactions to the Algerian presence on federal territory, see the author's PhD dissertation, which is currently being revised for publication: Mathilde von Bülow, "The Foreign Policy of the Federal Republic of Germany, Franco-German Relations, and the Algerian War," University of Cambridge, 2007, chaps. 2, 6. See also von Bülow, "Hôtes importuns: Des Algériens en République fédérale pendant la guerre d'Algérie (1957–62)," in *Migrations et Identités: L'exemple de l'Allemagne au XIXe et XXe siècles*, ed. Jean-Paul Cahn and Bernard Poloni (Lille: Presse Universitaire du Septentrion, 2009), 119–32.

10. There is a growing historiography on the impact of the Algerian War on the Algerian community in France. See, for instance, Linda Amiri, *La Bataille de France: La guerre d'Algérie en Métropole* (Paris: Laffont, 2004); House and MacMaster, *Paris 1961*, part 1; Neil MacMaster, *Colonial Migrants and Racism: Algerians in France, 1900–1962* (Basingstoke: Macmillan, 1997), chap. 11; Benjamin Stora, *Ils venaient d'Algérie: L'immigration algérienne en France (1912–1992)* (Paris: Fayard, 1992), part 2; see also Marc Bernardot, "Une politique de logement: La SONACOTRA (1956–1992)," PhD thesis, Université Paris I–Panthéon-Sorbonne, 1997); Raphaëlle Branche and Sylvie Thénault, eds., *La France en guerre 1954–1962: Expériences métropolitaines de la guerre d'indépendance algérienne* (Paris: Autrement,

2008); Peggy Derder, *L'immigration algérienne et les pouvoirs publics dans le département de la Seine 1954–1962* (Paris: L'Harmattan, 2003); Monique Hervo, *Chroniques du bidonville: Nanterre en guerre d'Algérie 1959–1962* (Paris: Seuil, 2001); Jacques Simon, *L'immigration algérienne en France des origines à l'indépendance* (Paris: Paris-Méditerranée, 2000), part 4.

11. On the conflict between FLN and MNA in metropolitan France, refer to the literature cited above in note 9 as well as Mohammed Harbi, *Une Vie debout: Mémoires politiques 1945–1962*, vol. 1 (Paris: La Découverte, 2001), chaps. 4–7; Harbi, *Le FLN: Mirage ou Réalité? Des origines à la prise de pouvoir (1945–1962)*, 2nd ed. (Paris: Jeune Afrique, 1985), 143–58; Ali Haroun, *La Septième Wilaya: La Guerre du FLN en France 1954–1962* (Paris: Seuil, 1986), esp. chaps. 1, 15, and 18.

12. MacMaster, *Colonial Migrants*, 195; Stora, *Ils venaient d'Algérie*, 206–9.

13. The term "sinister fratricide" was first used by the Algerian writer Kateb Yacine. See Benjamin Stora, "La Gauche et les minorités anticoloniales françaises devant les divisions du nationalisme algérien (1954–1958)," in *La Guerre d'Algérie et les Français*, ed. Jean-Pierre Rioux (Paris: Fayard, 1990), 63.

14. Amiri, *Bataille de France*, chaps. 6–7; Amiri, "La Répression policière en France vue par les archives," in *La Guerre d'Algérie: 1954–62, la fin de l'amnésie*, ed. Mohammed Harbi and Benjamin Stora (Paris: Laffont, 2004), 403–16; Jean-Luc Einaudi, *Octobre 1961: Un massacre à Paris* (Paris: Fayard, 2001); Jim House, "Contrôle, encadrement, surveillance et répression des migrations coloniales: Une décolonisation difficile (1956–1970)," *Bulletin de l'Institut d'histoire du temps présent* 83 (1er semestre 2004), 144–56; House and MacMaster, *Paris 1961*, esp. chaps. 3–6; House and MacMaster, "La Fédération de France du FLN et l'organisation du 17 Octobre 1961," *Vingtième Siècle* 83 (July–September 2004), 145–60; Raymond Muelle, *7 ans de guerre en France: Quand le FLN frappait en métropole* (Monaco: Grancher, 1994).

15. See, for instance, the case of Mammar D., who sought asylum for himself, his German wife, and their four children in order to escape payment of the revolutionary tax. Bundesarchiv, Koblenz (hereafter BA/K), B106/5350, Schreiben, Landesministerium des Innern (hereafter LMI) Baden-Württemberg an das Bundesministerium des Innern (hereafter BMI), 14 April 1958.

16. The German consulate in Lyon and Saarland provincial authorities reported a rise in the number of employment enquiries made by Algerians. Politisches Archiv des Auswärtigen Amts (hereafter PA/AA), Berlin, B25/7, Schreiben, Bundesministerium für Arbeit an BMI und Auswärtiges Amt (hereafter AA), 7 August 1956; BA/K, B106/63320, Vermerk, Referat VIB5/BMI, 10 June 1958.

17. Amiri, *Bataille de France*, esp. 56–61; MacMaster, *Colonial Migrants*, 196–97; House and MacMaster, *Paris 1961*, esp. 26–32 and chap. 1; House, "Contrôle," 147–48.

18. Harbi, *Vie debout*, 1:222; Gilbert Meynier, *Histoire Intérieure du* FLN *1954–1962* (Paris: Fayard, 2002), 534, 551.

19. Haroun, *Septième wilaya*, chap. 5; Muelle, *7 ans*, 122–37.

20. "Emigranten auf Zeit: 4000 Algerier leben in der Bundesrepublik," *Rheinischer Merkur* (Bonn), 3 March 1961; Perrenoud, "La Suisse et les accords d'Evian," 4; Stora, *Ils venaient d'Algérie*, 148.

21. Marcel Streng, "'Abrechnung under Nordafrikanern?' Algerische Migranten im Alltag der französischen Gesellschaft während des Algerienkriegs (1954–1962)," *Werkstattgeschichte* 35 (2003), 65.

22. "Die algerischen Nationalisten organisieren sich in West Deutschland," *St. Galler Tagblatt*, 23 September 1958; "Die algerischen Nationalisten organisieren sich in Bonn," *Luxemburger Wort*, 24 September 1958; MAE, Service Europe/République fédérale d'Allemagne (hereafter EU/RFA/1272, dépêche no. 148 du Quai d'Orsay au ministère de l'intérieur, 29 September 1958; BA/K, B106/15783, Aufzeichnung, Sicherheitsabteilung VIA an Staatssekretär (hereafter StS) im BMI Ritter von Lex, 26 June 1959.

23. MAE, MLA/2, Instructions de l'Ambassade de France à Bonn aux consuls français en République fédérale d'Allemagne (hereafter RFA), 21.1.1958; EU/RFA/1272, Dépêche no. 658 de l'Ambassade de France à Bonn au Quai d'Orsay, 8.4.1958; BA/K, B106/5350, Notiz an Breull, IB3/BMI, für die am 18./19.7.1960 stattfindende deutsch-französische Besprechung, undatiert. See also Spire, "Semblables," 58–59.

24. BA/K, B106/5350, Vermerk, Referat IB3/BMI, 2 October 1958; Stora, *Ils venaient d'Algérie*, 147; Cahn and Müller, RFA *et Guerre d'Algérie*, 197–98.

25. MAE, EU/RFA/1272, dépêche no. 658 de l'ambassade de France, Bonn, 8 April 1958. See also Cahn and Müller, RFA *et guerre d'Algérie*, 197.

26. MAE, MLA/2, dépêche no. 2 de l'Ambassade de France à Bonn au Quai d'Orsay, 21 January 1957; dépêche no. 1245 de l'Ambassade de France à Bonn au Quai d'Orsay, 29 July 1957.

27. PA/AA, B1/59, Aufzeichnung, Dr. Wolfrum, Bundesministerium für Flüchtlinge und Vertriebene, 24 March 1958; MAE, EU/RFA/1272, dépêche no. 902 de l'Ambassade de France à Bonn au Quai d'Orsay, 20 May 1958.

28. MAE, EU/RFA/1272, télégramme no. 472 de l'Ambassade de France à Bonn au Quai d'Orsay, 26 February 1958; "Algerier flüchten in die Bundesrepublik," FAZ, 25 February 1958.

29. "Die algerischen Nationalisten organisieren sich in West Deutschland,"

St. Galler Tagblatt, 23 September 1958; "Die algerischen Nationalisten organisieren sich in Bonn," *Luxemburger Wort*, 24 September 1958; MAE, EU/RFA/1272, dépêche no. 148 du Quai d'Orsay au ministère de l'intérieur, 29 September 1958; BA/K, B106/15779, Schreiben, Referat IB3/BMI, an Passkontrolldirektion Koblenz, LMIs, und AA, 30 September 1958.

30. BA/K, B106/5350, Vermerk, Referat IB3/BMI, 2 October 1958.

31. MAE, EU/RFA/1273, Bonn embassy tel. no. 503 to Quai d'Orsay, 11 March 1959.

32. Of these 2,992 Algerians, the geographical distribution was as follows: Bavaria, 232; Berlin, 30; Bremen, 44; Hamburg, 221; Hessen, 116; Niedersachsen, 90; Nordrhein-Westfalen, 864; Rheinland-Pfalz, 253; Saarland, 554; Schleswig-Holstein, 56; and Baden-Württemberg, 532. BA/K, B106/5352, Brief, BMI an UN High Commission for Refugees, Branch office for Germany, 5 January 1961.

33. PA/AA, B25/11, Schreiben, AA an BMI und Bundesministerium für Arbeit, 6 October 1959.

34. PA/AA, B25/11, Schreiben, BMI an AA, 26 November 1959; "Emigranten auf Zeit," *Rheinischer Merkur*, 3 March 1961; "Viertausend Algerier in Deutschland," FAZ, 29 March 1962; BA/K, B106/47459, Schnellbrief, AA an BMI, 20 July 1963.

35. The Quai d'Orsay was first alerted to the existence of such transit networks by the Interior Ministry in early January 1958, although such networks were thought to have been operational since August 1957. MAE, MLA/2, dépêche no. 326/1 du ministère de l'intérieur au Quai d'Orsay, 2 January 1958.

36. Spire, "Semblables," 59.

37. PA/AA, B25/11, Schreiben, Präsidenten der Bundesanstalt für Arbeitsvermittlung, 5 January 1960.

38. All information on foreigners residing in Germany was meant to be communicated by police authorities and border guards to the Federal Ministry of the Interior's Ausländerzentralregister (AZR—central registry for foreigners). The process of passing this information on was, however, highly cumbersome. Constant delays and procedural inconsistencies meant that the AZR's statistics were never complete or up-to-date. BA/K, B106/15779, Niederschrift, Besprechung mit den Vertretern der LMIs, 10 October 1958; PA/AA, B25/4, Schreiben, BMI an AA, 13 November 1958; B25/11, Schreiben, BMI an AA, 26 November 1959.

39. MacMaster raises the point that Algerian migrants during the colonial era generally shied away from official state authorities, especially the police. This meant that even in France, many led an underground existence. Algeri-

ans who sought to join the FLN or *Armée de Libération Nationale* in North Africa generally had their lodging in Germany organized and paid for by the FLN; other times Algerians would subsidize their rent by working underhand for their landlords. See MacMaster, *Colonial Migrants*, 12; PA/AA, B25/11, Schreiben, Präsident der Bundesanstalt für Arbeitsvermittlung, 5 January 1960; "Viertausend Algerier in Deutschland," FAZ, 29 March 1962; former ALN fighter, anon., interviewed by author, 10 January 2002, Cambridge UK.

40. PA/AA, B25/11, Schreiben, BMI an AA, 26 November 1959.

41. Cited in Spire, "Semblables," 57. See also BA/K, B106/15779, Aufzeichnung, Referat 1B3/BMI, 21 October 1958.

42. Service Historique de la Défense–Terre (hereafter SHD-T), Vincennes, 1R/352/D2* (files marked * are accessible only *sur dérogation*), Synthèse de renseignements no. 6060, 2ème bureau de l'Etat-major des Armées (hereafter EMA/2), 28 March 1956. See also MAE, MLA/2, dépêche no. 184 du service d'Europe centrale à l'ambassade de France, Bonn, 28 December 1957; EU/RFA/1272, dépêche no. 408 de l'ambassade de France, Bonn, 27 February 1958.

43. Haroun, *Septième wilaya*, 90–91; Harbi, *Vie debout*, 1:239.

44. Haroun, *Septième wilaya*, esp. chap. 12. The question of FLN arms trafficking is discussed further in von Bülow, "Foreign Policy," chaps. 4, 8.

45. Service des Archives et du Musée de la Préfecture de Police de Paris (hereafter SAMPP/P), H1B/16*; fiche d'interrogatoire technique concernant B.A.M., sans date; 11 November 1961; H1B/18*, Service de Coordination des Affaires Algériennes, section de renseignements (hereafter SCAA/Ren), audition du nommé R.Z., 27 January 1961; SCAA/Ren, audition du nommé H.A., 25 January 1961; SCAA/Ren, audition du nommé H.B.A., 27 January 1961; SCAA/Ren, audition du nommé C.S., 25 January 1961; SCAA, audition du sieur B.M., 11 February 1961; SCAA/Ren, audition du nommé B.B.K., 1 February 1961; H1B/19*, SCAA/Ren, audition du nommé C.S., 31 January 1961; SCAA/Ren, audition du nommé R.Z., 30 January 1961; SCAA/Ren, audition du sieur F.M., 30 January 1961; SCAA/Ren, audition du nommé H.A.A., 1 February 1961.

46. French intelligence began to report the presence of an organized and permanent "Algerian committee" located within the premises of the Tunisian embassy as early as June 1958. SHD-T, 10T/528/D2*, notice d'information no. 8389 du Service de Documentation Extérieure et de Contre-espionnage (hereafter SDECE), 17 June 1958.

47. SHD-T, 1H/1753/D1, note anonyme, 21 January 1958; MAE, EU/RFA/1272, note du service d'Europe centrale, 6 September 1958; 10T/525*, notice d'information no. 11838/SDECE, 20 October 1958; 10T/528/D2*,

notice d'information no. 29648/SDECE, 5 April 1960; 1H/1743/D1, étude no. 3450 du 2ème bureau de l'Etat-major Interarmées (hereafter EMI/2), 23 June 1960; Mémento no. 1878 du Bureau d'Études de la Délégation Générale du Gouvernement en Algérie (hereafter DGGA/BE), 22 August 1960; étude, EMI/2, January 1961; étude no. 1937, EMI/2, 1 June 1961; Mémento no. 40/DGGA/BE, January 1962.

48. BA/K, B106/5350, Niederschrift, Aussprache mit Vertretern des französischen Innenministeriums, 18 November 1958; Jean-Émile Vié, *Un Préfet au XXème siècle* (Paris: Harmattan, 2002), 130–31.

49. SHD-T, 1R/352/D2*, synthèse de renseignements no. 6060/EMA/2, 28 March 1956; SHD-T, 1R/333/D1*, rapport no. 1868 du service de sécurité de la défense nationale et des armées (hereafter SSDNA), 6 September 1958; rapport no. 2140/SSDNA, 8 October 1958; rapport no. 20888/SSDNA, 6 November 1958, rapport no. 2707/SSDNA, 2 December 1958; 1R/214/D5*, rapport no. 19346/SSDNA, 14 October 1958; MAE, MLA/4, rapport no. 22204/SSDNA, 28 October 1959; SHD-T, 10T/550*, synthèse mensuelle no. 842 du 2ème bureau du Commandement en Chef des Forces Françaises en Allemagne (hereafter CCFFA/2), 2 May 1960; rapport no. 750/SSDNA, 4 June 1960; synthèse mensuelle no. 1327/CCFFA/2, 16 July 1960; synthèse mensuelle no. 1498/CCFFA/2, 10 August 1960; synthèse mensuelle no. 1749/CCFFA/2, 20 September 1960; synthèse mensuelle no. 2111/CCFFA/2, 21 March 1961; 1R/333/D1*, rapport no. 6370/SSDNA, 27 March 1959; note anonyme sur les désertions entre janvier et septembre 1959; rapport 1778/SSDNA, 6 October 1959. See also Harbi, *Le FLN*, 229–30.

50. For a discussion of the impact of the Algerian War on German public opinion and foreign policy, refer to Cahn and Müller, *RFA et guerre d'Algérie*; Nassima Bougherara, *Les rapports franco-allemands à l'épreuve de la question algérienne (1955–1963)* (Bern: Peter Lang, 2006); as well as von Bülow, "Foreign Policy."

51. MAE, EU/RFA/1272, dépêche no. 658 de l'ambassade de France, Bonn, 8 April 1958. See also MAE, MLA/2, dépêche no. 184 du Service d'Europe Centrale au Quai d'Orsay à l'Ambassade de France à Bonn, 28 December 1957.

52. The use of counterfeit French identity cards was exposed when German police uncovered a forgery workshop run on behalf of the FLN in Osnabrück in June 1960. See BA/K, B131/198, Wochenbericht der Sicherungsgruppe Bonn des Bundeskriminalamts, 1 July 1960; PA/AA, B25/11, Schreiben des Generalbundesanwalts beim Bundesgerichtshof an das Bundesministerium für Justiz, 21 July 1960. The use of passports issued by Arab governments was considered a common practice by French authorities. See BA/K, 106/15783, Note et aide mémoire par les Renseignements Généraux pour le docteur Toyka au ministère fédérale de l'intérieur, 1959.

53. MAE, MLA/2, note 2 du service de liaison avec l'Algérie au Quai d'Orsay à la DGGA, 7 January 1958; EU/RFA/1272, Bonn embassy tel. 2299 to Quai d'Orsay, 15 October 1958.

54. BA/K, B106/5350, Vermerk, Referat IB3, 30 September 1958.

55. PA/AA, B25/10, Vermerk, Referat 502, über eine Ressortbesprechung im BMI vom 6.10.1958, 8 October 1958; BA/K, B106/15779, Niederschrift über die Besprechung mit den Vertretern der LMIs über ausländerpolizeiliche Fragen im Sammellager für Ausländer in Nürnberg, 10 October 1958.

56. BA/K, B106/5350, Niederschrift, 18 November 1958; MAE, MLA/2, Compte-rendu, 18 November 1958; télégramme no. 2876 de l'ambassade de France, Bonn, 21 November 1958; dépêche no. 1921 de l'ambassade de France, Bonn, 26 November 1958; EU/RFA/1272, dépêche no. 1997 de l'ambassade de France, Bonn, 9 December 1958.

57. BA/K, B106/5350, Vermerk, Referat IB3/BMI, 2 February 1959.

58. BA/K, B106/15779, Vermerk, Abteilungsleiter VI/BMI, 4 December 1958; Vermerk, Referat VIA3/BMI, 16 December 1958.

59. BA/K, B106/5350, Vermerk, Referat IB3/BMI, 29 August 1962.

60. BA/K, B106/5350, Vermerk, Referat IB3/BMI, 2 February 1959; B106/15783, Vermerk, Unterabteilungsleiter VIB/BMI, 20 August 1958; Spechzettel, Referat VIA3/BMI, 3 October 1959; B106/5351, Schreiben, BMI an AA, 9 September 1959; Vermerk, Referat IB3/BMI, 12 December 1959.

61. See, for instance, BA/K, B106/15783, aide mémoire pour le Docteur Toyka, BMI, sans date; B106/15778, Vermerk, Unterabteilungsleiter VIA/BMI, 26 May 1959; B106/63320, Niederschrift, deutsch-französische Sitzung, 18 November 1960.

62. PA/AA, B25/11, Schreiben des Präsidenten der Bundesanstalt für Arbeitsvermittlung und Arbeitslosenversicherung an das Bundesministerium für Arbeit und Sozialordnung, 5 January 1960; "Die Lage der Algerischen Studenten: Aus dem Arbeitsmaterial des Verbandes deutscher Studentenschaften," *Freies Algerien* 3:5 (May 1960), Dokumentarbeilage.

63. The French Interior Ministry had placed a travel ban on all Algerians listed on the Fichier Z, which was to be applied even retrospectively. BA/K, B106/15783, aide mémoire au BMI, sans date (1959).

64. BA/K, B106/15783, aide mémoire au BMI, sans date (1959); BA/K, B106/15778, Vermerk, Unterabteilungsleiter VIA/BMI, 26 May 1959; Note du directeur Vié au Colonel Duchène, Bonn, 30 November 1959.

65. PA/AA, B25/4, Aufzeichnung, Referat 204/AA, 16 September 1958; B15/14, Vermerk, Referat 204/AA, 23 October 1958; B25/10, Aufzeichnung, Abteilungsleiter West, AA, 24 October 1958.

66. "Algerier flüchten in die Bundesrepublik," FAZ, 25 February 1958.

67. MAE, EU/RFA/1272, dépêche no. 52 par le Service d'Europe Centrale du Quai d'Orsay à l'ambassade de France à Bonn, 21 March 1958.

68. MAE, EU/RFA/1272, dépêche no. 52 par le Service d'Europe Centrale du Quai d'Orsay à l'ambassade de France à Bonn, 21 March 1958; see also MAE, EU/RFA/1272, télégramme no. 472 de l'ambassade de France à Bonn au Quai d'Orsay, 26 February 1958; dépêche no. 408 de l'ambassade de France à Bonn au Quai d'Orsay, 27 February 1958; note par la Direction des affaires administratives et sociales du Quai d'Orsay au Service d'Europe centrale, 18 March 1958; PA/AA, B25/4, Aufzeichnung, Referat 302 des AA, 26 February 1958; Schreiben Nr. 134 des BMI an das AA, 26 February 1958; Informationsfunk der Bundesregierung nr. 58, 28 February 1958.

69. MAE, EU/RFA/1272, télégramme no. 2299 de l'ambassade de France, Bonn, 15 October 1958.

70. MAE, MLA/4, instructions de l'ambassade de Bonn à M. les Consuls Généraux, Consuls de France et Chef de Chancellerie détachée à Düsseldorf, Francfort, Hambourg, Munich, Stuttgart, Berlin, Mayence, Hanovre, et Kiel, le 8 août 1959, au sujet du rapatriement de Français Musulmans en RFA.

71. BA/K, B106/5350, Niederschrift über die vertrauliche Aussprache mit Vertretern des französischen Innenministeriums über das Algerier-Problem am 18 November 1958 im BMI (emphasis added).

72. SAMPP/P, Ha/66*, Instructions du directeur Vié no. 4085, 12 September 1957.

73. MAE, MLA/2, compte-rendu de la conférence entre représentants français et allemands au sujet de l'activité des rebelles algériens en RFA, 18 November 1958 (emphasis in the original).

74. MAE, EU/RFA/1272, Bonn embassy dépêche no. 103, 12 July 1958.

75. Unsurprisingly, this memorandum was written by members of the police prefecture's Service d'Assistance Technique, staffed heavily by former colonial officials from Algeria. SAMPP/PHa/68*, Quelques suggestions sur la lutte à mener contre le FLN en France, sans date, PP, Cabinet, SAT.

76. PA/AA, B25/4, Aufzeichnung, Referat 204, 16 September 1958 (emphasis added).

77. BA/K, B106/15779, Punkt 4 der Tagesordnung einer Besprechung zwischen dem Bundeskriminalamt und dessen Landesvertretungen über die Bearbeitung von schweren Rechtsbrüchen, die von Algeriern in der Bundesrepublik verübt sind, 23–24 November 1959.

Conclusion

The Colonial Past and the Postcolonial Present

ROBERT ALDRICH

In the subtitle of their edited 2004 collection, Mohammed Harbi and Benjamin Stora announced the "fin de l'amnésie" about the Franco-Algerian War, and other commentators, including English-language scholars such as the late William Cohen, David Schalk, Herman Lebovics, and the contributors to volumes edited by Alec G. Hargreaves and Patricia Lorcin have written about the "anamnesis" that has taken place in France in regard to the history of the Algerian War of Independence and, by extension, colonial history in general.[1] Have we indeed now seen the end of what, in a well-known paraphrase of Henry Rousso's term for the Vichy years, had come to be known as the "Algerian syndrome" and, once again by extrapolation, the general syndrome of postcolonial forgetting or *occultation*, particularly in regard to questions of colonial violence?[2] What are the reasons for the rediscovery of the colonial past, the *retour du colonial*? What are the uses and the limits of the much hailed *devoir de mémoire*? And what does this project say about contemporary French identity and political action?

The theme of history and memory has been a boom area in historiography in the last couple of decades, and debates about historical memory—the way it is recorded, recovered, commemorated, contested, and even put on trial—are not unique to France. The "British world," for instance, also confronts its colonial past. The events in Britain in 2007 marking the bicentenary of the abolition of the slave trade are proof positive of the demand by various groups for an accounting for the past; books, exhibitions, public manifestations such as a service at Westminster Abbey, and other gestures testify to the ever-present legacies of the colonial era in the United Kingdom and its former outposts.[3] Australia, to take the example of one former British outpost, has seen intense debate about that country's colonial past; the "history wars" pitted what former prime minister John Howard branded a "black armband" view of colonial history against what his opponents labeled a "white blindfold" version of the past. The wars were fought in the lecture halls and seminar rooms of universities on such issues as the legal and philosophical foundations of the doctrine of *terra nullius*, whether there were indeed "frontier wars" in the nineteenth century, and how many Aboriginals and Europeans perished in them, as well as about responsibility for the "stolen generations" of Aboriginals forcibly removed for their "protection" from 1910 to 1970.[4] However, these debates produced great impact, as well, outside the sandstone towers of the universities, linking to questions of Aboriginal land rights and the implementation of the Mabo decision by the High Court to allow compensation for the "stolen generations," and to the way Australia's past is presented in such institutions as the National Museum in Canberra. Particularly volatile was the question of whether the government should officially say "sorry" to Aboriginal Australians for the treatment of the "stolen generations" and other ill effects of colonialism. Howard resolutely refused to do so, but the public apology given by then new prime minister, Kevin Rudd, in a 2008 statement in Parliament, with Aboriginals watching from the gallery and a public riveted to television screens, will no doubt count as one of the defining moments of Australia's modern history.[5]

Similar "colonial history wars" have raged elsewhere. In Belgium a 2004 film titled *White King, Red Rubber and Black Deaths* and then a retrospective exhibition of Belgian colonialism at the Royal Museum for Central Africa in Tervuren provoked argument at home and abroad.[6] In the Netherlands, the four-hundredth anniversary of the founding of the VOC (United East Indies Company) led to competing reassessments of Holland's long history of engagement with the outside world.[7] A book published in 2005 by the dean of Italy's colonial historians, Angelo Del Boca, *Italiani, brava gente?*, brought into question the

Italians' perception of themselves as a basically benign people at war and peace; Del Boca catalogued exactions and violence in Italy itself, in the Italian actions during the Boxer Rebellion, and in Italian Abyssinia, Somalia, and Libya.[8] In the case of Germany, in 2004 a minister of state, speaking in Namibia, officially apologized for the massacre of the Herero people (which most historians now refer to as a "genocide") in the early years of the twentieth century in what was then German South West Africa.[9]

These examples represent various types of reevaluation of the past, debate about the past, and gestures attempting to "come to terms with the past" (what Germans call *Vergangenheitsbewältigung*) or "working through the past" (a phrase that many prefer to "coming to terms with the past"), and they could be multiplied.[10] The Truth and Reconciliation Commission in South Africa offered a forum for public examination of the apartheid era, in often painful fashion. Contrarily, in Japan the government has avoided questioning that country's war record and such issues as the "rape of Nanjing" and the sexual exploitation of thousands of "comfort women"; conservatives stoutly defend Japan's actions, while war victims (and countries such as China and Korea) accuse Japan of refusing to face up to its past. Debate has been relatively more intense concerning the Yasukuni War Memorial in Tokyo, where the souls of Japan's soldiers, including convicted war criminals, are enshrined, particularly with the controversial visits of former prime minister Junichiro Koizumi to the site.[11] The degree to which former colonizers, and the former colonized, engage in a serious and critical analysis of their past, it should be said, varies widely. Many former colonies, as independent states, have been less than eager to depart from an orthodox and nationalist narrative of anticolonialism and state building generally used to validate postcolonial regimes. A case in point: any visitor to the fascinating historical museums in Hanoi quickly apprehends the unquestioned nature of resistance to French rule, the beneficent role of the Communist Party, and the "great man in history" status of Ho Chi Minh.[12]

Rather than discussing the public memory of empire in the former outposts of Greater France, let us return here to France itself. Few would deny that colonialism was hardly the central topic in public debate or in historical research in the years after decolonization, and President de Gaulle pioneered a new post-empire orthodoxy in word and deed. An amnesty saved from prosecution those who might be accused of illegal actions during the Algerian War, *anciens combattants* returned unthanked and largely unrecognized, and the *harkis* were shamefully parked in hostel camps left over from the Second World War.[13] The white *rapatriés* managed economic and social reintegration with great speed, though the mounting number of postcolonial migrants from the Maghreb and sub-Saharan Africa, like the *harkis*, found it less easy to make a real home in France. Through an immensely successful effort at "spin-doctoring," de Gaulle and his successors championed France as the great decolonizer, the liberator of slaves, advocate of the Third World, and critic of neo-imperial campaigns such as the American war in Vietnam, conveniently ignoring France as colonizer, enslaver, fighter of colonial wars, and staunch defender of imperial enterprises.

Why did things begin to change in the mid-1980s, and then move forward with greater acceleration in the 1990s? One reason lies in blackletter historiography. By that time some of the old historical paradigms had lost their force; the triumphant Annales School of social history no longer seemed avant-garde, and the themes dear to many Marxist historians (though not only those historians), such as the Revolution, workers' movements, and socialism, no longer commanded the same sort of attention in the wake of the disintegration of traditional Marxism. The new cultural history, with research strategies influenced by Foucault but developed outside of France, boomeranged back to France, where the provocative ideas and methods of Edward Said and others gradually began to build on local interest in Orientalism and "the other." Anniversaries, as always, provide a precipitant for the organization of academic work and public debate, as occurred with the bicentenary of 1789 and volumes on the colonies in the Revolution, then with the sesquicentenary of the abolition of slavery in 1848, and the fiftieth anniversary of Dien Bien Phu in 2004. Research on the colonial past was facilitated, too, by the opening of archives thirty years after decolonization and by the consolidation of the Archives d'outre-mer in Aix-en-Provence. Writers in the 1970s, seeking to distance themselves from a colonial history writing that in the age of empire provided ideological support for imperialism, had embarked on "regional studies," "development studies," or specialism in the "Third World," research strategies that intentionally displaced colonialism from its key spot in the history of extra-European countries.[14] Scholars such as Charles-Robert Ageron, Pierre Brocheux, Catherine Coquery-Vidrovitch, Gilbert Meynier, Marc Michel, and various others had nevertheless kept the discipline of colonial history alive and have contributed mightily to the understanding of colonial and postcolonial societies in Africa and Asia. They led the way for a more nuanced view of colonialism that now began to replace some of the old colonialist and indeed anticolonialist verities. The historiographical context of the 1980s and 1990s thereby provided a congenial environment for French imperial history.

The public—readers of novels, cinemagoers, and visitors to exhibitions—have also played their part in the return of colonial history. The *grand public*, when it did not wish to forget colonialism altogether, often gazed upon an empire misted with the haze of nostalgia for the "good old days." Though they could not be judged apologias for empire, such books as Marguerite Duras's best-selling *L'Amant* (1984) and Régis Wargnier's film *Indochine* (1992), both fine artistic achievements, presented the colonies in terms of the French experience of adventure, love and loss, and the tragic end of a perhaps ill-guided but nobly intentioned effort overseas, a point even more clearly made in Pierre Schoendoerffer's *Dien Bien Phu* (1992). A revival of interest in colonialist and Orientalist art—marked by a series of exhibitions on Provence and the colonies held in Marseilles and a signal exhibition of colonialist artworks in Boulogne-Billancourt in the 1980s, accompanied by soaring prices on the art market for these previously demeaned works—centered on the picturesque exoticism of renditions of life in the harem or souk, on the Mekong or the Congo, rather than on the dynamics of the colonial situation. Yet this wider interest in colonialism both mirrored and provoked more rigorous analysis of empire, especially colonial iconography, the cultural import of imperialism and the ways that stereotypes (e.g., "Y'a bon, Banania") persisted in the French *imaginaire* and spread across genres ranging from painting and film to advertising.[15]

Another reason for the recall of empire lay in the efforts of particular groups connected with the colonial era, a trend that has certainly continued into the present. The French may dislike a communitarianism that sits uncomfortably with the ideals of republican egalitarianism, but interest groups have nonetheless shown great restiveness across the ideological spectrum. Many pieds-noirs, an aging community, have seemed anxious to tell their stories, secure their legacies, and pass on their identities to a new generation through Cercles algérianistes and countless other organizations. The prominent place occupied by pieds-noirs in the Front National and their antimigrant stances promoted a certain idea of national identity that inevitably valorized France's colonial past. The often incendiary remarks of Jean-Marie Le Pen ought not to be underestimated as a catalyst for debate on French colonialism, the imperial legacy, and the complexion of French society.[16] More moderate groups, such as FNACA, the main association of returned soldiers from Algeria, campaigned for pension rights denied to those who served in campaigns for the "maintenance of law and order" and promoted the naming of streets and squares for "19 mars 1962."[17] Representing a different heritage of the colonial past, the Beur movement in the 1980s evoked a colonial past that many compatriots did not wish to recall. Groups such as DiversCités, localized in Bordeaux, called for a reexamination of the history of slavery, a campaign seconded by activists in France's *départements d'outre-mer* in the West Indies and in La Réunion.[18] More recently, Les Indigènes de la République, in more polemical fashion, has riveted attention on the colonial past as a major cause of the disenfranchisement of "nonwhites" in present-day France. In the interstices between the broader public and the strictly academic, the noteworthy group Les Anneaux de la Mémoire in Nantes revealed and explored the taboo subject of slave trading, and the wealth accumulated from it, in one of the major slave-trading entrepôts of Europe. A generation after decolonization—perhaps the thirty-year rule works for collective memory as well as for archival regulations—the French seemed receptive to the excavation of colonial memories and eager for new "sites of memory" symbolized by the Mémorial des Guerres en Indochine in Fréjus, the Musée du Nouveau Monde in La Rochelle, and the Musée de la Compagnie des Indes in Lorient.[19]

A third reason for the "archaeological" work on the colonial experience was firmly grounded in contemporary politics, both in France and elsewhere. The general debate on what it means to be French—"être

Français, ça se mérite," read one of the Front National's slogans, although paradoxically Le Pen argued for Frenchness as a birthright of those with ethnically untainted French ancestry—often concerned the sequels to colonial migrations and the arrival of large numbers of Maghrebins and black Africans in France. Debate on migration and the status of migrants (and their descendants) has animated politics since the presidency of Giscard d'Estaing. The continued interlinking of "metropolitan" and "colonized" people and their cultures beyond the era of decolonization and the increasingly contested nature of these connections lie in the background of the revival of colonial studies.

Yet several specific developments have galvanized discussion of colonialism among historians and in the general public.[20] One is that in the 1980s and afterward France confronted several dramatic problems linked to colonialism and its aftermath overseas. The civil war in Algeria provided a vivid and bloody reminder of postcolonial problems in a country where France has maintained substantial interests, though with which—because of their entangled histories and the presence of so many Algerians and their descendants in France—it enjoys very fraught relations. Algeria remains familiar territory for the French, and while the bloodshed made the country a no-go area for tourists, it brought to newspapers and television screens the spectacle of a country tearing itself apart, with violence committed by militants of the Front Islamique du Salut and by a government under the control of the Front de Libération Nationale that had emerged victorious in 1962 and has garnered French support since independence. Attacks on some of the few remaining French residents of Algeria, such as the massacre of seven monks of Tibéhirine in 1996 (subject of the award-winning film *Of Gods and Men*), coupled with rising ethnic tensions in France, hardly seem to advance reconciliation between the old foes.

Another, slightly earlier national and "colonial" precipitant merits mention as well: "events" (as they were euphemistically called in the official terminology) in New Caledonia in the 1980s brought one of the "confetti of empire" to public attention.[21] France's role in its remaining "colonies"—a term hotly contested by supporters of continued French sovereignty—sparked much debate in the 1970s and 1980s with calls for independence in several of these "possessions," movements demanding redress of grievances centered on cultural and political marginalization, and such new cultural movements as *créolité*. French "use" of its *départements et territoires d'outre-mer* for natural resources, geopolitical leverage, and nuclear testing in French Polynesia evinced criticism at home and abroad. Violent episodes erupted in several territories.

Nowhere did the strife become more antagonistic than in New Caledonia, conquered by France in 1853, used for three decades as a penal colony, and a profitable source of one of the world's largest deposits of nickel. The situation in New Caledonia had become very tense by the 1980s. Indigenous Melanesians, now a minority of the territory's population, had lost much of their land and occupied a marginal position in the territory's economy and society, and the first calls for independence had already sounded. The Caldoches, descended from both convicts and free settlers, held the reins of commercial and political power through their monopoly over the nickel mines, tourism, and pastoralism; though they chafed at the arrival of increasing numbers of *métropolitains*, they bitterly feared independence. A large number of Tahitians and Wallis islanders, imported as cheap labor, also expressed concern about their future in an independent New Caledonia, and the presence of smaller populations of Asians, the descendants of Indonesian and Vietnamese indentured laborers, further complicated a social situation that nevertheless divided along immovable fault lines of supporters and opponents of independence. For some commentators Calédonie française in the 1980s replayed Algérie française in the 1950s and early 1960s: a population of settlers enracinated in a distant territory defending their rights against an indigenous people that had suffered the despoliation of land, economic exploitation, political disenfranchisement, and cultural alienation. The struggles of the evocatively named Front de Libération National Kanak et Socialiste (FLNKS) to achieve independence were countered by the efforts of the French state (with the support of the Caldoches) to keep control of the territory. Such tactics as attempts to create a "third force" between *indépendantistes* and *loyalistes*, the *nomadisation* of troops, the discrediting of indigenous nationalists as dangerous rebels under the sway of foreign forces, and the refusal of France to accept internationalization of the conflict at the United Nations seemed eerily reminiscent of strategies in North Africa in the 1950s. The violence that accompanied the independence efforts and the repression of them also recalled, at least in jagged outlines, the Algeria of just twenty-five years earlier. Debate in France between *engagé* supporters of the FLNKS and their opponents also harked back, though without the virulence, to the ideological clashes of the Algerian War.[22]

One of the main players in the struggle over New Caledonia was Jacques Chirac, leader of the political party most closely associated with the largely Caldoche anti-independence movement in New Caledonia. Chirac, as cohabiting prime minister (1986–88) and then president (1995–2007), contributed markedly to the reappearance of colonialism on France's national agenda. Chirac's political career displayed his continuing keen promotion of France's overseas presence, both contemporary and historical, and Chirac's experiences as a lieutenant in Algeria in the late 1950s proved formative of his perspectives on France's role in the world and a Gaullist sense of its national mission.[23] Chirac's pronouncements and programs in the 1980s left little doubt about his support for Calédonie française and the other remnants of France's empire, and statements by his ministers—Charles Pasqua remarked that the defense of Corsica began in New Caledonia—underlined the point.[24]

As president, Chirac, in addition to his backing for the *départements et territoires d'outre-mer* as integral parts of the Republic, showed a great interest in France's recent past, including but not limited to its colonial past.[25] Chirac, to his credit, also made greater overtures to coming to terms with some of the more difficult moments in the past than had his predecessors from de Gaulle through Mitterrand. Most notably, he acknowledged the responsibility of the state for the actions of the Vichy government, which François Mitterrand had argued represented an illegitimate regime that thus did not implicate the Republic in the crimes committed during the war years. Chirac also addressed colonial issues. He promulgated laws that, in 1999, declared the Algerian conflict a "war" and in 2001 declared slavery and slave trading crimes against humanity.[26] He instituted a *journée nationale* in honor of the *harkis* in grandiose ceremonies at the Invalides and the Élysée Palace. He made an official state visit to Algeria, the first president to do so since the end of the war, returning a ceremonial artifact taken by the French conquerors and long reclaimed by Algerians. In 2003, on the banks of the Seine in Paris, he inaugurated a memorial to French soldiers killed in Algeria. In

2006 he unveiled a plaque to colonial soldiers who served in the First World War at Verdun, speaking movingly about the contributions of *Tirailleurs Sénégalais* and other troops from the empire. He commissioned the new Musée du Quai Branly (on the other side of the river from the Algerian monument), and the government offered financial and moral support for a project (later abandoned) to construct a Mémorial National de l'Outre-Mer in Marseilles.[27] He appointed a high-level commission on the memory of slavery convened by the novelist Maryse Condé and dedicated a monument to slaves in the Luxembourg Gardens in 2007.[28] Chirac also became involved in an infamous piece of legislation, a law promulgated on 23 February 2005 that mandated the teaching of the "positive role" of French colonial actions in North Africa; the president's silence on the introduction and adoption of the text seemingly gave tacit consent, but his annulment of the act's pedagogical clause in the wake of enormous protests from educators and others represented a withdrawal of his benediction.[29]

Space is lacking here to examine in detail Chirac's *instrumentalisation* of colonial history (and the "troubles" in New Caledonia), but more than any previous president of the Fifth Republic forebears, Chirac was involved, in diverse ways, in commemoration of the *outre-mer* and valorization of the actions of France's settlers and soldiers in the empire. His acknowledgment of the evils of slavery and the belated recognition that he offered to the *harkis* undeniably rectified political avoidance of two aspects of the colonial heritage, yet Chirac's gestures also suggested that colonialism ought to be viewed in a more favorable light than often presented by anticolonialists (both activists and historians). This interpretation fits into the general context of Chirac's policy, with efforts to reaffirm traditional French identity, control migration (in ways his opponents judged discriminatory against non-Europeans), and rewrite provisions for the granting of citizenship.

The 2005 law, especially its directive on the teaching of "positive" aspects of colonialism, became an *affaire* in good French fashion with petitions, books, and manifestos that brought colonial history more dramatically into the public sphere but also underlined the dangers (said many historians) of the imposition of state-sanctioned interpretations of the past.[30] This episode followed on other *affaires* that, taken together, constitute another congeries of explanation for the new prominence of the colonial past in the French present: contemporary political instigation for rediscovery of colonialism and its heritage.

Colonial ghosts have returned to haunt the French on several occasions in the past decade. In 1997–98, the French belatedly put Maurice Papon on trial in connection with his activities in the Second World War, especially his responsibility for deportation of French Jews from Bordeaux to Nazi extermination camps. The trial also revealed aspects of Papon's activities as a prefect in Algeria and as the de Gaulle-appointed prefect of police in Paris in the early 1960s. The last years of the Algerian War saw the transposition of the conflict to French soil with increasing protests by both sympathizers with Algérie française and those favoring an independent Algeria. Supporters of the nationalists, including the famous *porteurs de valises*, who secretly transported funds to the Algerians, and advocates of independence, such as Jean-Paul Sartre among many other intellectuals, confronted defenders of a dying colonialism. Unrest became increasingly intense in France, especially in light of the diehard pro–Algérie française position and actions of the Organisation de l'Armée Secrète (OAS).

Defenders of the maintenance of French rule at all cost damned FLN activists in France, as well as "treasonous" politicians willing to "abandon" Algeria. Police reaction against demonstrations of pro-Algerian sentiment encompassed surveillance of Algerians and the harassment and physical abuse of North Africans in France. When Papon, as prefect of police, ordered a curfew for Algerians in Paris in October 1961, following a summer of muscular actions against Algerians in the *métropole* (who, after all, were full French citizens), matters came to a head. Algerians organized a peaceful demonstration with unarmed marchers—FLN leaders absolutely forbade any weaponry—silently converging on declared rallying points on 17 October 1961. The police responded violently; several dozen protesters (the number remains disputed) were killed, their bodies often thrown into the Seine, while thousands were arrested and herded into detention centers.[31] The crackdown sparked much opposition at the time, but Papon's trial thirty-five years later—though he stood in the dock because of Second World War deeds, not ones from the Algerian War—reminded the French of the way that a colonial conflict had spilled over into France and how authorities had reacted.

Another reminder of old wounds came with new revelations about wartime torture by one of the victims, Louisette Ighilhariz, and one of the perpetrators, General Paul Aussaresses (and others), in 2000. Writers and activists had alerted the French public to torture by soldiers and police in Algeria in the 1950s, with some commentators even making comparisons to Gestapo tactics. Authorities had justified such actions as necessary to discover plots endangering French lives and to counter the insurgency; they pointed, too, to similar bloody practices undertaken by the FLN, both against the French and against Algerians who ranged themselves alongside the colonizers. Although the new government of de Gaulle, coming to power in 1958, affirmed that it had ceased such practices, most knew that various strategies of interrogation, detention, and punishment that might well be considered torture endured. Nevertheless, with the end of the war, debate about torture drifted into silence. The exposés in 2000 brought the issue to public attention, just as it asked questions about general French culpability for misdeeds in the colonial era. Opinion, not surprisingly, divided among those who charged that any further discussions impugned the integrity of the French military, including the memory of soldiers *morts pour la patrie*, those who demanded full revelations, political acknowledgment, judicial actions, and even compensation, and those who argued that the issue should remain confined to the academic domain of historians.[32] Scholars, with access to newly declassified archives, ultimately showed that the French government and the judiciary had colluded in various extralegal procedures, including torture.[33] The 2005 law on the "positive" effects of colonialism represented one response to this debate, an attempt to burnish the tarnished reputations of the French military, administration, and settler community.

Yet another postcolonial *affaire* overlapped with these debates on the French record in Algeria, though centering on Algerian migrants to France. The affaire du foulard concerned the right of Muslim girls to wear Islamic head coverings in state schools (and, by extension, in other state institutions). Muslims argued that the covering of heads was part of the right to practice their religion and an integral aspect of cultural identity. Opponents based their arguments on the ironclad separation of church and state in France, consecrated in legislation in 1905, and the maintenance of state schools (and other institutions of the Republic) as strictly secular. Defense of the *école laïque* remains as a central pivot of French republicanism, its antecedents stretching back to revolutionary disestablishment of the Catholic Church, underlying social currents of secularization and de-Christianization, anticlericalist campaigns by liberals and republicans against the overweening power of the church in the nineteenth century, and the idea of a direct civic allegiance to the Republic unmediated by religious, ethnic, or other sectarian divisions. The practice of Muslim girls wearing head coverings in state schools, many felt, contravened the sacrosanct principles of *laïcité*. Since most of the Muslims, however, were the descendants of migrants from former colonies, the *affaire* assumed aspects of an ethnic and a "colonial" issue, touching on the general position of migrants and the capacities, willingness, or desirability of France to become a multicultural society. After intense debate—with supporters of *laïcité* branded as either defenders of Republican equality or as closet neocolonialist racists—Parliament in 2004 enacted legislation prohibiting the wearing of any "ostentatious" religious symbols, of whatever denomination, in state schools. Though not connected with colonialism per se, the *affaire* underlined the role of colonial links in paving the way for migration, the historically ambivalent attitude of the French toward Islam, and the nature of collective French identity undergoing ineluctable metamorphosis.[34]

A final reminder of the colonial heritage came with the riots in the *banlieues* that erupted in autumn 2005. The precipitants lay in the large-scale unemployment, poor living conditions, limited avenues for advancement, and general social frustration evident in the suburbs. Journalists and the public often perceived the violence in ethnic, or indeed racial, terms as it erupted in areas with large "ethnic" populations. Indisputably, many protesters came from Arabic or Islamic backgrounds, the second or third generation of migrants with anger fueled by marginalization and discrimination. The heritage of migration, the legacy of violence that featured so prominently in the Algerian War (on both sides), and, for many, links to other social conflicts, such as the affaire du foulard, provided ingredients in the pot that boiled over in the *banlieues*. Sociologists, while underlining the complex nature of the mix of causes in the disturbances, have looked in particular at the connection between the "social question" and a new "racial question" in a country that has long tried not to view problems in racial terms. Partly because of experiences in the Vichy years, "race" has been a taboo subject in contemporary France. The French state's interpretation of egalitarianism has meant that issues of race and religion have often been elided—census forms are not allowed to ask questions about ethnicity. "Immigration," indeed, has often been a code word for race or ethnicity, though many of African, Asian, or West Indian background, of course, are not first-generation migrants. Though by no means all migrants to France have come from its former colonies, there is a particular visibility to those from North Africa and sub-Saharan Africa who arrived via a conduit built in the colonial era; the riots dramatically showed that not all feel fully a part of the body politic, and some do not share the principles generally proclaimed to contour the French way of life. They pointed out, in spectacular fashion, what other indicators have made patently evident: postcolonial France does indeed face issues revolving around "race," an issue hardly unconnected with the colonial experience.[35]

The French rediscovery of empire in the 1990s, and its continuing prominence in public life, therefore reflect various developments: changing historiographical paradigms that fostered new research on the history of imperialism; communitarian interventions (whether by *anciens combattants*, migrant groups, or others); general interest in the old imperial days whetted by films, books, and exhibitions; debates about migration, French identity, and citizenship in the Republic; and a constellation of *affaires* from an independence movement in distant New Caledonia in the 1980s to civil strife in the suburbs of Paris in the early 2000s. These have primed a new confrontation with the colonial past and demands for a Vergangenheitsbewältigung, a *devoir de mémoire* that involves public debate, commemoration and political gestures, and French-style "history wars." Both arcane scholarly disputes and clearly politicized actions by legislators and lobbyists seeking electoral advantage (or extraparliamentary clout) have erupted into the public arena, and colonialism has sounded with great resonance among the French population.[36] A notable example is the attention given in 2006 to the film *Indigènes*, portraying the role of North African soldiers in the liberation of France in the Second World War, a film that highlighted the war service of the Maghrebins (and others), largely unknown to many spectators, and also the often unequal treatment the French military and state meted out to the soldiers.

Arguments about the colonial past and its legacy show no signs of abating. President Sarkozy, visiting Dakar in 2007, made a speech that was interpreted by some as an apologia for colonialism, provoking angry retorts by Africans and several books by scholars criticizing what their authors judged a misuse of history. Further criticism came when the new president set up a Ministère de l'Immigration, de l'Intégration, de l'Identité Nationale et du Développement Solidaire, with its jumbling of responsibilities and concepts, and when he initiated a debate on "national identity," which has failed to produce clear outcomes. In 2010 the Sarkozy government, considering a ban on the wearing of the burqa in France, seemed to be reviving debates on religion and *laïcité* and on the relationship between private behavior and public life. The plan to build a museum of French national history, Sarkozy's key *grand projet*, raises questions about how the colonial aspects of France's history will be treated. Meanwhile, public interest groups and political parties of all ideological positions continue to mobilize the record and heritage of colonialism in marking out their territory.

What does this "rediscovery" mean? It would be satisfying to offer a simple answer, but as undergraduate essays often conclude, more work needs to be done—in this case, by the historians *and* by the French population. A spate of recent books has addressed colonialism in French life and memory—a "black book" of French colonialism and the retort that France has little of which to be ashamed in its colonial record. Some have argued that France risks self-mutilation by wallowing in postcolonial culpability, and others that France must face up to its colonial past in order to get on with its future. Yet others have deciphered the ways various individuals and groups have manipulated and used colonial issues. Scholars, *engagé* or indifferent to political disputes, generally lambast interference from politicians and interest-group lobbyists in academic research. Historians, however, are far from unanimous on the place colonialism occupies in the national narrative and the role of empire in the formation of national identity.[37]

The Colonial Past and the Postcolonial Present

Colonial history remains contested terrain over which scholars and activists scramble; memories clash and commemorations conflict. Monuments and museums testify to efforts to work through colonialism, though often with less than consensual outcomes. The Paris municipal council put up a plaque on the Seine in memory of the demonstrators of October 1961 and named a square after the anticolonialist Maurice Audin (killed in Algeria at the hands of the French police), while the city council of Marignane, in the Midi, erected a monument in memory of executed members of the OAS. West Indians in Paris successfully pushed for a street bearing the name of a slave trader to be renamed for a Guadeloupean composer, while an Alsatian town named a street for General Bigeard, a controversial figure of the Algerian War. The municipality of Perpignan has sponsored a proposed *mur des disparus* to commemorate those who disappeared—focusing on pieds-noirs and *harkis*—during the Algerian conflict. The state has proposed creation of a museum of slavery and slave trading. The old colonial museum in Paris (transmuted in the early 1960s into the Musée des arts africains et océaniens) has been turned, somewhat curiously, into a museum and documentation center on immigration to France. In the age of the Internet, proliferating websites provide new genres of exhibitions, memorials, and forums for debate.

"Memory work" about the colonial past is thus a work in progress. Whose memories ought to be safeguarded, commemorated, and even celebrated? Who is the proper guardian of these memories—local governments, the state, community groups, organizations representing those who consider themselves victims of colonialism? (Who indeed are the victims, and is "victimology" the best approach to colonialism's workings?) Is "memory work" not also needed in the former colonies, and how can it be brought about? Is there a French exceptionalism in regard to the colonial past, or is the recovery of memory and the rewriting of that history part of a more general undertaking for Britain, Germany, the Netherlands, Italy, and other colonizing countries? How should the colonial past be acknowledged in monuments, museum displays, and even such banal manifestations as the names of streets and squares? Should the guardians of memory, and should historians, aim at a consensual perspective, or was colonialism a phenomenon with clear rights and wrongs—and should those deeds be subject to present-day legislative and legal action or moral judgment? Can this anamnesis improve the lot of marginalized groups in France or of the former colonized people overseas? Ought the colonial past to be dug up or laid to rest? To what extent are contemporary issues in France inextricably tied to the colonial past? Could a reassessment of that past help France to redefine its national vocation, confront its present-day challenges, and find its way in a globalized world? Perhaps, for the moment, it is better to leave the questions without answers, but to monitor closely the way in which the French—scholars and curators, public officials, private organizations and the *grand public*—grapple with the questioning.

History, both France's record in its empire, on the one hand, and the continued discovery, analysis, and interpretation of that record on the other, has been central to the *retour du colonial*. Historians have unearthed new sources, rethought standard topics such as imperial governance and the processes of conquest, administration, and decolonization, and ventured into new areas—colonialism and its connections with the history of gender, the environment, medicine, and popular culture. Their studies have shown that colonialism had a broader and more long-lived impact on French society than was often thought, even though there are differences of opinion about how deep the impact was. As various individuals and lobby groups mobilize their own interpretations of colonialism to forward their particular campaigns, and as the public becomes increasingly aware of the multiple legacies of colonialism, scholars have tried to decipher and understand the very complex encounters between France and the countries and cultures over which it ruled. Those efforts, such as the chapters in the present collection, help to comprehend the place of the empire in the construction of the French nation and state but also help to guard against the abuse and the misuse of that history in debates about contemporary problems that, whether closely or distantly, are related to the colonial heritage.

Notes

1. Mohammed Harbi and Benjamin Stora, eds., *La Guerre d'Algérie: 1954–2004, la fin de l'amnésie* (Paris, 2004); William B. Cohen, "The Algerian War, the French State and Official Memory," *Historical Reflections* 28:2

(2002), 219–40; David Schalk, "Of Memories and Monuments: Paris and Algeria, Fréjus and Indochina," *Historical Reflections* 28:2 (2002), 241–53; Herman Lebovics, *Bringing the Empire Back Home: France in the Global Age* (Durham NC: Duke University Press, 2004); Alec G. Hargreaves, ed., *Memory, Empire, and Postcolonialism: Legacies of French Colonialism* (Lanham MD: Lexington Books, 2005); Patricia Lorcin, ed., *Algeria and France, 1800–2000: Identity, Memory, Nostalgia* (Syracuse NY: Syracuse University Press, 2006). On the notion of "anamnesis" see Michel Laronde, "'Effets d'Histoire': Représenter l'histoire coloniale forclose," *International Journal of Francophone Studies* 10:1–2 (2007), 139–55.

2. Henry Rousso, *The Vichy Syndrome: History and Memory in France since 1944* (Cambridge MA: Harvard University Press, 1991), first published in France in 1987. The standard work on the amnesia is Benjamin Stora, *La Gangrène et l'oubli: Mémoire de la guerre d'Algérie* (Paris: Découverte, 1991). See also Raphaëlle Branche, *La Guerre d'Algérie: Une histoire apaisée?* (Paris: Gallimard, 2005).

3. On the imprint of empire, and Britain's memories of colonialism, see Andrew Thompson, *The Empire Strikes Back: The Impact of Imperialism on Britain from the Mid-Nineteenth Century* (Harlow UK: Longman, 2005).

4. Stuart Macintyre and Anna Clark, *The History Wars* (Melbourne: Melbourne University Press, 2004).

5. "Mabo" was a landmark decision by the High Court of Australia in 1992, which ruled that British colonization of the Australian continent had not extinguished the land rights of the indigenous population; subsequent legislative acts and court decisions have recognized the land claims, which must be proved largely in terms of continued occupation or use, of a number of Aboriginal and Torres Strait Islander peoples. The "stolen generation" refers to Aboriginals removed from parental care and placed in state-run institutions.

6. See the review by Adam Hochschild, "In the Heart of Darkness," in the *New York Review of Books*, 6 October 2005, and the reply by Jean-Luc Vellut, the historical adviser to the Royal Museum for Central Africa in Tervuren for the exhibition, in the issue of 12 January 2006.

7. Gert J. Oostindië, "Squaring the Circle: Commemorating the VOC after 400 years," *Bijdragen tot de Taal-, Land-en Volkenkunde* 159 (2001), 135–61; Leonard Blussé, "Four Hundred Years On: The Public Commemoration of the Founding of the VOC in 2002," *Itinerario* 27:1 (2003), 79–91.

8. Angelo Del Boca, *Italiani, brave gente?* (Turin: Laterza, 2005).

9. Reinhart Kössler, "La Fin d'une amnésie? L'Allemagne et son passé colonial depuis 2004," *Politique Africaine* 102 (2006), 50–66; see also Vincent

Bertout, "Mémoires et stratégies politiques: Les commémorations culturelles Herero en Namibie," *Politique Africaine* 102 (2006), 67–84.

10. See Robert Aldrich, "Coming to Terms with the Colonial Past: The French and Others," *Arts: The Journal of the Sydney University Arts Association* 28 (2006), 91–116. On memory in France more generally, see Sarah Blowen, Marion Demossier, and Jeanine Picard, eds., *Recollections of France: Memories, Identities and Heritage in Contemporary France* (Oxford: Berghahn, 2000). The importance of historical memory is also underlined by Rod Kedward in a chapter titled "Memory and Identity, 1990s–2000s" in *La Vie en bleu: France and the French since 1900* (London: Penguin, 2005).

11. Franziska Seraphim, *War Memory and Social Politics in Japan, 1945–2005* (Cambridge MA: Harvard University Asia Center, 2006); and Sheila Miyoshi-Jager and Rana Mitter, eds., *Ruptured Histories: War, Memory, and the Post-Cold War in Asia* (Cambridge MA: Harvard University Press, 2007).

12. On Vietnam's memory of its past, see Hue-Tam Ho-Tai, ed., *The Country of Memory: Remaking the Past in Late Socialist Vietnam* (Berkeley: University of California Press, 2001); and Patricia M. Pelley, *Postcolonial Vietnam: New Histories of the National Past* (Durham NC: Duke University Press, 2002); and on the French side see Alain Ruscio and Serge Tignères, *Dien Bien Phu, myths et réalités, 1954–2004: Cinquante ans de passions françaises* (Paris: Les Indes Savantes, 2005); and Nikki Cooper, "Dien Bien Phu—Fifty Years On," *Modern and Contemporary France*, 12:4 (2004), 445–58.

13. The *harkis* were soldiers who fought under French command in the war; on their "repatriation" and status in France, see Géraldine Enjelvin, "Les Harkis en France: Carte d'identité française, identité harkie à la carte?" *Modern and Contemporary France* 11:2 (2003), 161–73.

14. Catherine Coquery-Vidrovitch provides an overview of the writing of colonial history, as well as the role of history writing in the debates and policics that have arisen with the *retour du colonial*. Coquery-Vidrovitch, *Enjeux politiques de l'histoire coloniale* (Marseille: Agone, 2009). Another orientation to research on colonial history in France is offered in "L'Écriture de l'histoire de la colonisation en France depuis 1960," co-ordinated by Sophie Dulucq, *Afrique et Histoire* 6:2 (2006), 235–74.

15. Raymond Bachollet, ed., *Négripub: L'image des noirs dans la publicité depuis un siècle* (Paris: Somogy, 1992); and Pascal Blanchard et al., *Images et colonies* (Paris: Syros-ACHAC, 1993), were two of a large number of books on colonial iconography. In English, see Martin Evans, ed., *Empire and Culture: The French Experience, 1830–1940* (London: Palgrave-Macmillan, 2004).

16. During the last World Cup Jean-Marie Le Pen remarked that the

French soccer team was too black; Lilian Thuram, a West Indian, retorted that Le Pen needed to learn his colonial history, and Thuram pointed out that several players, including himself, come from islands whose residents have lived under the French flag for more than 350 years, and that other black players are French born and bred.

17. The Fédération nationale des anciens combattants en Afrique du Nord FNACA) chose the date of the Algerian War ceasefire agreed by the Évian accords, but many veterans objected not only because this represented the end of Algérie française (and the forced "repatriation" of pieds-noirs) but also because of the killing of some Frenchmen, and tens of thousands of *harki* auxiliaries, after that date.

18. On commemoration of slavery, see Catherine A. Reinhardt, *Claims to Memory: Beyond Slavery and Emancipation in the French Caribbean* (Oxford: Berghahn, 2006); Françoise Vergès, *La Mémoire enchaînée: Penser l'esclavage aujourd'hui* (Paris: Albin Michel, 2006); Jean-Luc Bonniol, "Échos politiques de l'esclavage colonial, des départements d'outre-mer au coeur de l'État," in *Politiques du passé: Usages politiques du passé dans la France contemporaine*, ed. Claire Andrieu, Marie-Claire Lavabre, and Danielle Tartakowsky (Aix-en-Provence: Presse Universitaire de Provence, 2006), 39–46; Chris Bongie, "A Street Named Bissette: Nostalgia, Memory, and the *Cent-Cinquantenaire* of the Abolition of Slavery in Martinique (1848–1998)," *South Atlantic Quarterly* 11:2 (2001), 215–57; and Nelly Schmidt, "Commémoration, histoire et historiographie: A propos du 150e anniversaire de l'abolition de l'esclavage dans les colonies françaises," *Ethnologie française* 29:3 (1999), 453–60.

19. See Robert Aldrich, *Vestiges of the Colonial Empire in France: Museums, Monuments and Colonial Memory* (London: Palgrave-Macmillan, 2005).

20. The notion of "acceleration" comes from Benjamin Stores, "1999–2003, guerre d'Algérie, les accélérations de la mémoire," in Harbi and Stora, *La Guerre d'Algérie*, 501–14.

21. The phrase "confetti of empire" was coined by Jean-Claude Guillebaud, *Les Confettis de l'empire* (Paris: Seuil, 1976). See Robert Aldrich and John Connell, *France's Overseas Frontier: Départements et Territoires d'Outre-Mer* (Cambridge: Cambridge University Press, 1992).

22. See Robert Aldrich, *France and the South Pacific since 1940* (London: Macmillan, 1993); Stephen Henningham, *France and the South Pacific* (Honolulu: University of Hawaii Press, 1992); and the earlier volume by John Connell, *New Caledonia or Kanaky?* (Canberra: Asia-Pacific Press, 1987); more recently see Nathalie Mrgudovic, *La France dans le Pacifique Sud: Les*

enjeux de la puissance (Paris: L'Harmattan, 2008); and Sarah Mohamed-Gaillard, *L'Archipel de la puissance? La Politique de la France dans le Pacifique Sud de 1946 à 1998* (Brussels: Peter Lang, 2010).

23. Bernard Droz, "Lieutenant en Algérie," *L'Histoire* 313 (October 2006), 52–53.

24. Chirac in the 1980s, for instance, appointed a Guadeloupean ally, Lucette Michaux-Chevry, as junior minister for Francophonie, and another ally from Tahiti (a staunch opponent of independence for French Polynesia and New Caledonia), Gaston Flosse, to a short-lived portfolio as minister for the Pacific.

25. See Jean-François Tanguy, "Le Discours 'chiraquien' sur l'histoire," in Andrieu, Lavabre, and Tartakowsky, *Politiques du passé*, 133–46.

26. The orthodox nomenclature had been that the French had been engaged in a "conflict" with "operations for the maintenance of order"; Algeria, as a set of *départements*, was not a foreign country against which war could be waged. The refusal to admit the fact of a "war" not only reduced the Algerian nationalists to the status of insurgents but—of importance to old soldiers—deprived veterans of certain entitlements and recognition of their war service. Failure to use the word "war" was part of the "Algerian syndrome."

27. The Musée du Quai Branly, however, has not escaped controversy and critical appraisal. See Sally Price, *Paris Primitive: Jacques Chirac's Museum on the Quai Branly* (Chicago: University of Chicago Press, 2007); and Dominic Thomas, "The Quai Branly Museum: Political Transition, Memory and Globalization in Contemporary France," *French Cultural Studies* 19:2 (2008), 141–57. The long-standing project of the Mémorial National de l'Outre-Mer—part museum, perhaps also part memorial—evoked considerable dispute concerning the purpose and program for the site, the participation of interest groups (such as pieds-noir associations) and the historical texture of its proposed displays. Arguments also occurred about funding and administrative possibility. In 2007 the director of the project announced that plans for the memorial had been suspended, and it appears the proposal is effectively abandoned.

28. The report of the Comité pour la mémoire de l'esclavage, and various documents concerning their activities, can be accessed on their website (http://www.comite-memoire-esclavage.fr/).

29. Robert Aldrich, "Colonial Past, Post-Colonial Present: History Wars French-Style," *History Australia* 3:1 (June 2006).

30. Some historians also therefore objected to the 2001 law declaring slavery and slave trading as a "crime against humanity."

31. Jim House and Neil MacMaster provide the most comprehensive—and

indicting—account; House and MacMaster, *Paris 1961: Algerians, State Terror, and Memory* (Oxford: Oxford University Press, 2006).

32. Neil MacMaster, "The Torture Controversy (1998–2002): Towards a 'New History' of the Algerian War?" *Modern and Contemporary France* 10:4 (2002), 449–60; see also Joshua Cole, "Intimate Acts and Unspeakable Relations: Remembering Torture and the War for Algerian Independence," 125–41, and Sylvie Durmelat, "Revisiting Ghosts: Louisette Ighilahriz and the Remembering of Torture," 142–159, both in Hargreaves, *Memory, Empire, and Postcolonialism*, as well as several other chapters in this collection.

33. Raphaëlle Branche, *La Torture et l'armée pendant la Guerre d'Algérie* (Paris: Gallimard, 2001); Sylvie Thénault, *Une Drôle de guerre: Les magistrats dans la Guerre d'Algérie* (Paris: La Découverte, 2004).

34. Bronwyn Winter, *Hijab and the Republic: Uncovering the French Headscarf Debate* (Syracuse NY: Syracuse University Press, 2008).

35. Among other works on the riots see Didier and Éric Fassin, eds., *De la question sociale à la question raciale: Représenter la société française* (Paris: La Découverte, 2009).

36. One indication is the special issues of popular history journals devoted to the topic, including numbers on "Le Temps des colonies," *Les Collections de l'Histoire* 11 (April 2001); "L'Esclavage: Un tabou français enfin levé," *Historia* 80 (November–December 2002); "Indochine—Vietnam: Colonisation, guerres et communisme," *Les Collections de l'Histoire* 23 (April–June 2004): "L'Indochine française," *La Nouvelle Revue d'Histoire* 2 (May–June 2004); "La Colonisation en process," *L'Histoire* 302 (October 2005); and "La fin des colonies—Afrique—1960," *L'Histoire* 350 (February 2010); as well as dossiers in other magazines, such as "La Chute de l'empire français," *Marianne* 401–2 (25 December 2004–7 January 2005); and "Colonies: Un débat français," *Le Monde* 2 (hors série), no date.

37. Among a growing stack of works, see Marc Ferro, ed., *Le livre noir du colonialisme: De l'extermination à la repentance, XVIe–XXIe siècles* (Paris: Laffont, 2003); Pascal Blanchard, Nicolas Bancel, and Sandrine Lemaire, *La Fracture coloniale: La société française au prisme de l'héritage colonial* (Paris: Autrement, 2005); Claude Liauzu and Gilles Manceron, eds., *La Colonisation, la loi et l'histoire* (Paris: Syllepse, 2006); Romain Bertrand, *Mémoires d'empire: La controverse autour du "fait colonial"* (Paris: Editions du croquant, 2006); Daniel Lefeuvre, *Pour en finir avec la repentance coloniale* (Paris: Flammarion, 2006); Sébastien Jahan and Alain Ruscio, eds., *Histoire de la colonisation: réhabilitations, falsifications et instrumentalisations* (Paris, 2007); and Coquery-Vidrovitch, *Enjeux politiques de l'histoire coloniale*. See also the special issue on "Passés coloniaux recomposés" in *Politique Africaine*

102 (2006). On specific themes and regions, see, e.g., Patricia M. E. Lorcin, ed., *Algeria and France, 1800–2000: Identity, Memory, Nostalgia* (Syracuse NY: Syracuse University Press, 2006); Alain Ruscio and Serge Tignères, *Dien Bien Phu: Mythes et réalités, 1954–2004 — cinquante ans de passions françaises* (Paris, 2005); and Françoise Vergès, *La mémoire enchainée: Questions sur l'esclavage* (Paris: Albin Michel, 2006).

Contributors

ROBERT ALDRICH is professor of European history at the University of Sydney. He has written extensively on the French in the South Pacific and is also the author of several works on French colonialism and its legacies, including *Colonialism and Homosexuality* (London: Routledge, 2002), *Vestiges of Colonial Empire in France: Monuments, Museums and Colonial Memories* (Basingstoke: Palgrave-Macmillan, 2004), and, as editor, *The Age of Empires* (London: Thames and Hudson, 2007).

MARTIN S. ALEXANDER is professor of international relations at Aberystwyth University in Wales, where, from 2007 to 2009, he was director of the Centre for Intelligence and International Security Studies. His books include *The Republic in Danger: General Maurice Gamelin and the Politics of French Defence, 1933-39* (Cambridge: Cambridge University Press, 1992) and, as editor, *Knowing Your Friends: Intelligence in Alliances and Coalitions* (London: Cass, 1998), along with books coedited with John Keiger and Martin Evans, *The Algerian War and the French Army: Experiences, Images, Testimonies* (Basingstoke: Palgrave Macmillan, 2002), and coedited with John Keiger, *France and the Algerian War, 1954-62: Strategy, Operations and Diplomacy* (London: Cass, 2002). He is writing a reassessment of French civilian and military responses against the Blitzkrieg in 1940, on which he has published a preview article in *War in History* (14:2 [April 2007], 219-63).

JOSHUA COLE is associate professor of history at the University of Michigan. He is the author of *The Power of Large Numbers: Population, Politics, and Gender in Nineteenth-Century France* (Ithaca NY: Cornell University Press, 2000), as well as other articles on French social and cultural history in the nineteenth and twentieth centuries. The selection for this volume comes from his current book project, provisionally entitled "The Empire of Fear: Violence and the Politics of the Colonial Situation in Eastern Algeria, 1930-1940."

Contributors

WILLIAM GALLOIS is reader in history at Roehampton University, United Kingdom. He is the author of *Zola: The History of Capitalism* (Bern: Peter Lang, 1999); *Time, Religion and History* (London: Longman Pearson, 2007); and *The Administration of Sickness: Medicine and Ethics in Colonial Algeria* (London: Palgrave Macmillan, 2008). His next book is provisionally entitled "A History of Violence in the Early Algerian Colony."

SAMUEL KALMAN is associate professor at St. Francis Xavier University in Antigonish, Nova Scotia. He is the author of *The Extreme Right in Interwar France: The Faisceau and the Croix de Feu* (London: Ashgate, 2008), along with numerous articles that have appeared in a variety of periodicals, including *French History, Historical Reflections/Réflexions historiques*, and *French Historical Studies*. He is currently working on a book entitled "Colonial Fascism: The Extreme Right in French Colonial Algeria, 1919–1939."

JOE LUNN is professor of African and modern European history at the University of Michigan–Dearborn. He is the author of *Memoirs of the Maelstrom: A Senegalese Oral History of the First World War* (Portsmouth NH: Heinemann, 1999), as well as numerous journal articles and book chapters. He is presently working on "African Voices from the Great War: An Anthology of Senegalese Soldiers' Life Histories," which will further explore the First World War's impact on the lives of the Senegalese.

NEIL MACMASTER, honorary reader at the University of East Anglia, is author of several books, including *Colonial Migrants and Racism: Algerians in France, 1900–62* (London: Palgrave Macmillan, 1997); *Racism in Europe, 1870–2000* (Hampshire: Palgrave, 2001); with Jim House, *Paris 1961: Algerians, State Terror, and Memory* (Oxford: Oxford University Press, 2006); and *Burning the Veil: The Algerian War and the "Emancipation" of Muslim Women, 1954–62* (Manchester: Manchester University Press, 2009). He is currently writing a book on peasant society, anthropology, and French counterinsurgency in Algeria ca. 1945–60.

KIM MUNHOLLAND is professor emeritus at the University of Minnesota–Twin Cities and is a specialist in French and French colonial history. His publications include several articles on French imperial expansion in Southeast Asia. He recently published a book on French-American relations in a colonial setting, *Rock of Contention: Free French and Americans at War in New Caledonia, 1940–1945* (New York: Berghahn, 2006).

BERTRAND TAITHE is professor of cultural history at the University of Manchester and a director of the Manchester Humanitarian and Conflict

Response Institute. He has published on war and medicine and the history of humanitarian aid. His most recent book, *The Killer Trail: A Colonial Scandal in the Heart of Africa*, is with Oxford University Press (2009).

MARTIN THOMAS is professor of colonial history and director of the Centre for the Study of War, State, and Society at the University of Exeter. His publications include *The French Empire between the Wars: Imperialism, Politics, and Society* (Manchester University Press, 2005) and *Empires of Intelligence: Security Services and Colonial Disorder after 1914* (University of California Press, 2007). His comparative study of policing and interwar political violence in European colonial empires, *Violence and Colonial Order: Police, Workers, and Protest in the European Colonial Empires, 1918–1940*, will be published by Cambridge University Press.

MICHAEL G. VANN is an assistant professor at California State University, Sacramento, vice-president of the California World History Association, and immediate past president of the French Colonial Historical Society. He specializes in the French colonial empire, with attention to the construction of racial identity in Southeast Asia. In addition to several articles and book chapters on topics as diverse as race, film, disease, murder, and rats in the empire, he recently published *"The Colonial Good Life:" A Commentary on Andre Joyeux's Vision of French Indochina* with Joel Montague (Bangkok: White Lotus Press, 2008). He is currently preparing a book manuscript on colonial whiteness in French Hanoi. He teaches a variety of courses on world, Southeast Asian, and colonial history. He divides his time between Sacramento, Santa Cruz, and Southeast Asia.

MATHILDE VON BÜLOW is a lecturer at the University of Nottingham, where she teaches colonial and international history. Her research examines the role of security and intelligence services in the suppression of anticolonialism and colonial nationalism during the late colonial era, with a particular focus on French Algeria. She is currently completing her first monograph on Federal Germany and the internationalization of the Algerian war of independence.

OWEN WHITE is associate professor of history at the University of Delaware. He has written several articles on colonialism in West Africa and is the author of *Children of the French Empire: Miscegenation and Colonial Society in French West Africa, 1895–1960* (Oxford: Oxford University Press, 1999). He is now researching a history of the wine industry in French Algeria.

Index

Abbas, Ferhat, 118, 121, 149, 150
Aboriginal people (Australia), 335, 351n5
Abyssinia, 336
"accommodation" (word), 218n29
Action Française, 215
The Administration of Sickness (Gallois), 7
aerial warfare, xxiv, 259, 265, 268, 273
Afekane, Henri, 124
Affaire des Grottes, 3–4, 9–20; in fiction, 22–23n2
Affaire du Foulard, 345–46
Afghanistan, 285–86
African Americans, 242n21, 299n8
African emigrants: France, xxxviii. *See also* Algerian emigrants
Afrique Occidentale Française (AOF). *See* French West Africa
Agathon, 202, 204
age of consent, 192
agricultural workers. *See* farmworkers
agriculture, xvii; Algeria, 120, 124, 125, 129, 142–43, 157, 160–61, 164; destruction of crops, xxviii, 6
Agriculture Ministry. *See* Ministry of Agriculture

aid, international. *See* international aid
airplanes: military use. *See* aerial warfare
Akli, Amar, 117
Albert, Phyllis Cohen, 79
alcohol, 299–300n16, 300n17, 300n19
Algeria, xxxi–xxxiv, 3–25, 112–39, 182; anti-Jewish riots (1934), 77–112; civil war (1990s), xli; conquest of, xxvii–xxviii, 5–6; conscription in, 222; North African soldiers and, 254; West African soldiers and, 159, 232, 233, 234. *See also* Algiers; Blida; Bordj-bou-Arréridj; Constantine; Dahra; Guelma; Oran; Sétif
Algerian emigrants: France, xxxix, 308, 309; West Germany, xxxix–xl, 304–33
Algérianiste movement, 112–13, 114, 120, 130, 131
Algerians: psychological disorders of, xii
Algerian War of Independence, xiii, xvi, xxxix–xl, 131, 140, 283–303; amnesties and, 337; euphemism and, 354n26; histo-

361

Index

Algerian War of Independence (*cont.*)
  riography, 334; West Germany and, 304–33. *See also* Palestro "massacre"
Algiers, 81, 84, 116, 117, 147, 155, 162
Allard, Jacques, 287
Allen, Chris, 143
ALN. *See* Armée de Libération Nationale (ALN)
Alsace-Lorraine, 222
Altmayer, Robert, 183, 184–90, 192–93
Amant, L', (Duras), 338
Americanism, 213
Amiens, 259–61
Amirouche Aït Hamouda, 293
Amis du Manifeste et de la Liberté (AML), 149, 150, 154
Amitiés Africaines, 275
amnesties, 337
Amour, L' (Djebar), 23
Angoulvant, Gabriel, 181
Annales School (historiography), xl, 337
Anneaus de la Mémoire, 339
anniversaries. *See* commemorations
anthropology, 229–35
anti-Communism, 115, 122, 129
anti-Semitism, xxx–xxxi, xxxii, 77–112, 115–16, 119, 121, 125, 133n19; Psichari on, 203
AOF. *See* French West Africa
Aouizerat, Ruben, 110n38
apologies, state, 335, 336
Appel des Armes, L' (Psichari), 207, 208, 209, 213, 215
Arabic language, 6, 89, 188, 209
Arabization, 127

Arab League, 152
Archinard, Louis, 37, 223, 234
Archives nationale d'outre-mer, 337
Arendt, Hannah, 43, 284
Armée Coloniale. *See* French Colonial Army
Armée d'Afrique (XIXth Army Corps), xxviii, 148–49, 163, 257
Armée de Libération Nationale (ALN), 283, 293, 298n1
art, 338
assassination, 56, 58, 288, 293, 294, 296, 297
assimilation, 60, 210; Algeria, 5, 80, 86, 126, 128, 129, 130; anti-Semitism and, 107n27; hostility toward, 63; West African soldiers and, 232
"assimilation" (word), 139n85
"association" (concept), 130, 139n85
Association of Algerian Muslim Scholars, 89
Association of Reformist 'Ulamaʿ, 118, 119, 121, 122, 123, 134n33, 135n35, 150–51; Algerian food crisis and, 146, 161; Algerian War and, 288; surveillance of, 149
asylum, 318, 319, 320, 327n15
atrocities, 3–4, 6, 9–20, 35, 36, 37; rumors of, 40; Vigné d'Octon and, 45n6; World War II, 248–49, 273–74. *See also* massacres
attentisme, xxxix, 283–303
Aublet, Marcel, 270
Audéoud, Marie, 223
Audin, Maurice, 349
Aussaresses, Paul, 345
Australia, 335, 35n5
Azzedine, Si, 288, 297

Index

Bachir Ben Saadi, Taleb. *See* Brahimi, Bashir
Balearic Islands, 255
Bambara people, 30, 226, 231, 236, 237
bandits and highwaymen, 58
bans of smoking, drinking, etc. *See* prohibition (of smoking, drinking, etc.)
Barbier, Johannes, 37
Barkatz, Émile, 86, 87
Barlon, Daniel, 253–54
Barot, Louis Joseph, 190
Barrès, Maurice, 202
Basch, Victor, 118–19
Battle of Algiers (1957), 284, 287
Battle of France (1940), xxxvii–xxxviii, 248–82
Battle of Hanoi (1946-1947), 69–70
Baudet, Joseph-Antoine, 267
Baudouin, Marcel, 257
Baule people, 180–82, 195n14
Bazelaire de Ruppiére, Joseph-Maurice de. *See* De Bazelaire de Ruppiére, Joseph-Maurice
Bazin, Alfred-François, 58, 61
beatings: of Algerian news vendors, 124; of colonial administrators, 68; during Constantine riots, 94; interracial unions and, 187; of servants, 54, 56
beheadings, 35, 36, 66
Behr, Edward, 16–17
Belgium, 309–10, 335. *See also* Congo Free State
Ben Badis, Abd al-Hamid, 89, 93, 118, 121–22, 129
Bendjelloul, Ahmed ben Salah Bach-Mohaden, 91
Bendjelloul, Mohamed-Salah, 87–90, 92, 93, 94–95, 98, 99, 100, 109n31; CDF/PSF and, 118, 119, 124, 138n77; demonization of, 129; election collusion and, 117
Benelmouhoub, Mouloud, 91, 92
Benhoura, Mohamed, 118
Béni-Koufi tribe, 19
Benôt, Yves, 65
Berbers, 80, 113, 116, 119, 123, 124, 125; family disputes and, 293; French West African population stats, 227. *See also* Kabyle Berbers; Tuareg people
Bergson, Henri, 208
Berque, Jacques, 150, 160, 163, 164, 297
Bertrand, Louis, 112, 113, 120; *Le Sang des Races*, 131n2
Beteuil, Arsène, 18
Betts, Raymond, 139n85
Bigeard, Marcel, 349
Billotte, Gaston, 252
biological determinism, 229
Birnin Konni, 34
black Americans. *See* African Americans
blaming the victim, 11, 12, 19, 100
Blanc, Captain, 9–13, 22
bleus de chauffe, 288–89
Blida, 6
Blum, Léon, 82
Blum-Viollette bill, 126, 127–28, 130, 131
Bodichon, Eugéne, 14
Bolis, Ernest, 35
bombs and bombings, xxx, 55; aerial, xxiv; Hanoi, 56, 61, 66–67
Bonnafort, Louis, 68
Bonnal, Henri, 234
Bordès, Pierre, 120

363

Bordj-bou-Arréridj, 115, 117, 124
boredom, 186
Boulanger, Georges Ernest, 30
Bou-Maza, 20
bounties, 66
Bourbaki, Charles Denis, 19
Bourdieu, Pierre, xvi–xvii, xviii, 127
boycotts, 90, 116, 300n17
Brahimi, Bashir, 149
Brazza, Pierre Savorgnan de, 191
Brentano, Heinrich von, 315, 320
bride-price, 181, 188, 189, 197n28
Bringard (Algiers police chief), 162–63
Britain. *See* Great Britain
British Army, xxii
British Sudan, 45n2
Broca, Paul, 232
Brooke, Alan, 257
Brower, Benjamin, xii
Brussaux, Édouard-Octave, 270
Buffon, Georges Louis Leclerc, comte de, 228
Bugeaud, Thomas, xxviii, 3, 4, 6, 11, 12–16, 22; *colonnes* and, 45n1; Voulet-Chanoine affair and, 32
burqa, 348

café bombings, 56, 61, 66–67
Cahiers de la quinzaine, 204
Caldoches, 341, 342
Cameroon, 250
Camus, Albert, 173n75
Camus, Auguste, 273
cannibalism, 230
Canrobert, Marshal, 17, 18
"Cao Bang disaster," xiv–xv
capital, xvii
captives, 31, 36, 37, 191. *See also* prisoners of war; slaves

Caribbean islands. *See* West Indies and West Indians
Carlès, Émile-Jean, 257, 268
Carnets de Route (Psichari), 206, 208
Catholic Church, xxxvi, 202, 346; Psichari and, 202, 203, 205, 209, 215
Catholic missionaries, 180, 189, 215
Catholics: Islam and, 188–89
Cavaignac, Louis-Eugène, 9–10, 14, 15
cavalry, 185, 257
caves as redoubts, 3, 9–13, 15, 16–17, 20
Cazedmajou, Marius Gabriel, 31, 47n19
CDF. *See* Croix de Feu (CDF)
censorship, xiv, 17, 35, 37; avoidance of, 39. *See also* self-censorship
Centre d'information et d'études (CIE), 148, 149, 151, 154
Chad, 28, 29
Chanoine, Julien, 26–51
Chapman, Guy: *Why France Collapsed*, 249
Chapon, Lieutenant-Colonel, 259, 260, 265
Charles X, 120
Chasselay massacre, 248–49, 275
Chataigneau, Yves, 146, 155, 156, 161–62, 164
chiefs and headmen, 33, 36, 191, 290, 296
children: Australia, 351n5; Côte d'Ivoire, 192; massacre of, 31, 34, 35; in Voulet-Chanoine mission, 29, 30. *See also* girls; métis children

Index

China, 302n48, 336
Chinese in Hanoi, xxx, 55, 66
Chirac, Jacques, 342–43, 354n24
Christianity: Muslims and, 210; Psichari and, 211. *See also* Catholic Church; conversion to Christianity
church and state, 345–46
CIE. *See* Centre d'information et d'études (CIE)
"collaboration" (word), 218n29
citizenship: Algerians and, 80, 83, 88, 97, 115, 126, 129, 306, 319, 343; "Manifesto" and, 149
"civilizing mission," 38, 56, 130, 202, 205, 215
civil rights, 149, 323
civil service entrance requirement, 113
civil war, xxxix, xli, 283–303, 305, 308, 340
"civil war" (term), 298n1
Clauzel, Bertrand, 6
Clemenceau, Georges, 28, 39, 255
Clermont-Tonnerre, Stanislas, comte de, 97
Clozel, François-Joseph, xxxv, 180, 195n12
Cluseret, Gustave Paul, 20
Code de l'indigénat, 80, 85, 88, 108n29, 113, 127
cohabitation, interracial, xxxiv–xxxvi, 177–201
Cohen, William, xxxviii
Cold War, xxvi, xxvii
collective violence, xix, xx
Collingham, Elizabeth, xliii(n18)
collusion, 117, 345
colonial administrators: assassination, 56, 58; boredom of, 186;

demotion and transfer, 190; relations with native women, 177–201
Colonial Army. *See* French Colonial Army
Colonial Union. *See* Union coloniale française
The Colonizer and the Colonized (Memmi), xx
colonnes, 45n1
Comité de l'Afrique du Nord, 151, 152
Comité de l'Afrique Française, 28, 38, 230
Commission Criminelle (Vietnam), 64
commemorations, 334, 337, 349
Commission interministériel des affaires musulmans (CIAM), 88
Commission on Africa, 7
Communist Party of France. *See* Parti Communiste Français (PCF)
concentration camps. *See* prison camps
"concubinage" (word), 194n7
Condé, Maryse, 343
Congo, French. *See* French Congo
Congo Free State, 71n4
Conklin, Alice, 114, 139n85
Conrad, Joseph: *Heart of Darkness*, 40
conscience, 178, 184, 187
conscription, xxxvi–xxxvii, 221, 222
conspiracy theories, 18, 138n77
Constantine, 163; riots of 1934, xxx, 77–112, 115, 121, 148
Constantine (department), Algeria, xxxii–xxxiii, 114, 117, 154
conversion to Christianity, 205, 212, 214

Coquelin, Henri, 92
Coquery-Vidrovitch, Catherine, 43, 338
corporal punishment, xxii, xxx
Côte d'Ivoire, xxxv, 192, 195n12; Colonial Army and, 257; interracial marriage and sex in, 180–81
counterviolence, xiv–xv
country marriage. *See* marriage *à la mode du pays*
coups: Hanoi, 55, 56
court cases, 335
craniology, 232–33
Crémieux decree, 80, 97, 101, 115, 119, 137n70
Crewe, Lord. *See* Milnes, Robert Offley Ashburton, Marquess of Crewe
criminal justice: Algeria, 80, 85; Vietnam, 65
Croix de Feu (CDF), xxxi, xxxii, 77, 87, 89, 94, 114–39
curfews, 308, 309, 344
customary law, 80, 105n10
Cuttoli, Paul, 126

Dagneau, Colonel, 198–99n53
Dahomey, 29, 31, 39
Dahra, 3–4, 9–20, 22
Dakar, 212, 213, 215, 348
Dakar Cathedral, 213, 215–16
Daughton, J. P., 215
Debay, Alfred, 120–21, 122, 125
de Bazelaire de Ruppière, Joseph-Maurice, 252, 259, 260
decapitation. *See* beheadings
deculturization, 60
de Froissard-Broissia, Colonel, 266
de Gaulle, Charles, 216, 237, 336–37, 342

de Lacroix, Henri, 223, 234
Delafosse, Maurice, xxxv, 180, 195n14, 225
Del Boca, Angelo: *Italiana, brava gente?*, 335–36
Delcassé, Théophile, 29
Délégation générale du gouvernement en Algérie, 310
de Monpezat, Henri, 68
demonstrations, protests, etc.: Algeria, 92–93, 150; France, 301n22, 309, 344, 349
deportation, xxv, xxxix, 64, 308, 318, 324
Déroulède, Paul, 43
Derrécagaix, Victor, 13, 17, 20
Desjoberts, Amédée, 7
destruction of economic resources, xiii, xxviii, 6, 14. *See also* razzia
detention, 64, 345. *See also* captives; penal colonies; prisoners of war
De Tham, 62, 65–66, 68
de Torcy, Louis. *See* Torcy, Louis de
de Trentinian, Colonel, 38, 40
Devaud, Stanislaus, 115, 116, 118, 125, 126, 128, 129, 130
diaries, 179, 183–90, 197n33, 206, 208, 253–54
Dien Bien Phu, 286, 337
Dien Bien Phu (1992 film), 338
discipline, xxii, 289
disease, 42. *See also* "Soudanite" (pathology); venereal diseases
disappeared people: commemoration, 349
distribution of land. *See* land distribution
DiversCités, 339
Djebar, Assia, 22–23n2
doctors. *See* physicians

Dol, Jean, 59, 69
Dominican Order, 203, 214–15
Dongo (Songhai deity), 51n69
Douglass, Frederick, 71n5
Doumer, Paul, 58
drama. *See* plays
dress codes, 346–47, 348
Dreyfus, Alfred, 40
Dreyfus affair, 28, 30, 38, 40, 42; Algeria and, 81; Psichari and, 203–4; purges and, 234
drinking. *See* alcohol
droit de jambage, 192
drought, 154
Drumont, Eduard, 131
dumdum bullets, xxiv
Dunkirk, 259, 262
Duras, Marguerite: *L'Amant*, 338
Dussaulx, Émile, 183–84, 199n54
Dutailly, Henry, 251–52
Dutch East India Company. *See* United East Indies Company

Echenberg, Myron, xxxviii, 276
École Etz Haïm, 86
education and education policy, xvii–xviii, 343; Algeria, 85. *See also* Islamic education; schools
Eisenbeth, Maurice, 86, 111n49
elections: Algeria, 81, 97, 115, 117, 124
electoral college systems, 83, 101, 127
emigrants, African. *See* African emigrants
emigrants, Algerian. *See* Algerian emigrants
emigration and immigration. *See* immigration and emigration
enfranchisement. *See* voting and voting rights

ethics and morality. *See* morality and ethics
ethnic violence. *See* inter-ethnic violence
Étoile nord-africaine (ENA), 117, 118, 121, 122
eugenics, xxxiv
euphemism, 340, 354n26
European Convention on Human Rights, 319
"européenne" (label), 79
execution and executions, 36–37; Algeria, 11, 140, 290; Hanoi, 56, 64, 65; monuments and, 349; Voulet-Chanoine affair and, 29, 31, 35; World War II, 265. *See also* public execution
exiles, 162, 173n72
expulsion. *See* deportation

Fadel, Mohammed, 210, 218n27
Faguet, Émile: *Le libéralisme*, 186
Faidherbe, Louis, 32, 231
famine: Algeria, 1945. *See* food supply crisis, Algeria, 1945
Fanon, Frantz, xii, xiii, xiv, 57, 182, 188, 193; *Black Skin, White Masks*, 177–78
farming. *See* agriculture
farmworkers, 115, 141, 157, 160–61
fascism, 112–39
Fashoda Incident, 30, 38
Faucon, Georges, 118
Faure, Félix, 43
Favre, Julie Velten, 205, 214
fear: Algeria, 95, 122, 123, 142, 148, 295; Hanoi, 57, 62, 70; Rhodesia, 166n9
fear, inculcation of. *See* terrorism

fear of capture and torture, 8
fear of colonists, 192
fear of Muslims and Islam, xxxii, xxxvi, 114, 115, 121
fear of poisoning, 69
Fédération des élus indigènes, 118
Fédération des élus musulmans Algériens (FEM), 117, 118, 150
Fédération des élus musulmans de Constantine (FEC), 87, 88, 90, 95, 109n31–32
Fédération des Scouts Musulmans Algériens (FSMA), 151, 170n43
Fédération nationale des anciens combattants en Afrique du Nord (FNACA), 339
Feraoun, Mouloud, 287, 289, 290–92, 293–95, 296, 301n32, 303n53, 303n55
Ferro, Marc, 43
feuds, 293, 294, 296
Fichier Z, 316–17, 324
films, historical, 335, 338, 347–48
Finance Ministry. See Ministry of Finance
fire as a weapon, 11–12, 14, 19. See also burning of villages
Flamme, La, 115, 119, 128
FLN. See Front de Libération Nationale (FLN)
FLNKS. See Front de Libération Nationale Kanak et Socialiste (FLNKS)
Flosse, Gaston, 354n24
FNACA. See Fédération nationale des anciens combattants en Afrique du Nord (FNACA)
food supply crisis, Algeria, 1945, xxxiv, 140–73
football. See soccer

forced labor, xvii, xxii, 31, 38
Force Noir, La (Mangin), 223, 255
Foreign Affairs Ministry. See Ministry of Foreign Affairs
forgetting. See memory and forgetting
Fort Bonnier, 198–99n53
Fort Hugueny, 185
Fort National (Algeria), 291, 293, 296
Foucault, Michel, 33, 337
Foureau-Lamy expedition, 29
Fourniau, Charles, 65
Franco-Vietnam War, xv, 286, 337; in films, 338
Fraser, William, 255
Frédéric-Dupont, Édouard, 290
freedom of movement, restriction of. See travel restriction
Frémanger, Colonel, 258
French-Algerian war. See Algerian War of Independence
French Army, xxvii–xxviii, 8, 256; Affaires des Grottes and, 3–4, 9–21; Algerian War and, 287, 288, 289–93; street fighting in Hanoi, 69–70; West African conscripts, xxxvi–xxxvii, 221–47; West Germany, 314. See also Armée d'Afrique; Battle of France; French Colonial Army; harkis; soldiers, North African; soldiers, West African
French-British relations, 31
French Colonial Army, 223, 230, 239, 257; Psichari and, 205–7; Soudan, 182–83, 186–87. See also Voulet-Chanoine affair
French Colonial Union. See Union coloniale française

French Congo, 29, 40, 191; Messali Hadj and, 162, 173n72; Psichari and, 202, 204, 205–8
French Equatorial Africa, xxvii, 173n72. *See also* Cameroon; Chad; French Congo
French-German relations, 40, 222, 224, 237, 251; Algeria and, 304–33. *See also* Battle of France
French Guinea, 183, 190, 200n72
French Polynesia, 341, 354n24
French Right. *See* Croix de Feu; Front National; Parti Social Français (PSF)
French Sudan. *See* Soudan
French Union, 142
French West Africa, xxv, xxvii, 193–94n4, 221–47; interracial cohabitation in, xxxv–xxxvi, 177–201. *See also* Côte d'Ivoire; Dahomey; French Guinea; Mauritania; Niger; Senegal; Soudan; Voulet-Chanoine Affair
French women, 180, 187, 195n12; on interracial marriage, 182; viewed with disfavor in Vichy, 184
Frère, Aubert, 259
Freydenberg, Henry, 257
Front de Libération Nationale (FLN), xxix–xl, 286–90, 292–97, 320–23; bibliography, 165n1; "bloody practices" of, 345; fines of, 303n53; France, 301n22, 308, 309, 344; Ramadan and, 299–300n16; West Germany, 305, 306, 311, 312, 313, 314–15, 316, 317, 319. *See also* Armée de libération nationale (ALN)
Front de Libération Nationale Kanak et Socialiste (FLNKS), 341, 342
Front Islamique du Salut, 340
Front National, 339, 340
Front Popular. *See* Popular Front
FSMA. *See* Fédération des Scouts Musulmans Algériens (FSMA)

Gallieni, Joseph-Simon, 38, 178, 196n21
Gallois, William, 7
gambling, 186, 188, 189; prohibition of, 288, 300n19
Gamelin, Maurice, 252, 279n32
Garets, M. L. Gamiers de, 234
Gazagne, Pierre-René, 162, 163, 173n72
general strikes, 287–88
Geneva Conventions, 319, 320
genocide, 20, 25n39, 336
Georges, Alphonse, 251, 252, 253
German scholarships, 317
German Southwest Africa, 40
Germany, xxxvi, 336; World War II, xxxviii, 153–54, 248–82. *See also* French-German relations; Nazis and Nazism; West Germany
girls: marriage and cohabitation, 126, 128, 181, 183, 201n77. *See also* Muslim girls; virgins
Giscard d'Estaing, Valéry, 340
Goody, Jack, xxi
Gosnell, Jonathan, 113
gossip, 57
Gouin, Félix, 163
Gouraud, Henri, 215–16, 218n27
Gouvernement Provisoire de la République Algérienne, 313
Grandin, Commandant, 13, 18
Grandmaison, Olivier Le Cour, 7

Great Britain, xliii(n18), 285; African colonies, xxii, 61; Arab League and, 152; Australia and, 335, 351n5; "concubinage" and, 200; historiography, 334–35; India and, 57–58, 144; World War II, 251. *See also* French-British relations
Great Depression, xxvi, 87, 125
Greek Civil War, 296
Greffon, Said, 117
group violence. *See* collective violence
Guelma, xxxiii, 121, 147, 157–58, 163
Guha, Ranajit, 57
Guinea, French. *See* French Guinea
Günter, Hans, 238

Habich, Bel, 116
habitations bon marché (HBM), 85–86
Haddour, Azzedine, 112–13
Hadj, Messali. *See* Messali Hadj
Haiphong, 58, 65
Hamoumou, Mohand, 289, 290, 294, 295
Hanoi, xvi, xxix–xxx, 52–76, 336
Hanoi Hotel, 61, 66–67
Hanotaux, Gabriel, 29, 38
Hansen, Christian, 262
Harbi, Mohammed, 300n19, 334
harkis, 293, 294, 301n34, 337, 349, 352n13; Chirac and, 342, 343
headmen. *See* chiefs and headmen
head scarves: banning of, 345–46
Heart of Darkness (Conrad), 40
Henrikson, Alan, xi
Herero people, 336
historical films. *See* films, historical

historiography, xl, 21, 35, 53, 65, 100–101, 334–56; North African, 89; *la repentance* (trend), 43; West African soldiers and, 249
hoarding (alleged), 159–60
Ho Chi Minh, 336
Holland. *See* Netherlands
homosexuality, 190, 199n53
Horne, Alistair: *To Lose a Battle*, 249
Houphouët-Boigny, Félix, 196n18
housing, 85–86, 127
Howard, John, 335
hunger, 153, 155, 161, 164
hysteria, 57, 62, 68

Iba-Zizen, Augustin, 129–30
identity cards. *See* national identity cards
Ighilhariz, Louisette, 345
Ihler, Marcel, 263
"immigration" (word), 347
immigration and emigration, 340; forced, 221. *See also* African emigrants; migrant workers; refugees
indexes, 249
India, 57–58, 144
"indigène" (label), 79, 80
Indigènes (2006 film), 347–48
Indigènes de la République, 339
"*indigénophiles*," 181
indigenous Australians. *See* Aboriginal people (Australia)
Indochina War. *See* Franco-Vietnam War
Indochine (1992 film), 338
Indochinese soldiers. *See* soldiers, Indochinese
inequality, 53, 253; Algeria, 81, 113, 126, 143, 153, 156–57, 294

Index

informers and informing, 283–84, 293, 294–95, 301n27
insanity. *See* sanity and insanity
insurrections. *See* revolts
intelligence gathering, 147–48, 149, 164; during civil war, 283–303; West Germany and, 315–16
inter-ethnic violence, 54, 77–112. *See also* interracial violence
Interior Ministry. *See* Ministry of Interior
international aid, 155, 158
interpreters. *See* translators and translation
interracial children. *See* métis children
interracial cohabitation. *See* cohabitation, interracial
interracial marriage, 179, 180–81, 182, 190–91
interracial sex, xxxiv–xxxvi, 177–178, 180
interracial violence, 52, 53, 54, 55, 56, 57, 61, 68, 69
interrogation, xxii, 96, 288, 308, 313, 345
Iraq, 285
irrationality, xii, xv, xx, xxxiii
Islam: Psichari and, 202, 206–7, 208–14. *See also* Catholics: Islam and; Muslims; Ramadan. *See also* Qur'an
Islamic education, 88, 151
Islamic law. *See* Qur'anic law
"israélite" (label), 79
Italiana, brava gente? (Del Boca), 335–36
Italy, 255, 335–36
Ivory Coast. *See* Côte d'Ivoire

Jalabert, Monsignor, 212–13, 215–16
Japan, 68, 336
Jarty, Captain, 268, 271
Jaurès, Jean, 234
Java, xxxiii
Jeannel, Joseph, 262
Jesuits, 18
Jews, xx, 40; Algeria, xxx–xxxi, 77–112, 115–16; Papon and, 344
Joalland, Paul, 27, 29–30, 34
Jonnart Law, 83–84, 102, 106n18, 127
journals (diaries). *See* diaries
Jouvencourt, Captain, 9, 10, 18, 19
Jurgenson, Jean, 319, 322–23
justification of violence. *See* violence: justification and rationalization

Kabyle Berbers, xvi, 3, 9–20, 293–94
Kaddache, Mahfoud, 84
Kafi, Ali, 300n19
Kalyvas, Stathis, 283–84, 296, 298n1
Kennedy, Dane, 53, 61
Kenya, 61, 300n17
Khalifa, Elie, 91–92, 99–100
Khodja, Hamdan, 5–7, 21
kidnapping, 66, 190
King Charles X. *See* Charles X
Klein, Martin, xxxv, 182
Klobb, Jean-François, 26, 27, 29, 38, 40, 42–43
Koizumi, Junichiro, 336
Koran. *See* Qur'an
Koranic law. *See* Qur'anic law
Korea, 336
Koulibaly, Mamadou, 36
Kounta people, 187–89, 198n51

labels and labeling, 79–80, 96–97, 99, 101; of Jews, 115–16. *See also* names and naming

Index

labor, xvi, xviii, xxxvi–xxxvii; Algeria, 124, 126; coercion and, xxii; Vietnam, xvii; violence and, xxx, 42. *See also* forced labor; slavery; unemployment; wages
Labor Ministry. *See* Ministry of Labor
Labruyère, Jacques, 125
Lacheroy, Charles, 287
Lacroix, Henri de. *See* De Lacroix, Henri
Laffon, Émile, 146, 147, 168n22
Laloum, Maurice, 86
Lambert, Gabriel, 114
Lamoudi, Lamine, 118
Lamy-Foureau expedition. *See* Foureau-Lamy expedition
land distribution, 125, 143
land grants (proposed), 125
land seizure, 113
Langlois, Hippolyte, 234
La Rocque, François de, 114, 117, 119, 126, 128, 130
Latinité (Bertrand concept), 120
law, customary. *See* customary law
laws, 53, 63–64, 85, 113, 343, 346, 354n30. *See also* Blum-Viollette bill; Code de l'indigénat; Jonnart Law
Lebanon, 143
Le Beau, Georges, 148
Le Bon, Gustave, xix, 225, 233, 241n16
Lebovics, Herman, xv
Lebu people, 228
Lecache, Bernard, 138n77
Leclerc, Marius, 190–91
Lecoq, Louis, 130
Léger, Paul, 288–89
legislation. *See* laws

Lellouche, Henri, 86, 93, 99
Le Pen, Jean-Marie, 339, 340, 352–53n16
Leroy-Beaulieu, Paul, 38
Lesort, Paul-André, 268
Lestrade-Carbonnel, André, 148
Letourneau, Charles, 233, 241n14
Levas, Paul, 119
Libya, 255, 336
Ligue des Droits de l'Homme, 64, 118
Ligue internationale contre l'antisémitisme (LICA), 124, 138n77
The Logic of Violence in Civil War (Kalyvas), 283–84
Lorraine, 222–23
Lunn, Joe, 30, 275
Lyautey, Hubert, 204, 207, 235
lynch mob mentality. *See* mob mentality

Mabo decision (Australia), 335, 351n5
MacMaster, Neil, 113, 308
Madagascar (Malagasy), xxvi, xxvii, 38, 178, 253, 256
Ma' al 'Ainin, 211
Malagasy soldiers. *See* soldiers, Malagasy
Mali, 184. *See also* Timbuktu
Mandel, Georges, 255
Mangin, Charles, xxxvii, 223–33, 235, 255
Manifesto of the Algerian People, 149
Mann, Gregory, xxxviii
Mannoni, Octave, 178
Manouvrier, Léonce, 232–33
Marbaud, Pierre, 18
Marchand, Theodore Paul, 28, 30

Marignane, 349
Maritain, Jacques, 202, 204, 208, 212, 214
marriage, interracial. *See* interracial marriage
marriage *à la mode du pays*, 182, 190, 191
Marseilles, 310
Marxism, 337
masculinity, xvi, xxxiv–xxxv
massacres, 8; Algeria, 3–4, 6, 9–20, 284, 340; compared to urban violence, 56; German South West Africa, 336; Greece, 296; of West African soldiers, 238, 248–49, 265, 273–74; of women and children, 31, 34, 35
Massis, Henri, 202, 204, 208, 216, 220n48
Maugham, Somerset, 254
Mau Mau insurrection, 300n17
Mauritania: Psichari and, 202, 204, 208–12
Maurras, Charles, 215
McDougall, James, xxxiii, 121, 150
media, print. *See* press
Mediterranean High Committee, 122, 151
Meifredy, Françoise, 248–49, 275
Memmi, Albert, xx, 130
Memoirs of the Maelstrom (Lunn), 275
memorials and monuments, 336, 339, 342–43, 349, 354n27
memory, xl, 334
mental health. *See* sanity and insanity
"mental maps" (Henrikson concept), xi
Messali Hadj, 88, 109n33, 117, 120, 122, 129, 287; detention of, 149; exile of, 162, 173n72. *See also* Mouvement pour la Triomphe des Libertés Démocratiques
métis children, 179, 188–89
métissage. *See* interracial marriage; interracial sex
Meuse (river), 267–72
Mévil, André, 36
Michaux-Chevry, Lucette, 354n24
Michel, Marc, 250, 338
Michel, Marcel, 153
Midlarsky, Manus, 143
migrant workers, 54, 101, 125
militarism and military technology, xxiv. *See also* aerial warfare
military draft. *See* conscription
Milnes, Robert Offley Ashburton, Marquess of Crewe, 200n70
Minart, Jacques, 255–56
mining, xvii. *See also* nickel mining
Ministère de l'Immigration, de l'Intégration, de l'Identité Nationale et du Développement Solidaire, 348
Ministry of Agriculture, 145
Ministry of Finance, 145
Ministry of Foreign Affairs, 144–45, 154, 315, 319, 320
Ministry of Interior, 141, 144, 146–47, 148, 152, 163, 313; Algeria subdivision, 151, 152–53, 162; North African affairs service, 153; West Germany and, 315
Ministry of Labor, 145
Ministry of National Economy, 145, 158
Ministry of Prisoners of War and Refugees, 154
Ministry of War, 3, 148, 152, 153
Miquel, René, 91, 92, 110n37–38

Miroir, Le (Khodja), 5–7
miscegenation. *See* interracial marriage; interracial sex
misogyny: purported, 126
missionaries, Catholic. *See* Catholic missionaries
mission civilisatrice. See "civilizing mission"
Mitterrand, François, 342
mixed-race children. *See* métis children
mixed-race cohabitation. *See* cohabitation, interracial
mob mentality, 57, 63. *See also* vigilantism
Moinier, Charles, 235
Montaner, Raymond, 290, 292, 301n34
Montangerand, Colonel, 267, 272
Monteil, Parfait-Louis, 31, 47n19, 48n42
monuments. *See* memorials and monuments
morale of troops, 251, 258, 259
morality and ethics, 21–22
Morinaud, Émile, 81, 84, 87, 91, 97, 100, 106n22
Morlat, Patrice, 65
Moroccan regiments. *See* Régiments de Tirailleurs Marocains (RTM)
Morocco, 254, 257, 313
mosques: Algeria, 91, 92, 99, 107n23
Mosse people, 28, 30, 33
Mouvement National Algérien (MNA), 287, 293, 298n1, 308, 309, 314; West Germany and, 312, 313, 316
Mouvement pour la Triomphe des Libertés Démocratiques, 308

murder: Algeria, 96; of employers, 59, 73; Hanoi, 56, 58, 58, 59, 61; West Africa, xxxix, 26, 27, 42–43, 47n19; of West African soldiers, 265. *See also* massacres
Musette, 112, 113
museums, 335, 336, 339, 348, 349, 354n27
"Muslim French citizens from Algeria" (FMAS), 306, 310, 312; guaranteed electoral seats for, 83
Muslim girls: dress codes and, 346
Muslims: Algeria, xxxiii, xxxiv, 112–39, 147–48, 157, 285, 340; *attentisme* and, 285; Chanoine and, 32; Constantine riots of 1934 and, xxx–xxxi, 77–112; French West African population, 227
Muslim Scouts. *See* Fédération des Scouts Musulmans Algériens (FSMA)
mutinies, 58. *See also* Voulet-Chanoine affair

names and naming, 349
Namibia, 336
Narboni, Elie, 84, 86, 87
National Front. *See* Front National
national identity: Algerian, 118; French, xxiii, xxv, 339
national identity cards, 310, 312, 314, 331n52
nationalism: Algerian, 121–22, 125, 129, 150, 151, 308; Muslim, 126, 150, 151; pan-Arab, 108n29; Psichari and, xxxvi, 204, 216
naturalization, 80, 81
Nazis and Nazism, xl, 120, 154; massacres and, 249–50, 265;

Papon and, 344; pseudoscience and, 238
Nebout, Albert, 180, 187, 195n12, 195n17
Netherlands, xxxiii, 61, 72n15, 335
New Caledonia, xl, 340–42, 343, 354n24
nickel mining, 341
Niger, 31
Niger valley, 38
Noiret, Louis-Émile, 259, 260, 262, 267
Noiriel, Gérard, 101, 107n27
North African Committee. *See* Comité de l'Afrique du Nord
North African culture, 89
North African soldiers. *See* soldiers, North African
N'Tchoréré, Charles, 265, 280n53
nurses, 249, 275
Nye, Robert A., 231

"official mind," 193n1
Olié, Jean, 291
Olivier de Sardan, Jean-Pierre, 44
Oran, xxxi–xxxii, 81, 114, 155
Oran (department), Algeria, 118
Organisation de l'Armée Secrète (OAS), 344, 349
Organisation politico-administrative (OPA), 283, 286, 287
Orléans, 265–67
Osborne, Milton, xxix, 53
Other (concept), 53, 59, 337
Ottoman Empire, 6, 20
Ouagadougou, 28, 37
Ouled Riah tribe, 3–4, 9–20
Ouvrard, Colonel, 258

Pallier, Lieutenant, 29, 34
pan-Arabism, 108n29

Papillault, Georges, 231–32
Papon, Maurice, 289; Algeria and, 162, 163, 164, 290, 309, 323; war crimes trial of, xli, 344
Paris, 301n22; *banlieu* riots, 346; strikes, 287
Parisian Society of Anthropology. *See* Société d'anthropologie de Paris
Parti Communiste Français (PCF), 64, 87, 108n29, 138n77
Parti du Peuple Algérien (PPA), 109n33, 117, 118, 120, 123, 149, 150; food supply crisis and, 154
Parti Social Français (PSF), xxxi–xxxii, 114–39
Pasqua, Charles, 342
passports, 315, 331n52
paternalism, xxxviii, 253
PCF. *See* Parti Communiste Français (PCF)
Péguy, Charles, 202, 204, 208, 216, 219n48
Pélissier, Jean Jacques, 3–4, 9–20
penal colonies, 341
Perreaux, Charles, 223
Péteau, Lieutenant, 39–40, 49n51
Petiet, Robert-Marie, 263
Petitbon, René, 162, 163, 164, 173n73
Phan Boi Chau, 61–62
"phony war" (1939–40), 250, 254, 258
photographs, 37, 41, 94
physicians, 27, 243n33
pieds-noirs, xxxi, 112, 114, 120, 125, 127; economic dominance and privilege, 124, 126, 130; forced "repatriation," 353n17; historiography, 339, 349

pillage, 29, 58
pirates, 58, 62
Pitts, Jennifer, 5
plays, 66
poisoning, xxx, 59, 61–63, 69
police, xii; Algeria, 162, 163, 164, 294, 345; brutality, 113, 309; Code de l'indigénat and, 85; Constantine, Algeria, 91, 92–94, 100, 110n37–38; food hoarding and, 159; France, xxxix, 309, 344; Java, xxxiii; surveillance by, xxv, 88, 148; West Germany, 312, 315–16, 317. *See also* Sûreté
political asylum. *See* asylum
polygamy, 126, 128
Polynesia, French. *See* French Polynesia
Ponty, William, 195n12, 223, 230
Popular Front, 82, 89, 115
popular opinion. *See* public opinion
porters, xxxvi–xxxvii, 31, 37
poverty, 124, 125, 160, 163
POWs. *See* prisoners of war
PPA. *See* Parti du Peuple Algérien (PPA)
prayer, 209
press, 3–4, 14, 17, 18, 35, 37, 39, 40; Dreyfus affair and, 40; food supply crisis and, 155; *force noire* and, 229; Hanoi and, 57, 59, 68, 69
press sensationalism, 37, 73, 94
Principles of Sociology (Spencer), 225
prison camps, 68, 238, 304
prisoners. *See* captives
prisoners of war, 153–54, 265; West African soldiers as, 238, 265, 275
prohibition (of smoking, drinking, etc.), xxxix, 288, 289, 299–300n16, 300n18–20
propaganda, 35, 113, 123, 313, 314; Algeria, 295, 296; Nazi, 154, 275; pan-Arab, 152
Prouteaux, Maurice, 191–92, 201n77
protests, demonstrations, etc. *See* demonstrations, protests, etc.
provocation and provocateurs, 82, 94
pseudoscience, 230, 236, 241n14
PSF. *See* Parti Social Français (PSF)
Psichari, Ernest, xxxvi, 202–20
psychiatry, xii, xv, xxix, 28, 41–43
psychological violence, xiii, xxxix, 284
public execution, xxx, 56, 65
public opinion, 4, 148, 285, 286
public schools. *See* state schools
punishment, xxiii, 61, 345; Code de l'indigénat and, 85; collective, xxvii. *See also* corporal punishment
punitive raids. *See* razzias

Quai d'Orsay. *See* Ministry of Foreign Affairs
Qur'an, 207
Qur'anic law, 113, 126, 128, 129

Rabah of Burnu, 28, 29
race and race theory, xii, xxi, xxiii, 130, 188, 221–47, 347
racial violence. *See* interracial violence
racism, xiii, xviii, xxi, xxxii, xxxvii, xxxviii, 224–25, 323; Algeria, 292, 307; Arendt on violence and, 54; of Chanoine, 32; in U.S. Army, 242n21
raids, punitive. *See* razzias

railroads, 38
Ramadan, 299–300n16
Randau, Robert, xxxii, 130; *Les Colons*, 112, 113
rape, 53, 190. *See also* droit de jambage
Rassemblement national d'action sociale, 114
rationing, 144, 153, 154, 156–57, 159
razzias, xxvii, xxviii, 6
reading, 186–87, 198n46
rebellion and rebellions. *See* revolts
Rédares, Marcel, 125
refugees, 101, 304, 320
Régiment de Tirailleurs Sénégalais (RTS), 267, 269–72
Régiment d'Infanterie Coloniale Mixte Sénégalais (RICMS), 259–63, 265–67
Régiments de Tirailleurs Marocains (RTM), 257
relief, international. *See* international aid
religious wars, xv, 151
renaming of streets, 349
Renan, Ernest, 203, 206–7, 210, 214
Renseignements Généraux (RG), 148, 162–63, 316
repression, xiii, xv, xix, xxii–xxiii, 313; Algeria, xxxiii, xxxiii–xxxiv, 140, 142, 297; France, 42, 308, 309, 344; Vietnam, 52, 58, 61, 64
resistance to colonialism, xix, 8, 69; Algeria, 114, 283–303; retribution for, 31, 35
restriction of travel. *See* travel restriction
retribution, 295, 296, 297
retributive violence, 31, 35, 36, 37,
55; Algeria, 140; Vietnam, 55, 58, 59, 62–63, 65–66, 68
Réunion, 339
revenge. *See* retribution
revolts, xiii, xxvi, xxxiii–xxxiv, 52, 54, 57, 57–58; compared to urban violence, 56. *See also* Sétif uprising (1945)
Reynaud, Paul, 251, 279n32
RG. *See* Renseignements Généraux (RG)
Rhodesia, 61, 166n9
RICMS. *See* Régiment d'Infanterie Coloniale Mixte Sénégalais (RICMS)
riots: Constantine, xxx, 77–112, 115, 121, 148; Paris, 346
River Meuse. *See* Meuse (river)
River Somme, 259–61, 263–65
robbery, 58, 59
Robinet, Auguste. *See* Musette
Rommel, Erwin, 263, 264
Rosenberg, Clifford, 101
Roubaud, Lieutenant-Colonel, 153, 154
Roucaud, Charles, 258, 267, 269, 270, 271
Roume, Ernest, 190–91, 200n72
Rousso, Henry, 334
Roy, Jules, 124
RTS. *See* Régiment de Tirailleurs Sénégalais (RTS)
rubber industry, xvii, 58, 72n15
Rudd, Kevin, 335
Rundstedt, Gerd von, 269

Saar and Saarland, 252, 310–11
Sadoul, Georges, 273
Said, Edward, 337
Saint-Arnaud, Armand Jacques Leroy de, 15, 16–17

salafiyya movement, 89, 118
Salaman, Lieutenant, 36
Samori Touré, 29, 32, 33, 37, 44
sanity and insanity, xxii, xv, xxviii, xxix, 27, 40, 41–42, 43
Sansané Haoussa, 31, 34, 36
Sarkozy, Nicolas, 348
Sarraut, Albert, 68
Sartre, Jean-Paul, 344
Sbéah tribe, 9, 10, 14, 15
scalpings, 35
SCANA. *See* Service central des affaires nord-africaines (SCANA)
scandals, 343–46, 347; Algeria, 3–25; West Africa, 26–51
Scheck, Raffael, xxxviii, 249, 274–75
Schein, Edgar, xii
Schmidt, Rudolph, 262
scholarships, German. *See* German scholarships
schools: Algeria, 86, 123, 151. *See also* state schools
Schreier, Joshua, 97
Sciulli, David, xviii
Scott, James C., liii(n96), 286, 299n8
Séchet, Félix-Pierre, 263
secrecy, 322, 323
secularization, 346
self-censorship, 296, 303n55
self-defense, 83, 86, 121
Senechal de la Roche, Roberta, xviii, xix–xx
Senegal, 190, 206, 228, 257. *See also* Dakar
"Senegalese troops" (term), 236
sensationalism by press. *See* press sensationalism
Serer people, 228, 236

servants, 60; beating of, 54, 56; fear of poisoning by, 69; murder by, 59, 73; theft by, 58–59
Service central des affaires nord-africaines (SCANA), 153, 154
servicemen, Indochinese. *See* soldiers, Indochinese
servicemen, Malagasy. *See* soldiers, Malagasy
servicemen, North African. *See* soldiers, North African
servicemen, West African. *See* soldiers, West African
Sétif, xxxiii, xxxiv, 106–7n23, 118, 121
Sétif uprising (1945): economic aspects, 140–73
sex, interracial. *See* interracial sex
sex slaves, xxxv, 36–37, 182
sexually transmitted diseases. *See* venereal diseases
sexual violence, xxviii, xxxiii. *See also* rape
Seydoux, François, 315, 320
sharecroppers, 157, 159, 160
shea butter, 188
Siddiya Baba, 210–11, 218n25
siege, 11, 15
Sivan, Emmanuel, 130
slavery, xxvii, 337, 339, 343, 349, 354n30; abolition commemoration, 334, 337; effect on owners, 71n5; interracial marriage and, 191; Mangin and, 228
slaves, 26, 35–36; massacre of, 31, 36; United States, 299n8. *See also* sex slaves
smoking, 288, 289, 299–300n16, 300n17–20
soccer, 352–53n16

social control, xii, xiv, xviii–xix; Algerians and, 313–14, 318, 321, 324; food supply and, 143; laws and, 63; power and, 53; urban planning and, xxiii. *See also* travel restriction

Société d'anthropologie de Paris, 222, 230–34

Sociétés indigènes de prévoyance, 144, 157

Society of Jesus. *See* Jesuits

sodomy, 183, 196n27

Sokoto (West African sultanate), 29, 47n19

soldiers, Indochinese, 256

soldiers, Malagasy, 262

soldiers, North African, 253, 254, 256, 257, 266; in films, 347–48; West Germany, 314. *See also* veterans, Algerian

soldiers, West African, xxxvi–xxxviii, 30, 221–47; Algeria, 159, 232, 233, 234; Altmayer and, 185; Chanoine Affair and, 29; Chirac and, 343; Psichari and, 210; World War II, 248–82. *See also* Régiment de Tirailleurs Sénégalais (RTS); Régiment d'Infanterie Coloniale Mixte Sénégalais (RICMS); "Senegalese troops" (term)

Somalia, 336

Somme. *See* River Somme

Somono people, 183, 196n26

Songhai Empire, 31, 33, 44

Sonni Ali Ber, 44

Soudan, xxxv–xxxvi, 45n2, 182–83, 184, 186; *force noire* and, xxxvii; Voulet-Chanoine Affair and, 26, 29, 30–31, 33–43. *See also* Timbuktu

"Soudanite" (pathology), 41–42, 198n47

Soult, Nicolas, 13, 14–15, 16

South Africa, 336

"space of death" (Taussig concept), 7–8, 20–21

spectacles (displays), 65

Spencer, Herbert, 224, 225, 226, 233

Spillman, Henri, 151–52

Spire, Alexis, 306, 312

state apologies. *See* apologies, state

state repression. *See* repression

state schools: France, 345–46

STDs. *See* venereal diseases

Steel Shirts, 170n43

Steiner, Zara, xxiv

stereotypes, xvi, xxx, xxxii, 59–60, 338; of Africans, xxxvii, 230, 233, 239, 250; of Algerians, 322; in drama, 66; of interracial relationships, xxxvi; of Muslims and Jews, 98

Stoler, Ann, xii, xxxiii, 61, 72n15

Stoller, Paul, 44

Stora, Benjamin, 334

Stovall, Tyler, xxv

street fighting, 69–70

strikes, general. *See* general strikes

student scholarships, German. *See* German scholarships

subsidized housing, 85–86

Sudan, 45n2

Sudan, French. *See* Soudan

Sumatra, 61, 72n15

Sûreté, 64–65

surveillance, xxiii, xxv, 88, 98, 142, 163; France, 344; West Germany, 313, 318, 321, 324–25

Switzerland, 309

symbolic violence, xvii, xviii, 113
Syria, 143, 170n43

Tahitians, 341, 354n24
Taillardat, Ferdinand, 153
Tarde, Alfred de, 202
Taussig, Michael, 7–8, 21, 52, 70n1
taxation, 6, 88, 192, 309, 327n15; resistance to, 20
Tchad. *See* Chad
technology, 211. *See also* militarism and military technology
Terres de Soleil et de Sommeil (Psichari), 206
Terrier, Auguste, 38
terrorism, xiii, 7–8, 20–21, 284; Algeria, xxviii, xxxix, 287–88; Hanoi, 66–67; Voulet-Chanoine affair and, 32, 33
theater. *See* plays
theft, 58–59
Thomas, Martin, 133n16, 139n88, 250–51
Thompson, Elizabeth, 143
Thuram, Lilian, 353n16
Tilly, Charles, xix
Timbuktu, 183, 184–90, 198–99n53
"Tirailleurs Sénégalais" (term), 257
Tirailleurs Sénégalais Regiment. *See* Régiment de Tirailleurs Sénégalais (RTS)
Tixier, Adrien, 146, 147, 163, 168n22
Tocqueville, Alexis de, 5, 22
Togo, 40
Togoland, 250
To Lose a Battle (Horne), 249
Tonkin campaign, 35
Torcy, Louis de, 235
torture, xli, 8, 293, 297, 345

Toucouleur people. *See* Tukulor people
Touré, Samori. *See* Samori Touré
translators and translation, 36, 48n33
"trauma learning" (Schein concept), xii
travel restriction, 85, 108n29, 308, 310, 315, 322, 332n63. *See also* curfews; passports
trials, 96
troop morale. *See* morale of troops
Truth and Reconciliation Commission, 336
Tuareg people, 33, 185, 189, 226; French West African population, 227
Tukulor people, 231, 236
Tunisia, xx, 254, 255, 313
Turkey, 250

'Ulamaʿ. *See* Association of Reformist 'Ulamaʿ
Umar Tall, 32
unemployment: Algeria, 120, 124, 125, 160
Union coloniale française, 230
United East Indies Company, 335
United Kingdom. *See* Great Britain
United Nations, xxii, 341
United States, 155, 158, 285–86, 337. *See also* African Americans
Upper Nigeria, xxix
uprisings. *See* revolts
urban space and urbanism, 56, 64; Algeria, xxx, 98–99, 123, 125, 160; social control and, xxiii

Vacher de Lapouge, Georges, 238
vengeance. *See* retribution
Verdier, Jean, 316, 321, 322, 323

Vernillat, Jean, 257
veterans: Algerian, 114, 116, 125, 127, 153; French, 339; memorials to, 343; West African, 275
Vichy empire, xl, 101, 114, 151, 152; *attentisme* and, 298n3; Chirac and, 342; postwar purges and, 146, 162; Psichari and, 216; West African soldiers and, 237, 275
victims and "victimology," 349. *See also* blaming the victim
Vié, Jean, 316, 317–18, 321–22
Vietminh, 69–70
Vietnam, xvii–xviii, 337; colonists in, xxiii; famine in, 144. *See also* Hanoi; Tonkin campaign
Vietnamese: as conscripts (proposed), 239–40n2; in New Caledonia, 341
vigilantism, xxxiii, 68
Vigné-d'Octon, Paul, 28, 39, 42, 45n6
village burning, 33, 35
violence: definition, xii; justification and rationalization, 5, 22, 32, 113. *See also* collective violence; counterviolence; inter-ethnic violence; repression; psychological violence; retributive violence; sexual violence; symbolic violence
Viollette, Maurice, 109n32, 127
Viollis, Andrée, 65
virgins: defloration, 192, 199n54
Voix qui crient dans le desert, Les (Psichari), 215
voting and voting rights, 81, 83, 88, 97, 106n18
Voulet, Paul, 26–51
Voulet-Chanoine affair, xxviii–xxix, 26–51, 186

Voyage du Centurion, Le (Psichari), 208–9, 213, 214, 215
Vrolyk, Pierre, 147, 156, 164, 172n58

wages, 126, 129
Wallis islanders, 341
"war" (word), 354n26
warfare, aerial. *See* aerial warfare
Wargnier, Régis, 338
War Ministry. *See* Ministry of War
Warnier Law, 113
wars, religious. *See* religious wars
Waterfield, Gordon, 262, 273
water supply, 31
Weil, Patrick, 101
Weinstein, Jeremy, 144
Weisgerber, Charles Henri, 231
West African soldiers. *See* soldiers, West African
West African women: relations with French men, 177–201
West Germany, xxxix–xl, 304–33
West Indies and West Indians, 339, 349, 353n16, 354n24
Weygand, Maxime, 255, 262, 279n32, 279n33
wheat, 145, 155, 156, 159
whistleblowers, 39–40
white identity, xxv, 52, 70
White King, Red Rubber and Black Deaths, 335
Why France Collapsed (Chapman), 249
winter: African soldiers and, 253, 278n22
Witthöft, Joachim, 271
Wolof people, 228, 236, 237
women: banning from French forts, 198–99n53; brutalization of, 35;

women (*cont.*)
    massacre of, 12, 31, 35; in Voulet-Chanoine mission, 29, 30. *See also* French women; misogyny; sex slaves; West African women
work. *See* labor
workers, agricultural. *See* farmworkers
workers, migrant. *See* migrant workers
work permits, 315
World War I, xxiv, xxxvi–xxxvii, xxxviii, 127, 222–23; West African soldiers and, 235–37, 257
World War II, xxvi, 192, 304; Algeria, 140–73; in films, 347–48; West African soldiers and, 237–39. *See also* Battle of France; "phony war" (1939–40)

xenophobia, 112, 113, 114

Yasukuni War Memorial, 336
Young, Robert J., 251

Zaborowski-Moindron, Sigismond, 232
Zenati, Rabeh, 118
Zinder (West African sultanate), 26, 29
Zouaves, 9, 91, 92, 232

In the France Overseas series

To Hell and Back:
The Life of Samira Bellil
Samira Bellil
Translated by Lucy R. McNair
Introduction by Alec G. Hargreaves

Colonial Metropolis:
The Urban Grounds of
Anti-Imperialism and Feminism
in Interwar Paris
Jennifer Anne Boittin

The French Navy and the
Seven Years' War
Jonathan R. Dull

I, Nadia, Wife of a Terrorist
Baya Gacemi

Transnational Spaces and Identities
in the Francophone World
Edited by Hafid Gafaïti,
Patricia M. E. Lorcin, and
David G. Troyansky

French Colonialism Unmasked:
The Vichy Years in
French West Africa
Ruth Ginio

Bourdieu in Algeria:
Colonial Politics, Ethnographic
Practices, Theoretical Developments
Edited and with an introduction
by Jane E. Goodman and
Paul A. Silverstein

Endgame 1758:
The Promise, the Glory, and
the Despair of Louisbourg's
Last Decade
A. J. B. Johnston

Cinema in an Age of Terror:
North Africa, Victimization,
and Colonial History
Michael F. O'Riley

Making the Voyageur World:
Travelers and Traders in the
North American Fur Trade
Carolyn Podruchny

A Workman Is Worthy of His Meat:
Food and Colonialism in Gabon
Jeremy Rich

The Moroccan Soul:
French Education, Colonial
Ethnology, and Muslim
Resistance, 1912–1956
Spencer D. Segalla

Silence Is Death:
The Life and Work of Tahar Djaout
Julija Šukys

The French Colonial Mind,
Volume 1:
Mental Maps of Empire and
Colonial Encounters
Edited and with an introduction
by Martin Thomas

The French Colonial Mind,
Volume 2:
Violence, Military Encounters,
and Colonialism
Edited and with an introduction
by Martin Thomas

Beyond Papillon:
The French Overseas
Penal Colonies, 1854–1952
Stephen A. Toth

Madah-Sartre:
The Kidnapping, Trial, and
Conver(sat/s)ion of Jean-Paul Sartre
and Simone de Beauvoir
Written and translated by
Alek Baylee Toumi
With an introduction by
James D. Le Sueur

To order or obtain more information
on these or other University
of Nebraska Press titles, visit
www.nebraskapress.unl.edu.

www.ingramcontent.com/pod-product-compliance
Lightning Source LLC
Chambersburg PA
CBHW021814300426
44114CB00009BA/168